A

COMMENTARY ON THE PSALMS:

FROM

PRIMITIVE AND MEDIÆVAL WRITERS;

AND FROM THE

Various Office-books and Hymns

OF THE

ROMAN, MOZARABIC, AMBROSIAN, GALLICAN, GREEK, COPTIC,
ARMENIAN, AND SYRIAC RITES.

BY

THE REV. J. M. NEALE, D.D.,

SOMETIME WARDEN OF SACKVILLE COLLEGE, EAST GRINSTEAD,

AND

THE REV. R. F. LITTLEDALE, LL.D.,

SOMETIME SCHOLAR OF TRINITY COLLEGE, DUBLIN.

VOL. II.

PSALM XXXIX. TO PSALM LXXX.

LONDON:

JOSEPH MASTERS, ALDERSGATE STREET,

AND NEW BOND STREET.

NEW YORK: POTT AND AMERY.

MDCCCLXVIII.

PREFACE.

THE circumstances under which this second volume of the Commentary on the Psalms is issued seem to call for a few words of explanation.

The long interval which has elapsed since the appearance of the earlier portion is due in part to the necessarily slow progress involved by the complicated plan of the work, in part to the unceasing activity of Dr. Neale in other fields of literary toil, and in part, unhappily, to the failure of physical power which began to tell upon him several months before his fatal illness disclosed itself.

He had reached only to the fifth verse of Psalm lix. when he was struck down, and the fragment thus prepared was scarcely large enough for separate publication.

It was his earnest desire that his plan should not remain incomplete, and he indicated an accomplished friend, poet and scholar like himself, as his successor in the task. That friend was obliged, by the pressure of other claims, to decline the undertaking; and the call was next made upon me.

I believed that I should better carry out the wishes of my dear friend by attempting to continue those labours which had so often formed the subject of discussion between us, than by declining the responsibility, as I well might have done, on the double ground of the inherent difficulty of the task, and my own very inadequate powers of grappling with it. But I was engaged, at the time of my acceptance of the proposal, with literary work of my own, which occupied all my

available time. Further, it was essential for me to
accumulate the necessary books, as only a few of them
were in my possession, and Dr. Neale's library was no
longer accessible to me. By the time that this obstacle
was overcome, and that I was ready to begin my
part of the work, the autumn of 1867 was already
far advanced; and the portion now laid before the
public has been completed, amidst many long inter-
ruptions and incessant ill-health, since that date.

My editorial duties began with the tenth sheet of
the volume, at p. 217, as the earlier part had all
been worked off at press before I was called upon.
They continued only to the close of that sheet, for
Dr. Neale's MS. ceases abruptly on the first page of
the succeeding one; and I alone am responsible for
what thenceforward follows.

My account of my stewardship, however, is not
yet ended. I have to remark upon the non-appear-
ance of a Dissertation promised several times in the
first volume, and once again in this, to be the fourth
in order. It was to have treated the whole subject
of the divisions, diction, and mystical character of
the Psalter, and to have discussed the causes of the
frequent discrepancies between the Hebrew, Greek,
and Vulgate. Of that Dissertation, so far as I can
ascertain, no part has ever been put into writing; nor
am I capable of supplying its place from my own stores.
In its stead appears a table of the supposed chronological order and occasion of the Psalms, which I have
printed in discharge of my editorial duty, but not from
any belief in its critical value. My dear friend, un-
surpassed in several departments of theological learning, unrivalled in not a few, and profoundly intimate
as he was with the letter, and still more with the
spirit, of Holy Scripture, had yet given but slight
attention to that part of Biblical study, for which we
have no definite name, but which German scholars
call *Einleitung*. I have therefore not hesitated to
depart widely from the conclusions of this Dissertation whenever I have had occasion to discuss the date
of any Psalm.

One other Dissertation he had projected, and had

even written its introductory paragraphs. It was
to have described the English metrical versions of
the Psalter. I do not know whether he was aware
that the task had already been (in some degree, at
least) accomplished, nor if he had fully realized the
extent of the undertaking. The number of these
versions is not much under three hundred, and a dissertation upon them must therefore be either a mere
bibliographical catalogue, or a larger book than a volume of the Commentary itself. I have, consequently,
determined to leave this also unessayed, and to content myself, should a further instalment of this work
be called for, with a liturgical discussion of the use of
the Psalter in the Sacraments and Occasional Offices
of the Eastern and Western Churches, as a pendant
to the first Dissertation, which treats of its employment in the daily recitation of the Canonical Hours.

With regard to my own portion of the book, I am
fully conscious of its marked inferiority to the model
I have attempted to follow. Continuations are pro-
verbially unsuccessful, even when the artist himself
makes the effort, and even when that artist is a Cer-
vantes, a Bunyan, or a De Foe. Much more is
failure to be expected when a feeble copyist takes up
the pencil of a great master. It is true that as this
Commentary is chiefly a mosaic from old writers,
the peril seems at first sight less. But it is not really
so. Two jewellers may have identical piles of gold
and gems given them as materials, and the one will
produce with them a wonder of art, while the other
obscures their beauty by coarse and tasteless work-
manship. Here, moreover, the heaps are not equal.
The vast stores of Dr. Neale's learning were hardly
less remarkable than the readiness and certainty
with which he could draw on them, the ease with
which he could illustrate any subject he treated, with
apt classical allusion, parallels lying hid in history
or legend, hymn or song, of ancient or modern times.
Any one coming after him in the many paths of his
labours is at a disadvantage in comparison, but especially in a field so peculiarly his own as the mystical interpretation of Scripture.

Yet, as I have not attempted to bend the bow of
Ulysses out of any spirit of boastfulness or rivalry,
but in fulfilment of the wishes of the departed, I
may commit my work to the lenient consideration of
those who will not expect a mere student to equal
in a few months' labour that which cost a great
teacher more than as many years. The chief merit
of my work is that there is so little original matter
in it. Some there is, for I have thought it desirable
to follow the example of my predecessor, who admitted, though sparingly, in the latter part of his
labours, passages not drawn from the text-books
before him. They are introduced in the following
three cases only: (1.) When they are really ancient,
but cannot be identified (at least by me) for want of
reference. (2.) When they are natural deductions
and expansions of trains of thought already set down.
(3.) When, as sometimes happens, all the commentators simultaneously become jejune and prosaic in
the treatment of a passage capable of better things.

I have used several authorities which were either
unemployed by Dr. Neale, or which he began to quote
after the Second Dissertation was printed, and which
are thus omitted there. They are as follows:

(1.) Arnobius of Gaul, (+ circ. 460) whose Commentary on the whole Psalter is published in the
eighth volume of the Bibliotheca Maxima Patrum.

(2.) Peter Lombard, Bishop of Paris, (+ 1164)
the famous Master of the Sentences, compiled a
Commentary on the Psalms, chiefly from S. Augustine, Cassiodorus, Venerable Bede, and Haymo of
Halberstadt, not without occasional pithy remarks of
his own. This is commonly known as the "Gloss,"
and is cited more than once under that name by Dr.
Neale. My copy bears date, Paris, 1541.

(3.) S. Bonaventura (+ 1250) has scarcely maintained his high reputation in his Commentary on the
Psalms, which is brief, and more didactic than mystical. But a few gleanings from it will be found in
these pages.

(4.) Hugo of S. Cher, Cardinal of S. Sabina,
(+ 1268) to whose industry the first division of the

Bible into chapters, and its result, the first concord-
ance, are due, has left Commentaries on the whole
Bible, amongst which those on the Psalms, frequently
quoted in this work, hold the foremost place.

(5.) Richard Rolle of Hampole, (+ 1349,) the
Yorkshire hermit, preacher, poet, and saint, author
of the "Pricke of Conscience," wrote a terse mystical paraphrase of the Psalter, which often comes
very little short in beauty and depth of Dionysius
the Carthusian himself. I have cited it with frequency proportioned rather to its merit than its bulk.

(6.) Richard of Le Mans, a Franciscan, and Doctor
of Theology of Paris, (+ circ. 1550,) in editing the
Gloss of Peter Lombard, has added several notes of
his own on each Psalm, often of value, and display-
ing a knowledge of Hebrew as rare as it was credita-
ble in those days.

(7.) Simeon de Muis, Archdeacon of Soissons, and
Professor of Hebrew at Paris, (+ 1654,) has left a
Commentary mainly critical, exhibiting the version
of S. Jerome, the Vulgate, and a new translation of
his own in parallel columns, with copious notes bearing chiefly on the Hebrew text, and on Rabbinical
interpretations of the Psalter. The work is still cited
with respect by critics, and the edition I use, (2 Vols.
4to. Louvain, 1770,) is further enriched with comments by the famous Bossuet.

(8.) Reinhard Bakius, a Lutheran, and Pastor of
the Cathedral of Magdeburg, (+ circ. 1660,) compiled a Commentary which, though violently contro-
versial, and full of reference to mere passing politics
and gossip, yet contains some more valuable ore, to
which I have been sometimes indebted. I quote the
second edition, fol. Frankfort, 1683.

(9.) Thomas Le Blanc, a Jesuit, Professor at
Rheims and Dijon, and Provincial of Champagne,
(+ 1669,) produced three immense double-columned
folios of Comment on the Psalter, (Cologne, 1744,)
which I have used a little, though deterred by their
homiletic prolixity and ponderous learning.

Of more modern books, it will suffice to say that
I have freely availed myself of the works of De Wette,

Olshausen, Hupfeld, and Delitzsch, though as the
scope of this book is to show the current of mystical
interpretation of the Psalter in the Church, and not
to discuss the critical exegesis of the original text,
most of their matter is beside my purpose. I have
drawn more than one useful hint from Mr. Thrupp's
work on the Psalms, and have consulted also, with
less result, Archdeacon Wordsworth's rapidly executed Commentary. My perfect unacquaintance with
Slavonic has made it impossible for me to continue
Dr. Neale's occasional references to that version, but
I have endeavoured to make amends by citing other
and earlier ones, wherever their variants seemed important for the object in hand.

Should my labours in this unaccustomed field meet
with approval, I will endeavour to complete the task
I have undertaken, but if an unfavourable verdict be
recorded, I will content myself with having done
what I could to give effect to the dying wishes of
him to whom the conception of this work is due, and
will gladly consign its fulfilment to abler and worthier hands. I am not without hope that the sweet
perfume of many of the flowers I have culled here,
(however I may have overlooked lovelier blossoms,
and unskilfully wreathed the garland,) may prove
grateful to those who delight in the pleasaunce of
Holy Writ, and I would fain usher in my attempt to
show how Saints of old found their Master in the
songs of His great ancestor, with the quaint words
of a mediæval poet:

Rithmis et sensu verborum consociatum
Psalterium Jesu, sic est opus hoc vocitatum.
Qui legit intente, quocunque dolore prematur,
Sentiet inde bonum, dolor ejus et alleviatur;
Ergo pius legat hoc ejus sub amore libenter,
Cujus ibi Nomen scriptum videt esse frequenter.

R. F. L.

London,
Feast of S. Augustine of Hippo, 1868.

A
COMMENTARY ON THE PSALMS.

PSALM XXXIX.

TITLE.—Vulgate: To the end; to Idithun himself. A song of David. English Version: To the chief musician, even to Jeduthun. A Psalm of David. Others: To the Supreme. Upon his dispensation. A Psalm of David.

ARGUMENT.

ARG. THOMAS. That CHRIST corrects and emends us for our iniquity. The Prophet blames the Jews, who, having the riches of the Scriptures, know not to whom they leave them; and the Church upbraids them that heap up riches, and cannot tell who shall gather them. The Prophet blames those who have riches, and know not to whom they shall leave them. The voice of the just against his enemies.

VEN. BEDE. The name Idithun signifies that his choir sang this hymn. Now the name Idithun is, by interpretation, *He that leaps* 1 Chron. *by them.* It therefore signifies him who in his spirit passes by xxv. 3. earthly things, and leaps by them that, cleaving fast to the ground, and bowed down to earth, have no thoughts save for those things that are most terrene; him that, dwelling in the lofty habitation of the mind, freely philosophises concerning the vanity of worldly occupations. And lest you should think that this, because it speaks of difficulty, is a Psalm of penitence, he adds, A song of David. Now a song sometimes pertains to them that are joyous, sometimes to them that mourn, but never has to do with them that are penitent. And note that those Psalms which are called in their titles songs, always celebrate the joys of victory in adversity. . . . This Idithun —he that leaps over vices, affording us the type of a righteous man— testifies from the first part of the Psalm how he, with much advantage, kept silence against the enemies that leapt upon him to attack him, asking to know the end of his life, if perchance he might merit to behold the Incarnation of the LORD, even with his bodily eyes: *I said, I will take heed to my ways.* Next, he proveth that the fear of mortals is vain, because all things are given into the power of the LORD: *Surely man walketh.* Thirdly, he maketh request that his sins may be forgiven, and that his life may be concluded with a happy end: *Hear my prayer, O Lord.*

II.   B

SYRIAC PSALTER. A prayer and exhortation to refrain the tongue from evil words, and to set a guard over the sight and the other senses.

VARIOUS USES.

Gregorian. Tuesday. Matins.
Monastic. Tuesday. II. Nocturn.
Parisian. Thursday. Compline.
Quignon. Monday. Sexts.
Ambrosian. Wednesday of the First Week. III. Nocturn.

ANTIPHONS.

Gregorian. That I offend not * with my tongue.
Monastic. The same.
Quignon. In GOD * is my salvation and my glory.
Mozarabic. None.
Parisian. Save me, O GOD, * for the faithful are minished from the children of men.

1 I said, I will take heed to my ways : that I offend not in my tongue.

The story is well known how Pambo, a recluse of the Egyptian desert, when about to enter on his novitiate, betook himself to an aged monk, and requested from him instruction for his new course of life. The old man opened his Psalter, and began to read the present verse. "That is enough," said Pambo; "let me go home and practise it." And long, long after, being asked by one of his brethren whether he were yet perfect in his first lesson, the saint, now in his turn an aged man, replied, "Forty and nine years have I dwelt in this desert, and am only just beginning to learn how to obey the commandment." They well say that S. James has almost taken away the office of a commentator from any one else : "If any man offend not in word, the same is a perfect man, and able also to bridle the whole body. . . . And the tongue is a fire, a world of iniquity : so is the tongue among our members, that it defileth the whole body, and setteth on fire the course of nature, and it is set on fire of hell." And notice the double duty contained in this verse : *That I offend not with my tongue,* in speaking when I ought to be silent, or saying that which I ought not to say : and *that I offend not with my tongue* also in being silent when I ought to speak ; in having never a word on GOD's side, when the world and the devil have advocates more than enough. There is a time to keep silence, says the wise man, and he puts that first ; but there is a time to speak also. And the order is well set. There is a time to keep silence—namely, in this world, where silence is often our best safeguard ; there is a time to speak in the world to come, when, as it is written, "I will sing and speak praises unto the LORD." But chiefly as we repeat this verse do we see the Word of the FATHER standing silent

(margin notes:) Palladius. Lausiac. c. 10.
S. James iii. 2.
S. Greg. Moral. vii. 17.
Eccles. iii. 7.
Rupert.

before the judgment-seats both of Herod and Pontius Pilate; "insomuch that the governor marvelled greatly." And compare here the Saint of all saints with one of His most glorious followers: the one, "as a sheep before his shearers is dumb, so He opened not His mouth;" the other was but too ready with his "GOD shall smite thee, thou whited wall." *I said.* And they observe that any one who can thus set down his resolution with the feeling and certainty that it will be kept, is not far from the kingdom of GOD. *I said:* nothing easier generally; "They say, and do not:" but *I said* as one who is in earnest,—one who knows that by our words we shall be justified, and by our words we shall be condemned,—one that remembers Who it was that from our words took the title of His own Incarnate Godhead, THE WORD,—this is a kind of speech indeed which is worth being reported by the Psalmist.

Rupert.

Acts xxiii. 3.

Cd.

2 I will keep my mouth as it were with a bridle : while the ungodly is in my sight.

In the Vulgate we have no mention of the bridle: it is simply, *I set a guard about my mouth.* But the other early translations give it as we have it. And notice this : here we have the resolution of one who is striving to keep GOD's law, that he will close his mouth; whereas, in the description of the virtuous woman as we have it in the Book of Proverbs, it is, "She openeth her mouth with wisdom." And they behold in this a deep mystery. Up to the time of her who was blessed above women, the Word of GOD was, as it were, sealed up; "The mystery was hid from ages and from generations." But from the time that she exclaimed, "Behold the handmaid of the LORD," the mouth of those that declared the will of GOD was indeed opened with wisdom. For so it follows: *while the ungodly is in my sight.* As if he, the ungodly,—he, the source and fountain of all ungodliness,—was openly in the sight of the world, was the lord and ruler of that world before the Incarnation. Therefore, up to that time the prophecies were sealed, the types were hidden, the parables were dark ; but after that the ungodly had lost the empire of this world,—after that Satan had, as lightning, fallen from heaven,—then no more occasion for this repression of the truth, this keeping the mouth, as it were, with a bridle. And notice also, that even more exactly than the former verse, this applies to Him who stood silent before the seat of the ungodly. S. Bernard, preaching to a secular congregation, uses a metaphor which they must all have understood. The falconer does not dismiss the hawk unless the heron be in sight; so neither will the good man permit a word to fly from his tongue, unless there be that which may be struck and transfixed by it. S. Chrysostom observes that GOD, as the most wise Architect of the human body, has inclosed the tongue with a deep fortification—the teeth, namely, and the lips; as if knowing how liable that member is to the

Ay.

S. Bernard. in Col. iv. 13.

S. Chrysost. in loc.

B 2

assaults of our great enemy. And how often might the true GOD say to us, what the false deity of Homer exclaims,

τέκνον ἐμὸν, ποῖόν σε ϝέπος φύγεν ἕρκος ὀδόντων;

And again: *While the ungodly is in my sight.* But we know for how short a time the ungodly will be out of the sight of the servant, even as he was of the Master. When the devil had ended all his temptation, he departed from Him for a season. And so this season, and so this period in which the mouth need not be kept as it were with a bridle, is but for a little moment; is but, so to speak, the time in which Satan

C. is preparing himself for new attacks.

3 I held my tongue, and spake nothing : I kept silence, yea, even from good words; but it was pain and grief to me.

L. And there are two senses, entirely opposite to each other, in which we may take the verse; the one applying to David, the other to the Son of David. To David: He *kept silence* in those long months in which, after the death of Uriah, the king had taken Bathsheba to be his wife, and of which the

2 Sam. xi. 27. only record is, "Nevertheless, the thing which David had done displeased the LORD :" the other, to the Son of David, when He also kept silence, as was just now said, before the tribunal of Pilate and Herod. The Chaldean has : *I kept silence from the words of the law, therefore my grief was renewed :* a plain enough sense as applied to David himself.

De Offic. lib. S. Ambrose takes it to signify, that the duty of the good
i. 5. man, who, when falsely accused, would follow the example of his LORD, is sometimes altogether to be silent, without any attempt to make manifest his innocence; which he shows by the example of Joseph, when accused by Potiphar's wife, and by that of Susanna, when slandered by the elders. But

S. Hieron. S. Jerome remonstrates vigorously against such an interpre-
in loc. tation, and dwells at great length on the duty of not letting our good be evil spoken of. There are nine interpretations of *keeping silence from good* which have been more or less

L. in vogue among the interpreters of the Church : of these the strangest is that which tells us that *good* is here put for *ill,*

S. Cyril. in the Psalmist not being willing to mention wickedness; and
S. Joan. lib. that David here, therefore, only tells us how assiduously he
xii. strove against every idle word. But it is much better to refer the phrase altogether to our dear LORD; and that in His own sense of not casting our pearls before swine. Seeing

Vitalis Zu- that one of His good words was distorted into "This Man
colius. Hom. calleth for Elias," good need there was that He should keep
in S. Marc.
63. silence from such.

4 My heart was hot within me, and while I was thus musing the fire kindled : and at the last I spake with my tongue,

They see in this the secret operation of the HOLY GHOST, *Hugo Card.*
by which the heart of each of His servants is itself kindled
with the full fervour of His love, before he endeavours to
impart to others that which he himself has received. They
see, for example, S. Augustine in his narrow cell at Rome,
before he proclaimed CHRIST Crucified under that old oak in
Kent. They see S. Francis stripping himself of all his
earthly possessions in his Italian home, before offering to
enter the furnace, if the Egyptian soldan would by that
miracle be converted to his LORD. They see S. Francis
Xavier in prayer and meditation in his Portuguese monas-
tery, before bringing in thousands to JESUS; truer pearls
than those of the Pearl coast, a sweeter savour before the
throne of GOD than that of the Spice islands. *The fire kindled.* *Origen. in S.*
This is the fire which CHRIST came to send upon earth; the *Luc. xii. 49.*
fire which sprang from Himself, even as when the angel
touched the rock with his staff, the flame rose up out of it, *Judg. vi. 21.*
and consumed the sacrifice. This is the fire of which GOD
spoke to Jeremiah, "Behold, I will make My words in thy
mouth fire, and this people wood, and it shall devour them." *Jer. v. 14.*
This is the fire of which the LORD speaks when He tells of
the candle that is lighted, not to be put under a bushel, but
on a candlestick, to the end it may give light to all that are
in the house, the universal house of GOD, the Catholic Church.
S. Bernard well says that the coming of GOD into the heart
of each of His saints is thus described: "There shall go a *S. Bernard.*
fire before Him, and burn up His enemies on every side." *Serm. 31, in*
And at the last I spake with my tongue. They gather from *Cant.*
hence how the preacher ought long, as well as deeply, to
have been kindled with the fire of GOD's love, before he endeavours to kindle others with the same. *At the last.* Not
in the first glow of a heart turned from darkness to light,
and from the power of Satan unto GOD; not in that early
stage of love, when the difficulties have scarcely been weighed,
—when the cost has hardly been counted,—when nothing
seems certain but this, that anything, that everything must
be done for Him Who has done all for us. That great *S. Thomas*
preacher,—that saint, of so deep insight into the human *de Villanov.*
heart,—perhaps, on the whole, the most remarkable saint of *i. 311.*
the sixteenth century,—S. Thomas,—dwells at great length
on the subject. *At last I spake with my tongue:* when I
not only knew what has to be done, but the difficulties which
lie in the way of doing it; not only man's duties, but his
weakness; not only GOD's requirements, but also Satan's
temptations. When, in short, the preacher can enter into
the full spirit of that most merciful Spanish proverb, "You
see what I drink, but not the thirst I suffer," then it should
follow, *At the last I spake with my tongue.*

5 LORD, let me know mine end and the number of
my days: that I may be certified how long I have to
live.

It is not so easy to apply this verse to the Eternal Word of God. For He did know from the beginning His end and the number of His days: as it is written by that Apostle who had drunk most deeply into His Divine secrets, "JESUS, knowing all things which should come upon Him." But they take it rather of the voice of the Church before the coming of the LORD. "Let me know how long I have to endure this darkness, and long for the light; this tyranny, and long for liberty; this time, when many prophets and righteous kings desire to behold the coming Salvation, and are not yet permitted to see it." And in this sense also they take those words of Job, "Who can bring a clean thing out of an unclean? Not one. Seeing his days are determined, the number of his months are with Thee, Thou hast appointed his bounds which he cannot pass; turn from him, until he shall accomplish, as an hireling, his day." "The number of his months are with Thee,"—that is, the allotted time before the tyranny of Satan shall be riven in sunder, the four hundred and thirty years before Israel shall go free from the tyranny of Pharaoh. This was the study of Daniel, when, in the Babylonian captivity, he prayed to be taught how long would be the time ere Israel yet returned to their own land. S. Chrysostom, as most of the Greek Fathers, ignoring this mystical signification, take the verse in its more ordinary sense. "Let me, let each of Thy servants, know the number of our days, that I may be certified (not as we read it—how long I have to live, but) *quid desit mihi :* τί ὑστερῶ ἐγώ; how much I yet lack, or come short in: come short in, that is, to the working out my own salvation." And thus also the Angelic Doctor explains the passage most emphatically. And here they dwell at great length on those remarkable warnings of diminished life, "The bloodthirsty and deceitful man shall not live out half his days:" that though GOD has appointed a time which man might reach, if he would, sin cuts it short. Hear what Vieyra, in one of his most fearful sermons, has written with respect to this very subject. "GOD most manifestly declares and teaches us, says S. Augustine, that He has assigned to each man a certain measure or number of sins, until the completion and consummation of which He waits for their conversion; but as soon as that measure is fulfilled, that number accomplished, GOD waits no longer, and remediless condemnation ensues. S. Ambrose affirms the same thing, where he comments on that passage, 'The iniquities of the Amorites are not yet full.' And because this is the common opinion of all the expositors of Holy Scripture, the most learned of all shall suffice for the rest. Cornelius à Lapide, writing on the ephah of Zechariah, says thus: 'The ephah is the measure of the sins of each, be it man or people; on the completion of which GOD's anger will be worked out in revenge.' And there is no difficulty in the fact that this measure of sins is greater for one man, less for another; because this very inequality, as we in our poor in-

Margin notes: L. Ay. / S. Greg. Moral. in loc. / Job xiv. 4. / S. Johan. Chrysost. in loc. / S. Thomas Aquin. / Serm. do Quarto Sabbado da Quaresma. tom. iv. 31. / Gen. xv. 16. / Zech. v. 6.

telligence call it, is in Divine Providence the highest justice.
For answer me this: God also measures the days of the life
of each man, as David tells us, 'Behold, Thou hast made a
measure to my days.' And this measure is so certain and
determined, that, when the last day has arrived, there is no
help for it; as Job affirms, 'Thou hast set him his bounds
which he cannot pass.' Well, then; as no man complains of
God, nor thinks it strange that the measure of one man's
days should be so much less than that of another, much less
should it seem strange that the measure of sin should also be
unequal, especially when we consider that one, and that the
very first sin, is sufficient to induce God, if He judged us
according to strict justice, to damn us. The reason is the
supreme dominion of God, Who is equally the Author of
grace and of nature; and thus since, so far as He is Author
of nature, He can limit life to a certain number of days
without injustice to the individual man, so, without injustice
to the same man, can He limit His pardon to a certain number of sins. Whence it follows that, as the day which fills
up the number of all our days is necessarily the last,—so that,
when it has ended its course, die we must,—so, in like manner,
the sin which fills up the number of our sins is also the last,
and once committed, leaves no escape from condemnation, because there is no longer any place for pardon."

*"Ecce men-
surabiles po-
suisti dies
meos."*
Job xiv. 5.

6 Behold, thou hast made my days as it were a
span long : and mine age is even as nothing in respect of thee; and verily every man living is altogether vanity.

Or as it is in the Vulgate, *Behold, Thou hast made my
days measurable.* That is, they say, Time against action: so
much to be done, so long to do it in : a race of such a length
to be run, such a space of time allowed for its completion.
They finely compare with this verse, that saying in Isaiah,
"Who hath .... meted out heaven with the span, and comprehended the dust of the earth in a measure, and weighed
the mountains in scales, and the hills in a balance?" See how
beautifully the two respond to each other. *Thou hast made
my days as it were a span long.* Yet also: "Thou hast
meted out the heavens with the span," with this very span,
the span of human life. That is, however high those heavens,
however glorious that reward, however infinite and eternal
that blessedness, it is not above my span; it is not past my
strength. And take the word *days* in a good sense. My
days, those works which I do, those efforts that I make, by
the light of the Sun of Righteousness, they shall end in the
true Day:

Ay.

Villalpan-
dus. Tom. 3.
pars 2. lib. 3.
cap. 16.
Isa. xl. 12.

L.

> The Light that hath no evening,
> That needs nor moon nor sun :
> The Light so new and golden,
> The Light that is but one.

Mine age is even as nothing in respect of Thee. And so had Job pleaded before: " Spare me, O LORD, for my days are vanity." As David here : *And verily every man living is altogether vanity.*

Job vii. 16.

Exigua pars est vitæ quam nos vivimus,

Attius.

said the old Roman poet. Will you take the *vanity* as man's misfortune or his fault? Most mediæval writers explain it of the former : Apollinarius, I think, of the latter.

Apollin.

καὶ μάλα ῥίζαν ἐμῆς βιστῆς ἀχρήϊον ἔγνως.

S. Hiero-
nym. ad S.
Damas. Ep.
57.

S. Greg.
Mor. ix. 10.

W.

Hence they dwell, by way of contrast, on the glorious title, I AM THAT I AM : that man cannot properly be said to *be* or *exist :* that real and very existence is the property of GOD alone. *Every man.* Some have taken it *whole man ;* that is, *man in his most perfect state.* And they say that He—to speak it with all reverence—Who became perfect Man, that He might redeem man, may thus be called by the title of vanity, even as He says Himself in another place, "As for Me, I am a worm, AND NO MAN."

7 For man walketh in a vain shadow, and dis-quieteth himself in vain : he heapeth up riches, and cannot tell who shall gather them.

How *in a vain shadow?* Some say, the valley of the sha-dow of death, through which the saints must pass all the days of their mortal life.

Seq. de S.
Germano.

> In hoc *loco tenebrarum,*
> In hac valle lacrymarum,
> In hac solitudine,
> Suspirabas et plorabas
> Et ad lucem aspirabas
> Quæ caret caligine.

S. Basil.
S. Cyril.
Hug. Card.

Others take it that he walks like an unreal phantom, or ap-pearance in a mirror, or the unsubstantial shade of a real object. But others, more beautifully take the shadow—*in imagine pertransit homo :* ἐν εἰκόνι διαπορεύσεται ἄνθρωπος—to refer to that Image in which he was at first created, and which however much broken and debased, has never wholly been lost. Here we must take *but* rather than *for.* " Every man living is altogether vanity :" *but*—nevertheless—*he walketh in the Image* of GOD, poor, and vain, and miserable as his present life may seem. *And disquieteth himself in vain.* Surely, they say, for the Great King will not permit His Image to perish : for the Creator must needs have com-passion on the works of His hands. And there is yet an-other sense in which we may take the two verses, and that, perhaps, the most striking of all. *Man walketh in a vain shadow :* namely, a shadow of good things to come : every

A.
S. B. C.
S. Greg.
Mor. x. 13.
D. C.

external appearance of nature, every human occupation, See it admirably worked out by
leading onward and upward to something higher and better.
So our LORD taught in many of His parables: of the fields
ripe to the harvest, of the city set upon an hill, of the lilies Cd.
that neither toil nor spin. He that would desire to see this
whole idea worked out, has only to consult Bellarmine's Biblioth.[1] Mystic. et Ascetic. Tom. vi.
Ascensio mentis in Deum per scalam rerum creatarum. He
then that might thus be led by visible to invisible beauty,
does disquiet himself in vain, if he sets much store by the
things of this world. *He heapeth up riches.* The later
writers give us all the commonplace of the uncertainty of
wealth, and the certainty of death, and rightly quote the
sermon of S. John Chrysostom on this text, delivered to S. Chrysost. Hom. l. in loc.
those rich and luxurious Antiochenes. But I confess, the
mediæval interpretation to me is far lovelier: He, Whose
every action or suffering was the acquiring of merit; He, Who
whether He laboured or rested, still was working out our
salvation; He, Who completed and enhanced all His merits
by the Death of the Cross; He heaped up riches indeed, the B.
infinite abyss of His deserts, *and cannot tell,* in so far as Man
alone, *who shall gather them,* what poor guilty sinner shall
find healing, what glorious saint shall there acquire victory.

But, returning to the former sense: "Now," says Ger- G.
hohus, "Idithun beholding celestial things above, terrestrial
things below, having overleapt the one, and still stretching
forth to the other, continues and exclaims:

8 And now, LORD, what is my hope: truly my
hope is even in thee.

O LORD JESUS, Who has not hoped for Thee? whether as Origen. Hom. in S. Joan. xix.
the Doctor of Thy people, Who shalt show them the way of
wisdom; or as their Redeemer, Who shalt purchase them Hos. x. 11.
from all bondage; or as the Liberator, Who shalt set free Ps. cxl. 9.
the spirits in prison; or as their Cleanser, Who shalt purify Zech. ix. 11.
them from sin; or as their Illuminator, Who shalt disperse
the darkness from their hearts; or as their Protector, Who Isa. ix. 1.
shalt guard them against their enemies; or finally, as their Isa. xix. 20.
exceeding and eternal great Reward. These seven expectations are the groundwork of the seven O's; the glorious
Antiphons and Magnificat, sung in the week of the LORD's
Expectation:

Draw nigh, draw nigh, Emmanuel, *Veni, veni, Emmanuel.*
And ransom captive Israel!
That mourns in lonely darkness here,
Until the SON of GOD appear.
Rejoice! rejoice! Emmanuel
Shall be born for thee, O Israel!

[1] This little library of the best mystical works of the Middle Ages, at a most reasonable price, cannot be too strongly recommended to the English Priest. It may be procured at Nutt's.

B 3

G.

What is my hope? Truly this: that though I now sit, as a stranger in a strange land, vainly endeavouring to satisfy my ravening hunger with the husks that the swine do eat, the day will come when I shall arise and go to my FATHER, even when He calls me to depart from this world, and that then He will give me a place and an inheritance among His hired servants, among those who have well borne the labour and heat of the day for the penny of eternal salvation; yea, even among His sons; yea, even with His First-Begotten SON, my Elder Brother JESUS CHRIST.[1] Lo, David's prayer is heard! He had said above, "LORD, let me know mine end;" that is, the thing which should be my aim, my goal, my scope, the one object of my life; and here he has found it. This his hope, or aim, is GOD, and GOD only. And he has not only obtained his petition, but he has won a benediction: as it is written, Blessed is he that waiteth for the LORD. The second clause of the verse is different in the Vulgate.

D. C.

S. Thomas Aq.

A.

G.

And now what is my expectation? is it not the Lord? and my[2] substance is with Thee. That is, that in Him we have our true essence; in Him we live, and move, and have our being; what we are, in and by Him we are. Gloriously Gerhohus: "*My substance is with Thee.* For *my substance,* not my guilt, was assumed by Thy SON; and in this Thine Only-Begotten, my nature, my very flesh, *is* before Thee. Less than Thee in nature, but not less in glory: because the glory of the Only-Begotten, which my nature possesseth in CHRIST, is not inferior to the glory of the FATHER; nor didst Thou, when Thou madest Him a little lower than the Angels, subtract anything of Thy glory from Him, Who is altogether and eternally consubstantial with Thee. . . . . Thus singing with Idithun, we pass above all things which are lower than GOD, and in the most highest glory of the very Deity we venerate the human substance, and say, *What is my hope?* Mine, who am a servant? *Is it not the Lord?* Is it not that I shall enter into the joy of my LORD? But whence is this to me, the servant, that the joy or glory of my LORD should come unto me? Thence it is, because, O my LORD, *my substance is with Thee:* there in Thy highest glory, O King of Eternal Glory, O GOD the FATHER! Now in the end of the world, I have intercession with Thee, when the Man-GOD intercedes for me: Consubstantial with me, in

---

[1] We have here a very curious example of that which "Idithun" is to leap over and pass by. "In extremo nunc tempore Antichristo vel aperte regnante, præcipue in officiis Clericorum synodaliter interdictorum, cum talium Missas interdictas transibo, et solas Catholicorum Missas libenter audio, et ob hoc oppro-bria sustineo, *quæ* tunc *est expectatio mea?*"

[2] The Roman has: *and my substance is as nothing in respect of Thee,* which is only taken from ver. 6. The LXX. give, like the Vulgate, ὑπόστασις, but Symmachus has ἀναμένων, and Aquila καραδοκία. And it is the true force of תוֹחַלְתִּי.

that He is Man; consubstantial with Thee, in that He is GOD."

9 Deliver me from all mine offences : and make me not a rebuke unto the foolish.

From all mine offences. They fall eagerly on the scholastic question, whether GOD can, by His infinite power, in accordance with His justice, forgive one mortal sin without forgiving all. But rather look at the faith which instigates this pleading. Let not me, O LORD, for whom Thou didst die, ever have this cast in my teeth by Satan, that Thou didst die for me in vain! **L.** **S. Johan. Chrys.**

> Quærens me, sedisti lassus :
> Redemisti crucem passus :
> Tantus labor non sit cassus.

And we may boldly put the words into our dear LORD's mouth, when overwhelmed with the weight of all the sins of all the world, He was hanging on the Cross. *A rebuke unto the foolish.* First, to those that passed by, wagging their heads, and saying, "If Thou be the SON of GOD, save Thyself, and come down from the Cross!" Then from him who, in his mad folly, would be like the Most High; would exalt his throne above the stars of GOD. And in their degree, every martyr, of whom it is written, They fools counted his life madness, and his end to be without honour, prays to be delivered from the load of cruel mockeries. And doubt not this; that, of all the bitter agony which will be the portion of the lost soul at that *Depart, ye cursed,* not the least will be the bitter reproaches and derision of those evil spirits who have seduced him to his ruin. " For this morsel of meat to have sold thy birthright! For the fleshly pleasures of a few days to have bartered thine eternal jewel! For a few grains of yellow earth to have missed the city with streets of gold, and gates of several pearls! O fool beyond all folly! O madman beyond all insanity !" Truly we have need to pray with all earnestness, *Make me not a rebuke unto the foolish.* **Procop. in Isa. cap. liii.** **Theophylac. in loc.** **Origen.**

10 I became dumb, and opened not my mouth : for it was thy doing.

Who can dare[1] to take these words of any but of the spotless LAMB? or at least only of others so far as they typify His patience and silence? So Eli: "It is the LORD; let Him do what seemeth Him good." So Job: "What? shall we receive good at the hand of GOD, and shall we not receive **L.** **1 Sam. iii. 18.** **Job ii. 10.**

---

[1] Natural as this interpretation is, it is singular how very few of the commentators refer to it. If I am not mistaken, only S. Thomas Aquinas and Lorinus, of those who are interpreting this Psalm do so, though Procopius, in writing on Isaiah liii., refers to the verse here.

1 Maccab.
ii. 60.
evil? So the Maccabees: "Nevertheless, as the will of GOD is in heaven, so let Him do." But rather see the Martyr of Martyrs, when He answered never a word, insomuch that S. Cosmas:
Great Thurs-
day. the governor marvelled greatly. "For Thou wast silent, innocent LAMB, that Thou mightest atone for our evil speeches. Thy tongue spoke not at all, because the tongues of this world are worlds of iniquity. Thou, when reviled, reviledst not, that we might bridle our lips with the remembrance of Thy forbearance. Thou, the Word, archetypal and consubstantial, didst now surround Thyself with silence. LORD and lover of men, glory be to Thee!" *For it was Thy doing.* O true answer to all suggestions and temptations to impatience! Reply which David himself made in another 2 Sam. xvi.
11. place, touching Shimei: "Let him alone, and let him curse, for the LORD hath bidden him." Or you may take it in another sense, equally true: I was enabled thus to remain silent, for it was Thou that gavest me grace to remain so.

Apollin.   ἔτλην κωφὸς ἄναιδος· ἐπεὶ σύ με τοῖον ἔτευξας·

says Apollinarius.

11 Take thy plague[1] away from me: I am even consumed by the means of thy heavy hand.

Ps. xxxviii.
18.
"*Take Thy plague away,*" exclaims S. Ambrose, "'And I truly am prepared for the plague.' How can the two be reconciled?" And he affirms the explanation to be, that he had now, by his sufferings of shame and pain undergone the chastisement that GOD had thought necessary for him; and the cause having ceased, the effect might also be removed. But does not the Son of David Himself give us another interpretation? In that He at one time said, "I have a Baptism to be baptised with, and how am I straitened till it be accomplished;" and yet at another, "If it be possible, let this cup pass from Me," did He not show that these variations of feeling are only a proof of His perfect Humanity: the same variation which will lead His true servant sometimes to be full of joy at the approaching conflict, sometimes to desire that, were GOD's will so, he might be spared it? Agnes Ar-
nauld, Lettre
CDXIV. "But one stroke," cries a loving saint, "one stroke we will not ask Thee to take from us; nay, rather, we will implore Thee that Thou wouldest never take from us, the reflection of and participation in, Thine own wounds, so that we with Paul may say, 'From henceforth let no' evil spirit venture Gal. vi. 17. nigh me to 'trouble me; for I bear in my body the marks of the LORD JESUS.'" This is the higher love, doubtless: Harphius. just as when the Bride makes petition, "Awake, O north wind, and come, thou south; blow upon my garden, that the

---

[1] Observe that here *plague* is the simple translation of *plaga:* there never has been, nor could be, any difference as to the meaning of the word.

spices thereof may flow out:" it is placed first, as the higher
act, to ask for the cold, nipping, north wind, if that be necessary, than for the sweet sunny southern breeze, however
for that also he may make supplication. *I am even consumed.*
And who could more truly say so than the Only-Begotten
SON? To others, the FATHER's hand deals not with them
after their sins, nor rewards them according to their iniquities: to Him, the Beloved One, it was unmixed heaviness. It is a curious sense in which some take the *defeci*, the
ἐξέλιπον, as if David had intended to say that he failed from,
that he had renounced, sin, because he had thus suffered; in
other words, that this is a parallel to the verse, "Before I
was troubled I went astray: but now have I kept Thy law."

D. C.

Ay.

12 When thou with rebukes dost chasten man for
sin, thou makest his beauty to consume away, like as
it were a moth fretting a garment: every man therefore is but vanity.

With rebukes. As that *Mene, Mene, Tekel, Upharsin,*
written on the wall of the Babylonian palace—as the hand-
writing on the sand, which caused the accusers of the adulteress to be convicted by their own consciences. Let us by all
means hear the scriptural S. Albertus: "And note, that the
rebukes of GOD are to be endured patiently. First, on account of the example of CHRIST: 'I hid not My Face from
shame and spitting.' Also for the avoiding evil; and first,
the evil of guilt. 'How have I hated instruction, and my
heart despised reproof! I was almost in all evil.' Also of
sudden death: 'He that being often reproved hardeneth his
neck, shall suddenly be destroyed, and that without remedy.'
And of ignorance: 'He that hateth reproof is brutish.' And
of the fear of hell: 'He that hateth reproof shall die.' Also
for the obtaining divers kinds of good things. Firstly, knowledge. 'He that heareth reproof getteth understanding.'
And again: 'The rod and reproof give wisdom.' And life:
'Reproofs of instruction are the way of life.' Again: 'So
wilt Thou correct me, and make me to live.'"

L.

S. Albert. M.

Isa. 1. 6.

Prov. v. 12, 14.

Prov. xxix. 1.
Prov. xv. 10.
Prov. xv. 32.
Prov. xxix. 15.
Prov. xvi. 23.
Isa. xxxviii. 6.

The next clause is difficult enough. *Even as it were a moth
fretting a garment.* The sense is clear, but the three last
words are not in the Hebrew. *Thou causest his soul to consume like a spider:* so is the Vulgate and the LXX. But it
is *a moth* in the original; and they discover many ways in
which the likeness applies.

Grossa retro: succincta: brevis: virus: timet ignem.
Pro muscis: pendens: viscere texit opus.

Hugo Card.

But this translation—the spider—reminds us of a curious
tradition of the Hebrews: That David, in his youth, desired
to know from GOD why He had created three things that appeared most useless—madmen, spiders, flies. The Divine

Abulens.
in 1 Reg.
xxiv. q. 6.
L.

answer was, that at a future time David should learn by finding that they were all useful to himself. And so it came to pass. The first—when he himself feigned madness in the palace of Achish. The fly: when he took the spear from Saul while asleep, he became so pent up behind Abner, that he could not retreat; a fly stung that warrior, and, without waking, caused him to move, and so liberated David. The spider: when, flying from Saul in the desert of Ziph, a web was spun over a cave in which he rested, and thus the band in search of him were led to believe that none could be there. And notice that in the Chaldaic paraphrase of Psalm lvii., instead of, "I will cry unto the Most High God, even unto the God That shall perform the cause which I have in hand," it is, "I will cry unto the most high and mighty God, Which sent the spider, that she should spin her web in the mouth of the cave to preserve me."

Ps. lvii. 2.

13 Hear my prayer, O LORD, and with thine ears consider my calling : hold not thy peace at my tears.

14 For I am a stranger with thee : and a sojourner, as all my fathers were.

W.

"I know that Thou hearest Me always." O Thou Only-Begotten Son, what would become of us if this were not so? If Thy prayers, once offered as the Victim, slain from the beginning of the world—now as the Great High Priest That by His own Blood has made entrance into the Holy of Holies—were not always heard, were not of infinite and prevailing merit ! *My tears.* The strong crying and tears of which S. Paul speaks: the tears, when He was troubled in spirit, saying, "FATHER, if it be possible, let this cup pass from Me : nevertheless not as I will, but as Thou wilt." It is a beautiful idea of Gerhohus, that the tears may be future as well as past. I cannot tell what I yet have to suffer. Thou knowest. I cannot tell how my future road lies. Thou knowest. Thou canst pity all. Thou canst counsel for all ; Thou canst provide for all. *I am a stranger with thee.* They see in this a reference to Jacob—how he was a stranger in a strange land ; how he, while yet a stranger, was comforted with that glorious vision ; how such a pillow of stone, how such a dwelling—Luz—thus helped him forward on his road. *I am a stranger.* But how? *with Thee.* O LORD, what matter the more or less of my strangeness on earth, if one of the many mansions is prepared for me in heaven? And oh what misery were that, had it been written, *a stranger to Thee !* But no—a stranger on earth, a denizen of heaven : a stranger with the weakness and infirmity of the flesh, at home in all the longing and expectation of the spirit : a stranger, while I look at the things seen, a citizen while I look at the things unseen : then indeed is it *as all my*

Heb. v. 7.

G.

A.
q. 156 in
Gen.

S. Albert.
Mag.

fathers were. Then is it as all the Fathers of the Church— Rupert. let them be Martyrs or Confessors, that went home to Thee. Still I desire to be like them; still I shall one day be like them; still, some day—for me and for them—the sufferings of the present time are not worthy to be compared with the glory that shall be revealed in us.

15 O spare me a little, that I may recover my strength : before I go hence, and be no more seen.

There are few texts which have been more earnestly discussed. Whether the Psalmist is speaking of sin or of sorrow, whether the strength refers to the Baptismal power once given in full—so often weakened and so miserably lessened. And *spare me*—where? I will not be tempted away from my settled purpose of not entering on any polemical subject in the Psalms of Peace. Let those who choose see a reference to Purgatory here—I would rather see in it the sure consolation we can all lay hold of. Spare me, that I may show Thy grace, and its power to man. Spare me, that by G. conquering, and trampling down, the favourite sin of my own heart, I may make me fit to sit in the light of Thy Love. W. *Seen* I shall be, one day, the latter day when Thou, O LORD, shalt stand on the earth. *Seen* I must be when the wicked shall be severed from the good—the tares from the corn; but till then—while both grow together till the harvest—till then, while none shall dare to pronounce the definitive judgment— spare me! I have need to be spared now! Forgive me! Unbind me! Spare me for His sake Who was not spared! Forgive me, for His sake Who had no need of forgiveness Ay. for sin, and yet was condemned! Pity me now for His sake Who cried with an exceeding great and bitter cry, *Eloi, Eloi, lama sabacthani?*

And therefore:

Glory be to the FATHER, in Whose Image we are created; and to the SON, Who was chastened with rebukes: and to the HOLY GHOST, of Whom it is said, My hope is ever in Thee;

As it was in the beginning, is now, and ever shall be: world without end. Amen.

COLLECTS.

GOD, That art the only Hope of Thy servants, grant us so Ludolph. to kindle in our meditations, that our souls may be inflamed with Thy love, and our hearts on fire with Thy praise. Through. (11.)

O CHRIST, SON of the Living GOD, Who for our sakes Mozarabic. wast made the Bread of the universe; grant that we may never be led away by the temptation of our enemy, but may follow Thee in the true government of our tongue. Amen. Through Thy mercy. (11.)

Mozarabic.   We have walked long enough, O LORD, according to the old man: give us grace to be renewed daily according to the grace of Thy HOLY SPIRIT; that we may so watch over our words, and reckon our deeds, that we may finally attain to life everlasting. Amen. Through. (11.)

PSALM XL.

TITLE.—To the Chief Musician, A Psalm of David. [To the Supreme, A Psalm of David.]

ARGUMENT.

ARG. THOMAS. That CHRIST is the beginning in the head of the Old Testament. The patience of the people. The voice of the Church after the Resurrection of the LORD. Concerning the patience of Paul the Apostle, when he is the first to preach CHRIST. Read it with the Acts of the Apostles.

VENERABLE BEDE. We have often seen how by the title CHRIST is signified, by whose members the Psalm is begun, as it is finished by the head. In the beginning, the Church of the Gentiles returns thanks because, set free from the listless grief of the world, she has attained to the joys of the New Testament. Next the LORD speaks of His holy Incarnation and righteousness; He supplicates the help of the FATHER, that He may overcome the perils brought upon Him by the Jews: beseeching that all His enemies may be confounded, and that they all who hope in Him may rejoice.

SYRIAC PSALTER. In the literal sense it pertains to David when Shimei brought to him the names of those who ministered in the house of the LORD. But in the spiritual sense a thanksgiving to GOD by His worshippers in the Church.

S. JEROME. This Psalm hath in the beginning the voice of the Gentile people called to be a portion of GOD'S heritage, and then of the Mediator Himself to the FATHER.

VARIOUS USES.

Gregorian. Tuesday. Matins.
Monastic. Monday. II. Nocturn.
Parisian. Friday. Tierce.
Quignon. Wednesday. Compline.
Ambrosian. First Week. Wednesday. III. Nocturn.

ANTIPHONS.

Gregorian. That I offend not * in my tongue.
Monastic. The same.
Parisian. For innumerable troubles are come about me, * let it be Thy pleasure, O LORD, to deliver me.
Ambrosian. As the last Psalm.

Mozarabic. I waited patiently for the LORD, * and He inclined to me.

Gregorian Office of the Dead. Let it be Thy pleasure, O LORD, to deliver me, * make haste, O LORD, to help me.

1 I waited patiently for the LORD : and he inclined unto me, and heard my calling.

I waited for Him That is the expectation of the Gentiles, and so does He wait also. "And therefore will the LORD wait that He may be gracious unto you, and therefore will He be exalted that He may have mercy upon you." The Rabbis are fond of comparing those two texts : "the heathen say, Where is now their GOD?" and that triumphant reply, "Lo, this is our GOD, we have waited for Him, and He will save us." S. Athanasius makes a simpler use of the verse ; that we are not, as it were, to outrun the providential leadings of GOD, by exposing ourselves voluntarily to our persecutors, but are rather *expecting to expect* Him, till He shall make the way clear for us, whether it is His will that we should serve Him yet longer in this world, or should glorify Him once for all in the fires. But take it rather of the expectation of the Church after the promise of now four thousand years' standing ; "The seed of the woman shall bruise the serpent's head ;" expectation revived and renewed in every age by the types and prophecies, and at last fixed to a certain epoch by the seventy weeks of Daniel. *I waited patiently.* And "we are saved by hope ;" and what is hope but patient expectation, according to that saying of the Apostle, "Then do we with patience wait for it?" And if ever of any expectation, it may be said of that expressed by the Psalmist here. And so S. Bernard says—and no one has written better than he on hope—"Thou, O LORD, art my Hope : whatever I have to do, whatever to avoid, whatever to tolerate, whatever to wish, Thou, O LORD, art my hope : the only cause and reason of my expectation. Let another speak of his own merit ; let him boast that he bears the burden and heat of the day. Let him vaunt that he fasts twice in the week, let him glory that he is not as other men ; but as for me, I have no such ground of acceptance, *I expecting will expect the Lord,* and Him alone." And again, in another place, "If rewards are promised us to be obtained through Thee, I will hope : if battles rise up against me, I will hope ; if the world rages, if Satan attacks, if the flesh lusteth against the spirit, in Thee will I hope." *And He inclined to me.* Never so gloriously, never so lovingly, as when the King, now exalted on the throne of the Cross, inclined His Head to give the last kiss of affection to His Bride ; or, as others will understand it, to ask her leave to absent Himself for a little while, according to that saying, "I will come again and receive you to Myself." S. Thomas goes through the different stages of expectation, comparing them to the increasing

L.

Isa. xxx. 18.

Isa. xxv. 9.

S. Athanas. De Fugâ, sect. 11.

Lu.

Theodoret. Rom. viii. 25.

D. C.

S. Bernard, Serm. 9, super Qui habitat.

Wasimund.

S. Thom. Aquin.

brightness of a summer morning: the first greyness, when you can hardly tell whether the day has really broken or not —and that was the hope of the patriarch; the earliest streaks of colour which tell most undoubtedly of the approaching sun, and there we have the Mosaic types; the brightness diffused over the whole earth, and there we have the predictions of the prophets; and then, lastly, the one or two actual rays which shoot up from the horizon, and in like manner such manifest revelations as Daniel's seventy weeks, and Malachi's "The LORD Whom ye seek, shall suddenly come to His Temple."

2 He brought me also out of the horrible pit, out of the mire and clay : and set my feet upon the rock, and ordered my goings.

Out of the horrible pit : or, as it is in the Vulgate, *Out of the lake of misery.* That is a noble passage of S. Augustine's, where he speaks of the barrenness of that land where the rivers of justice flow not. Mediæval writers refer to the prophecy of Zechariah, "As for thee also, by the blood of the covenant, I have sent forth thy prisoners out of the pit, wherein is no water." *Out of the mire.* And they dwell, not only on the polluting nature of sin, but on its power of engulphing and swallowing up, like an abyss of mire. And they remind us how, here also, like cures like: how man, made of clay, and to be resolved into clay again, and engaged in the hard labours which the spiritual Pharaoh exacts from the clay-field, was cured from his blindness by that clay which our LORD made. S. Gregory says well: "By the name of *mire* in Holy Scripture sometimes we understand the cupidity of earthly possessions, sometimes filthy and polluting doctrines, sometimes the desires of carnal concupiscence." And so the Prophet cries out, "Woe to him that increaseth that which is not his !—how long ?—and that loadeth himself *with thick clay !*" Or they take the *horrible pit* on the one side, and the *mire and clay* on the other, to set forth to us the shame as well as the agony of the LORD's Passion. *Upon a rock.* "O true Rock !" cries a mediæval saint; "O glorious Rock, lifting itself so serenely above the storms and clouds of this lower world! Thou only firm abiding-place for the trembling feet! Thou only secure abode for the hunted conies! What thanks or praise can I give to Thee, Rock, to which I turn my eyes, Rock of my security, Rock whence burst forth the Living Water, the Water whereof, if a man drinketh, he shall thirst no more! Rock of ages! Rock of the elect!" This is the Rock so worthily figured by the smitten rock in the wilderness: we need fear no error when we have an Apostolic commentator, "That rock was CHRIST." And not water alone did that Rock send forth : " He made him to suck honey out of the rock, and oil out of the flinty rock."

De Civ. Dei. xviii. 35.

Zech. ix. 11.

L.

S. John ix. 9.

Moral. in Job. ix. 45.

S. Thomas Aquin.

Wasimund.

1 Cor. x. 4.

Deut. xxxii. 13.

Christus misit quod promisit
Pignus Sponsæ, quam revisit
Die quinquagesimâ :
Post dulcorem melleum,
Petra fudit oleum,
Petra jam firmissima.

Adam. Victorin. Seq. "Læs jucunda."

Or yet again: we may take the rock of that Mountain which shall be established on the top of the mountains and exalted above the hills; the utmost bound of the everlasting hills. A Rock indeed! For, let the foot once be set there, and what can remove it? let the house once be established there, and what can endanger it? And then it may well follow, *and ordered my goings.* For then we shall see how all our goings have been so *ordered,* as to lead us in safety to the Everlasting LORD; *ordered,* by means that we little thought; *ordered,* by many an affliction, many a fear, many an "all these things are against me;" but *ordered* right, for all that, all things working together for our good. Or, if we take the Hebrew, the sense is even still more applicable: כּוֹנֵן אֲשֻׁרָי, making good my success: that glorious, final success, where no more temptations have to be met, no more watch and ward maintained; where the armour may be laid by; where there is perfect peace! Therefore it well follows:

Isa. ii. 1.
L.
Rupert.
B.

3 And he hath put a new song in my mouth: even a thanksgiving unto our GOD.

They are full of the different meanings which the *new song* may have: whether it is to be taken of the *Gloria in Excelsis,* first heard at Bethlehem; or the *Nunc Dimittis,* with its extension of redemption to the Gentiles. But if we take the rock as we have just taken it, of the heavenly mountain, then this can only be the song of Moses and of the Lamb: of Moses, in that the Red Sea of this life is past; and of the Lamb, in that, in a higher and more perfect sense, peace is proclaimed to men of peace in that true Vision of Peace. S. Clement of Alexandria dwells at great length on this passage, comparing our LORD, in that half Pagan way of his, to another Orpheus. In the three new songs which the Church daily employs, the *Benedictus,* the *Nunc Dimittis,* and the *Magnificat,* they see a mystical application to each Person of the Blessed TRINITY, and the especial work of that Person in the salvation of man. But why does it go on—*even a thanksgiving unto our God?* Because, as Ruffinus observes, there are many who so take a hymn of praise into their mouths, as in real truth to glorify themselves, and not GOD. Not unfitly do they compare with this *new song* the old song of corrupt human nature, which, like the syren melody of Pagan lore, endeavoured to plunge men into a bottomless

S. Chrysost. & Eligius.
D.
Hugo Victorin.
Cohort. ad Gentes.
Ay.

D. C.

abyss. But if, as before, we put these words into our LORD's mouth, then what shall the *new song* be? And they well answer that still there are three. The first is, "I ascend unto My FATHER and your FATHER ;" the second, "Whose sins soever ye remit, they are remitted unto them;" the third, "I will send the promise of My FATHER unto you."

4 Many shall see it, and fear : and shall put their trust in the LORD.

Or, as S. Augustine reads it, *The just shall see it :* a reading for which there is no authority. But we may ask, How can we see a song? And why ought not the Psalmist rather to say, They shall *hear* it? And the answer is ready : Because the hymn of praise that GOD loves is that of deeds, and not of words. Hence it is set down as the character of the wicked, "Behold, they speak with their mouth :" that is, with their mouth only. Therefore also it is said that, when

Vieyra, iii. 121.

the evil spirit troubled Saul, it was the harp of David—not his voice—which drove it away ; for the harp needs the hand to make it sound. *And fear.* But why, if it be a thanksgiving, should they fear? And they happily refer to that first new song, "Glory to GOD in the Highest," concerning which it is said that the shepherds were sore afraid. *And shall put their trust in the Lord.* For so they did when they continued, "Let us now go even unto Bethlehem."[1] And they observe also how any example of great trust has been preceded by a time of fear. "Fear not : lengthen thy cords, and strengthen thy stakes." And so the Angel to the Blessed

S. Luke i. 30.

Virgin : "Fear not, Mary ; for thou hast found favour with GOD." So to the shepherds : "Fear not ; for behold, I bring

S. Luke ii. 10.

you good tidings of great joy, which shall be to all people." So to the holy women at the Sepulchre : "Fear not ye ; for I know that ye seek JESUS, Which was crucified." It is well

S. Matt. xxviii. 3.

said, "In the way of GOD we begin by fear, and advance to courage ; for, just as in the way of the world adversity is the

S. Greg. Mor. xi. 7.

parent of fortitude, so in that of the LORD boldness ends in debility, fear in strength." And how is this? Let an early writer explain : "The beginning of our salvation and of our

Cassian. Instit. Num. iv. 17.

wisdom is, as Scripture testifieth, the fear of the LORD ; from the fear of the LORD springs salutary compunction ; from compunction self-renunciation ; from that, humility ; from humility mortification of all our appetites : by that mortification every vice is uprooted, and withers ; and vice failing, then grace takes root, and flourishes." And so it follows here : *shall fear, and shall put their trust in the Lord.* Oh happy dread, so ending in happy love! Oh hard yet dear

---

[1] It is a singular physical illustration which is given by Ayguan : "Sic enim docet experientia, quod si aliquem videris a remotis ligna cædentem, visus prius percipit illum actum, quam auditus sonum illius."

schoolmaster, thus to bring us to the only Source of perfect
security! Who would not fear, who would not tremble,
with Esther? Who would not say, ' If I perish, I perish,' if
only Ahasuerus is about to stretch forth the golden sceptre,
and to welcome the timid suppliant?

5 Blessed is the man that hath set his hope in the
LORD : and turned not unto the proud, and to such
as go about with lies.

Or, as the Vulgate gives it, *Whose hope is the Name of the
Lord :* the difference arising from the various readings of
שֵׁם, *the Name,* and שָׂם, *he set.* It is curious to see how
every little redundancy of the Vulgate is made, by these
pious writers, to give its own instruction : as here—in *Beatus
vir* CUJUS *nomen Domini spes* EJUS, where the *ejus* is the
mere colloquial repetition, they beautifully see the hope set
on the LORD as the *Author* of Faith in the *cujus*—as its
Finisher in the *ejus.* But what Name is this, save the " New
Name, which the mouth of the LORD shall name?" as so it
was fulfilled, when the command of the Angel was, " Thou
shalt call His Name JESUS." *Unto the proud.* For to some
one we must turn. If we will not listen to that dear invitation, " Look unto Me and be ye saved, all the ends of the
earth," then we turn to Satan ; for we cannot stand alone.
The μανίας ψευδεῖς of the LXX., the *insanias falsas* of the Vulgate, lead the commentators to dwell at great length on the
Bacchic frenzy of the heathen festivals ; and so to the participation in heathen crimes by those Christians " whose god
is their belly." But our version is truer and better ; and its
mystical meaning is the higher. For who is *the proud* indeed but he who said, " I will exalt my throne above the
stars of GOD : I will be like the Most High?" And there
may also be a dim allusion to the " Lawless One,"—" who
opposeth and exalteth himself above all that is called GOD,
and that is worshipped,"—under the name *proud :* and in
them *that go about with lies* to the Beast, " who doeth
great wonders, and deceiveth them that dwell on the earth
by the means of those miracles." And, as it is here said,
*Blessed is he who hath set his hope in the Lord, and turned
not unto the proud, and such as go about with lies,* so S. John
tells us, " All that dwell upon the earth shall worship him,
whose names are not written in the Book of Life of the Lamb
slain from the foundation of the world." *Whose hope is the
Name of the Lord.* The great Carmelite expositor reminds
us that, as Romulus, by offering an asylum to all the evil
doers of other places, in a short time enormously increased
the population of the new city ; so the Church has a temple
to offer us, a hiding-place to all those who are grieved with
the burden of their sins ; and this temple is none other than
the Name of JESUS. " The Name of the LORD is a strong

W.

Hugo Vic-
torin.
Alex. Ha-
lens.

Isa. lxii. 2.

Rupert.

S. Ambros.
Serm. xvii.
de Kal. Jan.

Isa. xiv. 13.

Rev. xiii. 14.

Rev. xiii. 8.

Ay.

S. Aug. de
Civ. Dei, v.
17.

tower: the righteous runneth into it, and is safe." Of this
Church, in a higher than the original sense, the LORD saith,
2 Chron. "I have chosen Jerusalem, that MY NAME might be there."
vi. 6.
And it is the multitude of those who have fled to the refuge
of this Name which have made the Church so populous: as
In Cant. i. 3. S. Bernard says, "whence, think you, is so sudden and so great
a light, save from the Name of JESUS?"

6 O LORD my GOD, great are the wondrous works
which thou hast done, like as be also thy thoughts
which are to us-ward : and yet there is no man that
ordereth them unto thee.

The Vulgate is not better than our version. *Many marvellous things hast Thou done, O Lord my God : and in Thy
strength there is none like unto Thee.*
Ay.
It is the voice of the Church exulting in the Incarnation.
*Great are the wondrous works which Thou hast done in old
time*; the creation of the world, the overthrow of the five
cities, the deliverance of the children of Israel out of Egypt,
their introduction into the land of Canaan. But this is the
wonder of wonders; this is the miracle of miracles. For
Hugo Vic-   Hugh of S. Victor well observes, that though all things
torin.
which exist were made by GOD, yet in a more especial sense
He is said to have made those things which have to do with
the reconciliation of man to Himself; and of all these the
Incarnation must hold the first place. And if we are to take
the version, *yet there is no man that ordereth them unto Thee,*
then we can only understand how the scheme of redemption
is here said to have been GOD'S counsel from the very first,
suggested to Him by no inferior or created being, but the
D. C.   marvellous work of His own eternal mind.

7 If I should declare them, and speak of them:
they should be more than I am able to express.

It is almost wonderful that so much difficulty should have
been made in the interpretation of the word *them.* Some
Lyranus.   will have it as a parallel passage to that in S. John, where
he says that if the deeds of our LORD were written every
one, he supposes that not even the world itself could contain
the books which should be written. But surely he refers to
the works which he has before mentioned, those works which
preceded the Incarnation. For see how the contrast is continued. "*If I should declare* THEM . . . Then said I, Lo, I
come." These previous actions, whether of mercy or of judgment on the one hand, and the coming to save the earth on
Ay.   the other. In the Vulgate it is, *I have announced them, and
have spoken of them : they are multiplied beyond all number.*
And in this announcement of that which is to take place,
we have the prophecies of the Incarnation. That: "Behold,
a Virgin shall conceive and bear a Son." That: "There

shall come forth a Rod out of the stem of Jesse, and a _{Isa. xi. 1.}
Branch shall grow out of his roots." That: "Behold, a
woman shall compass a man." That: "This gate shall be
shut, it shall not be open, and no man shall enter in by it; _{Ezek. xliv. 2.}
because the LORD the GOD of Israel hath entered in by it,
therefore it shall be shut." S. Thomas takes care to draw
the practical conclusion: *If I should declare them, and speak
of them, they shall be more than I am able to express:* then
in return, What shall I render unto the LORD for all the
benefits He hath done unto me?

8 Sacrifice, and meat-offering, thou wouldest not:
but mine ears hast thou opened.

Here we have in the first place a great difficulty as to the
understanding of the passage. In the LXX. it is: *Sacrifice
and offering Thou wouldest not, but a Body hast Thou prepared.* So it is in the Italic. In the Vulgate it is as we
read it, *but mine ears hast Thou opened.* S. Paul quotes
it from the LXX.: "Wherefore when He cometh into the _{Heb. x. 5.}
world, He saith, Sacrifice and offering Thou wouldest not,
but a body hast Thou prepared Me." The reason of this
variation is, that the Hebrew אָזְנַיִם was derived from זן, *to
prepare :* whence it meant the substance or body provided.
Whereas in the other sense it was taken from אֹזֶן *an ear:*
whence the difference. This is one of the most curious passages in the Psalms ; S. Paul taking it one way, followed by
the Eastern Church: the Western, together with the Jewish
commentators, taking it the other. It is remarkable that
the HOLY GHOST speaking by S. Paul, should have been
pleased to put so much honour on a translation which we
cannot believe to represent the original meaning. Nevertheless we are bound to follow that which seems to be undoubtedly the sense of the Hebrew, and to explain that. *Mine
ears hast Thou opened.* The reference is to the law in the
Mosaic ritual, "If the servant shall plainly say, I love my _{Exod. xxi. 6.}
master, my wife, and my children, I will not go out free:
then his master shall bring him unto the judges; he shall
also bring him to the door, and to the door posts; and his
master shall bore his ear through with an awl, and he shall
serve him for ever." Now see how most divinely this applies _{Ay.}
to our LORD. He, as a good servant, did indeed say, "I love _{Guarric.}
My Master," namely that FATHER, the LORD of heaven and
earth, Who appointed Me this task of redemption, and
Who hereafter shall say to Me, "Well done, good and faithful servant:" "My wife," that is, the Church, betrothed to
Me on the Cross, though the marriage can only be con-
summated in the kingdom of heaven: "and My children,"
namely those of whom it is written that, having loved Mine
own that were in the world, I loved them unto the end.
Then it proceeds: "His Master shall bring Him unto the

Guarric.

judges :" and so the FATHER caused Him to be set before those most unrighteous judges, Annas, and Caiaphas, and Pontius Pilate. " He shall also bring Him unto the door or unto the door post :" where notice the two phrases which seem so clearly to denote the upright and transverse beams of the Cross. " And His Master shall bore His ear through with an awl :" the ear simply represents the organ of obedience ; and the LORD's ear was so bored with an awl, when His hands and feet were pierced and then fastened to the Cross, that true door to eternal felicity. " And He shall be His servant for ever :" and so we are reminded that His work on earth did not cease with the Cross, seeing He " ever liveth to make intercession for us." Whence we see how marvellously true a type was Jacob of our LORD. Jacob served seven years for his Rachel ; why then did the true Jacob serve only three years and a half for the true Rachel, namely, the Church? Because, when He died on the Cross, His work was but half complete ; His labour on earth formed the first half, His prevailing intercession in heaven the second ; just as seven years are the double of three years and a half.

Serm. v. 116.   It is worth while quoting the eloquent words of Vieyra. He takes the Vulgate literally : *But Mine ears hast Thou perfected.* " He would say, Thou, LORD, rather desirest the perfection of ears, than the oblation of Thy sacrifices. Whence it follows, that the Sacrifice and Sacrament of the Altar being the greatest thing that GOD can receive from us, *quà* Sacrifice, and that the greatest thing we can receive from GOD, *quà* Sacrament, yet that He desires, even more than this, our ears, and to that end makes them perfect : *aures autem perfecisti mihi.* See if I had not good reason to say that CHRIST had rather be heard than sacramentally received. But why? To communicate, is to receive that which CHRIST *is :* to hear CHRIST, is to receive what CHRIST *says.* How can it be better to hear that which He says, than to receive that which He is? The question seems difficult, but the answer is easy ; and it is here : *aures autem perfecisti mihi.* It is possible to hear CHRIST with perfect, and it is possible to hear Him with imperfect ears. To hear Him with imperfect ears, is to hear Him without doing His works : to hear Him with perfect ears, is to hear Him and to do that which He commands. And when He is heard after this fashion, it is better to hear Him than to receive Him. CHRIST says so Himself. The woman in the Gospel praised the Blessed Virgin that she had borne CHRIST in her womb : *Beatus venter qui te portavit :* and the LORD answered, *Quinimo beati, qui audiunt verbum et custodiunt illud.* Hence it follows : that it is better to hear CHRIST, doing what He says, than to communicate in CHRIST, receiving what He is."

9 Burnt-offerings, and sacrifice for sin, hast thou not required : then said I, Lo, I come,

10 In the volume of the book it is written of me, that I should fulfil thy will, O my GOD : I am content to do it; yea, thy law is within my heart.

First, let us hear the inspired commentator on the inspired Psalm : "Wherefore when He cometh into the world, He saith : Sacrifice and offering Thou wouldest not, but a body hast Thou prepared Me : in burnt offerings and sacrifices for sin Thou hast had no pleasure. Then said I, Lo, I come (in the volume of the book it is written of Me,) to do Thy will, O GOD. Above when He said, Sacrifice and offering and burnt offerings and offering for sin Thou wouldest not, neither hadst pleasure therein; which are offered by the law; then said He, Lo, I come to do Thy will, O GOD. He taketh away the first, that He may establish the second. By the which will we are sanctified through the offering of the body of JESUS CHRIST once for all." Hence some of the Fathers have taken occasion to argue, that sacrifices were not the ordinance, but simply the permission, of GOD, allowed by Him as the lesser evil of the two, to keep off the peril of idolatry. But this opinion is a grave error : only compare these passages. "The LORD had respect unto Abel and to his offering :" "And Noah builded an altar unto the LORD; .... And the LORD smelled a sweet savour:" and the express command given to Abraham for, and as to the materials of, a sacrifice. "We know," says the Apostle, "that the law is good, if a man use it lawfully;" that is, if he use it with the remembrance of Him Whom it sets forth; if, in offering its sacrifice, he fixes the eye of faith on the Great Sacrifice for the sins of the world. And in this belief, that the Jewish sacrifices were not merely permissive, but really, as inferior sacrifices, well-pleasing to GOD, the greatest of the Fathers agree.

But we have now one of the most difficult verses in the Psalms before us; one, the full meaning of which will perhaps not be manifested till we "know as also we are known" in the next world.

THEN said I. When? And hence they take occasion to discuss the question whether, if man had not fallen, the LORD would have been incarnate; or whether His determination to take upon Him our nature depended on His prevision of our sin. Surely of these questions we may say, "Such knowledge is too wonderful and excellent for me : I cannot attain unto it." Yet doubtless they who have written on it, seem, all but certainly, to have made their point good. And this has been the general opinion from the foundation of the Church : that, whether Adam had fallen or not, the Second Adam would nevertheless have been incarnate. *Then said I, Lo, I come.* And herein are the types of our LORD in old time fulfilled. Joseph, when Israel said to him, "Do not thy brethren feed the flock in Shechem? Come, and I

Heb x. 5.

L.

Gen. iv. 4.
Gen. viii. 21.
Gen. xv. 9, 10.
1 Tim. i. 9.
S. Aug. de Caritat. Dei. xvii. 5.
S. Chrysost. Hom. xviii. in Epist. ad Heb.
S. Bernard. Hom. lviii. in Cant.

Pet. Lomb. lib. iii. distinct. 2.

Gen. xxxvii. 30.

II. C

1 Sam. iii. 8. will send thee unto them. And he said to him, Here am I."
Samuel, when he said, "Here am I, for thou didst call me."

Isa. vi. 8. Isaiah, as it is written, "I heard the voice of the LORD, saying,

D. C. Whom shall I send, and who will go for us? Then said I, Here
am I, send me." And notice the *then*. *Then*, before all worlds.
then, long since in eternity; *then*, when it was predestined
that man should have his being, the SON of GOD offered Himself to become man. But now we come to the hardest point.
*In the volume of the book it is written of Me. In the head of
the book*, it is both in the Vulgate and Italic, also in the LXX.
But *volume* is perhaps nearer to the Hebrew. Then the
question arises, in what book was this written? In the book
of predestination, S. Thomas says, and with him, many of the

Z. chief schoolmen; and in this opinion agrees Venerable Bede.
Theodoret. In the book of GOD'S Providence, some of the late school-
S. Joh. Chry-
sost. men say, which seems to be only the same sense under differ-
S. Athanas. ent words. In the whole volume of the Prophets, say most
S. Ambros. of the early Fathers. S. Ambrose, following the interpre-
in loc. tation, *In the Head of the Book*, refers this prophecy to the
Book of Genesis. "In the beginning GOD created the heavens
and the earth:" that is, by Him Who is the Beginning, the
Alpha as well as the Omega, the First not less than the Last.
S. Isidor. in S. Isidore, though referring the words to Genesis, takes a dif-
loc. ferent verse towards the commencement of that book: "This
is now bone of My bone, and flesh of My flesh," which he
applies to the Incarnation. Some later writers, and more es-
pecially Jansenius, will have it that the death of Abel is the
Procopius in especial type to which reference is here made. Procopius,
loc. that the allusion is to the ram slain instead of Isaac. A whole
A. host of saints refer it to the Psalter, in the head of which
Cassiod., book we find "Blessed is the man that hath not walked in the
Hugo Vic-
torin. counsel of the ungodly." Others would rather take it of the
Head of the Gospels: "the book of the generation of JESUS
CHRIST:" "the beginning of the Gospel of JESUS CHRIST:"
and more especially, "In the beginning was the Word, and
the Word was with GOD, and the Word was GOD." If I had
myself to decide upon all these, I should without hesitation
adopt that interpretation which understands by the *Head of
the Book*, the first verse of the Bible. *That I should fulfil Thy
will, O My God.* Hence they take occasion to dispute how far
the will of our LORD concurred in His Passion: and this verse
Synod. La- became of course a celebrated quotation in the Monothelite
teran. Con-
sult. 2. controversy. Having given these various interpretations, I
Vieyra, xv. cannot bear to pass over a wonderful passage in Vieyra:[1]
95. "All that had been written by the Prophets, or that had been
represented by the patriarchs, that CHRIST had to suffer, He
saw and knew most perfectly in that hour of His agony; and
from that very instant He engraved the principle of the Cross
on His heart: *Yea, Thy law is within My heart. In medio
cordis*, not on one side; on one side He laid His own natural

---

[1] This is curious as being Vieyra's only Sermon preached in Spanish.

feelings, fears, thoughts, cares : the Cross took the central place. *Then said I, Lo, I come.* Then? When? When He came into the world : 'Wherefore when He cometh into the world He saith, *Lo, I come.*' When? When He was prepared for His Passion : when Jesus, knowing all things that should come upon Him, went forth. When? When He was nailed to the Cross, as it is written in the same Psalm, *Corpus autem perfecisti mihi.*"

11 I have declared thy righteousness in the great congregation : lo, I will not refrain my lips, O Lord, and that thou knowest.

12 I have not hid thy righteousness within my heart : my talk hath been of thy truth and of thy salvation.

In the great congregation. And when was that? Refer it, if you will, to the *great congregation* of the Angels, the nine orders of the celestial hierarchy, to whom, before the world was, the Son of God declared His purpose of atoning for the future sins of the future man. A *great congregation* was that also, when, having now taken our nature upon Him, He stood a Child of twelve years old in the temple amongst the doctors, both hearing them and asking them questions. The *great congregation* again sets before us the five thousand fed by the side of the Lake of Gennesaret, and that would fain have taken Him by force to make Him king, Who said, My kingdom is not of this world. Once more in a *great congregation* it was that "on the last day, that great day of the feast, Jesus stood and cried, If any man thirst, let him come unto Me and drink." But that was a greater congregation still, when hanging on the Cross in the sight, doubt it not, of those twelve legions of Angels, of whom He had the night before spoken ; in the sight too, of the Prince of the Power of the Air, with all his assembled hosts ; He so declared God's righteousness as never before had it been, never since could it be manifested, in those words, " It is finished." And, as others remind us, there is yet to be a *great congregation* in which all kindreds, and tribes, and people, and nations shall be assembled together, and the judgment shall be set, and the books opened, and once more the Son of God shall declare His Father's righteousness, with the "Come, ye blessed," and "Depart, ye cursed." *Lo, I will not refrain My lips.* But how is this, when it is said, "As a sheep before her shearers is dumb, so He opened not His mouth ?" Because it is written, "There is a time to keep silence, and a time to speak." Before Caiaphas and Pontius Pilate, He was silent: but at the tribunal of the Father day by day He pleads our cause, by His own Almighty words, not less than by the all-prevailing power of the Wounds to which He points. And notice herein a promise of His intercession for us, as

W.

S. John vii. 37.

D. C.

Eccles. iii. 7.

c 2

long as the Church militant shall need it; a promise confirmed in a certain sense by an oath, *and that Thou knowest.*

G.

Whatever be the danger, whatever the affliction,—in the ex-
tremest calamity, in those days, when, if it were possible,
the very elect should fall away, I, Who stood silent in My
own defence, will speak in the cause of My Bride. When she
is persecuted by the powers of the world, when she suffers
from the attacks of heretics without, or bleeds from dissensions within, then I, that am her Advocate, I, that have promised to be her Mediator, *I will not refrain My lips, O Lord,
and that Thou knowest. I have not hid Thy righteousness.*
They fail not to tell us how in this Melchisedec, the King of
Righteousness, is the great type of our LORD, and how S.

Rom. i. 17.

Paul reminds us of the righteousness revealed by the Gospel.

D. C.

My talk hath been of Thy truth, as when in the parable of the
Good Samaritan He promised, "Whatsoever thou spendest
more, when I come again I will repay thee;" as when He
made that declaration, "No man is able to pluck them out
of My FATHER's hand:" as when He so often promised,
"Ask, and ye shall receive:" "If ye shall ask anything in
My Name, I will do it:" "In My FATHER's house are many
mansions:" and a hundred other promises where mercy and

F.

S. Bruno
Carth.

truth meet together. Or they take it, understanding the
word righteousness in the sense of the price of our acquiring righteousness, and thus of our LORD's Blood: *I have not
hid Thy righteousness within My heart;* namely, when for
our sakes the Blessed LORD permitted that heart's Blood
not to remain within His heart, but to pour forth as a torrent,
when His side was pierced with a spear.

O cor, voluptas cœlitum !
Cor, fida spes mortalium !
En ! hisce tracti vocibus
Ad te venimus supplices.

Tu nostra terge vulnera
Ex te fluente sanguine :
Tu da novum cor omnibus
Qui te gementes invocant.

13 I have not kept back thy loving mercy and
truth : from the great congregation.

L.

Why does he say it twice? And they answer, in order to
contrast the two great assemblies: that in which the LORD,
after being unrighteously judged, ascended the tribunal of
the Cross; and that in which, with the same Cross, as the
sign of His glory, He shall come again, to judge righteously
the quick and the dead.
Of this we have just spoken, and need not repeat what was
then said.

14 Withdraw not thou thy mercy from me, O

LORD : let thy loving-kindness and thy truth always preserve me.

They take it as the prayer of our LORD, not for Himself in His own person, but in that of His Church. " As even in the time of My greatest desolation on the Cross, still, after a certain sort, Thou wast present with Me, so now let not the fruits of My Sacrifice be lost; be Thou with My Church in its several passions, as Thou wast with Me in Mine own. Because I have not hid Thy mercy and Thy truth from the great congregation, from the unity of the universal Church, look Thou on Thy afflicted members; look on those who are guilty of sins of omission, and on those who are guilty of sins of commission, and withhold not Thy mercy from them." The great Saxon theologian takes it in another sense : " Whoever feels that he is set afar off from GOD by an evil life; whoever feels that sins are strengthening into customs, and customs into habits, let him cry like Esau, with an exceeding great and bitter cry, *Withdraw not Thou Thy mercy from me, O Lord.* I have withdrawn myself from Thee, but withdraw not ·Thy Presence from me." And then S. Thomas comforts such a penitent by reminding him, " The LORD is nigh unto all them that call upon Him." " I call," as the Eastern Church says, " not on account of my merits, but of my demerits; not on account of the work of my hands, but for the sake of the Hands that were stretched out on the Cross. I call, the unjust on the Just, because the Just suffered for the unjust; I call, fixing my eyes on Thee, Who didst fix Thine eyes on Peter; on the GOD Who for me suffered, for me died, for me rose again, for me ascended. And thus it is that I offer up my Kyrie Eleison." *Let Thy loving kindness and Thy truth.* Notice how often he puts these two together, as knowing that they never could have been reconciled but by the Cross. These, they say, were figured by the upright and cross-beams ; these are the two sticks which the widow of Sarepta was gathering when salvation came to her; and was gathering for this end, that she and her son might live, and not die. And he has need to use the strongest plea to win GOD's mercy ; because it follows :

Margin notes: S. Thom. Aquin. — A. — Lu. — S. Thom. Aquin. — Cathisma of the Second Stichologia at Lauds on the second Tuesday of the Great Fast. — P.

15 For innumerable troubles are come about me; my sins have taken such hold upon me that I am not able to look up : yea, they are more in number than the hairs of my head, and my heart hath failed me.

Do not let us fear to put the words into His mouth, Who Himself took our infirmities and bare our sicknesses. *Innumerable troubles.* Who ever doubted it, O Thou Man of sorrows, Whose whole life was one long sorrow ! Thou, Whose vigils on the lonely mountains were for us, that did not watch for ourselves ! Thou, Whose many fastings were for

Margin note: Luiz de Granada, Opp. ix. 271.

us, that pamper the flesh with its affections and lusts; Thou,
Whose never-ending prayers were for us, and we, miserable
creatures! will not give one poor hour to prayer for ourselves,—*innumerable troubles came about Thee* indeed! Is it
not marvellous to think how these troubles have been the food,
and strength, and consolation of the Church of GOD in the
midst of her own? Has she ever educated any great saint,
some one or more of whose works do not touch on the Passion? Oh, how their words glow like fire, burn whenever
they draw nigh Calvary! Oh, how the driest, coldest dissertation on Canon or Rubric, on disputed date or involved
history, kindles at once, if incidentally it touches on the
LORD's sufferings! And for me, on whatever I may be employed, whatever task I have in hand,—more especially when
I interpret Holy Scripture, either now, as in writing, or by
preaching,—"if I forget Thee," O most sweet Passion,
Source of all confidence, Fountain of all peace, and therefore
most fitly to be called Jerusalem, which is by interpretation
the Vision of Peace, "if I forget Thee, O Jerusalem, let my
right hand forget her cunning!"

Vieyra, Serm. vii. 196.

My sins have taken such hold upon Me. Those sins which,
since I took them on Myself that I might save a perishing
world, are now really to be called *Mine:* those sins, on account of which the light of GOD's Countenance was withdrawn
from Me, and therefore could *I not look up;* and therefore
that was My cry, *Eloi, Eloi, lama sabacthani!*

Lævin. Torrent. De Christo in Cruce pen-dent. v. 98.

Quidquid enim proavi, quidquid commisimus ipsi,
    Committentque alii quos sua sæcla manent,
Hoc insons simul omne luit pro sontibus, æquâ
    Lance volens pœnas pendere pro meritis.
Adde quod ut doceat mala vincere cuncta ferendo,
    Prævius ipse ultro pessima quæque tulit.
Scilicet hæc duræ causa est pulcherrima mortis,
    Causa quod infamem non renuitque necem.

Or, if looking for a moment from the Cross to that illustrious band of penitents who have knelt, from the days of
the good thief and the pardoned Mary, at its foot, and taking
these as their words, can we apply them at one and the same
time to Him Who did no sin, and to them who have, save
Him, no refuge from sin, better than by quoting those verses
of one who came back after long wanderings?

Shirley.

It is no merit of mine own, but Blood of Him That died,
Our Elder Brother, and Thy SON, Whom my sins crucified;
For every drop of crimson dye thus shed to make me live,
Oh, wherefore, wherefore have not I a thousand souls to give?

16 O LORD, let it be thy pleasure to deliver me:
make haste, O LORD, to help me.
17 Let them be ashamed, and confounded toge-

ther, that seek after my soul to destroy it : let them
be driven backward, and put to rebuke, that wish
me evil.

18 Let them be desolate, and rewarded with
shame : that say unto me, Fie upon thee, fie upon
thee.

19 Let all those that seek thee be joyful and glad
in thee : and let such as love thy salvation say alway,
The LORD be praised.

20 As for me, I am poor and needy : but the
LORD careth for me.

21 Thou art my helper and redeemer : make no
long tarrying, O my GOD.

It will be better to consider these verses when, by GOD's
help, they occur again, where they form the 70th Psalm.
That, as the second edition, may be considered, if I may use
the expression without irreverence, as the more perfect, in
its verbal differences, of the two ; and for that therefore we
will wait.

And now :

Glory be to the FATHER, in Whose book it is written that
the Only-Begotten should do His will ; and to the SON, Who
saith, Lo, I come : and to the HOLY GHOST, Who openeth
our ears ;

As it was in the beginning, is now, and ever shall be :
world without end. Amen.

COLLECTS.

GOD, Which art the only expectation of Thy saints, Whose Ludolph.
Advent into this world is set forth in the Head of the Book,
graft, we pray Thee, Thy Law in our hearts ; to the end that
we, declaring Thy righteousness, may be saved from every
peril. (5.)

O CHRIST the SON of GOD, Whose sorrows at the time of Mozarabic.
Thy Passion were multiplied above the hairs of Thy Head, Passiontide.
deliver us from the multitude of our sins, which, in like
manner, exceed in number our own hairs ; that the punishment due to them may be remitted by the atonement of Thy
mercy. Amen. Through Thy mercy. (11.)

Let it be Thy pleasure, O LORD, to deliver us from the Mozarabic.
hand of our enemies, and let them be desolate that would Passiontide.
swallow us up ; that we may never be ashamed through the
deeds of our own pravity, whose trust is that we have been
renewed by the glory of Thy Passion. Amen. Through
Thy mercy. (11.)

PSALM XLI.

TITLE.—English Version: To the chief musician. A Psalm of David. Vulgate: In finem, Psalmus ipsi David. Italic: In finem, Psalmus David. LXX.: Εἰς τὸ τέλος, ψαλμὸς τῷ Δαβίδ.

ARGUMENT.

ARG. THOMAS. That CHRIST, for us made poor and needy, enricheth us that understand[1] Him with eternal riches. This Psalm is to be read with the lection of Isaiah[2] the Prophet. The voice of CHRIST concerning His Passion and Resurrection, and of Judas, the traitor; and concerning the conversion of all, and chiefly of the poor. Every Christian may take this Psalm into his own mouth. Against the unclean spirit; i. e., the man of his filth.

[Notice the singular reading, *homo fæcis suæ*, instead of *pacis suæ;* and which Vezzozi does not mention.]

The Prophet speaketh concerning them that give alms. Of communion with all men, or with the poor.

VEN. BEDE. These words are already familiar to us [he is speaking of the title]; but, to handle them briefly, all has to do with CHRIST. This Psalm is honoured by its position as standing in the 40th place; a number which is frequently adapted to holiness and purification.

[He would refer to the forty days in which Moses and Elijah fasted, as well as to the Lent of our LORD; to the forty years during which the congregation of Israel were purified, so to speak, from the unbelievers who had rebelled at the instigation of the spies; and to the like instances.]

At the outset the Prophet saith, that he who giveth alms is blessed, and that with a manifold benediction: *Blessed is he that understandeth.* Next, the LORD commemorateth His glorious Passion: *Mine enemies speak evil of Me.* Thirdly, to the end that He may confirm the hope of the faithful, He predicteth His Resurrection: *Raise Thou Me up again.*

EUSEBIUS OF CÆSAREA. A prophecy of CHRIST and the traitor Judas.

S. ATHANASIUS. A Psalm proclaiming beatitude.

SYRIAC PSALTER. A Psalm of David when he appointed overseers to take care of the poor; a prophecy concerning CHRIST and Iscariot.

ARABIC PSALTER. A prophecy of the Incarnation, and the salutation of Judas.

VARIOUS USES.

Gregorian. Tuesday. Matins.
Monastic. Monday. II. Nocturn.

[1] So the reading, as Thomasius gives it, is, *intelligentes se opibus ditet eternis.* But surely it were better to read *indigentes:* thus contrasting our LORD's poverty and our own.

[2] Probably the reference is to the 53rd chapter.

Parisian. Saturday. I. Nocturn.
Quignon. Tuesday. Vespers.[1]
Ambrosian. Wednesday of the First Week. III. Nocturn.

ANTIPHONS.

Gregorian. } Septuagesima. Heal my soul, * O LORD, for I have
Monastic. } sinned against Thee.
Parisian. When I am in my health * Thou upholdest me, and
shalt set me before Thy face for ever.
Ambrosian. Haste Thee to help me, * O LORD GOD of my salvation. Kyr. Kyr. Kyr.
Mozarabic. But Thou, O LORD, * have mercy upon me : raise
Thou me up again, and I shall reward them.

1 Blessed is he that considereth the poor and
needy : the LORD shall deliver him in the time of
trouble.

We may take it in either sense : *Blessed is he that,* as
the plague-struck Israelite the brazen serpent,—as the warrior fighting against Ai the outstretched spear of Joshua,—as
the thirsting wanderer in the wilderness the rod of Moses,
uplifted to smite the rock,—*considereth the poor and needy :*
Him that was so poor in His lifetime as not to have where
to lay His head; Him that was so needy in His death, as
that they parted His garments between them, and for His
vesture they did cast lots. For who would not thus consider
Him, the Fountain of all consolation, the Source of all
strength; Him, from Whom to turn away the eye is as surely
to perish, as they that were bitten by the fiery flying serpents, and would not fix their gaze on the brazen serpent,
left their carcases in the wilderness. Or—and it is the higher
and nobler sense—the GOD blessed for evermore is here
more blessed. *Blessed is He That,* amidst the songs of the
angels, from the beatitude of His own eternity, *considereth
the poor and needy,*—namely, us, of whom it is written,
"Because thou sayest, I am rich, . . . and knowest not that
thou art wretched, and miserable, and poor, and blind, and
naked." Blessed is He That so considered them, as to leave
the Throne of the FATHER, and to come into a world that
was to despise and reject Him; according to the hymn :

D. C.
Luiz de
Granada.

A.
B.
Z.

Rev. iii. 17.

Egressus ejus a Patre :
Regressus ejus ad Patrem :
Excursus usque ad inferos ;
Recursus in thronum Dei.

The hymn
*Veni Re-
demptor.*

And compare this with the 1st Psalm, that commences with
the benediction, "Blessed is the man that hath not walked in

[1] It is remarkable that Quignon—without any authority that
I can find—commences this Psalm, both in the text and in
the index, *Beatus vir qui intelligit.*

c 3

the counsel of the ungodly." See there, His holiness; here, His compassion. He, the eternally rich, had mercy on us, the poor; He, the all-sufficient in all things, undertook the salvation of us, the needy in everything. But then, how shall that be fulfilled, *The Lord shall deliver Him in the time of trouble?* "O, My FATHER, if it be possible, let this cup pass from Me!" But it was not possible; and how then can it be said, The LORD shall deliver Him? For this reason: He and His are one. For Himself, He was not delivered; in His people He was. Nay, rather, as the great Carmelite says, "To this very end He was not delivered in Himself, that He might be in His people." He asked life of Thee, "Let this cup pass," and Thou gavest Him a long life,—the eternity of His Church. He asked deliverance, and the cup had to be swallowed; but He was delivered in His martyrs from them that kill the body, and after that have no more that they can do; in His confessors, from a flesh that lusted against the Spirit, into that happiness where—

Freed from every stain of evil,
All their carnal wars are done;
For the flesh made spiritual
And the soul agree in one :

in His virgins, from the lures and pleasures of this world, into that blessing, where more are the children of the desolate than the children of the married wife. And in them He will be delivered till the end of all things; till that most glorious and perfect jubilee, which shall introduce the sometime captives of sin and prisoners of Satan into Jerusalem which is free, which is the mother of us all. And notice that in the Vulgate it is, *Blessed is he that understandeth the poor and needy.* And there we are brought at once to the length and breadth and depth and height of the love of CHRIST, which passeth knowledge. For this is the true understanding that *Poor and Needy*, which we must do if we would be transformed, as the Apostle says, into the likeness of His sufferings. And furthermore, observe how true that is, that they who have most entirely devoted themselves to the contemplation of the LORD's Passion, have been most completely delivered in the evil day; how they, like S. Bonaventura, S. Bernard, Luiz de Granada, Gretser, and others, who wrote most lovingly, and studied most deeply, the LORD's death, were themselves most notably blessed with the grace of euthanasy. This has passed almost into a proverb.

2 The LORD preserve him, and keep him alive, that he may be blessed upon earth : and deliver not thou him into the will of his enemies.

3 The LORD comfort him, when he lieth sick upon his bed : make thou all his bed in his sickness.

They see a sixfold blessing in these promises to him who "considers" the LORD's Passion. 1. Eternal life, which is indeed being delivered from all trouble. 2. Preserving grace: *The Lord preserve him.* 3. Quickening grace: *and keep him alive.* 4. Consummating grace: *that he may be blessed.* 5. Deliverance from temptation: *deliver not him into the will of his enemies.* 6. Deliverance from temptations of the flesh: *The Lord comfort him when he lieth sick upon his bed.* But much meeter is that interpretation which sees a distinct promise for each work of temporal mercy:

Hugo Vic-torin.

Visit; give meat; give drink; redeem the slave; Clothe; house the stranger; lay the dead in grave.

L.

He is preserved, who clothes; he is kept alive, who gives food; he is not delivered into the hands of his enemies, who redeems; he is blessed, who visits; he is comforted, who takes in the stranger; he has the sick bed made, who makes the last bed of death. Or, if we take the blessing as pronounced on our LORD, He had the seven works of mercy exercised on Him.

Halens.

He had food given Him: "There they made Him a great feast."
He had drink given Him: The woman of Samaria.
Visited when sick ...... This they explain by the unction of His feet, when He was weary and distressed.
Redeemed............. Gamaliel undertaking the defence of the Apostles before the Council.
Clothed.............. In the grave-clothes, by Nicodemus.
Housed .... A certain woman named Martha received Him into her house.
Buried .... In Joseph of Arimathea's new tomb.

P.

Deliver not Thou him into the will of his enemies. Hesychius quaintly says, that the soul, anointed with the oil of mercy, slips from and eludes, like a practised athlete, the hands of those that could wrestle with it. *Make Thou all his bed in his sickness.* They point to the bed of agony of S. Laurence, which yet was so marvellously *made*, that he uttered no word of complaint; and to Tabitha, whom GOD's Apostle raised, not from the bed of sickness, but from the bed of death. The Chaldee has it, *That God may appear to him on his bed of sickness.* May appear to him first by the influx of the Paraclete in the sufferer's heart; and afterwards, as his eyes close to this world, by opening them to the more true and more glorious visions of the next. Again, they explain it of the paralytic: and that very beautifully. He indeed "understood the Poor and Needy," acknowledging His

Hesych.

P.

S. John v. 8.
Hesych.
S. Ambros.
Serm. i. de
Adv.

power as GOD Who took upon Him the form of man; and therefore his bed was made for him in his sickness: "Arise, take up thy bed, and walk." I very much prefer these interpretations to that (it seems to me) unnecessarily harsh explanation of S. Jerome and S. Augustine, which would turn a most sweet promise of relief into a prophecy of affliction. *The Lord*, they explain it, *shall turn over*, that is, *make uneasy, all his bed in his sickness*: that is, shall not allow those things to which he looks for rest really to be any comfort; and this to the end that he may more earnestly desire the better rest of Paradise. Certainly, the words of the LXX. and Vulgate are *capable* of that sense: ὅλην τὴν κοίτην αὐτοῦ ἔστρεψας ἐν τῇ ἀῤῥωστίᾳ αὐτοῦ, *universum stratum ejus versasti in infirmitate ejus.* But how[1] much more loving is the other sense! and how prettily expressed by Apollinarius!

δέμνια οἱ μετέθηκεν, ἔλυσε δὲ κήδεα νούσων.

Nor does Duport turn it badly:

πᾶν δ᾽ οἱ πορσυνέεις λέχος, ἥν μιν νοῦσος ἔχῃσιν.

G.

Isa. xxxviii.
5.

In referring, as is natural, to the case of Hezekiah, and the promise, "I will add unto thy days fifteen years," the great German commentator sees in it a promise of the life that now is, and of that which is to come: $15 = 8 + 7$: in the number *seven* we have the seven days of this worldly life; in the number *eight* we have the octave of eternal blessedness.

Cd.

S. Albert. M.

Corderius very prettily turns the text into an encouragement to Sisters of Charity to persevere in their holy work, in which they are so manifestly fellow-workers with GOD. S. Albert says, in words not very easily translated: "In hoc lecto doloris gemunt sancti. 'Infelix ego homo, quis me liberabit de corpore mortis hujus?' . . . Quod si quæris, Unde hæc miseria?' Causam reddit: *Omne stratum ejus*, sensibilem et vegetabilem carnem, O Domine, *versasti* ipsam rationem supponendo, et ipsam quodammodo subjiciendo, *in infirmitate ejus*, quando homo primo est infirmatus."

4 I said, LORD, be merciful unto me: heal my soul, for I have sinned against thee.

C.
Gen. xlii. 9.

L.
S. Thomas
Aq.

Here our true Judah declares how He took upon Himself to be surety for us, His poor little Benjamin. "I will be surety for him; of My hand shalt Thou require him. If I bring him not unto Thee, and set him before Thee, then let Me bear the blame for ever!" This has formed the versicle and response at Tierce at least from the time of S. Gregory; because, as S. Thomas says, it is only through faith in the Blessed Trinity that sins can be remitted. *Heal my soul.* Observe that it is said without any restriction, as is even

---

[1] It is fair, however, to say, that the Master of Sentences quotes the meaning of the passage, iv. Distinct. 49 a.

the case in the chapter which goes along with this versicle at
Tierce, "Heal me, O LORD, and I shall be healed; save me, *Jer. xvii. 4.*
and I shall be saved." That is, "Cost it what it may—be
the cure as painful to flesh and blood as it will—yet heal me,
yet save me!" They quote the old physician Avicenna, who *Com. i.*
says that, to preserve good health in a city, it is necessary
that the windows and doors should face towards the east.
And so, if the city of our heart is to be *healed,*—if it is to be *Ay.*
healthy,—we must keep all its outlets open to the Man Whose *Zech. iii. 8.*
"Name is the East." As it is written, "O Jerusalem, look *Baruch iv.*
about thee to the east, and behold the joy that cometh unto *36.*
thee from GOD." And again: "Open the window eastward, *2 Kings xiii.*
and shoot." *I said, Lord be merciful.* Mercy, not justice! *17.*
The extreme of mercy, for the extreme of misery. Righteous- *S. Thomas*
ness as filthy rags,—a flesh in which dwelleth no good thing,— *Aquinas.[1]*
on the one side; on the other, it is "neither herb nor mollifying *Wisd. xvi.*
plaster that restored" to health; "but Thy WORD, O LORD, *12.*
which healeth all things." "O quam affectuosa," cries out
the holy Carthusian, "et sententiosa ac efficax est oratio *D. C.*
hujus versiculi, quam utinam dicamus non ore tantum sed
interno corde et penitentia humili!" It is a wretched translation of Symmachus, *Heal my soul, albeit I have sinned* *εἰ καὶ ἥμαρ-*
against Thee: running counter to the whole system of plead- *τον.*
ing which is the glory of David—penitence. "Be merciful
unto my sin, for it is great." And so constantly is that the
basis of supplication; never such glory for GOD's forgiveness, because never such an abyss of man's sins; deep calling
unto deep.[2] *Heal my soul.* Yet once again, see in this the
petition of our LORD, speaking as bowed down with the sins
of the whole world. And well says S. Augustine: "If He *A.*
were lanced, Who rottenness had none,—if He, our very
Medicine, despised not the medicinal fire,—ought we impa-
tiently to bear the Physician burning and cutting; that is,
by every tribulation exercising us, and from sin healing us?
Wholly let us commit ourselves to the Physician's Hand,

---

[1] Let those who are in the
habit of charging mediæval writers with reliance on their merits,
only just read this most humble
passage, Tom. i. 386, of the Ve-
nice edition of 1775, and never
again venture to repeat so foul a
calumny.

[2] Though it is incapable of an
English translation, yet it is
worth while to give the word
which they assign for the reason,
quia peccavi tibi, instead of, as
one should have expected, *in te.*
It is a writer of our own, Stephen
of Canterbury, who thus ex-

presses himself: he is commenting on Deut. xxxii. 5: "Aliud
est peccare Deo, aliud non peccare, et aliud peccare in Deum.
Dupliciter peccat quis Deo, id
est, ad honorem Dei, consecutive
scilicet per gloriam ignoscendi,
quia ex peccato sequitur sæpe
contritio, ex contritione remis-
sio, quæ est gloria Dei: unde,
Da gloriam Deo; item, *Tibi soli*
peccavi. Vel peccat quis Deo
per curam: quia qui peccat, curæ
Dei se subdit, quia ab eo sa-
lutem sperat."

for He errs not, to cut the sound for the gangrened; He knoweth whereon He looketh; He knoweth what is vicious, because Himself made our nature; what Himself created, what by our lust hath been added, He discerneth."

5 Mine enemies speak evil of me : when shall he die, and his name perish?

Wisdom ii. 20.

L.

"For if the Just Man be the Son of God, He will help Him, and deliver Him from the hands of His enemies. Let us examine Him with despitefulness and tortures, that we may know His meekness and prove His patience. Let us condemn Him with a shameful death, for by His Own saying He shall be respected." So said that Court, in which Caiaphas, speaking not of himself, prophesied it expedient that One Man should die for the people. *When shall He die, and His Name perish?* Notice the twofold attack. *He die*, on the Cross. *His Name perish*, in the Church. And they thought that the latter question had once been answered, and the medal of Diocletian, which boasted

Florez. Es-
pana Sagrad.
xxi. 67.

G.

of *Christianitas devicta*, still remains, as if to bear witness to the prayer, "So let all Thine enemies perish, O Lord!" This verse, no doubt, is one reason why this Psalm has been appropriated for the dead. *When shall He die?* And the answer is, Rejoice not against me, O mine enemy: when I fall I shall also rise; when I lay me down to my last long sleep, it will not last for ever: the *name* which thou desirest to perish, if it be but written in the Book of Life, all thy malice, all thy rage, all thy enmity, cannot destroy it. Well

S. Ambros.

says S. Ambrose, "*Mine enemies speak evil of me.* Fools, who thought that the Author of Life could die! The Church laughs them to scorn, believing that, though, according to the predetermination of God, He submitted for a while to the law of death, that very death would but increase His fame and glory; and therefore she turns to Him and saith, 'I will remember Thy Name from one generation to another.' And again: 'Thy Name is as ointment poured

G.

forth.'" And so the German commentator, not less beautifully, "Wherefore they hung Me, the Righteous, between two thieves, that together with My life they might also end My remembrance. But it fell out to the contrary. For, as a grain cast into the earth perisheth not, but, if cast into good ground, produceth a large increase; so also My Name, after My death, increased into a harvest of believers in Me. . . . . Yet the devil still continueth to stir up a persecution against the Church, that, even so, My Name may perish in that. But the bones of martyrs, committed to the ground, will bud and blossom, so that the faith, strengthened and nourished by their fertility, may bring forth the finer bloom and the riper fruit."

6 And if he come to see me, he speaketh vanity :

and his heart conceiveth falsehood within himself,
and when he cometh forth he telleth it.

And thus it was when that great enemy came to *see* Him,
an hungred in the wilderness, and said, "Command that
these stones be made bread;" for truly his heart conceived
falsehood within himself, when he thought so to tempt by
his three great snares for man Him Who alone was without
sin; and *when he cometh forth he telleth it*, for he put into
the hearts of his servants the Pharisees to "speak evil" of
Him when they said, "Behold a man gluttonous and a wine-
bibber, the friend of publicans and sinners."

S. Ambrose takes the verse more especially of Judas. He   S. Ambros.
did come to see the LORD: he did speak vainly, if not by the
words, at least by the kiss of the lips; and when he had gone
forth before, he told that which the most familiar and loving
converse of his Master had taught him. For it is a very
ancient tradition that the LORD was accustomed to salute
His disciples when they returned from their different missions with a kiss; whence it was simple and natural, so to
speak, of the traitor, so far as the Apostles were concerned,
to say, "Hail, Master!" when he gave that kiss. The same
S. Ambrose, dwelling on the contrast of David within, and
the multitude to whom David's secret enemies went forth
without, reminds us of Zachariah in the temple, the Jews S. Luke i. 21.
waiting outside: Moses and Elias in the cloud with our
LORD; the unbelieving scribes and elders at the bottom of S. Matt.
the mountain without; he tells us of Cain, who said to his xvii. 5.
brother, "Let us go out into the field;"[1] of Dinah, who went
forth to see the daughters of the land; and so he exhorts us
to act up to that commandment of GOD, "Come, My people,
enter thou into thy closet, shut thy doors upon thee, hide
thyself, as it were, for a little moment, until the calamity be
overpast;" and so he warns us to be at home in the depth of
our own hearts; to be at home with none but JESUS for our
companion: to be at home as the poor and faint shadow and
foretaste of that eternal dwelling which only and truly and
everlastingly is Home.

7 All mine enemies whisper together against me:
even against me do they imagine this evil.

8 Let the sentence of guiltiness proceed against
him : and now that he lieth, let him rise up no
more.

First let us take the Vulgate as it stands, so far as the last

---

[1] It is well known that in the | "And Cain said to his brother,
LXX. before the murder of Abel, | Let us go out into the field."
we have the inserted clause, |

verse is concerned : *They devised an evil word against Me :
what, shall he that sleepeth not add again that he shall rise ?*
And next, consider the literal sense, because it leads on to
the mystical. David, an exile because of Absalom, receiving
news every moment of fresh defections from his cause : as
Ahithophel, as Shimei, as the whole band of those that afterwards would have been called Sadducees, the half infidel
multitude to whom He so often refers, e.g., " The fool hath
said in his heart, There is no GOD ;" and then again those,
like Sheba, the son of Bichri, and Nebat, the father of
Jeroboam, who desired to bring about the separation of
the ten tribes from the house of David. And so in the
hour of His deepest earthly humiliation, those that had,
after a certain sort, followed our LORD while He was working His miracles, and going about doing good, fell off and
joined themselves to His adversaries. Otherwise of the
multitudes whom the Evangelists testify to have believed
in Him after all His great miracles : " Many believed in
Him there ;" " The whole world is gone after Him :" " If we
let Him alone, all men will believe on Him ;" how could
the numbers have so dwindled down, that when He manifested Himself on the mountain of Galilee, there should
have been but five hundred of His followers, and many of
them doubting ; that after His Ascension the number of
names together should have been but a hundred and twenty.
Then one may well say, *What, shall he that is asleep not add
again to arise ?* And, so explaining the passage, many see in
it the reason given by our LORD, why, just before, He said,
They devised an unjust word against Me, the unjust
word being, " That Deceiver said :" " So the last error shall
be worse than the first ;" and the proof of its injustice being
the fact of the Resurrection.

S. Isidor. de
Pass. et
Resurrect.
cap. 53.
Genebrard.

9 Yea, even mine own familiar friend, whom I
trusted : who did also eat of my bread, hath laid
great wait for me.

Euseb.
Ambros.
S. John xiii.
18.

The man of my peace, as the Vulgate more literally and
beautifully gives it. And Judas was indeed the man of *His*
peace, Who on the same night of His betrayal said, " Peace
I leave you, My peace give I unto you." And remember,
that this is no accommodation or mystical reference : it is
the explanation given by our LORD Himself, and that in the
strongest possible way, with a " that the Scripture might be
fulfilled." *Whom I trusted.* Trusted with the gift of the
keys ; trusted with power over devils, and to cure all manner
of diseases : trusted, in a more especial manner, in that he
alone dipped with Me in the dish : trusted, to the end My
people, in all ages, might learn to despair of none, however
far gone in sin : and trusted, finally, when grace was quite
quenched, with that awful commission, by which the salvation

Ruffinus.
A.

of man was assured,—THAT THOU DOEST, DO QUICKLY!—
Warning, as it were, against this, the Prophet had written long
before: "Take ye heed every one of his neighbour; and Jer. ix. 4.
trust ye not in any brother; for every brother will utterly
supplant, and every neighbour will walk with slanders." *Who
did also eat of My bread.* And this very expression might
be enough in itself to settle the disputed question, whether
Judas did or did not receive our LORD's Body and Blood.
The exhortation of the English Church manifestly assumes
it; perhaps the general sense of the Primitive and Mediæval L.
Church, though with many exceptions, is for it. It is a for-
midable list which they give of the authorities which take
such a view: Pseudo Dionysius,[1] Origen, S. Chrysostom, Ven.
Bede, S. Cyprian, S. Leo, S. Bernard, S. Cyril of Jerusalem,
S. Cyril of Alexandria, Hugh of S. Victor, Euthymius Zi-
gabenus, S. Hrabanus Maurus. To these we may add the
public offices of both East and West. In the West:

> Cibum turbæ *duodenæ*
> Se dat suis manibus.

And again:

> Turbæ fratrum *duodenæ*
> Datum non ambigitur.

The Eastern still more plainly:

νόμου φιλίας ὁ δυσώνυμος Ἰσκαριώτης γνώμῃ ἐπιλαθόμενος, οὓς Ode viii. Tro-
parion iii.
ἐνίψατο ηὐτρέπισε πρὸς προδοσίαν πόδας· καὶ σοῦ ἐσθίων ἄρτον, of the Canon
Σῶμα θεῖον, ἐπῆρε πτερνισμὸν ἐπὶ σὲ, Χριστὲ, καὶ βοᾷν οὐ συνῆκε· at Lauds on
Τὸν Κύριον ὑμνεῖτε τὰ ἔργα, καὶ ὑπερυψοῦτε εἰς πάντας τοὺς αἰῶνας! Great Thurs-
day.

I cannot help giving, as the best commentary on this part
of the Psalm, the Stichoi of Great Thursday with their
Stichera;—and I purposely do so in Greek, rather than in a
translation, in order to tempt my brethren to study those
glorious hymns for themselves, by—where I can—showing
them the beauty of Eastern hymnology.

Idiomelon. Σήμερον τὸ κατὰ τοῦ Χριστοῦ πονηρὸν συνήχθη Ps. ii. 1.
λαοὶ ἐμελέ-
συνέδριον, καὶ κατ' αὐτοῦ κενὰ ἐβουλεύσατο, παραδοῦναι Πιλάτῳ εἰς τησαν κενά.
θάνατον τὸν ἀνεύθυνον.[2] Σήμερον τὴν τῶν χρημάτων ἀγχόνην Ἰούδας
ἑαυτῷ περιτίθησι, καὶ στερεῖται κατ' ἄμφω, ζωῆς προσκαίρου, καὶ θείας.
Σήμερον Καϊάφας ἄκων προφητεύει· συμφέρει, λέγων, ὑπὲρ τοῦ λαοῦ
ἕνα ἀπολέσθαι· ἦλθε γὰρ ὑπὲρ τῶν ἁμαρτιῶν ἡμῶν τοῦ παθεῖν, ἵνα ἡμᾶς
ἐλευθερώσῃ ἐκ τῆς δουλείας τοῦ Ἐχθροῦ, ὡς ἀγαθὸς καὶ φιλάνθρωπος.

Stichos. Ὁ ἐσθίων ἄρτους μου, ἐμεγάλυνεν ἐπ' ἐμὲ
τὸν πτερνισμόν.

Idiomelon. Σήμερον ὁ Ἰούδας τὸ τῆς φιλοπτωχείας κρύπτει προσω-

---

[1] This passage I cannot find:
L. gives it as Eccl. Hierarch. § 13.
But my edition does not divide
that work into sections; and I
have vainly looked through it.

The other authorities have been
verified.
[2] Guiltless, because *not liable
to trial:* a very common hymno-
logical sense.

πεῖον, καὶ τῆς πλεονεξίας ἀνακαλύπτει τὴν μορφήν· οὐκέτι τῶν πενήτων
φροντίζει· οὐκέτι τὸ μύρον κιπράσκει τὸ τῆς ἁμαρτωλοῦ· ἀλλὰ τὸ οὐρά-
νιον μύρον, καὶ ἐξ αὐτοῦ νοσφίζεται τὰ ἀργύρια. Τρέχει πρὸς Ἰουδαίους,
λέγει τοῖς παρανόμοις· Τί μοι θέλετε δοῦναι, κἀγὼ ὑμῖν παραδώσω αὐτόν;
Ὦ φιλαργυρίας προδότου ! εὔωνον ποιεῖται τὴν πρᾶσιν· πρὸς τὴν γνώμην
τῶν ἀγοραζόντων τοῦ πωλουμένου τὴν πραγματείαν ποιεῖται· οὐκ ἀκρι-
βολογεῖται πρὸς τὴν τιμήν, ἀλλ᾽ ὡς δοῦλον φυγάδα ἀπεμπωλεῖ· ἔθος
γὰρ τοῖς κλέπτουσι ῥίπτειν τὰ τίμια· νῦν ἔβαλε τὰ ἅγια τοῖς κυσὶν ὁ
μαθητής· ἡ γὰρ λύσσα τῆς φιλαργυρίας κατὰ τοῦ ἰδίου Δεσπότου μαί-
νεσθαι ἐποίησεν αὐτόν· ἧς τὴν πεῖραν φύγωμεν, κράζοντες· Μακρόθυμε
Κύριε, δόξα σοι.

Stichos.[1] Ἐξεπορεύετο ἔξω καὶ ἐλάλει ἐπὶ τὸ αὐτό.

Idiomelon. Ὁ τρόπος σου δολιότητος γέμει, παράνομε Ἰούδα·
νοσῶν γὰρ φιλαργυρίαν, ἐκέρδησας μισανθρωπίαν· εἰ γὰρ πλοῦτον ἠγά-
πας, τί τῷ περὶ πτωχείας διδάσκοντι ἐφοίτας ; εἰ δὲ καὶ ἐφίλεις, ἵνα τί
ἐπώλεις τὸν ἀτίμητον, προδιδοὺς εἰς μιαιφονίαν ; Φρίξον, ἥλιε· στέναξον,
ἡ γῆ, καὶ κλονουμένη βόησον· Ἀνεξίκακε Κύριε, δόξα σοι.

Stichos. Λόγον παράνομον κατέθεντο κατ᾽ ἐμοῦ.

S. Ambros.
in loc. cit. &
Origen.

However, there are not wanting those, who denying that
Judas did eat of our LORD'S Body, see in the *Bread* here
merely a metaphor of having been a listener to the words of
CHRIST; as do some of those even who agree in the usual
belief. Lorinus rather understands, by the eating of the
bread, the dipping of the morsel in the dish; which, by the

Ay.

general consent of the Fathers, was not the Holy Eucharist.
So again the great Carmelite expositor. But yet I must
think that the more beautiful explanation, which understands
My Bread, of the Blessed Eucharist: *My Bread* most truly,
as not only *Mine*, but Myself.

> Verbum Caro panem verum
> Verbo carnem efficit.

Genebrard.

This sense is
originally
Richard of
S. Victor's :
it is given
briefly by S.
Bonaven-
tura, and
expanded
at great
length in
a very pious
sermon by
Philip de la
Grève : yet
neither
quotes Ri-
chard.

Others see in the *man of my peace* a plain reference to Absalom, whose name is, by interpretation, the *peace of the
father*. And there is yet another sense in which it is very
beautifully taken; namely, as the complaint of the new nature against the old Adam : in fact as a mystical amnesty in
the struggle which S. Paul describes in Romans vii. The
flesh *is the one familiar friend* of the spirit; the friend in
whom *it trusted* too much, and *great wait* indeed does the
one lay against the other. " For the flesh lusteth against the
spirit, and the spirit against the flesh : and these are contrary one to the other ; so that ye cannot do the things that
ye would." One remark yet remains to be made with reference to the Vulgate close of the verse : *hath magnified his*

[1] Notice the extreme beauty
of this Stichos. It is, of course,
simply the LXX. reading of ver.
6 of this Psalm : yet how admirably the ἐξεπορεύετο ἔξω of
Ahithophel answers to the εὐθέως
ἐξῆλθεν of Judas !

supplantation against me. Other sins may indeed to a cer- **Cd.**
tain extent be the betrayal of CHRIST: but the profanation
of the Blessed Eucharist in a most emphatic and most enormous degree; this indeed is not to betray only, but *to mag-*
nify our betrayal.

10 But be thou merciful unto me, O LORD : raise
thou me up again, and I shall reward them.

"Hitherto," says the great Carmelite, "the Psalm hath **Ay.**
spoken of the Passion of CHRIST, it now goes on to tell of His
Resurrection. And this Psalm is divided into four clauses. In
the first, He prayeth that He may be raised : *raise Thou Me up*
again. Next, He expresseth His certain assurance of being
heard : 'By this I know.' Thirdly, He showeth that He *hath*
been heard : 'Mine enemy doth not triumph.' And finally,
from all that has gone before, He resteth to praise : 'Blessed
be the LORD GOD of Israel.'" *Raise Thou Me up.* Here is an
example of a prayer offered for that which we have a promise of, Vieyra, ix.
whether we pray or not, like "Thy kingdom come." But yet 274.
it was a belief of some of the Fathers, and of more mediæval
writers, that whereas, when the prophecy was made, how the
Son of Man should be three days and three nights in the
heart of the earth, it was intended to be taken in its fullest
and most natural sense, according to which our dear LORD
could not have risen till three in the afternoon of the Monday, yet, in the mercy of the FATHER, and in compliance
with the prayer of the SON, the time was shortened, as much
as it could be, while the words of prediction remained sure.[1]
And I shall reward them. How? How, but by giving them
a crown of gold for a Crown of Thorns; by bestowing on **A.**
them the manna of His quickening Body for the gall which
they presented to Him that He might eat; by refreshing S. Hiero-
them with the River of Water of Life instead of the vinegar nym.
that they held to His dying lips : by writing their names in
the Book of Life, whereas His was only written by them as
the title of His accusation on the Cross. How, but by fulfilling His own prayer, "FATHER, forgive them?" when the

---

[1] With respect to the expression three days, the writer acci-
dentally met with an anecdote
which may be worth repeating.
It is contained in a letter from
Howard the philanthropist to
a Dr. Stennett, an Anabaptist.
After mentioning the capital punishment of a fraudulent trades-
man, and the sentence that his
body was to remain exposed three
days in a street of Constanti-
nople, he continues : "It being
very hot weather, August, I said
it was impossible to remain three
days in the street. 'Yes, it did,'
said my informant; 'for our
three days may be only five or
six-and-twenty hours. If one
half-hour before sunset, we call
it a day: if half an hour after
sunrise, we call it a day : it is
another day.'"—Ivimey's Hist.
of English [Ana]baptists, vol. ii.
p. 361.

Z.
S. Cyril.
Hieros.

Durandus.

Ay.

Philip de
Grève.

Isa. xxxviii.
1.

preaching of the Rock of the Church brought in three, and then five thousand to the True Rock. And notice how in this our LORD speaks both as GOD and as Man: *raise Thou Me up;* so He prays as Man: *and I shall reward them;* so He promises as GOD. This verse is one of the causes why the present Psalm forms a part of the Office for the Dead. *Raise Thou Me up again,* exclaims the corpse from which the spirit has gone forth, that we are now about to sow in dishonour, in weakness, in corruption; *and I shall reward them:* I shall have my revenge over those enemies who, during my sojourn upon earth, sought to make me the instrument of pollution and hindrance to the soul, by becoming in turn its great assistance, its everlasting helpmeet, in the unceasing service of GOD.

11 By this I know thou favourest me : that mine enemy doth not triumph against me.

12 And when I am in my health, thou upholdest me : and shalt set me before thy face for ever.

In the literal sense, probably, the meaning is, that the success given to the stratagem of Hushai, and the period thus put to the immediate hopes of Absalom, were sufficient to show the ultimate success of the enterprise; for no Saint ever seems so thoroughly, as David, to have trusted for the future because he had been blessed for the past: "Because Thou hast been my help, therefore under the shadow of Thy wings will I rejoice." And thou, too, poor trembling Christian, ready to give up all for lost, because thou art not always successful, ready to say, "I shall not see the LORD, even the LORD, in the Land of the Living," because He sometimes seems to shut His eyes from thee,—what are the triumphs of the enemy over thee? Are they more frequent than in times past? When he obtains for a while the victory, dost thou arm more quickly from the defeat? When thou hast truly fallen, art thou more grieved for the sin? Then say it with confidence, say it with truth, say it whatever may appear on the other side: *By this I know Thou favourest me : that mine enemy doth not triumph against me.*

And when I am in my health. As the hymn says;

> O how glorious and resplendent,
>   Fragile body, shalt thou be,
> When endued with so much beauty,
>   Full of health, and strong, and free,
> Full of vigour, full of pleasure,
>   That shall last eternally!

And where is it we can only truly say, *when I am in my health,* but in that city, whose inhabitant, as Isaiah speaks, "shall no more say, I am sick?" *Thou upholdest me.* *Upholdest me* that I can never more fall into sin which first brought pain and sickness into the world: *upholdest me*, or otherwise how should I ever support the glorious Beatific vision which is promised in the next clause, *and shalt set me before Thy face for ever?* Or we may take it of that dear LORD, Who after His death, rose again to life, never more to suffer pain or weariness, as when He "being weary with His journey sat upon the well, or slept through the storm on the Lake of Gennesaret, when His disciples took Him even as He was into the ship, but now in the same Body has ascended into heaven; *Thou upholdest Me, and shalt set Me before Thy face for ever:* when the FATHER said unto Him, "Sit Thou on My right hand, until I make Thine enemies Thy footstool;" and "The last enemy that shall be destroyed is death." But then also we may take this, if in a lower, still in a comforting sense. *When I am in my health.* Why *my* health? Because He speaks of the health, vigour, actual keeping of GOD's commandments, into which every Christian is put by Baptism: MY *health*, because Thou gavest it to me; but still even so, even then, taking it at its best, *when I am in* MY *health*; it is not by my own power, I have no strength to hold firm my position, much less to advance on in it; *When I am in my health*, THOU UPHOLDEST ME. It teaches us the same thing as that other Psalm, "Blessed be the LORD my strength .... Who subdueth *my* people that *is under* me." And again they take it in a nobler sense. *When I am in my health;* that is, when I shall have overcome all Mine enemies, when I shall have passed through all My tribulation, when the crooked shall have been made straight, and the rough places plain, then *Thou upholdest Me:* that is, Thou hearest My petition. "And I knew that Thou hearest Me always." And therefore here we have a prophecy, and an invaluable prediction it is, of the everlasting Priesthood of CHRIST. And the Vulgate answers such a meaning still more strikingly. *But Me hast Thou upheld because of Mine enemies.* And what can we add, O innocent, O gentle, O immaculate Lamb of GOD, to this, save the dying speech of the poor thief? "We indeed justly." I have no other plea, save Thy spotlessness, and mine own guilt. But Thou wast heard because of Thine innocence, and as for me, Thou wilt hear me because of my guilt: "pardon my iniquity, for it is great." *Shalt set Me before Thy face.* And they tell us the blessing of such a presentation before GOD; how it enlightens our understanding, how it purifies our will, how it humbles and keeps us humble before Him, in Whose sight not even the heavens are pure.

Margin notes: Ps. viii. 1. 1 Cor. xv. 26. Cd. Ps. cxliv. 2. S. Chrysost. Hesych. S. John xi. 41. L. Euseb. in Heb. vii. 23. D. C. Ay.

13 Blessed be the LORD GOD of Israel : world without end. Amen.

Here we end the first book of the Psalms. Of this division I shall have to speak at length in the First Dissertation of this volume. And here, too, in this Psalm we have

Ay.

G.

for the first time the word *Amen* : the word which from that time to this has been the seal of so many prayers, long since heard, long since fulfilled, and the many occasions of which have long since been forgotten in that land where mortality is swallowed up of life. As Gerhohus says, Who can add to such a plain and simple ascription of praise which comes in as the closing harmony after all the discord of a Psalm so equally divided between triumph and depression?

And therefore:

Glory be to the FATHER, Who raiseth up the SON again that He may reward His enemies; and to the SON, Who considereth the poor and needy: and to the HOLY GHOST, Who upholdeth us when we are in our health;

As it was in the beginning, is now, and ever shall be: world without end. Amen.

COLLECTS.

Ludolph.

O Everlasting GOD, Who dost forgive and pass by our sins, and in Whose promise to show mercy to the needy we put all our hope of escaping the evil day, have compassion we pray Thee, on our sorrows; so that while Thou gently concealest our casual faults, Thou mayest graciously give us the pardon of our souls. Through. (2.)

Mozarabic.

O CHRIST, SON of the living GOD, against Whom Thine enemies laid to Thy charge things which Thou knewest not; do Thou in every kind of temptation defend us with Thy guardian shield; that through Thee we may never yield to our adversaries, Who ever makest us to conquer by the Omnipotence of Thy Deity. Amen. Through. (11.)

PSALM XLII.

TITLE.—To the Chief Musician, Maschil, for the sons of Korah. Vulgate: To the end; an understanding for the sons of Korah. Or rather: To the Supreme; an instruction of the Sons of Korah.

ARGUMENT.

Here we have the first of the Psalms which are ascribed to the family of Korah, of which there are eleven, and all of them are singularly beautiful. It was to this family that the especial charge of the Temple gates was committed by David; and down to the time of Jehoshaphat they maintained their reputation for psalmody. For, in the great battle between Jehoshaphat and the Ammonites, before 2 Chron. xx. the conflict began we read : "And the Levites of the children of the 19. Kohathites, and of the children of the Korhites, stood up to praise the LORD GOD of Israel with a loud voice on high." There can be no doubt that this Psalm was written by some of the Levites who followed David when he fled from Absalom; and either the day before or the day after he passed over the Jordan. But more probably *2 Sam. xvii. 22.* after he had passed the Jordan; because, as we have seen, Psalm 41 appears to have been written after David had become acquainted with the success of Hushai's false counsel, which counsel necessitated his immediate crossing the Jordan. And, therefore, unless we arbitrarily imagine the 42nd to precede in order of time the 41st Psalm, the present one must have been composed after that passage. Besides, as we shall see at verse 6, the whole feature seems rather that of our looking towards Jerusalem, as would naturally have been the case when the Jordan was passed, than away from it, as if it still had to be crossed. Only this seems certain, that the present and the preceding Psalm were written, if not on the same day, at least on two succeeding days.

ARG. THOMAS. That CHRIST puts away our wickedness by the ablution of Baptism. The voice of CHRIST, and of penitence after Baptism, hastening to or desiring the fruition of tears. Before Baptism the voice of CHRIST and them who are about to obtain faith. Read it with Isaiah.[1]

VENERABLE BEDE. The sons of Korah, as Heman, Ethan, Asaph, Jeduthun, were not writers of Psalms, but singers. They were elected by David to psalmody, and, on account of the significance of their name, had their titles prefixed to their works. Kore, then, by interpretation is Calvary; in the place of which name our LORD was crucified: wherefore they are worthily called the sons of Kore, who under the banner of that Passion, serve with the whole devotion of their minds. This Psalm fits every Christian who is kindled with the flame of the LORD's love. We ought all to remember what blessed Jerome saith: "While I carefully examine the whole Psalter, I no where find that the sons of Kore were the authors of a melancholy Psalm; everything in their Psalms is glad and joyous; and while they despise earthly delights, and desire that which is celestial and eternal, they well agreed with the meaning of their name." The son of Kore, signed, as we have said, by the honourable mark of the Cross, at the very opening of the Psalms professeth that the whole desire of his heart is fixed on the LORD. *Like as the hart, &c.* In the second part he speaketh to his soul, and telleth her not to be troubled in the stormy sea of this world, because GOD is her certain and lifelong rest and support. *Why art thou so heavy, O my soul?*

SYRIAC PSALTER. A supplication of the Prophets; and it is the Psalm which David sang while he was an exile, and longing to return to Jerusalem.

EUSEBIUS OF CÆSAREA. A supplication of the Prophets over the rejection of the Jewish people.

VARIOUS USES.

Gregorian. Ferial: Tuesday. Matins. Office of the Dead. III. Nocturn.

Parisian. Wednesday. Tierce.

---

[1] No doubt reference is made to the 60th chapter, which is the prophecy for the solemn seasons of Baptism, both in the Mozarabic and Ambrosian rituals.

Ambrosian. First Week. Thursday. I. Nocturn.
Quignon. Wednesday. Sexts.
Monastic. Monday. II. Nocturn.

ANTIPHONS.

Gregorian. Office of the Dead. My soul * is athirst for the living GOD : when shall I come and appear before the Presence of GOD ?
Ambrosian. My soul * is athirst for Thee, O GOD. Kyr. Kyr. Kyr.
Monastic. (In Septuagesima.) Heal my soul, O LORD, for I have sinned against Thee.
Quignon. Hope * thou in the LORD, for I shall yet give Him thanks.
Parisian. Hope thou in GOD, * my soul : the salvation of my countenance, and my GOD.

1 Like as the hart desireth the water-brooks : so longeth my soul after thee, O GOD.

Numb. xv. 49.

The sons of Korah, as we are expressly told by Moses, died not when Korah perished ; and to them it was that the temple music became in great measure entrusted. The names of those sons who thus escaped when the earth opened, were Assir, Elkanah, Abiasaph ; and the tradition of the Jews is that their family was illustrious for the gift of prophecy, even down to the time of Solomon. To them are attributed Psalms 44, 45, 46, 47, 48, 49, 84, 85, 87, 88. Eusebius speaks of eight in all ; but he perhaps counts the 43rd as theirs, because although it is now called a Psalm of David, it has usually been considered a part of the preceding compositions. Mediæval writers remark how here, as so often, it was the will of GOD to raise up saints where they could have been least looked for. Who would imagine that from the posterity of him who said, " Ye take too much upon you, ye sons of Aaron," should have risen those whose sweet Psalms would be the heritage of the Church of GOD to the end of time ?

In Ps. xxii. & Ps. xxix. 8.

We have already seen how the hart, or hind, is a symbol of our dear LORD. Here, before entering again on the same type, it will be well to give the various proprieties of the hind, as seen by early commentators.

Hug. Card.

Clune natans portat : vocat Hydros : cornua mutat :
Cor senis ossescit : salit : et sitit ; et juvenescit :
Sylvester : sapidus : vivax : velox : sine caudâ :
Pes durus : fulvusque pilus ; venatio fœtus.
Pugnat ob uxores : fusâ pinguedine squallens.
Surdus demissis : bene rectis auribus audit.

Remember that it is the sons of the Cross, the true Crusaders against the world, the flesh, and the devil, who take this Psalm in their mouth. And who then shall we say is this *hart*, this morning hind, with whom their song begins? Who but He Whom we saw so lately as the hind persecuted to death by the hands of His pursuers? And during that chase, while on the one hand false witnesses stood up against Him, and laid to His charge things that He knew not, and on the other, Chief Priests and Scribes were exclaiming, "He saved others, Himself He cannot save," here we learn what that was for which during the long course of that weary day, this Hind thirsted. For so He had said Himself long before, "I have a Baptism to be baptized with, and how am I straitened till it be accomplished;" and so He said in the midst of His Passion, "I thirst."

> O JESU mirifice
> Quid est quod agebas?
> Tu de siti conquerens
> De cruce silebas:
> Non quod hoc doloribus
> Magis sentiebas:
> Sed salutem potius
> Nostram sitiebas.

Yes; it was for the salvation of the whole race of man which lay at the end of His course, that He then thirsted, when that prophecy of Job was fulfilled: "Is there not an appointed time to man upon earth?" That is, a time appointed for his salvation: "are not his days also like the days of an hireling?" Job vii. 1. That is, do not his days of eternal life depend on the days of Him Who is a true hireling, "Who for the joy that was set before Him endured the Cross, despising the shame, and is set down at the right hand of the throne of GOD." But as, of Judg. i. 15. old, Achsah desired the upper springs, so did our Hart pant not only after those waters of His Passion, but also after those upper springs which were to depend on them, the grace of the HOLY GHOST Which "was not yet given, because that JESUS was not yet glorified." And just as we saw in that verse where the voice of the LORD is said to "prepare the hinds," that they may be a type of CHRIST's people, as well as of CHRIST, so also we may understand it here. And what water-brooks do they pant for, save that most precious stream which floweth from their LORD's side for the cleansing of the whole world? And so again, if not for the water of Baptism now, because that has already taken place once that it might be for ever, yet at all events, for the every-day forgiveness of transgression, which is a part of the effect of Baptism. Wherein it is written so marvellously in the Nicene Creed: "I acknowledge one Baptism for the remission of"—not sin, but—"sins." And this, not as if those Fathers of Nicæa imagined that Baptism would be usually conferred on adults, but because, full of the HOLY GHOST as they were, they saw that there could be no forgiveness of actual sins, except that which is founded upon Baptism as upon a base; since none could

II.   D

Thomas.
Vol. i. 479.

receive the power of the keys unless he was baptized, any
more than the benefit of them could reach an unregene-
rate man. And therefore very meetly was this Psalm part
of the early Office of Baptism; and I have already quoted
that beautiful hymn in the Gregorian Antiphonary:

> Currite *sicut cervi ad fontes* vivos verbi :
> Bibite aquam vivam : habetis plenam vitam.

Well, then: *as* CHRIST Himself desired His Passion; *as* the
Confessors of old drank and were refreshed of the graces of
the HOLY GHOST; *so*, say the sons of Korah, *longeth my
soul after Thee, O God*. It is hardly worth while seriously
to refer[1] to that interpretation of S. Augustine, which nevertheless was the stock allegory of the Middle Ages. "It
destroys serpents, and after the killing of serpents, it is
inflamed with thirst yet more violent; having destroyed serpents, it runs to *the water-brooks*, with thirst more keen than
before. The serpents are thy vices; destroy the serpents of
iniquity, then wilt thou long yet more for the Fountain of
Truth."[2] And so again in that the hart is the only animal
which brings forth its young with pain, here they see a type
of that Passion by which our LORD, so to speak, brought the
Church, then not existing, into the world. S. Peter Damiani
makes a beautiful use of the metaphor in his "Rhythm on
the Glory and Joys of Paradise."

> Ad perennis vitæ fontem
> Mens sitivit arida,
> Claustra carnis præsto frangi
> Clausa quærit anima :
> Gliscit, ambit, eluctatur
> Exul frui Patriâ.

2 My soul is athirst for GOD, yea, even for the
living GOD : when shall I come to appear before the
presence of GOD?

First notice the very remarkable reference which there
here is to the Blessed Trinity. *For God: the living God:
the Presence of God.* And observe that here, as almost
always, it is the First Person of the ever-blessed Trinity

[1] Herman Hugo, who died of the plague in his charitable labours amongst plague-stricken men at Antwerp, has an elegy
in his *Pia Desideria* on this verse, where he does not fail to introduce the legend of the stag and the serpent.

Vis dicam mea lux quam te meus
    ardor anhelat?

Cervus ut irrigui fontis anhelat
    aquas.
Nempe venenifero pastas ser-
    pente medullas
Cervus agit totis hausta venena
    fibris.

[2] Of this passage and others like it I could say with Lorinus:
"Indico fontes talia sitientibus alia ipse sentiens et sitiens."

Who is mentioned without any epithet or qualification of Deity. And then, with respect to our LORD, it is well said, *the living God.* For, as we have just been hearing Him speak in the days of His Passion, so it is only fit that we should be reminded of His Resurrection. And yet once more. *When shall I come to appear before the presence of God?* That GOD, the Blessed SPIRIT, Who evermore dwells and manifests Himself in His regenerate people; when shall they who have hitherto been His hosts in His temple, go to be His guests in that temple which, as the love of the SON has prepared for them, so the love of the SPIRIT has prepared them for? As it is in the Vulgate: *My soul is athirst for the mighty, living God:* and some copies of it read, instead of *fortem, fontem.* *To God which is my living fountain.*[1] On this verse again the Belgian poet, Herman Hugo, has an elegy of such rare beauty that I cannot refrain from quoting some of its verses:

Præmonstr.

> O qui sidereas ducis fortissime turmas,
>   Qui cingunt decies millia mille latus,
> Quam tua regifico radiant prætoria luxu!
>   Mens stupet et tantæ languet amore domus.
> Stat placidus positis aquilonum flatibus æther,
>   Servat et æternus longa serena tenor.
> Sed neque flammantes liquido lavat æquore currus,
>   Nec subit occiduas sol fugitivus aquas:
> Nec præmit astra dies, neque sol fugat æthere stellas,
>   Nec premitur lassus nocte fugante dies.
> O qui sidereas habitas, Rex maxime, sedes,
>   Quot tua deliciis affluit illa domus!
> Jam flagrat et studio nimis inflammata videndi,
>   Mens desiderio deficit ægra suo.

But there can be no lovelier commentary on the verse than that of S. Bonaventura, when he says, "What would I not give to behold the multitude, composed not only of victors from among every tribe of men, but of Angels, of Archangels, of every dignity of the celestial hierarchy? Of these I may speak; of these I can perchance think: but of the King Who is in the midst of them,—but of the LAMB That liveth, and yet hath, as it were, been slain, what voice of man can say a single word, what heart of man can think a single thought? My soul is athirst for that city which is the dwelling-place of all Angels, all saints: where eternal salvation abounds as from an overflowing fountain; where truth reigns, where none deceives or is deceived, where nothing that is beautiful can be ejected, where nothing that is wretched can be admitted." It is not wonderful that most of those saints who have preached on the passion of S. Stephen, should have

---

[1] And so I find it in the *Psalterium Trilingue* (Basle: 1545), | which has been my handbook all through this work.

referred to this text. Let us end our commentary on it with
a quotation from the noble sequence of Adam of S. Victor:

Forward, champion, in thy quarrel!
Certain of a certain laurel,
  Holy Stephen, persevere :
Perjured witnesses confounding,
Satan's synagogue astounding
  By thy doctrine true and clear.

Lo, in heaven thy Witness liveth :
True and faithful proof He giveth
  That His martyr's cause is right :
Thou by name *a crown* impliest ;
Meet it is in pangs thou diest
  For a crown of glorious light.

For a crown of life unfading
Bear the torturer's brief invading ;
  Victory waits to end the strife :
Death thy heavenly birth revealeth ;
And thy latent pang unsealeth
  To thy soul a truer light.

3 My tears have been my meat day and night :
while they daily say unto me, Where is now thy
GOD?

Where is now thy God? It has been the question from
GOD's enemies from that time to this. "Who are they
among all the gods of these lands that have delivered their
land out of my hand, that the LORD should deliver Jerusalem
out of my hand?" "Then she that is mine enemy shall see
it, and shame shall cover her which said unto me, Where is
the LORD thy GOD? Now shall she be trodden down as the
mire in the streets." Where is thy GOD? It was the question demanded of those early Christians when their great
persecutor entered in the records and stamped on the medals
of the empire that the Christian superstition had been utterly
destroyed. But notice this. *They daily say unto me.* You
will observe that wherever time is thus reckoned by days in the
Psalms or in the Prophets, it is almost always in a prophecy
of good ; whereas if it be counted by nights or months, it is
almost always a denunciation of ill. Then how can it be said
that so blasphemous an inquiry of the enemy can in any sense
be good? Let S. Paul answer. "In nothing terrified by
your adversaries, which is to them an evident token of perdition, but to you of salvation, and that of GOD." *My tears
have been my meat.* Compare with this the promise in Ecclesiasticus of him that feareth the LORD, "With the bread of
understanding shall she feed him, and give him the water of
wisdom to drink." Thus we learn that true penitence is the
only way to true wisdom: and in this sense also is that reply

2 Kings
xviii. 20.

Micah vii.
10.

Ay.

G.

Philip. i. 28.

A.

Ecclus. xv.
3.

of S. Bonaventura admirable, who, when he was asked where
he had acquired all his marvellous wisdom, pointed to the
crucifix. The best food of the soul, says S. Gregory, is that Moral. v. 7.
sorrow for sin which it conceives within itself, when it understands the love that died for sin. And further observe *day
and night*. As the Carmelite says: It is easy enough to sor- Ay.
row for sin in the night of adversity: so Saul did when being
forsaken by Samuel, he cried out, "I have sinned." So Ahab 1 Sam. xv.
24.
did, when being threatened with destruction by Elijah, "he 1 Kings xxi.
rent his clothes and put sackcloth upon his flesh, and fasted 27.
and lay in sackcloth, and went softly." But to sorrow for
sin in the day of prosperity, that is the true repentance which
GOD loves: that explains the ancient proverb

ἀγαθοὶ δ' ἀριδάκρυες ἄνδρες.

"The good man is a man of many tears." Hugh of S. Victor, Hugo Vic-
one of the greatest masters of the ascetic life that there ever torin.
was, thus speaks: "I will be fed with grief, I will earnestly
seek by tears, I will call by groans, until the presence of Him
Whom I seek shall put an end to all. I will weep because He
Whom I long for is absent. I will weep because that which
I love not is present. I love not present infelicity; I desire
future beatitude; and so I love both the upper springs and
the nether springs: the upper, because my soul desireth to
GOD its living fountain; the lower, because it is said to me,
Where is thy God? The one pertains to the present misery,
because the rebukes of them that rebuked GOD have fallen
upon me: the other to future glory, because it is written,
'Blessed are they that mourn, for they shall be comforted.'"
I cannot help quoting a beautiful passage of Gerhohus
with reference to this, the last verse: "O my soul! O thou G.
that thirstest for the mighty living GOD, behold, thou
hast found the virgin flower full of Divinity, fortitude and
might, grace and truth! Draw honey from it, like the
sagacious little bee; draw honey for thyself, draw honey
for the whole Church, assiduously crying in thy prayer to
the same GOD; Holy GOD, Holy Mighty, Holy Immortal,
have mercy upon us. Holy GOD, to Whom frankincense,
Holy Mighty, to Whom gold, Holy Immortal, to Whom
myrrh is offered, have mercy on us who offer frankincense to
Thee, because we believe Thee GOD to be adored, and honoured with sacrifices: gold, because we confess Thee the
King of all wealth: myrrh, because we proclaim that Thy
Body, once mortal, is now embalmed with the myrrh of immortality and incorruptibility. Have mercy on us all and on
each: each, that Thy SPIRIT may dwell in the soul and body
of each one of us, to the intent that our whole spirit, and
soul, and body may be preserved blameless until the coming
of our LORD JESUS CHRIST: on all, that the whole priesthood of the whole Church may truly offer to Thee that most
lucid incense, pure and holy prayer: so that as the LORD's

Body was preserved from among the dead, the Body of His Church may, through the myrrh of continence, be kept free from the corruption and filth of sin." And then it follows, These things having been so done by the LORD, and done in the Church, and in every member of the Church, When, O when shall I appear before the presence of GOD?

4 Now when I think thereupon, I pour out my heart by myself : for I went with the multitude, and brought them forth into the house of GOD.

5 In the voice of praise and thanksgiving : among such as keep holyday.

I must first give the translation of the Vulgate on account of its marvellous beauty. *These things I call to remembrance, and I poured out my spirit within me: for I will pass over into the place of the admirable tabernacle, even to the house of God. In the voice of exultation and confession; the sound of him that feasteth.* The question is, to what *thereupon* refers.

D. C.

And most of them answer, to the panting of the hart after the water-brooks. That is: While I think of the LORD's Passion, *I pour out my heart* that I in my sufferings may in my poor measure be like Him in His. *By myself.* For, as S. Thomas says, then are we most with GOD, when we are without the company of man. But if we take in the first place the words in their literal sense, and in the future, as they ought to be, *I shall go forth to the tabernacle,* you must see David, having crossed the Jordan, in his flight from Absalom, looking back over the swelling waters of which we shall hear more presently, and comforting himself in the thought that, though the great river now rolls between him and Jerusalem, the day will come when he shall again return

Ay.

to the temple, and to the temple services. And then comes the remarkable mystical interpretation. Why should we speak of the tabernacle rather than the temple? For tent, though it still was, in his own time, yet he rarely so calls it, and could hardly be expected to do so, when he is contrasting the perpetuity of its services with his own exiled and fugitive condition. Why, but for this cause? that the Son of David, also, having passed the Jordan of death, would take up these words with reference to that which was in one sense the temple of His Body, but which in another view might well be called a *tabernacle,* seeing that like a tent it had now been taken down and laid aside. It is not wonderful that the words of the Vulgate have kindled some of the highest aspirations of mediæval poets: but of none more than of Bernard of Cluny in that glorious passage where he says :

> Est ibi pascua, mitibus afflua, præstita sanctis :
> Regis ibi thronus, agminis et sonæ est epulantis.

Gens duce splendida, concio candida, vestibus albis,
Sunt sine fictibus, in Syon ædibus, ædibus almis ;
Sunt sine crimine, sunt sine turbine, sunt sine lite,
In Syon ædibus editioribus Israelitæ.

Others again take the passage of the entrance of a Cate- A.
chumen into the Church militant, which certainly is only the
tabernacle of GOD, hereafter to be changed into the temple,
that Church triumphant, which can never be taken down.

6 Why art thou so full of heaviness, O my soul :
and why art thou disquieted within me?
7 Put thy trust in GOD : for I will yet give him
thanks for the help of his countenance.

As these two verses are triply repeated, I shall reserve
their consideration till we come to the last repetition, when
it will most conveniently fall under our notice.

8 My GOD, my soul is vexed within me : therefore
will I remember thee concerning the land of Jordan,
and the little hill of Hermon.

First, let us consider the literal sense. And the Bible version is : *O my God, my soul is cast down within me : therefore
will I remember Thee from the land of Jordan, and of the Her-
monites, from the hill Mizar.* But such a hill as Mizar never
existed : and the Vulgate gives the meaning most correctly ;
and of the Hermons,[1] *from the little hill,* or *from the lowest
descent ;* that is, the whole territory in which the victories of
the children of Israel over Sihon and Og had originally been
gained. And the way in which GOD is to be remembered
concerning the land of Jordan, has given rise to an infinite
number of mystical interpretations. How it was there that
the nether waters fell off to the Dead Sea, and the hither Ay.
waters stood up on a heap " very far from the city Adam :" that
is, that here, as it were, first, GOD made a division between
the righteous and the wicked, the latter being cut off from
the congregation of His people, and finding their just portion
in that sea where nothing living can exist ; whereas His true
servants, who remained joined to their source, rise up on a
heap, that is, are lifted up towards heaven : and all this very
far from the city Adam, that is, from the original fall of man.
That is one interpretation. Then again : they call to mind
the way in which first at the prayer of Elijah, and then at
that of Elisha, this same river gave a passage to the Pro- D. C.
phets of GOD. Whence they conclude how every servant of
GOD ought to be comforted by this thought, that no physical
hindrance can keep him from performing that work which is

[1] *Hermoniim, a monte modico.* | rect : *et Hermonis a monte mo-*
The old Roman is not so cor- | *dico.*

G.

appointed to him by his Master. And then again in a deeper sense still, " I will remember Thee concerning the land of Jordan, that territory of death, the " Jordan" which divides the desert of this world from the land of promise, and of which our LORD took possession, when He said, " It is finished." *The*

Agillius.

little hill. Some of the interpreters will have this to be the same with the mountain above the little city of Zoar, where Lot, seeking for safety, fell into his great sin. *I will remember Thee.* And therefore others, applying the whole text to our LORD see in the river Jordan the remembrance of His Baptism, and in Hermon that of His Transfiguration; the latter called a *little hill* not in itself, but because He, Who made it the scene of His glory, was, nevertheless, a little lower than

S. Thomas Aquinas. S. Bruno.

A. Cd.

the Angels. And yet again: others see in Jordan a type of Baptism; in Hermon, which by interpretation is " cursing," or an " anathema," the renunciation therein made of the devil and all his order, and in the *little hill,* that grace of GOD which is only given to the humble; as it is written, " GOD resisteth the proud, and giveth grace unto the humble."

9 One deep calleth another, because of the noise of the water-pipes : all thy waves and storms are gone over me.

First let us take the literal sense. And no doubt David was looking down on the river which he had just passed in the time when it was swollen into *cataracts* of water, which is the word that both the Vulgate and the LXX. give. And any one who has seen the *bore* either in the Severn or the Seine, the roar of which can be heard for many miles off, may have a fairly clear comprehension of that which the exiled king then saw ; and to which he compared the state of the Jewish Church then, as others have done that of the Catholic Church from then till now. But the great meaning eagerly seized on by the writers of both the Eastern and Western Church, for those words, *Deep calleth unto deep,* or as it is in their versions, *Abyss calleth to abyss,* has been one and the same : the depth of our misery calls to the deep of GOD's mercy. If I were to quote those who have thus employed the verse, I should be quoting well nigh all penitential writers from the time of our LORD. But there is also another ex-planation, which, if it be brought forward by fewer, has at least great authorities, which would see in both these abysses,

S. Leo. S. Thomas Aquin. S. Hiero- nvm. Epist. 150.

that which S. Paul expresses: " O the depth of the riches, both of the wisdom and knowledge of GOD !" That is : in the first place an abyss which would seem utterly to ruin and overwhelm the Church, was it not that a contrary miracle of mercy comes to set her cause right: a providence which fol-lows a Diocletian with a Constantine, a Constantius with a

Arnobius.

Theodosius. In another sense, Arnobius takes the first abyss to signify the SON, the second the FATHER ; the SON, Who when He called on the FATHER, immediately the cataracts of heaven were open, and the HOLY GHOST came down. Others *Ven. Bede.* understand the first abyss of the infinite wisdom laid up in the prophecies of the Jews; the second abyss, of the vast multitude of the Gentiles, and one inviting another to become a part of the future Church. In a sadder sense one depth of *Hugo Card.* sin involves another and a still deeper abyss, hurrying on the sinner from this to that. But no doubt the true mystical sense is the first, that of man's misery and GOD's mercy: and this on account of that which follows. *Abyss calleth abyss in the voice of Thy cataracts:* that is, in the midst of that wrath which Thou pourest out against sin and as a propitiation to which I have given Myself up to the Cross. And then it well follows; *All Thy waves and storms have gone*   D. C. *over me.* For on Him, on Him the Only-Begotten, on Him the only-beloved, GOD poured forth not this or that suffering, not this or that denunciation of anger, as against individual sinners; but all at once, as all being poured forth on Him, on Whom the whole weight of the sins of all the world was laid. It is very well said by Hugh of S. Victor in reference *Hugo Vic-* to the Vulgate: *All Thy lofty things and Thy waves have* *torin.* *passed over me:* "Tribulations are called high things, because they raise us up on high. Terrene felicity causes us to cleave to the earth. Adversity and tribulation disjoin us from perishable things, and raise us to those which shall last for ever: just as S. Chrysostom says on S. Matthew: As the rain which descends on the earth raises up the tender plants, so tribulation, falling upon the soul, causes it to spring up towards heaven."

10 The LORD hath granted his loving-kindness in the day-time : and in the night-season did I sing of him, and made my prayer unto the GOD of my life.

And first, what is the day-time and what is the night-sea-*Ruffinus.* son? They give innumerable explanations; why GOD's loving-kindness should be confined to the former, as if it were not equally shown in the darkness of adversity: and again why any praises should only be sent up to Him in tribulation, and not in the time of prosperity. But it is better to take it with Gerhohus. The day-time was the period in   G. which our LORD JESUS CHRIST dwelt on earth: the words are the words of the Church: and the night-season is the long track of years from then till now, in which our LORD has been absent, and the hope of His second appearance must make up for the joy of His actual presence. And how did He not *grant His loving-kindness in that day-time?* By what miracles, by what parables, by what labours, by what sufferings did He not express His love to that world which He came to save? *And in the night-season will I* (1) *sing of Him* *S. Thom.* *and* (2) *make my prayer.* But why in this order? Is not *Aquin.*

prayer to precede praise? Does not the supplication for deliverance from evil come before the thanksgiving for preservation from it? Are we not taught first to say, "Deliver us from evil," and *then*, "For Thine is the kingdom, the power and the glory?" For this reason : that, after the time of praise such as this world can allow, there will come a period when thanksgiving must be silent altogether, and there can be nothing but prayer. That is, they look forward to that time of Antichrist when the daily sacrifice shall be taken away, and so the great oblation of the Church's thanksgiving will come to an end : when from those few scattered servants of GOD who remain without a priest and without a temple, what can there be but earnest prayer, that, for the elect's sake, those days may be shortened? *And to the God of my life.* For see how even then, GOD will show Himself as the GOD that has power over death, and the quickener of all things. For when His acknowledged worshippers on earth will be reduced to the two witnesses, and they shall have been slain, then it follows with respect to Him Whom the Church calls *The God of my life :*

Rev. xi. 11. "After three days and a half, the spirit of life from GOD entered into them, and they stood upon their feet ;" just as, long

Ezek. xxxvii. 5. before, we read in the typical vision of Ezekiel ; "Thus saith the LORD GOD . . . . behold, I will cause breath to enter into you, and ye shall live, and ye shall know that I am the LORD."

11 I will say unto the GOD of my strength, Why hast thou forgotten me : why go I thus heavily, while the enemy oppresseth me?

S. Greg. The translation of the Vulgate is quite different : *With me is a prayer to the God of my life : I will say to God, my upholder art Thou, why hast Thou forgotten me, &c. My upholder.* And how could He have upheld this weakness of our own, but by taking it upon Himself? How could He have enabled our body to rise at the last day victorious over death, unless He had Himself assumed that body? And therefore it

D. C. is well written : *I will say unto God.* That is, I will remind Him That is GOD, of what He has suffered as Man ; I will bring to the recollection of *Strength,* what it felt in the time

Hugo Victorin. of His weakness. And Hugh of S. Victor tells us how the two verses, this and the preceding, in their contrariety of assertions, show the true bearing of a loving soul: first it is, *The Lord hath granted His loving-kindness ;* and then directly after, *Why hast Thou forgotten me?*

12 My bones are smitten asunder as with a sword : while mine enemies that trouble me cast me in the teeth ;

13 Namely, while they say daily unto me : Where is now thy GOD?

In what sense are we to take this *sword?* Is it to be the sword of the SPIRIT, which pierces even to the dividing asunder of soul and spirit, and of the joints and marrow: that is to say, the conviction of sin? Or is it the attacks of Satan, the first part expressing the same as the last part? It is to be observed that in the Vulgate we have it, *While my bones are broken, mine enemies have upbraided me who trouble me.* (It is hard to say why the *sword* of the Hebrew original is in this version omitted.) Others take it as the complaint of the Church, how her chief saints, the *bones*, as it were of her strength, are smitten asunder, are destroyed by the power of Satan. *While they daily say unto me.* This upbraiding we have so often met with before, that it need not detain us now.

Ay.

14 Why art thou so vexed, O my soul : and why art thou so disquieted within me?

15 O put thy trust in GOD : for I will yet thank him, which is the help of my countenance, and my GOD.

As we shall have occasion to consider these verses again at the end of the next Psalm, we need say nothing on them here.

And therefore:

Glory be to the FATHER, in Whose presence we shall come to appear; and to the SON, the Hart That desireth the water-brooks of our salvation: and to the HOLY GHOST, the GOD of our strength;

As it was in the beginning, is now, and ever shall be : world without end. Amen.

COLLECTS.

O GOD, the health of our countenance, after Whom the souls of Thy servants do ardently long; grant, we beseech Thee that while we are nourished with the food of our visible tears, we may set Thee invisibly within the tabernacle of our hearts. Through. (1.)

Ludolph.

O GOD, Who in the day-time commandest Thy mercy, and in the night-season manifestest Thyself, we pray Thee that Thou wouldest both in the day defend us for our salvation, and in the night protect us for our rest. Amen. Through Thy mercy. (11.)

Mozarabic.

PSALM XLIII.

TITLE. A Psalm of David.

ARGUMENT.

Most modern critics have imagined this a mere part of the preceding Psalm; the subject being so completely the same, and the chorus or refrain which was twice repeated in the 42nd, again concluding this.

ARG. THOMAS. That CHRIST is the Light of the world, the Way, the Truth, and the Life: the voice of the Church praying that she may be divided from them that believe not. To them who have obtained the faith of CHRIST [that is, the recently baptized], the voice of the Church praying that the good and the bad may be severed in the last day.

[This Psalm is,—in one point of view,—so nearly the second portion of the preceding; and in another, so appropriated to the service of the altar rather than of the choir; that we may proceed to it without further preface.]

1 Give sentence with me, O GOD, and defend my cause against the ungodly people : O deliver me from the deceitful and wicked man.

2 For thou art the GOD of my strength, why hast thou put me from thee : and why go I so heavily, while the enemy oppresseth me?

These two verses will better come under our notice in Psalm CXLIV.: for a reason there to be mentioned.

3 O send out thy light and thy truth, that they may lead me : and bring me unto thy holy hill, and to thy dwelling.

Ay.

S. John i. 9.
S. John xiv. 6.

Lib. iii. dist. 19.

S. Chrysost.
Hesych.

Here he sets forth the only way of his liberation :—and what way is that, but by the Incarnation? *Thy Light :* as it is written : "That was the true light, which lighteth every man that cometh into the world." *Thy Truth :* as He said Himself :—"I am the way, and the truth, and the life." And therefore, the Master of Sentences uses this verse formally, when writing "of the benefits of the Incarnation." *Light* indeed, after so many centuries that darkness covered the earth, and gross darkness the people! *Truth* indeed, when those things that were concealed from the wisest philosophers of Greece and Rome are now revealed to babes and sucklings! Others will have it that, by *Light,* the SON of GOD, by *Truth,* the HOLY GHOST, is more especially set forth.

That they may lead me. So our translation, and rightly. The
Vulgate has, *they have led me:* then, with reference to the
past benefits of the Incarnation: *Thy holy hill.* Take it of
the Church Militant, as almost all the commentators: not that
I would much blame those, who keeping our LORD's dear
Passion here, as always, before their eyes, see in the *holy hill,* Hesych.
Mount Calvary. It is to be observed that, in the "sending
forth," the Greeks, followed by S. Ambrose, generally see an
allusion to the First Advent; S. Augustine, with almost all S. Ambros.
the Latin Fathers, to the Second. And then truly the *light* de Spirit. S.
will be shown which clearly distinguishes the tares from the xix.
wheat; and the *truth,* which, however they may have been
mingled in this world, shall then definitively, and for ever,
set the sheep on the right hand, and the goats on the left. It
is a beautiful idea of Hugh of S. Victor that by *light* is meant Hugo Vic-
the faith by which we walk now; by *truth,* the reward which torin.
we are hereafter to possess:—as if the reality would so far
surpass all that faith can tell, or hope desire, here, as to make
their warmest aspirations little better than untruths. This
was one of the many verses used against the Arians:—the
TRINITY being set forth in Him Who sends: in the Light: S. Athanas.
and in the Truth. The Jews were in the habit of referring ad Serapion.
the truth to Elijah; the light to the Messiah. And no doubt in S. Joan.
there is a reference to the Urim and Thummim by which GOD's
Will was manifested on the stones of the High Priest's breast-
plate. *And to Thy dwelling.* Take the *holy hill* in what
sense you will, there can be no doubt that this *dwelling* is the
"habitation of GOD, the house not made with hands, eternal,
in the heavens." Therefore, the Incarnation: therefore that
holy hill up which the LORD bare the Cross: therefore also
that *holy hill* the Church Militant; all to this one end: that
Calvary might end in Mount Salem, that the Church of warfare might lead to the Church of peace!

4 And that I may go unto the altar of GOD, even
unto the GOD of my joy and gladness : and upon the
harp will I give thanks unto thee, O GOD, my GOD.

Never, surely, more glorious and comforting verse than
this. To see the Man of Sorrows,—now His warfare almost
accomplished,—now the sin He bare for us almost pardoned,
—approaching to the Great Altar of the Evening Sacrifice
of the world. And yet, drawing near to offer Himself to the
FATHER, that FATHER is the GOD of His joy and gladness.
O glorious example for His servants in all their sufferings! G.
See to it, Christian, that when thou art called to offer a sacrifice to GOD, He is the fountain of gladness. See to it that
thou draw nigh, not with fear, not reluctantly, nay, not even
acquiescingly,—but rejoicing that thou hast it in thy power
thus to sacrifice to Him Who sacrificed Himself for thee.
See to it that thou count nothing of any further worth than as

it may so be made the matter of sacrifice; and say with Him, the Priest and Victim, as thou drawest near the time of thy trial,—"I have a Baptism to be baptized with: and how am I straitened till it be accomplished!" This is well chosen as the introit to the altar of the Latin Church, though the Vulgate translation be different: "And I will enter in to the altar of God, to the God, Who giveth joy to my youth." That, albeit not the correct sense of the Hebrew, is not the less appropriate in our dear Lord's mouth; seeing that it was in the very prime and best estate of human youth, that S. Chrysost. He thus drew near to His altar. Or, taking the words in Hesych. another sense,—here *our* youth is indeed rejoiced and gladdened, because at that altar of the Cross, we put off the old man, corrupt according to the deceitful lusts, and put on the new man, renewed in knowledge after the Image of Him That created him. Others again take this altar of the golden altar on which the prayers of the saints are offered; so that Ruffinus. we do really and truly draw nigh that altar whenever we approach God in prayer. Or, as the Carthusian takes it, so may we,—of the Blessed Eucharist. *That I may go unto the* D. C. *altar of God;* yes, but that is the least part of our service; wherefore, not stopping at the altar, he continues, *even unto the God* Whose Flesh and Blood are there really and truly eaten and drunk. And notice the parallelism of the two passages: *even unto the God that rejoiceth my youth,* and that Ps. ciii. 5. other Psalm: "Who satisfieth thy mouth with good things," (and what are they but the food of angels?) "making thee young and lusty as an eagle."

And upon the harp will I give thanks unto Thee. I have Vieyra, iii. said before why on the harp. The harp gives forth no sound 117. till it is struck by the hand; and the only praise which God cares for is that which comes from the deeds, which satisfieth His goodness not only by the lip, but also in the life. And how in another sense the harp sets forth the peculiar offering of martyrdom, we have already seen in Vol. I. p. 460.

5 Why art thou so heavy, O my soul : and why art thou so disquieted within me?

6 O put thy trust in God : for I will yet give Him thanks, which is the help of my countenance, and my God.

The third time, in this, and the preceding Psalm, in which we have these verses. They see in this, a dependence on each Person of the Ever Blessed Trinity for and against our enemies; or, as others, we may see in the triple repetition,— the Thanksgiving for Creation, for Redemption, and for C. Glory. And Cassiodorus dwells at great length on the consideration: how precious, in the sight of God, must be the virtue of Christian joy,—when S. Paul twice,—"Rejoice in the LORD always, and again I say, rejoice,"—and David, as here, thrice commends it to us.

And therefore:

Glory be to the FATHER, Who sends out His Light and His Truth; and to the SON, the GOD of our strength: and to the HOLY GHOST, which is the help of our countenance, and our GOD;

As it was in the beginning, is now, and ever shall be: world without end. Amen.

COLLECTS.

Almighty GOD, fountain of perpetual light, we pray Thee that, sending forth Thy truth into our hearts, Thou wouldst lighten us with the new effulgence of Thy eternal light. Through. (1.) *Ludolph.*

O LORD, Only-Begotten SON of the FATHER, Who didst by Thy Passion judge betwixt Thy servants and the ungodly people, defend us, we beseech Thee, by the virtue of the same Passion from the power of the enemy: that Thou alone mayest receive the praises of Thy Church, Who alone didst pay the price of our Redemption. Amen. Through Thy mercy. (11.) *Mozarabic. Passiontide.*

Grant, O LORD, we beseech Thee, that we may be illuminated by Thee the Light, directed by Thee the Way, corrected by Thee the Truth, quickened by Thee the Life. Who livest. (5.)

PSALM XLIV.

TITLE.—Vulgate: In finem; Filiis Core ad intellectum. Bible Version: To the Chief Musician for the Sons of Korah, Maschil. Rather: To the Supreme. An instructive of the Sons of Korah.

This is evidently one of the Psalms which owe their origin to the period of the captivity; and the first of such which has come before us.

VEN. BEDE. The sons of Core, as is aforesaid, are the sons of the Cross, martyrs or confessors, who in this Psalm complain to the LORD that the ancient saints most easily triumphed over their enemies, but that their own way to victory lies through the grievous tortures of martyrdom. And it is well added, *for understanding;* because we need a very deep understanding, if we would comprehend the dispensations of the One and Selfsame Creator, whereby the then rude peoples were, by earthly rewards, stirred up to embrace the faith; who also received the land of Canaan for possession; and whereby also, now that faith hath increased, and the gate of the heavenly kingdom opened to all, the soldiers of CHRIST are to approve themselves in a harder fight, lest we should be willing to loiter along our earthly journey, and should with greater carelessness seek after those celestial rewards.

ARGUMENT.

ARG. THOMAS. That we are freed by the virtue of CHRIST, and not by our own arm. The Prophet expresseth repentance for all the people of Judah. This Psalm is to be read with the Epistle of Paul[1] to the Romans. The Prophet speaketh to the LORD concerning His works. The voice of the whole Church, asking for Divine help in persecution. For public confession of martyrdom.

VEN. BEDE. Whether we here have the words of martyrs or confessors: in the first part they affirm that they have heard how their fathers were victors over many nations, but that they are given over to be the prey of their enemies' revenge. In the next, they number up the various sufferings which they endure in this present world, and that through them all they remain mindful of GOD. In the third, they ask for help; that, grievously afflicted as they are, they may be assisted in the time of the Resurrection: *Up, Lord; why sleepest Thou?*

SYRIAC PSALTER. A Psalm of the Sons of Korah, which the people, together with Moses, sang in Horeb. Furthermore, a supplication of the Prophets, David and others. But to us, a hymn of victory against them that attack us.

VARIOUS USES.

Gregorian. Tuesday. Matins.
Parisian. Friday. Prime.
Monastic. Monday. II. Nocturn.
Quignon. Tuesday. Matins.
Ambrosian. Thursday of the First Week. I. Nocturn.

ANTIPHONS.

Gregorian. My heart is inditing * of a good matter.
Monastic (Septuagesima). My heart is inditing of a good matter.
Ambrosian. My soul longeth after Thee, O GOD. Kyr. Kyr. Kyr.

1 We have heard with our ears, O GOD, [2]our fathers have told us : what thou hast done in their time of old ;

Didymus.

With our ears. But what is the use of the phrase? *Can we* ever hear in any other way ? There is a deep meaning here. Unless GOD so purges our ears, that they are capable of imbibing the lesson He would teach, the tales of past deliver-

[1] Probably the reference is to Rom. v. 25—29.
[2] The LXX. and the Roman here insert καί, which is neither in the Hebrew, nor in the Vulgate.

ance may be repeated over and over again, without making
any impression on our hearts. " He that hath ears to hear, S. Matt. xiii.
let him hear." " By hearing ye shall hear, and shall not un- 15.
derstand." We hear of their deliverances, and doubt of our S. Ambros.
own; we see how GOD's Right Hand was then stretched out to
save, and think it is shortened now. Cardinal Hugo notices Z.
from this text three necessary requirements for learning Hugo Card.
well:—1. Intention and attention in him who learns: (*we
have heard with o u r ears.*) 2. Authority in him that teaches:
(*our f a t h e r s have told us.*) 3. Love between the teacher
and the taught: (*o u r fathers.*) *What thou hast done:* or,
more correctly, *The work that Thou hast done.* Why only
work in the singular, when such innumerable deliverances
had been wrought by Him, from the passage of the Red
Sea to the destruction of the hundred and eighty-five thousand in the camp of the Assyrians? Because all these were S. Ambrose.
but types of that one great work, that one stretching forth
of the LORD's Hand, when Satan was vanquished, death destroyed, the kingdom of heaven opened to all believers. I Ay.
like this better than the explanation of the Carmelite, who
sees, in the opening verses of this Psalm, the five great benefits wrought by GOD for the race of man.

This verse formed a part of some editions of the Sarum
Litany, as it does of the present English Litany.

2 How thou hast driven out the heathen with thy
hand, and planted them in : how thou hast destroyed
the nations, and cast them out.

That Hand, then nailed to the Cross for us and for our Eusebius.
salvation, nevertheless even then was beginning to burst the Hesychius.
bands by which the Prince of the powers of this world lorded
it over the whole earth.

> Manus clavis perforatas,
> Et cruore purpuratas,
> Cordi premo præ amore,
> Sitibundo bibens ore
> Cruoris stillicidium.

These are the Hands with which that patient dresser of the Rupert.
vineyard planted the Gentile Church on a very fruitful hill;
the hands with which, bleeding and torn from their combat,
He plucked up the briars and thorns that would have occupied their place, and *planted them in.* Take the two clauses,
if you will, as referring to the type and the antitype; the
first of the Jewish Church, the second of the Church of the
Gentiles. Hence they dwell on the seven Canaanitish nations L.
as types of the seven deadly sins: Folengius.

The Canaanite	. .	Avarice.
Amorite	. .	Luxury.
Hittite .	. .	Sloth.

Perizzite	.	.	Pride.
Hivite	.	.	Envy.
Jebusite	.	.	Ignorance.
Girgashite	.	.	Gluttony.

3 For they gat not the land in possession through their own sword : neither was it their own arm that helped them;
4 But thy right hand, and thine arm, and the light of thy countenance : because thou hadst a favour unto them.

It was probably with reference to this verse that Achior, in his speech to Holofernes, is made, in the Vulgate, to say, *Judith v. 16, Vulg.* "Everywhere they entered in without arrow and bow, and without shield and sword; for their GOD did fight for them, and overcame." And in this sense, too, S. Paul says, " The *L.* weapons of our warfare are not carnal." And perhaps also, with reference to this : " Blessed are the meek; for they shall inherit the earth:" that is, the Land of the Living.

By their own sword. And so one of their most miraculous deliverances was that when the watchword of the three hundred was, " The sword *of the Lord*, and of Gideon!" *Rupert.* *The land.* Take it, as we have already done, of the Land of the Living, if you will; take it also of the *land*, this little territory of the body which we have to hold in sub-*Arnobius.* jugation, and too often utterly to re-conquer, for GOD. *Thy Right Hand, and Thine Arm, and the Light of Thy Coun-*Hugo Vic-*tenance.* Some, but not perhaps very appropriately, see here torin. a reference to the Blessed TRINITY; others, the three prin-*Ay.* cipal offices of our LORD, as Consoler, Strengthener, Illuminator. *Light of Thy Countenance.* We may take it either of that clear bright Light which He is to the souls of His people, " *Thy Word* is a light to my paths,"—and again, in *2 Sam. xxiii. 4.* that loveliest of metaphors, " And He shall be as the light of the morning, when the sun riseth, even a morning without clouds; as the tender grass springing out of the earth by clear shining after rain:" or it may be applied to that terrible glory by which the LORD's enemies have so often been dismayed and overwhelmed; and which we considered at length in the 18th Psalm. And so Apollinarius seems to have taken it here :

ἀλλὰ τεὴ παλάμη, καὶ σῆς μέγα φέγγος ὀπωπῆς.

Because Thou hadst a favour unto them. It is[1] exactly the same phrase that was uttered at our LORD's Baptism : " In Him I am well pleased." Because in Him, therefore in them : " for Thy servant David's sake, turn not away the

---

[1] ὅτι εὐδόκησας ἐν αὐτοῖς is the expression of the LXX.; ἐν ᾧ εὐδόκησα, of S. Matthew.

presence of Thine Anointed." And this εὐδοκία it was which formed the subject of that first anthem of the Angels; εὐδοκία,[1] as the last MS. research seems to prove, manifested in, rather than to, men.

5 Thou art my King, O GOD : send help unto Jacob.

What help? The later commentators, such as Lorinus, here tell us that S. Augustine is to be "cautiously read," because he refers the entire fulness and consummation of that hope to the period following the Resurrection. We, perhaps, may be forgiven for believing, with those older doctors, that the Beatific Vision (except in the case of martyrs) will not be the portion even of saints, much more of the rest of GOD's elect, till death has been entirely swallowed up in victory; and then that the glorious completion of *help* will be of a verity *sent unto Jacob*, when all his tribes shall be gathered in, all his warfare accomplished, all his iniquity pardoned. *Thou art my King, O God.* The LXX. and the Vulgate, (but not the Hebrew,) *Thou art my King and my God.* But, as they ask, who can say this of a truth? Who has thus taken for his king Him That was crowned with thorns, Whose sceptre was a reed, Who reigned from the Tree? Who so poor of spirit as to choose the poor Monarch? Who so renunciant of the world, as to choose the Sovereign That had not where to lay His Head? And yet, *Send help unto Jacob.* Jacob, His true people, in that, as a Prince, they have power with Him, and prevail: in that they supplant the world, the flesh, and the devil. And notice, *Jacob* needs help: the supplanter cannot carry on his long and wearisome struggle without the assistance of his LORD: Israel, he that sees GOD, needs no help, warfare being at an end, danger impossible, temptation a thing of the past. *Send help.* In the Vulgate it is, *salvations.* And S. Ambrose takes occasion to say how, not this or that help, this or that deliverance, we owe to the GOD of our salvation; but *all* help, *all* mercy, *all* loving kindness: according to that saying of the Apostle, "And the LORD shall deliver me from every evil work, and will preserve me to His heavenly kingdom." S. Albert asks by what authority can man call GOD *his* King, when He is rather the King of Angels?—when those blessed spirits might say, with the men of Israel in old time, "We have ten parts in the King, and we also have more right in David than ye." And he answers, "Because it is written, 'Verily, He took not on Him the nature of Angels, but He took on Him the seed of Abraham.'" And there is another sense to be elicited from the plural, *salvations.* Esau had but one

L.

G.

Ay.

S. Ambrose.

2 Tim. iv. 18.
S. Albert. M.

2 Sam. xix.
43.

Heb. ii. 16.

G.

---

[1] I refer to the Codex Sinaï-ticus, which, by giving *ἐν ἀνθρώ-ποις εὐδοκίας*, seems to make it | certain that this reading, fol-lowed by the Vulgate, is the true one.

blessing, and that the earthly and the (in itself) worthless one; plenty of corn and wine, richness of the earth, abundance of dew. Jacob had this; but he had the other and better blessing, the heavenly blessing, also: so that the *qui mandas salutes Jacob* is emphatically true.

6 Through thee will we overthrow our enemies : and in thy Name we will tread them under, that rise up against us.

Overthrow scarcely gives the force of the Hebrew. *Rebut* comes nearest to it: בְּךָ צָרֵינוּ נְנַגֵּחַ the metaphor being taken from the battles of horned animals. So in the LXX.: ἐν σοὶ τοὺς ἐχθροὺς ἡμῶν κερατιοῦμεν: in the Gallican, *ventilabimus cornu:* in the Roman, *ventilabimus* only. *Arietare* would be, perhaps, the nearest Latin expression; and its force is dwelt on by most of the commentators. They take these horns of Him Who was indeed, like the bullock of old times, our Sacrifice; or of the unicorn, to whom our mighty Deliverer is so often likened. Or again, they see in the horns themselves, with which we are to push, the arms of the Cross; and so Tertullian and S. Cyprian. Not like those lying horns made by the false prophet Zedekiah, with the message, "Thus saith the LORD: With these shalt thou push the Assyrians, until thou have consumed them:" nor yet like those four horns seen by Zechariah, of which the Prophet was told, "These be the horns which have scattered Judah, Israel, and Jerusalem:" nor, again, like those of which Amos upbraids the possessors, "Ye which rejoice in a thing of nought; which say, Have we not taken to us horns by our own strength?"

And in Thy Name. How, over and over again, does that Name of all glory come before us! Surely, as with S. Bernard, so with David: "Whatever I read, it is unsavoury, except I there find that Title; it is insipid, unless it be savoured with that Name!" And here, more, S. Cyril will have us remember GOD's declaration to Pharaoh, one of those that did indeed "rise up against us:" "In very deed for this cause have I raised thee up, that My Name may be declared throughout all the earth." To return again to the *horn:*[1] they lay a great stress on the kind of horn—the oneness of it—"My horn is exalted as the unicorn's:" that one Horn of our strength, that one Name under heaven given

Margin notes:
A.
S. Ambrose.
S. Hieronym.
Ricard. Victor.

Hesychius.

L.

1 Kings xxii. 11.

Zech. i. 19.

Amos vi. 13.

S. Cyril. Alex.

Exod. ix. 16.

---

[1] S. Albert's mystical interpretation of the Horns, by far too long to be here quoted, is an admirable example of the use to which the fancies of mediæval natural histories were symbolised; each particular in the horn of an animal, as given by them, being parallelised with some characteristic of the Horn of our salvation.

among men, whereby they may be saved. And no doubt it   Ay.
was in great measure from this text that those early emperors carried the ☧ on their standards.

> Christus purpureum gemmanti textus in auro   Cd.
> Signabat Labarum.

That rise up against us. In *nos* it is in almost all the
Fathers, and so in the Roman; but in the Gallican[1] version
we have *in nobis*, which the other commentators, if they mention it at all, mention it to blame. But deep S. Thomas ob-   S. Thomas
serves, "Most truly said; for what injury could our spiritual Aquinas.
enemies do us, unless they could rise up *in us* as well as
against us? 'The prince of this world cometh, and hath no- S. John xiv.
thing in Me:' but *in* us, or *against* us, or both, in *His* Name 30.
we shall tread them under, Who subdued them in His own
strength."

**7 For I will not trust in my bow : it is not my
sword that shall help me;**

"Lay the stress," says S. Ambrose, "on the *my; for there s. Ambros.
is a bow in which must be all our salvation and all our desire."
That Bow set in the clouds of tribulation; that Bow given
by the promise of the LORD, in Whom the seven graces of   L.
the HOLY GHOST reside fully; that Bow which we, as faithful
watergalls, are to imitate. And this was the favourite lesson
of the wonder-working ascetics of the desert,—

> "Holy Macarius and great Antony,"

that none can obtain a victory who knows not that he cannot Cassian.
obtain it. O glorious Christian paradox! foolishness to them Coll. v. 14.
that are beginning the race, but of what perfect comfort to
those that have nearly attained the goal?
    Or, in another sense: the bow, which sends to, and smites Id. de re-
at, a distance, is prayer. And still the emphasis is on *my.* nunc. instit.
Not in *my* prayers, as mine, but as presented with the much xii. 13, 14.
incense by the Angel; yea, rather, as made His own by the
LORD of the Angels. And hence it is well said, "Also he bade
them teach the children of Israel the use of the bow;" which, 2 Sam. i. 18.
indeed, we have need to learn by diligent use, if ever we seek
to prevail by it. And there is no more striking exhortation
to the employment of this bow than the fourth sermon of S.
Macarius. Well did those ancient ascetics of the desert
know how to send up their prayers to the GOD That heareth

---

[1] I must ask the reader to remember (as this expression so
often occurs) that by the Gallican Version I mean that which
is now the authentic translation
of the Roman Church, except
only in S. John Lateran: by the
Roman, that former version,
about which see the first volume
of this Commentary, p. 75.

Cassian. prayer, and mightily did they succeed in their petitions. *My sword.* They take it of good works, the fittest weapon wherewith to fight against Satan; and yet *it is not my sword that shall help me* neither, because " of Him, and through Him, and to Him are all things."

8 But it is thou that savest us from our enemies : and puttest them to confusion that hate us.

Ay.

Jer. xxiii. 6.

This and the preceding verse are, in the Vulgate, in the past. *Savest us :* and how? In three ways, says the Carmelite. First, by penitence from our sins; as it is written, " In His days Judah shall be saved;" but Judah is, by interpretation, *Confession.* Secondly, the innocent shall be saved by the purity of his actions. The patient shall be saved by long-suffering in tribulation. But they all—knowing how much yet remains before our salvation shall be complete— with one accord take the past or present of the future. So S. Augustine : "Da prophetam cui non tantum certum sit præteritum sed futurum : et quemadmodum tibi quod meministi factum non potest fieri ut non sit factum : sic ille quod novit futurum, non potest fieri ut non fiat."

9 We make our boast of GOD all day long : and will praise thy Name for ever.

We shall be praised is the Vulgate, unless, indeed, the *laudabimur* is a mere deponent. The LXX. have ἐπαινεθησό- μεθα· answering fairly enough to הִלַּלְנוּ of the Hebrew. *We will glory* is perhaps the nearest expression. But that is a beautiful sense which takes the passive meaning, as Apollinarius does :

ἡμάτιων κλέος ἄμμι παρ' ἀθανάτῳ βασιλῆι.

Ay.

That He Who gives the power will give the reward; He Who bestows the grace will guerdon that grace with glory; that He Who conquers in us will crown in us that victory which He has bestowed. *We make our boast of God.* As it is written in the Prophet, " Let not the rich man glory in his riches; let not the mighty man glory in his might :" exactly that which David over and over tells us, " Hold not Thy tongue, O GOD of my praise:" "The LORD is my strength and my song." *And will praise Thy Name for ever.*

> Ave Nomen [1] dulce JESUS!
> Tu de monte Lapis cæsus,
> Et vitalis mentis esus,
> Ad te clamet homo læsus.

[1] "Edidit hoc carmen quidam monachus Grissorum, Ad laudem Domini JESU, studiumque bonorum."

Ave Nomen admirandum,
Orbe toto prædicandum,
Jesu dulcis ad narrandum,
Nos accendas ad amandum.

Ave, dives tu diei!
Adsis mihi, Fili Dei:
Ne me vincant Amorrhæi
Recordare, Jesu, mei!

10 But now thou art far off, and puttest us to
confusion : and goest not forth with our armies.

11 Thou makest us to turn our backs upon
our enemies : so that they which hate us spoil our
goods.

But now. This, then, is that season, in which, as S. Peter
says, "if need be," we must be in heaviness through manifold temptation. And, remembering this, it is pleasant to
translate that *and now*, as some do by *although.* True, we
have these troubles, but we know them to be the only way to
rest; true, for awhile we suffer, but, "if we suffer, we shall
also reign with Him."

1 S. Pet. i. 6.

Aquila has
καιπερ :
S. Chryaos-
tom reads,
καιγε.

12 Thou lettest us be eaten up like sheep : and
hast scattered us among the heathen.

This is the first time that the word *sheep*, in a metaphorical meaning, afterwards so favourite a metaphor, occurs in
the Psalms: we may as well therefore, in this place, hear the
mystical reasons which Cardinal Hugo gives for the selection
of that animal as the type of God's people.

Fœta bidens: dormit vestita: lupum timet: imbres
Carne juvat; pelle; vellere; lacte; fimo.
Cernit humum balans: edit herbas: hostia: velox
Pastorem sequitur: in grege sola dolet.
Ruminat: innocuo cornu: pede, vertice duro:
Tonsa tacet: maculat morbida peste gregem.

As sheep of slaughter. That is, they explain, because devoured by the roaring lion that goeth about; and, so devoured
by him, turning into a part of his substance, and increasing
his strength. Or, in another sense, martyrs thus destroyed
by their enemies became to them the means of eternal life;
and most truly of all, the Lamb, the Lamb of God, in the
same night in which He was accounted to be slain did indeed
in truth give His Flesh to be the life of the world. That
which His people do only mystically, and in a far off type, He
does really and substantially, and in no figure of speech.
And scattered us among the heathen. Manifestly the Psalm

A.

L.

was written at a very late period of the Jewish history:—and how marvellously it applies to the young Christian Church.

Acts viii. 59. *Thou lettest us be eaten up like sheep:* "They stoned Stephen, calling upon GOD:" *and scatterest us among the heathen.* "Now they that were scattered abroad upon the persecution that arose about Stephen travelled as far as Phenice," &c.

Acts xi. 19. (whence the Gospel preached to the Gentiles.) *Thou lettest*

S. Albert. M. *us.* The scriptural S. Albert will have us remember, that, unless GOD permitted, the enemy could have no advantage. "Who gave Jacob for a spoil, and Israel to the robbers?

Isa. xlii. 24. Did not the LORD, He against whom we have sinned?" And

Amos iii. 6. again: "Shall there be evil in a city, and the LORD hath not done it?" *Eaten up like sheep.* And notice: those sheep are only fit to be eaten, that are barren. So they only are permitted to fall a prey to the spiritual Lion, who bring forth no good works. S. Albert also curiously enough compares the being *scattered among the heathen* like sheep with that

Heb. xi. 37. passage in the Hebrews, "They w a n d e r e d about in s h e e p skins and goat skins, being destitute, afflicted, tormented; of whom the world was not worthy."

13 Thou sellest thy people for nought : and takest no money for them.

The Hebrew is quite plain; but a various reading of the LXX. has given rise to a considerable discrepancy of interpretation, and a beautiful variety of meaning. There can be no doubt that the original Greek was—καὶ οὐκ ἦν πλῆθος ἐν τοῖς ἀλλάγμασιν αὐτῶν· there was no multitude,—was no advantage or enrichment, in their commutations,—in the sale or barter of GOD's people. But through the carelessness of some transcriber, ἀλλάγμασιν became ἀ λ α λ ά γ μ α σ ι ν—there was no multitude nor quantity of their *exultations:* that is, the Church was plunged into grief which allowed no triumphal strain. S. Augustine[1] therefore reads: *et non fuit multitudo in exultationibus eorum;* all the others, *in commutationibus eorum;* except the Ambrosian which has *in commutationibus nostris.* The Greek Church (using the word in its peculiar signification) agrees with the Western, in reading ἀλλάγμασι, but the Slavonic, curiously enough, follows the other reading. This is also alluded to by the Master of the Sentences,—S. Cyril, Euthymius, S. Nicephorus, S. Alcuin.

G.   *For nought:* that is, for no earthly price;—no sum that a worldling can understand. That which the Martyr sells himself for,—or is sold by his LORD for, is what? Truly, "an inheritance incorruptible, and undefiled, and that fadeth not away"—but it is *reserved.* Truly an habitation in that City whose gates are of twelve several pearls, and whose streets

[1] But not the Roman, as Lorinus says: that agrees with the Gallican.

of pure gold like transparent glass; but then it is invisible
to human eyes.

Cœlestis Patriæ mens inhians bonis
Mundi spernit opes, fluxæque gaudia :
Vitæ quin etiam, præ Domini lucro
Jacturam facilem putat.

The hymn Christi Martyribus.

Thou sellest Thy people for nought. So it seemed then;
and now, we take up those glorious words of the Eastern
Church :

Προπατόρων, Πατέρων, Πατριαρχῶν, Ἀποστόλων, Μαρτύρων, Ἱεραρ-
χῶν, Προφητῶν καὶ Ὁσίων σου, Ἀσκητῶν καὶ Δικαίων, καὶ παντὸς
ὀνόματος ἐγγεγραμμένου ἐν Βίβλῳ Ζωῆς, τὴν ἁγίαν μνήμην τελοῦντες,
Χριστὲ ὁ Θεὸς, πάντας συγκινοῦμεν, εἰς πρεσβείαν δεόμενοι· Εἰρήνευσον
τὸν κόσμον σου δι᾿ αὐτῶν, ὡς φιλάνθρωπος, ἵνα πάντες βοῶμεν σοι· Ὁ
Θεὸς ὁ ἐνδοξαζόμενος ἐν βουλῇ Ἁγίων σου, σὺ ὑπάρχεις ἀληθῶς ὁ δοξάσας
ἀξίως τὴν μνήμην αὐτῶν. *And takest no money for them.* "Forasmuch as ye know that ye were not redeemed by corruptible things, as silver and gold, but with the precious Blood
of CHRIST, as of a Lamb without blemish and without spot." 1 S. Pet. i. 18.
In the literal sense, as regards the Jews, they quote most
happily that passage from Tacitus, where he is speaking of
their banishment from Rome : Et si ob gravitatem cœli inte-   Cd.
riissent, *vile damnum.* The Jews themselves speak of thirty Tacit. Annal.
captives sold after the siege of Jerusalem for one silver piece : ii. 85.
meet retribution, says Hugh of Florence, to those who had
sold their One LORD for thirty pieces of silver.

But it is pleasanter still to raise one's eyes to the martyrs,
and see how the LORD sold them—how He gave them to the
horrible agonies, the miserable shame, the prolonged tortures
of the arena, for nothing less than the unspeakable glory
which they have thereby won.

Mundus pulcher ne placeret
   Deus traxit pulchrior :
Egit, mundus ne terreret,
   Deus terribilior.
O totius cœli luce
   Dignum certe prælium !
Cogitatâ Christi Cruce
   Dulce fit Martyrium.

14 Thou makest us to be rebuked of our neighbours : to be laughed to scorn, and had in derision of
them that are round about us.

15 Thou makest us to be a by-word among the
heathen : and that the people shake their heads at us.

We have spoken of the martyrs: let us turn our eyes to
the Martyr of martyrs on Calvary. *Rebuked* indeed! In S. Ambros.
the first and chief place, "*Thy* rebuke hath broken His
heart;" but *rebuked of His neighbours* also. *His neighbours*

II. .   E

in place: "the thieves also that were crucified with Him, cast the same in His teeth." *His neighbours*, in that "verily He took not on Him the nature of angels, but He took on Him the seed of Abraham;" and the cry was, "Let CHRIST, the King of Israel, come down now from the Cross, that we may see and believe!" And therefore, rightly afterwards were the Jews rebuked of—deserted for—passed over in exchange for—the Gentiles—as it is written: "Seeing ye . . . . judge yourselves unworthy of eternal life, lo, we turn to the Gentiles." And thou, O Christian, disquiet thyself not when herein thou art called to drink of thy LORD'S cup. "If they have persecuted Me, they will also persecute you; and in like manner, If they have derided Me, they will also deride you." *A by-word.* Marvellously said: first *Christian*, then *Nazarene*, and now *Saint*. In the LXX. and the Vulgate it is yet more: *in similitudinem*, εἰς παραβολήν. And they tell us truly how, as the proverbs of the True Solomon are verily "to know wisdom and instruction, to perceive the words of understanding," so the devil's proverbs are plentiful, and (in their way) sparkling with a kind of earthly wisdom, fit to captivate the simple believer: to be a proverb or similitude:— that is, when we have suffered in GOD'S cause, that Satan or the world should pervert our sufferings to our ruin; or, miserably worse, when we, professedly GOD'S servants, have fallen deeply, and thereby brought dishonour on our Master and on our side,—is always spoken of in Scripture as the greatest of evils. And especially, as the Saints particularly warn us, no worse *parable* or *proverb* can the servants of GOD be made to His enemies, than by their intestine quarrels. Nestor speaks truly:—

Margin references:
S. Matt. xxvii. 44.
Heb. ii. 16.
Acts xiii. 46.
S. John xv. 20.
S. Greg. Moral. viii. 39.
L.
Deut. xxviii. 36, 37; xxix. 24; 1 Kings ix. 7; 2 Chron. vii. 20; Job xvii. 6; Jer. xxiv. 9; Ezek. xiv. 8; Numb. v. 25, 27.

> Verily, great is the woe that shall fall on the land of Achaia;
> Verily, Priam himself shall rejoice, and the children of Priam;
> While on the Trojan army shall rest the gladness of spirit,
> When they shall hear that ye, who are first in the war of Achaians,
> First in their counsels of peace, thus strive and wrangle together.

Our neighbours. I think that the Hebrew gives a truer picture of the war in which we are engaged. "For we wrestle not against flesh and blood, but against principalities, against powers, against the rulers of the darkness of this world, against spiritual wickedness in high places." These truly may be, and are, our *neighbours;* but they are more than that: *we are made a reproach* לִשְׁכֵנֵינוּ *to our* INVADERS: those who are continually pressing forward us,—trying to get more than they have,—taking the ell for the inch. So in another Psalm, הָיִינוּ חֶרְפָּה לִשְׁכֵנֵינוּ, to our *invaders*, again.

Margin references:
Eph. vi. 12.
Ps. lxxix. 4.

16 My confusion is daily before me : and the shame of my face hath covered me;

17 For the voice of the slanderer and blasphemer: for the enemy and avenger.

And now it is no longer the Church, but the Head of the Church, Who speaks. *Daily:* for those long periods of *shame* and misery on the Cross formed an age, to be reckoned S. Thomas by a long succession of days. *My confusion:* that out of the Aquinas. twelve, My elect band, My chosen warriors, the men of My countenance, the men whom I had strengthened, comforted, warned,—in whose mouths had been but a few hours ago, "Though all men, yet not I,"—they have all forsaken Me at the first struggle. So the Saints who followed the Luiz de Passion represent the LORD of the Passion. And notice Granada, I.[1] this: *My confusion is before Me.* So it must have been, when those that ought to have been His most valiant soldiers, so foully fell away; *and the shame of My face hath covered Me,* when all but one of them *kept* away. "Woe, that the Triodion; Face," cries out the Eastern Church, "the Joy of the Angels, Tuesday in the Glory of the Blessed, should thus be marred and dis- Week. figured by the sins of the daughter of my people! O JESUS, *my* JESUS, O perishing One for the perishing, O shamed One for the shamed, O Head degloried that I may henceforth be glorified, what sacrifice of love have I to offer?—what vessels can I prepare for my Joseph: my Joseph, Whom an evil beast hath devoured,—my Joseph, That without doubt is rent in pieces?—but yet Whose shame shall be rolled away, Whose glory shall return to His Countenance, when it shall be proclaimed by the Voice of the Archangel and the rending of the rocks, 'Joseph is yet alive, and is governor over all the land!'" Or, taking it in another sense, "O glorious S. Ambros. shame," says S. Ambrose, "which is for CHRIST's sake! O miserable shame, which is against Him! Glorious shame, if the law be that, in thee, CHRIST be scourged, be fettered, be imprisoned, be brought before the magistrate! Wretched and forlorn shame if then thou say, with Pharaoh, 'I know not the LORD,'—with Peter, 'I know not this man of whom ye speak.'" *From the voice.* And S. Thomas most appo- S. Thomas sitely compares the most subtle device of the arch per- Aquinas. secutor Maximin, when gathering together those miserable women, the greatest and most notorious sinners in every principal city, he made them add to all their iniquities this abominable rest,—that the followers of CHRIST had been the most guilty, the most abandoned, of their followers in sin. Gerhohus,—let us imagine that his commentary on the G. more immediately preceding Psalms was written in the time of some deep trouble,—has now of a long season said nothing worthy of himself. Let us attend to him here, where he developes that which I just now quoted from S. Ambrose:— "But note, that there are two kinds of confusion; whence

---

[1] Where I quote this beautiful writer, I do so from the edition of Gabriel de Leon, Madrid, 1676.

Ecclus. iv.
21. the Wise Man saith, 'There is a shame which bringeth sin, and there is a shame which is glory and grace.' Shame[1] is sinful when we are ashamed of things in which there is no shame : for example, the humble ministration to our brethren in their necessities, the washing their feet, or when we are ashamed to have that sin animadverted on in the presence of men, when we have not been ashamed to contract the vile guilt of its commission in the Presence of GOD. But shame *then* brings glory, when we so blush in the Presence of GOD for our sins, that we are in no wise confounded regarding the fact of their purgation ; as Mary, who blushed not at the guests, when, to the end that she might be washed by the LORD, she washed His feet with her tears : that she might be cleansed, she cleansed ; that she might be anointed,[2] she anointed ; and endured the ridicule and exprobation of the Pharisee and his companions, not without a certain confusion. But this confusion won for her great glory ; for her many sins were remitted to her, with all their true shame, because she so dearly loved as to undertake that humble ministry of washing in the presence of the guests. . . . But this humble ministry raised her to a lofty and glorious one, since afterwards it is written that she anointed His head with very precious ointment of spikenard. What more glorious than this ? The Baptist, though sanctified from the womb, dared not to touch the holy Head of GOD, save at the LORD's express command. But this woman, uncommanded, not in presumption, but in love and a good conscience, anointed a Head venerable to the Angels themselves. Great is the glory to have ascended from the Feet to the Head of CHRIST, whether any one, through belief in His true Humanity, rises to the cognition of His true Divinity, or by ministering through almsdeeds to His least ones on earth, is raised to the altitude of His super-celestial Godhead."

18 And though all this be come upon us, yet do we not forget thee : nor behave ourselves frowardly in thy covenant.

19 Our heart is not turned back : neither our steps gone out of thy way ;

[1] Notice how here the tenets, as so often, of this great theologian would have been called *Rigorist* in the age which was occupied in endeavouring to reconcile the love of GOD with the pursuit of the world.

[2] Gerhohus is no doubt remembering the beautiful *English* hymn :—

Jesum quærens, convivarum
  Turbas non erubuit ;

Pedes unxit, lacrymarum
  Fluvio quos abluit :
Crine tersit, et culparum
  Veniam promeruit.

Suum lavit Mundatorem ;
  Rivo fons immaduit ;
Pium fudit flos liquorem ;
  In ipsum refloruit :
Cœlum terræ dedit rorem ;
  Terra cœlum confluit.

20 No, not when thou hast smitten us into the
place of dragons : and covered us with the shadow
of death.

And as they well observe, we here have the fourfold use of
affliction. 1. Humiliation—*Thou hast humbled us in the*
place of dragons; 2. Remembrance of GOD—*if we have for-*
gotten; 3. Hatred of sin—*Shall not God search it out?*
4. Self-mortification—*And are counted as mortified sheep.*
Into the place of dragons. And according to our translation,
that is dangerous enough; but tenfold dangerous as most of
the mediæval commentators have taken it, *Into the place of*
syrens. For if it be perilous to be attacked by open and malicious enemies, it is a thousand times more dangerous to be
lulled into security, or enticed to sins of sloth and pleasure
by those friends of which the syrens were only the too true
type. This is what Bernard of Cluny means when he says,

Ay.

L.

> The miserable pleasures
> Of the body shall decay;
> The bland and flattering struggles
> Of the flesh shall pass away.

And so they quote that verse in Isaiah, "And owls shall
dwell there, and syrens shall dance there." And again in
Micah, "I will make a wailing like the syrens, and mourning
as the owls." Then from this same verse S. Ambrose draws
well the contrast between the human nature of our LORD and
our own: how His Body was not a body of death, but of
life; how, so far from casting the shadow of death, it was resplendent with the glory of true existence; that its afflictions
brought our consolation, its humiliation our exaltation: nay,
and further, that, as the face of Moses drew a certain effulgence
of glory from the full blaze of the Divine Majesty, so our
flesh, dark, weak, and sinful in itself, has, from its contact
with, or rather co-incorporation into, our LORD's human nature, received the seeds in the present life of that which will,
in the life to come, be its perfect and eternal glorification.

Isa. xiii. 21.

Micah i. 8.

21 If we have forgotten the Name of our GOD,
and holden up our hands to any strange god : shall
not GOD search it out? for he knoweth the very
secrets of the heart.

22 For thy sake also are we killed all the day
long : and are counted as sheep appointed to be
slain.

Whence observe that adversity causes us to remember
GOD. And they make a very ingenious remark on the so
frequent negative use of the word *if*, as here : that he who
once begins to parley with temptation, to question IF he shall

Ay.

follow GOD's will or his own, to ask IF he shall tread in our
LORD's steps or in the path of his private fancy, is as good as
lost. *And holden up our hands*—or, as it is in the Septuagint and the Vulgate, *stretched forth our hands.* How can
we, they ask, stretch forth our hands to any one save to Him
Who stretched forth His hands for us on the Cross? The
very fact of stretching forth the hands shows the profession.
It is the Cross that makes the Christian. *If we have forgotten the Name of our God.* There is a passage of such rare
beauty in Ayguan on this subject, that—though over and
over again I have had occasion to speak of this Blessed
Name, and GOD forbid it should ever be otherwise—I cannot refrain from quoting it here :—" Next, as Peter of Ravenna says, this is the Name which gives hearing to the deaf,
power of walking to the lame, speech to the dumb, life to the
dead, and which chases the whole power of the devil from
those whom he has possessed : whence this Name appears to
be that theriac, of which the physician Avicenna says that it
is the most sublime of all medicines, and is serviceable in the
most desperate cases. He adds, that those who employ it in
the hour of their health can be hurt by no poison, and are
subject to no plague. And true it is that this Name of
JESUS avails not only to expel present, but to repel future
ills : whence Bernard saith, ' Thou hast an electuary, O my
soul, enshrined in the vessel of this Name, efficacious against
all pestilence.' And therefore it is written in the 4th of the
Acts, ' For there is none other Name under heaven.' Then,
too, this Name is our comfort. S. Isidore says that the wild
olive is a tree bitter, unfruitful, and uncultivated ; in which,
however, if a branch of the true olive be inserted, it changes
the very nature of the tree, and converts it to its own likeness. So also that unfruitful olive of sinful human nature,
which may well be called bitter, seeing that it goes softly all
its years in the bitterness of its soul ; seeing also that, as
Jeremiah saith, ' It is an evil thing and bitter that thou hast
forsaken the LORD thy GOD.' Into that sad and bitter tree,
I say, let the sprig of olive be inserted, which the dove bare
back in her mouth at evening. And what is that sprig but
the NAME of JESUS? This is the proper nature of that
branch, whence saith Richard of S. Victor, ' JESUS, O Name
of sweetness, O Name of delectation, O Name of comfort to
the soul, O Name of most blessed hope. Therefore, O JESUS,
be Thou my JESUS !' " *The secrets of the heart.* S. Ambrose
will rather have it from the version of Aquila, *the visions of
the heart.*[1] He would say that GOD sees and pays attention
to the passing fancies,—the castle-buildings as we should now
speak,—which occupy so much time and so many hearts.
Shall not God search it out? Not, as it is very well said,

L.

S. Greg.
Moral. vi. 16.

Jer. ii. 19.

[1] The Roman agrees with the Gallican translation, in sense, if not in letter ; the former having it *occulta*, the latter *abscondita cordis.*

that He may Himself learn, but that He may teach us: not
that He Who foresaw every secret or vision of our heart
from eternity, has occasion to be informed of it now, but
that we, remembering the Eye that is always upon us, "may
live soberly, righteously, and godly in this present world."
And are counted as sheep appointed to be slain. Or, as the
hymn tells us—

C.

> Cæduntur gladiis more bidentium :
> Non murmur resonat, non querimonia ;
> Sed corde tacito mens bene conscia
> Conservat patientiam.

And they take the metaphor of sheep to signify the fruitfulness of the sufferings of the martyrs, according to that proverb, so dear to primitive times. Or others understand the
metaphor of the utter helplessness of the sheep, having
neither arms of offence nor defence. And lastly, from these
sheep appointed to the slaughter, who would not raise his eyes
to the LAMB of GOD That taketh away the sins of the world?

L.

C.

23 Up, LORD, why sleepest thou : awake, and be
not absent from us for ever.

24 Wherefore hidest thou thy face: and forgettest
our misery and trouble?

Shall we take it of the voice of the Apostles during the
time that their dear LORD was sleeping in the grave? or (as
others) of the martyrs pleading as S. John heard them ; "How
long, O LORD, holy and just, dost Thou not avenge our blood
on them that dwell on the earth?" They do not fail to
notice the sleep of many of GOD's saints, taking it in connection with that verse, "I sleep, but my heart waketh," that
is, waketh to, and trusteth in, GOD. So Jacob, when he fled
from his brother; so Elijah, when he escaped from Jezebel ;
so Jonah, while the idolaters were in terror; so Peter, in the
prison; so Adam, while yet innocent; so Abraham, before
one of his most remarkable visions. And they may well
compare this apparent sleep of our LORD (actual, on the lake
of Galilee ; metaphorical, as the great historian of the Church
applies it to the infamous lives of the successors of S. Peter
in the tenth century) with that sleep with which Elijah
taunted the worshippers of Baal, " Peradventure he sleepeth,
and must be awaked :" all the more bitter irony, if we believe,
as no doubt the truth is, that on other occasions the demon
whom they worshipped had enabled his priests to perform
the very same miracle which his worshippers were expecting
then. *Up, Lord, why sleepest Thou?* And is it not a reflection on the faith of the Apostles, that David in the darker
dispensation should have asked so plain a question, when the
two that went to Emmaus could believe no further than
this; "We trusted that it had been He Which should

C.

A.

Rev. vi. 10.

Gen. xxviii. 11.
1 Kings xix. 3.
Jonah i. 5.
Acts xii. 6.
Gen. ii. 21.
Gen. xv. 12.

G.

S. Ambros.
in Heb. xiii.

Heb. i. 3.

have redeemed Israel;" and even S. Mary Magdalene could
only say, "They have taken away my LORD, and I know
not where they have laid Him." *Wherefore hidest Thou
Thy face?* S. Ambrose takes this as the complaint of the
heathen world before the Advent of our LORD. *Wherefore hidest Thou* as yet Him Who is the brightness of Thy
glory, and the express image of Thy Person? It is the
same complaint that we have before now so constantly heard;
the sound which, finding its utterance in a Gentile mouth,
could say,

> Adgredere, O magnos, aderit jam tempus, honores,
> Cara deum soboles, magnum Jovis incrementum!
> Adspice convexo nutantem pondere mundum;
> Terrasque tractusque maris coelumque profundum:
> Adspice, venturo lætantur ut omnia sæclo!

25 For our soul is brought low, even unto the
dust : our belly cleaveth unto the ground.

26 Arise, and help us : and deliver us for thy
mercy's sake.

A.

It is not ill-observed by S. Augustine how this expression,
Our soul is brought low even unto the dust, is merely an am-
plification of that verse in the first Psalm, where the wicked
"are like the chaff" or dust "that the wind scattereth away
from the face of the earth." And so in another Psalm it is
written, "Thou shalt bring me into the dust of death." So,
take it in which sense you will, with reference to the wicked
in this life, or with reference to the corruption of death, they
do not fail to see the complaint of our LORD in His Passion.
And with respect to the nature of dust, mediæval writers
give it us—

Ps. xxii. 16.

Auctor
operis de
Salutaribus
Documentis
apud S.
Augustin.

> Aridus, instabilis, sterilis, levis, innumerosus,
> Sordidus, excæcat, pulices facit, imbre lutum fit.

Cleaveth. But the word is a great deal stronger than
this: it is almost, as S. Jerome translates it, *Is glued to the
ground.* And so they all, those great masters of spiritual
learning, tell us how utterly impossible a thing it is of ourselves to rise from those earthly trammels and desires to
which we are thus bound. But yet, from these very words
they bid us take comfort; reminding us of Him Who might
most truly have used them in the moment of His agony,
which agony was, nevertheless, only the beginning of His
victory. And that which happened to its Head may, save
through their own fault, also befall the members; more especially if they only take in their hearts, as well as on their
lips, the prayer which follows in the last verse. Of that verse
I have only to observe, that where we read *for Thy mercies'
sake,* the Vulgate and the LXX. give it *for Thy Name's sake.*

Ay.

G.

C.

Of that most blessed Name we have spoken so often and so
lately, that we will not repeat the same thoughts now.

And therefore:

Glory be to the FATHER, of Whom our fathers have told
us what He hath done in their time of old; and to the SON,
Who is the King That sends help unto Jacob: and to the
HOLY GHOST, Whom we make our boast all the day long;

As it was in the beginning, is now, and ever shall be:
world without end. Amen.

COLLECTS.

Arise, O LORD, and help us, and deliver us from all tempt- Ludolph.
ations of Satan; and do Thou, Who in the days of our
fathers didst overthrow the machinations of Thine enemies,
deliver us by the light of Thy countenance from the snares
of the devil. Through our LORD. (1.)

O LORD JESUS CHRIST, Whom we confess to be the LORD Mozarabic.
and King of ages, Who workest salvation in Jacob, and art
the sweet contemplation of Israel; implant salvation in our
hearts, and so blot out all offence of sin from our conscience,
that our spirits may receive Thee, the Light of Truth, and
being illumined by Thy splendour, may proceed from strength
to strength in Thy faith. Amen. Through Thy mercy. (11.)

O GOD our King, Who sendest salvation to Jacob, over- Mozarabic.
throw, by the majesty of Thy Name, the attacks of every
temptation. Make our faith firm, of Thy mercy condescend
to our humility; and ever be present in our defence. Amen.
Through Thy mercy. (11.)

PSALM XLV.

TITLE.—LXX. and Vulgate: To the end: for them that shall be
changed: for the Sons of Core, to understanding. A Song for the
Beloved. English Bible; To the Chief Musician upon Shoshannim,
Maschil, a Song of Loves. Rather: To the Supreme: for the Hexachord, (or, upon the Lilies,) by the Sons of Korah : an instructive
of Loves.

No title seems more obscure than this, or has given rise to a greater
number of interpretations. How the LXX. ὑπὲρ τῶν ἀλλοιωθησο-
μένων is derived from the Hebrew על־ששנים seems impossible to say.
But the mystical interpretation is easy : *To the End*, the Omega as
well as the Alpha, the Last as well as the First : *for them that shall* Ay.
be changed, either by the death to sin and the new life to righteousness; or *that shall be changed*, when this corruptible must put on
incorruption, and this mortal must put on immortality : "for the
trumpet shall sound, and the dead shall be raised incorruptible:
AND WE SHALL BE CHANGED." And all this is for the *Sons of Core*,

the sons or followers of the Cross. *To understanding :* that is, for
the interpretation of so great a mystery as that which occurs in the
next phrase,—*a Song for the Beloved :* a Hymn to CHRIST as the
Bridegroom, and to the Union, never to be separated, of the Word
with our nature.

To the end. As before, Aquila has τῷ νικοποιῷ : as before, our
Version inserts the word *musician :* while we will retain our old version,—To the Supreme.

On Shoshannim. Aquila has it, ἐπὶ τοῖς κρίνοις : Symmachus,
ὑπὲρ τῶν ἀνθῶν. The lily has this name, as a six-leaved flower : it
lingers in the Spanish *açucena.* I wonder that this was not the
favourite mediæval version. In a Psalm that speaks of the glories
of the Virgin Church, of the glorious Virgin of Virgins, and of
"the Virgins that be her fellows," the allusion to the lilies among
whom the Lamb feedeth would have been so exquisitely beautiful.

> Tu pascis inter lilia,
> Septus choreis Virginum ;
> Sponsus decorus gloriæ,
> Sponsisque reddens præmia.

And again :

> Liliis Sponsus recubat, rosisque
> Tu, tuo semper bene fida Sponso,
> Et rosas Martyr, simul et dedisti
> Lilia Virgo.

*Santol. Vic-
torin.*

*In hunc
Psalm.*

*S. Greg.
Nyss. in loc.*

*Vatablus.
Nebrensis.
Calmet.
Dr. Good.*

*S. Petr.
Chrysol.
Serm. 143.*

S. Basil connects the *breve lilium* with the *pro iis qui commuta-
buntur,* as if the quickly fading life of man was set forth literally by
the one translation, and mystically by the other. He will have the
change also taken of the daily renewal for which each member of
the Church prays : and S. Gregory Nyssen, expanding his brother's
remarks, symbolises this by the petals of the lily, once mere damp,
foul mould of the earth, now vying with snow in purity and bril-
liance. And with reference to this, I may quote those noble words,
In carne præter carnem vivere non terrena vita est, sed cœlestis : et
si vultis scire, Angelicam gloriam acquirere majus est, quam habere.
Esse Angelum, felicitatis est : Virginem esse, virtutis. Still, I think
that the *hexachord,* which is supported by great authorities is, on
the whole, the better interpretation, and seems to accord more easily
with the titles of Psalms IV. and V.

A Song for the Beloved. Here, for the first time, that dear title of
the New Testament is made the heritage of the Church : Rex vir-
tutum, dilecti dilecti : and well may it be so at the commencement
of the loveliest description of love that the Old Testament contains,—the Book of Loves being left out of the question.

ARGUMENT.

ARG. THOMAS. That CHRIST, fairer in form than the children of
men, joined by GOD the FATHER to the Church, is to be blessed.
[The Psalm] must be read to understand Matthew. The Prophet
speaketh concerning the Queen of the South. The Voice of the
FATHER concerning the SON by the Prophet, setting forth the repentance of His people. The Prophet speaketh concerning CHRIST
to the Church. The Church is described as the Bride of CHRIST.

VEN. BEDE. The Prophet, replenished with celestial meats, promiseth that he will announce the tidings of the LORD's Incarnation; that thence, whence he himself was satiate, others also might be fed. The first part of this epithalamium contains the praises of the Bridegroom: that is, of the LORD the SAVIOUR, in four ways. In the first, *My heart hath indited a good Word.* In the second part, the Bride the Church is praised for a like number of mystic virtues: *Hearken, O daughter, and consider.*

SYRIAC PSALTER. A Psalm written by the Sons of Korah in the time of Moses. The apparition of CHRIST, and concerning the Church, and of the glorious virtue of the LORD.

S. JEROME. The whole Psalm is referred to CHRIST, of Whom the FATHER saith in the Gospel: "This is My Beloved SON, in Whom I am well pleased." Or the Psalm contains the Sacrament of spiritual marriage; that is, the union of CHRIST with the Church: it begins then with the Voice of the FATHER.

VARIOUS USES.

Gregorian. Tuesday. Matins.
Parisian. Saturday. Tierce.
Ambrosian. Thursday of the First Week. II. Nocturn.
Monastic. Monday. Matins.

SPECIAL. *Little Office of B. V. M.* II. Nocturn.
Christmas Day. I. Nocturn.
Common of Virgins. I. Nocturn.
Common of Apostles. I. Nocturn.
English. Christmas Day. Matins.
Quignon. Thursday. Tierce.

ANTIPHONS.

Gregorian. Ferial. My heart * is inditing a good matter.
Ambrosian. Thy seat, O GOD * is for ever and ever. K. K. K.
Little Office of B. V. M. Hail, full of grace * the LORD is with thee: blessed art thou among women.
Christmas Day. Full of grace are Thy lips, * because GOD hath blessed Thee for ever.
Common of Apostles. Thou shalt make them princes over all lands; they shall remember Thy Name, O LORD.
Common of Virgins. According to Thy worship * and renown ride on.

1 My heart is inditing of a good matter : I speak of the things that I have made unto the king.

Auster veni, perfla mentem,
Et accende torpescentem
Aquilonis frigore!
Surge tepor Aquilonis,
Novo rore, novis donis
Fœcundato pectore!

So *he* may well pray, who takes in hand this most marvellous, most mysterious, most burning of all Psalms to interpret. *My heart is inditing. Eructavit cor meum verbum bonum.* Here, more clearly than ever yet, we have the ineffable Name of the Logos bestowed by the FATHER on the Only-Begotten SON. O insuperable clause, proof sword of the Church against all heresies on the Incarnation! So Tertullian hews down Marcion and Praxeas: so S. Cyril of Alexandria, his Arian opponent; so S. Ambrose: so again and again and again S. Athanasius[1] fought and conquered. Hence that great saint shows the Word[a] to be Only-Begotten; hence Nazianzen demonstrates Him[b] to be Consubstantial; hence Augustine and Jerome speak at length on the Only FATHER of the Only SON. That the saying is from the FATHER is the teaching of by far the larger part of Ecclesiastical doctors; yet there are not wanting those who assign it to David.[c] It is almost impossible to enter into the very strict explanations of the *Eructation* of the good word, without falling into coarseness that modern taste will not endure. "Confert ructus externi generatio, quæ necessitate quâdam fit, ad intelligendum quomodo generatio divina sit omnino necessaria et naturalis, et ex fœcunditate divinitatis: et quasi ex plenitudine intra ventrem Patris absque projectione, divisione, sectione, diminutione, aut aliâ quâpiam ejusmodi ratione, cujusmodi cernitur in aliorum viventium generationibus." *A good Word* indeed: That same Word That spake and it was done; That commanded, and it stood fast: That Word That was in the beginning, and was with GOD, and was GOD: That Word which was preached by the Angel Gabriel in the cottage at Nazareth, and has from that time to this been proclaimed to every kindred, and tongue, and people, and nation. *I speak of the things I have made unto the King,*—or, as the Vulgate,—*I tell my works to the King.* And so the FATHER tells all the secrets of His own eternity to that King anointed by Him upon the holy hill of Sion; told Him the plan of human redemption; laid out before Him the mystery of death destroyed by death, and the Tree atoned for by the Tree. And do thou in another sense, O Christian, tell thy works also to the King; thy works of sin and misery to the King That suffered for them on the Cross; thy works of weakness, to the King Omnipotent; thy works that have any sweet savour of His grace in them to the King That will unite them with His Own Royal Merits, and plead these merits for thine.

My heart hath produced a good Word. And therefore: Βηθλεὲμ ἑτοιμάζου· εὐτρεπιζέσθω ἡ φάτνη· τὸ σπήλαιον δεχέσθω. Ἡ Ἀλήθεια ἦλθεν· ἡ σκιὰ παρέδραμε· καὶ Θεὸς ἀνθρώποις ἐκ Παρθένου πεφανέρωται, μορφωθεὶς τὸ καθ' ἡμᾶς, καὶ θεώσας τὸ πρόσλημμα. Διὸ Ἀδὰμ ἀνανεοῦται σὺν τῇ Εὔᾳ, κράζοντες· ἐπὶ γῆς εὐδοκία ἐπεφάνη, σῶσαι τὸ γένος ἡμῶν.

2 My tongue is the pen : of a ready writer.

Lib. ii. cap. 4, and Lib. ii. cap. 7, 11.
S. Cyril. Alex. in Tim. ii. 14.
S. Ambros. de benedict. Patre.
[a] De Decret. Conc. Nic.
[b] Orat. 49, de fide.
[c] C. Arnobius. S. Laurent. Justin.

L.

G.
S. Ambros. de Filii Divin. cap. 2.
Euseb. de Præp. Evang. vii. 5.
S. August. de Gen. Lib. imperf. cap. v.

Idiomela for Lauds on Christmas Day.
S. Sophron.

[1] Cont. Arian. Orat. iii.; Orat. iv. Serm. *de Deo Deus.* Serm. *omnia mihi tradita sunt.* Epist. ad Marcell. Epist. de sententia S. Dionysii. Epist. de Decret. Conc. Nicen.

And still they refer it to the Divinity of the Son of God. In itself a word may sound and pass; but this good Word is lasting[1] as the sentence graven with an iron pen and lead in the rock for ever. It is the Father, then, Who continues; it is the Son Who is the Tongue by Whom the Father speaks to the world,—the enduring Voice, one jot or tittle of which can never pass away. And this is the more ordinary explanation of primitive commentators; and the *ready writing* of this Divine Pen, they say, pierced three thousand to the heart in one sermon of S. Peter's; in one moment converted Saul the Persecutor into S. Paul the Apostle; writes its laws on the fleshly tables of innumerable hearts, daily and hourly, from East to West, and from pole to pole. But others will have it that David now speaks; he the pen held by God, he the ready writer, to chronicle the glories of the heavenly nuptials to which we are invited to draw near. And S. Augustine[a] that, just as the tongue, when it speaks, must pass between the two lips, so the prophetic tongue speaks under the guidance of the Two Testaments. They are rich in their references to these two portions of Holy Scripture. The two[b] points of a pen, that form any one letter,—that verse, " The Lord spake once, and these two things we have heard,"—the didrachm found for tribute money in the mouth of the fish,—the two pence given by the good Samaritan to the host,—the rod and the staff of which David tells,—the ladder of Jacob, with its two uprights and many rundles,—the tongs of Isaiah, which between them held the burning coal of the Holy Ghost. And again, in the double split of the pen, they see the Divine and Human Natures of our Lord: the ink is the Blood of Calvary; the pen, expressing the meaning of the holder, sets forth Him Who is the Express Image of the Father's Person, and renders Him visible to human eyes. Or, if we take the words as said by David of himself, most fully do they stand forth, as the true theory of inspiration, in these days of trouble, and rebuke, and blasphemy. The human author merely the pen; God the writer. A faultless pen, too, as Albertus says, writing so quickly, so clearly, without blots, without erasures. Yes: let who will talk of the human element in the composition of Scripture, not so did those holy men of God, who spake as they were moved by the Holy Ghost, teach of themselves.

Marginal notes: S. Greg. Moral. xxxiii. 3. — S. Cyril. Alex. in Isa. cap. 29. Euseb. Demonst. Evangelic. cap. 3. Procopius, præf. in Gen. S. Hieronym. in Esech. cap. xl. — [a] Vel potius S. Eucherius; *de formulis.* — Hildebert. deAdv.Dom. Serm. 3. [b] Zeno Veron. de somn.Jacob. Ps. lxii. 12. S. Matt. xvii. 23. S. Luke x. 35. Ps. xxiii. 4. — S. Ambros. — S. Albert. Magn.

3 Thou art fairer than the children of men : full of grace are thy lips, because God hath blessed thee for ever.

[1] Quia quod lingua dicitur sonat et transit : quod scribitur manet: cum ergo dicat Deus Verbum, et Verbum quod dicitur non sonat et transeat sed dicitur et maneat, scriptis hoc maluit Deus comparare quam sonis. S. August.

> Salve Jesu, Candor Lucis,
> Thronum tenens summi ducis!
> Qui es passus pœnas crucis,
>   Nobis sis propitius!
>
> Salve Jesu, Fons amoris!
> Qui es totus, intus, foris,
> Plenus maximi dulcoris
>   Et superni luminis.

Yes: in spite of the whole phalanx of Eastern Doctors, take this verse of that dear LORD's external beauty as Man. If with one voice, and basing their opinion on Isaiah's " He hath no form nor comeliness, and when we shall see Him, there is no beauty that we should desire Him," S. Cyril of Alexandria,[a] S. Athanasius,[b] S. Basil, Hesychius, Euthymius, S. Gregory[c] Nazianzen, followed by Remigius and Arnobius, deny that the Incarnate WORD possessed human beauty, let us rather follow the more pious opinion of all the great teachers of the West, that of this Son of David also is that saying true, "in all Israel there was none so much to be praised for His beauty : from the sole of His Feet even to the crown of His Head there was no blemish in Him." It is the general tradition of the Church; it is the almost[1] universal representation of the schools of Christian art. S. Bernard,[d] in many and many a passage of ravishing beauty, tells us of the exquisite glory of our LORD's Humanity. S. Anselm expressly blames a vision of S. Bridget[e] for denying it. S. Isidore[f] breaks forth with a rapture of admiration at the earthly glory of the Incarnate WORD: and S. Thomas seems almost to claim such a belief as part[g] of the Catholic Faith. I pass over the most uncertain authority of the Epistle to Abgarus, and that of Lentulus. But yet I firmly believe, that a certain type of the Face of our Blessed LORD would not have been so universally received in Eastern, and early Western art, unless it had possessed some real foundation. Every one must be acquainted with the general idea of That Countenance as given in Byzantine icons, and crystallized, if we may so speak, in the West under the name of the *Dieu d'Amiens*.[2] But, even towards the end of that weary thirty-three years, His Face was so marred more than any man's, that the Jews asked, "Thou art not yet fifty years old, and hast Thou seen Abraham?" And then, when it had been smitten by the soldiers,—when that Divine Head

Marginal notes:
a Glaphyr. Lib. 9.
b Orat. de Hum. suscept.
c In 1 Sam. cap. 1.
2 Sam. xiv. 25.
d Serm. 70 in Cant. Serm. 1 de omnibus SS.
e In Rev. Lib. i. cap. 19.
f In Gen. cap. xxx.
g In hunc Psalm.

---

[1] I say *almost*, because there was undoubtedly a local school of art, which seems confined to the central South of France, which represented our LORD as deficient not only in Divine Majesty, but in ordinary human grace. See on this subject Didron, Hist. de Dieu, p. 179. How far this view, though undoubtedly held by some Catholics, might not have its origin in the teaching of the Albigenses, is a question far beyond the limits of a Commentary to decide.

[2] See the excellent remarks of Viollet le Duc on this subject. Gloss. iii. 245.

had been crowned with thorns,—when it was brought into
the dust of death, then was not that prophecy of Isaiah fulfilled: " And when we shall see Him, there is no beauty that
we should desire Him?" *Full of grace are Thy lips.* " Thy Cant. iv. 11.
Lips, O my Spouse, drop as the honeycomb; honey and milk
are under Thy Tongue." Blessed Lips indeed, that spake as
never man spake; that said to the poor paralytic, " Thy sins
are forgiven thee;" that comforted the woman taken in
adultery with " Neither do I condemn thee;" that on the s. Bernard.
evening of a stormy day again showed to the longing eyes of
man the Eden whence he had been banished for four thousand
years, saying, " To-day shalt thou be with Me in Paradise;"
that by one word made Himself known to her that loved most,
" Mary!" that first gave a blessing to the little band of
Apostles, ere they said aught further, " Peace be unto you!"
But how *full* for us *of grace,* how blessed for us beyond all
power of conception, if those lips shall one day, after all our
errors, in spite of all our sins, notwithstanding all our wander- L.
ings, pronounce to us the *Venite, benedicti! Because God hath
blessed Thee for ever.* They inquire what is the force of the
διὰ τοῦτο, the *propterea*; and there seems an equal difficulty
in the *because* of our English Version. It were better to
take it, *Verily, God hath blessed Thee.* " I have blessed him,
yea, and he shall be blessed." " He shall see of the travail
of His soul, and shall be satisfied." Blessed, even in those
hours of Agony on the Cross: for then the LORD of Hosts
was reigning on Mount Zion and in Jerusalem, and before Isa. xxiv. 23.
His Ancients gloriously: *blessed* even when reduced by the
Ecce Homo to the lowest condition of earthly misery; for in
the precious Blood that then poured from Him the great
multitude that no man can number, out of every kindred,
and tongue, and people, and nation, were afterwards to wash
their robes, and make them white, even as His own raiment
had been white on Mount Tabor. They dispute whether this S. Basil.
blessing is spoken of our LORD according to His Divinity or S. Chrysost.
His Humanity. But, though some Greek Fathers apply it S. Cyril.
Hieros.
to Him as Man, the general voice of the Church takes it of
that *ab eterno* benediction which by right of inheritance per-
tained to the Co-Eternal Word. And thus David, having in
a rapture of holiness unveiled the King of kings as He is in
His own eternity, now proceeds to arm Him for His wars on
earth, saying:

4 Gird thee with thy sword upon thy thigh, O
thou most Mighty : according to thy worship and
renown.

5 Good luck have thou with thine honour : ride
on, because of the word of truth, of meekness, and
righteousness; and thy right hand shall teach thee
terrible things.

"The sword of the SPIRIT, which is the Word of GOD," says S. Paul. And though there, no doubt, in the highest and noblest sense, that Word is the Co-eternal and Consubstantial Word, yet here, most of the commentators agree in applying to the message of the Gospel this sword of which the Psalmist speaks. And in that this sword is bound on the thigh, they see that these glad tidings, wherewith, as by a mighty weapon, the enemies of the human race are to be hewn down, are the doctrine of the Incarnation. With this they compare the adjuration of Abraham to his faithful servant, "Put, I pray thee, thy hand under my thigh;" and that of Jacob in his last command to Joseph. And to the same effect we read, in the Apocalypse, that He—He, the King to Whom this psalm is indited—"hath on His vesture and on His thigh a name written, King of kings and LORD of lords." Here also they take the "vesture" of the glory of His Divinity; the "thigh" of the humility of His Humanity: in both, evermore to be victorious. *With Thy sword.* There are not wanting those who would see in this sword the Cross; that bitter pang which, as it pierced the heart of His Blessed Mother, so His own, when He cried, "Oh, My FATHER, if it be possible, let this cup pass from Me!" yet still in reference to the Incarnation, because, had He not first been true Man to suffer, He could not thus have proved Himself True GOD to save. And of this Cross He said Himself, "I came not to send peace upon earth, but a sword;" when the son shall be divided against the father, and the daughter against the mother. S. Augustine works these sayings out to a marvellous extent: how our LORD Himself is the son, the Christian Church the daughter, and the Synagogue the mother. But according to what *worship and renown?* What is the chief glory of Him Who has just before been addressed as *Most Mighty?* And, as the Carmelite well replies, the Church teaches us, where she says, "O GOD, Who declarest Thy Almighty power most chiefly in showing mercy and pity." It is this sword, then, the proclamation of His mercy, whereby He makes His way among His enemies; not in the storm, not in the earthquake, not in the fire, but in the still small voice. *Good luck have Thou with Thine honour : ride on, because of the Word of truth, of meekness, and righteousness.* Remarkable are the varieties of translation here. The LXX., καὶ ἔντεινον καὶ κατευοδοῦ καὶ βασίλευε: the Gallican and Roman, *Intende, prospere procede et regna:* the Chaldaic, *He shall multiply children, therefore shalt thou be prosperous : as horsemen upon the throne of the kingdom :* our Bible version, *And in Thy Majesty ride prosperously,* which is the nearest to the original. The sense of ἔντεινον, *intende,* made out of the Hebrew הֲדָרְךָ, was taken by mediæval writers of intense care and strife, which it cannot possibly signify. And the variety of ways in which, under that idea, it has been interpreted, are more puzzling than profitable. To me, the

best commentary on this most noble verse is that much mis- Apoc. vi. 1—
understood passage in the Apocalypse, where the Four Living 8.
Creatures address[1] their LORD in four different characters,
with COME! and He accordingly appears successively as the
Rider, on the White Horse; as the Conqueror, on the Red
Horse; as the Warrior, on the Black Horse; as the Judge,
on the Pale—or rather, Ghastly (χλωρὸς) Horse, with Death
and Hell led in triumph behind Him. This is indeed *riding
on in His Majesty.* And why? *Because of the Word of
truth, of meekness, and righteousness.* Here they find a
glorious application to the three orders of saints: the *truth,*
of the martyrs; the *meekness,* of the confessors; the *righteousness,* of just men. The *truth,* of the martyrs; they,
faithful and true witnesses to Him—He, the true and faithful
Witness to them:

Testis tuus est in cœlis,
Testis verax et fidelis,
Testis innocentiæ:

Adam. de S.
Victor.

the *meekness,* of the confessors; as the Church sings—

The day that crowns with deathless fame
This *meek* confessor of Thy Name:

and the *righteousness,* of the just; "for the fine linen is the
righteousness of saints." These, then, fill the ranks of that
heavenly city: ἡ ἄνω Ἱερουσαλήμ, ἡ μὴ βλεπομένη, νοουμένη δὲ S. Greg.
πόλις, ἐν ᾗ πολιτευόμεθα καὶ πρὸς ἣν ἐπειγόμεθα, ἧς πολίτης Χριστὸς, Naz. Orat.
καὶ συμπολῖται πανήγυρις καὶ ἐκκλησία πρωτοτόκων ἀπογεγραμμένων xi.
ἐν οὐρανοῖς, καὶ περὶ τὸν μέγαν πολιστὴν ἑορταζόντων τῇ θεωρίᾳ τῆς
δόξης. *And Thy right hand shall teach Thee terrible things.*
So also S. Jerome; but the LXX. and the Vulgate, and so
the Slavonic, *Thy right hand shall lead Thee wondrously;* it
should rather be, *teach Thee wonders.* Both senses are true,
according to the many-sided fulness of the Hebrew. *Terrible things* indeed that Right Hand suffered on the Cross:

Manus sancta, te complector,
Et gemendo condilector:
Grates ago plagis tantis,
Clavis diris, guttis sanctis
Dans osculum cum lacrymis.

Salutatio
aurea.

Terrible things that Right Hand inflicted on its foes: "Thy Tertull.
right hand, O LORD, hath dashed in pieces the enemy." cont. Jud.
c. 10.

---

[1] Our Version makes the four Living Creatures say, "Come *and see.*" But (1) observe that the words "and see" are not in the best MSS.; (2) that the Living Creatures never elsewhere address a created being; (3) that as the Conqueror on the White Horse certainly represents our LORD, so by analogy should the succeeding appearances, which come forward at the call of the three other ζῶα.

In the other sense: *Thy right hand*—that is, the works of
Thy right hand—*shall lead Thee wondrously*; from the form
of a Servant and the Death of the Cross to the express Image
of the FATHER, and the participation of the Throne. For
here the Psalmist gives as it were the summary of that most
Phil. ii.   Divine theology of S. Paul, where he shows how the sufferings of the Incarnate WORD merited the elevation of the
consubstantial Humanity.

6 Thy arrows are very sharp, and the people shall
be subdued unto thee : even in the midst among the
King's enemies.

And here, too, the versions widely differ. The LXX.,
after *very sharp*, add δυνατέ, *O Thou puissant!* So does the
Slavonic, CИЛНЕ, with the same meaning. The Roman gives
34 Moral. c. *potentissime*, which S. Augustine recognises, and S. Gregory
5.
ᵃ Epist. cxlv. quotes. S. Jerome, in one[a] place, observes that it is a mere
ᵇ In Isaiam, addition from verse 3; but in another he quotes the inser-
c. xlix. tion.[b] Our version is the only one which translates *in the
midst*: instead of *the heart*, which is the undoubted meaning.
The Bible Version: *Thy arrows are sharp in the heart of the
King's enemies.* The Vulgate, following the LXX., reads *in
corde*; the Gallican, better, *in corda*, except that the Hebrew
is not plural.
    And verily sharp are those *arrows* of love, which *subdue*
the hardest *heart* among the *people* that "imagine a vain
thing against the LORD'S Anointed." "O glorious wound,"
cries Nyssen, "O sweet stroke, whereby life and love penetrate into the inner man!" *Thy arrows* in very deed : Thou
2 Kings xiii. art the true Elisha, that must command to take bow and
16. quiver; Thou must lay Thy Hands, Thy Wounded Hands,
on his to strengthen them, before each Joash among Thy
Priests can shoot the arrow of the LORD'S deliverance. And
all their virtue comes from Thy bed of death, the hard bed of
the Cross. These were the arrows that pierced the hearts of
the martyrs,

Propert. ii.   Nec quisquam ex illo vulnere sanus abit :

S. Cyril. and therefore "we fools counted their life madness, and their
Alex. in end to be without honour." S. Cyril explains the properties
Zach. c. ix.
§ 60, 61. of these Divine arrows, and how the people fell under them ;
and Cardinal Hugo gives their mystical characteristics neatly
enough :—

> Lignea (1), recta (2), rigens, gracilis (3), capitata (4), rotunda,
> Ferro (5) barbato lato, pennata (6) secante,
> Arcu (7) jacta rotat, volat (8) eminus, et pharetratur (9) :

characteristics which, as applied to the message of the Gospel, the reader may work out at his leisure with the texts in the note :[1] the "verba," as S. Jerome says, "cor transfigentia, amorem excitantia." And it is because wounded with these arrows that the Bride says, "Stay me with flagons, comfort me with apples; for I am sick of love." S. Hieronym. in Cant. ii. 5.

7 Thy seat, O GOD, endureth for ever : the sceptre of thy kingdom is a right sceptre.

"Unto the SON He saith" it : the HOLY GHOST, therefore, teaches Who it is That addresses, as well as Who it is That is addressed. It is not wonderful that the Jews and the Arians should have been perpetually pressed with the commencement of the verse : a formal proof of the MESSIAH's Divinity which no art of the devil or man can gainsay. So Tertullian,[a] so Eusebius,[b] so S. Cyril of Alexandria,[c] so S. Athanasius,[d] so S. Gregory Nazianzen,[e] and S. Cyril of Jerusalem.[f] They dispute of what throne the Prophet speaks; whether of that Judiciary Seat which, at the consummation of all things, the SON, according to that most deep theology of S. Paul, will resign to the FATHER,—or the seat of Kingly authority, which will last for ever and ever. And of this latter it seems better to take it. "He shall reign over the house of Jacob, and of His kingdom there shall be no end." *The sceptre of Thy kingdom :* or *rod,* as it is in the versions. This is the rod that devoured the serpents of the spiritual Pharaoh, itself esteemed as one of them, when they said, "He hath a devil." This is the rod which divided the Red Sea into two parts, and made its depths a way for the ransomed to pass over. This is the rod which stretched out against Pharaoh and his hosts, overwhelmed them in the mighty waters. This is the rod that smote the stony rock, and the waters gushed out, and the streams flowed withal. This is the rod that, laid up in the Tabernacle, bloomed blossoms and yielded almonds. This is the sceptre which every trembling Esther, if she can only venture to touch, shall live. This is the rod that we must hold in our hands while we eat the spiritual passover. This is the rod wherewith we must pass, with Jacob, over the Jordan. This is the rod that breaks "the staff of his shoulder, the rod of his oppressor;" that shatters the "Assyrian, the rod of his anger," through which the "rod of the ungodly shall not rest upon the lot of the righteous;" that causes the wicked to exclaim, concerning the spiritual Moab, "How is the strong staff broken, and the beautiful rod!" that overthrows the "rod of pride" in the mouth of the foolish.

Heb. i. 8.
[a] Cont. Prax. 13.
[b] Demonstr. Evang. iv. 15.
[c] In S. Joann. ii. 14.
[d] Orat. ii. contr. Arian.
[e] Orat. 1. de Filio.
[f] Cateches. xvi.
Virga, ῥάβδος, שֵׁבֶט.

L.

Isa. ix. 4.

Isa. x. 5.

Ps. cxxv. 3.

Jer. xlviii. 17.

8 Thou hast loved righteousness, and hated ini-

[1] (1) Prov. xv. 4; (2) Prov. iv. 25; (3) Isa. xlix. 2 m.; (4) Eph. iv. 15; (5) Dan. ii. 40; (6) Isa. xl. 31; (7) Isa. xlix. 2, 1. All these are from Ay.

quity : wherefore God, even thy God, hath anointed
thee with the oil of gladness above thy fellows.

Thou hast loved righteousness. " *Dilexi justitiam, et odivi
iniquitatem,*" (they were the last words of S. Gregory VII.,)
" *et ideo morior in exilio.*" But it was well answered by one
that stood by, though whether the reply was understood by
the parting spirit is not certain, " In exile, servant of Christ,

**Baron. An-
nal. xi. 587.**
thou canst not die, seeing that God hath given thee the
heathen for thine inheritance, and the uttermost parts of the
earth for thy possession." The Chaldee paraphrast applies

L.
the verse thus : " Thou, O Christ the King, hast loved righteousness;" and to Whom else should we address it? And
how dearly He loved it He showed by the fulfilment of the
promise made as soon as the earthly Paradise was lost, that
the heavenly Eden should be won by His own sufferings;
that promise on which so many prophets and righteous men
so strongly and so securely anchored their golden hopes;
that promise which, tested so fearfully in Gethsemane, in the

W.
Pavement, at Calvary, was triumphant over all agony, endured all shame, lived through and prevailed by death.
Therefore. And that, S. Thomas says, either as a final or
effective cause. Therefore hast Thou wrought righteousness, that God might anoint Thee: or, To this end God
anointed Thee, both as King, Priest, and Prophet, that Thy
sceptre might be the golden sceptre of mercy, or the iron one
of severity; that Thy rod, as the True Aaron's, might ever-

**S. Thomas
Aquinas.**
lastingly blossom; that Thy staff might bring forth living
waters for Thy people, as did that of Moses; and, as did *not*
that of Elisha, raise the corpse—the human race, dead in
trespasses and sins—to a better life. *The oil of gladness.*
We may take this clause in two senses. The first, *Wherefore,*[1] *O God, Thy God hath anointed Thee;* where we have a

**S. Hilar. Lib.
4, de Trinit.
S. Ambros.
c. 2, Lib. 1,
de Fide.**
manifest reference to the Blessed Trinity : the address being
to the Son, *O God;* the action from the Father, *Thy God;*
and the Holy Ghost represented by the *oil of gladness* : as
it is written, " How God anointed Jesus of Nazareth with

Acts x. 38.
the Holy Ghost;" and as the Church says,

Tu spiritalis Unctio.

**S. Athanas.
de Un. Deit,
1.**
But others see in the redoubled nominative the Father and
the Holy Ghost, taking the oil of gladness rather for the
grace of that Blessed Spirit than Himself; and considering our
Lord's Person sufficiently expressed, though not absolutely
named. But how are we to take the *unction* itself? Are we to

---

[1] The Greek, ὁ Θεός, ὁ Θεός
σου, is ambiguous ; but the Slavonic gives the vocative : **ПОМА-
ZATA, БЖЕ, БГЪ ТВОИ.**

understand it of that manifestation of the Grace and Divinity of the Hypostatic Union, when, in His Baptism, the Three Glorious Persons were revealed together? If we do, we shall follow S. Chrysostom,[a] S. Hilary,[b] S. Ambrose.[c] S. Augustine sees a type of this in the stone which Jacob anointed; an unction which clearly possessed some deep mystical meaning, since it was repeated by Jacob on the occasion of his second visit to Bethel. Or shall we rather take it of the sanctifying grace bestowed on the Human Nature of the LORD, both by Himself,—"For their sakes I sanctify Myself,"—and by the FATHER and the HOLY GHOST? Then we follow S. Athanasius.[d] Or we may, if we will, understand this unction of the glory of His Resurrection and Ascension; and then we have S. Jerome on our side. They who take it of the sanctifying, inherent grace which CHRIST, so far as Man, received,—so far as GOD, gave,—see in another Psalm a lovely type of this interchange: "it is like the precious ointment upon the Head"—the Divinity—"that went down the beard, even Aaron's beard, and ran down to the skirts of his clothing"—His Humanity. Hence they proceed to discuss the difficult question, whether the soul of CHRIST can be said to have merited the Incarnation and the Hypostatic Union. And they reply, Not in an ordinary and strict sense, because the Human Soul of CHRIST had no existence before the very moment of the Hypostatic Union, which was the exact instant of the Conception; and before its existence could have merited nothing. Yet still they allow that, in a certain sense, GOD willed to bestow on that Soul the grace of the Union, in prevision of the merits that it would thereafter acquire. And this is the general opinion of the Schoolmen, based on the deepest teaching of S. Augustine. S. Hilary, indeed, in one place seems to speak of antecedent merit in the Human Nature; but it is probably rather from an obscurity of language than from obscurity of thought. Observe, too, that the blessed company of heaven ascribe to the Death of our LORD His principal merit,— "Worthy is the Lamb *That was slain* to receive glory," &c.; and this is exactly according to the Pauline theology in Phil. ii. 1—9. *Above Thy fellows. Thy participators—præ participulis tuis,* S. Jerome reads; and so does the Vulgate in the quotation to the Hebrews; and the Council of Frankfort, and Lactantius. And who are these *fellows* or *peers?* And it is better to take it in the sense of a comparison of the Human Nature of our LORD with that of all those who have been made partakers of the same grace, angels as well as men; they partly and imperfectly, He in plenitude from the beginning; though its manifestation grew more and more glorious, as S. Luke formally teaches. S. Cyril of Alexandria even goes so far as to say that the title of *Christotocos,* which only would Nestorius allow to the Blessed Virgin, is common to the mothers of all that have GOD's grace.

[a] Hic in Ps.
[b] Lib. 2, de Trinit.
[c] In Ep. Heb. c. i. v. 9.
Cf. Gen. xxviii. 18, and xxxiv. 14.
[d] Orat. 2, in Arian.
In S. Joan.

A.

Ps. cxxxiv. 2.

De predest. SS. c. xv.
De Bono Perseverantiæ, c. ult.
S. Hilar. de Trin. Lib. 4.

S. Hieronym. Ep. 140.
Hugo Card. in Heb. i. 9.
S. Athanas. Serm. ii. cont. Arian.
Epist. ad Solitar.

9 All thy garments smell of myrrh, aloes, and
cassia : out of the ivory palaces, whereby they have
made thee glad.

Myrrha, et gutta, et cassia—so the Gallican and Italic :
σμύρνα καὶ στακτὴ καὶ κάσσια—so the LXX. and the Slavonic.
We need not here enter into the precise nature of these gums :
it is enough to observe that מִנִּי, which our Version translates, without any particular sense, *whereby*, should rather be
Armenian, as in Jer. li. 27. *From palaces*—or rather cabinets—*of Armenian ivory they*—the garments there laid up
—*have rendered Thee glorious.*

Ay.

And what is myrrh but the bitterness of self-mortification
and self-denial? "A bundle of myrrh is my Beloved unto
me," exclaims the Church : "He shall lie all night"—all the
night of this world—"betwixt my breasts." Count up this
bundle, O Christian, and reckon all the sufferings, all the re-
jections, the fasts, the vigils, the doing good and bearing ill
of thy LORD : "My soul is exceeding sorrowful, even unto
death;" "Now is My soul troubled, and what shall I say?"
Aloes, good, say the physicians, against tumours and swell-
ings, what should they set forth but the humility which is in-

S. Matt. xi.
29.

deed the antidote to the swelling of pride? "Take My yoke
upon you, and learn of Me; for I am meek and lowly of
heart." And cassia, a reed that grows by running brooks,
and increases to an immense size, is a type of that faith which
begins at Baptism, and fills the whole world. Not that our
Bridegroom, in the strict sense, possessed or could possess
that faith, because that cannot be believed which is known
and seen ; but, as being the Author and Finisher of our faith,
He may be said thus to set it forth to us. And it is well
said, *All Thy garments.* For the garments represent the
Humanity of the LORD : and it was from His Humanity that
we are to take the example of self-mortification, of humility,
of faith. *Out of the ivory palaces.* Hear S. Augustine :

A.

"Would you understand the spiritual sense of *ivory palaces?*
Understand by them those magnificent houses and tabernacles of GOD, the hearts of the saints." He, however, joins
the commencement of the next verse with the conclusion of

Ay.

this : *whereby Thy daughters have made Thee glad.* The
Carmelite commentator takes the word *palaces*, as I have

Pyxides.

translated it above, in the sense of *caskets*, or *cabinets*.[1] Then

---

[1] In the LXX. it is ἀπὸ βά-
ρεων ἐλεφαντίνων. This some
translators mistook for βαρέων,
and turned it, without any possible sense, *a gravibus eburneis* ;
which got corrected, it appears,
into *a gradibus eburneis.* The

word, as used by the Greek Tra-
gedians, means a kind of flat-
bottomed Egyptian boat :

Ξέρξης δὲ πάντ᾽ ἐπέσπε δυσφρόνως
βαρίδεσσι ποντίαις.

But afterwards, and especially,

he sees in the King's daughters the ointment-bearers that were
very early at the sepulchre; and in the *casket* the vessel in which
they brought the precious ointments to anoint the Body of
that dear LORD. Gloriously does the Eastern Church exclaim,
τὰ μύρα τῆς ταφῆς σου αἱ Γυναῖκες κομίσασαι λαθραίως, πρὸς τὸ Μνῆμα
παρεγένοντο ὄρθριαι, τῶν Ἰουδαίων δειλιῶσαι τὴν αὐθάδειαν. καὶ στρα-
τιωτῶν προορῶσαι τὴν ἀσφάλειαν· ἀλλὰ φύσις ἀσθενὴς τὴν ἀνδρείαν
ἐνίκησεν· ὅτι γνώμη συμπαθὴς τῷ Θεῷ εὐηρέστησε· προσφόρως οὖν
ἐκραύγαζον Ἀνάστα, Κύριε, βοήθησον ἡμῖν, καὶ λύτρωσαι ἡμᾶς, ἕνεκεν
τοῦ Ὀνόματός σου !

Cathisma at the II. Stichologia of the Ointment-bearers.

10 Kings' daughters were among thy honourable
women : upon thy right hand did stand the queen
in a vesture of gold, wrought about with divers
colours.

On the whole, I believe this to be the correct division,
though that which connects the first clause of this verse
with the last verse is the more common. The Western
Church, S. Augustine, the Italic Version, S. Jerome, and
many of the Greek Fathers take that view: our Prayer
Book and Bible Versions follow the Hebrew and Chaldee.
However, as Lorinus very truly says : "Ad sensum parum
refert." We lose the beauty however of the original : *Kings'
daughters were among Thy jewels* בִּיקְרוֹתָיךְ : and compare
the promise ; "And they shall be Mine, saith the LORD of
Hosts, in that day when I make up My jewels." *The gold of
Ophir :* the Vulgate, less exactly, *in vestitu deaurato.* But
both in the LXX. and the Vulgate is the singular addition, not
in the Hebrew, περιβεβλημένη, πεποικιλμένη *circumdata varie-
tate.* They are quoted by S. Basil, S. Clement[a] of Alexandria, S. Ambrose,[b] S. Augustine, S. Cyprian, and are in the
Ethiopic and Arabic Versions. Where could they have come
from ?

S. Hieromyn. in Ezek. xxvii. Id. in Amos iii.

Mal. iii. 17.

[a] 6 Strom. cap. 5.
[b] 1 de Virgin.

Kings' daughters were among Thy honourable women.

> Lüstlich, solt du spazieren
> Mit froïd und jubilieren
> 　In gruner hymels ow,
> In gilgen und in rosen
> Solt du mit gotte kosen
> 　Dz er dich freuntlich schow.

> Gar warm solt du dich halten
> Und dich nit lon erkalten
> 　Noch diser mynne bad.

S. Jerome says, in Palestine, it came to mean an enclosed house, or tower. The Slavonic Version falls into the mistake I have just alluded to—ѠТѦЖЕСТЄН СЛОНОВЫ : *out of the ivory heavinesses :* to the subversion of all sense.

Din baden bulen sye
Die allerschönst Marie;
Ein Gott und namen drye
Mit andoch zu der lad.

Wacker-
nagel. p. 621.

As the mediæval poet says so lovingly, if a little too rap-
turously for our cooler taste, in his quaint *Platt-Deutsch.*
But *Kings' daughters?* Because if He Whom they follow
is King of kings and LORD of Lords, the Apostles are the
Kings over and by whom He rules, as it is written, All kings
shall fall down before Him. And it was through their
preaching that these lovely ones were gathered into the
Church; first heard of the place and the name better than
of sons and daughters; were appointed to seek a portion
among the hundred and forty and four thousand, and sharers
in the New Song. *Upon Thy Right Hand did stand the
Queen.* And to whom are we to give that glorious title?
Some will behold the Church Triumphant, the Jerusalem
that is the Mother of us all, the Happy Assembly, so glorious with the blood of the Martyrs, so illustrious with the
Confessions of snow-white Virginity! O former humility,
present sublimity! O once earthly tabernacle, now celestial
palace! O house once of clay, now temple of light! O
slave, once defiled and miserable with Egyptian bondage,
now glorious, now peerless, now beautiful, now all beauty,
now onely! Yet the tide of mediæval commentators, and
primitive writers also, runs strongly in here beholding not
the Church, but the Blessed Mother of GOD. So Athanasius,[a] so Hugh of S. Victor,[b] so the angelic Doctor, so S.
Peter Damiani.[c]

A.

Ps. lxxii.

S. Cæsarius
Arelat. Hom.
1.
S. Antoni-
nus. Proleg.
in iii. Part.

S. Bernard.

a Serm. de
Deiparâ (si
revera sit S.
Athan.)
b Erud.
Theol. ii. 125.
c 1 Serm. de
Assumpt.

The Se-
quence *Salve
Mater spe-
ciosa.*

O Maria, tu cœlorum
Intrans sedes, angelorum
Sociata es sanctorum,
Regina, agminibus :
Vidisti, quem diligebas,
Ad quem ire cupiebas,
Et quo frui sitiebas
Angelis cantantibus.

But S. Gregory and others in this Queen behold every faithful soul, but more especially those blessed ones who having
embraced the religious life here, are nearest to the Bridegroom of the Virgins there. So S. Ambrose, so S. Jerome
also, who, from his hard struggle at Rome in defence, or
rather in the foundation, of that life, had cause enough to
study and to quote this Psalm. *Upon Thy Right Hand.*
O happy estate, cries a mediæval writer, which we know is incapable of change! O most blessed place, which so many
saints have gone through fire and water to attain; which so
many martyrs have, after the manner of men, fought with
beasts at Ephesus to come at, which so many Confessors have
wandered about in sheepskins and goatskins if they might

S. Greg. in 1
Reg. 6. 1.
De virgini-
bus. 1. 6.

but possess at last. And behold, by one effort of virginal purity, it is held at last. Or, to return again to that interpretation which here beholds the Church, well says Richard of S. Victor, "O most sweet light of the purified mind, O wisdom of all the sciences, which are, as it were, *honourable women* to the Queen, that queen who always standeth on the right hand of GOD *in a vesture of gold.* Sometimes as a herald before a king, sometimes as a sound before the articulate word, sometimes as righteousness before the face of GOD, sometimes as the law in the presence of the Judge, so are these her handmaids to her, the Queen. But thou, O Queen, art thyself the immaculate law, the faithful testimony of the LORD, the lucid precept, the right judgment, the holy fear of GOD, the sweet meditation, herald and interpreter of the entire GOD." *Philip. Gisbrins. in loc.*

11 Hearken, O daughter, and consider, incline thine ear : forget also thine own people, and thy father's house.

And they see two persons who speak: they who interpret the *daughter* of Mary. It may be David, speaking according to the flesh, to her who was his last descendant except the greater Son of David: or it may be GOD the FATHER, speaking to her, the Immaculate Bride. But truly this is one of the passages which, above all others, show how utterly boundless are the meanings of the Psalter. Take it of the Church; and you see the exhortation to forget her Judaic origin, to cast behind her the oldness of the letter, and to enter into the liberty of the spirit. They who see in it every penitent soul, find a magnificent exhortation to the same effect as that of the Apostle,—" Old things are passed away; behold, all things are become new:" the old desires, the old pleasures, the old hopes; and after the struggle such as S. Paul tells us of, arrayed with that beauty in which the King delights. S. Chrysippus calls this verse and the following the bridal song of the Mother of GOD. S. Athanasius, comparing the words of the Archangel Gabriel with those of David, dwells on the *daughter* of the one contrasted with the Mary of the other. "Yes," as a mediæval saint exclaims, " as Abraham forgot Ur of the Chaldees with its dangers; as the Jews returning from Babylon thought no more of the house of bondage; as Lot, delivered from the hand of Chedorlaomer, entered into the companionship of Abraham; so now, O once afflicted Church, in Babylon is nothing but confusion; in Egypt is the darkness, and the terror, and the storm; in Sodom is the fulness of sin : in Canaan only is there liberty, and light, and abundance. In thy former habitation were the husks that the swine did eat; in thy father's house bread enough and to spare : there the mighty famine; here the Angels' food." *Forget also thine own people.* It is *S. Ambros. ad Virginem lapsam. S. Hieronym. Epist. 140. A. S. Chrysost. Hom. 41. S. Pet. Chrysologus : Serm. 14.*

II.   F

Serm. 6, in
Vigil. Nati-
vitat.
well said by S. Bernard, that the Christian soul must not
take pattern by the tribe of Manasseh : half that tribe, enticed by the pasture lands and corn-fields of the eastern side
of Jordan, petitioned to remain there ; only half pressed on
into the Land of Promise. And that petition to be allowed
to remain among the good things of this life is almost always
heard in wrath ; just as when the Gadarites, having lost their
swine, requested the destroyer of them to depart out of those
coasts, He yielded at once, and never returned.

12 So shall the King have pleasure in thy beauty :
for he is thy LORD GOD, and worship thou him.

And here they take occasion to dwell—those mediæval
writers, who lived in the times of our LORD as in their native
home—about the beauty, according to the flesh, of the Incarnate WORD and His Blessed Mother. But, undoubtedly,
there is a certain type of beauty handed down, from whatever original source derived, which has been retained in the
East to this day ; and which, as I have said before, completely refutes the idea held by some of the Fathers that the
prophecy in the 53rd of Isaiah signifies that our LORD, in
external appearance, had no beauty in Him. It would seem
that, in the twelfth century, the latter interpretation obtained
almost everywhere : whence we have those crucifixes in
which our LORD is, in a way to us now scarcely comprehensible, represented as deformed. But we shall have a better
occasion of entering on this question when we come to the
Ay.98th Psalm. It is a singular interpretation which many
mediæval writers have entertained, that *thy beauty* means
the Blessed Sacrament of the Eucharist, the Sacrament of all
beauty as well as of all love. And truly it is a very loving
thought, that that which is given to the Bride is so much her
own, that He Who gave it should, as it were, desire it and
have pleasure in it. So they compare the two texts : " With
desire I have desired to eat this Passover with you ;" and *So
shall the King have pleasure in thy beauty.* That is, this
Passover, this better than Passover, which is the source of
every great act of endurance or of daring,—this Passover,
which has prepared every elect soul for the marriage supper
of the LAMB,—this belonging now rather to the Bridegroom
to be His special beauty,—this I have pleasure in. As how
should He not, when such a multitude of petitions, arising
from every corner of the earth,—petitions for earthly help
and for spiritual aid, petitions against evil and for good, petitions alike for the whole and for the wounded, for the quick
and for the dead, are accepted in heaven by the beauty of
that Sacrifice in which, though CHRIST being risen from the
dead, dieth no more, yet He still vouchsafes to offer Himself
under the hands of sinful priests, and as the great High
Priest to offer that same Sacrifice at the Throne of GOD the
FATHER.

13 And the daughter of Tyre shall be there with a gift : like as the rich also among the people shall make their supplication before thee.

First notice that in the Septuagint and the Vulgate, though not in the Hebrew, it is, ALL *the rich among the people.* *Omnes* divites plebis. And so is our LORD's prophecy fulfilled, "It shall be more tolerable for Tyre and Sidon than for thee:" far more than fulfilled, when here, she that in the one passage is the type of all iniquity, in the other is to be the first-fruits of the Gentiles. And the whole verse turns on the same contrast. Our LORD teaches, "It is easier for a camel to go through the eye of a needle, than for a rich man to enter into the kingdom of GOD." It is not the poor, of whom, speaking generally, is the kingdom of heaven; but the rich, the very class to whom its entrance is so hard, that, as the LORD's greatest glory, *shall make their supplications to Thee.* It is worth quoting, the use S. Augustine makes of this passage : "They," he says, "who came from the East to bring their offerings to CHRIST, were not its daughters, but its sons. Why, then, here does it speak of *the daughter of Tyre,* the meaning being the same? Because, as the Apostle teaches, ' In CHRIST there is neither male nor female.'" And.again, Why the daughter of Tyre? Because. Tyre, as the empress of the sea, is a type of the powers of this world, seeing that in the next there shall be no more sea. So says the great Carmelite expositor; but more truly, I think, the Carthusian, who beholds in the daughter of Tyre, famous for its purple, the self-oblation of the martyrs ; according to that saying, "The shield of his mighty men is made red, the valiant men are in scarlet." And again, why the *gift,* when, as we know, there were three gifts that were offered to the infant King? Let the seraphic doctor answer : "Because, in addition to the ordinary sense, these three gifts are to be interpreted of the three cardinal virtues, which every faithful soul, made a king as well as a priest to GOD, must offer to its LORD,—faith, hope, and charity ; which yet may all, in another sense, be resolved into one—charity—the sum as well as the source of all graces."

A.

A.

Ay.

D. C.

S. Peter Damian. in loc.

Nahum ii. 3.

S. Bonaventura.

14 The King's daughter is all glorious within : her clothing is of wrought gold.

And first observe how the King, who made the marriage for His Son, here calls the bride of that Son His daughter. "O happy soul," so speaks Psellus, "who, raised from the dust of carnal affection, lifted above the miserable cares of this world, changed from Leah into Rachel, having the inheritance of Israel instead of the toils of Jacob, is received in the loving arms of such a Bridegroom, is made partaker of the inheritance of such a Father! And why should it be said

F 2

that *the King's daughter*, rather than the King's bride, is all-glorious? Truly, because that most loving Bridegroom wooed and obtained His Bride, not on the throne of His glory, but in the depth of His humility: this new Eve was created from the side of an Adam, Who slept no sleep of rest but the hard slumber of the Cross." S. Chrysostom lays his emphasis on the word *within:* he contrasts the glorious earthly buildings reared in his time, when the Church was being corrupted by contact with the world,—their jewels, their vestments, their outward array,—with the poverty and simplicity of those who were serving GOD in countries which were yet given to the worship of idols. And mediæval writers see in this verse a prophecy of the history of the Church, *The King's daughter is all glorious within:* there you have the original purity of the Church, when she was so glorious with her martyrs, so illustrious with her confessors, so resplendent with her ascetics. *Her clothing is of wrought gold:* and there you have the more dangerous age, in which the world forced her treasures on the Church, and the Church by receiving them became in part infused with the spirit of the world. Never to be forgotten is that speech of S. Gregory of Tours: "In the days of old there were wooden chalices and golden priests; now there are chalices of gold and priests of wood." *Her clothing is of wrought gold.* And thus one is sent to the character of the virtuous woman: "She maketh herself coverings of tapestry, her clothing is silk and purple." For consider what is that glorious outside of the Church militant, which is not only the typical representation of her triumphant sister, but also the safeguard of her own internal graces; as it is written, "Upon all the glory shall be a defence." Call to mind all the beauty of her buildings made after the pattern of heavenly things, her marvellous cathedrals, her abbeys, her countless parish churches, her chapels, hallowing every corner of the earth, the peaks of desolate mountains, the recesses of woody valleys, imprinting her own holiness on bridges, and castles, and lonely sea rocks; then her music, which we may piously believe to be but the echo of the Song of Moses and the Lamb; further, her marvellous system of antiphons, transfiguring the Psalms of the Jewish Synagogue to her own more celestial meaning. And if we are to take the Vulgate translation, *surrounded about with a variety*, there is nothing more glorious than the difference in oneness, and the unity in multiplicity of the Liturgies, and Offices, and Hours, of the whole Catholic Church. And, on the contrary, they observe that the chief glory of the synagogue was not from within, but from without; the symbols of her worship looked forward to better things than she herself possessed: whether you look at the tabernacle or the temple, the case is the same,—the Law had a shadow, not of good things present, but of good things to come. And they further contrast the *clothing of wrought*

Marginal notes:

S. Chrysost. in 1 Cor. iv. 15.

Ay.

A.

Ay.

gold,—that is, of such gold as will pass current in the judgment of the King,—with the phylacteries of the Pharisees, which have no balm except in the eyes of the world. S. Basil explains the text in a different way still. If *the King's daughter is all glorious within,* and also *her clothing is of wrought gold,* then the inside and the outside are in accordance with each other. As a much later hymn says, S. Basil in loc.

> Voci vita non discordet ;
> Cum vox vitam non remordet
> Dulcis est symphonia.

15 She shall be brought unto the King in raiment of needlework : the virgins that be her fellows shall bear her company, and shall be brought unto thee.

And, as S. Peter Damiani observes, every word of the sentence has to be pondered. In the first place, *She shall be brought.* What? she, the King's daughter, not able to come of herself? Surely not. You might as well ask, when David says, "Turn away mine eyes, lest they behold vanity," what? could not the man after God's own heart turn away his own eyes from beholding that which displeased God? Truly, no. All is *from* Him, and *of* Him both first and last : unless she be brought to the King, she will never go to the King of herself: unless our Lord after His Resurrection say, "Peace be unto you," He will never be asked to say it. *Of needlework.* That is, that the preparation which is to make her fit to appear before her Lord is not the work of a moment, but is to be precept after precept, line upon line ; just as it is stitch after stitch makes up needlework. *The virgins that be her fellows.* "O Lord," exclaims S. Bernard, "how am I to interpret this fulness of meaning?" (He was then preaching to a set of Cistercian sisters.) "Am I to say that these my children are her fellows, her equals, who is the fulness of Him That filleth all in all? Or, how can I say that they are equals of her who is the Mother of my Lord and my God? So let us rather take that *she* to be the type and representative of every faithful soul; the likeness and pattern of them, as Abraham is called the Father of the faithful. *The virgins,* then, and what a multitude they are, who follow her, as she follows the King and Lord of the Virgins, *shall bear her company.* O sweet society of them that are called by the same name! of them that profess the same desire! O most foul reproach and ignominy of them who, while they profess the same wish, are yet torn asunder by the various lusts of this world, of their own hearts, or of him that is the father and founder of all division, namely, Satan! Consider this, then, ye that live doing no good works; ye that live disjointed amongst each other, and insomuch as his is the operation of division, obeying Satan ; how

S. Pet. Damian. in loc.

Ay.

S. Bernard. in Cant. v. 5.

is that needlework which is not the patient labour of every day, every hour, every minute? How is that Tyrian needlework, for so it is promised a little above, unless this daily work would be sealed by her blood, if need be? How should her fellows bear her company, unless they and she were at one in Him Who hath made all things one?"

16 With joy and gladness shall they be brought : and shall enter into the King's palace.

<small>Crucius in loc.</small>

And oh, what joy will that be, says a mediæval writer, when they who have so struggled among the thorns here, shall be so transfigured by Him Who now wears the Crown of gold there! What, when they who have trod in the King's footsteps below, shall be received to the King's embraces above! What, when they who have thought it so much but to see the prints of His Feet upon earth, shall be kissed with the kisses of His Lips in the heavenly kingdom! What words can express, what heart can devise, those good things which the true Solomon hath prepared for the soul that, like another Queen of Sheba, comes from a far country to behold His glory! And, brethren, what shall we say of them who, because of the six miserable lions that wait on this side and on that, according to the six footsteps of the throne, shall be afraid to approach to His excellency, Who, the Lion of the tribe of Judah, Himself sitteth upon the Throne!

17 Instead of thy fathers thou shalt have children ; whom thou mayest make princes in all lands.

A.

Here we have the comparison of the Synagogue with the Church, the Law with the Gospel, the letter with the spirit. *Thy fathers*, the types, the prophecies, the histories, the miracles ; everything that might lead forward to Him in Whom all types find their antitypes ; in Whom all histories find their fulfilment ; in Whom all miracles are turned into that chief of all miracles, GOD Incarnate. Or, if you take it in another way, the Apostolical succession is here set forth. As the Wise Man says, One generation passeth away, and another generation cometh ; and all these are *princes* to carry on the government of the Church, chiefs to extend its dominion among those that serve other gods ; and yet children obedient to the immutable faith, and carrying out the unchangeable liturgies of the Church. It has been well said by S. Augustine, "Think not thyself deserted because thou canst not behold Paul, because thou canst not behold Peter, because thou seest not those through whom thou wast born. Out of thine own offspring has a multitude of *Fathers* been raised up to thee. See how widely diffused is the Temple of the King, of which we read before. This is the universal Church ; this is she whose children so go forth ; whose children go to the uttermost islands of the seas, call men to

Ay.

come to the one body, and be led to the glorious Temple of the King." *Fathers.* And on this they raise a question in connection with the command of our LORD, "Call no man your father upon earth." Hence they ask, how can that title be rightly attributed to Bishops? S. Augustine writing against the Donatists, They answer once for all; and if the authority of a Western doctor be not sufficient, S. Chrysostom will tell the same thing. *Princes in all lands.* In the first and lowest sense, of the preaching of the Gospel by the Apostles, through the different provinces of the civilised world that then fell out to them. But it is curious to observe how, as the physical knowledge of the earth increased, the interpreters of the Church spread also their sphere,—"enlarge," as the prophet speaks, "the place of their tents, and stretch forth the curtains of their habitations;" how lands of which mediæval missionaries never heard they by degrees brought into the fold of CHRIST; how, when the petition in the Litanies of so many centuries was, "From the fury of the Tatars, good LORD, deliver us," those very Tatars, joined with the people among whom they are mixed, form nearly a third part of the Catholic Church. It is marvellous, too, to see how the newly-discovered capes, and islands, and bays, of lands unknown to the earlier Church, have received the name of her saints and of her festivals; nay, and not only so, but whereas the constellations of the Northern and first-known hemisphere are dedicated, as it were, to all the gods of the heathen, which are but idols; so the Southern, discovered by expeditions sent forth with the blessing and under the patronage of the Church, have the names which she gave, culminating in the glorious Southern Cross.

(margin: De Unitat. Eccles. c. 8.)

(margin: Hom. quod Christus sit Deus.)

(margin: Isa. liv. 2.)

18 I will remember thy Name from one generation to another : therefore shall the people give thanks unto thee, world without end.

Thy Name. And so all the ascetic writers take it: that Name which was prefigured in Joshua, who led the children of Israel into the promised land; still further honoured by Joshua the son of Josedech, him who stood before the LORD, Satan standing at his right hand to resist him; and lastly, as foretold by the Angel to Joseph, as of Him Who should save His people from their sins. It is of this that the bride speaks in the Canticles, "Let me hear Thy voice: for pleasant is Thy Name." Often and often have we already heard of it in the Psalms; and the only difficulty seems to be, under which of all the dear verses which teach of it they should pour forth their full love of its attributes, and their full knowledge of its mysteries. *The people :* that is, the ransomed people,—*the people* who are wholly the LORD's people, —the people who have cast off the dross and the dregs of this world. Here is fulfilled that which is written of the

(margin: D. C.)

(margin: Cant. ii. 14.)

(margin: Ay.)

Ecclus. xlix. wise man: "The remembrance of Jesus is like the compo-
1, 12. sition of a perfume that is made by the art of the apothecary:
it is sweet as honey in all mouths, and as music at a banquet
of wine." Or, in the same chapter, "This was Jesus, who
in his time builded the house, and set up an holy Temple to
the LORD, which was prepared for everlasting glory."

And therefore:

Glory be to the FATHER, the GOD Who anoints the
CHRIST; and to the SON, the King that has pleasure in the
beauty of His Bride: and to the HOLY GHOST, the Spirit of
Whom the "Good WORD" was Incarnate;

As it was in the beginning, is now, and ever shall be:
world without end. Amen.

COLLECTS.

Ludolph.   O CHRIST, the WORD of the FATHER, by Whom all things
were created; keep, we beseech Thee, Thy Church gathered
together from the various nations of the Gentiles; that while
we love Thee with a pure heart, we may merit the participation of Thy eternal kingdom. Who with. (3.)

Mozarabic.   Grant, LORD, that we may love righteousness and hate
iniquity, so that, advancing by Thee, the Way, to Thee, the
End, we may be led by Thy wonderful Right Hand to the
kingdom of eternal beauty. Amen. Through. (11.)

O GOD, Whose seat endureth for ever and ever, grant that
Thy Church may be enriched by the excellent beauty of all
virtues; while, nevertheless, she is far more glorious within,
through the indwelling of Thy ever-present Spirit, Who
livest and reignest. (3.)

PSALM XLVI.

TITLE: To the Chief Musician for the sons of Korah; a song
upon Alamoth. [More probably: To the Supreme, by the sons of
Korah.] [Symmachus, Ὑπὲρ τῶν αἰωνίων: For all future ages.]
Others: For the virgins. It is in the last sense that the Western
Church seems to have taken it.

ARGUMENT.

ARG. THOMAS. That CHRIST causeth the mind to rejoice by His
spiritual strength. This Psalm is to be read with the lection of the
Acts of the Apostles, and with the Gospel or lection of S. Mark.
The Prophet speaks of CHRIST to the Church, and the same LORD
CHRIST speaks to the same Church. The Voice of the Apostles.
The Voice of the faithful.

VEN. BEDE. [After explaining the title.] That CHRIST appears in the midst of the Church, Who hath founded her as on a most solid rock. And from that—*the rivers of the flood thereof*—the multitude of them that believe are invited to behold the miracles of Divine power; of that might which breaketh the bow, and knappeth the spear in sunder.

S. ATHANASIUS. A Psalm of thanksgiving.

SYRIAC PSALTER. A Psalm which David sang concerning his affliction and that of his people in the great plague. Mystically, the preaching of the Apostles.

S. JEROME. The Psalm teacheth that we ought to put our hope in Him Who only can deliver us from our afflictions.

VARIOUS USES.

Gregorian. Tuesday. Matins.
    Epiphany. Nocturn I.
Monastic. Saturday. Sexts.
Parisian. Saturday. Sexts.

ANTIPHONS.

Gregorian. Ferial. A very present help * in trouble.
    Epiphany. The rivers of the flood thereof, Alleluia, shall make glad the city of GOD, Alleluia.
Mozarabic. He chose out an heritage for us * even the Great King over all the earth.

1 GOD is our hope and strength : a very present help in trouble.

Well exclaims one of the Fathers, on the flight of our LORD into Egypt, "What! shall our hope and strength fly? what! shall our very present help leave us? what! shall our only source of courage fear?" *Our helper in the troubles which have heavily fallen upon us.* So the LXX. and the Vulgate. But the *very present* help is the truer, as well as the dearer sense; and so some of the Greek Fathers. They take these *troubles* of sin : and so the present help is our "Advocate with the FATHER, JESUS CHRIST the righteous." *Our refuge,* the Vulgate says; and there we have the Rock in Whose cleft side we may hide ourselves, until this calamity be overpast : according to that saying, "The high hills are a refuge for the wild goats, and so are the stony rocks for the conies;" and again, "The conies are but a feeble folk, yet make they their houses in the rock." *[right margin: S. Peter Chrysolog. S. Chrysost. Z. S. Nicephorus. A. Ps. civ. 18. Prov. xxx. 26.]*

2 Therefore will we not fear, though the earth be moved : and though the hills be carried into the midst of the sea;

3 Though the waters thereof rage and swell : and though the mountains shake at the tempest of the same.

F 3

S. Greg.
Moral.
xxxiii. 1.

Well may they give this Psalm to the festivals of many martyrs; going through such deep waters of affliction, tossed by such an Euroclydon of misery, only to pass into the eternal calm and the quiet harbour. But they see in these *moun-*

Ay.
but in rather
a different
sense.

tains the Apostles. They did indeed *shake at the tempest* when "they all forsook Him, and fled;" the highest and most glorious summit of all troubled at the voice of one poor maid-servant: and much more have lesser saints been for the while utterly carried away with some sudden outburst of tempest, and *carried into the midst of the sea* of doubts and

Eusebius.
S. Athana-
sius.

temptations. Others will have the mountains cast into the sea to be difficulties swept away by prayer; more especially evil spirits cast out by the mighty hand of GOD. And in this general confusion they liken the faithful soul to the halcyon, that not only brings her own peace into the rage of the storm, but there also nourishes her young, cradling them as it were on the foaming waves. So have the billows of persecution

S. Ambros.
Hexaem. v.
13.
S. Thomas
Aquinas.
Isa. xxix. 14.
1 Cor. i. 19.

cradled many a martyr and confessor, till the time came that he should go home. S. Thomas takes it very mystically: *waters*, he says, signify prophecy: their being troubled is interpreted of the frustration and confusion of heathen prophets and soothsayers, according to that saying, "I will destroy the wisdom of the wise, and bring to nothing the understanding of the prudent."

    4 The rivers of the flood thereof shall make glad the city of GOD: the holy place of the tabernacle of the most Highest.

נָהָר פְּלָגָיו

It is a noble idea, that of our Prayer Book version: that these very storms and billows—*the flood thereof*—*shall make glad* that Church which cannot fall, for she is founded on the Rock. But the Hebrew cannot bear that signification, nor does any other translation so render the passage. So rather take the contrast between the flood of violence and uproar and destruction, and the peaceful river-flood of beauty, and green meadows, and smiling pastures. This is

Ezek. xlvii.
1, &c.

that flood which Ezekiel beheld in vision: the waters that came down from the right side of the house, and rising first to the ancles,—then, as the Prophet passed onward, to the knees,—then to the loins,—became afterwards a river that he could not pass over; for the waters were risen, waters to swim in, a river that could not be passed over. Shall we see

S. Thomas
Aquinas.

in this, with the Angelic Doctor, the river of grace which burst forth from Mount Calvary?—streams branching off

Job xxxviii.

hither and thither, the *pelagim* of the Hebrew—"to satisfy the desolate and waste ground, and to cause the bud of the

Cant. iv. 15.

tender herb to spring forth." O "fountain of gardens," "well of living waters," "streams from Lebanon!" how do you, "the nether springs" of this world, bring to us somewhat of the everlasting loveliness and peace of those "upper

springs" by which the beautiful flock now feed and lie down,
none making them afraid.   Or, with S. Ambrose and S. Ber- S. Ambros.
nard, understand the verse of the "River of Water of Life, De Spiritu S.
clear as crystal, proceeding from the Throne of God and of cap. 20.
the Lamb."   And then the rivers of that flood shall indeed
make glad the city of God, the house not made with hands,
eternal in the heavens, where is the Tree of Life, that beareth
twelve manner of fruits, and yieldeth her fruit every month;
that country and that river of which the old Liturgies say,
" They who rest in the bosom of Abraham are in the tabernacles of joy and rest, in the dwellings of light, in the world
of pleasure, in the Church of the True Jerusalem, where
there is no place for affliction nor way of sadness,—where
there are no wars with the flesh, and no resistance to temptation,—where sin is forgotten, and past danger is only remembered as a present pleasure."   The day on which he writes S. Jacob.
causes him who thus endeavours to enter into the meaning of Interpr.
the Psalms to remember one who, as he firmly believes, now
knows far more about those habitations than human tongue
can tell or human thought can conceive; "those habitations."
to continue the words of the Liturgy, "where they who
fought against sin in this world shall be far from it there, expecting the resurrection of the body, when both body and
soul shall be joined together in the unwearied service of Him
Who is both God and Man, Jesus Christ."

5 God is in the midst of her, therefore shall she
not be removed : God shall help her, and that right
early.

God is in the midst of her.   So He was in the beginning, S. Ambros.
in that which was then His Church—" the Tree of Life in
the midst of the garden;" then, when Paradise was lost.   So
He was afterwards, when the second and better Tree of Life
was set up between the penitent and the impenitent on
Mount Calvary ; then, when Paradise was regained.   So in
the ancient Tabernacle, when the Shekinah rested between
the cherubim ; so also in that Temple, of which it is said,
" The glory of the latter house shall be greater than the
glory of the former," where His blessed Feet walked, Who,
as the Prophet says, was born for our salvation in the midst
of the earth.   *And that right early.*   Therefore notice that Ay.
all the great deliverances wrought in Holy Scripture were
wrought *so early*, as to have been brought to pass in the
middle of the night.   So Gideon, with his pitchers and lamps
against the Midianites ; so Saul, when he went forth against
Nahash the Ammonite; so Joshua, when he went up to
succour Gibeon ; so Samson, when he carried off in triumph
the gates of Gaza ; so also the Associate Kings, under the
guidance of Elisha, in their expedition against the Moabites,
when they, according to God's command, filled the wilder-

ness with ditches, and then beheld their enemies drawn to
their destruction by the reflection of the rising sun upon the
water. But as they explain it in a deeper and truer sense,
the *earlier* prophecies of that eternal morning to which there
shall be no night; that eternal spring to which there shall be
no autumn. And, as the Angelic Doctor tells us, here is the
difference between the help of GOD and the help of man: the
one *in* time, though not before the time; the other so often
late,—late in hope, late in promise, late in effect.

Ay.

*S. Thomas
Aquinas.*

6 The heathen make much ado, and the kingdoms
are moved: but GOD hath showed his voice, and
the earth shall melt away.

L.

D. C.

*Hom. 2, in
Pentecost.*

D. C.

And notice here the two external enemies of man,—*the
heathen*, that is, the world; *the kingdoms*, that is, the powers
and principalities of the evil one. But GOD hath showed His
voice. And first, they refer it to the Day of Pentecost: then
GOD showed His voice, not as in Mount Sinai, *from* afar off,
from the summit of the mountain, but *in* the room where the
Apostles were gathered together; showed it, not in the
dreadful lightnings, but in the quiet tongues of flames;
showed it, not so as to terrify the surrounding multitudes—
"Let not GOD speak to us, lest we die"—but so as to allure
them to the unity of the faith. Well says S. Chrysostom:
"The penalty of tongues dispersed men; the gift of tongues
brought them, when dispersed, together again." And if we
ask why it should be said, *God hath showed His voice*, rather
than GOD hath caused His voice to be heard, they give this
for the answer: that with Him to speak is to act; to utter a
command is to be obeyed:

Prudentius.

> Ipse jussit et creata: dixit ipse, et facta sunt;
> Terra, cœlum, fossa ponti, trina rerum machina.

*Distinct.
xxxiii. 91.*

*S Hiero-
nym. in
2 S. Pet. iii.*

So that His order may be as truly said to be seen as to be
heard. And then, most truly of all, as the Master of the
Sentences teaches, we speak of a visible WORD,—a WORD
That "was made flesh, and dwelt among us." *And the earth
shall melt away.* And herein those mediæval writers who
have looked forward to the consummation of all things seem
to themselves to find, not the destruction of the present
world, but its regeneration and transfiguration into that new
earth wherein dwelleth righteousness. *It shall melt away.*
But that which melts is not lost, only re-cast. And granting
that the early belief of the Church is true,—that this very
earth in which we now live, purified indeed by fire, (and so the
baptism of water by John preceded the Pentecostal baptism by
fire of the HOLY GHOST, as the earth, once overwhelmed by
the deluge, will a second time be cleansed by flame,) but not
destroyed, will be the future abode of the blessed, how
gloriously fulfilled will be that petition in the LORD's Prayer,

"Thy will be done in earth, as it is in heaven." How many millions of times has that petition been offered by hundreds and thousands of voices! and what a poor answer, according to our lower conception of the Church, will it have met with! But once look to the new earth as well as the new heaven of S. John, wherein dwelleth righteousness, and then the will of GOD will be done as well in the one as the other to ages of ages, and the supplications of time will be heard in the fulfilment of eternity.

7 The LORD of hosts is with us : the GOD of Jacob is our refuge.

We shall have better occasion to speak of this in the last verse of the Psalm.

8 O come hither, and behold the works of the LORD : what destruction he hath brought upon the earth.

9 He maketh wars to cease in all the world : he breaketh the bow, and knappeth the spear in sunder, and burneth the chariots in the fire.

They notice the difference of the two invitatories—this, and that of the 95th Psalm : the one to come and behold, the other to come and sing. "The two," says a mediæval writer, " are separated on earth, and only to be joined in heaven. *To behold* here is to see sadness, iniquity, faithlessness, impurity ; every sin, no goodness. *To behold* there is to see not only the gates of twelve several pearls, not only the streets of gold and the sea of glass, but to hear the universal song of all the ransomed, and that more especial anthem of them that are more especially redeemed ; to hear it and to join in it, as who would not unite in that strain which knits together the unformed spirits of heaven, and those who, not only through much tribulation, but also through much sin, have been redeemed from the earth." And notice that the invitation is only to those who shall be counted worthy to enter into that blessed place : *Come hither.* And it may be well said, *Come hither :* for in what other place can the works of the LORD be so fully seen as in that where they are perfectly glorious, gloriously perfect ; where they know neither limit to their efficiency, nor measure to their beauty ? And who are they that shall be counted worthy of that invitation ? Read further, and observe how he limits the call. What destruction hath He brought upon the earth ? This : that these present bodies, formed out of clay, moulded from earth, must one day say to corruption, Thou art my father ; to the worm, Thou art my mother and my sister ; must utterly be taken to pieces ; must be like the grain of wheat, which, except it die, yieldeth no fruit. And hence we learn why this verse is

Ay.

S. Leo in Marc.

used in the Antiphon to one of the Psalms in some Office for the Dead. At first sight we might not catch the connection between it and that glorious 15th chapter of the first Epistle to the Corinthians. But this *destruction* so *brought upon the earth,* so consuming the corruptible, will bring to pass the future glory of the incorruptible; the tabernacle, as of old time, must be taken down, in order that the temple of the truer Solomon, King of everlasting Peace, may arise. *He maketh wars to cease.* And therefore is He rightly called the Prince of Peace; therefore rightly at His birth was peace proclaimed by the Angels; at His departure was peace bequeathed to the Apostles. *The bow: the spear : the chariots.* A trinity of evil, here as so often. They differ as to the separate sense of each of the three; while the LXX. and the Vulgate, instead of *chariots,* translate it *shields. The bow* some take of the fiery darts of temptation, injected, as it were, from a distance by evil spirits into the fancy: *the spears,* of the hand to hand fight with the world that every faithful soul must carry on : *the chariots,* which it was forbidden to the Jews to multiply, of those carnal means of safety on which all are so apt to lean, forgetful of the GOD from Whom alone true help can come.

Missal. Ravenna.

Tertullian. contra Marc. c. xii.

Bruno.

L.

10 Be still then, and know that I am GOD : I will be exalted among the heathen, and I will be exalted in the earth.

S. August. Serm. de Marth. et Mar.

Be still: like Mary at the LORD'S feet, go, with the Hebrews, three days' journey (by the contemplation of the Blessed TRINITY) into the solitude, before thou offerest sacrifice : like the Apostles, refuse to serve the tables of carnal appetites, that thou mayest give thyself wholly to the ministry; keep Sabbath, as Rupert so beautifully says, not one day only out of seven, but every day of thy life.

Rupert. in Exod. xx. 4.

S. Prosper. Epigr. 14.

Est et in hâc vitâ requies multis data Sanctis,
   Quorum animas mundus non tenet occiduus ;
Quos desideriis nullis peritura fatigant,
   Et quibus omne bonum est Christus, et omnis honor ;
Utuntur terrâ ut cœlo : fugientia temnunt ;
   Quod credunt, quod amant, quod cupiunt, Deus est.

S. Ambros. Hugo Card.

They nobly compare this double exaltation to the double declaration of our LORD, " All power is given unto Me in heaven and in earth." Or, still more finely, " I will be exalted among the heathen,"—namely, by the preaching of that Cross whereon the Son of Man was lifted up—" and I will be exalted in the earth,"—the new earth, that is, the land of the living ; the earth where the saints shall reign; the earth where there shall be no more sea: and that by means of CHRIST'S exaltation to the Right Hand of Power, in that Ascension of which the next Psalm is about to tell us.

11 The LORD of hosts is with us : the GOD of
Jacob is our refuge.

He, the Captain of the LORD's host is with us, that we Josh. v. 13.
may smite our Jericho, in that case to become a true "City of
Palm Trees" to us by the victory it enabled us to win; He,
the LORD, Who caused the mountains round Dothan to be
"full of chariots of fire and horses of fire" for the defence of
His Prophet; He, one of Whose hosts smote in one night, in
the camp of the Assyrians, a hundred fourscore and five
thousand. But notice under what character as regards ourselves. *The God of Jacob.* Now Jacob is by interpretation
a supplanter or wrestler. Our refuge He is not, then, unless
we have wrestled with Him in prayer, as the Patriarch;
wrestled in the night of affliction, as he in the darkness;
wrestled by the brook of penitence, as he by the ford of
Jabbok; wrestled alone, as he, when he had sent his family
forward; wrestled, and said, as he of old, "I will not let Thee S. Hiero-
go, except Thou bless me." *The God of Jacob.* Others nym.
take it in another sense : that we must be "supplanters" of V. Beda.
wickedness,—strugglers against and conquerors of tempta- Ay.
tion,—if *the God of Jacob* is *to defend* us. This has the D. C.
stronger authority, but I confess the other seems the dearer Ludolph.
meaning.
And therefore:
Glory be to the FATHER, our Hope and Strength; and to
the SON, Whose City the River of Life maketh glad; and to
the HOLY GHOST, the GOD Who is in the midst of her;
As it was in the beginning, is now, and ever shall be:
world without end. Amen.

COLLECTS.

O most merciful LORD, our consolation and refuge, sanc- Ludolph.
tify with the river of Thy grace the tabernacles of our hearts,
that Thou, the GOD of Jacob assisting us, we may overthrow
every earthly enemy. Through. (1.)
O GOD, be Thou to us in adversity a refuge, in battle a Mozarabic.
consolation, to the end that when Thou shalt come to judge
the earth, they may be sharers with Thee in joy, who have
been followers after Thee in sorrow. Amen. Through Thy
mercy.
O GOD, our Refuge and Strength, be present with us in Mozarabic.
all our troubles, that every adverse sword may be sheathed,
and every heart may be enriched with the blessings of peace;
so that in tranquillity we may behold Thee, and beholding
Thee may possess Thee for ever. Amen. Through.

PSALM XLVII.

TITLE.—To the end : for the Sons of Korah : a Psalm.   [On the
Supreme : by the Sons of Korah : a Psalm.]

ARGUMENT.

ARG. THOMAS. That CHRIST, having obtained the heathen for
His inheritance, spake, in His own city, with the glory of the FA-
THER. CHRIST hath ascended to the FATHER. It is the voice of
the Apostles. This Psalm is to be read with the Acts of the Apostles, after the history how CHRIST ascendeth to the FATHER.

VEN. BEDE. Although the entire Psalm be sung in the person of
the Sons of Korah, nevertheless it is divided by the interposition of
a Selah. In the first section the heathen are admonished to give
praises to the LORD, because He hath acquired to Himself a people
of inheritance, and hath set them in His heritage. In the second,
the Ascension of the LORD is described, and the Kingdom which the
Saints are to enjoy, world without end.

EUSEBIUS OF CÆSAREA. The vocation of the Gentiles.

SYRIAC PSALTER. Of the glory of GOD in Mount Sinai : also it
is referred to the vocation of the Gentiles.

VARIOUS USES.

Gregorian. } Tuesday. Nocturns. { Epiphany.   Ascension.
Monastic. }   { Common of Apostles.
Parisian. Tuesday.   Sexts. [It is very curious, that hardly
any of the Gallican Breviaries, except the Amiens, appropriate this
Psalm to Ascension Day.]

ANTIPHONS.

Gregorian. Ferial. O sing unto GOD * with the voice of melody.
Ascension. GOD is gone up * with a merry noise : the LORD with
the sound of the trump. All.
Monastic. He shall choose out * an heritage.
Parisian. For GOD * is the King of all the earth.

1 O clap your hands together, all ye people : O
sing unto GOD with the voice of melody.

We have said before that the sons of Korah, by whom this
Psalm was written, are, by interpretation, the sons of the
Cross. In spite of that, the world would say,—because of
that, the Church would say, the first verse begins as it does :
O clap your hands together. And notice further. This, by
the consent of the whole Church, is an Ascension Psalm.
And by whom should such a hymn of praise be written, and
to whom should it pertain, save to those who, like their dear
LORD, by the Cross on earth, hope to attain to the throne of
heaven. *O clap your hands.* As we have had occasion to
notice before now, the *voice of melody* is not so much to be

uttered with the tongue, as with the hands : that is, it is our
deeds, not our words, by which GOD is here to be praised. Even
as it was in Him, Whose pattern we are to follow :
JESUS began both to do and to teach.

2 For the LORD is high, and to be feared : he is
the great King upon all the earth.

And why is He most *high ?* Because, first of all, He was
most low. There is nothing more wonderful than the manner in which mediæval writers work out the doctrine of S.
Paul : that it was because our LORD according to the flesh
was so humbled, that, according to the flesh, He is now so
exalted. It has been well said, He is thy LORD, if thou   Ay.
seekest Him ; He is *high*, if thou believest in Him ; He is   Hugo Card.
to be *feared*, if thou fearest Him ; He is the *King*, if thou
fightest for Him ; *great*, if thou humblest thyself before
Him ; *over all the earth*, that is, over the earth of thy flesh,
since thy body should be subject to thy spirit. Or you may   D. C.
take it in another sense. Happy earth, one says, that shall
be so subjected to CHRIST the King. How happy that new
earth and those new heavens wherein dwelleth righteousness ! And again : they notice that the first time in which ·   B.
the Apostles are said to have been *afraid*, was the season of
our LORD's greatest exaltation, namely, when He was trans-   ·
figured : " They feared as they entered into the cloud." To   S. Luke ix.
which they add, that the next time in which it is recorded   34.
that the same Apostles were afraid, was that in which He
was about to enter on His great humiliation : " As they followed Him they were afraid." Whence we may gather that   S. Luke xii.
there is equal occasion for fear, whether it pleases our LORD   47.
that we should tread in the steps of His humiliation, or be
counted worthy of the vision of His glory : lest we should
despair, or lest we should be puffed up. And as the remedy
to that danger, they further bid us notice that *He is the*   A.
great King upon ALL *the earth ;* that, not only from one
danger is He able to deliver us, but from all : that there
cannot be so many temptations which the first Adam has
brought upon his seed, as there are deliverances which the
Second Adam has wrought out for His children.

3 He shall subdue the people under us : and the
nations under our feet.

He shall subdue : or, as it ought to be, both according to
the Vulgate and the Hebrew, *He hath subdued.* *The people,*
in the first place ; *the nations,* in the second. Now observe :   Ay.
these people are the same of whom it is written in another
place : " Who subdueth *my* people that is under me :" that is, the   Ps. cxliv. 2.
evil passions and weaknesses of my own heart : " my people,"
inasmuch as they belong to me : but, *He shall subdue,* because none save Him, Who is infused into us by regenera-

Ay.

tion, can tread down in us that old and evil nature. *He shall subdue the people;* that, in the first place, *and the nations,* that, in the second. And who are the people, but those indigenous to our own hearts,—our own evil affections, and lusts, and concupiscences? And *the nations,*—the word nations being used as of those external to us,—who should they be, save the legions of evil spirits armed for our destruction? And observe, also, the difference of the triumph to be obtained over the two. *The people under us:* then we are brought back to that other text, "Who subdueth my people that is under me;" *under us:* because, in a certain sense, they belong to us, they are our own; we and they are bound together. But, those who are extraneous to us, those evil spirits who attack us from without, those we may more thoroughly trample on; yes, even though they may have overthrown us; though they may, in times past, have overcome us; according to that saying, "Thou shalt lead them captives, whose captives ye were."

Hugo Card.

Isa. xiv. 2.

4 He shall choose out an heritage for us : even the worship of Jacob, whom he loved.

B.

An heritage; or rather *the heritage;* that is to say, the possession for which the Church had been longing during those long four thousand years; *an heritage,* because from its very beginning that which was promised to Adam became the birthright of all his descendants, to the full as much as that other miserable heritage of original sin, the promised Seed of the woman who was to bruise the serpent's head. Not that *heritage,* of which, as she imagined it to be at first, she said at the birth of Cain, "I have gotten a man, even the Lord;" but Him Whom every maiden of Israel from the time that the holy race possessed the promised land, till the visit of the Archangel to Nazareth, hoped to be her own descendant : for Whose sake Hannah lamented her barrenness, for Whose sake Jephthah's daughter asked leave for those two months to bewail her virginity upon the mountains. Some of the fathers take *the worship of Jacob* to mean those prophecies which Jacob on his death-bed uttered with regard to his sons; and thus, in a certain sense, with regard to the whole Church for ever. And so we see why *whom He loved* should thus follow. In that meaning, as the twelve tribes of Israel were chosen out from the whole world to be the witnesses and carriers on of the knowledge of God in the world; and so among those twelve tribes, first of all the tribe of Ephraim, and then, after four hundred years, the tribe of Judah ("He refused the tabernacle of Joseph, and chose not the tribe of Ephraim,") was God's elect inheritance; so, out of the whole world, that Church was to be chosen by and for Him, whose very name in almost all languages, thus expresses *Ecclesia* the manner of her selection. And why

S. Chrysost. in Act. iv. 35.

S. Greg. Moral. 18, 19.

Jud. xi. 37.

B.

ἐκκλησία.

rather *the worship of Jacob* than of Israel? For this rea- D. C.
son: because, as He speaks in the future at the beginning of
the clause, so also He uses the name which pertains not to
that which shall be, but to that which is. *The worship of
Jacob*, the supplanter, or wrestler against powers of evil
now; but it will be the worship of Israel, of " him that sees
GOD," by-and-by. It would be as much out of place to
speak of the worship of Israel in this world, as it would be G.
to allude to *the worship of Jacob* in the next, where, through S. Thomas
GOD's goodness, there will be no enemies to supplant, no Aquinas.
victories to win, no temptations to struggle against, no
mountains to ascend, no "miry places and marishes" to
struggle through, no valleys to go down into; but "the
utmost bound of the everlasting hills" to behold, "the water
of the river of life" to drink of, "the tree of life" from
which we may pluck the fruit, the glorious "new heaven and
new earth," wherein righteousness may and shall dwell.

5 GOD is gone up with a merry noise : and the
LORD with the sound of the trump.

One can scarcely understand this verse of anything but
His Ascension, Who went up from Mount Olivet. But we
shall enter into the mystical meaning the better, if we first
realize to ourselves the literal signification; how David, after
first failing in his design of bringing up the Ark to Jerusalem
from Shiloh, after that went-up literally, as well as spiritually,
to the city of David, where the Temple was thereafter to
stand; to that same Mount Moriah, to which GOD had commanded Abraham to take Isaac before his sacrifice. And
though, in a certain sense, Elijah's ascension to heaven is the D. C.
type of our Blessed LORD's going up from Mount Olivet,
yet, even a truer symbol of that same glorious going up is to
be found in the Ark, when, from the house of Obed-Edom, on
the shoulders of the Levites, it was brought up to its own
dwelling in the city of David. Therefore, in primitive times, S. Leo.
as now,—therefore, from the furthest east to the furthest Serm. de
west, this has been the key-note, the key-stone, the very An- Ascen.Ment.
tiphon of the day; and we cannot do better than interpret censionis.
the verse according to the richest of all the many explanations given to us by the spotless Bride of Him that then
went up, the Mozarabic Office. Listen to it: for it is scarcely
possible to find at once a piece of devotion so rapturous and
yet so sober. "It is meet and right, Omnipotent FATHER,
that we should render thanks to Thee, through JESUS CHRIST
Thy SON, Who, after the most true Sacrament of His Second
Nativity,[1] after the glorious triumph of His Passion, in so
far as He was Man, after His going down into hell, because
He had taken man's death upon Himself, after His ascent
from hell by the quickening power of that resurrection which

---

[1] The first being His eternal generation by the FATHER.

He worked out for Himself, after His might, worked out by miracles, after the unmeasured healing which He poured forth on the sick, after the teaching which was to become so famous, because it was so common to all the Apostles,—when He carried back the prey, snatched from the jaws of the foe, to that seat of Thy majesty, equal to Himself and Thee, He made the captive of the devil and his companion, Thy guest. He made *him* worthy of the habitation of heaven, who had not power to remain in the enjoyment of Paradise. Thy work, His labour.[1] He, Who amidst the depths of darkness paid the things which the corruption of another had owed,—He, far above the clouds, has freely bestowed on His servants the reward of incorruptible purity. It did not suffice to His superabundant goodness that, to the end He might show His power over the conquered enemy, and His dominion over subject elements, unless He also gave His trembling disciple power to change, so far as regarded Himself, the nature of the same elements, and the law pertaining to the water on which He walked."

6 O sing praises, sing praises unto our GOD : O sing praises, sing praises unto our King.

7 For GOD is the King of all the earth : sing ye praises with understanding.

And first we notice the triple repetition of the Name of GOD, and under each repetition the double ascription of praise. Why? Because each Person of the Blessed Trinity is to be adored and exalted by the twofold choir of men and Angels. *O sing praises*, ye whom GOD so loved that He sent His Only-Begotten SON into the world to redeem you: *sing praises*, to whom GOD gave such grace that ye should never need redemption, *unto our God*, the FATHER Almighty. *O sing praises*, ye, whose Elder Brother has undertaken the work of your salvation. *O sing praises*, ye than whom your LORD was made a little lower, *unto our King*: the King over Whose Head that superscription was set up; the King Who had that reed for His sceptre, that purple vestment for His royal apparel, that crown of thorns for His diadem. *For God is the King of all the earth* : even as it is written, " The Spirit of the LORD hath filled the world." *Sing ye praises with understanding;* because in the full light of the new dispensation, the darkness of the patriarchal ages, the seeing as through a glass of the Levitical law, are turned into the vision of full and very reality.

Hugo Victorin.

8 GOD reigneth over the heathen : GOD sitteth upon his holy seat.

They dispute whether this is to be taken in the past or the

---

[1] *Opus tuum, onus suum.*

future tense. GOD *hath* reigned, or GOD *shall* reign. Here, as so often, the fulness of the Hebrew admits of either; and the meaning is equally true either way. He does reign now, according to that saying, "The earth is the LORD's:" He shall reign more gloriously when that same "earth shall be filled with the knowledge of the LORD, as the waters cover the sea:" He shall reign most gloriously when "He hath put all enemies under His feet." *God sitteth upon His holy seat.* In the first place, that throne which He has set up in the hearts of all His servants; a throne often assaulted by that rebellious faction, the "I yet the not I," of S. Paul; the throne only to remain firm to the end in those to whom GOD gives His last best grace of perseverance. And to this they also refer that saying in Daniel: "I beheld till the thrones were set, and the Ancient of days did sit."[1] But next, GOD *sitteth upon His holy seat.* That *holy* seat whence arises the continual intercession that to him that overcometh may be granted to sit with the Prince of Life in His throne, even as He also overcame, and is set down with His FATHER in His throne. Again: *God sitteth upon His holy seat,* so often as the immaculate Lamb, Who once reigned from the Tree now reigns from the Altar. And lastly, as one mediæval commentator says nobly, it may well be put in the present, *He sitteth,* because when we look forward to the everlasting throne, there is neither past nor future, in the sense of time, in eternity.

S. Thomas Aquinas.
Isa. xi. 9.
1 Cor. xv. 25.
D. C.
Dan. vii. 9.
Pierius. Hieroglyph. xliii. 1.
S. Jerom. in loc.
Rupert.

9 The princes of the people are joined unto the people of the GOD of Abraham: for GOD, which is very high exalted, doth defend the earth, as it were with a shield.

First, let us give the different versions. In the Vulgate: *The princes of the people are gathered together with the God of Abraham; for the gods, the mighty ones of the earth, are vehemently exalted:* the Italic is the same, except that, instead of *Congregati sunt,* it reads *Convenerunt.* Our own Bible version: *The princes of the people are gathered together, even the people of the God of Abraham: for the shields of the earth belong unto God: He is greatly exalted.* But the meaning should rather be, taking מָגִנֵּי in the sense of *beshielders,* rather than *shields. The chiefs of the people are assembled before the God of Abraham, for with God are the mighty of the earth: transcendently is He exalted.* Having broken the nutshell we may now come to the kernel.

And who are the *mighty of the earth* that are assembled before the GOD of Abraham? In the first place, the long and glorious procession of Old Testament Saints, "who through

Ay.

Ay.

[1] Till the thrones were cast down, it is in our Version; but the Vulgate, as indeed the Hebrew, will have either meaning.

Heb. xi. 33. faith subdued kingdoms, wrought righteousness, obtained promises, stopped the mouths of lions, quenched the violence of fire, out of weakness were made strong, waxed valiant in fight, turned to flight the armies of the aliens." Next, those valiant ones, who at this present moment are fighting the good fight of faith, both with the ill within them and without; with only GOD and the Angels as their spectators *now*, but

A. with the whole world to be the witnesses of their reward by-and-by. Then, quite in an opposite sense, *the mighty ones of the earth*, of the earth as distinguished from the valiant spirits in heaven, are gathered together, and also against *the God of Abraham;* the GOD of Abraham, because the Father of the faithful stands out as the first example of one, who for the faith that was in him, resisted the idolatrous nations around him, and a very Antipas was found the one true among so many false.[1] Wherefore it is that the Western Church prays by the death-bed of her children, " Deliver, O LORD, the soul of this Thy servant, as Thou didst deliver Abraham from Ur of the Chaldees ;" whereas, Haran

Gen. xi. 28. was not so delivered, but " died before his father Terah in the land of his nativity," it is generally thought by martyrdom. One cannot but notice the wonderful lesson which arises from the contrast of the Vulgate with the genuine Hebrew : the former, *For the Gods, the mighty ones of the earth, are vehemently exalted :* the latter, of the true GOD,

2 Kings vi. *transcendently is He exalted.* And our thoughts go back
16. to the prophet's " Fear not, for they that be with us are more
2 Chron. than they that be with them ;" and to the monarch's, " There
xxxii. 7. be more with us than with him : with him is an arm of flesh, but with us is the LORD our GOD to help us and to fight our battles." And what resulted to the " people" then may well be the consequence of this whole Psalm to GOD's true people now : we also may " rest" ourselves upon the words of our true Hezekiah.

COLLECTS.

Ludolph.   O GOD, the King of all ages, Whose empire extendeth over all people, enlarge, we beseech Thee, our dominion over the different tribes of vices that are to be put under our feet ; to the end that while we sing praises to Thee, our GOD, with understanding, we may tread them down through Thy help. Through. (2.)

Mozarabic.   O GOD, the King, both great and terrible, grant that, in all nations, true faith may bring forth to Thee her joyful fruits : and grant that we may sing, not only with our voice, but also with our heart, to Thee, Who art our GOD, that we

---

[1] *Antipas,* as it is so well known, probably not the name of an individual, but as Antichrist is he that opposes CHRIST, so this "faithful martyr" stood up against every one around him of the heathen city. (ἀντὶ-πᾶς.)

may live with Thee, world without end. Amen. Through
Thy mercy. (11.)

CHRIST JESUS our LORD and terrible GOD, in Whose Na- Mozarabic.
tivity the Angels offered praises together with the shepherds;
to Whom, after the author of death had been conquered, all
the people clapped their hands together and lifted up their
hearts; Thou Whom, when Thou didst carry back to heaven
the victorious trophies of Thy triumphs, the faith of the
Apostles also followed; grant that we may both celebrate
the mysteries of our redemption, and the glories of Thine
Ascension, with the jubilations of faith, and may, together
with the princes of the people, be well-pleasing by means of
our faithful service to Thee, the GOD of Abraham. Amen.
Through Thy mercy. (11.)

PSALM XLVIII.

TITLE.—Bible Version: A Psalm or Song for the Sons of Korah.
Vulgate: The Psalm of a Song for the Sons of Korah, for the
second day of the week.

ARGUMENT.

ARG. THOMAS. That CHRIST our great GOD shall rule us to
eternal ages. The type of the future Jerusalem. This Psalm is to
be used with the Apocalypse of S. John the Apostle. The voice of
the priests to the people concerning CHRIST, and concerning the
heavenly Jerusalem, which is both present and is to be: then also
the voice of the Apostles: the voice of the Church that praises
GOD: it is to be read with Jonah the Prophet.[1]

VEN. BEDE. The second day of the week is the day in which, as
we read in Genesis, GOD made a firmament in the midst of the
waters, and called it heaven. Here the loftiness of holy Church is
prefigured; which, suspended as it were between the lower and the
upper waters, is inferior to the sublimity of the Angels, but more
sublime than worldly conversation. As then the title of the 24th
Psalm, the first day of the week, on which light was made, shows
that the subject of that Psalm is to be the LORD's Resurrection, so also in the present Psalm, the second day of the week, on
which the firmament was made in the midst of the waters, sets forth
to us the edifice of the Church: and to this the Sons of Korah,
that is of the LORD's Passion, sing the praise of this Canticle. In
the first part they tell the glory of GOD: on which, while the
Church dwells at length, she manifests His glory to all the kings of
the earth. In the second, they render thanks for the Advent of the
LORD the SAVIOUR, to set *stiles*[2] in the Church, by which that SA-

---

[1] The reference will be seen
to explain the sixth verse, with
perhaps some reference to the
fourth.

[2] Ven. Bede is referring to the
Roman version: *distribuente gra-
dus ejus*, which our translation
gives as *set up her houses*.

VIOUR may be known, Who guards His servants with His eternal protection.

EUSEBIUS OF CÆSAREA. A Hymn to GOD of the Church, and the destruction of the persecutors.

S. JEROME. The whole Psalm hath to do with the holy people: the whole dwells on Ecclesiastical Mysteries.

VARIOUS USES.

Gregorian. Tuesday. Matins.
Monastic. Saturday. Sexts.
Both. Common of Virgins. Dedication of a Church. Christmas. Epiphany.
Parisian. Saturday. Sexts.

ANTIPHONS.

Gregorian. Ferial. Great is the LORD * and highly to be praised.
Common of Virgins. Many waters * cannot quench love.
Dedication. Moses built * an altar unto the LORD GOD.
Christmas ⎫ We have waited * for Thy lovingkindness, O GOD,
Epiphany ⎭ in the midst of Thy temple.

1 Great is the LORD, and highly to be praised : in the city of our GOD, even upon his holy hill.

S. Chrysost.   *Great is the Lord.* This, they say, is the ladder set upon earth, whose top reacheth unto heaven. *Great;* there we have natural religion: *and highly to be praised;* there we have the thanksgiving to be paid to Him in His earliest Church, namely, the synagogue: *in the city of our God;* there we descend to the Church militant here on earth: *even*

Ay.   *upon His holy hill;* and for the last step we arrive at that mountain which is exalted above all mountains, where the throne of the Eternal SON is established for ever. *In the*

S. Hiero-nym. in Esai. ix. 14.   *city of our God.* And in how many senses do they understand this saying! First of all, in that city which has not only its gates of pearls, and its streets of gold, and its houses of all manner of precious stones, but which is so compacted together that, as S. Jerome, himself accustomed to the most orderly and regular footing in this world, says, there needs nothing else to convince us of the celestial disposition of the heavenly promises than this; that the manifold arrangement of the heavenly hierarchy should be so wonderfully set in

Guarric. Ab. Serm. iii. de S. Joan. Baptist.   order. Or, as others will have it, this city of our GOD is His dear home in this world. And I do not wonder that one, so tossed about from this to that country, over stormy seas, through lands which obeyed four or five different lords, all of them at enmity one with the other,—that one in short, so situated as was Guarric, should have found his greatest comfort in this sense of the verse. "Be it so," he seems to say; "however miserable be the turmoil of this present condition, however Simon Magus seems to have seated himself in the chair of Simon Peter, nevertheless *great is our Lord:* He once before His Passion drove out those that sold sheep and doves from His temple on earth; He will again drive out those who make a traffic of the Blessed Sacraments, whereby we eat the Flesh of the Immaculate Lamb, and receive the influence of the heavenly Dove, from the Church which is now His temple.

2 The hill of Sion is a fair place, and the joy of the whole earth : upon the north side lieth the city of the great King; GOD is well known in her palaces as a sure refuge.

And here we have one of those classical places, so to speak, which tell us how the hill of Sion is to be taken of the Church militant, of the Church in the state of expectation, of the Church which still looks forward to those blessed things which are to be revealed.[1] But here is one of the most remarkable passages in the whole of Scripture. Interpret the original how you will, whether as we do, *upon the sides of the north, the city of the great King;* or as other versions, of the palace of the King in that city, being on its northern side. And why? Because the north, all through the Old Testament, is taken, even as village tradition has made it in our churchyards, the especial possession of Satan. "For thou hast said in thine heart, I will ascend into heaven, I will exalt my throne above the stars of GOD; I will sit also upon the mount of the congregation, upon the sides of the north." What does this show but that, even now, and even however much it may at this present moment appear to be the inheritance of Satan, "the earth is the LORD's and all that therein is?" Or, if we like to follow the Vulgate translation: *Mount Sion is founded with the exultation of the whole earth;* that Mount Sion which pertains to the sides of the north, *the city of the great King.* They observe how, if not the first, yet nearest to the first of all the graces of the SPIRIT, joy is reckoned : and here we have that original joy, when, even at the foundation of this world, miserable as it was thereafter to be from sin, " all the sons of GOD shouted for joy;" and so also when the new and lovelier Church arose on the ruins of the old, when the true corner-stone of that Church was truly laid in the resurrection of our dear Master, thus it is written: " Then were the disciples glad when they saw the LORD." So then, the foundation of the world in its first creation, and the foundation of the new world in its regeneration are one and the same thing : the WORD, the Creator, is the one; the WORD, the Redeemer, is

D. C.

Isa. xiv. 13.

D. C.

Job xxxviii. 7.

S. Thomas Aquinas.

S. John xx. 20.

Rupert. in Job. xxxviii. 17.

[1] We must not find any great fault with a most earnest writer, Ayguan, because he takes the hill of Sion, coupled with the north side, to mean the city of Rome, lying, as he, however mistakenly, thought, to the north of Italy.

II. G

the other. *In her palaces.* But what are her palaces? and in how many senses have they not been taken? In the first place, her Martyrs, who are of a verity the noblest of those dwellings in which the HOLY GHOST makes His habitation; then the Confessors, who dwelt in that mansion, as S. Cyril says, of charity, of faith, and of hope: then the Virgins who dwelt in the golden house of chastity; then the ordinary generation of Christians who, amidst all their various trials, have kept the faith undefiled; in all their *palaces* GOD is known as a sure refuge. Ah! it matters little whether you read with S. Jerome, *Agnitus est;* or with Arnobius, *Cognitus est:* or with the Roman and Ambrosian version, and with Cassiodorus, *Dignoscetur:* or with the Complutensian manuscripts, *Cognoscitur:* the thing is the same. Then it is, as a saint of later times says: "It is in these *palaces,* in one or other of them, that we must be found: different palaces in this world, but one and the same in that. For thither, as from so many varying regions, so also from as many different states, shall they all enter in, to whom, in their varying ages, the LORD has been indeed a *sure refuge;* whether Apostles, Martyrs, or Confessors; whether virgins, widows, or continent, all shall be received into those many mansions which are but one, all shall be found acceptable where they have merited a place in that Mount *Sion* which is founded with the *joy of the whole earth.*"

margin:
A.
Photius.
Bibliothec.
num. 14.
In Ephes. ii.
12.

S. Thom. à
Villanovâ.
ii. 157.

3 For lo, the kings of the earth : are gathered, and gone by together.

4 They marvelled to see such things : they were astonished, and suddenly cast down.

Are gathered and gone by together. But to what purpose? As friends or as foes? Is it the marshalling of foes drawn up in battle array, kings of the earth against the King that reigned from the Cross? Or, are these kings they who pass as in triumphal procession, casting down their crowns before the King of kings and LORD of lords? In this case, not as gone by or to pass away; but rather to pass on to that eternal kingdom which, unlike earthly sovereignties, shall never be removed. So say the later writers. But there is still another interpretation, and it is that which finds greater favour with the earlier saints. *The kings of the earth,* the three wise men, *are gathered,* seeing that they came not from the same region, but from lands far apart, and led by the star, *are gone by;* gone by Jerusalem where Herod might reign, but not the King of that Jerusalem which is free : gone by the hill-country of Judæa, then all alive with the tidings of that wonderful Birth : gone by Bethlehem too, when, being warned of GOD that they should not return to Herod, the wise men departed into their own country another way. And there is yet another interpretation, by

margin:
S. Eusebius
in loc.
S. Athanas.
tom. ii. 427
C.
Theodoret.
in loc.
S. Joan.
Chrysost.
Homil. 25.
Z.
S. Nicepho-
rus in loc.
Rev. iv. 10.
S. Remig. in
loc.
Haimo.
V. Bed.
B.
Cajetan.
S. Thomas
Aquinas (but
more doubt-
fully).
A.
S. Ambros.
Ruffin.
S. Hie-
ronym. in
S. Matt. ii.
Ludolph.

which we are taught that the kings of the earth,—that is, the kings chosen by GOD to rule the one nation upon earth which was His inheritance,—have gone by together in the sense of S. Peter, when he says that David, after he had served his people according to the will of GOD, fell on sleep and saw corruption; and so also the descendants of David, in like manner gathered to their fathers, passed by, as David had done: whereas He, the second and truer David, the only Child of that Royal line, He in Whom the posterity of the kings of Judah ended, He never went by, but remaineth, as S. Paul says, not only a Priest, but a King for ever, after the order of Melchisedec. *They marvelled to see such things. They marvelled*, those kings as they followed the star, *to see such things;* to see Him That upheld the earth, Himself hanging on His Mother's breast; *such things*, as that He, Who spreadeth out the heavens like a curtain, should Himself be sheltered by no better a covering than the roof of a stable; *such things*, as that He, Whose are all the beasts of the forests, and so are the cattle upon a thousand hills, should only have one ox and one ass to do Him homage; but, more than all, they marvelled to see such things as that the LORD of the world should come to His own, His own not receiving Him; and while that poor ox knew his owner, and that untaught ass his master's crib, Israel, rich with so many types, and parables, and instructions, would not know; the people, taught by so many prophecies, would not consider. *They were astonished, and suddenly cast down:* as it is written, "When they saw the young Child with Mary His Mother, they fell down and worshipped Him."

Marginal notes: Nicolas Lyranus. Cassiodorus. — Ay. — Ps. l. 10.

5 Fear came there upon them, and sorrow : as upon a woman in her travail.

And when did not fear fall upon those to whom any supernatural revelation of our LORD, or of His Angels, was vouchsafed? When, from the time that Manoah and his wife beheld Him Who gave them those good tidings of the deliverer of Israel,—from the time that Gideon, when he saw the messenger who announced the deliverance of his people from the Midianites? even as the three Maries when they stood at the tomb, and heard those tidings more blessed than had ever before entered into human ears. The great doctor of the Western Church tells us, that where there is no fear, there can be no hope; and so the great doctor of the Jewish Church had said long before: "The fear of the LORD is the beginning of wisdom." *As upon a woman in her travail.* And thus the Son of David repeats what David himself said long before: "A woman when she is in travail hath sorrow because her hour is come; but as soon as she is delivered of the child, she remembereth no more the anguish, for joy that a man is born into the world." Well may the Church take

Marginal notes: S. August. de Civit. Dei, xv. 12. — Prov. xv. 16. — S. John xvi. 21.

that discourse of our dear LORD to be her Gospel for Roga-
tion-tide; for then all the longing, all the yearning, all the
anxious expectation, which the Greek so marvellously expresses, (ἀποκαραδοκία,) then at last comes to an end: and the
fear and the sorrow of that long travail came so blessedly
to its conclusion.

6 Thou shalt break the ships of the sea : through
the east-wind.

Or, as it is in the Vulgate, *In a vehement wind Thou shalt
break the ships of Tarshish.* There are three things here
which are to be taken in connection with each other, or else
we shall fail of the meaning of each. First, consider at once
"the sorrow as of a woman in her travail," which the last
verse tells us of, and the *ships of the sea* which are to be
broken ; and with all these also compare the text: the ships
"went not" which were made to go to Tarshish, "for they were
broken at Ezion-geber." And what are these ships, except
those Holy Innocents,[1] who were sent forth as it were in search
of the true gold of salvation in Tarshish ? But they "went
not" in one sense; they were spared all that voyage over
"the waves of this troublesome world;" and yet, without it,
they obtained the true gold from the Land of Ophir. There
were, indeed, not only the ordinary sorrows of mothers ; there
was also the agony of mothers thus bereaved. As the great
Christian poet says—

O barbarum spectaculum!
Illisa cervix cautibus
Spargit cerebrum lacteum,
Oculosque per vulnus vomit.

Aut in profundum palpitans
Mersatur infans gurgitem,
Cui subter arctis faucibus,
Singultat unda et halitus.

Through the east wind. And notice, when the children of
Israel were to be delivered, and that for ever, from the
Egyptians, and when Moses had stretched out his rod, "the
LORD caused the sea to go back by a strong east wind all that
night, and made the sea dry land, and the waters were
divided." And so says the greatest of mediæval theologians ;
that Wind, namely, the SPIRIT of GOD, sent by the SON, as
proceeding from the FATHER, divides all seas of difficulty,
casts down all mountainous waves of temptation, makes both
the Red Sea and the Jordan a highway for the ransomed to
pass over. How can it be otherwise, when He, Whose
Name is the East, rules and governs that wind, causing it to
blow wheresoever and whensoever He will ?

Margin notes:
1 Kings xxii. 48.
Cathem. in Epiphaniam. 132.
Exod. xiv. S. Thomas Aquinas.

[1] *Non est nostrum,* as Ayguan says, where he thinks the inter- pretation to be rather better than usual.

7 Like as we have heard, so have we seen in the city of the LORD of Hosts, in the city of our GOD : GOD upholdeth the same for ever.

It is this text which was the great comfort of the Confessors, in that which later ages have thought so little of—the Iconoclastic persecution. *Like as we have heard, so have* S. Johan. *we seen.* For that reason, and in defence of the Incarna-Damascen. tion, because what they had heard from the prophets, what ubique. had been seen by apostolic and isapostolic eyes, that they were resolved to confess, even through torture, even to death, —therefore it is that the martyrology of the Eastern Church has received fully a third part of its names. It was not the cause of icons, but the belief in the Incarnation, that was at stake. *So have we seen.* But where? *In the city of the* Lorinus. *Lord of Hosts.* And here the later commentators notice, that which the primitive and mediæval writers could scarcely in the nature of things have seen, how the Church is the only communion of Christians in which symbolism is the foundation of her ornaments and of her rites. *Like as we have heard, so have we seen.* Is there a Holy of Holies, a heavenly kingdom, into which they only shall enter who have been made perfect through suffering, and not they till after the consummation of all things? So has the earthly Church her sanctuary as well as her choir and her nave. Is there a Church—so to speak—in Paradise, waiting for the perfect consummation of all things? So also has the earthly Church her choir, separated from the nave by that marvellous screen, the emblem of death ; separated also from the sanctuary less visibly and less actually, but still really. *Like as we have heard, so have we seen.* And notice this also, the double repetition, *In the city of the Lord of Hosts, in the city of our God.* Why *the* in one case, and *our* in the other? Because, speaking of Him in this world, He is not only the GOD of the elect, but the GOD of those that fight against Him, and the LORD of Hosts now ; whereas the simple word of worship, GOD, is applied to the future Kingdom, because *there* can be no battles, *there* can be no need of armies, *there* the true King of Salem—which is by interpretation the King of Peace—shall reign. *God upholdeth the same for* A. *ever.* It shows how strongly the revelation of oracles had power to influence even Christians, that S. Augustine, writing on this verse, should be at the pains to prove, at great length, how false was the common Pagan belief, that the Christian C. Religion should endure only six hundred years. And yet, as it has well been observed, his elaborate argument on this question, now rendered so utterly needless, ought to be an example to priests, how they are bound to put out their full strength against heresies and mistakes, however ludicrous in themselves, which carry away a certain number at the time then present, although they may be fully aware that, after a short period, the confutation will seem almost as trifling as the assertion. And, if for one moment we may turn away from those primitive and mediæval authors to our own time, may not such of us as have to do battle against the follies and heresies which, like Jonah's gourd, came up in a night, and will perish in a night, take all the more comfort in this, that, as we can work for no future reward in this world, so our recompense will be all the more laid up when our Master shall return from the far Country, whither He has now departed?

8 We wait for thy loving-kindness, O GOD : in the midst of thy temple.

L.

Or rather, as it is in the Vulgate, *We have received Thy loving-kindness, O God.* Here—and how happy would it be if only in other places *as* here—the Eastern and Western Churches are fairly arrayed against each other. The former takes the verse as a prophecy of the future, the latter as a history of the past: the one as typical of regeneration, the other of final election: the one as telling of the Blessed Eucharist, the other as of Him Who, no longer under signs and symbols, but in His Own dear Self, will manifest Himself to His people. We might reckon up, were it worth while, the commentators on each side: S. Athanasius, S. Cyril, S. Theodoret, on the Eastern; S. Remigius, S. Bruno, and the great S. Thomas, on the other. But, after all, both in the past, and present, and future, this dear verse has to do with us. *We wait.* But why? says the great Carmelite commentator. "Because Thou hast been my help, therefore

S. Thomas Aquinas.

under the shadow of Thy wings will I rejoice." "My help?" Let me quote Manoah, and his wife; his wife, when the weaker in sex, but the stronger in faith, said to her husband,

Judg. xiii. 23.

"If the LORD were pleased to kill us, He would not have received a burnt-offering at our hands." So also, because Samson, when he had so wonderfully conquered the Philistines, pleaded that former victory as a kind of reason why the second should be granted to him: "Thou hast given this

Judg. xv. 18.

great deliverance into the hand of Thy servant, and now shall I die for thirst, and fall into the hand of the uncircumcised?" And, latest and noblest of all, David, when he left this on record: "Because Thou *hast* been my helper, therefore under the shadow of Thy wings *will* I rejoice;" and, "Thou, O GOD, *hast* taught me from my youth up until now; therefore *will* I tell of Thy wondrous works." But they take the

D. C.

sense in a truer and deeper way. It is, perhaps, rather bold to understand our LORD'S Temple as consisting of those three crosses on the summit of Mount Calvary: He Himself in the midst; those that were crucified with Him, Dymas on the right, Gesmas on the left. And in the midst of these, even

Ludolph.

then pretypifying His own setting forth the Day of Judgment, He so waited for God's loving-kindness, He so waited, as that after He had said, "I knew that Thou hearest Me always," He should afterwards receive the full blessing of that waiting in "Lazarus, come forth;" Who so waited as regarded Himself, that the same loving-kindness was shown Him; firstly, in the ministrations of the daughters of Jerusalem; then in those Who stood round about His Cross; then in those who, having been so tremblingly afraid to confess Him while He yet dwelt among men, so gloriously paid their homage to Him after He had died the death of a malefactor. However physically untrue, one cannot wonder that the love of those mediæval saints should thence have gathered, as a philosophical dogma, that the city of Jerusalem was the centre of the earth. And to me it is a noble thought, that they should so bravely have taken God's Temple to mean this whole world, which not only ought to be His in fact, but is His by right.[1] *In the midst of* that *Temple*, then, that loving-kindness, for which, even in those old times, David waited, was poured forth both to David's seed according to the flesh, and to the truer seed of David according to the Spirit.

S. John ii. 42.
S. John v. 43.

B.

Pet. Abæ-lard. in loc.

A.

9 O God, according to thy Name, so is thy praise unto the world's end: thy right hand is full of righteousness.

According to Thy Name. And, as one says, how could there be a greater proof of the humility of the Only-begotten Son than this? *According to Thy Name*—that Name which has not only healed diseases, cast out devils, raised the dead, but in and by which the worlds were framed: what, after so glorious a beginning, might one not expect as a conclusion of the sentence? Was there ever, so it would seem to us, so miserable an apodosis? *So is Thy praise.* That praise to man so utterly worthless; that praise which has given glory to tyrants and the vilest of sinners? Even so: as it is written in another place, "Whoso offereth Me thanks and praise, he honoureth Me." *So is Thy praise.* So? So, by the blood of the martyrs was His praise Who was the Martyr of martyrs; so by the testimony of the Confessors was His praise, Who before Pontius Pilate witnessed a good confession; so by the love of the Virgins was His praise, Who so drew them that they should run after Him; so by the confession of every righteous man, that He, the only True, the

L.

Ps. lxii.
Vitriacus, in loc.

Cant. i. 4.

[1] And therefore, perhaps, if those old saints were better known to the writers of the present day, who, like Mr. Kingsley, are perpetually, in season and out of season, bringing forth this most great and noble truth, that "the earth"—not *will be*, but—"*is* the Lord's," they might, perhaps, a little draw back from their assumption of being the first Christian doctors who have proclaimed the same verity.

only Righteous, should have this testimony borne of Him; "This Man hath done nothing amiss." These were the four parts into which our LORD's garments were divided: divided, but not till He had made good His Name, the Name of JESUS, and that Name could only be made good on the Cross. *Thy right hand is full of righteousness.* And here they ask two questions: the one, why that *right* hand should be full of righteousness or justice, rather than of mercy? the other, why it should be the right rather than the left hand? S. Chrysostom says that, since the execution of justice is rather the active, the performance of mercy the passive, grace, therefore the right hand, the symbol of strength and action, has that attributed to it. But mediæval writers have found out a higher meaning, basing their interpretation on that saying of S. Paul, "that He should be just, and yet the justifier of him that believeth in JESUS." *Thy right hand,* they would say, (whatever multitudes shall be placed thereon at the last day to be received into Thy heavenly kingdom, miserable sinners though they were in themselves,) is, nevertheless, not only full of mercy, but full of justice also. Others, again, take the clause in the same sense in which, through so many Eastern monasteries, one sees the verse interpreted, "The souls of the just are in the hand of GOD:" a Divine hand, that is, surrounded with the nimbus of glory, holding within its grasp the liberated spirits of the righteous; and so an interpretation founded partly on the parable of our LORD, and partly on the saying of the Wise Men.

L.

In Jacob. ii. 13.

Ludolph.

10 Let the mount Sion rejoice, and the daughter of Judah be glad : because of thy judgments.

Ay.

And here they bid us notice how often David calls us to rejoice; which the SON of David never did. And why? Because David himself was a type, not of his suffering, but of his triumphant SON and LORD. "Never but once," says S. Thomas, with that most beautiful modesty which distinguishes writers who, like him, were imbued with, and, so to speak, steeped in, Holy Scripture; "never but once, *so far as I remember,* was Sion called on to rejoice, during our LORD's sojourn upon earth. And when," he continues, "was that? Just before that same *daughter of Sion* exclaimed, 'Crucify Him, crucify Him!' So hard," he says, "is it to indulge safely even in spiritual joy." "They were more whom the wood devoured that day than the sword devoured." That is, they were more who, by a false trust in the Cross, threw away their salvation, than they who, by the open assault of Satan, fell into unconcealed and deadly sin. And so, as S. Fulgentius says: "never let us think ourselves more near to some desperate ambush of Satan, than when we have obtained some signal victory over him—only let it have been an easy one: never let us be more afraid of falling into an

S. Thom. iii. 30, 37.

Lib. ii. distinct. 24, cap. 8.

2 Sam. xviii. 8.

S. August. de Trin. xii. 3. De Fide ad Petrum ii. 14.

ambush, than when the host of the Philistines was repelled
from us in a way which we cannot understand."

11 Walk about Sion, and go round about her:
and tell the towers thereof.

12 Mark well her bulwarks, set up her houses:
that ye may tell them that come after.

"Now, then," as says a holy writer, "now, then, all ye Drexelius.
that are weak in faith, ye that think the City of our solemni-
ties, after all, to be conquerable by the enemy; come and
behold what are its walls, what are its bulwarks; come and
observe how, set face to face over against Babylon, the one
in its calm and eternal strength, the other in its hurried and
pretentious weakness, it, and it alone, shall endure not only
the wind and the storm, but the attack of the enemy also.
I have set watchmen upon thy walls, O Jerusalem. And
who are they? The time, as blessed Paul saith, would fail
me to reckon who they are that are first mounting the walls, 2 Sam. v. 6.
not of the spiritual Jebus, but of the true Jerusalem. Who
are they"—for the writer lived in that terrible time of the
thirty years' war, when every Priest in Germany was almost
as conversant with the stratagems of a battle-field, and the
art of fortification, as with his own ecclesiastical rites—"who
are they, save the Martyrs, that are posted on the barbican,
awaiting the first onset of the foe? Who are they save the
Confessors who, on the outer walls, do their best to repulse
the more general assault? While the keep is held out, as
the heart of the whole fortress, by those who have taken the
vow of religion; while obedience, poverty, and chastity
mount their triple banner thereon." *Go round about her.* S. Hiero-
But it is a far dearer sense, that which the Hebrew allows, nym.
and which S. Jerome approves, *embrace her:* and so the S. Chrysost.
Greek Fathers understand the phrase in a meaning somewhat S. Basil.
between the two—so *go round about her,* as to be in love Z.
with her, as to take in all her beauties at one glance; while
there are not wanting mediæval writers who, taking it in a
higher sense still, would bid us understand the phrase of em-
bracing it with our arms. And again; many of the Fathers
would interpret the two clauses of the two different estates of Theodoret.
Christian men: *Walk about Sion*—there you have the se- Z.
cular life; *embrace her*—there you have the religious rule.
And then, in the three next phrases, *tell the towers—mark well* S. Nice-
her bulwarks—set up her houses, may we not be well said to phorus.
have the hundred, and sixty, and thirty-fold of the parable? Hugo de S.
exactly as in the prophet, "They shall mount up with wings Victor.
as eagles; they shall run, and not be weary; they shall walk, Isa. xl. 31.
and not be faint." And now for the reason why these three
divisions are chosen as the types of—to say it with all reverence—the earthly Trinity of all faithful souls. Highest of S. Ambros.
all are they who mount up by most closely following, in their in S. Matt.
ii. 6.

G 3

typical representation of the Cross, Him Who died on the Cross; so, and so only, as Euthymius says, they can mount. Run you may, and walk you may, without so exact a conformity to the Crucified One; but to be transformed into His most perfect image, three things are needful: the first, eyes like eagles, that can look at the full blaze of the sun; the second, extended wings, like those of the same birds, so as more fully to represent the sign of the Cross; the third, that as the chief characteristic of eagles, as distinguishing them from other birds of prey, is the rapid, decided, intent manner in which they swoop upon their quarry, so that not only while they pounce on it, but while they give it to their young, they never for one moment alight from their wings: so each particular makes them the truer representative of Saints. Next to them we have those who shall run and not be weary, namely, those who, whether in the estate of widowhood, or of the enforced service of our LORD, have given themselves up to Him. And then, lastly, "And shall walk, and not faint;" and that, as one says who himself did not strive after the highest life, involves a thousand graces, each several one being fraught with a victory over some one sin. I might well say, the time would fail me to tell of those who have thus summed up the various gifts set forth in this Psalm. And, fortified by all these interpretations, we ought, as S. Jerome says, to believe that which follows:

13 For this GOD is our GOD for ever and ever: he shall be our guide unto death.

And, GOD be thanked! there is but one difficulty in this verse, and that, on what the word *for* depends. And they most of them take it as a prophecy of the Church triumphant, as well as the years yet to come of the Church militant: "that ye may tell them that come after." Why? Because by the victories of the past they may understand the expectations of the future. So speaks the greatest doctor of the

Church, and a noble passage it is. *Them that come after.* And who are they? who but those who, having passed through great tribulation, have washed their robes and made them white in the Blood of the Lamb; those who shall

neither hunger any more for the vain joys of this world, nor thirst any more for the parching temptations of Satan; but the Lamb, the true Paschal Lamb, as of old time He led forth the tribes of GOD from Egypt, so now also shall lead them, no longer to the rock whose waters failed, but unto living fountains of waters. *He shall be our guide unto death.* And there we have a singular variation in the Chaldæan version, where it is, *He shall be our guide all the days of our*

youth. And, as one of the earlier commentators says, What is the difference? All the days of a Christian's life in this world,—are they not the days of his youth, and of that only,

so far as regards the next? *Our guide unto death.* So be it. Ludolph.
He Who went up to His own death carrying the Cross,
would have us in that, and in no other way, follow Him also.
Our guide unto death; because He Himself bare the Cross; B.
beyond it, because He Himself rose again from the dead;
for ever and ever, because it is written, "I am He that liveth Rev. i. 18.
and was dead, and, behold, I am alive for evermore."

And therefore:

Glory be to the FATHER, the LORD highly to be praised; and
to the SON, the GOD Who is well known in the earthly and
heavenly palaces as a sure refuge: and to the HOLY GHOST,
for Whose loving-kindness we wait in the midst of His
Temple;

As it was in the beginning, is now, and ever shall be:
world without end. Amen.

COLLECTS.

O GOD, Thou That art great and terrible, Who art adorned Ludolph.
as the glorious Prince in the heavenly Jerusalem, expand our
souls with spiritual intelligence, that Thy mercy tabernacling
within our breasts, we may be made worthy to set forth Thy
Holy Name. Through.

O most glorious LORD, magnify the joys of all the earth; Mozarabic.
to the end that faith, being spread abroad, may fill the whole
world, and that, according to the glory of Thy Name, Thou
mightest enable us to glorify Thy praise. Amen. Through
Thy mercy.

O Thou That art great and highly to be praised, spread Mozarabic.
abroad the faith of Thy Church into all realms; to the end
that as, in all its degrees, Thou art acknowledged to be GOD,
Thou mayest also be praised in the united devotion of her
people: receive of Thy mercy, her prayers, and in the midst
of the tempests of this world, be Thou her diligent pilot: so
that we may by Thy mercy enter that City which Thou hast
founded for ever and ever, and may be received therein, and
may tell within its towers Thy marvellous works. Amen.
Through Thy mercy.

PSALM XLIX.

TITLE.—To the Chief Musician. A Psalm for the sons of Korah.
Vulgate: To the end: for the sons of Korah a Psalm. Or rather:
On the Supreme; a Psalm for the sons of Korah.

ARGUMENT.

ARG. THOMAS. That CHRIST is the Wisdom of the FATHER, by
Whom the Prophets speak. He blameth the rich who, when they

are dead, go down into the pit. He blameth the rich, both for their possessions and for their vices, who, when they have once gone down into the pit, have no more power. The voice of the Church concerning Lazarus, and the rich man that was clothed in purple. The voice of CHRIST regarding the merits of the righteous and the punishment of the wicked.

VEN. BEDE. All the words of this title draw us to the LORD, and all who have been redeemed by His Blood. Through the whole Psalm they are the words of the Omnipotent SON. In the first part He tells what He shall say or shall give to the faithful during the period of His Incarnation : " *O hear ye this,*" &c. In the second He prophesieth that which will happen to the fools, "*for He saith,*" &c. In the third He foretelleth those things which will be alike common to the righteous and to the unrighteous : " *Be not thou afraid when one is made rich,*" &c.

SYRIAC. A prophecy concerning the might of the nations, and a document of divine judgment.

S. JEROME. The HOLY GHOST spake this Psalm through the Prophet in the person of preachers : or, that it might teach the rich men of this world to despise their wealth and to beware the guile of the serpent, and that it might call earnestly on the whole earth to hear the Word of GOD.

VARIOUS USES.

Gregorian. Tuesday. Nocturns.
Parisian. Saturday. Nocturns.
Monastic. Tuesday. I. Nocturn.

ANTIPHONS.

Gregorian. Great is the LORD, * and highly to be praised.
Parisian. And when I am in my health * Thou upholdest me, and shalt set me before Thy Face for ever.
Monastic. Great is the LORD, * and highly to be praised.

1 O hear ye this, all ye people : ponder it with your ears, all ye that dwell in the world :
2 High and low, rich and poor : one with another.

Strange it is that two Psalms so near together, as this and the 45th should, and should alone, imitate, or be the forerunners of, two works of David's son : this, Ecclesiastes, the former, the Canticles. Then the great question is : who it is that here speaks ? Is it an Evangelist or Apostle ? so seem the great doctors of the Eastern Church to think. Is it the HOLY GHOST Himself ? Who else, asks S. Basil, could have the right to address such an august audience as *all ye that dwell in the world ?* Is it, as S. Augustine would teach us, prophecy personified, and thus indeed speaking to all people, and that not of one generation only, but to those who should afterwards rise up as long as the world lasts. Learn one lesson, says S. Peter Chrysologus ; learn one lesson, O thou

preacher : be thine audience never so large, if thou hast a Serm. 39.
message from GOD,—then call to mind the saying of Ehud :
"I have a message from GOD unto thee, O king;" say with Judg. iii. 20.
David, "I will speak of Thy testimonies even before kings, Ps. cxix. 46.
and will not be ashamed;" obey the command given to Ezekiel; "They, whether they will hear, or whether they will Ezek. ii. 5.
forbear, for they are a rebellious house, yet shall know that
there hath been a prophet among them." *High and low,
rich and poor.* And first notice that, if it be our dear LORD
Who is speaking, as other mediæval Saints have taken it—
who has a better right than He to call on each class, on every S. Bernard.
rank ? He, so highly exalted in the bosom of the FATHER ; in loc.
He, so lowly tabernacling in the womb of the Virgin ; He, so
rich as the LORD of the City whose streets are of pure gold ;
He, so pure, that He had the wood of the manger for His
cradle, the wood of the boat's stern for a pillow in His troubled
life, the wood of the Cross for His last bed. Well may the
Eastern Church exclaim, "Thou wast high, O CHRIST, and
yet Thou didst condescend to my humility ; Thou wast lowly,
and Thou didst raise me up to Thy glory : Thou didst sleep, Second Sta-
—and Thou didst arouse the sleepers : Thou didst pray for sis of the Blameless ;
the unity of Thy Church, and Thou didst rend asunder the on the Great
veil of the temple. Thou wast buried in the tomb, and Thou Sabbath.
didst raise all men from all tombs. Glory be to Thee, CHRIST,
our GOD."

3 My mouth shall speak of wisdom : and my heart
shall muse of understanding.

4 I will incline mine ear to the parable : and shew
my dark speech upon the harp.

There is very little doubt how the two first clauses are to
be taken. *Wisdom*—we can understand that of none save of
Him Who is the true Wisdom, the Eternal Wisdom of the
FATHER. *Understanding*—and almost with one accord they
take that of the types and parables in which That Wisdom is
concealed in the Old Testament; beginning from the riddle S. Hiero-
of Samson, down to the last chapter of Malachi. And in nym. in 1
this sense this same verse might be the motto of all the Cor. i. 30.
Psalms. For, as says one of the greatest preachers of modern Cassio-dorus.
times, "Worthy is the Lamb Which was slain to receive Rufinus.
riches." And what riches does that Divine Lamb desire ? Vieyra, tom.
Search, and you will find. "The law of Thy mouth is dearer vii. p. 235.
unto me than thousands of gold and silver." These, then,
are the riches which He is worthy to receive, and worthy to
receive on this account, that He *was* slain. And, looking
forward to the continuation of this Psalm, the same preacher
teaches us, and that so nobly : *wisdom*, according to him,
being the condescension of GOD to man ; *understanding* the
upraising of man to GOD ; both one and the other meet in a

single doctrine and in that only ; the doctrine of the Incarnation as being the base of that of the Sacraments. "By the Incarnation, GOD, Who was incomprehensible, vouchsafed to be comprehended in one place ; by the Sacrament of Sacraments, CHRIST, Who was, according to His human Nature, comprehensible, becomes as it were infinite, and is at one time in all the places of the world. By the Incarnation, GOD, Who was invisible, became visible, and was thus seen of the eyes of men : by that Sacrament, CHRIST, Who was visible, becomes invisible, because neither do we, nor can we, therein see Him. By the Incarnation, GOD, Who was immortal and impassible, becomes mortal and passible ; not only became passible, but of a verity, suffered and died : in the Sacrament, though He thus humbles Himself, He can die no more, He can suffer no more, He can become subject to the ordinary circumstances of that material under which He is received, no more : at once so glorious and so lowly ; at once so exposing Himself to, and yet so incapable of, corruption."

My dark speech upon the harp. What dark speech? Surely this, that "it is better to go to the house of mourning, than to the house of feasting ;" that, "out of the eater cometh forth meat ;" that out of the lion honey is to be obtained : that only by the rod is the honeycomb to yield its strength : that only by casting (and that truly is a proverb in most modern nations,) the helve after the hatchet is the iron to swim. And see how gloriously it is said, *I will incline mine ear to the parable.* As if there were but one parable worth the attention of man ; as if in that parable—and indeed it is so,—lay hid all the treasures of wisdom and knowledge.[1] And why is the *dark speech* to be shown upon *the harp*, rather than upon any other instrument? For the old reason, or rather, the old double reason. The first, let Adam of S. Victor give in his own words ;

Margin: Vieyra, tom. vii. p. 234.

Margin: 1 Sam. xiv. 27.

Margin: Ay.

Clichtoveus, p. 208.

Sicut chorda musicorum
Tandem sonum dat sonorum
Plectri ministerio,
Sic in chely tormentorum
Melos Christi confessorum
Martyris dat tensio :

Or, if you prefer it in the words of S. Hildebert :

Margin: S. Hildebert. p. 1259.

Sicut corda solet dare tensa sonum meliorem,
Sic pœnis tensus dat plenum laudis honorem.

[1] I cannot help giving here the interpretation which Ayguan— the first in my opinion of mediæval Commentators of the Psalms,—gives of the word parable. Says he, It is derived from *para*, which in Greek means *near*, and *bole* which means *an opinion :* as not being an opinion or judgment in itself, but something near to one, and which may lead others to form one.

That, then, is the first reason; the other, the old explanation of the Acts, how JESUS began both to do and to teach: teaching by doing, just as the harp can only give forth its sound when struck by the hand.

5 Wherefore should I fear in the days of wickedness : and when the wickedness of my heels compasseth me round about ?

In the first place let us see the different meaning attached to the verse by varying translations. The Vulgate: *wherefore should I fear in the evil day? The iniquity of my footstep shall surround me.* The LXX. the same; except *heel* instead of *footstep*. But in all probability : *why should I fear, in the days of evil, that the iniquity of my supplication should overthrow me?* And so in Psalm xli. 9. All mediæval commentators are agreed in this : that the present verse is one of the most difficult in the whole Book of Psalms. Some take it—looking at the *heel* as the extremity of the body—as if the sense were: Wherefore should I fear even though the enemy gathered together against me all his instruments of mischief, assembled all his squadrons, did (as we say) his worst? Others take it in the sense; that for every sin we have committed, and of which we have, as it were, left an impression in the road over which we have travelled, there ought —if there were nothing but our own righteousness to be depended on,—to be a swift retribution? So then, the *wherefore* leads us to the Cross at once, and to the Agony in the Garden of Gethsemane, therefore undergone that to us there might be the eternal joy in a Paradise of pleasure. And others again would interpret the phrase of that great enemy who is always so watchful,—always so persevering in remembering and dragging out to light the sins of past years : that just as an Indian in the forest or in the prairies, tracks out the impression of the footsteps of his enemy, invisible to any eye—save to one practised in such schemes of vengeance,—so Satan, when he stands to accuse us, as he did Joshua, the son of Josedec, in the presence of the Angel of the LORD, will set forth every false step we have taken, every deviation from the King's highway that we have made,—and that indeed *in the evil day*, that day, as S. Joseph of the Studium says,

> That evil day, that day of speechless dread,
> When Thou shalt come to judge the quick and dead,
> I shudder to foresee,
> O GOD, what then shall be.

It will be unnecessary to go through the eighteen explanations which mediæval Commentators have given; it is not wonderful that the Fathers of the Greek Church, well versed in the conceptions of their tragic poets, and therein having learnt the terror of an Erinnys always dogging the footsteps

Marginal notes: Ay. Orosius, Serm. de Omnibus Sanctis. Ludolph. Zech. iii. 1.

of the sinner, till she had hunted him down, should take, in preference to other interpretations, the last mentioned one of the footprints followed up in the sand.

6 There be some that put their trust in their goods : and boast themselves in the multitude of their riches.

7 But no man may deliver his brother : nor make agreement unto GOD for him :

Genebrard ; also S. Nicephorus.

It is a very bold idea which some of the earlier mediæval writers bring forward. The wickedness of my heels in the foregoing verse, they take to mean that of which our LORD speaks, "They pierced My feet." Then, what are the *wealth and the multitude of the riches* of which these in the Psalms boast themselves? What, but our dear LORD's vestments, some of which the soldiers parted; for one of which they cast lots among themselves? "Ah," as one says, "if we could but have in reality, what they had in parable, if we could but have in antitype, what they had in type, what more abundant, what more ineffable riches could there be !" For notice : That glorious LORD clothed Himself with the vesture of our mortality to the end that we might be clothed with the golden garment of His righteousness : not according to that later heresy of which mediæval times knew nothing, as superseding our own, but as co-incorporating our poor deeds with His most perfect work and thereby rendering them acceptable to His FATHER. And here, whatever may be said of the true sense of the Hebrew original, there can be no doubt that that meaning on which the Church of GOD, Eastern or Western, has built all its interpretations for a thousand years, is true in the deepest and truest sense. *A brother redeemeth not, man shall redeem.* They try—those Latin Commentators—those words under every different aspect of interrogation, of assertion, of admiration. *Brother,* (to take it in the indicative meaning) that is brother according to our natural humanity cannot offer himself as a sacrifice for the whole race of Adam : *Can man redeem ?* that is, can any one so take upon himself our common nature, as to atone for that guilt which in the same nature was committed? As I have often said, our work here is not to investigate what the precise and critical meaning of the Hebrew may be, but to interpret each Psalm in the sense in which the Church, not the Synagogue, has received it ; ay, and received it too, for eighteen instead of ten centuries. Can man redeem? Nature says, no. Every Pagan religion says, no.[1] The Synagogue itself says, no. But man

B.

S. Hieron. in Jon.

S. Bernard. in Cantic. ii. 9.
Ludolph.

---

[1] It need hardly be observed that S. Bernard was not, and could not have been, acquainted with Satan's masterpiece (in one sense) in heathen countries, when a mortal like Krishna, in Hindooism, becomes first suffering and then triumphant : is first encircled by the serpent, and then sets his heel on its head.

can redeem. That Man, that Elder Brother, that Man Who so took the nature which was then Satan's prey, that He might exalt it to the throne of GOD: Who so assumed the human soul beset with outer darkness, that He might give it a portion in the inaccessible light: Who so took our weakness that He might make it victorious over thrones, and dominions, and principalities, and powers; That Man shall redeem, and That Man shall redeem, not *though*, but *because* He is our brother.

8 For it cost more to redeem their souls : so that he must let that alone for ever;

9 Yea, though he live long : and see not the grave.

Although the meaning is the same in all the great translations, most surely the beauty and the emphasis remain with ours. *It cost more*—than what? As S. Bernard says: More than all the sufferings of all the Martyrs, more than all the life-long patience of all the Confessors, more than all the purity of all the Virgins. But not more than one hour, nay, nor more than one minute of Calvary; of that courage, of that patience, of that purity. "Ye are bought with a price:" and as S. Paul continues, "Be not ye therefore the servants of men:" that is, of the flesh: of that flesh, of which it is written, "The adulteress will hunt for the precious life." "Precious!" cries S. Fulbert; "and oh, how precious ought that to be to us, O LORD JESUS, which stood Thee in such a cost! How precious that, for the sake of which the tree was cast into the pool of Mara; the helve caused the iron to swim; the water, the salvation of Israel, was turned into the appearance of the blood which tempted the Moabites to their destruction:* a redemption which cost no less than the betrothal of the thistle that was in Lebanon to the cedar that was in Lebanon.[1] On the other hand, it is curious to observe how the interpreters of the tenth and eleventh centuries, that time of most horrible corruption in the Church, see here, as they always do when they can, rather the threatening of Eternal punishment than the promises of Eternal salvation. I will not here take it so, because I know that this sense in this passage was never intended by the HOLY GHOST: but you may easily understand how terribly saints like S. Peter Damiani, like S. Bruno, like S. Gregory VII., work out the

S. Bernard. in S. Luc. 8.

1 Cor. vii. 23.

B.

Prov. vi. 26.

Ex. xv. 25. 2 Kings vi. 6. 2 Kings iv. 23.

[1] Here, in treating on the Incarnation,—or, as he himself expresses it, on the third Article of the Creed, composed by S. John the Evangelist, Ayguan dilates at great length on the third foundation of New Jerusalem, the chalcedony. I do not know that, in any other particular, does the mediæval Church seem so to have acted out the Apostolic doctrine, "of Him, and through Him, and to Him, are all things," than in the 'mythology' of those precious stones which encircled her chalices, and crosses, and ecclesiastical vestments.

translation of the Vulgate, *and he shall labour to eternity, and yet shall live for ever, and shall never see death.*   Most true is it, that which a great Portuguese preacher tells us, that this passage is one of those which, taken one way, is the savour of life unto life ; in the other, the savour of death unto death.   *So that he must let that alone for ever,* he of whom the sentence is gone forth that the harvest is past, the summer is ended, and he not saved ; *yea, though he live long,* namely, in the punishment prepared for the ungodly ; *and see not the grave,* the grave, that is, as a place of rest : or, *He must let that alone for ever,* He, namely, Who had taken the work of our salvation upon Himself, if the cup had passed from Him, if He, in His human nature, had lived without dying, if He had never ascended the Cross, if He had never lain in the new tomb, if He had never become the first-fruits of them that sleep.   If all this had been, then indeed, He must have left the salvation of man *alone for ever :* at the very possibility of which God forbid any Christian should hint without immediately adding, as S. Paul does in the like case ; " but now *is* CHRIST risen from the dead : for since by man came death, by man came also the resurrection from the dead."

R. de Jesus. Serm. p. 199.

1 Cor. xv. 20.

10 For he seeth that wise men also die, and perish together : as well as the ignorant and foolish, and leave their riches for other.

Ay.

Truly, as says the great Carmelite doctor, we all see,—see every day of our lives,—see as a spectacle both to angels and to men, the Wise Man, the GOD only wise, die ; that by death He might overcome death, that by the crown of pain, and the title of derision, and the sceptre of scorn, He might reign from the tree.   Truly the earth saw and owned that this Wise Man died, when the earth did quake and the rocks rent, and the veil of the temple was rent in twain.   Truly the heavens saw that this Wise Man died, when there was darkness over all the earth from the sixth hour until the ninth hour ; just as the same heavens had borne witness to the Birth of that same Wise Man, when the star stood in the east, and drew the three wise men to worship Him.   Or take it in a wider sense.   *He seeth that wise men also die and perish together.*   Verily they do, as long ago it was written in the Wisdom of Solomon : " We fools accounted his life madness, and his end to be without honour ; how is he numbered among the children of GOD, and his lot is among the saints."   And therefore, as S. Augustine says—and his saying has been amplified by his followers, and therefore were they wise, because they died and perished together ; because they, sometimes singly, but more often by twos or threes, and sometimes by tens and hundreds, died for Him Who died for them ; perished for Him Who never will suffer one hair of their heads to be lost at the last day.   And so Prudentius gloriously speaks :

B.

Wis. v. 4.

Prudent.
Peristepha-
non iv. 5.

Plena magnorum domus angelorum
Non timet mundi fragilis ruinam,
Tot sinu gestans simul offerenda
Munera Christo.

·Cum Deus, dextram quatiens coruscam,
Nube subnixus veniet rubente,
Gentibus justam positurus æquo
Pondere libram :

Orbe de magno caput excitata,
Obviam Christi properantis ibit
Civitas quæque, pretiosa portans
Dona canistris.

11 And yet they think that their houses shall continue for ever : and that their dwelling-places shall
endure from one generation to another; and call
the lands after their own names.

And yet they think. And what thought was ever, in the
eyes of the world, a thought of greater folly than this? That
He Who, for three years and a half, had with great difficulty,
and barely, notwithstanding all His miracles, set up His
house on earth, should, when He came to that most shameful death of malefactors, even the death of the Cross, imagine
that His house should continue for ever! Be it so : yet He
had a participator in that which this miserable world called
folly :—a participator? Yes: and one that spake, not of a
house, but of a kingdom that should be everlasting: "LORD,
remember me when Thou comest into Thy kingdom." *And
that their dwelling places shall endure.* And so observe how
it has hardly ever been known that one especial dwelling-place,
that one particular Church, should be swallowed up by Satan.
Unhappily, we cannot now say, as those mediæval saints
could, that there is not one single example in which—the
fight between the two being fair and hand to hand—the
Church was overthrown : for, we must remember too sadly
the examples of Japan and Cochin China. But yet on the
whole, see how gloriously the last clause of the verse belongs
to our LORD; that He should call the lands after His own
Name. See how even thus His words are gone out unto the
ends of the earth. Take it of Him alone, and how many
a city and province, by its very title, has owned its subjection
to Him Who is King of kings and LORD of lords. Take it
in the plural; and what colony on the mainland, what island
in the sea, is there, which has not some province, some cape,
some river, some city, baptized with a name from those of
His saints? And so, O LORD JESUS, do Thou go forth conquering and to conquer! changing into the title of Bethel
the place which was called Luz at the first; setting up altars
to Thyself,—altars on which should be sacrificed Thine own

S. Gregor.
Pastor. 3.22.

B.

D.C.

Ay.

Gen. xxviii.
19.

most precious Body and Blood,—altars on which also shall
be presented the oblation of the bodies and souls of Thy
faithful people as a holy and reasonable service.

12 Nevertheless, man will not abide in honour :
seeing he may be compared unto the beasts that
perish ; this is the way of them.

Ay.

Gen. iii. 5.

They well compare the idea which Adam entertained of
himself in the moment of the fall, with that knowledge which
GOD had concerning the result of the fall. Adam believed
him who said, " Ye shall be as Gods, knowing good and evil."
GOD says, *He may be compared unto the beasts that perish.*
Thus Satan's exhortation to divinity is GOD's degradation to
brutality. *Man will not abide in honour.* And well says the
same Carmelite : " Oh, sad and tearful mutation ! That man,
the inheritor of Paradise, the Lord of the earth, the Citizen
of heaven, the servant of the LORD of Sabaoth, the co-heir
of celestial spirits, the co-equal of heavenly virtues, should,
by a sudden conversion, have need of a Redeemer, Who, because of the weakness it was necessary He should bear, took
on Himself human infancy ; because of the rejection it was
needful that He should suffer, lay in the manger ; because of
the example He would set in trampling down pride, had no
better courtiers than the ox and the ass : the ox to acknowledge Whom man denied ; the ass to adore, in the stable,
Him from Whom Adam would have fled in Paradise. Wherefore, O man, adore His cradle, Whose empire thou didst at
first contemn : acknowledge Him as the poor Infant Whom

D.C.

thou didst refuse as the Almighty King." Or, if you will,
take it in another sense, *Man will not abide in honour.* Why
not ? And let the verse of the mediæval hymn answer :

> What love of Thine was that which led
> To take our woes upon Thy head,
> And pangs and cruel death to bear
> To ransom us from death's despair ?

13 This is their foolishness : and their posterity
praise their saying.

L.

Ay.

And now see whether any more true description could have
been given of that which was then, and that which is now,
of the life of the saints. *This is their foolishness.* This :
their struggles against themselves, their battles against the
world, their life-long warfare against Satan. But after all,
when the battle is over, when the crown is won, when the
pilgrimage is at an end, then *their posterity praise their saying :* then their descendants build the tombs of them to
whom their fathers gave the crown of martyrdom.

14 They lie in the hell like sheep, death gnaweth

upon them, and the righteous shall have domination over them in the morning : their beauty shall consume in the sepulchre out of their dwelling.

Is it not better, is it not dearer, is it not more like Him Who is Love, that of two opposite senses in these many-sided Psalms, we should take that which best represents that love ? In each separate diamond, out of all the facets, we may at all events choose that which sets forth His glory the most, to Whose worship all the Psalms and all their parts minister. Therefore we will not take this verse in its darker and sadder meaning, but rather see in it how even out of the depths of misery   L.

Vexilla regis prodeunt.

As He Who was dumb before His shearers like a sheep, so His servants giving their lives for Him as He for us, *lie in hell*, are received in the grave as a sacrifice well pleasing to Him. *Death gnaweth upon them.* And notice the force of the word, so true in its symbolical sense. It gnaws ; it does not devour or destroy ; but does its little worst, and that for a season only : *and the Righteous,*—He Who only is righteous, He Who alone is King of kings and LORD of lords, He Whose holiness shall atone for the sins of the whole world, *He shall have domination over them in the morning ;* in that morning of the resurrection when He, now standing on the shore of everlasting peace, shall call those who have been toiling all the night of this world, to gird to them those vestments of good works which, save for Him they never would have possessed, and without which they must have been that which S. Paul so earnestly prays against—" not that we would be unclothed, but clothed upon." *Their beauty shall consume in the sepulchre.* And it is well said, *Their beauty.* For there was One Whose beauty, so far as human eyes beheld it, first had its existence out of, and because of, *the sepulchre.* Till He was therein laid, He had no form nor comeliness, and when men saw Him, there was no beauty that they should desire Him. So then it follows very well :   D.C.

   2 Cor. v. 4.

   S. Chrysost.

15 But GOD hath delivered my soul from the place of hell : for he shall receive me.

Even the Jewish commentators here saw our LORD : and how shall not His own servants see that glorious redemption on the third day ? first in the Head, and then in the members. He is speaking of the redemption which CHRIST now showeth in Himself. For He hath descended into hell, and hath ascended into heaven. What we have seen in the Head we have found in the Body. For what we have believed in the Head, they that have seen have themselves told us, and by their means have we seen : " For we are all one body." But   Galat. vi. 6, 7.

   A.

are they better that see, we worse that have been told? Not
so, saith the Life Itself, our Shepherd Himself. For He
rebuketh a certain disciple of his doubting, and desiring to
handle His scars; and when he had so handled them, and
had cried out, saying, "My LORD and my GOD," seeing His
disciple doubting, and looking to the whole world which believe, "Blessed," saith He, "are they that have not seen, and
yet have believed."

16 Be not thou afraid, though one be made rich :
or if the glory of his house be increased;

17 For he shall carry nothing away with him when
he dieth : neither shall his pomp follow him.

So *one*, that One Great Enemy, was enriched by his first
conquest of Eden : enriched by the spoil of countless souls,
all, in that one action made over to him; so the glory of his
house was increased, when the creature made by GOD so very
good was so infinitely marred; when Adam, created himself in the Image and likeness of GOD, begat a son in his
own image and likeness. But these spoils shall be won back
from him again : the stronger than the strong man will bind
him and spoil his house: the prey shall be taken from the
mighty, and the lawful captive delivered.

Gigas noster, gigas fortis,
Victor fregit postes mortis :
Nuda gemunt Tartara.

Foleng.

Neither did his pomp follow him, when after he had showed
the LORD all the kingdoms of the earth in a moment of time,
he himself was put to flight with one "Get thee hence,
Satan:" *Neither did his pomp follow him* when the oracles
gradually ceased to give their responses, when the garlanded
hecatombs no longer crowded the temple doors, when the
stones and pillars mouldered into decay, when the temple of
Apollo itself, in the last Pagan struggle of Satan, under his
apostate servants could only offer, instead of the thousand
victims that once attested its fame, one poor fowl to its
false god.

S. Cæsar. Arel. Hom. i.

Sozomen. vi. 6.

18 For while he lived, he counted himself an happy
man : and so long as thou doest well unto thyself,
men will speak good of thee.

Marvellously true as is our own translation in itself, worthy,
if we may so speak, of inspiration, it is not the sense of the
Hebrew. The Vulgate is nearer. *Quia anima ejus in vitâ
ipsius benedicetur, confitebitur tibi cum benefeceris ei :* or,
nearer still, *Though, while he lived, he rejoiced his own soul,
then shall he praise thee for doing well to thyself. Then :*
then when the things that are seen have passed away before

the invisible world; *then* they who rejoiced their own souls, who said, "Soul, thou hast much goods laid up for many years, take thine ease, eat, drink, and be merry," then they *shall praise thee; thee*, the poor servant of the Poor King; *thee*, who didst bravely take up thy cross and follow thy Master; *thee*, who didst lay up thy treasures where thief cannot steal, nor moth nor rust consume; *then* they *shall praise thee* for thus doing well to thyself. "*Then* shall the righteous man stand in great boldness before the face of such as have afflicted him, and made no account of his labours. And they repenting and groaning for anguish of spirit, shall say within themselves, This was he whom we had sometimes in derision, and a proverb of reproach; we fools accounted his life madness, and his end to be without honour: how is he numbered with the children of GOD, and his lot is among the saints." *For doing well to thyself.* Oh, how well they did to themselves, those Martyrs who gave their bodies to the wild beasts, to the racks, to the scourge, to the stake, to the *equuleus*, to the scorpions, to all the torments which Satan devised for CHRIST's athletes! Oh, how well they did to themselves, those Confessors whose whole life was one long struggle with the world, and the flesh, and the devil: how well, when they were in perils often, in hunger and thirst, in cold and nakedness. Oh, how well they did to themselves, those Virgins, who for CHRIST's sake bartered all the love and joy and softness of this world, for the midnight service, and the cold cell, and the rough garment, and the discipline!

Wisd. v. 1, 3, 4, 5.

> O pulchras acies, castraque fortia,
> Quæ spes, una fides, unus amor regit,
>   Omnes lege sub unâ,
>   Uno sub duce militant!
> Heu! quantis rapiunt astra laboribus!
> Pulsant perpetuis quæstibus æthera;
>   Per jejunia longa
>   Vires corporis atterunt.

Santol.
Victor.

19 He shall follow the generation of his fathers: and shall never see light.

What light, save that light like to a stone most precious, even like a jasper stone, clear as crystal—that most glorious light of the Beatific Vision? *He,* Who did good to himself while he lived; he, who never for CHRIST's sake bore shame or reproach; he, who never endured hardness, as a good soldier of his LORD; he, who following *the generation of his fathers*, even from the time of Adam's fall, obeyed his own heart's lusts rather than His LORD's law: not for him is that blessed abode, where

Rev. xxi. 11.

L.

> Sole solis illustrata
> Semper est meridies.

20 Man being in honour hath no understanding :
but is compared unto the beasts that perish.

See ver. 12.
And therefore:
Glory be to the FATHER, Who shall deliver my soul from
the place of hell: and to the SON, Who showeth His dark
speech upon the harp: and to the HOLY GHOST, by Whom
the mouth speaks of wisdom ;
As it was in the beginning, is now, and ever shall be :
world without end. Amen.

COLLECTS.

Ludolph.

Fill, O LORD, our mouths with Thy wisdom ; that we,
being always mindful that Thou didst become man, and didst
redeem us from the power of the grave, may be filled with
the light of Thy Countenance: Who livest and reignest.

Mozarabic.

Let wisdom, we beseech Thee, O LORD, open our mouth,
and let prudence dwell on our tongue: and, to the end we
may not be compared unto the beasts that perish, instruct us
in the discipline of Thy Divine laws ; that so our understanding may comprehend Thee on earth, and may enjoy
Thee for ever in heaven.   Through.

PSALM L.

TITLE.—A Psalm of Asaph.

ARGUMENT.

ARG. THOMAS. That CHRIST is the GOD of Gods, and severs
the righteous from the unrighteous. This Psalm is to be read with
S. Matthew.[1] The Prophet speaketh concerning the advent of
CHRIST and the future Judgment. A rebuke of the Jews. Concerning martyrdom.

VEN. Bede. [After explaining who Asaph was.] In the first
part of the Psalm, the synagogue of the faithful speaks[2] concerning
the First and the Second Advent of the LORD CHRIST: *The Lord
even.* In the Second, the LORD JESUS CHRIST Himself admonishes
the people that, leaving such victims as bullocks and goats, they
offer to Him the sacrifice of praise: *Hear, O ye people.* And in the

---

[1] That is, with the description
of the Last Judgment in chap.
XXV.

[2] Venerable Bede has been endeavouring to explain why the

word synagogue may also be applied to the Christian Church ; as
it once, and only once, is in the
New Testament.

third, the synagogue replies, imputing our iniquities to the sinners in the midst of her : *But not the ungodly.*

SYRIAC PSALTER. Named from Asaph the Prophet, this Psalm treateth of the legal sacrifices in the law of Moses, and how they have been done away. And *as* it admonishes that, unless we follow out GOD'S commandments, we shall be held in abomination by Him.

S. JEROME. This Psalm divides the righteous from the wicked, the celestial from the terrene, saints from sinners : the Prophet protesteth that he speaketh not from himself, but that the LORD speaketh by him.

VARIOUS USES.

Gregorian. Tuesday. Matins.
Parisian. Tuesday. Tierce.
Monastic. Tuesday. Tierce.

ANTIPHONS.

Gregorian. The LORD * even the most mighty GOD, hath spoken.
Parisian. I will not sit among the ungodly * I will wash my hands among the innocent, O LORD.
Monastic. The same.

1 The LORD, even the most mighty GOD, hath spoken : and called the world, from the rising up of the sun, unto the going down thereof.

Here, in the first place, we have once more a marvellous witness to the mystery of the HOLY TRINITY. *The Lord :* there we have the incommunicable Name : *even the most mighty God :* there we have the operation of the HOLY GHOST in the human race ; *hath spoken :* but how ? And we have the answer in the second clause : *From the rising of the sun.* That is, in those thirty-three years, at the commencement of which the true Sun arose, take it as you will, in Nazareth or in Bethlehem. *Unto the going down thereof :* that going down on Mount Calvary, after that the created sun had been darkened from the sixth hour until the ninth hour. *Hath called the world :* as Adam so magnificently says : [Pinto in Ezech. cap. 23. Bredem. B. in Dan. cap. 1.]

> Lux jucunda, lux insignis,
> Quâ de throno missus ignis
> In Christi discipulos,
> Corda replet, linguas ditat,
> Ad concordes nos invitat
> Linguæ cordis modulos.

Called the world. Or as it is in the Vulgate, *earth.* The Prophet Jeremiah will tell us how. " O earth, earth, earth, hear the word of the LORD." When GOD calls man whom He has made, man whom He has redeemed, man whom He [Jer. xxii. 29. Hugo de S. Victore in loc.]

II.   H

Ps. cxiii. 3.

Ay.

has regenerated. And if you ask in what order the earth is called, another Psalm sets it forth: "The LORD's Name is praised from the rising up of the sun unto the going down of the same:" that is, that the faith first preached in the East, thence spread to the West:[1] only a repetition of what the present verse tells us.

2 Out of Sion hath GOD appeared : in perfect beauty.

L.
S. Aug. de
Unit. Eccle-
siæ. cap 10.
Isa. liii. 2.

And as they say most truly, here is one of the glorious contradictions in which Holy Scripture delights. Of one and the same Man it is written : "He hath no form nor comeliness, and when we shall see Him, there is no beauty that we should desire Him:" and also *out of Sion* He *hath appeared in perfect beauty*. The Prophet is not now speaking of His appearance from Jerusalem :

> Where in the land of beauty
> All things of beauty meet,

as Bernard says ; no ; nor yet of His glory on Mount Tabor, the earnest and foretaste of that imperishable light and incorruptible beauty. This *perfect beauty* was made manifest in the Pavement, on the *Via Dolorosa*, on the Cross ; just as another Prophet tells us : " Then the moon shall be confounded, and the sun ashamed, when the LORD of Hosts

Isa. xxiv. 23.

shall reign in Mount Sion" (notice the parallel expression,) "and in Jerusalem, and before His ancients gloriously." Hugh of S. Victor will have it that the *perfect beauty* is spoken of our LORD's sinless humanity.

3 Our GOD shall come, and shall not keep silence : there shall go before him a consuming fire, and a mighty tempest shall be stirred up round about him.

Or, as it is in the Vulgate, *Our God shall manifestly come.* And in this sense the present verse is beautifully selected for the Psalmellus of the First Sunday in Advent in the Ambrosian Office Book. This Coming of our LORD,—is it to be taken of His First or Second Advent? And the Fathers

Lib. v. cap.
18.

are almost equally divided. S. Irenæus takes it to refer to both. S. Chrysostom understands it of the Second Advent, and in favour of that interpretation compares the two verses :

S. Matt.
xxiv. 27.
In Esai. cap.
30.
De bono pa-
tientiæ.

There shall go before Him a consuming fire : and, "For as the lightning cometh out of the east, and shineth even unto the west, so shall also the coming of the Son of Man be." So also S. Jerome, so S. Cyprian. On the contrary, S. Cyril

In Schol. de
Incarn. cap.
2.
Thesaur. iii.
cap. 1.

[1] Ayguan hence draws an argument that the Catholic faith had left the East: it is curious to read the words with which he continues : *In parte occidentali hodie fides remansit ; ut in Italiâ, Franciâ, Alamaniâ, Angliâ, et hujusmodi.*

of Alexandria and Nicetas understand it of the First. *There shall go before Him a consuming fire.* And notice that this is the first place in which the Last Day is spoken of as to be accompanied with fire. After this time indeed we hear of that fire again and again : " Their fire shall not be quenched;" "A fire devoureth before them, and behind them a flame burneth;" "His throne was like the fiery flame, and his wheels as burning fire;" "The LORD GOD called to contend by fire, and it devoured the great deep and it did eat up a part." So again : "The day shall declare it, because it shall be revealed by fire;" "In flaming fire taking vengeance on them that know not GOD." "Do we fear? Be we changed and we shall not fear. Let chaff fear the fire: what has *it* to do with gold? What thou mayest do is now in thine own power: thou canst not say that, for want of being warned, sin has overcome thee against thy will." But we may take it in another sense, and that a dearer: and that is, of the fire of love. *A consuming fire* indeed: for we know how, through the strength of that love, all tortures have been despised, all contempt contemned, all death counted but as the porch to eternal life.

Isa. lxvi. 24.
Joel ii. 3.
Dan. vii. 9.
Amos vii. 4.
1 Cor. iii. 13.
2 Thess. i. 8.

A.

S. Thomas Aquin:

4 He shall call the heaven from above : and the earth, that he may judge his people.

He shall call. So undoubtedly it is in the Hebrew: so also in the LXX., προσκαλέσεται. But by a very easy mistake of the original, we have in the Latin the perfect for the future : *Advocavit* instead of *Advocabit*. This is the reading of the best manuscripts ; and S. Gregory the Great so quotes it five times ; and especially S. Bruno so cites it. But the Ambrosian Psalter gives it rightly ; though on the other hand S. Cyprian takes the perfect. Oh, how happy for the Church, if controversies like these made the sum total of all her disagreements ! Then mediæval writers take occasion to discuss the question why, the resurrection of the body having been promised, it should not take place at once, as our dear LORD's did, but should be reserved for the Last Day. Their discussions on such an abstract question could not possibly be given in brief here ; but the Carmelite compresses the difficulties and the replies to those difficulties into the smallest space.

De bono patientiæ.

Ay.

5 Gather my saints together unto me : those that have made a covenant with me with sacrifice.

With sacrifice. And first of all we think of that great Sacrifice, offered, the One Victim for the whole world, on the Cross on Mount Calvary.

O quam felix, quam præclara,
Fuit hæc salutis ara

H 2

Rubens Agni sanguine;
Agni sine maculâ,
Qui mundavit sæcula
Ab antiquo crimine!

But not in a higher, but in a more prolonged sense than this, it is that of the most blessed Sacrament; the continuation and the transfiguration of that first Sacrifice, made in the upper room by our LORD Himself. S. Augustine is poor in a singular degree in his interpretation of this text; so poor, that not one of those who have followed him have thought it worth while to enter into his explanation. But there is a most glorious sense in which mediæval saints have taken these words. *Gather My saints together.* So they do. So, first, in the commemoration of those more glorious martyrs, who—like him on whose festival these words are written—endured tortures almost beyond the imagination of man to conceive: but all saints in that most Divine festival, which unites together from one end of the world to the other, all the most illustrious servants of our LORD; *those that have made a covenant with Me,* first in the Blood of the Lamb, and who have then renewed that covenant, and, so to speak, graven it more deeply by their own blood. There are few passages to be found in any modern divines which, to my mind, speak with a truer eloquence than the following passage of the great Portuguese theologian, Vieyra: " It is not because, in that most dreadful day, the sun and the moon shall be darkened, and the stars shall not give their light; it is not because upon the earth there shall be perplexity, the sea and the waves roaring; it is not because men's hearts shall fail them for fear, and for looking for the things that shall be coming upon the earth: all this is little. All this is little? All this is absolutely nothing. This is it which makes that day so full of terror to the best (best, that is, so far as in this corrupt state of the world we call best), so utterly full of entire despair to such as have permitted things to run their own course,—have not in that deluge stretched forth their hands to escape from the general flood,—have not in that fire, at the cost of any limb, and that limb given up with whatever amount of pain, delivered themselves from the general conflagration. But so it is: so men will do: so, for a miserable and momentary pleasure here, they will run the risk—the risk? they will incur the certainty—of such a punishment hereafter. The body? yes: and for gluttony, or, as in other countries it may be said, for drunkenness;[1] and what, whether in the new world or the old world, is, I more than fear, an equal temptation—impurity. These are indeed the great

S. Vincent.

Tom. v. p. 329.

---

[1] The great Portuguese theologian, the great politician of his day, had seen drunkenness enough in other nations, and could not but have felt thankful that the crime was one which was then, as it is now, almost unknown to his own country.

affliction; these are the waves of the sea, that terrible sea of damnation, roaring; these ought to be the cause of (and oh, would to GOD they were!) men's hearts failing them for fear."

6 And the heaven shall declare his righteousness: for GOD is Judge himself.

And first of all we look to the nineteenth Psalm, where we find who these *heavens* are. They did indeed *declare His righteousness* when they stood forth at the day of Pentecost "to declare His righteousness; to declare, I say, as at this time, His righteousness"—how He should "be just, and yet the Justifier of them that believe in JESUS." They did declare His righteousness when, east, west, and south, and by-and-by, north, they went out, more clearly preaching Him Who, by the prophets of old, was afore spoken of as 'the LORD our righteousness.' And, just as these earthly heavens are not always equally clear to an earthly eye, but sometimes overshadowed with vapours, sometimes glorious, in the pure brightness of a summer's morn, so sometimes more clearly, as in those downright discourses of S. Peter at Jerusalem; sometimes more inductively, as when, in the bright starlight, S. Paul stood forth in the midst of Mars' Hill. S. Thomas, in a sermon on Advent, discusses the question, why He, Who condescends here to be a party in the trial, should declare that He, in that very trial being Judge, should therefore give the world occasion to admire His righteousness. And the magnificent passage in which he speaks of justice in the abstract, one of the most glorious dissertations of mediæval times, should certainly have been quoted here, did space allow. *(S. Basil. in loc. S. Cyril. S. Thomas, Serm. 52 in loc.)*

7 Hear, O my people, and I will speak: I myself will testify against thee, O Israel; for I am GOD, even thy GOD.

I will speak: or rather, *I will speak out:* putting one in mind of that saying of S. Paul's, "About the time of forty years suffered He their manners in the wilderness." After that indeed He spoke out; after that He spoke out in that threat, which the Western Church repeats daily (save on those two days when the superabundance of the love that flows from Calvary forbids even the repetition of any threat), "Unto whom I sware in My wrath, if they shall enter into My rest." *Will testify against thee:* rather, *will bring thee forward as a witness.* Our version, with the Roman, reads *for:* the LXX. and the Vulgate, more literally, *I am God, even thy God;* that is, this proposition it is that Israel is to bear witness to. Mediæval and primitive writers have here seen a reference to the I AM THAT I AM of the bush; but mistakenly, however beautifully. *Even thy God.* Oh happy *(S. Bonav. Acts xiii. 18. L. So S. Thom. Aquinas. Hugo de S. Vict. S. Augustin. S. Bruno.)*

Pseudo-
Hieronym.[1] warrior, who thus can appropriate infinite strength! Oh
safe penitent, who thus is received by infinite purity! *Thy
God* now, in the battle; *thy God* then, in the peace; *thy God*
here, under types and shadows; *thy God* there, in the Beatific
Vision!

8 I will not reprove thee because of thy sacrifices, or for thy burnt-offerings : because they were
not alway before me.

9 I will take no bullock out of thine house : nor
he-goat out of thy folds.

10 For all the beasts of the forest are mine : and
so are the cattle upon a thousand hills.

11 I know all the fowls upon the mountains : and
the wild beasts of the field are in my sight.

12 If I be hungry, I will not tell thee : for the
whole world is mine, and all that is therein.

13 Thinkest thou that I will eat bulls' flesh : and
drink the blood of goats?

Now we come to the glorious preparation for the Great
Sacrifice; the truer and nobler *Parasceue* of the truer and
nobler Passion. But not now proclaimed for the first time.
Four hundred years before, on those mountains of Moab,
had the question been asked by Balak, "Wherewithal shall
I come before the LORD, or bow myself before the Most
High GOD?" and answered by that unhappy prophet, who
indeed "beheld Him, but not nigh." *Because they were not*
always before Me. The Vulgate, with the same sense, *Thy*
burnt-offerings were always before Me. Not, then, for this
art thou to be blamed. But others will have the sense
similar with that of Isaiah, "They are a trouble unto Me; I
am weary to bear them." But, in a dear mystical sense,
Thy whole burnt-offerings are ever in My sight. The *whole*
body, and soul, and spirit, consumed with the burning fire of
love; that is the precious sacrifice in His eyes, Who is Love
Himself. And here they take occasion to argue the question, whether the Jewish Sacrifices were permitted, as the
less evil, when compared with the danger of idolatry; or
enjoined as a real, though less perfect, good. And, notwithstanding the names of S. Chrysostom and Hesychius,
who affirm the former, the Angelic Doctor, followed by a
multitude of later authorities, unhesitatingly maintain the
latter. *I will take no bullock.* Very remarkably it is in the
Chaldaic, *From the day of the destruction of the House of My*
Divinity, I have not received bullocks from thy hand : thus
transporting us at once to the "full, perfect, and sufficient

Ay.
Lyranus.

Hugo de S.
Vict.

A.

L.

Prim. Sec.
Q. cii. Art. 3.

[1] "Qui tamen Hieronymus non esse vel hinc intelligitur," as L.
very truly says.

Sacrifice" then made, when the Temple of the LORD's Body was destroyed. *Bullock: he-goat.* Mystically, the sins of pride or disobedience in the one, of impurity in the other; and then it is spoken to the Church. Such as these, however they boast themselves to be in My house, and to be occupied in My service, "Then will I profess unto you, I never knew you." *For all the beasts of the forest are Mine.* And as S. Bernard says, "Take comfort, O man, when thou findest the beasts may, after a certain sort, call GOD their GOD. When thou hearest how GOD had care for cattle in that great threatened destruction of Nineveh,—when thou readest in the New Testament how not one sparrow falleth to the ground but your Heavenly FATHER careth for it, take comfort for thyself. He Who said, 'Ye are of more value than many sparrows,'—He Who appointed so many sacrifices, wherein innocent creatures bled for thy sake,—what of His care for thee, what of His providence over thee?" *I know all the fowls.* And now then we must take that higher sense: how those saints, born, as fowls, of water, soaring, like fowls, above the earth,—thus soaring, also like fowls, only by virtue of the sign of the Cross,—how they are indeed known, so dearly known by that GOD Who, in a certain sense, knoweth all His works from the beginning of the world. *And the wild beasts of the field are in My sight.* Or, as it is in the Vulgate, in so very lovely a sense, *The beauty of the field is Mine.* No doubt the true meaning of the original is, *And the stock of the field is Mine:* thereby approximating much more closely to our own version. Nevertheless, we may be allowed for one moment to dwell on the mediæval interpretation. Those saints in their monasteries, whom we are apt to regard as utterly careless about physical beauty, here one and all show in words, what indeed the choice of situations for religious houses might also teach, how dear it was to them. S. Bernard, forbidding, as he did, the slightest ornamentation in his churches, forbidding towers, nevertheless taught his Cistercians to choose the loveliest situations for their houses. I wonder whether it were the romantic situation of his father's castle—Fontaines-lèz-Dijon—that taught him the instinctive love of natural beauty, which found their places, for Clairvaux itself, for Rievaulx, in our own Yorkshire, for Batalha, in Portugal, and for hundreds of other situations, showing how that Order was determined to make good our verse here, *The beauty of the field is Mine.* The *beauty,* κατ' ἐξοχήν, for sublimity and savageness attracted other orders; as who that has looked upon Whitby, or the Grande Chartreuse,[1] can ever forget? And no nobler illustration of the verse can be found than that most glorious of

Marginal notes: Serm. de Divers. 73. — Hesychius, S. Thomas Aquinas, S. Bruno.

[1] Perhaps the reader will forgive me for mentioning that it was in descending, on my return from the Grande Chartreuse, the tremendous gorge of Gresivaudan, that the commentary on which I am engaged first suggested itself to my mind.

sequences, the Alleluiatic. Think, again, how the beauty of
the field forms no inconsiderable portion of the loveliness of
the Song of songs. The roses of Sharon and the lily of the
valleys; the flowers appearing on the earth; the time of the
singing of birds come; the voice of the turtle heard in our
land; the garden enclosed; the orchard of pomegranates
with pleasant fruits; the fountain of gardens; the well of
living waters and streams from Lebanon; the getting up
early to the vineyards; the seeing that the vine flourish,
and the tender grape appear. No marvel if the mediæval
saints are lavish, as in their writings on our present verse,
in their transferring the beauty of the field from this worn-
out to the new earth.

S. Bernard. (margin)

> Hiems horrens, æstas torrens, illic nunquam sæviunt;
> Flos perpetuus rosarum ver agit perpetuum;
> Candent lilia, rubescit crocus, sudat balsamum.
>
> Virent prata, vernant sata, rivi mellis influunt;
> Pigmentorum spirat odor, liquor et aromatum;
> Pendent poma floridorum non lapsura nemorum.

If I be hungry, I will not tell thee. "Neither didst Thou,"
as S. Bernard says, "neither didst Thou, O dear LORD JESUS,
tell of Thine hunger either to man or to Satan: only Thou
didst permit Thine angels, when the forty days' fast was
over, to minister unto Thee. But of Thy thirst Thou didst
speak twice: once, when Thou didst, by the side of Jacob's
well, ask the woman of Samaria to give Thee to drink; once,
when Thou, Who hadst never uttered one complaint concerning the sufferings of the Cross, didst nevertheless say, 'I
thirst.' In the one setting forth the Baptism which Thou
shouldst ordain; in the other, the Absolution which Thou
shouldst bequeath." Tertullian—not that his authority is
very great in such a matter—quotes as a saying of the LORD's,
"The Eternal GOD shall neither hunger nor thirst." *The
blood of goats.* Hugh of S. Victor, in a series of verses which
I have before quoted, thus mystically symbolizes the goat:

S. Bernard. Serm. 48 in Cant. (margin)

Lib. 2 contra Marc. (margin)

> Lana, cibus, visus, sanguis, caro, cornua, fœtus,
> Hostia, mons, vitis, dens, pes, vox, barba, libido,
> Corda brevis, corium sotularibus usibus aptum,
> Lacte caret, fœtet, emissus ruminat hircus.

14 Offer unto GOD thanksgiving: and pay thy
vows unto the most Highest.

15 And call upon me in the time of trouble: so
will I hear thee, and thou shalt praise me.

Offer unto God thanksgiving: or, as it is in the Vulgate,
the Sacrifice of praise: and so the LXX. in the true sense of
the Hebrew. Are we to take this of the One Oblation then
accomplished for ever, of CHRIST on the Cross? Then we
shall agree with S. Chrysostom. Shall we rather interpret

it of the continuation of that Sacrifice of the Blessed Eucharist? Then we have on our side S. Zeno of Verona, and the later commentators. But, in whatever way we explain the exhortation, the second clause of the verse will retain the same emphasis on the *thy*. First, as one of the holiest of that great society advises, first, O sinner, plead the merits of those infinite sufferings; first, lay before the FATHER (if I may so express myself) the wanderings in this world of the well-beloved SON—that SON, so acknowledged, first of all in His Baptism, which was the beginning; next, in His Transfiguration, which was the consummation of His earthly course—first offer unto GOD, to His FATHER and to thy FATHER, these vows, and then *pay* THY *vows unto the Most Highest.* Which vows can these of thine be, save those that are most like to His own oblation of Himself? Or, as another mediæval writer puts it: first His, then thine; and thine only secondly, because His firstly; and thine only with any degree of acceptation before the FATHER, because in Him that same FATHER was so entirely[1] well pleased. *And call upon Me in the time of trouble.* And then what S. Bernard says is a saying for all ages: Had He said, Call upon Me in the time of prosperity; had He exhorted thee, Invoke Me when all seems to go outwardly well with thee; had He said, When everything around thee rejoices and is glad, call upon Me; then I should have perceived how He, the LORD both of joy and sorrow, the King both of life and death, would have had the best of thy heart's affections, or none at all. But here observe His great love: Call upon Me when thou hast none else to flee to,—when all earthly helps have proved themselves miserable comforters indeed,—when every worldly idol has shown the true property of an idol, and has failed its worshippers in their greatest strait, *Call upon Me in the time of trouble, so will I hear thee. And thou shalt praise Me.* They seem, those primitive saints, to lay the stress on the word *Me.* So *will I hear thee, and thou shalt praise* ME. Me, that is, Who for thy sake was led out into the wilderness to be tempted; for thy sake did for so many years have My habitation among men; for thy sake did choose not them that were valiant-hearted, and therefore ready to follow Me whithersoever I might lead them, but rather did out of the weak make the strong, out of the contemptible the glorious, out of death raised up to perfect life. In the same way do thou *call upon Me in the time of trouble:* so *will I hear thee, and thou shalt praise Me.* And that help and that praise are well set forth in the hymn, late though it be:

Side notes:
In his treatise: That CHRIST is true GOD.
Ay.
Hesych.
D. C.
Agell.
Valentia.
Ay.
Serm. 162.
This is taken from my manuscript Waay-mundus.

---

[1] Observe how, both in the Latin and Greek (and therefore in all the languages derived from the Latin as well), the "I am well pleased" of our version falls so infinitely short of the *Mihi complacui* of the Vulgate, of the ἐν ᾧ εὐδόκησα of the Greek.

H 3

Thy good name suffers from the tongue
  Of slanderers and oppressors?
JESUS, as on the Cross He hung,
  Was reckoned with transgressors!
More than the nails and than the spear
  His sacred limbs assailing,
Judea's children pierced His ear
  With blasphemy and railing.

Fear'st thou the death that comes to all,
  And knows no interceder?
O glorious struggle! thou wilt fall,
  The soldier by the Leader!
CHRIST went with death to grapple first,
  And vanquished him before thee;
His darts, then, let him do his worst,
  Can win no triumphs o'er thee!

16 But unto the ungodly said GOD : Why dost thou preach my laws, and takest my covenant in thy mouth;

17 Whereas thou hatest to be reformed : and hast cast my words behind thee?

18 When thou sawest a thief, thou consentedst unto him : and hast been partaker with the adulterers.

19 Thou hast let thy mouth speak wickedness : and with thy tongue thou hast set forth deceit.

20 Thou satest, and spakest against thy brother : yea, and hast slandered thine own mother's son.

And all the mediæval writers teach us, even from the Mosaic law concerning the leper, how the writer of this Psalm only put into words what those statutes expressed in fact. For so it is written : " The leper in whom the plague is, . . . he shall put a covering upon his upper lip." As *Homil. in loc.* they all, following Origen, say : let them who themselves are of polluted lips, take good heed not to teach others. Or, to take it in the opposite way, see how Isaiah would not speak to his people, because he was a man of polluted lips, and he dwelt among a people of polluted lips, till they had been touched with the living coal from the altar; and by that, as *Turrianus : de dogm. char. Lib. 3.* by a Sacrament of the Old Testament, a sentence of Absolution had been pronounced upon them.[1] *And takest My covenant in thy mouth.* And they see in it a warning against

[1] And here the mediæval commentators raise one of those questions in which they so delight. A priest, in mortal sin, is he, or is he not, to say the Hours? If he does not, he disobeys the command of GOD, repeated to him by the Church; if he does, most certainly he incurs the condemnation pronounced in this verse. And here, as always, the great Carthusian commentator lays down the conditions, on the one hand so

sacrilegious communions: the Holy Mysteries being not only our strength and life here, but the *covenant* of our eternal heritage there. *Whereas thou hatest to be reformed:*[1] or better, as the Vulgate has it, *disciplined.* It is worth while to reduce the ways in which, according to Holy Scripture, man rejects the salutary correction of which the Prophet speaks. Sometimes "they have refused to receive correction;" sometimes "he that refuseth instruction despiseth his own soul;" sometimes man "despises the chastening of the LORD;" sometimes "faints when he is corrected of Him;" sometimes, as here, *hates discipline:* and so in the Prophet Amos. *"Tu vero odisti disciplinam,* verberum et verborum," adds S. Bonaventura, with an ingenious play upon words. *Thou consentedst unto him.* There is a classical passage in S. Chrysostom on the guilt of sinning by proxy, or even by will; the condemnation of such as, if they do not themselves, as S. Paul says, commit things worthy of death, at all events have "pleasure in them that do them:" just as it is written in Hosea, "They make the king glad with their wickedness, and the princes with their lies." Manifestly from this verse of our present Psalm were the memorial lines partly framed concerning theft:

Jer. v. 3.

Prov. xv. 32.
Heb. xii. 3, 5.

S. Bona-
ventura.

In Isa. xvi.
11.
Rom. i. 32.
Hos. vii. 3.

> Jussio: consilium: consensus: palpo: receptus:
> Participans: mutus: non obstans: non manifestans.

Mystically, *they* consent to thieves who steal the words of Holy Scripture to, or accept them in, an heretical sense. *And hast been partaker with the adulterers.* The passage of S. Chrysostom, in which he recommends the communicant to give information to the deacon, if any one of impure life is presenting himself to receive the Holy Mysteries, is deeply valuable, as proving that the custom in his day was that which we now have in the English Church, of receiving the LORD'S Body in the hand. Then most marvellous is the concluding part of the clause, as applied to the Jews. *Thou hast let thy mouth speak wickedness,* O Synagogue, when thou didst exclaim, "Say we not well that Thou hast a devil, and art mad?"—when thou didst clamour forth, "Not this man, but Barabbas"—when thou didst pour out thy taunts, "Let Him deliver Him, if He will have Him." *And with thy tongue thou hast set forth deceit.* What else spake the two false witnesses, when they gave their testimony about the destruction of "His Temple?" what else, when thou dost teach, "Out of Galilee ariseth no Prophet?" And yet, all this while, *thou satest and spakest against thy Brother.* "Sitting down, they watched Him"—Him, the Elder Brother of the whole race of man—"there," and so sitting they

S. Cyprian,
Ep. lxiii.

S. Ambros.
in Ps. cxix.
88.

In loc.

S. Hie-
ronym. in
Dan. vii. 4.

---

strictly, on the other so tenderly, which reconciles the apparent contradiction.

[1] Is there a polemical *arrière pensée* in the somewhat unusual use of this word in this place?

mocked Him with their "He saved others, Himself He cannot save. Let CHRIST, the King of Israel, descend now from
the Cross, that we may see and believe." *Yea, and hast
slandered thine own Mother's Son.* For He, O children of
the Synagogue! was her Son as much as yourselves were;
and a cruel stepmother indeed she proved herself to Him, in
the day when she crowned Him, day though to our true Solomon it were of the joy, and day of the gladness of His heart!

21 These things hast thou done, and I held my
tongue, and thou thoughtest wickedly, that I am
even such a one as thyself : but I will reprove thee,
and set before thee the things that thou hast done.

These things hast thou done, and I held My tongue. And
here we see our LORD still before the judgment-seat, as a
sheep before her shearers, dumb; answering not a word, insomuch that the governor marvels greatly. The LXX. and
the Vulgate, and other early translations, make, and that
most rightly, a pause after *I held My tongue;* as if the Pro-
De Passione. phet would tell us of the first stage in that procession to
Calvary: when the WORD, as S. Bernard says, refused to
utter a single word before those whom He had made, and
who, now judging Him, were hereafter by Him to be judged.
*Thou thoughtest wickedly that I am even such a one as
thyself.* But, says S. Thomas Aquinas, when we think, O
LORD JESUS, that Thou art altogether such as ourselves, (sin
only excepted,—sin only, O ye Nestorians, excepted,) are we
therefore mistaken? Do we therefore do Thee wrong? Do
we therefore comfort ourselves with false consolation? Of a
verity, Thou art even such a one as myself; bone of my bone,
flesh of my flesh : fed as an infant with the milk of that most
spotless breast; hushed to rest with the lullaby of those most
blessed lips; suffering when a child as I, working for Thy
daily bread as I; and (had it not been so written I had never
dared to say it,) increasing in wisdom and stature, and in
favour with GOD and man. These things, O LORD, I think—
that Thou art even such a one as myself; but do I think
them wickedly? Then, how shouldest Thou be our Elder
Brother? How shouldest Thou be the First-Begotten brought
into the world? How should it have behoved Thee in all
things to be made like Thy brethren, that Thou mightest be
a merciful and faithful High Priest in things pertaining to
GOD, to make reconciliation for the sins of the people?
And set before thee the things that thou hast done : that is,
they say, as in a mirror: "thou didst it secretly; but I will
do this thing before all Israel, and before the sun." *The
things that thou hast done,*—one unrestrained glance of the
eyes : the setting before the king his sin, that enormous iniquity of Absalom, on the same house-top, in the sight of all
Israel. I dare not translate those words, words that, as it

were, burn with fire, of S. Chrysostom, when commenting on S. Chrysost, in loc.
this text, he teaches how every hidden iniquity of this world
will be dragged out into the full and terrible blaze of the
next: and how more especially, as indeed that luxurious age
more especially needed, he branded sins of impurity in language which our century is far too delicate-eared to hear,
though certainly not too delicate-handed to act. *And set
before thee the things that thou hast done.* Let us hear S.
Thomas once more, for we shall not have much longer in
which to hear him. "How are those things to be set before
us? How? And who can tell? Are we to imagine that
they will be proclaimed to all the assembled tribes of earth,
—to the kindreds, tongues, peoples, and nations, that shall
stand before the great white throne? Or, must we not rather realise this to ourselves, that that setting before us will
be in one moment, brought to pass in the secret recesses of
our own breasts? There so burnt in—if that, which GOD
forbid, should nevertheless happen—that it can never be
erased: then if in the moment of that terrible judgment we
stand acquitted, yet nevertheless remembered for ever, as the
most tremendous contest between mercy and judgment, the
most terrible equipoise between life and death." And, as S. S. Pet. Damian.
Damiani says: "Think, O my soul, what thou art, and what
are thy powers, amidst which this tribunal is to be set,—such
an accusation and such a defence to be heard, and such an
acquittal or condemnation finally and for ever to be pronounced."

22 O consider this, ye that forget GOD : lest I pluck
you away, and there be none to deliver you.

O consider this. And it is most remarkable how all, both
primitive and mediæval commentators, pass over the first
clause of this verse; as if they would forget those who forget Him. My people hath forgotten Me days without number. Jer. ii. 32.
There is a difference in the various translations between *Lest
I pluck you away*, and *lest He pluck you away*. And again, L.
some, like Arnobius, and S. Augustine also, read, *Lest He
pluck you away like a lion.* This is either a mere gloss, or
else it has crept into the present verse from the seventh
Psalm. And then in another and a dearer meaning: that I Ps. vii. 3.
may pluck you away, and that there may be none to wrest
you out of My hand. That is, in the sense: "My FATHER
Which gave them Me is greater than all; and no man is able
to pluck them out of My FATHER'S Hands." So S. Chrysostom and Euthymius take the passage. Notwithstanding
—so they understand it—all your past sins; notwithstanding
your many backslidings, though the remembrance of past
mercy was on one side, and the fear of future judgment on
the other. *Consider this, ye that forget God, lest* he, he, the
great enemy of souls, pluck you away, and then there be

Euthymius. none to deliver you; when the Lamb once slain for you shall have become the terrible and avenging Lion.

23 Whoso offereth me thanks and praise, he honoureth me : and to him that ordereth his conversation right will I show the salvation of God.

The Vulgate and Septuagint take it in quite a different sense : *The sacrifice of praise shall honour Him : and there is the way by which I will show him the salvation of God.* (Or, as the LXX. has it, herein at variance with all our present texts, *my salvation*.) But whether one translation or the other, the offering of thanks and praise, *the sacrifice of praise*, can only in its highest sense mean the Great Oblation for quick and dead. And see in how lovely a way the following clause joins in : *and there is the way where I will show him the salvation of God ;* how can it be taken otherwise than of the Viaticum? They point back with pride,—those writers who have defended the verity of that Blessed Sacrament,—Turrianus more especially,[1] to that Name in the first [a]Œcumenical Council, in the [b]second of Arles, in the [c]third of Orleans, in the [d]fourth of Carthage, in the [e]first of Toledo, and as used by Paulinus in his life of S. Ambrose. Neither are there wanting those who take that *way* of the Incarnation : the marvellous *way* by which He, the Virgin-born, came down alone, to the end that, to that blessed place whence He came, He might return with many :

De Dogmat. charact. lib. 3.
[a] Canon 12.
[b] Canon 12.
[c] Canon 34.
[d] Canon 77.
[e] Canon 14.
S. Hieronym. in Isa. cap. 56.
S. Cyprian. cont. Jud. i. 16.
S. Chrysost. Hom. 16 in S. Matt.

> Et cum multis illic scandit
> Unde solus venerat.

And therefore :
Glory be to the FATHER, even the Most Mighty GOD, Who hath spoken; and to the SON, GOD the Word, Who shall not keep silence : and to the HOLY GHOST, with Whom His Saints have made a covenant by sacrifice ;
As it was in the beginning, is now, and ever shall be: world without end. Amen.

COLLECTS.

Ludolph. O LORD, GOD of Gods, we beseech Thee, that Thou wouldest receive from us the sacrifice of praise ; so that we, being set free from the burden of our sins, may patiently run the race that is set before us. Through. (1.)

---

[1] When I refer to the Canons acknowledged by the whole Church, as here, I take them according to their enumeration in the last and best collection, that of Kalle and Potte, Athens, 1853, which appeared with the imprimatur of the H. G. S. of Athens.

O God, Who wilt manifest Thyself as the Righteous and Mozarabic. Almighty Judge, we beseech Thee to reveal Thyself first as the most merciful and Omnipotent Saviour; that as, when Thou sittest on Thy judgment-seat, Thou wilt be severe, so as often as Thou presentest Thyself to us here on the Throne of Thy mercy, Thou mayest be loving and gentle. Who. (5.)

We call on Thee, O Lord, in the day of our trouble, that Mozarabic. Thou wouldest give us the increase of faith and hope, to the end that we may obtain the everlasting inheritance of love. Amen. Through. (11.)

PSALM LI.

We have now reached the Psalm of all Psalms; that which of all inspired compositions has, with the one exception of the Lord's Prayer, been repeated oftenest by the Church. And there are almost as many mysteries in its position as there are in its structure.

As to the way in which the Church has repeated it. Till the last reformation of the Roman Breviary, it was said at every Hour, concluding the service, with the exception of Christmastide and the Great Forty Days. So, for some thirteen hundred years, this Fifty-first Psalm, in thousands of congregations, was repeated seven times daily. As S. Augustine says—and what small cause had he, compared to ourselves, thus to exclaim—"O most blessed sin of David, so gloriously atoned for! O most happy fault, which has brought in so many straying sheep to the Good Shepherd." And further notice the position of this Psalm as the L.[1] The Psalm, then, as the year of jubilee: so they all, those great lights of the Church, Origen, S. Hilary, S. Ambrose, S. Thomas, Cassiodorus, S. Jerome. Hom. 5 in Num. Compare with this, as the same saints have done, the law given on the fiftieth day after the people had departed from the land of Quest. Utriusque Test. 112. Egypt; compare the parable of our Lord about the two debtors, the one that owed five hundred pence, and the other fifty; espe- Apolog. cially remembering the sin of David, which you will, in this Psalm; David. cap. viii. compare the penalty of fifty shekels of silver inflicted on him who, S. Luke vii. 41. among the Israelites, had dishonoured a virgin. Think also of the fifty just men with whom Abraham's petition began; think of the Deut. xxii. 28. width of the Ark, fifty cubits, that ark which was to save all those who *were* saved from the general ruin; further, of the breadth of the Jer. xviii. 24. tabernacle which Ezekiel in vision beheld: and lastly of the freedom Gen. vi. 15. of Levites from the servile works of the tabernacle when their fiftieth year had been attained. But above all, the year of jubilee, when all Numb. viii. 25. debts were remitted, all manors returned to their original owners, all slaves were liberated, all prisoners were set free,—this, above all

---

[1] That is, except in the mere Hebrew: the LXX. and Samaritan, and other almost contem- | porary versions reckoning it as the Vulgate.

other interpretations, sets forth to us the mystery of this glorious fifty, which yet may be worked out, as we shall proceed to see, into many other senses.

Vol. i. p. 48.   To give the various Antiphons said to this Psalm, would be simply to give all those of the day hours in the Church's year: and of its quotidian use at all the latter, except in Eastertide, we have spoken not only above, but in the First Essay.

TITLE: To the chief musician. A Psalm of David, when Nathan the Prophet came unto him, after he had gone in to Bathsheba. "Where sin hath abounded, grace did much more abound." For consider how for nearly three thousand years that sin of David, that one momentary glance from the house-top, has given occasion to the enemies of the LORD, in each successive age, to blaspheme, down from the Lucians and Porphyries of primitive times, to the Voltaires and Humes and Paines of our own. And yet, no doubt the encouragement it has given to those who otherwise would have despaired, may be known to the Searcher of all hearts, far to outweigh the mischief and the blasphemy. So S. Augustine said in his time: so S. Bernard taught in his: so the latest of those who have any claim to the title of a mediæval teacher, S. Thomas de Villanova more than once asserts: so the great schools which have their rise on the one hand from S. Vincent de Paul, on the other from De Hauranne, differing as far as Catholics can possibly differ on the subject, are nevertheless agreed in this. One can only remember S. Augustine's words, with respect to a still sadder fall, and apply them to this: "O sin of Adam, certainly necessary, which merited such and so great a Redeemer."

This is taken out of Mazarin's Commentary on this Psalm.   Here, too, we may observe how many theological terms have their first origin in this Psalm. The *Kyrie Eleison* at the beginning; the *clean heart*; the *broken and contrite heart*; the *sinner shall be converted*; and above all, here is first to be noticed, the first faint foreshadowing of one of the foundation truths of the Catholic faith. *Take not Thy Holy Spirit from me.* Never before had the HOLY SPIRIT been made known to the Jewish Church; nor yet again was the Paraclete spoken of to them till Isaiah, now about to conclude his prophecies by his martyrdom, said of the generation in the wilderness: "They rebelled and vexed His HOLY SPIRIT."

a Hom. v. in Num.
b Quæst. Utriusque Test. 112.
c Cap. 8.
d In loc.
e In Esai. Cap. 42.
L.   Then as to the recitation of it. Never has Psalm, whether by Priest in Confession, or by Synod in Canon, been so often put into the mouth of Penitents as this. And thus Origen;[a] S. Hilary;[b] S. Ambrose,[c] more especially in his apology for David; Cassiodorus;[d] S. Jerome;[e] they all dwell strongly on this point. And again; it has been well observed that there is scarcely one great theological verity which is not in this wonderful Psalm set forth. Here you have—the Incarnation; the calling of the Gentiles; sin, both original and actual; the nature and effect of preaching; grace, both justifying and sanctifying; the Atonement; the Institution of the Church; the Mission of the HOLY GHOST.

In S. Luc. lib. 1.   *When Nathan the Prophet came unto him.* They enter largely into the various opinions on this seer; some holding with many mediæval writers that he is the same Nathan with the son of David mentioned at the beginning of his reign; some with S. Ambrose, with S. Augustine, and others, that he was a natural son of Uriah,

and afterwards adopted by David. The wonderful tale related by S. De con-
Epiphanius no reasonable critic will now believe. Only this is to be sensu Evan-
observed: that the "king's prophet," Gad, was not now made the gelist. lib. 2.
messenger of GOD to David; any more than two centuries later,
when GOD had a message of life and death to Ahab, Elijah was not
the prophet chosen; but the message which determined Ahab's
fate was given to one of far less note, Micaiah. As to Bathsheba, S.
Thomas most wonderfully observes how she is mentioned in the
genealogy recorded by S. Matthew. Her name is not given; her
husband's name *is* recorded; and so, in the genealogy of our LORD,
her sin is stamped on the whole history; whereas, of the honour that
she might have rightly claimed of being a progenitress of the Messiah, she is deprived by her name being withheld.

Before we enter on this Psalm, I may remark as a proof how dear
it has been to the Church, from the most primitive time till now, that
I know of a hundred and fifty-nine Catholic Commentators who have
explained it, either in treating of the Psalms generally, or of the
Penitential Psalms, or of this especial Psalm. One of these, whom
I have not, however, had the means of referring to, Alfonso de Tor-
tado, has published a folio volume of 1200 pages on this one Psalm.
And even for those beyond the Church, this Psalm has still had its
own charm; and the great Lutheran dictionary of the writers of
that Communion mentions twenty-seven who had written separate
volumes on it. I have no means of learning how many Calvinistic
authors have also made it the matter of an especial treatise; but I
believe that certainly not fewer than those of the Lutheran Communion. Take notice then, how, as one of the late Catholic Commentators says, the precious ointment of this Psalm not only ran
down the beard, but went down to the skirts of Aaron's clothing;
but was diffused even among the other sheep which were not of the
fold.

L.

ARGUMENT.

ARG. THOMAS. That CHRIST, without sin, for the sins of His
people, was judged and overthrew His judges. The voice of the
penitent. This Psalm is to be read at the lection of Isaiah the
Prophet, and of the Acts of the Apostles, where Paul is chosen.
The voice of CHRIST for penitent people, and the voice of Paul,
and of every one that believeth and doeth penitence. The doctrine
of Confession, and a prophecy of the Church. Of martyrdom.

VEN. BEDE. The history is known . . . . . Where we must
earnestly observe, that to this end have the greatest saints been
sometimes permitted to fall into such crimes, and their faults and
penitence are recorded in Scripture, that to us, poor weak creatures,
and following them at such a distance, fear and caution may be
commended; and in their reformation an example of penitence and
a hope of life may be given. But since even the evil deeds of saints
work out the mystery of salvation, David signifies CHRIST: Bathsheba (which by interpretation is the *Well of Satiety*) figures the
Church: Uriah (which by interpretation is *My Light of God*) sets
forth the devil, who desired fraudulently to seize the Light of the
Godhead, but being overthrown by the LORD, lost the kingdom of
the world, and put away the Church of the faithful to be governed
by CHRIST.

[The usual mediæval interpretation is more ingenious. Hildebert thus writes:

Ed. Beaugendre, p. 1217.

Bersabee Lex est; Rex David, Christus; Urias,
    Judæus;—regi nuda puella placet.
Nuda placet Christo Lex non vestita figuris;
    Aufert Judæis hanc, sociatque sibi.
Vir non vult intrare domum, nec spiritualem
    Intellectum plebs Israel ingreditur.
Scripta gerit, per scripta perit deceptus Urias;
    Sic et Judæus scripta sequendo perit.]

This Psalm is divided into five clauses. The first is the satisfaction of most perfect humility (1—6). The second, the confidence of heavenly mercy (7, 8). The third, that the LORD may turn away His Face from David's sin (9—12). The fourth, that other sinners will be encouraged if his terrible iniquity should be pardoned (13—17). The fifth, he commemorates the rise of the Church, which even then he looked for (18, 19).

EUSEBIUS OF CÆSAREA. The doctrine of Confession.

S. JEROME. This fiftieth Psalm echoes the voice of him that is penitent; showing, how he who has fallen into sin, may, by confessing that sin, rise again to good.

1 Have mercy upon me, O GOD, after thy great goodness : according to the multitude of thy mercies do away mine offences.

I can only begin, as Hugh of S. Victor begins, with this prayer: that what I should have felt of the evil of sin, standing under the cross of the penitent thief on Calvary, and seeing the penalty of man's guilt in that central Cross, and understanding the actual existence of human malice from the mockers and blasphemers around,—*that*, so far as is possible,
Annot. in Psalm. cap. 58.
I may feel in writing of that Psalm concerning which it may of a truth be said : "Put off thy shoes from off thy feet, for the place whereon thou standest is holy ground." And first of all they observe,—they, the theological commentators, in their way,—just as they, the mediæval artists in their way,—that in the very origin of this Psalm, we have the trinity of evil; that diabolical parody in working out iniquity of the operations of the GOD Who saw everything that He had made, and behold it was very good. David abused the power of a king, by giving command that Uriah should be slain. He abused the wisdom of a wise man by plotting the deceit which gave him over into the hands of the Ammonites. He took advantage of the goodness and purity of a righteous man, when he sent Uriah back again to the camp without allowing him to enter into his house. So we have the Omnipotence of the FATHER; the Wisdom of the SON; the Holiness of the HOLY GHOST, betrayed; and by each and all great occasion given to the enemies of the LORD to blas-

L.

pheme. *According to the multitude of Thy mercies.* And
they almost all, those great primitive and mediæval writers
take it of the Incarnation. And they well argue that sins,
those sins of which David's were the type, were utterly inex-
piable under the old law; that S. Paul spoke most simply
the entire truth of these, when he said that for such there
remained only a certain fearful looking for of judgment and
fiery indignation. But, on the other hand, they delight, those
heralds of GOD's mercy, to heap up the different promises by
which that mercy is assured to penitents, even in the Old,
how much more in the New, Testament. "Thou hast magnified Thy mercy," so Abraham says. "The LORD is longsuffering, and of great mercy," Moses pleads, when the
spies returned. "He is gracious and merciful, slow to anger,
and of great kindness," says Joel. "Thou hast shewed great
mercy unto David," says Solomon, in the beginning of his
reign. "Thy lovingkindness is better than the life itself,"
David tells us. "Mercy rejoiceth against judgment," as S.
James teaches us. And the 136th Psalm finds on the one
side those like S. Ambrose who would principally see in it
the Incarnation; on the other, those who like Innocent III.,
S. Thomas, S. Chrysostom, S. Cyril, and Hugo Cardinalis,
would take it of the Passion. *The multitude of Thy mercies.*
And they observe from this; that, although the one sin
was now that which was the hardest to bear, which, to
use the saint's own expression, bit the hardest, yet many
and many another sin, when once he was roused to a
sense of his guilt, also, as S. Hildebert says, fastened on
him like fiery serpents, he having made way to their in-
cursion by that first original venom of the ancient guile.
And how could one pass over this verse without quoting the
words of S. Bernard? "*Do away mine offences.* How
shouldst Thou not, O good JESUS, do them away? How
should we not run after Thee? when we perceive that Thou
despisest not the poor, abhorrest not the evil-doer, didst not
keep off from the penitent thief, didst allow Thy feet to be
kissed by her that was a sinner, didst receive the Syrophe-
nician woman, didst accept her that was taken in adultery, in
the very act; didst turn Levi the publican into Matthew the
Evangelist; didst, out of the very spectators of Thy crucifixion, call one who was to be among the very chiefest of
Thine Apostles." This is what S. Bernard takes as the innermost meaning of our first verse; and all the saints, and
all the holy commentators whom I might reckon up by hundreds, have but repeated, have but diluted, his words; have
but, knowing what they know of the terrible struggle between
the new and the old nature—between the first and the Second
Adam, said something, each according to his own capability,
which might throw some small light on the first verse of the
most wonderful of Psalms.

[Of all single Commentators on the Psalms, Ayguan is, I

S. Ambros.
Cassiodor.
Innoc. III.
Hugo Car-
dinal.
Origen.
Chrysost.
Cyril.

Gen. xix. 19.
Numb. xiv.
18.
Joel ii. 11.
2 Chron. i. 8.
Ps. lxii. 4.
S. James ii.
13.

S. Ambros.
Apolog. Da-
vid. Lib. ii.
cap. 12.

will not say the lengthiest, because that involves the idea of tediousness, but, the fullest. His work is included in two folio volumes, of a thousand pages each. But were he to dwell on the whole Psalter at the same length as he does on the verse of which we have now been speaking, forty folio volumes would not be sufficient to carry out what he had thus begun.]

2 Wash me throughly from my wickedness : and cleanse me from my sin.

L.

S. Ambros.

2 Sam. xii. 10.

And here, notice first : how, great as David's sins were, lust to begin with, adultery to go on with, murder to end with : yet, it is not from these great sins, but also from the small transgressions which the world would think little of that he,—he, with all the enormous weight of that former guilt,—prays to be freed. And observe further, that it is from the guilt, and not from the punishment, that he thus asks deliverance. That the sword should never depart from his house ; that the sin, begun, not only secretly even in its full accomplishment, but far more secretly in the recesses of David's heart, should be punished before all Israel and before the sun ; that the child so dear to David should be made one great punishment of his offence ; these things, so far as this Psalm is concerned, might, or might not be. It is of the offence against GOD ; of the defiling, although it were not then so expressly declared, GOD's temple by impurity, that David speaks,—speaks, as S. Fulbert says, commenting on that word *throughly*, as if, more or less, longer or shorter, to him who is of purer eyes than to behold iniquity, it were one and the same thing. And we must not wonder if, in these latter days, when the love of many is waxed cold, and because it has so waxed cold, every possible excuse is looked for, every possible palliation is found in, the Old Testament ; we must not wonder if that which was written by GOD to preserve from despair, is turned by Satan into the means to lead on to presumption. " So David sinned ;" thus Hildebert speaks : " So David, having sinned, is pardoned. And I, I, may I not sin as far as David in impunity, and stop short of him in bloodthirstiness ? May I not with him break the seventh, and yet keep the sixth Commandment ? And, if I break both, the man after GOD's own heart, did the same." And, as the same S. Hildebert says, " Ah, King of Israel, ah, ancestor of the CHRIST, is not this of GOD's infinite mercy toward thee, that, since thou hast occasioned, and wilt occasion, to the end of the world, so many, and so horrible, blasphemies, that thou shouldst also be the channel, through whose words the grace of GOD has descended to so many penitents ; by whose teaching the GOD who is Himself a consuming fire, should draw His followers on to the eternal light of heaven ; through whose attraction, the lamp to guide the feet of His servants in *this*, should become the same which never can go down or withdraw itself in *that* world?"

3 For I acknowledge my faults : and my sin is ever before me.

The heathen philosopher said : "What great truth is there in acknowledging the faults that a man has committed?" But here we have a more real appreciation of the difficulty. As S. Augustine says : if there be one madness greater than another, it is this,—not to be ashamed of the wound, but to be ashamed of the bandage. They collect together the passages of Holy Scripture in which men confess that they have sinned; none better or more earnestly than S. Bernard. On the one side—S. Peter, S. Mary Magdalene, the Penitent Thief, the Prodigal Son, the King of Nineveh, the Jews at S. Peter's first sermon, the jailor at Philippi, Saul, afterwards S. Paul. But others have confessed like the former Saul ; again like Antiochus. Thence they go on to show how the power of confession first of all depends on the power of spiritual sight; first of all you must perceive yourself guilty, before you can own that you are. For Satan, like Nahash the Ammonite, is wont to put out the eyes of those whom he leads captive. And then those deep writers on turning from sin, and the love of GOD, warn us of this, that the latter part of the verse, *my sin is ever before me* is, in and by itself, a very questionable kind of repentance. They may be so remembered as to be taken pleasure in again; they remark how many and many a prisoner has remembered his sins in prison, lived in them again, acted them over again, longed for the time when he might repeat them. Whereas the most perfect example of deep penitence, namely, that of S. Peter, is one as entirely separate from every re-inducement to sin. On the other hand, however much that blessed Apostle would grieve, without any mixture of any feeling but sorrow, when he remembered that crowing of the cock, and the more he dwelt on each particular circumstance of this sin, the self-assertion in presence of his dear Master on the preceding evening,—the presence of a cock in Jerusalem when, save by accident or negligence none could be there,—the hearing it once and not even then remembering, nay, the hearing it again, and not even so calling to mind what his LORD had said, till the same dear "LORD turned and looked upon Peter ;" the more he followed out (as no doubt in those, to him, miserable hours, he did) the whole series of his fall, most certainly, the truer repentance. But, as Pinusius says, whoever should have advised David to go through all the steps of his sin in the same way and with the same detail would only have shown how little he knew of the human heart. Therefore, they proceed; here is one of the great lessons to be—taught in the first place, learnt in the next—*when* the committed

S. Ambros. Apol. David. cap. 12.

A.

Serm. de S. Andrea.

1 Sam. xv. 24. 2 Macc. ix. 30.

L.

1 Sam. xii. 2. Judg. xvi. 21. Those especially of the school of Ghent, Giort, and Thomas à Kempis. S. Gregor. Moral. 22, capp. 2 & 3. Cassiodor. Coll. 20, cap. 9.

Pinusius in Cass.

Cæsarius
Arel. Hom.
2, de Pasch.
sin should be *ever before* the sinner in its details; *when* only
in its general substance and weight. *My sin is ever before
me*; or, as it is in the Vulgate, though not in the LXX.,[1] *my
sin is ever against me.* And therefore in that phrase the
fathers of the Western Church have exercised themselves in
exploring the full meaning. And again; S. Jerome takes
the words: *my sin is ever against me;* in this sense, that sin
separates GOD and man; therefore, that as man to be the
true servant of his LORD, must seek Him by prayer, so "those
Isa. lix. 2. iniquities which," as the Prophet says, "have separated between you and your GOD," and "that sin which hath hid His
face from you that He will not hear;" these are indeed
against us.

4 Against thee only have I sinned, and done this
evil in thy sight : that thou mightest be justified in
thy saying, and clear when thou art judged.

And first of all we ask, in what sense it can be said that he
had only sinned against GOD, when he had sinned both against
Bathsheba and Uriah; and to this they add a different ques-
S. Hieron.
Epist. 22, et
46.
Cassian.
Collat. 20.
S. Cyprian.
ad Novat.
128.
S. Clem.
Alex. Strom.
4, cap. vi. tion: whether he sinned most against her or him. And this
is to be observed beyond everything else; and so they who
lived in the earlier and in the mediæval ages of the Church,
seem to have felt most strongly how far higher the law that
our LORD came to lay down soars above even his law, whose
present Psalm has been the support, comfort, guide, guardian,
of so many thousand penitents. Take it in the words of a
mediæval saint. "O my GOD! Thou knowest how often, how
innumerable times, I myself, with ten thousand-fold the grace
of this Thy saint,—of this, the man that was well-pleasing to
Thee, have given Thee thanks for this Psalm. But this also:
for this I thank Thee, that Thou hast given to the meanest
of Thy servants now, the power to do,—the wisdom to know
this in the Church, as compared to that in the synagogue—
that which Thy servant and saint, only did not, because he
knew not. I thank Thee, O LORD, that to us it is not allowed,
to enjoy that which we have unlawfully coveted, when possession becomes lawful. I thank Thee that Thou hast from
S. Bonaven-
tura. Thy true and faithful servants, in this Thy better kingdom,
closed that which, had it been still allowable to them, might
have been a further incentive to sin." He means of course
that to a Christian man, after the previous sin, Bathsheba
would have been forbidden; and yet that, so far from this,
she, of all David's wives, to the very last, had the greatest
influence over him; and which they most truly observe, seems
Anselm. to have been, in that most corrupt generation, one of GOD's
truest servants. But there are several ways in which the

---

[1] And the Roman version fol-
lows the LXX. *Delictum meum* | (not *contra* but) *coram me est
semper*, and so also the Slavonic.

difficulty is resolved. *Against Thee only.* Some will have it
that we only learn from the parable of the infinite ten thousand talents, and the poor hundred pence, how a sin immediately committed against his neighbour may yet be man's infinitely more terrible accusation before his GOD. Others look
at David's anointing; and there see a special grace given, and
therefore a special power received; and therefore a special
sin in the neglecting the inward strength which that bestowed
power gave. Others—later in the mediæval Church—remembering how the dear Bridegroom and the dear Bride are one,
will have it that a sin against the latter is equally an offence
against the former. To which it is answered: that the synagogue can scarcely claim the same love from, the same union
with our LORD, that His Church now can.[1] And perhaps on
the whole, the parable of the ten thousand talents most probably gives the true meaning: murder, as regards Urias; pollution, as regards Bathsheba; but what, either one or the other,
as respects the LORD of Life, or the GOD of Purity? Then there
comes a still greater difficulty: how the fact of David's having
sinned against GOD alone should justify Him in His sayings.
And therefore it is not wonderful that they should have attempted a different reading, which the Chaldee paraphrase
gives rise to: *that Thou mightest justify me in,* or *with respect
to, Thy commandments.* And again, some will have it: *so
that Thou art just in Thy decree, unspotted when Thou judgest.*
That is, that the sin of David, though not followed up by the
avenger of blood, as, according to the Levitical law, it ought
to have been, was nevertheless rightly, according to that law,
punished by the GOD Who gave it. But, as those deeper
interpreters teach us, here faintly and weakly, the great sacrifice for sin is set forth. David has committed a sin which
must be punished by death; according to the Mosaic law,
not even, were the avenger of blood pacified, might the murderer live. Then next; by the mouth of GOD's prophet,
GOD gives His pardon; "the LORD also hath put away thy
sin; thou shalt not die." But not absolute and uncon-
ditional pardon; the sentence of death on the child follows.
We must not here work out that type; but over and over
again it has been shown how the Child of Bethlehem, born to
this end, that He might take on Himself the sins of the whole
world, was faintly and afar off typified by this, whose death
was so involved in his father's prolonged life.

S. Gregor.
Moral. ii.
cap. 19.

W.

Rupert.

Caietan.

V. Bed.

Deut. xix.
13.

2 Sam. xii.
13.

5 Behold, I was shapen in wickedness : and in sin
hath my mother conceived me.

[1] It is well worth observing how S. Augustine, though other-wise entering deeply into the mystical, as well as literal, sense of this Psalm, says not a word on the present difficulty in this exposition; nor, so far as I am aware, does he enter on the sub-ject in any of his works.

Origen.
Hom. viii.
in Levit.
Cyprian. lib.
iii. cont.
Julian.
Augustin.
cont. 2 Epis.
Pelag. cap.
10.
Isidor.de Pe-
nitent. de
arca Noe.
cap. ii.
Thauler de
Pass.
Christi. p.
194.

On this verse the whole multitude of early and mediæval Commentators have diverged this way and that into all kind of questions regarding the soul and body of man : when each was first created ; when the two joined together.   For my own part, leaving for this time those who have thus disputed,—their names are in the margin—and a host of others, I will only quote what Tauler in his commentary on the Passion says : " Let others, O LORD, dispute how sin entered into the world —how sin entered into man ; this, rather, this only would I ask Thee, that Thou Who, of a very truth, didst take our perfect nature, albeit without sin, on Thyself,—that Thou, Who knowest whereof we are made, and rememberest that we are but dust, wouldst have pity on all mine infirmities, wouldst compassionate all my weaknesses, wouldst, even in this body of sin, as Thy Church has learnt to say, not weighing my merits, but pardoning my offences, frame such a spirit as may be found worthy to enter the gates of Paradise ; such a body as may have part in the first resurrection : so that body, soul, and spirit, renewed, transfigured, reinstated ; I say not in their first, but in their more than first dignity, may together rejoice in the ineffable glory of the Beatific vision."[1]

6 But lo, thou requirest truth in the inward parts : and shalt make me to understand wisdom secretly.

L.

I cannot but see with Lorinus ; the more deeply we enter into this Psalm, the more utterly we feel how unworthy we are to penetrate into the shrine of his heart, who, sinner though he were, yet, nevertheless, was the man after GOD's own heart.   But first ; we must notice the difference of the Vulgate from our own translation. *But lo, Thou requirest truth : the uncertain and hidden things of Thy wisdom Thou hast made manifest to me.*[2] We ought the more diligently to listen to S. Thomas, seeing that he will be so soon taken away from helping us. So I cannot do better than quote his own words : *Behold thou hast loved the truth.* Here —this being taken in connection with the whole history of repentance, as written in this Psalm,—you have the sum of each portion, and of the whole put together. *Thou hast loved the truth.* *The truth* in true sorrow as regards thyself : *the truth* in true confession as regards thy priest : *the truth* in true restitution as regards thy neighbour. *The uncertain and hidden things of Thy wisdom Thou hast made known unto me.* *Of Thy wisdom ?* And who am I, O LORD GOD, that

[1] I quote from the edition of Lammertz. Cologne. 1851.

[2] Here we come (as we shall have occasion in a future dissertation to see,) to the sixth stone, the sardius ; the twelve stones divided, as it were, between, and shining on, each several portion of the Psalms, as there we shall more fully learn.

Thou shouldest make manifest "to me" that wisdom Who
saith, "I dwell in the highest, and My throne is in the
cloudy pillar." Thou hast made manifest to me[1] in the triple Ecclus.xxiv.
way of prophecy: the supernatural is when the prophet
speaks, "I saw the LORD sitting upon a throne, high and
lifted up:" the next, supernatural, and yet revealed to the
bodily eye, as well as to the spiritual sight, of which we hear
where that is written; "The LORD came down in a cloud,
and spake unto him, and took of the spirit that was upon
him, and gave it unto the seventy elders:" and lastly, when, Numb. xi.
without any revelation supernatural either to bodily or 25.
mental sense, the manifestation was only to the deepest and
inmost spirit, as where it is so often written in the Prophets,
"The word of the LORD came unto me, saying." Thus it is
that the greatest doctor of all saints, the greatest saint of all
doctors, teaches us on this matter; and were there any especial reason why we should value what he thus writes, it is
to be found in this—that his commentary on the Psalms
was the latest of all his works; was, as his immediate follower so loved to say, his swan's song; and that, while engaged in composing it,—most probably, in writing the very
portion of which we have just heard the abstract,—he fell
into that fainting fit which his dear sister, the Countess of
Grandella, prophesied would end his work on earth.

7 Thou shalt purge me with hyssop, and I shall
be clean : thou shalt wash me, and I shall be whiter
than snow.

Here, they all say, that which was merely confession by Pet. Natal.
word before, becomes confession in action. Any one can Lib.vii.c.14.
submit to the former; it requires a far greater grace, though
still not the crowning grace of all—that we shall come to
by-and-by—to receive the latter. Look at all the ritual puri-
fications of the Jews : the cleansing of the leper, that of the Lev. xiv. 7.
Lev. xiv. 51.
leprous house, the water of separation by the ashes of the Numb. xix.
red heifer: and then see how, even so early as the great 2.
doctor of the Western Church has taught,—even amidst a A.
people who had been educated in the belief that temporal De Doctrin.
promises, that earthly pleasure, were the heritage of those Lib. ii. c. 16.
who truly served GOD,—how even they were, in the types
and parables of their offices, shown—according to that far
higher Christian teaching, that it is by suffering, not by
pleasure, that we may hope to draw nearest to Him That
was the Man of Sorrows, and acquainted with grief.

8 Thou shalt make me hear of joy and gladness :
that the bones which thou hast broken may rejoice.

Or, as it is in the Vulgate,—and therefore this Psalm has

[1] This is the sense of S. Thomas : I am rather shortening the words.

II.　　　　I

its especial force, as one of those for the dead,—*the bones which Thou hast humbled.* But those words are taken in more senses than one: each of them so precious; each of them, in this or in that way, having reference to the Incarnation. *And the bones which Thou hast humbled. Humbled,* in the fall of man; that is which Thou hast permitted—as the type of the endurance of man against temptation—so to feel their own weakness: they—in that day known to Thee —they, in the regeneration of all things, shall, as the Prophet says, "rejoice and flourish as an herb." It shows what was the depth of meaning believed by the early and mediæval Church to lie concealed under these words, with different interpretations of them, that the references which they have been supposed to bear to our LORD's miracles and sayings in the Gospels should so entirely vary. But perhaps what S. Clement of Alexandria says is the most striking. They are to be *humbled* by faith and repentance, not to be broken by despair; they, the bones, shall hereafter rejoice— not the flesh, the seat and type of earthly passion and luxury. And he proceeds: "In the first and second Adam the case was thus far the same. In the first Adam, his bones were humbled by the loss of one of them, in order that out of it the help meet for him might be made. In the second Adam so humbled, that they might all be told: in the one case, by GOD's especial miracle of creation; in the other by (as with all reverence we may say it) the yet more especial and foretold miracle of His Providence." Let us hear, at the end of this verse, a noble passage of S. Jerome, in a work in which he certainly did not always write nobly:—" *The bones which Thou hast humbled shall rejoice.* I honour, in the flesh of the martyr, the scars received for the Name of CHRIST; I honour the power of Him That liveth for ever and ever in the everlasting memorial of His servant; I honour the ashes hallowed by the confession of the LORD; I honour, in those ashes, the seeds of eternity; I honour the body which hath showed me how to love my LORD,—the body which hath taught me, for my LORD, not to fear death; I honour the body which CHRIST hath honoured on earth,—the body with which CHRIST will reign in heaven." There cannot be a better commentary on that word *rejoice.*

Marginal notes: S. Athanas. C. S. Remig. Parænesis. c. 6. Ps. xxii. 17. In Vigilantium.

9 Turn thy face from my sins: and put out all my misdeeds.

Marginal note: Ay.

They say very well how here David rightly asks that which S. Peter, intending to ask rightly, so made request for as, had his petition been granted, it would have proved his eternal ruin. David says, *Turn Thy face*—not from me, but—*from my sins.* S. Peter, mixing the two together, petitioned, "Depart from me, for I am a sinful man, O LORD." Rather, as they teach us, the prayer of the centurion comes far nearer to this:

"LORD, I am not worthy that Thou shouldest come under S. Luke v. 8.
my roof." And they remind us of that ancient type of turning away the face from sin, when Shem and Japheth, turning
their backs on their father, so sympathized with his weakness,
so suffered for him in his sin. And in like manner they quote Ezek. xxviii.
21.
—and the reader may at his leisure refer to them—those pas- Gen. xxxi.
sages which tell of Ezekiel's vision, and of Rachel's artifice. 13.

10 Make me a clean heart, O GOD : and renew a
right spirit within me.

It is wonderful—or rather, perhaps, considering the malice
of Satan, it is not wonderful—that the great texts which
ought to be, and in themselves are, the greatest comfort for
the earnest servants of our LORD, are the chief battle-fields of
scholastic divinity. On this verse, as every scholar knows,
the Scotists and the Thomists find, each of them, a principal argument for their respective tenets about the mediate
source of grace. Volumes would not suffice even to give an
abstract of their arguments ; and perhaps, as a commentator
on this Psalm who lived very near to GOD says, were the Covetanus.
matter settled, the decision on one side or on the other would
neither bring to pass the conversion of one sinner, nor the
edification of one saint. The difficulty, of course, lies in the
word *create : Create in me a clean heart, O God :* how far,
and in what sense, that spirit can be said to be created which
is only turned from darkness to light; given over from the
power of Satan into that of GOD ; regenerated in baptism, if it B.
so be—otherwise, after baptism, turned round in conversion
from the slavery of Satan to the light yoke and easy burden of
its dear LORD. That is, how the poor kine, with their affections in the Philistines' country, may nevertheless, lowing as
they go, be—not forced, but—drawn, to bring up the ark of 1 Sam. vi. 12.
GOD to its own place : how, as another mediæval commentator Zech. ii. 2.
tells us, the man with the measuring line in his hand may
see what is the length as well as the breadth of Jerusalem.
It is a fault rather of our language than of our teaching, that
the identity of *spirit* and *wind*, or *breath*, is not at once per-
ceptible. For in connection with this verse we should otherwise at once catch those : "He bloweth with His *wind*, and Ps. cxlvii.
the waters flow;" "What manner of man is this, that even 18.
the *wind* and the sea obey Him?" and, "Whither the spirit
was to go, they"—the Living Creatures—"went, thither was Ezek. i. 20.
their spirit to go;" and, to sum up the whole, "As many
as are led by the Spirit of GOD, they are the sons of GOD."
Then this also has to be observed, to which I for one should
never have dared to allude, did not almost all the saintly
commentators on the Psalms point it out—*renew a right
spirit* : "Take not Thy HOLY SPIRIT;" "Stablish me with
Thy free Spirit." And so they say, taught, in the first
place, (so far as I know,) by S. Bernard, that the HOLY

SPIRIT is, according to His proper Name, the Third Person of the Blessed Trinity; the right Spirit is spoken of the SON; the free, or princely, or royal Spirit, of the FATHER: of the FATHER, because He only is not GOD of GOD, Light of Light, very GOD of very GOD, but GOD of Himself, Light of Himself, very GOD in and of His own eternal essence: the self-existent JEHOVAH, a title which, in these days, so many, with more zeal and love than knowledge, would apply to our Blessed LORD. How this verse is the seventh foundation of the Church, and answers to the Chrysolite, I may well leave to those whose studies lie in that direction.

11 Cast me not away from thy presence : and take not thy HOLY SPIRIT from me.

From this verse the Church has taken one of the most common and most encouraging petitions. If we ask that the HOLY SPIRIT may not be taken from us, it follows that we must have received Him. " Now, then," as one of the great preachers of the seventeenth century says, "now, then, ye who say that the HOLY GHOST is not given in Baptism, what will ye? If He is not, then are our children manifestly in a worse condition than those of the Jews. *Take not*, saith David, *Thy Holy Spirit from me.* How had David that HOLY SPIRIT? Will you answer that it was as GOD's Pro- phet, as GOD's Psalmist, as GOD's vicegerent upon earth? And what poor miserable culprit, standing even before an earthly tribunal, would remind the judge of the especial reasons there were that he should not have fallen into the crime for which he now stood in peril of his life? And David now was capitally condemned, according to the law of the Jews, on a double charge—adultery and murder; and would he then have pleaded, Take not That HOLY SPIRIT Which has so taught me to sing Thy praises—take not That HOLY SPIRIT by Which I have been anointed king over this great people—from me? Verily, what would this have been but to stir up the hot anger of GOD even to a higher degree than it had been before kindled? No, thus it is: Because I, the son of Abraham, was, as an infant, admitted into the fellow- ship of Thy children, take not That HOLY SPIRIT from me, which, outwardly, at all events, then sealed me to be Thine own. Now, therefore, O disciple, not of the Catholic Church, but of Calvin,—now, then, O follower, not of the confession of the Apostles, but of that of Augsburg,—are thy children to be better or worse off than those of the Jews? If worse, whereto serves the New Testament? If better, thank that LORD Who died for thee and for all men, that verily and truly they are regenerate; and that the multitude who died in their infancy, having received Baptism which is not that of the Church, found that That HOLY SPIRIT was not taken from them in the hour of their death, and now follow the LAMB whithersoever He goeth."

12 O give me the comfort of thy help again : and stablish me with thy free Spirit.

And here they say—why need I make a list of those who merely reiterate what every Priest knows, or ought to know? —how much that comfort is needed by those who either awake to a sense of their own sins, or have to bear the sins of others. No one can speak better than S. Eucherius : "Who would undertake that most terrible office of announcing the mercy of GOD to men, if they knew what was that office of standing in the place of GOD to men? There are the four Beasts round about the Throne, there are numberless beasts on earth; men like beasts; men worse than beasts; men learned in that of which beasts are altogether ignorant. I know not how this office could be undertaken, were it not that the LORD saith, 'Ask, and it shall be given unto you; seek, and ye shall find; knock, and it shall be opened to you.' To ask implies learning; to seek implies devotion; to knock implies self-denial. All these things must meet in the person of a Priest : the seeking, the asking, the knocking. And observe how. How, dost thou say? Both from heaven and from earth. What that seeking, asking, knocking of the sinner is, ye, brethren," (for he was addressing a synod of his Priests,) " are not ignorant. What it is as regards the great High Priest—knowledge must ask, love must seek, operation must knock; the beginning of the work is from necessity; its perseverance is in love; its action in rest; its rest in labour : this is what we owe as Priests, on the one hand, to penitents; on the other, to the great High Priest." *And stablish me with Thy free Spirit.* And *free* is such a poor translation of the word. *Liberal*, or *royal*, or better still, which the Vulgate has, *princely spirit.* They discuss, those great Doctors both of the Eastern and Western Church, what especial grace—if one may use the expression without irreverence—what favourite grace is signified by this epithet of the HOLY GHOST. It is singular to observe, by all the commentators on the Psalms, reaching down from almost Apostolic ages to this, how that especial grace, which the world then chiefly set at nought, is the Princely Spirit signified. For example : in an age of heresy, S. Ambrose will have it to be the true faith; in an age of luxury, S. Chrysostom understands it of the grace of purity; later down, in an age of feudal tyranny, it is interpreted of the freedom which, in spite of earthly bonds and fetters, the servant of GOD enjoys; the foretaste of that Jerusalem which is free; and still later, in an age of scholastic disputation, the Spirit of Wisdom is the *Princely* Spirit. In the same way that, during the many centuries of the Church's existence, *that* doctrine has been, above all others, *the* Catholic doctrine which the world, for the time being, agreed to hate : as in the fourth century, the CONSUBSTANTIAL; in the fifth, the Incarnation; in the present, all Sacramental teaching.

A.
Ruffin.
S. Gregor. in Hom. 20, in Ezek.
Cassiodor.
S. Remig.
V. Bede.
Haimo.
S. Innocent.
S. Athanas.
S. Cyril.
In 2 Kings xxvii. p. 155.

Apolog. David. cap. viii.
Hom. iii. de Spiritu Sanct.

S. Thomas Aquin.

13 Then shall I teach thy ways unto the wicked :
and sinners shall be converted unto thee.

And why should he set forth this as one great end and aim
of his life? And they all with one consent answer, Because,
after his sin, till his repentance, he had taught to all his sub-
jects, and to all the nations round, as he has taught to all future
generations, by that one sin, Satan's ways. So the stress is to
be laid on THY *ways*. Up to this time I have taught any ways
but Thine; up to this time I have given great occasion to
Thine enemies to blaspheme; but *then—then*, when Thou
shalt have not only bestowed on me, but stablished me with
Thy Princely Spirit, *then shall I teach Thy ways*. A Spirit
so Princely in forgiveness as to remit my own transgressions;
a Spirit so Princely in strength, as to trample under foot all
future assaults of the enemy. *And sinners shall be converted
unto Thee.* "How little he thought," so says the Carthusian,
"what thousands and hundreds of thousands of sinners should
learn repentance from this Psalm, who when," the words
are worth noting, "they see Priests, highly educated, prepared with all the array of this world's learning, professing
to give up themselves and their lives to the instruction and
conversion of others, find them all so utterly fail; because
they speak not with the fire of the HOLY GHOST, but so
coldly, so drily, so wretchedly; instead of those sharp, pene-
trating, red-hot words, which they who have taken in hand
to bring men from darkness to light—from the slavery of
Satan into the liberty of the LORD—ought to have. As saith
the Apostle, 'Thou art confident that thou thyself art a
guide to the blind. . . . Thou, therefore, which teachest another, teachest thou not thyself?'" *Sinners shall be converted
unto Thee.* They ask, Who are the three great Doctors of
the Catholic Church? Surely, take them all in all, we should
answer, David, the murderer; Peter, the denier; Paul, the
blasphemer. And here is fulfilled what so long before the
Mosaic dispensation had been written for our learning;
how the Unicorn *is* now willing to serve us, *will* bring home
our seed, and gather it into our barn. "See," says S. Gregory the Great, "what remission of sins this is, which not
only frees the converted, but converts the bondsman. See
what wisdom this is which turns the serpent's malice on himself, and out of which his very venom produces the saving
efficacy of redemption as theriac out of poison."

14 Deliver me from blood-guiltiness, O GOD, thou
that art the GOD of my health : and my tongue shall
sing of thy righteousness.

We must not take this text—for, except in the Vulgate, it
never could be interpreted in that lovely sense—*Deliver me
by means of blood-shedding :* that is, by the one Offering of

Marginal notes:
L.
Ludolph.
D. C.
Innocent. III.
Job xxxix.9.
Hugo de S. Victor.

Calvary. They give eight other interpretations : all of them, except this, connected with the Jewish law ; whether as having to do with the punishment of death inflicted, under the Mosaic dispensation, both for murder and for adultery, or the vengeance which had been threatened, that the sword should never depart from the house of David, might be removed from his family. And it would be useless to dwell on the senses which the ingenuity of the middle ages affixed to this petition. But perhaps that which will come more nearly and dearly home to the heart of those who most frequently recite this Psalm, is this: Deliver me from the guilt of the Blood of Calvary. Where notice this : that the petition of the Jews, as they intended it, the most awful that human lips ever uttered, " His Blood be on us and on our children," is, in another sense, that one supplication on which all our dearest hopes hang—" Not by water only, but by water and blood." And so now, *Deliver me from blood-guiltiness :* that is, not, GOD forbid ! from having any interest in that most precious Blood poured forth for us on the Cross ; but from having, as S. Paul says, crucified that same LORD afresh, and put Him to an open shame. *[S. Athanas.]*

15 Thou shalt open my lips, O LORD : and my mouth shall show thy praise.

Marvellous verse, which has merited to begin so many myriads of services, since the Church first began to lead a liturgical life !

> Ut queant laxis resonare fibris
> Mira gestorum famuli tuorum,
> Solve polluti labii reatum,
> Sancte Redemptor.

L.

Say, as of old, *Ephphatha :* touch my lips with the burning coal from off the altar; give me an elect tongue, a "pure language, that" I "may call upon the Name of the LORD;" give me a learned tongue, that I may "speak as the oracles of GOD;" "O let my mouth be filled with Thy praise, that I may sing of Thy glory and honour all the day long." They call to mind those noble African confessors, who, when their tongues were cut out by the persecuting Arians, spoke none the less plainly : they point to the cloven tongues as of fire, which had no sooner sat on the Apostles, than they began to speak in divers languages the wonderful works of GOD. *[S. Mark vii. 34. Zeph. iii. 9. 1 S. Pet. iv. 11. S. Gregor. Dial. iii. 32.]*

Thou shalt open my lips : the Chaldee adds, *in Thy law.* They find a singular allegory in the history of the five kings hid in the cave of Machpelah. The cave is the mouth: the five kings are the sins of taste, smell, touch, sight, hearing. Our True Joshua commands us to open our mouths in the confession of them ; and when we have done so, then, and not till then, He bids us be of good courage, and put our *[Ay.]*

A.

"feet on the necks of those kings." *And my mouth shall show Thy praise.* S. Augustine: "*Thy praise,* because I have been created; *Thy praise,* because, sinning, I have not been forsaken; *Thy praise,* because I have been admonished to confess; *Thy praise,* because, in order that I might be succoured, I have been cleansed."

S. Thomas
Aquin.

And finally, O LORD, so *open my lips,* that I may come to Sion with songs, and everlasting joy.

16 For thou desirest no sacrifice, else would I give it thee: but thou delightest not in burnt-offerings.

17 The sacrifice of GOD is a troubled spirit: a broken and a contrite heart, O GOD, shalt thou not despise.

A.

Hence in many places, though not especially in his commentary on this verse, S. Augustine takes occasion to write gloriously concerning "the New Sacrifice of the New Law;" all his teaching being so marvellously bound up by S. Thomas in that almost first of Christian hymns, the sequence for *Corpus Christi.* One could, in spite of history, long to believe the story, (which, however, is not so undoubtedly a legend but that even at the present day it finds critical supporters), that when the new feast was instituted against the rationalising heretics of the time, Peter Abælard, Peter the Eater, and the rest, the composition of the service was entrusted equally to the Angelic and to the Seraphic Doctor: that to the former we owe those hymns, beyond all earthly praise—*Pange Lingua gloriosi Corporis; Verbum supernum prodiens, Nec;* and *Sacris solemniis:* while to the latter we are indebted for that noble sequence, *Lauda Syon Salvatorem.* But, in point of fact, Thomas proved himself as much the first Christian poet of his age, as—it may be with the single exception of S. Augustine—he is *the* Christian doctor of all ages.

Horæ Talmud.

From this verse even the Rabbis take occasion to teach us how there is a higher Sacrifice than that of sacrificed victims. For David's sin, wilfully carried on from that first eye-glance from the house-roof, to the bloody death under the wall of Rabbath, the LORD provided no remedy: it was a hopeless offence. This is what the great mediæval writers, in their Passion sermons, so loved to dwell on: this is why, like S. Thomas, they so constantly, with reference to the Levite that "came and looked upon the wounded man, and passed by upon the other side," point us to the "certain Samaritan,"

L.

The hymn,
Adoro te devote.

> Cujus una stilla salvum facere
> Totum mundum quit ab omni scelere.

Galatinus,
ii. 9.

A Rabbi Jehoshua had enough insight into the true meaning of the law, to teach his disciples that a truly contrite heart was more acceptable to GOD than one million of lambs. And notice this: David, after his sin, never—so

far as we are told—offered any sacrifice for it. He felt, no
doubt, that he must let that alone for ever. Yet, as we
have seen, it was a not unusual subject of disputation,
whether his great fall, taken together with its consequences,
had, on the whole, been a hindrance or a help to the Church.
This we must remember: that the injury is far more visible
and palpable. We partly know how, from the very begin- Jansen.
ning of the Church till the present time, the reproach has Gaud.
always been; "What! *this* the man after GOD's own heart!
the man who, to adultery, added murder, and that murder at
second hand, involving himself in the guilt, but putting off
the odium to another?" As S. Ambrose says, "O David, O
David, so glorious a saint, so miserable a sinner, of a verity
thou hast given great occasion to the enemies of the LORD to
blaspheme!" More than S. Ambrose knew, more than he
could have imagined: fifteen hundred years' longer scandal,
and in the latest of them the pencil employed as well as the
pen to scandalise those who, from the Psalms of David, have
learnt to come to the Son of David. But then, on the other
side, as one well worthy of his name has taught, *golden-worded* S. Pet.
indeed in this respect. Who can tell how many penitents, all Chrysolo-
but driven to desperation, all but entering into the pains of gus. Serm.
hell, all but ready to rush out of this world into the next,— 107.
who can tell how many that have despaired of GOD's pardon,
lost all trust in His love, all but cast away the latest remnant
of hope, have not taken these most divine words into their
mouths, and been turned again? have not been baptized in
this Jordan, and recovered from the leprosy? have not bathed
in this Siloam, and received their sight? O most dear, most
precious words; words, if any, worthy to be written in letters
of gold; words meriting to be inscribed with an iron pen
and lead in the rock for ever! It is not so much in the
public mouth of the Church,—it is not so much in the great
congregation,—it is not so much when the priests, the ministers of the LORD, have stood between the porch and the
altar, that ye, as sweet-smelling frankincense, have gone up
to heaven. No: it was when she of old wiped those Blessed
Feet with the hairs of her head, after she had anointed them
with her ointment; it was when a greater sinner than even
this rejoiced to offer the body so polluted with guilt to the
stake, in the presence of the heathen judges; it was when
merciless men, steeped up to the lips in blood, have, with all
the strength and agony of their repentance, appealed to the
Blood of Calvary; it was then, and in a thousand thousand
like cases, that ye, O most blessed, O most glorious words, O
words that none save He, in all points tempted like as we are,
yet without sin, could have inspired,—it was then that ye
have merited to prevail!

18 O be favourable and gracious unto Sion: build
thou the walls of Jerusalem.

19 Then shalt thou be pleased with the sacrifice of righteousness, with the burnt-offerings and oblations: then shall they offer young bullocks upon thine altar.

L.

Up to this time David has prayed for himself: now, as every true penitent ought to do, he ends by interceding for others. And here we have one of the examples which, to a casual view, would seem to confuse the two terms: nay, and even if we take the literal sense, may seem confined to that. For consider how David had, at the time when this Psalm was written, but just fortified himself in Sion; while the walls of Jerusalem, long ago ruined in more than one siege, had not so much to be built, as to be rebuilt. But, keeping to that rule, so infallible in the enormous majority of cases, that we are bound to believe it our failure in understanding when one instance out of fifty seems not to obey the law; and then, what is the lesson?[1] And surely this most glorious one: that, in proportion as our LORD helps forward His earthly Church, in the same degree does He build the walls of that Jerusalem, concerning which it is written,

S. Bernard.
Serm. i. De
Sancto Mi-
chaeli.

> "Many a blow and biting sculpture,
> Polished well those stones elect."

Mazzarin.
disc. 93.

And why two epithets to that same dear LORD's dealings with Sion? *Be favourable and gracious:*[2] *favourable,* in every little help that He gives His servants in this world militant; *gracious,* in the entire manifestation of Himself to those in that world triumphant; *favourable,* and there may be still much of sin, more of infirmity; *gracious,* and there shall be what the schoolmen call the blessed necessity of sinlessness on the one hand, and on the other, "The inhabitant shall not say, I am sick." *Be favourable:* so now That LORD is, to all who are taking up His Cross, following His banner, fighting the good fight; *gracious,* so He now is to those blessed ones who are at all events nearest—not here to debate the question whether the martyrs at once enjoy the Beatific Vision—to His Throne. *Build Thou the walls of Jerusalem.*

[1] I know very well how those reviewers of my first volume, against whom I would not be willingly found to stand, have thought that, without a most violent pressure, Jerusalem and Sion cannot be always interpreted as mediæval Saints have taught us. I trust that the essay at the end of the present volume, if God permits me to write it, may explain some of the difficulties which yet hang about this question. I need hardly add, not of myself, but from the Saints and Doctors whose commentary this is.

[2] It is the same contrast, though not exactly expressed in the same way, both in the LXX. and in the Vulgate. In the former, ἀγάθυνον, Κύριε, ἐν τῇ εὐδοκίᾳ σου· in the latter, *Benigne fac Domine in bona voluntate tua Sion.*

I know not that a heathen poet has ever been to my mind quoted with more exquisite beauty than Virgil here: **L.**

> "O fortunati, quorum jam mœnia surgunt."

And what kind of walls those shall be, let Tobit tell us. "Jerusalem shall be built up with sapphires, and emeralds, and precious stones; thy walls, and towers, and battlements with pure gold; and the streets of Jerusalem shall be paved with beryl, and carbuncles, and stones of Ophir; and all her streets shall say, Alleluia." *Tobit xiii. 16.*

> Hierusalem! Hierusalem!
> God grant I once may see
> Thy endless joys; and of the same
> Partaker aye to be.
>
> Thy walls are made of precious stones,
> Thy bulwarks diamonds square;
> Thy gates are of right orient pearl,
> Exceeding rich and rare.
>
> Thy turrets and thy pinnacles
> With carbuncles do shine;
> Thy very streets are paved with gold,
> Surpassing clear and fine.
>
> Thy houses are of ivory,
> Thy windows crystal clear;
> Thy tiles are made of beaten gold;—
> O God, that I were there!

Then shalt Thou be pleased with the sacrifice of righteousness. They ask, Why is it said *then?* why not *now?* And they, in the first place, who take this sacrifice of the Holy Eucharist, see the fulfilment, entire, eternal, perfect, of that Sacrifice in the sight of the Lamb as it had been slain. They who would rather take the sacrifice of righteousness to refer solely to that of Calvary, see in this prophecy, the end and aim of our dear Lord's Passion. Therefore He tasted of death, that we should never taste of it; therefore He died, that we might live; therefore the Cross to obtain the Crown.[1] *Then shall they offer young bullocks upon Thine altar.* And the third among the Evangelistic symbols tells us of the highest sense in which we are to take the promise: *D. C. Pet. Vega. S. Ambros. Paul. Bergens. Scrut. iv. 1. Mazzarin. 95. Ay.*

> Rictus bovis Lucæ datur,
> In quâ formâ figuratur
> Nova Christus hostia;
> Ara crucis mansuëtus
> Hic mactatus, sic et vetus
> Transit observantia.

---

[1] It would be too long, and would lead us too far from our subject, to see how mediæval writers, and especially the Carthusian, dwell from this verse on the virtues of the Crucified as a foundation of the heavenly Jerusalem.

L.

And in the plural, as they tell us, we are to see those followers of the One True Victim who, for His sake, and keeping the two thousand cubits behind the very Ark, nevertheless, in their time, and after their degree, were sacrifices to GOD of a sweet-smelling savour: firstly and chiefly, the Martyrs; then, the Confessors; then, the Virgins; then, the Doctors; then, every righteous soul that shall have had the grace of perseverance to the end; among which GOD grant both those that shall read, and him that writes this book, to find a place, for JESUS CHRIST'S sake.

And therefore:

Glory be to the FATHER, Who, according to the multitude of His mercies, does away our offences; and to the SON, That is the GOD of our health: and to the HOLY GHOST, the Free Spirit by Whom we are established;

As it was in the beginning, is now, and ever shall be: world without end. Amen.

COLLECTS.

Mozarabic.   We beseech Thee, O LORD GOD, to turn Thy face from our sins, and to put out all our misdeeds; and as the publican, who stood afar off, was heard for the sake of his humility, so hear us for the merits of our Humility, that is to say of Him Who, being co-equal with Thee, His FATHER, yet for our sakes vouchsafed to take upon Him the form of a servant, our LORD JESUS CHRIST. Through.

Mozarabic.   O GOD, Who, the more we hide our sins, the more bringest them into open day; Who out of doubt dost bring certainty, out of error, truth; visit us with the dew of Thy mercy: so putting out all our misdeeds, as to make us a new heart by the infusion of Thy HOLY GHOST, to the end that we, rejoicing in such an indweller, may have our mouth opened for the declaration of Thy praise. Amen. Through.

Mozarabic.   O LORD JESUS CHRIST, GOD of our salvation, Who by Thy salutary Passion dost extinguish all our evil Passions; give to us Thy servants forgiveness of our sins and remission of our guilt, to the end that from Thee, O LORD, we may one day receive eternal life. Amen. Through.

PSALM LII.

TITLE: To the chief musician, Maschil. A Psalm of David, when Doeg the Edomite came and told Saul, and said unto him, David is come to the house of Abimelech. [Rather: On the Supreme. An Instructive of David; when Doeg the Edomite went and told Saul, and said unto him, David is gone to the house of Abimelech.]

ARGUMENT.

ARG. THOMAS. That CHRIST will exterminate and excommunicate every man that thirsteth after impiety from the riches of His goodness. The voice of CHRIST concerning Judas. The voice of the Prophet through the HOLY GHOST, against the devil, and Judas the traitor, and the insanity of all the companions that cannot be called back from his fellowship. The voice of CHRIST to Judas the traitor.

VEN. BEDE. Let CHRIST, as ever, be represented by David; let Saul be the persecuting Jews; let Doeg the Edomite, which by interpretation is the motion of blood, be Judas the traitor; let Abimelech the Priest be the elect disciples, in the midst of whom he hath both beheld and betrayed the LORD. Some say that Doeg is Antichrist, of whom Judas was a member; because, as the same Doeg slew eighty[1] priests, so will Antichrist destroy all those who hold the faith of CHRIST. In the first part the Prophet inveighs against Judas, or against Antichrist; warning them not to be puffed up because of their sins, seeing that so heavy a retribution awaits them: "Why boastest thou thyself," &c. In the second part he prophesies his speedy destruction, "Wherefore GOD shall destroy," &c. In the third he saith that the saints who now marvel at the rage of the ministers of Satan, shall then wonder at their utter destruction. "The righteous shall see it," &c. In the fourth, the Prophet looketh for himself, in common with the saints, for the fruition of the Beatific Vision: "As for me, I am like a green olive tree," &c.

EUSEBIUS OF CÆSARÆA. A reproval of evil habits and the end to which they lead.

S. ATHANASIUS. A Psalm accusatory of the wicked and evil doers. When it is sung, it may be taken against the words of Rabshakeh, otherwise the voice of CHRIST against Judas Iscariot.

VARIOUS USES.

Gregorian. Tuesday. Matins.
Monastic. Tuesday. Matins. I. Nocturn.
Parisian. Friday. Matins.

ANTIPHONS.

Gregorian. The LORD, even the most mighty GOD hath spoken.
Monastic. The same.
Parisian. My heart is disquieted within me : and the fear of death is fallen upon me.
Mozarabic. When the LORD shall bring again the captivity of Sion, then shall Jacob rejoice and Israel shall be right glad.

1 Why boastest thou thyself, thou tyrant : that thou canst do mischief;

[1] I know not on what translation Venerable Bede founded this interpretation. In the Hebrew, as we have it now, it is, as in the English version, four-score and five persons: in the Septuagint, followed therein by the Slavonic and other translations dependent on the LXX., it is 305 persons.

2 Whereas the goodness of GOD : endureth yet
daily ?[1]

Here, right or wrong, our English version has, as in not a
few other places, a beauty of its own. The *tyrant* on one side,
the goodness of GOD on the other; the *boast* of the tyrant
in doing mischief, the power of GOD exhibited in being kind
to the unthankful and evil. He can *do mischief* indeed. He
is a *tyrant* indeed. From that first mischief, that primeval root
of all mischief, down to the saying of Caiaphas, by which this
tyrant hoped to have won his complete victory; mischief in
the sinner who followed his suggestions; mischief in the
saints who yielded to his temptations; mischief against the
innocent ones who suffered by his instigation. *Why boastest
thou thyself?* For this reason: because thou canst kill the
body; canst kill it by miserable torments; by such tortures
as make the blood run cold to read of, and the mind almost
refuse to believe. *Why boastest thou thyself, thou tyrant?*
Because thou hast stirred up heresy after heresy, to vex and
to harass the Church; scarcely ever giving her one year of
peace, so devising that when there are not " fightings without," there should be " fear within." *Why boastest thou
thyself, thou tyrant?* Because thou hast so prevailed even
amongst the greatest saints; as with David in the matter of
Bathsheba; as with Hezekiah in the matter of the ambassadors from Babylon; as with Martin when he gave in to
the threat of an insolent and usurping king. But notice how
it is written. Not simply, *Why boastest thou thyself?* but,
Why boastest thou thyself that thou canst do mischief? Therefore take courage, O servant of the LORD, whosoever thou
art. He has prevailed against thee, thou wouldest say, a
thousand times. I in no wise doubt it. He has a thousand
times caused thee to cry out, " The good that I would I do
not, but the evil which I would not, that I do;" a thousand
times to say, " O wretched man that I am, who shall deliver
me from the body of this death?" But what *mischief* so long
as that promise remains, " Blessed is the man that endureth
temptation, for when he is tried he shall receive the crown of
life ?" while that command stands fast, " Count it all joy
when ye fall into divers [and horrible] temptations." And as
S. Bonaventura says, though not on this verse, The malice

Ay.

D. C.

S. Thomas
Aquin.

S. Bonav.

---

[1] Here we have an utter diver-
gence of our own version from
the Vulgate and the LXX. The
Vulgate has, *Why dost thou glory
in malice : thou who art powerful
in iniquity? All the day long
hath thy tongue devised unrighteousness: like a sharp razor thou
hast worked deceit.* Where, as
is evident, all reference to the
goodness of GOD is omitted. The
LXX. and the Vulgate omit אֵל
altogether, probably as not knowing what to make of it : others
alter the order in which it stands,
changing חֶן to חֵם, and taking
the אֵל as a preposition.

of Satan is indeed multipresent, but is not omnipresent; may be multipotent, but is not cunctipotent; he may be the strong man (and yet, oh, how weak to the weakest Christian that stands to his arms!), but yet This is the stronger than he, Who once beheld him like lightning fall from heaven, Who now has bound him, like a chained beast, fast; Who will finally, utterly, once and for ever, bruise him under our feet: yes, and that shortly. Rom. xvi. 20.

3 Thy tongue imagineth wickedness : and with lies thou cuttest like a sharp razor.

4 Thou hast loved unrighteousness more than goodness : and to talk of lies more than righteousness.

All those who have much to do with the commentaries of the saints, must notice what we have had occasion to notice more than once in this poor commentary, how they pass over with scarcely a word, denunciations of wrath against the wicked, on which, had they been promises to the righteous, they would have dwelt at such enormous length.[1] But, as mediæval writers say, This is the true and beautiful meaning: Hugo Cardinal. *With lies thou cuttest like a sharp razor.* If there is any sin to be discovered, discovered it will be, just as a razor removing superfluous hair, shows the very flesh itself. But, as a Haymo. razor, rightly held, does not really wound, so GOD keeps back the malice of the ungodly from really injuring, however much —witness the case of Shimei, as regarded David—it may lay the secrets of the heart bare. And, as they remind us, that advice, "Tarry at Jericho until your beards be grown, and then return," (however kindly in the historical sense given,) is exactly, in a mystical sense, the counsel which Satan would give. A man has had some conviction of sin, and would fain at once get rid of it. But, the great Tempter so prevailing, the poor sinner tarries in Jericho, the accursed city, mixes in and with the world, till those feelings are lost, till in the man's own eyes the sin is covered over, and then he returns; returns to his original sin, returns, and the evil spirit brings back those seven spirits more wicked than himself, and—we all know the terrible ending.

5 Thou hast loved to speak all words that may do hurt : O thou false tongue.

Omnia verba præcipitationis, as the Vulgate has it, and

---

[1] For want, I suppose of some higher topic, Lorinus, who always will say something, here enters into a dissertation as to the first Christian author in whom we find mention of a razor. It is in S. Sidonius Apollinaris, Lib. i. Epist. 2. But, as he also observes, *Non refert.*

the LXX. even more forcibly,[1] κατακοντισμοῦ, of "plunging in the sea." The LXX. gives, and correctly, the latter clause in the accusative, *false tongue*, i.e. language of guile. Are we to take it of the Jews, and then, "we have no king but Cæsar," as some of the earlier fathers? Or shall we rather see in it that primæval deceit, "Ye shall not surely die?" Then surely WERE *all words that* might *do hurt* wrapped up in that one NOT. That was a κατακοντισμός indeed, when man "came into deep waters, so that the floods ran over him." And yet again they explain it mystically: how, although Satan did not mean it so, nor for one moment think of the possibility that it should be so, but, in that fierce clamour of the Jews, in that unjust sentence of Pilate, we have the true κατακοντισμός of the Gospel sweep-net, or *seyne*, which shall, when drawn to shore, be the salvation of the good fish, the casting away for ever of the bad.

S. Hilar.

L.
Lindanus,
de Opt. Gen.
Interpr. iii.
11.

S. Matt. xiii.

6 Therefore shall GOD destroy thee for ever : he shall take thee, and pluck thee out of thy dwelling, and root thee out of the land of the living.

For ever : or, as it rather is, *at last :* the lying tongue is but for a moment. And therefore, as S. Gregory nobly says, that lying tongue was but for a moment which said, "Thou shalt not surely die." He meant it to deceive : deceive it did : he meant man to fall, and man did fall : but, in the long future, man had a better life prepared for him than that of the earthly paradise : man so surely lived, if he willed to live, that "whosoever overcometh shall not be hurt of the second death." This, of a verity, shows THE false tongue, the tongue of him who is a liar and the father of it, destroyed for ever : destroyed in its intended meaning, but ratified, as was that saying of Caiaphas, in that meaning which was not intended. In the same way that our LORD's bitter mockery, His coronation, His investiture with a robe, first of white, then of purple ; His adoration ; His reed-sceptre, were, in one point of view, those words which the false tongue, because they should do hurt, therefore *loved :* but in the truer and everlasting meaning, they were prophecies, long ago prophesied *of :* prophecies, which, for a short time might have given the hosts of Satan joy, but which, in the end, point to one of the dearest possessions of the legions of the LORD of Hosts. *Shall pluck thee out of thy dwelling.* They inquire what dwelling that is, out of which this deceitful tongue is to be plucked. *Tabernacle,* as it is in the Vulgate ; and that surely is the precise expression for the shortness of life, whether in everyday life a lie, or in the life of the Church, a heresy. Some will have it of the ejection of those lying Jews from the once holy city after the terrible siege : some, of the Jews still, but in a less ter-

In Gen. iii.

Rupert.

S. Paulinus
Aq.

Cassiodor.
S. Bruno.
Herbip.

---

[1] The Slavonic still more forcibly, ВСА ГЛАГОЛЫ ПОТОПНЫА.

rible sense, of their dispersion from their own land: others
in a very matter-of-fact interpretation of the excommunica-
tion of the wretch, to whom primarily this Psalm applies
after his murder of the fourscore and six that ware ephods,
Doeg the Edomite. *Out of the land of the living.* And here
almost for the first time, we have that dearest of all titles
given to our future home. It is marvellous how even thóse
who protest to study Holy Scripture, ay, and those who have
studied it, and that earnestly too, miss one of the most glorious passages in connection with this verse, that are to be
read in the Pentateuch. GOD pronounced Adam's curse,
beginning with the malediction, for man's sake, of the earth
—" In sorrow shalt thou eat of it,"—and culminating in " till
thou return to the ground, for out of it wast thou taken: for
dust thou art, and unto dust shalt thou return." And what
is Adam's reply? A reply, truly, as S. Thomas says, evincing
the greatest faith which man ever showed except—if, indeed
except,—the confession of the penitent thief. " And Adam
called his wife's name Eve, because she was the mother of all
living." All living? And GOD had just pronounced the
sentence, " Dust thou art, and unto dust thou shalt return."
It is marvellous, as a theologian of the seventeenth century
says, how many and many a Christian soul, whose whole hope
is nailed to the Resurrection, yet nevertheless passes over
that marvellous declaration of Adam as if it were something
put in, because it must be said somewhere, and by-the-by.
Whereas, here, just at the very moment when that sentence
had been pronounced on man,—ashes to ashes, dust to dust,
—Eve is called, and that more than called; is entitled, as it
were, by law; the mother of all; not mortals, but, of all living. This is the antitype in the first Adam, of the victory
through which death by death was overthrown in the second
Adam.

7 The righteous also shall see this, and fear : and
shall laugh him to scorn ;

8 Lo, this is the man that took not GOD for his
strength : but trusted unto the multitude of his
riches, and strengthened himself in his wickedness.

Here, as we might expect, our mediæval commentators are
full of the blessings of poverty, and the temptation of riches.
One or two, and only one or two, have the courage to apply
that general dogma to the state of the Church in their own
days, so far as this world went, " rich and increased with
goods, and having need of nothing." And it must always be
remembered that the very first sign of decay in the Western
Church—taking the Western Church (which is always to be
remembered) as a very different thing from the Roman Court,
—was the way in which this very question of poverty and

Marginal notes:
S. Greg. II.,
which also
S. Hilary
seems to say.
S. Greg.
Nyssen.

L.

Master of
the Sen-
tences. II.
Distinct. 39.

Avrillon.

riches, settled as it was, militated against the strict rules of
the then strictest and holiest of orders. There is nothing
which so illustrates that saying of the Apostle's, "How un-
searchable are His judgments, and His ways past finding out,"
than the conflict between those who held to the first fervour
of their rules, the genuine, primitive Franciscans, and who
yet so holding, fell into all kind of mystical heresies; and on
the other, those who from Rome obtained licence to receive
any amount of riches, and who therefore became what we unhappily know that the followers of S. Francis did become, a
by-word and reproach to mediæval Europe. If any one
thinks that this remark has nothing to do with the Psalm, let
him rather take it in this point of view: as to each phase
of our own individual lives, temptation, of whatever kind,
from the world, the flesh, or the devil; whether ending in
victory or defeat, or drawn out into a long conflict. In these
things, every Christian man can find in the Psalms that which
in the particular moment suits his particular need: in the
same way that they fit into, they dovetail in with, the history
of the Church.

9 As for me, I am like a green olive-tree in the
house of GOD : my trust is in the tender mercy of
GOD for ever and ever.

10 I will always give thanks unto thee for that
thou hast done : and I will hope in thy Name, for
thy saints like it well.

Ay.
L.

They have, those mediæval writers, much to say on the
colour of *green*, the daily colour of the Western Church;
how it is the most refreshing to the eyes, how it gives the
dearest hope of the coming spring, how, besides the gems
which are of that hue, and which always have been believed
to have possessed especial virtue, the various shades and dis-
tinctions of the colour, in which they say there are more
diversities than in any other colour, may be seen the infinite
variety of the graces of the HOLY GHOST. *I will hope in
Thy Name.* That Name of which we have so often spoken :
that Name which is, as it were, the Antiphon to so many
Psalms : that Name, the dear love to which is so feebly expressed either in our own version, or in the LXX., or in the
Vulgate, the Hebrew giving, *I will hope in Thy Name, for it
is the chief good of Thy saints.*

And therefore :

Glory be to the FATHER, Whose goodness endureth yet
daily; and to the SON, the Righteous, Who shall see His
reward; and to the HOLY GHOST, in Whose trust is our
tender mercy for ever and ever;

As it was in the beginning, is now, and ever shall be :
world without end. Amen.

COLLECTS.

Only-Begotten WORD of the Unbegotten FATHER, Thou Mozarabic. Who art long-suffering towards the people that rise up against Thee, and of Thine infinite love dost endure the tyrant who boasteth that he can do mischief; grant of Thine infinite goodness that we may, at however great a distance, follow Thine example of pardon; and may also, however far below Thee, have our portion among those that have been forgiven. Through. (11.)

O GOD, Almighty SAVIOUR, vouchsafe, we beseech Thee, Gregorian. that we who do confess that the SON of GOD is Co-equal and Consubstantial with Thee, the FATHER, may merit like a fruitful olive to be planted in the heavenly Jerusalem, for His merit's sake. Who. (1.)

PSALM LIII.

TITLE: To the Chief Musician upon Mahalath, Maschil. A Psalm of David.

LXX.: To the end over Macleth. Of understanding to David.

Rather: on the Supreme; for the flutes, an instructive of David.

ARGUMENT.

ARG. THOMAS. That which CHRIST bestoweth on Israel, by His coming. The prophet blameth the Jews and the infidels. This Psalm is to be read with the Gospel of S. Matthew.[1] The voice of the HOLY GHOST blaming Judas and the unbelieving Jews, and all those who deny[2] the works of GOD. The Advent and monition of the SAVIOUR.

VEN. BEDE. In the first clause of the Psalm, the Church speaks, blaming those who, whether in word or deed, fear not to be corrupted: *the foolish body.* In the next he speaketh of the evils which they will receive, the same evils which they have inflicted on Christians, "Are they not all," &c. In the third, he warneth the faithful to bear with good courage the hardships of this world, till the judgment-seat of Majesty shall be set, when it shall be given to

---

[1] Are we to think that this refers to S. Matthew xxiii.? In the original there follows (and it shows how imperfectly these headings have come down to us): the Prophet finds fault with—

[2] Here we have some clue to a date as to these most valuable headings. The original is, *Atque* *omnes operibus Deum negantes increpantis.* The use of the ablative after the verb, is a kind of foretaste of that same ablative taking the place of the nominative or accusative. This alteration is a mark of the fourth, or at latest of the fifth, century.

all those that have done righteously, to receive good things. *Who shall give.*

S. ATHANASIUS. A Psalm that accuseth the impious and iniquitous.

ARABIC PSALTER. A prophecy of David concerning Babel and Sennacherib, ver. 15 (that is, the last clause of our eighth verse).

VARIOUS USES.

Gregorian. Wednesday. Matins.
Parisian. Monday. Nones.
Monastic. Tuesday. II. Nocturn.

ANTIPHONS.

Gregorian. The LORD turned again the captivity of His people.
Parisian. The same.
Monastic. The same.

1 The foolish body hath said in his heart : There is no GOD.

2 Corrupt are they, and become abominable in their wickedness : there is none that doeth good.

3 GOD looked down from heaven upon the children of men : to see if there were any that would understand, and seek after GOD.

4 But they are all gone out of the way, they are altogether become abominable : there is also none that doeth good, no not one.

We have already spoken of these verses in Psalm xiv. 1—4.

5 Are not they without understanding that work wickedness : eating up my people as if they would eat bread? they have not called upon GOD.

6 They were afraid where no fear was : for GOD hath broken the bones of him that besieged thee; thou hast put them to confusion, because GOD hath despised them.

7 Oh, that the salvation were given unto Israel out of Sion : oh, that the LORD would deliver his people out of captivity !

8 Then should Jacob rejoice : and Israel should be right glad.

See Psalm xiv. 8—11.
And therefore :
Glory be to the FATHER, Who looked down from heaven

upon the children of men; and to the Son, Who is in the generation of the righteous; and to the Holy Ghost, by Whom the salvation is given unto Israel out of Sion;

As it was in the beginning, is now, and ever shall be: world without end. Amen.

COLLECTS.

See Vol. I., p. 167.

<hr>

PSALM LIV.

Title: To the chief musician on Neginoth, Maschil. A Psalm of David when the Ziphims came and said to Saul, "Doth not David hide himself with us?" Otherwise: to the Supreme: for the stringed instruments: an instructive of David, when the Ziphites went and said, "Doth not David hide himself with us?" The literal sense is given in the words: "Then came up the Ziphites 1 Sam. xxiii. to Saul to Gibeah, saying, Doth not David hide himself with us 19, 23. in strongholds in the wood, in the hill of Hachilah, which is on the south of Jeshimon? See therefore, and take knowledge of all the lurking places where he hideth himself, and come ye again to me with the certainty, and I will go with you: and it shall come to pass, if he be in the land, that I will search him out throughout all the thousands of Judah." S. Augustine gives the mystical sense thus: Saul, the persecutor of David, as bearing the figure of a temporal kingdom, belonging not to life but to death, is a type of Satan. David, hiding from his persecutors in a certain village, Ziph, is a type of Christ, or of the Body of Christ. What then of the Ziphites? These Ziphites, when they had learned that David had hidden himself among them, betrayed him to the king his persecutor, saying, "Doth not David hide himself with us?" The word Ziphites is by interpretation, *men flourishing*. Certain enemies, then, to holy David, were flourishing while he was hiding. We may find them in mankind, if we are willing to understand this Psalm. First find David hiding, and we shall find his enemies flourishing. "For ye are dead," saith the Apostle to the members of Christ, Col. iii. 3. "and your life is hid with Christ in God." These men that are hiding, when shall they be flourishing? "When Christ Who is Col. iii. 4. your life shall appear, then shall ye also appear with Him in glory." Or we may take it of our Lord, Who chose rather to hide among the Jews, and when questioned by Pontius Pilate answered, "My S. John kingdom is not of this world." Therefore here He was hidden; xviii. 36. and all good men are hidden here; because their good is concealed, within, in the heart, where are faith, charity, hope, where also is their treasure.

1 Save me, O God, for thy Name's sake : and avenge me in thy strength.

That *Name*, and the salvation by that Name, often and often we have heard of before; often and often shall we in these self-same Psalms; and, as S. Peter Chrysologus says, GOD forbid there ever should be a time when, if we have not that Name in our mouths, at all events when we have it not in our heart of hearts! It may well go on, *Avenge me in Thy strength*. Because as those loving mediæval writers tell us, Of all strength love is the greatest: "Many waters cannot quench love, neither can the floods drown it: if a man would give all the substance of his house for love, it would utterly be contemned." *In Thy strength*. And what is that strength save the weakness of the Cross! where defeat is victory, where shame is glory, where reprobation is coronation, where, finally, death is life.

Ay.

Hugo Vict.

2 Hear my prayer, O GOD : and hearken unto the words of my mouth.

3 For strangers are risen up against me : and tyrants, which have not GOD before their eyes, seek after my soul.

D. C.

It is well said, *Hear my prayer*. *Hear*, the weaker word: but *hearken*: that is, so hear as to listen to, so listen to as to grant, *the words of my mouth* : my Mouth, indeed, my Mediator, my Daysman, my Advocate, hearken unto the words of The WORD ; to the words of Him the true Aaron, of whom Thou hast said, "Is not Aaron thy Brother? I know that He can speak well." *For strangers*. Here that word, as we know from the title of the Psalm, means those of David's own people. So join the two expressions together in their higher sense; strangers, my own rebellious will and passions, *have risen up against me* : a word which one never could use except of a civil war or domestic rebellion. *And tyrants* : tyrants as being all the servants of, as all deriving their strength from, that one tyrant ; *the* tyrant in opposition to THE King ; *the* rebellious chief of Babylon in contradistinction to the peaceful Monarch in Jerusalem.

Exod. iv. 14.

B.

S. Bonaventura.

4 Behold, GOD is my helper : the LORD is with them that uphold my soul.

In which sense shall we take it? Of the synagogue, looking for, and yearning after, in the midst, and in spite of, all her troubles, the Advent? Or of our LORD Himself, staying Himself on the love of the FATHER, as with that thought of the twelve legions of Angels ; as with that declaration, "I know that Thou hearest Me always?" Or lastly, shall we take it of the Church, knowing that, as the FATHER was the Helper of the LORD, so That FATHER and That LORD will be her aiders, and against whatever enemies will *uphold her soul?*

S. Gregor. Moral. 22. 18.
S. Matt. xxvi. 53.
S. John xi. 42.
Valencio in loc.

5 He shall reward evil unto mine enemies : destroy thou them in thy truth.

S. Augustine probably using a bad copy of the Latin translation, reads *in virtute* instead of *in veritate;* and therefore gives an interpretation which, however true in itself, is not the meaning of the Psalm.[1] *Destroy Thou them in Thy Truth.* That dear truth on which my present Christian life S. Hilar. hangs ; " Resist the devil, and he shall flee from you ;" that future dear truth, "And the GOD of all grace shall bruise Satan under your feet shortly."

6 An offering of a free heart will I give thee, and praise thy Name, O LORD : because it is so comfortable.

7 For he hath delivered me out of all my trouble : and mine eye hath seen his desire upon mine enemies.

And so again here, those ponderous commentators of the sixteenth century, Lutherans and Calvinists, who yet from the old stream of tradition derive so much beauty, find an argument against vows of any kind ; because, as it seems, day by day, and hour by hour, the offering is to be *free,* which L. it cannot be if it is compelled. But with a deeper truth, Doctors and Councils of the Middle Ages use the same verse Greg. Pap. against those who devoted children to the religious life before vii. 5. they had the power of understanding what such a life meant. And S. Jerome, the strongest advocate of that life among all the primitive Fathers, who sometimes, with respect to marriage almost trembles on the verge of heresy, dwells in the same sense on this Psalm.

It is a verse that seems fated to be fought over ; for a totally different controversy finds it a battle field ; in the widest sense, Jansenism and Pelagianism ; in the narrower, Augustinianism and semi-Pelagianism. It is a verse very De Vitâ Contemplativâ. dear to S. Prosper. And one cannot but remark, that of all templativâ. the translations which could express the meaning of the last ii. Opera, clause of the sixth verse, our own only Prayer Book version 1609. p. 289. is so much the most telling. Who would set the *For it is good* of the Authorised translation, the *quoniam bonum est* of the Vulgate, the ὅτι ἀγαθόν of the LXX., even the Slavonic ІАКѠ БЛГѠ, compared to that word which is not only so perfectly English, but which shows how the English language gives the dearest and deepest senses of inspired writings— *comfortable ?* And then, for the conclusion, let us hear our

[1] It is very curious to see how Lorinus takes occasion from this verse to attack a certain Scotchman Hume, of whose name, but from this exposition I am utterly ignorant, as drawing from the latter clause of the verse an argument for the worst, the *supra lapsarian,* scheme of Calvinism.

D. C.

dear LORD speak in His own Person. Thou hast delivered Me. Thou hast delivered Me indeed from the false witnesses that agreed not together; Thou hast delivered Me from Annas, from Caiaphas, from Herod, from Pontius Pilate; Thou hast delivered Me from the scourging and coronation, and the shame, and the Crucifixion; *and Mine eye hath seen his desire upon Mine enemies.* And what was that desire?

S. Bruno.

What save that petition, "FATHER, forgive them, for they know not what they do." And yet the word itself is even stronger in the original: *Thou hast banqueted mine eyes.* And only remember how many of those that then stood round the Cross and mocked, will hereafter be found written among the number of them that have been invited to sit down at the eternal marriage feast.

And therefore:

Glory be to the FATHER, Who is our Helper; and to the SON, for Whose Name's sake we are saved; and to the HOLY GHOST, in Whose strength we are avenged;

As it was in the beginning, is now, and ever shall be: world without end. Amen.

COLLECTS.

Mozarabic.

Save us, O LORD, for Thy Name's sake, and avenge us in Thy strength; bring us out of tribulation, and fill us with gladness, to the end that while Thy salvation is fully bestowed on us, Thy glory may joyfully be chanted by us. Through Thy mercy. (11.)

S. Jerome.

We beseech Thee, O LORD JESUS CHRIST, that we by Thy help being saved from our enemies, may both in will and deed follow Thee, our Head Which art in heaven. Who livest.

PSALM LV.

TITLE: To the chief musician on Neginoth, Maschil. A Psalm of David. Or, To the Supreme. For the stringed instruments. *Vulgate.* To the end. In the songs. An understanding of David.

ARGUMENT.

VEN. BEDE. *For the end,* CHRIST: *in the songs,* in spiritual joys: an instructive of David: to instruct us that *He* was to be incarnate through Whom the Prophet expected to be delivered from trouble. Through the whole Psalm they use the words of the LORD. In the first part He asketh that, in His tribulation His prayer may not be overlooked, His petition may be speedily despatched. In the next place, that the iniquities of the Jews may be put an end to, because in their city was the contradiction of truth. Thirdly, He predicted the evils which He foreseeth to impend over the Jews. After this a pious consolation is introduced.

EUSEBIUS. A Revelation of those things which were cruelly done against CHRIST.

S. JEROME. This Psalm contains the words of the Mediator, Who, being GOD, took on Himself for our freedom the form of a servant.

VARIOUS USES.

Gregorian. Wednesday. Nocturns.
Parisian. Friday. I. Nocturn.

ANTIPHONS.

Gregorian. The LORD turned * the captivity of His people.
Parisian. I mourn in my prayer * and am vexed : the enemy crieth so.
Mozarabic. Hide not Thyself from my petition, * take heed unto me, and hear me, O LORD.

1 Hear my prayer, O GOD : and hide not thyself from my petition.

2 Take heed unto me, and hear me :

And first they notice how many have uttered that same prayer, and have been heard, not from the mercy, but from the anger of GOD. So it was with the people that desired the quails; so with those who asked for a king: so even with Satan himself. Again, of some who asked and were not heard, and yet of whom it cannot truly be said that GOD hid Himself from—or, as the Vulgate translates it, despised—their petition. So with Moses, and with S. Paul; while, again, some are both despised and not heard, as the five foolish virgins. S. Basil speaks of the reasons why men who ask are not heard. Sometimes the unworthiness of the asker, as David, when he besought that he might build the temple; sometimes that of those for whom the petition is made, as when Jeremiah was forbidden to pray for the Jews; and sometimes because of the listless way in which the petition was made, as when the Apostles failed to cast out the devil from the lunatic child. Most mediæval writers take the difference between the prayer and the petition, or, as it is in the Latin, deprecation, to be, that the one asks for that which is good, but the other prays against that which is evil. But, as we shall have occasion to see, and as S. Euthymius here says, these words are as often as not used in exactly the opposite sense.

Ruffinus. Ex. xvi. 23. 1 Sam. viii. 22. Job l. 12; ii. 6. Hugo Vict. Deut. iii. 25. 2 Cor. xii. 8. Reg. 262. 2 Sam. vii. 5. Jer. vii. 16, and xiv. 11. S. Matt. xvii. 21. Hugo Vict. S. Bruno.

How I mourn in my prayer, and am vexed.

3 The enemy crieth so, and the ungodly cometh

II. K

on so fast : for they are minded to do me some mischief; so maliciously are they set against me.

But henceforth we must drop all allusion to the petition of sinners, yes, and even of saints, and see only the offering made by the LORD, of strong crying and tears, unto Him That was able to save Him from death, when He was heard in that He feared. And the Western Church shows that she receives this Psalm in this sense by reading the commentary of S. Augustine on it, for the three middle Lessons of Matins on Maundy Thursday. *The enemy crieth so,* as when they all cried, "Not this Man, but Barabbas :" as when "they that passed by reviled Him, wagging their heads, and saying, Thou That destroyest the Temple, and buildest it in three days, save Thyself."

Heb. v. 7.
Cassiodor.
S. Remig.
S. Hilar.
S. Bruno.
D. C.
Ludolph.

4 My heart is disquieted within me : and the fear of death is fallen upon me.

5 Fearfulness and trembling are come upon me : and an horrible dread hath overwhelmed me.

And as they say, there can be but One, one time, one scene to which these words can truly apply. S. Hilary, while he takes them in the sense of that Agony which was suffered once, but can never be suffered again, nevertheless is careful to show how all this pain, misery, and shame was the portion of the WORD made flesh, in that He was Man, could not have been, so far as He was consubstantial with the FATHER, and with the HOLY GHOST. That passage, and this text (not that I am fond of dwelling on polemical discussions from dear verses in the Psalms,) have nevertheless given rise to long arguments as to how, in what sense, and how far, the *fearfulness and trembling* did come on our Blessed LORD.[1] It is believed that notwithstanding, in so far as He was GOD, He knew that He must suffer many things of the Jews and the third day rise again; still, in His Human Nature, He was *overwhelmed* with *an horrible dread,* insomuch that His sweat was, as it were, great drops of blood falling down to the ground. For in that fearful hour came upon His righteous Soul all the sinful thoughts and words and deeds that had been since man gave heed to the Tempter, and that should be till His Second Coming, when sin should be at an end; all the impenitence of desperate sinners, to whom His Passion would only be an increase of condemnation; all the

L.

S. Hilar.
Lib. x. de
SS. Trini-
tate.

[1] All these questions are discussed by the Master of the Sentences, Lib. iii. Distinct. 15, on the *Infirmities of Man, which* | *Christ in His Human Nature assumed;* and 16, *whether there was in Christ a necessity to suffer and to die.*

coldness and want of faith of those, who would not, so far as in them lay, in their own persons, fill up that which remained behind of the sufferings of CHRIST.

6 And I said, O that I had wings like a dove : for then would I flee away, and be at rest.

7 Lo, then would I get me away far off : and remain in the wilderness.

8 I would make haste to escape : because of the stormy wind and tempest.

And in the first place we think of that Dove which once endeavoured to flee away from the ark, the only place of rest. No doubt, as so many mediæval writers explain it, thinking that rest might be found on the whole wide face of the earth which it was impossible to obtain in the narrow prison of the ark. And see the result. The raven did find rest ; rest, probably, on some of the carcases floating on the surface of the water. But, as they go on to remark, the dove wished for some rest, as David here wishes : the dove found none in leaving her home, nor yet could David have found, nor yet will any true servant of GOD find, quiet and peace, by forsaking that home of duty which GOD has given him. *Hugo de S. Vict. Rupert. S. Pet. Chrysologus, Serm. 84.*

But there is a more beautiful sense which is dearer to the mystical writers. It is to be taken in connection with that verse in Hosea: " They shall seek to flee[1] as a bird out of Egypt, and as a dove out of the land of Assyria : and I will place them in their houses, saith the LORD." And see in how lovely a manner this prophecy applies to our dear LORD : how He indeed desired to escape to His FATHER and to His Home from the hands of His twofold enemy,—the Jews on this side, the Romans on that, both leagued together against Him. And then observe how it proceeds : " I will place them in their houses, saith the LORD." Them : Him in the first place, Who died that He might open the passage; them, in the next, Who, through His sufferings shall have a portion in the many mansions which He died to secure for them.[2] S. Hilary speaks very touchingly here on the yearningness of this petition—for petition it is—for deliverance. It is, he truly observes, a kind of prayer from the human to the Divine nature of our LORD; which, hypostatically united to- *S. Hilar. S. Hieronym. B. D. C. Haimo. Hosea xi. 11. Serm. xiv. Ps. cxix. v. 6.*

[1] It is in our version *tremble.* But that given above, which is also that of the Vulgate and the LXX., is the truer interpretation.

[2] It is worth while to quote the mystical verses in which Hugh of Saint Victor compre- hends the characteristics of the dove :

Grex, visus, pulli, fel, oscula, pugna, capilli, Grana, latex, nidus, turris, gemitus, color, et pes, Nuncia, simplicitas, fimus, ova, Venus, fuga, cervix.

gether, yet nevertheless could and did, the one petition, as it were, the other: the latter strengthens and comforts and supports the former.

9 Destroy their tongues, O LORD, and divide them : for I have spied unrighteousness and strife in the city.

In the first place: their tongues were truly destroyed and they themselves divided, when the testimony of the two false witnesses agreed not so together. Then, secondly, when the contradictory account of the soldiers that kept watch at the

Ay. sepulchre, which, in itself was sufficient to condemn itself, received the promise of confirmation—a confirmation, the original expression for which shows by what means it was to be brought to pass—from the governor. And there is a wonderful beauty, except that the use of the lower word, (a very rare fault in our translation,) rather obscures it, in that *I have seen unrighteousness in the city.* For, as our LORD when He ascended the Cross had His Face turned to-ward the Temple, so He perceived, not only the unrighteous-

S. Hilar. ness of those who thirsted after His Soul, but also the *strife* between those Psalms which they constantly recited, and those words which they were then taking in their own

Moral. in Job xxxiv. 3. mouths. S. Gregory applies the text to S. Paul's conduct with respect to the Pharisees and Sadducees, during his ex-amination by the Sanhedrim : and not unreasonably observes that, in this respect, the master and teacher of the false wit-nesses against our LORD and the calumniators of His saints, excelled his agents. For of leviathan it is written : " The

Job xli. 23. scales of his flesh are joined together; they are firm in them-selves; they cannot be moved." Whereas the defensive armour of his adherents is anything but firm in its jointure, piece into piece, and can so easily be pierced by that sword of the SPIRIT.

10 Day and night they go about within the walls thereof : mischief also and sorrow are in the midst of it.

11 Wickedness is therein : deceit and guile go not out of their streets.

Sà. *Day and night.* For, as they say well; just as in the day of prosperity, and the night of adversity, the Captain of our salvation is ready to help; and not only ready to help, but His work is to take advantage of each separate characteristic either of the day or the night :

As darkness shows us worlds of light
We never saw by day;

so also is the ancient enemy ready to avail himself of every
advantage which the especial difficulty of day or night may
put into his power against us. But there is a very beautiful
antithesis which the love of mediæval writers has attached
to this verse. They see in it the diabolical caricature of one
of the greatest miracles in the Old Testament, the march
round Jericho before its walls fell down. For always be this
remembered, that it seems to be one of Satan's chief delights
to parody the works of GOD: as the ritual, the chancels,
the chants, the monasteries, the vows of chastity, the cross
fylfott of Buddhism are but a ghastly parody of the Catholic
Church ; and, which is so remarkable, a parody, it is to be
believed, older than its original. In like manner, that which
those saints who most deeply studied the Apocalypse tell us, of
the probable Incarnation, the Resurrection from the dead, of
the Antichrist. And so here they take the procession round *S. Bruno.*
Jericho, of our LORD, as the true Ark, attacking the city of *S. August.*
this world by the seven virtues of the HOLY GHOST, by His
seven words on the Cross; by the seven days, so to speak, in
which He prepared for the glorious octave of the Resurrection. And with hatred only less than love, in the same
degree that finite cannot compass the infinite power, does
Satan in the seven deadly sins, *day and night go about the
walls* of our souls. *Deceit and guile.* They interpret it of the
guile by which our LORD was sold for thirty pieces of silver,
betrayed by a false kiss, condemned on the testimony of lying
witnesses. And therefore *go not out of their streets,* because *S. Ambros.*
that same falsehood continued even after our dear LORD's *in Tobit.*
Passion, continued when the chief priests gave large money *cap. 4.*
to the soldiers, finally continued until those streets of Jerusalem, up one of which the Man of Sorrows passed to His
Passion, became, as its prophesiers had foretold, a ploughed
land, a place for flocks to lie down in.

12 For it is not an open enemy, that hath done
me this dishonour : for then I could have borne it.

13 Neither was it mine adversary, that did magnify himself against me : for then peradventure I
would have hid myself from him.

14 But it was even thou, my companion : my
guide, and mine own familiar friend.

And, referring, as it was impossible not to do, this whole
passage to Judas Iscariot, they dwell on the horror which *S. Ambros.*
from the very beginning his treachery has impressed, not *Euseb. De-*
only on the doctrine, but on the ritual of the Church. How *monstr.*
not only the greatest doctors of primitive ages, have dwelt *Evangel.*
on the progress of his crime from his first call to the Apos- *cap. 2.*
tolate to his suicide : but how in various laws and canons *S. Prosper.*
de Promis.
iii. 18 (the

chapter is
well worth
reading).
Origen.
Tom. xxxii.
in S. Johan.
S. Isidor.
de Pass.
Dom. cap.
22.

that no Christian should be baptized by the name[1] of Judas, so that if any one had any special devotion to the other S. Jude, he must christen his child Thaddeus : how, though Judas was a hundred times more guilty than Pontius Pilate, yet the Church abhors the sin of the one in her creed, but will not pollute her mouth with the utterance of the other : and how in the popular ceremonies of Easter Eve, in both the Eastern and Western Churches, as in being hung from the yard-arm in ships at sea, and the like, Judas yearly receives his meed of ignominy. *My companion.* And in all the versions used by the Church, it is much stronger than that : *one of a like soul with me ; unanimous :* ἰσόψυχος. Per-

Snoyg.

haps *one of an equal rank with me,* comes nearer to the original. And notice, as they well say, how here also, to quote His own teaching with all reverence, " the first shall be last, and the last first." " Greater works than these shall ye do." And Judas among the rest. Of the same rank with the other Apostles in miracles ; with the other Apostles in the same rank, so far as the world could tell, with their Almighty LORD. It is singular to observe how chary the primitive Church was of applying these verses to Judas ; I suppose because they feared that the putting them into our dear LORD's mouth, with reference to the traitor, might give some advantage to the Arians. But, as

Euthym.
Niceph.
Hugo Card.
Ay.

centuries swept away that heresy, the truer, the more comforting, the deeper meaning, was worked out more and more. *For it is not an open enemy.* And here all the ascetic writers refer with one consent to religious houses. As needless, thank GOD, as it would be miserable, as it would be incredible to such as love to image those convents of the Middle Ages at their best, that is at their saintliest ; no need to dilate for one moment on the horrible miseries, the tremendous wickedness, the fearful violation of all human and Divine law, of which those holy writers speak. This was,

S. Vincent.
Ferrer.

and good reason why, a favourite text among the itinerant reformers of the fourteenth and fifteenth centuries : *even thou, My companion,*—My companion daily in the Seven Hours of My Passion,—*and Mine Own familiar friend. My guide.* It is not so in the Hebrew. But the dear love

Placidus.

of the Mediæval Church explained even this difficulty. He " was guide unto them that took JESUS." And even in another sense, as they fear not to say, he was the guide of our LORD Himself : that is, he, the infinite wisdom of Divine foresight so permitting it, resolved on all those tortuous ways

S. Bruno C.

by which the Immaculate Lamb was led to the judgment-seat, and was therein offered as the evening sacrifice of the whole world.

[1] Lorinus, curiously enough, compares the decree of the French Parliament, passed the very year before that in which he wrote, which forbad, in horror of the murder of Henry IV., that the name of Ravaillac should ever be given in baptism.

15 We took sweet counsel together : and walked in the house of GOD as friends.

Or as it is in the Vulgate, with a deeper meaning, *who together with me didst receive sweet food :* and although that cannot be borne out by the Hebrew, yet no wonder that thousands of mediæval priests saw in the expression a prophecy of him who was to dip his hand in the same dish with our LORD.[1] S. Ambrose, interpreting the Hebrew words in the same sense, nevertheless understands their mystical meaning differently. According to him, the *sweet food* was our dear LORD'S own discourses, those sermons and parables of which Judas was equally a hearer with the rest of the Apostles. *And walked in the house of God as friends.* So all the authorised translations give, and that rightly : S. Jerome alone, by some extraordinary misunderstanding, or wonderful false reading, translates it, *walked in the house of God in terror.* And the Carthusian draws this good lesson, which I will give in his own words : Hence it appears that those persecutions and injuries are the harder to bear which are inflicted on us by our acquaintances and friends, especially when we have made sure of their love, and have deserved nothing but good from them. As therefore, the Passion of CHRIST was the more bitter, in that He was sold by a disciple, and put to death by His elect and peculiar people. And therefore He saith by Micah, "O My people, what have I done unto thee, or wherein have I wearied thee?" And again, "What could have been done more to My vineyard, that I have not done unto it?"

Ay.

And so S. Bruno.

D. C.

Micah vi. 3.

Isa. v. 4.

16 Let death come hastily upon them, and let them go down quick into hell : for wickedness is in their dwellings, and among them.

We have already spoken of these, the so-called imprecatory clauses of the Psalms. And here Dathan and Abiram stand forth as the type of those sinners,—sacrilegious in like manner,—of whom David speaks. *And among them.* But it is more than this. In their very texture, inwoven into the whole fabric of their existence.

L.

17 As for me, I will call upon GOD : and the LORD shall save me.

Have I called : so it is in the LXX., and in the Vulgate, though not correctly. The Carmelite says well : He cried in the country, when He sowed the good seed among the multi-

Ay.

S. Luke viii. 8.

[1] And in the same way they take the house of GOD, of that "large upper room," which, in one sense, was undoubtedly the first Christian house of GOD, inasmuch as it contained the first Christian altar.

S. John vii.
28.
S. John xi.
43.
S. Matt.
xxvii. 46.
S. Luke
xxiii. 46.

tudes: He cried in the Temple, when He preached the law: He cried in the place of death, when He raised the dead: He cried on the Cross, when He tasted of death: He cried to the FATHER, when into His Hands He commended His own Spirit. And the same writer well puts it, that we are to call upon GOD for the support of our corporeal life, for our deliverance from temporal pain, for the consolation of our innermost heart, for our escape from eternal punishment, for the remission of sin, both original and actual.

18 In the evening, and morning, and at noon-day will I pray, and that instantly : and he shall hear my voice.

And here we have the first authorization of the Canonical Hours : and therefore this one verse might supply the material for a large volume. But the earliest interpretation spoke of our LORD, and of Him only. *At evening*, that is, in that evening of the Passion wherein the evening sacrifice of the world was accomplished ; *at morning*, namely, that moment, when before the rising of the sun, the stone was rolled away from the entrance of the sepulchre ; *at noonday*, namely, that noon, when "He led them out as far as to Bethany, and lifted up His hands and blessed them ; and it came to pass that, while He blessed them, He was parted from them, and taken up into heaven." Then in the earliest commentators we find Vespers, Matins, and the Liturgy shadowed out. It would be endless to go through all the Scriptural illustrations of these especial times of prayer, from Daniel down to S. Paul and Silas. But it is worthy of notice, that the Jews from a very early period of their history, kept Tierce, Sexts, Nones: Tierce, because the law, they say, was then given ; Sexts, because the brazen serpent was then reared up: Nones, because the smitten rock then poured forth its waters. It is most marvellous that the synagogue should so have foreshadowed the Church. For what responds to the giving of the Law, but the Descent of the HOLY GHOST, as at our Tierce? What answers to the erection of the serpent on the pole, but the lifting up of CHRIST on the Tree of Life, as at our Sexts? What is the antitype of the stream gushing from the rock, but the water that flowed from the pierced Side of His People's True Rock, as at our Nones? And they find many an admirable reason why these three hours, rather than the seven (on which we shall also have hereafter to dwell,) should be named. Because of the three ever-blessed Persons of the Trinity ; because of the three theological virtues of thought, word, and deed ; because of the three classes into which all sins fall, the lust of the flesh, the lust of the eyes, and the pride of life ; because of our three great enemies, the world, the flesh, and the devil. There is a remarkable sense which some early mediæval writers elicit. They say that by *the evening*, we are to un-

A.

S. Hiero-
nym.
Ven. Bede.
Haimo.
S. Prosper.
S. X.
S. Augustin.
203.

Ven. Bede.

·derstand those things which as the conclusion of the day, now gone by, are already past: the Nativity, the Passion, the Resurrection,—in short, our dear LORD'S whole work on earth. By *the morning*, the glorious morning of the Resurrection; that time when the morning being now come JESUS shall stand on the shore of everlasting peace. By *the noonday*, the perfect and unclouded splendour of eternal blessedness:

> Endless noonday, glorious noonday
> From the Sun of suns is there.

And therefore truly *He shall hear my voice* follows the noonday, because the prayers of His people partially and imperfectly heard and answered before, shall then be fully accepted, shall then be more than ten thousand times realised.

19 It is he that hath delivered my soul in peace from the battle that was against me : for there were many with me.

As they very well observe, they are two almost opposite, and yet both lovely senses in which we may take the last clause. *For there were many with me.* On the one hand: the many, who took my part, were only the means by which Cassiodor. He delivered my soul: by their prayers, or by their physical help, He assisted me; and *in peace*, because our alliance was the effect of peace. Thus, it is only what S. Paul says: "I know that this shall turn to my salvation, through your prayers, and the supply of the Spirit of JESUS CHRIST." Or, Philip. i. 19. on the other hand: they take *with me* to mean: encamped on the same field of battle, and fighting against me. And Arnobius. then the verse is explained by that: "Though an host of S. Hilary. men were laid against me, yet shall not my heart be afraid." Ps. xxvii. 3. *In peace.* "For He is our peace, Who hath made both S. Hilar. one."[1] The Chaldaic explanation gives also a beautiful sense: Eph. ii. 14. *because in many afflictions His Word was with me.* Yet one more interpretation. It is the wheat speaking of the tares: Ay. it is Elijah, complaining of his standing alone, while the 1 Kings xix. prophets of Baal were so many. 14.

20 Yea, even GOD, that endureth for ever, shall hear me, and bring them down : for they will not turn, nor fear GOD.

The most noble explanation is that of a Greek saint: S. Euthymius. which sees our dear LORD, *even God that endureth for ever*, That is the same yesterday, and to-day, and for ever, That

---

[1] About this verse S. Augustine has written admirably in his forty-eighth Epistle, Ed. S. Maur., but the passage is too long to quote.

must be true, though every man be a liar, called on by the remembrance of that which He condescended to suffer from human falsehood—even now, according to the poor merits of His servants, to *bring them down*, the fighters against justice, the haters of the righteous, the lovers of a lie. Here, in our version, we have the word *me* inserted: and that most rightly. Some of the mediæval commentators interpreted the *hear*, the hearing *them*, not *me*, and puzzled themselves in what sense the enemies of David, and of the truer David, could be said to be heard.

21 He laid his hands upon such as be at peace with him : and he brake his covenant.

22 The words of his mouth were softer than butter, having war in his heart : his words were smoother than oil, and yet be they very swords.

And perhaps there is not another verse in the Psalms which has had so many different explanations—not of the original meaning, which is most perfectly clear—but of the deeper and truer sense. In the first place : *he*, the traitor of Agellius. traitors—*he*, who afterwards repented after a sort—*he* laid his hands on Him That was at peace with him. He, so at peace with the only man of whom it is said, "Good were it for that man if he had never been born," that He permitted the fallen Apostle to lay his hands on His Own most sacred Body, when he gave Him the kiss of peace, where-with He was wont (so tradition tells) to receive His disciples, Jer. xx. 10. returning from their various missions. *He laid his hands— upon such as were at peace with him.* As they most truly quote from that prophet who was the closest and most exact type of the "Man of Sorrows," of the "acquainted with grief"—so exact a type that modern Judaism interprets the 53rd chapter of Isaiah of him—from Jeremiah: "I heard the defaming of many, fear on every side. Report, say they, and we will report it." Although we have not now to do with the prophecy of Jeremiah, is not this most wonderful? The command to report the circumstances of His death Who was betrayed, as we have seen, by His friends. Report, say they : say the chief priests and elders, after they had taken counsel, to the soldiers that had kept watch at the sepulchre S. Matt. of the LORD; report: "His disciples came by night, and xxviii.12,13. stole Him away while we slept." And we *will* report it. Exactly : so you will. And that report in the miserable times, when the whole history of the Resurrection was searched, inquired into, as a witness might be under cross-examination, was the terror of infidels ; was the support of such as needed such an external kind of witness.

23 O cast thy burden upon the LORD, and he

shall nourish thee: and shall not suffer the righteous
to fall for ever.

There are two different senses in which they took this
casting the burden. The one—that which I suppose would Marcus Na-
be generally taken; *thy burden*—the heavy load of sin, rinus.
sorrow, temptation, let it be what it may, the Man of Sorrows will bear them all. Or, in another sense; *Cast thy* S. Basil. de
burden on Him in the same way that the ship in a storm Predicat.
casts her burden on the anchor, which anchor holds on to its
sure fixing place. And to my mind, that is the more beautiful sense of the two: a sense which, once entered into, may
be followed out in these glorious verses:—

And I see the good ship riding, all in a perilous road;
The low reef booming on her lee; the swell of ocean poured,
Sea after sea, from stem to stern; the mainmast by the board:
The bulwarks down; the rudder gone; the boats stove by the
chains:—
But courage still, brave mariners! the ANCHOR yet remains:
And he will flinch—no, never an inch—until ye pitch sky high;
Then he moves his head, as if he said: "Fear nought! for here
am I."

And He shall nourish thee. And look in what different
ways. How will you have it? Of Joseph nourishing his Gen. xlv. 11.
father and his brethren: or of the widow woman commanded
—though she little knew it—to sustain Elijah; or, of the 1 Kings xvii.
miraculous provision of manna, or of quails, or of that in the 9.
great famine of Samaria, when the spoilers were spoiled? 2 Kings vii.
All this against famine. Or shall we take it of that dear 18.
love which can bring nourishment out of bitterness, as in the
waters of Marah—or, out of absolute poison, as from the Exod. xv.25.
springs of Jericho—or from downright venom, as from the 2 Kings ii.
viper in Melita, which beast was the occasion of the sus- 21; iv. 41.
tenance of S. Paul and his company after the inhabitants of 5, 10.
the island changed their minds, and said that the Apostle
was a God.

It is remarkable how Arnobius, who interprets the word
burden of all thoughts—*care* would be the nearest interpretation of all—dwells on the infinite mercy which allows us—
not only *allows,* but commands us to commit all those troubles
which haunt us, either from sin, or from temptation, or from
bodily suffering, to Him Who therefore fell beneath the load
of His Own Cross, that we might never fall under the weight Serm. v. de
of ours. And so also says S. Leo. Quadrages.

24 And as for them: thou, O GOD, shalt bring
them into the pit of destruction.

25 The bloodthirsty and deceitful men shall not

live out half their days : nevertheless, my trust shall
be in thee, O LORD.

The most noble sermon, perhaps, which was preached in
that century of sermons, the seventeenth, though not taken
from, was yet, to a great extent, based on this verse : that of
Vieyra's, from the text, "Go and sin no more." Thus he
shows how there is a certain amount of sin, known only to
Him Who knows all things, and differing in different persons,
which once heaped up, the day of mercy is at an end. After
having dwelt on those prophecies in Amos—"For three
transgressions of Damascus, and for four"—"for three transgressions of Gaza, and for four"—and so on, he turns to this
text as his proof that man's term of life is not so absolutely,
determinately appointed, but that it may by his own wickedness be cut short. That sermon, to my mind, has a solemnity
which can hardly find a parallel. They interpret the words
of the Psalm, it is true, in other ways.[1] It is a more curious
than plausible interpretation of the *shall not live out half
their days*, which S. Gregory gives. Every sin, he says,
must be repented of : the life of a Christian, therefore, is
made up of falls and penitence : therefore, he who is guilty
of the falls, but knows nothing of the penitence, lives but
half that which he ought to live : of such David speaks. It
may perhaps be said, without any irreverence to one of the
greatest Doctors of the Church, that, had all his interpretations been of the same character, he would scarcely have
stood as high both in the East and West, as he does now.

And therefore :

Glory be to the FATHER, That endureth for ever, and shall
hear me, and bring mine enemies down ; and to the SON, the
LORD, on Whom our burden is to be cast, and Who shall
nourish us with His Own Body and Blood ; and to the HOLY
GHOST, Who, when its tongues were destroyed and divided
of old time, gave us that first Pentecost, the gifts of divers
languages to His Apostles, for the propagation of the faith ;

As it was in the beginning, is now, and ever shall be :
world without end. Amen.

COLLECTS.

Ludolph.   LORD JESUS, Who wast before all ages with the FATHER
and the HOLY GHOST, and yet didst in the latter days take

---

[1] Though I should hope not
many, as Thomas Bozius, who,
a Latin himself, turns this verse
against the Eastern Church, and
observes—which is perfectly true
—that no Emperor of Constan-
tinople reigned more than forty
years, except one who held the
sceptre for forty-three, and two
who ruled for fifty-six. One
can only be sorry that so good a
man as Lorinus should have
given a kind of endorsement to
this interpretation.

Side notes:
Vieyra, tom. iii. Serm. 1.

S. Gregor. Mor. v. 28.

upon Thyself the nature of man, and wast betrayed by Thy companion and own familiar friend; grant, we beseech Thee, that we, praising Thee at morning, and evening, and noonday, and that instantly, may hear Thy Voice, because Thou art pleased to hear ours. Who livest. (1.) Mozarabic.

God, Which perceivest us to be afflicted by the temptations which Thou permittest to attack us, give to us, we beseech Thee, that most powerful help, the victory of the holy Cross; to the end that we, who, by Thy example, strive to overcome the world, may also, because Thou hast gone before us into heaven, merit to follow Thee. Amen. Through S. Jerome. Thy mercy. (11.)

We beseech Thee, Almighty God, that we, being heard by Thee, nourished by Thee, and by Thee set free from the billows of this world, may live out the full number of our days in Thy eternal kingdom. Through. (1.)

PSALM LVI.

TITLE: To the Chief Musician upon Jonath-elem-rechokim, Michtam of David, when the Philistines took him in Gath. In the Vulgate: To the end; for the people which is put far away from the saints; David in the inscription of the title, when the Philistines detained him in Gath. Or rather, perhaps: To the Supreme, in the oppression of the band of exiles; a golden Song of David, when he was a captive by the Philistines of Gath.

ARGUMENT.

ARG. THOMAS. That CHRIST hath drawn us out from the depths of our sin, and from the abyss of perdition. The voice of the prophet concerning the elders of the Jews. The voice of CHRIST to the FATHER concerning the princes of the Jews. Every faithful soul prays against the sins of the flesh, and the flesh itself. The prophet speaketh of CHRIST, and concerning Judas the traitor, and a prayer for enemies.

VEN. BEDE. In the Hebrew we read thus: For the mute dove: the exile of David, humble and perfect: when the Philistines detained him in Gath. The mute dove, and David, humble and perfect, signify CHRIST in His Passion. As to our translation [i.e., the Vulgate] for the people which is put far off from the Saints; that is, for the companions of David who, while exiled in Gath were put far off from Judæa where was the Holy of holies, this signifies that the Psalm hath reference to the Disciples of CHRIST who were scandalized at the time of His Passion; and for whose faith, that it might not fail, the LORD Himself beareth witness that He made intercession. David, in the inscription of the title, signified the LORD in His Passion,—when the title set over Him was, the King of the

Jews : that is, of all that believe in, and *confess* GOD. *When the Philistines held him captive in Gath:* when the Jews and the soldiers of Pilate had crucified Him : for Gath, which by interpretation is a winepress, setteth forth the hard torture of the Cross. In another way we may in the mute dove, and in the people far off from the Saints, understand all the faithful; who, being in exile from the eternal joy of the Saints, say with the Apostle, " While we are present in the body we are absent from the LORD :" for whom David ceaseth not to pray, That David in very deed, Who sitteth at the Right Hand of GOD, Who also maketh supplication for us. Likewise the Psalm may be understood in the person of the Church ; which never ceaseth in this world to suffer trouble, being laden with divers afflictions. In the first section of the Psalm the Church, our mother, prays in the confidence that she will be delivered from our enemies : *Be merciful.* In the second she enumerates her own sufferings, returning thanks for that she hath been delivered from so many perils, and professes that she will never fear those evil things which must of necessity pass swiftly away. In the third place, she promises to sing the perpetual praises of the LORD in that future beatitude, when He shall have delivered us from the adversities of this world. *Unto Thee, O God, &c.*

SYRIAC. The just man's rendering of thanks because he hath been delivered from the enemy.

VARIOUS USES.

Gregorian. Wednesday. Matins.
Parisian. Friday. Compline.
Monastic. Tuesday. II. Nocturn.

ANTIPHONS.

Gregorian. Be merciful * unto me, O GOD.
Monastic. Be merciful unto me, O GOD, * for man goeth about to devour me.
Mozarabic. In Thee, O GOD, are my vows, * the praise which I will return to Thee.

1 Be merciful unto me, O GOD, for man goeth about to devour me : he is daily fighting, and troubling me.

2 Mine enemies are daily in hand to swallow me up : for they be many that fight against me, O thou most Highest.

We must take the whole Psalm, S. Augustine says, but more especially these first two verses, in connexion with the title : " When the Philistines took him in Gath ;" for Gath, by interpretation is a winepress. And according to that very favourite mediæval metaphor, that spices only give out their strength when they are bruised,—as the strings of the lyre require to be strung to their full extent before they

can give out their sweetest melody,—so and even more plainly,
the grape cannot yield that juice which maketh glad both
GOD and man, until it has been exposed to, and so to speak
suffered in, the winepress. So Adam of S. Victor:

> Parum sapis vim sinapis,
> Si non tangis, si non frangis;
> Et plus fragrat quando flagrat
> Thus injectum ignibus.

Thus taught by the title, the whole Psalm so applies itself
to the Son of David, simply and exclusively that not only the
literal interpretation seems almost impossible, but that scarcely
any other mystical explanation is allowable—*For man goeth
about to devour me.* It is not wonderful that they should
here make such a point of that parable where, though enemy
in the original, yet in the Vulgate, it is said, that the MAN the
enemy, soweth tares also. Every one who is acquainted in ^{Ay.}
the slightest degree with the most ordinary ecclesiastical cor- ^{S. Matt. xiii. 25.}
respondence, to say nothing of the commentaries, of the
middle ages, knows that the *homo inimicus*, occurs over and
over again, wherever any temptation of the individual, or
trial to the Church, is in question. And as it is well said by
Jerome,—if Satan transforms himself into an Angel of Light,
much more may he, and does he, transform himself into the
image of that "man" whose whole race he, as far as he could,
made like to himself in the disobedience of Adam. But then;
of all Psalms that most dearly apply to our LORD's life in the
years of His ministry, none surely can match with this.

3 Nevertheless, though I am sometime afraid:
yet put I my trust in thee.

It is quite different in the Vulgate: *From the height of the
day shall I fear: but in Thee will I put my trust.* In all
likelihood, the two verses have been wrongly divided; as so
often: so that the "O Thou most Highest" of the former
verse, is indeed rightly joined with it in our translation, so ^{Aquila.}
far as its division goes: and, literally, the interpretation
should be this, "Mine enemies are daily in hand to swallow
me up, for they be many that fight against me out of pride."
Where the *Out of pride* is expressed in our translation by, *O
Thou most Highest:* in the Vulgate it is carried over into the
next verse, and appears in *height of the day.* It is our work,
not so much to inquire into the meaning of the Hebrew, as
into the sense in which the Western Church took her own
translation. Out of the twelve mystical interpretations,—
which it is needless to go through,—these, perhaps, are the
most striking. *From the height of the day will I fear.* "And ^{S. Bruno.}
it was about the sixth hour, and they crucified Him." So

during that darkness which fell on the earth, surely if ever
fearfulness and trembling came upon—it is not true as yet to
say, the Church, but—the LORD's few followers, that was the
place, so then was the time. And the words, so taken, have
a higher meaning even than these. The more we study the
four histories of the Passion, the clearer it is that towards the
afternoon of that day, what we should now call the popular
feeling as regarded the Crucified One, had entirely changed.
They passed by wagging their heads: true: but that was
before noon: after the confession of the Good Thief, and the
darkness, and the earthquake,—not one word more is recorded of insult: but everything to the contrary. We are
far too apt to pass over one clause of one verse in S. Matthew.

S. Luke
xxiii. 47.
S. Matt.
xxvii. 54.

That the Centurion said: "Certainly this was a righteous
man," "Truly this was the SON of GOD," every child can
tell us. But we scarcely realise all that is meant by that
expression of S. Matthew,—"Now when the Centurion, AND
THEY THAT WERE WITH HIM, WATCHING JESUS, saw the
earthquake, and those things that were done, THEY feared
greatly, saying, Truly this was the SON of GOD." It was at
the *height of the day*, at that sixth hour when they crucified
Him, that the faith of the little band of His followers must
have been most shaken; whereas after that time, each succeeding event, if it could work a kind of belief in the mere
by-standers, much more must have aided in restoring or
strengthening the faith of disciples.

4 I will praise GOD, because of his Word : I have
put my trust in GOD, and will not fear what flesh can
do unto me.

It is rather remarkable that the first, the striking, mystical
sense of *Because of His word*, should find so very slight
recognition in the earlier Commentators. They rather take

1 S. Pet. iv.
11.
Euthymius.

it in the sense of S. Peter: "If any speak, let him speak as
the oracles of GOD:" whether that the word so preached to
the Gentiles brings them in from darkness to light; or because that word teaches whatever we might otherwise think
good, and be ready to extol in ourselves, of a verity is all His:

Bredemba-
chius.
Ay.

("Not unto us, O LORD: not unto us, but unto Thy Name,")
—but this seems rather a far-fetched meaning; though the
Carmelite seems to approve of it: or again; as if David were
saying,—let others praise, and, in a certain sense, rightly
praise, earthly actions, *I will praise God*. But in truth it
must be That Word Which was in the beginning, Which was
with GOD, Which was GOD, that the Psalmist will praise.[1]

---

[1] The excuse for these Commentators, so great and holy, who
yet took this particular verse in a
low sense, is clear. The Vulgate
has: *In Deo laudabo sermones
meos.* The plural, in the first
place, set them wrong; in the
next, the employment of *Sermo*,

I have put my trust in God, namely, in GOD the Word Who was made Flesh to this end; that we might not be afraid what flesh can do to us. Made Flesh in the Incarnation, that the weariness and the hunger, and the thirst, and the coronation, and the scourging, might teach us S. Peter's lesson : "Forasmuch then as CHRIST has suffered for us in the flesh, arm yourselves likewise with the same mind." Made Flesh in the Blessed Sacrament, to the end that, that dearest of all verses might in us be fulfilled;

1 S. Pet. iv. 1.

> Se nascens dedit socium
> Convescens in edulium
> Se moriens in pretium
> Se regnans dat in premium.

And therefore it may well follow, I, for whom that most precious Flesh was torn on the Cross, I, by whom that most glorious Flesh, the more glorious because of its humiliation, has been again and again eaten, *I will not be afraid what Flesh* can do unto me.

This is rather the interpretation of the more recent Commentators, such as Placidus.

5 They daily mistake my words : all that they imagine is to do me evil.

Mistake : or, as it is in the Vulgate, *execrated.* The servant is not above his lord. If the Scribes and Pharisees sent out them that should feign themselves just men, for the sake of purposely mistaking His words, like to Whom never man spake, what great marvel if from that time till the end of the world, the poor, feeble, faltering words of His servants, should again and again sometimes purposely, sometimes really, be mistaken? If His enemies could pervert the "Destroy this temple, and in three days I will raise it up;" if His friends could misunderstand His, "Our friend Lazarus sleepeth;" what wonder if they who speak in His Name should have their sayings in like manner distorted. *They daily execrated my words.* What marvel, then, if they called the Master of the house Beelzebub, that by the same name they should term them of His household. And then, in a higher sense still: they did indeed refuse and were scandalised at His words, when "from that time many of His disciples went back, and walked no more with Him :" when

S. John ii. 19.

S. John xi. 11.

S. John vi. 66.

instead of the name consecrated by the Church, *Verbum.* It would be a curious monograph which should detail the transient struggle for mastery between the two words, *Sermo* and *Verbum*, as the correlative of the Logos. It is singular how the former was always the Arianising term; the latter was finally crystallized in the teaching of the Catholic Church. On a smaller scale,— in Portuguese, Protestant translations have *Palavra;* Catholic, always *Verbo*, and *Verbo* only.

to them, as to many now, even of those who call themselves
His followers, His doctrine concerning the eating His own
Flesh, and the drinking His own Blood, met only with the
response : "This is an hard saying, Who can hear it?" *All
that they imagine is to do me evil.* And, as they well say, how
they imagined to do Him evil, almost every chapter of every
Gospel teaches. By tempting Him : by lying in wait to observe Him : by sending forth spies that should feign themselves just men : by endeavouring to cast Him down from the
precipice on which Nazareth was built; by taking up stones
again, (wherefore, not for the first time,) to stone Him; all
this before we enter on the Passion. But they of whom it
might be said, *All that they imagine is to do me good;* how
many are they? Some did imagine to do Him good, during
His most holy life, forsaking Him in His most bitter Passion :
other some, having held aloof from Him during that life,
braved all shame and danger for His sake, during that death.
S. Peter, and the other nine Apostles that forsook Him, an
example of the one class; Joseph and Nicodemus of the other.
But of men, not one from first to last clave to Him, unless it
may be said that S. John did. Of women, besides the Blessed
above women, two at least, most probably three, as they had
ministered to Him in His life, so they were not afraid or
ashamed to, as that strong Greek expression has it, "be
glued" to Him in His Passion and Death. Thus it was that,
here also, "the LORD chose new wars."

6 They hold all together, and keep themselves
close : and mark my steps, when they lay wait for
my soul.

In the Vulgate, the mystical sense comes out far more
deeply and earnestly; not indeed of the LORD and Master,
to whom hitherto we have turned our thoughts, but of the
servants who are not to be above that LORD, of the disciples
who are not to be above that Master. *They shall inhabit
and hide.* O most wonderful description of the sin that doth
so easily beset us! Most marvellous antitype of that saying
of old : "The Canaanites WOULD dwell in that land." And
again, Judah "could not drive out the inhabitants of the
valley, because they had chariots of iron :" and how it came
to pass that even "when Israel was strong they put the
Canaanites to tribute and did not utterly drive them out."
And hide themselves. "Take us the foxes, the little foxes,"
skulking and hiding themselves by nature, because they are
foxes; concealing themselves the more easily, because they
are *little* foxes.

Ay.
S. Hilar.
Arnobius.

7 Shall they escape for their wickedness : thou, O
GOD, in thy displeasure shalt cast them down.

The Vulgate is entirely different: thus: *They shall inhabit and hide themselves: they shall observe my footsteps. As they have waited for my soul, Thou shalt make them of no regard: in Thy anger, O God, Thou shalt break the people. O God, I have announced to Thee my life, Thou hast put all my tears in Thy sight.* The two last verses form the Verse and Response on Wednesday. *Shall they escape.* And we are immediately reminded of Caiaphas's advice, that one man should die for the nation, and yet for all that, they did not escape; but the Romans came, and took away their place and nation. *For nothing Thou shalt save them,* is taken by S. Augustine in a very curious way. " *With not any merit of theirs going before shalt Thou save them.* I that before was a blasphemer, he saith, and a persecutor, and injurious. Therefore, of this man, not any good merits had gone before, nay, such things had gone before on account of which he would be condemned. Nothing of good he brought in, and saved was he. For nothing Thou shalt save them: that is, with the free gift of Thy grace. What had that robber brought to the Cross? From the lurking place to the judgment; from the judgment unto the tree; from the tree into Paradise. He believed, and therefore he spake. But even that very faith Who did give, but He that by him hung?"

8 Thou tellest my flittings; put my tears into thy bottle : are not these things noted in thy book ?

Thou tellest my flittings. So they notice twelve flights of David; and so the flittings of the Son of David were not only through Judæa, and Samaria, and Galilee, but also in times of greater danger, as when "they took up stones to cast at Him, but Jesus hid Himself, and went out of the Temple, going through the midst of them, and so passed by:" or when on the Mount of precipitation, "He passing through the midst of them, went His way." *Put my tears into Thy bottle.* And we think of that strong crying and those tears which, unrecorded in the Gospels, were, nevertheless *noted in God's Book* by the great Apostle. Or, as they well say, if to Hezekiah God sent the message, "I have heard thy prayer, I have seen thy tears;" if Jeremiah could so plead his own tears for Jerusalem, of how much more effect must those tears be, which together with the Blood of Calvary, were poured forth for the salvation of the world? In mediæval times, the pilgrimage to Vendôme was one of the most famous in Europe: for there was the relic enshrined in a crystal vessel, of a tear of CHRIST. *Put my tears into Thy bottle.* And what becomes of those tears afterwards, the hymn may tell us.

L.

S. John viii. 59.

S. Luke iv. 30.

D. C.
Isa. xxxviii. 5.

> Bright with pearls the portal glitters,
> It is open evermore.

that is, tears which cannot be carried into heaven, are trans-figured into the decoration of its external gates. *Are not these things noted in Thy Book?* The text will come in very well: "He said unto them, What things? And they said unto Him, Concerning JESUS of Nazareth, which was a Prophet mighty in deed and in word." *In Thy Book.* Even as it is written in another Psalm: "Lo, I come, in the volume of the book it is written of Me, to do Thy will, O GOD."

S. Luke xxiv. 19.

9 Whensoever I call upon thee, then shall mine enemies be put to flight : this I know ; for GOD is on my side.

Whensoever I call upon Thee. And we are at once carried on to the "FATHER, I thank Thee, that Thou hast heard Me, and I know that Thou hearest Me always." *For God is on my side,* is, in the Vulgate, *For Thou art my God.* See, S. Augustine, how the one thing follows the other. If Thou art my GOD, then, whensoever I call, I shall be heard. There was but one, and there never shall be but that one, who saying, and not only with truth, but in the very highest and intensest sense, My GOD, was not heard, namely, in that cry on the Cross, "My GOD, My GOD, why hast Thou forsaken Me?" And yet even here, in a truer sense, and in the fulness of time, as S. Paul says, "He was heard in that He feared." *Then shall mine enemies be put to flight.* As they gloriously were by that last "It is finished:" Satan vanquished, the bars and gates of hell burst, the kingdom of heaven open to all believers. *Whensoever I call upon Thee, then shall mine enemies be put to flight.*

Ay.

10 In GOD's word will I rejoice : in the LORD's word will I comfort me.
11 Yea, in GOD have I put my trust : I will not be afraid what man can do unto me.

So he had said before : and the reason of the repetition they take to be, that whenever the first expression of trust succeeded one of fear, this was necessary, lest the certainty that His enemies should be put to flight might savour of presumption. The great Carmelite, following S. Jerome and others, sees in this verse another manifestation of the Trinity, but surely less conveniently. They notice also that the difference of the expression, *God's Word* and *the Lord's Word,* may refer to His mercy and His justice, as much as to say that in one, not less than the other, would David put his trust. Notice further, that in the fourth verse, it is "what flesh," here it is, *what man, can do unto me :* the old distinction of the battle from within and from without.

Ven. Bede.

L.
Ay.

12 Unto thee, O GOD, will I pay my vows : unto thee will I give thanks.

13 For thou hast delivered my soul from death, and my feet from falling : that I may walk before GOD in the light of the living.

And gloriously was this promise kept when the vow that the good Shepherd had made to give His life for the sheep, was accomplished on Calvary. *Unto Thee will I give thanks.* Not only in that "FATHER, I thank Thee that Thou hast heard Me," before the Passion was yet accomplished, but even more gloriously after the Resurrection, when He, returning from His exile, brought back the thank-offering of a ransomed world, as an oblation to His FATHER and our FATHER, to His GOD and our GOD. *For Thou hast delivered my soul from death :* even according to that saying, "Thou shalt not leave my soul in hell, neither shalt Thou suffer Thy Holy One to see corruption." *That I may walk before God in the light of the living :* Himself the Light that not only lightens this world, but that is the brightness of the celestial kingdom : "for the LORD GOD doth lighten it, and the Lamb is the Light thereof:" Himself the Light: "In Him was Life, and the Life was the Light of men." In another sense they take it of the conversion of heretics, translated out of the darkness and death of their former ignorance, into that light first of all implanted by Baptism and manifested in the Church militant now, hereafter to be more gloriously brilliant when her warfare is accomplished. It is well said, that in the deliverance of the *soul from death,* we have the work of the FATHER; of the *feet from falling,* that of the SON; of the walking in the *Light of the Living,* that of the HOLY GHOST, the LORD and Giver of life.

S. Bonaventura.

Ludolph.

S. Hilar.

Hugo de S. Victor.

And therefore:

Glory be to the FATHER, in Whose Word we will rejoice; and to the SON, Who paid His vows in the evening sacrifice of the world; and to the HOLY GHOST, through Whom we trust to walk in the Light of the living;

As it was in the beginning, is now and ever shall be: world without end. Amen.

COLLECTS.

Almighty GOD, the Preserver of Thy people in their invisible wars, Who permittest not them that put their trust in Thee to be oppressed by their enemies, wipe away, we beseech Thee, the tears of sin from the eyes of Thy servants; to the end that, we through Thy grace may both now conquer in every carnal battle, and may finally walk before Thee in the Light of the Living. Through.

Ludolph.

Mozarabic.   O GOD, we set forth to Thee, our Life, that Life which by death destroyed death ; so that Thou, regarding not our merits, but His love, may both put our tears into Thy bottle in this life, and may everlastingly wipe them away in the Land of the Living.   Amen.   Through Thy mercy.

S. Jerom.   We beseech Thee, Almighty GOD, that we, suppressing all carnal desires, and conquering all the allurements of the world, may be found worthy to behold Thy SON JESUS CHRIST in the Land of the Living.   Through the same.

DISSERTATION IV.

HAVING now reached that part of the Psalter in which the references to the details of David's life become more particular and express, it will be well if we endeavour to form a chronological table of their sequence. It is evident that any such attempt must of necessity be involved in a good deal of uncertainty. That which follows is based on the scheme proposed by my late grandfather, Dr. Mason Good, in his introduction to his translation of the Psalms. It has been familiar to me for many years, and the more I have had occasion to study it, the more I am convinced that in its main features it is correct. Some of the passages, in which allusions to historical details in the books of Samuel and Chronicles are seen have not, to the best of my knowledge, been noticed by any other writer. It will be interesting to trace the parallel, so far as it holds good, between the Psalms, as composed in the consecutive periods of David's exile, humiliation under Absalom, and final triumph, with the words spoken by the Son of David, followed also consecutively: nothing would perhaps bind the Psalms and Gospels more firmly together, than such a parallelism.

PERIOD OF MOSES.

Psalm.	Author.	Occasion.
90	Moses*	(?) After the fiery serpents. Compare Numb. xxi. 7.
91	Moses	(?) After the condemnation of the man twenty years old and upwards. Numb. xiv. 29.

PERIOD OF SAMUEL.

Psalm.	Author.	Occasion.
(?) 115	(?) Samuel	(?) After the victory over the Philistines at Mizpeh. 1 Sam. vii. 8.

PERIOD OF DAVID.

1. *His early Pastoral life.*

1	David	
26	David*	
23	David*	Soon after his unction by Samuel. 1 Sam. xvi. 13.
19	David*	
(?) 139	David*	
8	David*	At Winepress-tide, and after his victory over Goliath. Ver. 2.

2. *His outset in Political life.*

35	David*	
64	David*	
36	David*	
59	David*	"When Saul sent, and they watched the house to kill him:" hence address to the GOD of frustration, Saul's plot having been frustrated by Michal's stratagem.
140	David*	
143	David*	
141	David*	

3. *His Exile.*

131	David*	(?) On his march to Nob.
52	David*	"When Doeg the Edomite came and told Saul, and said unto him, David is come to the house of Ahimelech."
120	(?) David	(?) After the destruction of the Priests by Doeg. Compare ver. 3. "What shall be done unto thee, thou false tongue?"
86	David*	
40	David*	Probably in Keilah. Compare 1 Sam. xxiii. 2, "The LORD said unto David, go and smite the Philistines, and save Keilah. . . . So David and his men went to Keilah," with ver. 9, "Then said I, Lo, I come, in the volume of the book" (? Ahimelech's ephod, expressly said to have been brought to Keilah) "it is written of Me, that I should fulfil Thy will, O my GOD."
(?) 13	David*	
31	David*	Almost certainly after his departure from Keilah. Compare "Thanks be to the LORD, for He hath showed me marvellous great kindness in a strong city."
(?) 28	David*	
62	David*	

Psalm.	Author.	Occasion.
54	David*	"When the Ziphims came and said to Saul, Doth not David hide himself with us?" 1 Sam. xxiii. 19.
27	David*	
22	David*	"In the midst of gloom."
142	David*	"A prayer when he was in the cave." 1 Sam. xxiv. 3. That is, while Saul was sleeping at the entrance of one of the huge caves in the wilderness of Engedi, while David and his followers were in the interior. Compare ver. 9. "Bring my soul out of prison, that I may give thanks unto Thy Name."
57	David*	"When he fled from Saul in the cave." That is, evidently, when he had made his escape; and thence, like 59, addressed to the GOD of frustration.
11	David*	Almost certainly at this time. Compare ver. 1, "How say ye then to my soul that she should flee as a bird unto the hill?" with 1 Sam. xxvi. 20, "The King of Israel is come out to seek a flea, *as when one doth hunt a partridge upon the mountains.*"
56	David*	When the Philistines took him in Gath, probably towards the end of his four years' exile at Ziklag.
39	David*	Probably in his march after the Amalekites who had smitten Ziklag. 1 Sam. xxx. 6, "David was greatly distressed; for the people spake of stoning him." This was the day, or the day but one, before the battle on Mount Gilboa.

4. *His reign in Hebron.*

101	David*	Probably, by its whole tenour, the first after his unction at Hebron.
(?) 138	David*	
(?) 95	David* (Heb. iv. 7.)	
75	Asaph*	Probably after the murder of Ishbosheth. Compare ver. 5, "I said unto the fools, Deal not so madly," and ver. 8, "GOD is the Judge; He putteth down one and setteth up another."

5. *His reign in Jerusalem.*

80	Asaph*	Before his kingdom was firmly established. Compare ver. 2, "Before Ephraim, and Benjamin, and Manasseh," &c., (the three tribes that, next to his own, were then his warmest partizans,) with 1 Chron. ix. 3, "In Jerusalem"—that is, immediately after its capture—"dwelt of the

II.   L

Psalm.	Author.	Occasion.
		children of Judah, and of the children of Benjamin, and of the children of Ephraim and Manasseh."
(?) 33	David* (According to LXX. and Vulg.)	
83	Asaph*	Almost certainly during the danger from the great heathen confederation that attacked him at the beginning of his reign. Compare ver. 6, "The tabernacles of Edom and the Ishmaelites," &c.
125	(?) David	Perhaps on his march from Jerusalem against the allies. If so, "as for such as turn back unto their own wickedness" will apply to the tribe of Asher. Compare lxxxiii. 8, where Assur ought to be read Asher.
48	The Korhites	Almost certainly after the victory : "Thou breakest the ships of Tarshish with an east wind," referring to the storm which, Josephus tells us, dispersed the fleet which was to have assisted in the invasion.
(?) 144	David*	If this Psalm was composed at this time, then "Who subdueth my people that is under me" will again refer to the tribe of Asher.
(?) 9	David*	If on this occasion, the title is very appropriate : "To the Supreme, on the death-blow."
98	(?) David	Probably when the Ark was brought up to Jerusalem.
96	(?) David	On the same occasion.
48	The Korhites*	Probably on the second bringing up of the Ark.
68	David*	On the same occasion.
24	David*	When the Ark was brought into the sanctuary prepared for it.
47	The Korhites	About this period.
15	David*	At least after the ceremony of introducing the Ark into the sanctuary. The opening question of this Psalm seems more appropriate to this than to any other part of David's life.
27	David*	At the commencement of the great confederacy of the Syrians, Moabites, Ammonites, Philistines, and Amalekites. 2 Sam. viii. 12.
20	David*	The same.
60	David	"When he strove with the Syrians of Naharaim, and with the Syrians of Zobah ; when Joab returned and smote of Edom in the valley of Salt twelve thousand." That is, while David was attacking the Syrians in the north-east, the Edomites

Psalm.	Author.	Occasion.

took advantage of his absence, and made an irruption in the south; on which he despatched Joab and part of the army to meet them. Compare "Gilead is mine, and Manasses is mine," as being just delivered from the Syrians, and now it is, "Who will bring me into Edom?"

108 David* — This is only the latter half of Ps. 60, with several verses prefixed from Ps. 57.

76 Asaph* — Probably at the same time.

20 David — Probably before he marched against the united Syrians and Ammonites. 2 Sam. x. 16. Compare "Some put their trust in chariots, and some in horses," with 2 Sam. x. 18, "David slew the men of seven hundred chariots of the Syrians, and forty thousand horsemen."

6. Decline of David's power.

51 David* — "When Nathan the Prophet came unto him, after he had gone in to Bathsheba."

32 David* — One can hardly doubt that "when I kept silence" refers to 2 Sam. xii. 16, the seven days that he was interceding for the child.

21 David* — · After the fall of Rabbah. Compare "Thou shalt set a crown of pure gold upon his head" with 2 Sam. xii. 30, "And he took the king's crown from off his head, the weight thereof was a talent of gold . . . and it was set on David's head;" and again, "Thou shalt make them like a fiery oven," &c., with 2 Sam. xii. 31, "He made them (the Ammonites) pass through the brick-kilns."

18 David* — This is inserted, towards the end of David's reign, in Samuel; and yet this period, that of the last great success which he ever won, seems the latest to which it can be assigned.

97 (?) David — (?)

92 (?) David — This is the first Psalm in which mention is made of the infidel faction at court, which culminated in the temporary success of Absalom. See ver. 6, "An unwise man," &c.

16 David* — It speaks still more strongly of that faction.

25 David* — No doubt after the matter of Tamar: for it was not written at an early period of his life. See ver. 6. "O remember not the sins and offences of my youth:" while

Psalm.	Author.	Occasion.
		"the sorrows of my heart are enlarged" seems an expression very applicable here.
14	David*	The general wickedness still continues to gain ground.
53	David*	(A recast of Ps. 14.)
12	David*	The same.
10	(?) David	Here for the first time a complaint is made that the courts of justice were affected by the increasing wickedness. Compare 2 Sam. xv. 4, "Absalom said, moreover, O that I were made a judge in the land, that every man which hath any suit or cause might come unto me, and I would do him justice."
58	David*	The opening of this Psalm, "Are your minds set upon righteousness?" seems exactly to apply to that wish of Absalom's; and, probably, with reference to the troubles manifestly about to arise. It also is addressed to the GOD of frustration.
17	David*	Compare especially ver. 13 and 14, "Up, LORD, disappoint him," &c.
70	David*	"A recollection." A re-edition of part of Ps. 40.
73	Asaph*	
82	Asaph*	In both these we have the general profligacy, and especially the corruption, of the judges strongly set forth.
38	David*	"A recollection." We learn from Josephus that at this time David was seized with a dangerous illness. Compare ver. 3, "There is no health in my flesh."
30	David*	At the dedication—or, as it should be, the opening—of the house of David: the opening, that is, to his court after his recovery. "O LORD, my GOD, I cried unto Thee, and Thou hast healed me," &c.

7. Rebellion of Absalom.

Psalm.	Author.	Occasion.
7	David*	"Which he sang unto the LORD concerning the words of Cush the Benjamite:" or rather, the perfidious Benjamite—no doubt Shimei; the rather that no such name as Cush occurs elsewhere.
3	David*	"When he fled from Absalom with his son."
5	David*	This seems so completely the counterpart of 3, that it is impossible to doubt that it was written about the same time.
(?) 6	David*	As this comes in between 5, probably, and 7, certainly, composed in the wilderness, it may be referred to the same period.
42	The Korhites*	This was clearly written after the king

Psalm.	Author.	Occasion.

had passed over Jordan. 2 Sam. xvii. 22, "Therefore will I remember Thee concerning"—or rather, *from*—"the land of Jordan :" that is, from the tribe of Gad, where was Mahanaim. And doubtless, "One deep calleth unto another," refers to that very passage of Jordan, always a boisterous river, and then perhaps swollen by the equinoctial torrents.

43 David This is so clearly a continuation of 42, that it must of necessity come here.

41 David* This was manifestly written after the treachery of Ahithophel, ver. 9: "Yea, even mine own familiar friend," &c.: therefore it is extremely probable that the blessing on him that considereth the poor and needy refers to Barzillai, and the others, who with him assisted David at Mahanaim.

109 David* This also manifestly refers to Ahithophel; and therefore, like the preceding, must have been written on one of the two or three days which elapsed between David's knowledge of his treachery and the tidings of his suicide.

(?) 94 (?) David This has so much in it of the spirit of 109, that it is only reasonable to place it here.

88 Heman the Laureate* It would seem that like so many others of the king's friends, Heman remained in Jerusalem—and was there thrown into prison: "I am so fast in prison that I cannot get out." And this may account for 88 being the only Psalm which is unmingled gloom from beginning to end.

69 David* Observe how this is in the very spirit of 6 and 109, with the one exception, that no reference is made to any treachery. David having now probably heard of Ahithophel's death. Observe also the reference to "the waters," in the first verse, as if the writer was still by Jordan.

4 David* This would seem to have been written after Absalom's defeat. Both 3 and 4 are night Psalms: but notice the difference of the safety in one, and the danger in the other.

61 David* The expression, "From the ends of the earth," that is, the outskirts of the land,—proves that David was still on the east of Jordan; while "Thou shalt grant the King a long life," or rather, "Thou shalt prolong the King's life," and the general cheerfulness of the Psalm would lead us to think

Psalm.	Author.	Occasion.

that it must have been written after the victory in the wood of Ephraim.

63   David*   "When he was in the wilderness of Judah." Almost certainly at this time; the longing to be once more in the sanctuary; the reference to "those that seek after my soul to destroy it," and so manifestly pointing to Sheba, the son of Bichri; and the clause "all they that swear by him shall be commended," or, as it might be, "Every one that taketh the oath to him shall triumph:" all these can lead to no other conclusion.

8. *Close of David's monarchy.*

124   David*   The whole spirit of the Psalm would point out the time of David's return to Jerusalem; and notice (v. 4,) the reference to "the waters" again.

(?) 66   (?) David   Observe in ver. 5, "There did we rejoice thereof;" a very probable reference to the passage of Jordan at the very place where, under Joshua, "they went through the water on foot." And written at Jerusalem, because of ver. 12.

(?) 118   (?) David   The whole tenour of the Psalm answers admirably to this period; and compare ver. 5 with Psalm 66, ver. 12.

(?) 49   The Korhites*   (?)

110   David*   Here there seems a manifest reference to some crushed rebellion; while the last verse, "He shall drink of the brook," &c., would seem to point out David's triumphant passage over Jordan on his return.

50   Asaph* ⎤
65   David*. ⎟
99   (?) David ⎬   All that can be said of these Psalms is, that they were manifestly composed for the Feast of Weeks.
114   (?) David ⎦

81   Asaph* ⎤
84   The Korhites ⎬   These two Psalms, by their titles, were written for the winepress-tide or Feast of Trumpets.
  ⎦

130   (?) David   (?)

78   Asaph* ⎤
29   David* ⎟
67   (?) David ⎟
100   (?) David ⎟
103   David* ⎬   All that can be said of these Psalms is, that they appear to have been composed for the Feast of Tabernacles; and 29 manifestly refers to one of the equinoctial hurricanes, so common at that season, and to another, of which reference is made in Ezra x. 9, 13.
104   (?) David ⎟
111   (?) David ⎟
112   (?) David ⎟
117   (?) David ⎟
145   David* ⎦

Psalm.	Author.	Occasion.
119 120 122 133 134 37	David*	It is absolutely impossible to assign any period for these Psalms.
71	(?) David	If this Psalm be David's, it manifestly belongs to the close of his reign ; compare ver. 18, " Now also when I am old and grey headed," &c.
72	David*	The last Psalm, as we learn from the conclusion, of David's composition, and manifestly written, not only as the title tells us " for Solomon," but after his coronation.

REIGN OF SOLOMON.

132	(?)	This Psalm was plainly written after David's death ; compare vers. 10, 11, and before the dedication of the temple.
127	(?)	" For Solomon." And plainly referring (compare ver. 3,) to his marriage with Pharaoh's daughter.
45	The Korhites*	Acknowledged by all to have been composed for the same occasion.
128	(?)	This coming close to 127, and on the same subject, was no doubt written at the same time.

REIGN OF REHOBOAM.

74	Asaph	This exactly answers to the state of Judah after the invasion of Shishak. Compare vers. 4—8 with 1 Kings xiv. 25, 26.
77	Asaph	Being by the same author and in the same tone as the last, it may fairly be thought to belong to the same time.
79	Asaph*	The same remark applies to this Psalm.
89	Ethan the Laureate	This Psalm must have been written after David's death, in a time of great public sorrow, such as certainly did not occur during the reign of Solomon, nor till the invasion of Shishak, and it could not well have been later, because, reckoning Ethan to have been but twenty-one when his earliest Psalm was written, he must now have been ninety-eight.

REIGN OF JEHOSHAPHAT.

46	The Korhites*	This so exactly corresponds with the victory gained by Jehoshaphat over the allied Moabites, Edomites, and Ammonites,

Psalm.	Author.	Occasion.

| | | over the cliff of Ziz, that even from internal evidence alone, one could scarcely have doubted its place here. But when its composition is attributed to the Korhites in the title, and when we find in the history, 2 Chron. xx. 19, that the Korhites did actually compose a Psalm on that occasion ; its position here becomes morally certain. |
| 125 | (?) | All that can be said is, that this Psalm has very much of the tone of the other, while the reference to the hills standing round about Jerusalem, taking into connection that the great victory was won just beyond those hills, gives an additional likelihood to this being the right position of the Psalm. |

REIGN OF HEZEKIAH.

116	(?) Isaiah	Jewish tradition has always attributed this Psalm to the time of Hezekiah's recovery from his sickness. As the King's own hymn of praise is given in the Book of Isaiah, it seems only natural to conclude that this Psalm was not written by him ; and by none so likely as by the prophet himself.
135	(?)	This Psalm, at all events, corresponds very well with the repulsion of Sennacherib, and the destruction of his army.
87	The Korhites*	This is certainly of the time of Hezekiah ; because the only one period in which Babylon was on friendly terms with the Jews, was that of the embassy from Merodach Baladan to Jerusalem ; and the only one place in the Psalms where Babylon is mentioned in friendly terms is ver. 4, " I will think upon Rahab and Babylon," &c.

THE BABYLONIAN CAPTIVITY.

123	(?)	The whole tenour of this Psalm amply proves that it must have been written at this period : which may also be said of the next.
44	The Korhites*	
137	(?)	
126	(?)	Manifestly from its opening verse, "When the LORD turned again the captivity of Zion," written just before the return.
129	(?)	The same thing may be said of this Psalm.

THE RETURN TO JERUSALEM.

Psalm.	Author.	Occasion.
85	The Korhites*	The first verse fixes its own period.
136	(?)	Vers. 23 and 24 seem to have reference to the return from captivity ; and when we find from the history, Ezra iii. 12, 13, that a Psalm was composed for the Dedication of the Temple, of which the chorus was " For His mercy endureth for ever ;" there can be no reasonable doubt that this was it.
102	(?)	This almost fixes itself to the period when the Samaritans had obtained the counter edict which forbad rebuilding the walls of Jerusalem. Compare ver. 14, " Thy servants think upon her stones, and it pitieth them to see her in the dust ;" and again, " When the LORD shall build up Zion," which passages, taken by themselves, might refer to any time antecedent to the completion of the walls ; but taken in connection with the deeply penitential character of the whole ; and especially with ver. 10, " Thou hast taken me up, and cast me down,"—words so exactly applicable to the edict and the counter-edict—fix the Psalm with great certainty here.
146	(?)	The reference at vers. 7 and 8, and the " loosing of the prisoners," &c. would seem to point out the return from the captivity as the period of this Psalm.
147	(?)	During the rebuilding of the walls, or immediately after ; see ver. 2, " The LORD doth build up"—(literally, "is building up") " Jerusalem," &c. And again, ver. 13, " For He hath made fast the bars of thy gates."
148 149 150 }	(?) Ezra	As is well known, Jewish tradition ascribes these Psalms to the time when Ezra re-edited the Old Testament books and completed the Canon of the Psalms.

PSALM LVII.

TITLE: Bible Version: To the Chief Musician, Altaschith, Michtam of David, when he fled from Saul in the cave. Vulgate: To the end; destroy not; David for the inscription of the title. Or better: To the GOD of frustration; a golden Psalm of David when he fled from Saul in the cave.

VEN. BEDE. *To the end* signifieth the LORD, Who remaineth the perfection to us of all good things; because, when we shall have attained to Him, none occasion will there be for us to seek anything further. *Destroy not.* It is forbidden that David should be destroyed by Saul, seeing that he was ordained by GOD to the kingdom. *For the inscription of the title.* This applieth not to David, but to the LORD, that the title once written on the Cross should ont be changed. *When he fled.* As David, when he fled from Saul, hid himself in a cave, so the Divinity of CHRIST was hidden from the perfidious Jews within the Temple of His Body. It may also be said, that the LORD so long suffered from the Jews, till He entered into the cave of the Sepulchre, especially seeing that this Psalm pertaineth not only to His Passion, but also to His Resurrection.

ARGUMENT.

ARG. THOMAS. That CHRIST our King breaketh the teeth of demoniac damnation. The voice of the Church to CHRIST. The voice of CHRIST to His FATHER in His Passion. And the voice of Paul, after the LORD'S Resurrection; and of the Church against heretics; and a prayer against sin.

VEN. BEDE. The LORD CHRIST in the first part of the Psalm prayeth earnestly in His Passion as man: in the second, He commemorates the glory of His Resurrection as GOD: in the third He sets forth on that account the praises of His FATHER.

EUSEBIUS OF CÆSAREA. A thanksgiving of David, and a prophecy of the calling of the nations.

VARIOUS USES.

Gregorian. Wednesday. Nocturns.
Monastic. Tuesday. Lauds.
Parisian. Saturday. Lauds.
Ambrosian. Friday of First Week. II. Nocturn.

ANTIPHONS.

Gregorian. Be merciful * unto me, O GOD.
Parisian. My heart is ready, * O GOD, my heart is ready : I will sing and give praise.
Mozarabic. As preceding Psalm.

1 Be merciful unto me, O GOD, be merciful unto me, for my soul trusteth in thee : and under the shadow of thy wings shall be my refuge, until this tyranny be over-past.

Hugh of S. Victor says well that this is the third Psalm *Hugo de S.* which begins with *Miserere*—the 51st and 56th having al- *Vict.* ready done so; and this because of our threefold danger from the lust of the flesh, the lust of the eye, and the pride of life. " This," says S. Bernard, " is to me the one source of all *Serm. 9, in* my expectations, the one fountain of all promises : *Miserere Ps. xc.* mei, Deus, miserere mei.*" This hemistich was adopted as his motto by Pope Nicholas III. : *For my soul trusteth in Thee.*

2 I will call unto the Most High GOD : even unto the GOD that shall perform the cause which I have in hand.

It is a most remarkable explanation of this verse, as well **L.** as a singular example of the way in which mediæval writers felt their LORD to be one with them, and themselves one with Him, that they so dwell on the literal sense of the Vulgate : *I will cry unto the Most High God : even unto the God Who hath done well unto me.* So that, precisely as every Christian soul has a right to say, " Because Thou hast been my helper, therefore under the shadow of Thy wings will I rejoice ;" so, according to His humanity, it was with our LORD ; so, to say it with the most infinite reverence, because the place where we are standing is holy ground,—just as David said, " The LORD That delivered me out of the paw of the lion, and out of the paw of the bear, He shall deliver me out of the hand of this Philistine :" so the Son of David, according to His manhood, might say, " My FATHER, Who delivered Me out of the hand of Herod, and out of the hand of the Pharisees and Scribes, when they sought to tempt Me, and out of the hand of the enemy in the wilderness, He shall deliver Me out of the hand of this Philistine," that is, when our Master was approaching His last and hardest battle ; and when He almost seemed to take these words on His own· blessed lips, when He said, " FATHER, into Thine hands I commend My Spirit."

Unless saints had said it first, I should not, with all its *S. Bernard.* beauty, have dared to take such an interpretation. *Ven. Bede.*

S. Augustine, referring this text to ourselves, compares it **A.** with that in Isaiah : " I was found of them that sought Me *Isaiah lxv. 1.* not." In this sense : that if GOD was found of us, who (for the most part) neither did seek, nor could have sought, His grace in Baptism ; how much more, now that we have that *S. Augus-* grace, will He be found of them who, using it, seek Him in *tine, Serm.* a yet nearer way. *v.*

Neither must we omit those Commentators who, still understanding the passage of man, interpret it thus : *unto the God, Who is performing the cause which I have in hand. The cause* ; that is, the cause of my soul, For it is GOD that worketh in you, both to will and to do, of His good pleasure.

3 He shall send from heaven : and save me from
the reproof of him that would eat me up.

4 GOD shall send forth his mercy and truth :

Ay.

Thus, they say, our LORD, in the midst of the cause which
He had in hand, namely, our salvation on the Cross, encouraged Himself. He shall send from heaven; not now the
Angel who appeared unto Him, comforting Him in His
agony, but the Angel that rolled away the exceeding great
stone, and sat upon it. And S. Augustine shows how the
A.
reproof of the Jews was turned to their own shame ; so that
even the heathen were amazed to see the manner in which
the sometime people of GOD stood confounded by their own
D. C.
Scriptures. God shall send forth His mercy and truth. His
mercy, in that the GOD of all mercy came into the world to
redeem it; His truth, in that His promises, "The seed of the
woman shall bruise the serpent's head;" and "Behold, a
Virgin shall conceive and bear a Son," were, in the fulness
of time, accomplished.

My soul is among lions.

5 And I lie even among the children of men, that
are set on fire : whose teeth are spears and arrows,
and their tongue a sharp sword.

Ay.

S. Bruno,
Carthusian.

And still it is our LORD speaking from the Cross, even as
He spoke in the 22nd Psalm, "Save Me from the lion's
mouth." And notice also that the children of men are brought
in as worse than lions. In the Vulgate occurs a clause
which, though it cannot be fairly got out from the Hebrew,
yet is so true in itself, and affords such a lovely contrast with
another verse in the Psalms, that one cannot wonder at its
being so dwelt on by mediæval writers. I slept in trouble.
Compare this with the words that the same dear LORD puts
into the mouth of all His followers: "I will lay me down in
peace, and take my rest." He, therefore, slept in trouble,
that we might take our rest in peace; He, therefore, as
S. Paul teaches, tasted of death, that we might never taste
of it.[1]

6 Set up thyself, O GOD, above the heavens : and
thy glory above all the earth.

[1] It is worth while noticing
with what beautiful truth it is
that Shakespeare puts into the
mouth of a brave heathen an expression, to which he has never
given utterance in the person of
a Christian, as knowing how, to
them, death was, " of all terrible
things the most terrible :"

" Cowards die many times before
their deaths :
The valiant never taste of death
but once."

And here our Lord ceases to speak, and the Prophet tak
up His words. As one, long years after, when he beheld the
Man of Sorrows hanging on the Cross, addressed Him as
the Lord that was to come in His kingdom; so here that
same Man of Sorrows, having but now cried out, " I lie even
among the children of men," receives for answer, *Set up
Thyself, O God, above the heavens.* Thou art now, he would
say, set up high on the Cross; set up, a spectacle to men
and to angels; set up, to be the scorn and mockery of those
that are round about Thee, and that wag their heads in derision.
But henceforth *set up Thyself above the heavens.* Thou, to
Whom, according to Thy Godhead, the seat at the Right
Hand of the Father appertained from all eternity, go and
assume it according to Thy Manhood, in virtue of the merits
of Thy precious Death and Passion. *And Thy glory above* S. Greg.
all the earth. Because, exalted above the heavens, there to Moral. in
intercede for us, therefore shalt Thou have the *glory above* Job. xxvii.
all the earth: because Thou didst suffer, therefore, accord- 25.
ing to Thy humanity, shalt Thou reign till Thou hast put all
things under Thy Feet—those blessed Feet, once nailed for
us to the Cross, that they might, even by that very suffering,
bruise the head of the serpent.

7 They have laid a net for my feet, and pressed
down my soul : they have digged a pit before me,
and are fallen into the midst of it themselves.

They have laid a net for my feet. And they well notice
the marvellous type of one snare set for David and for the Ay.
Son of David. Saul, when his daughter loved David, said,
" I will give him her, that she may be a snare to him; and 1 Sam. xviii.
that the hand of the Philistines may be against him :" so, 21.
because the true David Himself loved humanity, (certainly
not loved by it, for it is written, " We love Him, because
He first loved us,") therefore, out of this very love, Satan
laid a net, as it were, for His feet; and exactly as by Michal
came David's after kingdom, so, by the love of His Church,
the time shall come when He shall, even in this world, reign
King of kings and Lord of lords. And furthermore notice:
They have laid a net for my feet—pressed down my soul— L.
digged a pit before me. Where, as Hugh of S. Victor teaches,
we have manifestly the lust of the flesh, the lust of the eyes,
and the pride of life, to which our Lord, as the Good Captain of our salvation, vouchsafed to be exposed in the wilderness. Some mediæval writers find an especial voice in the
preposition *before:* that whereas apostates, and backsliders, D. C.
and cowards would be more likely to be taken in a pit made behind them, He, Who ever went straight forward, had His pit
set in the right onward path. *And are fallen into the midst of*
it themselves. As those who went forth to tempt our Lord Ay.
by entangling Him in His talk, the elders who brought to

Him the woman taken in adultery,—the Pharisees and Herodians, who, diametrically opposed to each other on the very question, asked whether it be lawful to give tribute to Cæsar,—the Sadducees, with their interrogation about the woman that had seven husbands,—were all taken in their own snare, so that they marvelled and left Him, and went their way, and at last no man durst ask Him any more questions: so also, and in a far higher sense, Satan himself fell into his own pit; Leviathan, endeavouring to swallow the bait of our Lord's Humanity, was dragged out of the scene of his former dominion by the hook of the Divinity.

D. C.

8 My heart is fixed, O God, my heart is fixed: I will sing, and give praise.

S. Bernard, Serm. 1, in Quadragesima.

Take it rather, *My heart is ready;* and then interpret David's resolution with the last Western Father. Dost Thou desire me to be a king? Is it Thy will that I should be a shepherd? Wilt Thou have me to remain a fugitive? Thou, Who hast given all, wilt Thou take away all, so as to cause me to become a beggar? *My heart is ready.* S. Paul truly says, "I have learned, in whatsoever state I am, therewith to be *content.*" But David, or rather, our truer David, goes far

Hugo de S. Vict.

beyond. *My heart is ready: I will sing and give praise.* Hugh of S. Victor here sees the perfect pattern of a true and earnest confession. *My heart is ready*—there you have the true contrition for sin; *I will sing*—there is his open acknowledgment; *and give praise*—there the thankfulness

P.

for its pardon. Taking the words *give praise,* in another sense, as said of a musical instrument, in contradistinction to the *I will sing,* which refers to the voice,—and connecting this verse with the instrument of ten strings, they make these strings to be: our confession of the mystery of the Trinity; of the Incarnation; of the Nativity; of our Lord's life and miracles; of His Passion; His descent into hell, His Resurrection, His Ascension; the mission of the Holy Ghost; and the foundation and existence of the Catholic Church.

[We are to observe that this and the four following verses form the beginning of the 108th Psalm, where *My heart is fixed* is given, as we have just now taken it, *My heart is ready.*]

9 Awake up, my glory; awake, lute and harp: I myself will awake right early.

Ay.

Here, as they delight to point out, we have the gradual steps which conducted our Lord from His first to that which shall be His last victory, so far as redeemed humanity is concerned; as it is written, "The last enemy that shall be destroyed is death." *Awake up, my glory.* So might the Apostles have said, had they stood around the new sepulchre

in the garden of Joseph, towards the midnight of that first
Easter Eve. *My glory*, individually to each; *my glory*, inasmuch as we are members one of another, universally to all.
Origen compares well—and would that he had said *all* things   Hom. ii. in
as well!—our LORD's descent into that sepulchre with David's   Cantic.
entrance into the cave of Engedi. It was while He was there
that Saul also entered in; "and the men of David said unto   1 Sam. xxiv.
him, Behold the day of which the LORD said unto thee, Be-   4.
hold, I will deliver thine enemy into thine hand, that thou
mayest do to him as it shall seem good unto thee. Then
David arose." *Awake, lute and harp.* But yet a second,
before His final, triumph, awaited the Victor; that day in
which it was asked, and reply was made, "Who is the King
of glory? The LORD, strong and mighty; the LORD, mighty
in battle." And it is well said, *lute and harp;* that thereby   S. Jerome,
the concord of the Church Triumphant, *the lute*, and the   in S. Matt.
Church Militant, *the harp*,[1] should be set forth. *I myself*   xxv. 42.
will awake right early. "Then cometh the end." The final
seal, the essential consequence of our LORD's Resurrection, is
our own. Because He burst the bands of death, therefore
we also; and then, and not till then, shall He put down all
rule, and all authority and power.

And yet they also love to put these same words into our   S. Ambros.
LORD's mouth. How it is now He Who is exhorting those,   de Institu-
whom of His great love He condescends to call His glory,   tione Vir-
whether by the great things they shall do, or the greater   ginum, c. 1.
which, like S. Paul, they shall suffer for His sake, to awake   Col. iii. 1.
up. "If ye, then, be risen with CHRIST, seek those things
which are above." And then, as both setting the pattern
and giving the courage, He adds, "I, even I Myself, am He   Isa.
That comforteth you." *I Myself will awake right early.* So
early, that the saying aforehand concerning the three days   Zuccolius.
and the three nights was just, and only just, fulfilled. So   S. Mark i. 6.
eager was the Victor to return with the spoils of His triumph
to His own; so gloriously was that promise fulfilled, "While
they are yet speaking, I will hear."

10 I will give thanks unto thee, O LORD, among
the people : and I will sing unto thee among the
nations.

[1] Because, as the same saint observes, the *cithara* has six strings, whereby are signified the six corporal works of mercy. It is almost needless to observe that, according to the teaching of the Church for nearly a thousand years, there were only six; even as there are only six mentioned in our LORD's prophecy of the Day of Judgment. Even as late as Rupert of Deutz the old tradition is clung to, till it gave way to the analogy of the spiritual works of mercy, and to the argument that, whereas every other work of love rendered to our dear LORD during his earthly life could be referred to one of the six, His Burial could not, except in a very forced way, find a place there.

11 For the greatness of thy mercy reacheth unto the heavens : and thy truth unto the clouds.

12 Set up thyself, O God, above the heavens : and thy glory above all the earth.

Rom. xv. 9.
S. Bonaven-
tura.
Z.
S. Luke
xxiv. 47.
L.

Taught by S. Paul, we see a prophecy of the vocation, not of the Jews only, but also of the Gentiles. Where observe : he puts *the people*—the Jews—first ; according to that commandment of our LORD, "beginning at Jerusalem." And of this double apposition they see the parallel in the next verse : *For the greatness of Thy mercy reacheth unto the heavens : and Thy truth unto the clouds.* The *heavens,* namely, the Jews, on whom, however mistily, the light of the Sun of Righteousness had dawned. *The clouds,* namely, the Gentiles, of whom it was written, "Darkness shall cover the earth, and gross darkness the people :" (it being manifest that they who were comparatively clear as an unclouded sky before their rejection of their King, sank down afterwards into grosser darkness than the nations around them : " For even unto this day the veil yet remaineth untaken away.")

The last verse is only a repetition of the sixth.

Therefore :

Glory be to the FATHER, Who shall send from heaven and save me ; and to the SON, under the shadow of Whose wings shall be my refuge ; and to the HOLY GHOST, the Mercy and Truth sent forth to those whose soul is among lions.

As it was in the beginning, is now, and ever shall be : world without end. Amen.

COLLECTS.

Ludolph.

Take away, we beseech Thee, O LORD, the iniquity of this Thy family, which putteth its trust under the shadow of Thy wings ; to the end that, Thy mercy being sent down from heaven, we may be preserved from the snares of our enemies, and from the nets of them that do evil. Through.

Mozarabic.

Have mercy upon us, O LORD, have mercy upon us, and hear the prayers of them that trust in Thee ; break Thou the strength of our adversaries, destroy Thou the hopes of them that lie in wait for us ; that we, being ever guided by Thy light, may with a ready heart exalt among the people the mercy of Thy truth, Who for us didst endure the shame of the Cross. Through Thy mercy.

S. Jerome.

Grant, we beseech Thee, to us, O LORD, in all our troubles and adversities, the gift of Thy HOLY GHOST ; so that we, being guarded by Thy protection and bulwarks, may be in this world prepared for eternal joys, and in the world to come may possess them for evermore. Through.

PSALM LVIII.

TITLE: Bible Version: To the Chief Musician, Altaschith, Michtam of David. Vulgate: In finem, Ne disperdas, David in tituli inscriptionem. Or, perhaps: To the Supreme, the GOD of frustration; a golden Song of David.

ARGUMENT.

ARG. THOMAS. That CHRIST shall render to His saints, in righteous judgment, a revenge concerning the slaughter of the poor. The Prophet speaketh concerning the elders of the Jews. And the Voice of CHRIST to the Jews, judging Him unjustly; and against the Priests, perversely condemning His members.

VEN. BEDE. The word *end* and *David* in the inscription of the title signifieth CHRIST on the Cross; and Pilate is thereby admonished not to destroy that inscribed title which declared the LORD to be King. In the opening of the Psalm the LORD upbraideth the iniquity of the Jews: *Are your minds set upon righteousness?* In the second part He declareth, in most apt types, the vengeance that shall fall on them: *Break their teeth, O God.* In the third part He telleth what shall be the feeling of the just concerning the punishment of sinners: *The righteous shall rejoice when he seeth the vengeance.*

SYRIAC PSALTER. A Psalm of David, when Saul threatened the priests because they would not make known to him the hiding-place of the same David, though they knew it themselves; but to us it setteth forth a manifestation of the just judgment of GOD.

VARIOUS USES.

Gregorian. Wednesday. Matins.
Parisian. Friday. Tierce.
Monastic. Tuesday. II. Nocturn.
Ambrosian. Friday of First Week. II. Nocturn.

ANTIPHONS.

Gregorian. As for the preceding.
Parisian. Innumerable troubles have come about me; * let it be Thy pleasure, O LORD, to deliver me.
Monastic. Do ye judge the thing that is right, O ye sons of men?

1 Are your minds set upon righteousness, O ye congregation : and do ye judge the thing that is right, O ye sons of men?

Hence they gather, S. Jerome leading the way, that, even in the corrupted state of human nature, and without regeneration, the sense of moral right and wrong remained, and still remains, to man : wherein S. Jerome was only the disciple of S. Paul, when he teaches concerning the Gentiles S. Hieron.

that they " show the work of the law written on their hearts,
their consciences also bearing witness, and their thoughts
Rom. ii. 15. the meanwhile accusing, or else excusing, one another."
They lay, of course, the stress on *the sons of* MEN, as distin-
guished from the sons of GOD. It is well said by the great
French divine of his age, that, of all things, this is the most
Hugo de S. Vict. important to each individual man—that he should judge
rightly concerning these ten things: concerning faith, the
world, the devil, himself, GOD, the duty of each day, the
opportunities afforded by time, strife, death, and the dead.
And the Carmelite, equally well, compares the speech of
Ay. those Jews who feigned themselves just men: " Master, we
S. Matt. xxii. 16. know that Thou art true, and teachest the way of GOD in
truth," with our LORD's answer here: *Are your minds set
upon righteousness, O ye congregation?*

2 Yea, ye imagine mischief in your heart upon
the earth : and your hands deal with wickedness.

L. It is well said, *in your heart.* For, of a certainty, with
their mouths, both Jews and Gentiles sometimes uttered the
S. Matt. ii. 6. very truth concerning our LORD : as when the chief priests
declared that He should be born in Bethlehem ; as when
Caiaphas uttered that prophecy, that it was expedient that
S. John xi. 50. one man should die for the people; as when Pilate made
that reply, " What I have written I have written." But
further observe that the mischief they imagine is only upon
the earth. Take it in either sense : either, as they gene-
Ay. rally understand it, that the miserable and insulting lie
here becomes a glorious truth there—witness the crown of
thorns, and the purple robe, and the sceptre of mockery ; or,
as S. Gregory will have it, that by *the earth* he means the
S. Greg. in Job. ix. 6. Body of our LORD, which, in that He was consubstantial
with us according to the flesh, was, like our own bodies,
formed of the earth. And notice that here, in speaking of
S. Bruno. evil, the prophet begins from the thought, and proceeds to
the deed : *and your hands deal with wickedness ;* exactly as
our LORD taught the Pharisees, how it is out of the heart
that murders and adulteries come. But, when we are taught
anything concerning the propagation of good, the order is
Acts i. 1. reversed : " All that JESUS began both to do and to teach."

3 The ungodly are froward, even from their mother's womb : as soon as they are born, they go
astray, and speak lies.

A. · It was a favourite idea of the primitive Fathers that the
Serm. 20 de Sanctis. Jews are here especially specified, because they were froward,
Rupert. even from the womb of their mother the synagogue ; in that
S. John v. 46. the law was, so to speak, pregnant with the Gospel : " For
had ye believed Moses, ye would have believed Me." This

text was a great weapon in the armoury of the Church, against those followers of Origen who taught that the human soul, pre-existent to the body, had sinned before its union with its companion. And, not ill, they take the verse of the Jews, who, from their very origin as a nation, did go astray, as in the matter of the calf; did speak lies, as when they said, "All that the LORD hath spoken unto us we will do and obey." As in the beginning, so at the end—still the same lies: "He is guilty of death;" "Now we know that Thou hast a devil." And CHRIST tells of the reason where He saith, "Ye seek to slay Me, a man that doth tell you the truth."

D. C.

Ay.

4 They are as venomous as the poison of a serpent : even like the deaf adder that stoppeth her ears;
5 Which refuseth to hear the voice of the charmer : charm he never so wisely.

And we are at once reminded of that multitude, who stopped their ears and ran upon Stephen with one accord. Therefore, well might that repeated exhortation of our LORD be given: "He that hath ears to hear, let him hear." And of a truth, they did refuse to hear the voice of the charmer. He Who should have charmed them to submission by His miracles, by His parables, by His teaching, by all that He did and all that He suffered,—He Who charmed *never so wisely*, when the destroyer was destroyed, the deceiver deceived, Life brought out of death, everlasting joy from temporary agony, how many had He to hear His last seven words of wisdom? How many followers were to be found at the mountain of Galilee before His Ascension, and in the large upper room after it? But while we condemn the Jews, let us take heed lest that happen to us which the Wise Man testifies, saying, "When the ungodly curseth Satan, he curseth his own soul;" take heed lest we refuse *to hear the voice of the Charmer*, charming us now no less wisely than His own people then; charming us by threatenings or allurements, through others or by ourselves, by pleasure or by pain, by sudden events or by gradual leading; anyhow, charming us *never so wisely*.

D. C.

S. Bruno.

6 Break their teeth, O GOD, in their mouths; smite the jawbones of the lions, O LORD : let them fall away like water that runneth apace; and when they shoot their arrows, let them be rooted out.

It is an ingenious remark of S. Jerome, that as the terrible strength of lions lies principally in their teeth, which teeth, nevertheless, are not ordinarily visible; so the most

Com. in Joel i.

A.

Ay.

dangerous assaults of the roaring lion, that goeth about seeking whom he may devour, are those which he conceals the best. They also teach us that whereas we, in this Psalm, are first told of the venom of the serpent, and then of the rage of the lion, it was after the same sort that the various sects of the Jews first sent emissaries, feigning themselves just men, to tempt our LORD, before (now no longer dissembling their malice) they cried out, "Away with Him! away with Him! crucify Him! crucify Him!" And further that, as here there is no very decided victory asserted, or prayed for, over the serpent, the fulness of conquest is petitioned for against the lion, even as it was by the open rage of the Jews, and not by their secret guile, that the LORD's Right Hand wrought out our salvation. *Let them fall away.* Well says S. Augustine: Be not terrified by certain streams which are called torrents; they are filled up with winter-waters. Do not fear; after a little that water falleth away. For a time it roareth, but it will soon subside; it cannot hold out long. . . . The whole of this age for a time is roaring, and is seeking whom it may drag along. Let all ungodly men, all proud ones echoing against the rocks of their pride as it were with waters rushing along, in no wise terrify you: winter waters they are, they cannot always flow; it must needs be that they run down into their place, even unto the end. And, nevertheless, of this torrent of the world the LORD hath drunk; but in the way He hath drunk, in the passage over; for in the way of sinners He hath not *stood.* For of Him, what saith the Scripture? He shall drink of the brook in the way, therefore shall He lift up His Head: to wit, for this reason He hath been glorified, because He hath died; for this reason hath risen again, because He hath suffered. *When they shoot their arrows, let them be rooted out.* There is here a marvellous difference in the translations. The Vulgate has it, *He bendeth his bow until they be made weak.* The Bible translation, *When he bendeth his bow to shoot his arrows, let them be as cut in pieces.* And

Genebrard.

the interpretations are even more strangely different than are the versions. Some will have it that the *he* refers to the wicked; the sense then being, Let them shoot as long as they will, the only result will be that, without doing any harm to the righteous, they will simply weary themselves.

Gen. xix. 11.

Just as the men that sought to harm Lot, and were smitten with blindness, only "wearied themselves to find the door."

A.

Others, like S. Augustine, and, following him, the chief expositors of the Western Church, understand the *he* of GOD Himself; in the sense that *He will shoot His arrows,* whether of correction in love, or simply of love, into the hearts of those sinners whom He is drawing to Himself, *till they become weak,* with that weakness of sorrow for sin, and of distrust in themselves, which is indeed the truest strength.

So the latest of Eastern

Thirdly, almost all the Easterns, and among the Westerns

S. Hilary, also understanding the subject of the Psalmist to be GOD, take this sending forth His arrows in the sense of judgment, and not of mercy.

commentators, Anthemius, Patriarch of Jerusalem.

7 Let them consume away like a snail, and be like the untimely fruit of a woman : and let them not see the sun.

Here the versions entirely differ. The Vulgate gives it, *As wax that melteth, let them be taken away : the fire hath fallen from them, and they have not seen the sun.* But, except that *slug* would be a fitter translation than *snail*, our version is undoubtedly the right one. But, according to that version, S. Albertus Magnus explains the comparison thus : that as a snail or slug is destroyed by salt, so David asks, by that "good" salt of purity and holiness, his enemies—and, mystically, the enemies of the Son of David—might come to nothing and be dissolved. But the greater part of mediæval writers, interpreting the Hebrew word as signifying wax, find here a prayer for the conversion of sinners : that is, that their stony heart may be, according to the prophet's promise, turned into a heart of flesh.

S. Albert. Mag. de piscibus.

Ay.

Arnobius.

8 Or ever your pots be made hot with thorns : so let indignation vex him, even as a thing that is raw.

Here, again, the discrepancy is not less. The Gallican: *Before your bush shall bring forth thorns, as living ; so in his anger he shall swallow them up.* The Vulgate : *Before your thorns should understand the bush, as living ; so in anger he shall swallow them up.* Or, according to the modern translation : *Before they can breed revolt, set thorns in the midst of them ; as with force, as with fury, let them be scattered with a whirlwind.*

9 The righteous shall rejoice when he seeth the vengeance : he shall wash his footsteps in the blood of the ungodly.

10 So that a man shall say, Verily there is a reward for the righteous : doubtless there is a GOD that judgeth the earth.

And so *the righteous* did *rejoice*, not only when, reigning from the Tree, He saw the utter defeat of His enemies and ours by means of that very throne ; but when He beheld also that more glorious vengeance of love, by which, for every drop of the most precious Blood that He shed, myriads and myriads of elect souls should enter into His kingdom. *The righteous shall rejoice* when He seeth that, as it were in revenge of His Passion, the noble army of martyrs spring forward in His service ; in revenge of His weariness, and bearing all

A

L.

manner of evil, such an uncounted multitude of confessors took up their special cross, to the end they might follow Him; when, in revenge of His sorrow, even unto death—of His weakness, even to falling beneath the load of the Cross—so many of His servants have rejoiced in long illnesses, have triumphed under false accusations, have endeavoured to realise to themselves the glorious octave of His beatitudes. *So that a man shall say, Verily, there is a reward for the righteous.* And it is well said, *a man;* for it is the Centurion who first confessed this truth, so that once more Gentiles should put to shame Jews. *Doubtless there is a God that judgeth the earth.* And that also was fulfilled, when He, Who shall come to judge the quick and the dead and the world by fire, was pleased, as Judge no less than King, on the Cross, to set the good on His right hand, and the evil on His left. *Verily, there is a reward for the righteous.* "Certainly, this was a righteous man."

S. Bonaventura.

And therefore:

Glory be to the FATHER, Who hath prepared a reward for the righteous; and to the SON, the GOD That shall judge the earth; and to the HOLY GHOST, Who alone can set the minds of men on righteousness.

As it was in the beginning, is now, and ever shall be: world without end. Amen.

COLLECTS.

Ludolph.

Almighty GOD, Who settest men's minds upon righteousness, and causest them to judge the thing that is right; grant that there may be neither evil on our lips, nor iniquity in our hearts; so that righteousness in works may precede good speaking in tongue. Through.

Mozarabic.

GOD, Whose words are pure and Whose judgments are right; stretch forth Thy Right Arm for our defence; smite the jawbones of the lions, O LORD, which would devour us; that in Thee the multitude of the redeemed may rejoice, seeing that Thou art the Crown of the righteous, and that to Thee we may sing the psalm of joy, when we arrive at the fruit of well-doing. Amen. Through Thy mercy.

PSALM LIX.

1 Sam. xix. 11.

TITLE: Septuagint and Vulgate: To the end. Destroy me not. David, for the inscription of the title, when Saul sent and watched his house that he might slay him. On this title, S. Augustine and S. Hilary, among the western, and S. Gregory Nyssen, among the eastern doctors, have written the most fully. They show how the story of David, for whom, around his house, they laid wait, by night, is with the story of the Son of David, in the same night in which He was betrayed. And therefore S. Gregory Nyssen says boldly, that those words, *Destroy them not,* are the most sweet and gentle utterance of our LORD Himself: FATHER, forgive them, for they know not what they do.

Or perhaps, rather, *to the Supreme,* GOD of *frustration :* a golden song of David; on the sending of Saul when they watched about the house to kill him.

ARGUMENT.

ARG. THOMAS. That CHRIST, by means of His Resurrection in the morning, hath given to us a life turned from sorrow to joy. The Voice of CHRIST to the Jews.

VEN. BEDE. The title has been more than once explained before; when the Passion of CHRIST is described, and His kingdom that can never be removed. When Saul sent and watched his house that he might slay him: when the Chief Priests sent and watched the sepulchre of CHRIST, unto the end that they might, as it were, keep Him in death, having closed every door to His Resurrection. In the first place, the LORD makes His petition, that His enemies may not prevail against Him to hurt Him: *Deliver Me from Mine enemies.* Next, He prophesies how in the end of the world, the Jews shall be converted, and, with wonderful love, offers for them this petition; in the evening they will return. Thirdly, He prophesies what they will do after they have returned, and how He and His Saints will rejoice thereat: *As for me I will sing of Thy power.*

EUSEBIUS. The vocation of the Gentiles, and the rejection of the Jews.

SYRIAC PSALTER. David made this Psalm when he heard that the Priests had been slain by a sword; but to us it declares the conversion of the Gentiles to the true faith, and the reprobation of the Jews.

VARIOUS USES.

Gregorian. Wednesday. Matins.
Parisian. Friday. II. Nocturn.
Monastic. Tuesday. II. Nocturn.
Ambrosian. Friday of First Week. III. Nocturn.

ANTIPHONS.

Gregorian. As for preceding Psalm.
Parisian. From them that rise up against me * defend me, O LORD, for the mighty men are gathered against me.
Monastic. As for preceding Psalm.
Ambrosian. From them that rise up against me * defend me, O LORD.

1 Deliver me from mine enemies, O GOD : defend me from them that rise up against me.

2 O deliver me from the wicked doers : and save me from the bloodthirsty men.

A.

Hugo de S.
Victor.

L.

That, as S. Augustine says, which our LORD suffered, we must also suffer ; whether from the temptations of evil spirits, or of evil men, we have equal need to be delivered. The four petitions with which the Psalm begins, are interpreted of the four different stages to which the servants of Satan are allowed to proceed. *Mine enemies :* there you have the wish to hurt, even though the power be absent. *Them that rise up against me;* then, those who by their words or writings, do what harm they can to the cause of GOD. *The wicked doers*, made the confessors : and *the bloodthirsty men*, the martyrs.

3 For lo, they lie waiting for my soul : the mighty men are gathered against me, without any offence or fault of me, O LORD.

Ay.
Rufinus.
V. Bede and
D. C.
S. Bruno.
L.

Who *lie waiting?* They explain it differently. Some take it of the night in which the LORD was betrayed ; other some, of our LORD's descent into hell ; others, and probably in a truer way, take the *they lie waiting for my soul*, of all the reproaches, slanders, troubles, which He bore, Who, for our sake, not His own, was the Man of sorrows and acquainted with grief. There cannot, they say, be a better commentary on this verse, than the declaration of Pilate : "Take ye Him, and judge Him ; for I find no fault in Him."

4 They run and prepare themselves without my fault : arise thou therefore to help me, and behold.

Ay.

D. C.

2 Kings xix.
14.

How they ran, how they prepared themselves, those emissaries of Pharisees, Sadducees, and Herodians, may well teach us : especially in that matter of the tribute money, when the two sects meet in opposition with each other, united against Him. If He had said that tribute to Cæsar was lawful, the Pharisees would have cried out against Him : if He had said that it was unlawful, the Herodians would have done the same thing. *Arise Thou therefore to help me.* In the first and highest sense, it is the prayer of our LORD to the FATHER : but there is a clear sense also, for all those who, treading in His footsteps, are reaching forward to His promises. *And behold.* Just as when Hezekiah had received the blasphemous letter of Rabshakeh, he "went up into the house of the LORD, and spread it before the LORD."

5 Stand up, O LORD GOD of hosts, thou GOD of Israel, to visit all the heathen : and be not merciful unto them that offend of malicious wickedness.

Ay.

Stand up. In the first place from the grave ; then, in Thine Ascent into the kingdom of heaven, when Thou wilt not leave us orphans; (for Israel, as we have seen, is by interpretation, he that sees GOD;) and also *to visit all the heathen.*   We know not what,—we know not when,—the day of that visitation will be.   Take it as you will, either of the day of our own death, or of the Day of Judgment. And then,—then most truly,—will the prophecy be fulfilled; then, will the heathen be,—those that have seldom, or have never been, "visited:" and as regards such, "Shall not the Judge of all the earth do right?"

D. C.

Gen. xviii. 25.

Or, as regards the rest; see how David prays, with the whole force of his soul, for those enemies, only excepting *them that offend of malicious wickedness.*   "There is a sin unto death: I do not say that ye shall pray for it."[1]

1 S. John v. 16.

6 They go to and fro in the evening : they grin like a dog, and run about through the city.

Rather, with the Bible Version, the LXX., and the Vulgate, *They return at evening—convertentur ad vesperam.* And the commentators all interpret it of the conversion of sinners, and especially of the Jews, at the evening of the world.   For the doctors lay down that there are seven ages of the world : the first, from Adam to Noah; the second, from Noah to Abraham; the third, from Abraham to Moses; the fourth, from Moses to David; the fifth, from David till the carrying away to Babylon; the sixth, from the carrying away till CHRIST; the seventh, from CHRIST to the end of the world.   So, then, the last age of the world begins from CHRIST, and is therefore called the evening.   Up to that time the Gentiles abode in unbelief and idolatry; but at the Advent of CHRIST, and the preaching of the Apostles, they were converted.   And though the Jews are not yet obedient to the faith, still the Prophet foretells their late return : " For the children of Israel shall abide many days without a king, and without a prince, and without a sacrifice, and without an image, and without an ephod, and without teraphim : afterward shall the children of Israel return, and seek the LORD their GOD, and David their king; and shall fear the LORD and His goodness in the latter days."   That was the evening in which CHRIST brought peace to the world.   "The dove came in the evening, bearing an olive-leaf."   In that evening the light of grace was given to the Gentiles, as Zechariah foretold, "at evening time it shall be light."   Or it may be that last awful evening of the world, when the LORD is coming to judgment, and those who have refused to seek Him before, *must* soon behold Him.   They will then be moved to repentance, though they did not turn early in the

Ay.

D. C.

Hosea iii. 4, 5.

Gen. viii. 11.

Zech. xiv. 7.

G.

---

[1] At this point the Commentary of John Mason Neale ceases. The pen, fallen from the hand of the great scholar, poet, and divine, is henceforth taken up by the weak fingers of his disciple. R. F. L.

S. John i. 1, 4.

morning to see that "in the beginning was the WORD, the Life and Light of men;" nor at noon-day to behold the Sun of Righteousness in the mid-heaven of His brightness; that vision which is prepared for those elect who search for Him,

Cant. i. 7.

asking, "where Thou feedest, where Thou makest Thy flock to rest at noon." *They grin like a dog.* More, they howl, (הָמָה) and that for hunger, as the LXX., λιμώξουσιν, and the Vulgate, *famem patientur.* What that hunger is, let the Prophet tell us: "Behold, the days come, saith the LORD

Amos viii. 11.

GOD, that I will send a famine in the land; not a famine of bread, nor a thirst for water, but of hearing the words of the LORD." Dogs the Jews called the Gentiles, as if being un-clean. For even the LORD Himself, when after Him there

A.

cried a certain woman of Canaan, saith, "It is not meet to take the children's bread, and to cast it to dogs." "Truth,"

S. Matt. xv. 25.

she saith, "LORD," surely a true thing Thou sayest, a dog I am, "yet the dogs eat of the crumbs which fall from their masters' table." And immediately the LORD: "O woman, great is thy faith." Therefore the nations are dogs, and for this reason they are hungry. *And will go about the*

H.

city. S. Hilary and Euthymius explain this of the Jews, mourning over the desolate ruins of Jerusalem, and seeking to trace the remains of its sacred places. But others more

B.

happily take it of the Church, and of those who go up and down in it, guarding it from visible enemies by preaching the Word, and from invisible ones by prayer, who are in-

Cant. iii. 3.

deed "the watchmen that go about the city." Even if these dogs be dumb and not preachers, yet they can go about the city

G.

with prayers for all, and especially for the afflicted members of the Church; in teaching whom they are like the dogs which licked the sores of Lazarus, not wounding them afresh with the tooth of calumny, but soothing and healing them with gentle words of consolation, teaching, warning, and prayer.

7 Behold, they speak with their mouth, and swords are in their lips : for who doth hear?

Not merely believing in their heart, nor recording in their writing, but preaching the Word boldly. *And swords are*

Isa. xlix. 2.

in their lips. So Isaiah: "He hath made my mouth like a sharp sword." Here is that sword twice whetted, whereof

Eph. vi. 17.

the Apostle saith, "And the sword of the Spirit, which is the

A.

Word of GOD." Wherefore twice whetted? Because smiting

Acts x. 13.
Rev. i. 16.
Ricard. Victorinus in
Apoc. i. 16.
Heb. iv. 12.
S. Albertus
Magnus.
S. Matt. x.
34.

out of both Testaments. With this sword were slain those whereof it was said to Peter, "Kill, and eat." This is that sharp two-edged sword which goes out of the mouth of the Son of Man, "piercing even to the dividing asunder of soul and spirit," cutting away carnal sins in the Old Testament, and spiritual ones in the New, and parting the bad from the good. And of it the LORD spake, saying, "I am not come to send peace on earth, but a sword." And again: "He that

hath no sword, let him sell his garment, and buy one." And S. Luke xxii.
spoken of the Passion, these words fitly apply to those chil- 35.
dren of Israel who killed the Paschal Lamb at evening, with G.
their wicked cry, "Crucify Him." *For who doth hear*—to believe? That is, the preachers shall be wroth with men that are Z.
slow to believe. Thou seest a man slow before he is made
Christian; suppose him to be converted, and then he would A.
have all men to be Christians, and wondereth that not yet
they are. It hath chanced to him at evening to have been
converted; but because he hath been made hungering like a
dog, he hath also on his lips a sword; he saith, *Who doth
hear?* What is, *Who doth hear?* "Who hath believed our Isa. liii. 1.
report, and to whom is the Arm of the LORD revealed?"
The Jews did not believe, and nevertheless, through believing
Jews, the Gospel went round about the city; and they said,
For who doth hear?

**8 But thou, O LORD, shalt have them in derision :
and thou shalt laugh all the heathen to scorn.**

Not only the unbelievers shall be derided, but those
preachers who are discouraged, and doubt the spread of the G.
Gospel; since far more will hear and believe than they suppose. *Thou shalt laugh all the heathen to scorn.* Because a
most easy thing it will be for all nations to believe in Thee.
And the chief reason why the heathen shall be laughed to H.
scorn is, that while in the folly of worldly wisdom they reproach Him Who was crucified, dead, and buried, not understanding the mystery of His great loving-kindness, they
do not believe Him to be the SON of GOD rising again from
the dead, and the LORD of Majesty.

**9 My strength will I ascribe unto thee : for thou
art the GOD of my refuge.**

The Hebrew is rather, *I will wait on Thee, my strength.*
But the LXX. and the Vulgate both render it, *I will keep
my strength to Thee.* And it is expounded of CHRIST, Who L.
would not use His power against His persecutors, but delayed
their punishment according to the FATHER'S dispensation.
That He could have punished them, yet did not, He showed, S. John
by making the soldiers fall to the ground by a single word, xviii. 6.
and yet praying on the Cross for His enemies. And He kept S. Luke
His strength, says S. Hilary, by taking again His life which xxiii. 34.
He laid down, but which no man took from Him, and because H.
His might and refuge were of Him into Whose Hands He
commended His Spirit. And we may take it primarily of
David, who, though entitled to the kingdom on the death of Z.
Saul, is content to leave the issue of events in GOD's hands.
It holds, too, observes S. Augustine, of every soul of man. A.
For those strong men have fallen for this reason; because

M 2

their strength to Thee they have not kept: that is, they that upon me have risen up and rushed, on themselves have relied. But I *my strength to Thee will keep*, because, if I withdraw, I fall; if I draw near, stronger I am made. For see, brethren, what there is in a human soul. It hath not of itself light, hath not of itself powers, but all that is fair in a soul is virtue and wisdom; but it neither is wise for itself, nor strong for itself, nor itself is light to itself, nor itself is virtue to itself. There is a certain origin and fountain of virtue, there is a certain root of wisdom, there is a certain region of unchangeable truth: from this the soul withdrawing is made dark, drawing near is made light. "They had an eye unto Him, and were lightened," because by withdrawing ye are made dark. Therefore, *my strength will I keep to Thee:* not from Thee will I withdraw, not on myself will I rely. For where was I, and where am I? Whence hast Thou taken me up? What iniquities of mine hast Thou remitted? Where was I lying? To what have I been raised up? I ought to have remembered these things: because in another Psalm is said, "When my father and my mother forsake me, the LORD taketh me up." *My strength to Thee will I keep.* And we are not left to seek for the cause of this confidence: *for Thou art the God of my refuge.* My *high place*, as the Hebrew; my *lifter up*, as the LXX. and Vulgate. And either truly, for it is spoken in the person of CHRIST, Whom the FATHER took up to the highest place, even the hypostatic union with Godhead. And because He hath so gone up on high, Who is our Head, we, His members, know that we shall follow. So runs the hymn of the Paris Breviary:

Ps. xxxiv. 5.

Ps. xxvii. 12.

Ay.

Santol. Victorin. in Ascens.

Nos membra, quo nostrum caput,
Quo dux praeivit, ibimus;
Si jungat una mens simul,
Nos una junget gloria.

10 GOD showeth me his goodness plenteously: and GOD shall let me see my desire upon mine enemies.

The Bible Version here agrees more nearly with the LXX. and Vulgate, *The God of my mercy shall prevent me.* And S. Augustine, arguing against the Pelagians, explains it of prevenient grace, saying, "What good thing have I brought, that Thou shouldest have mercy on me, and shouldest justify me? What in me hast Thou found, save sins alone? Of Thine there is nothing else but the nature which Thou hast created; the other things are mine own evil things, which Thou hast blotted out. I have not first risen up to Thee, but to awake me Thou hast come: for *His mercy shall prevent me.* Before that anything of good I shall do, *His mercy shall prevent me.*" And S. Bernard draws the same con-

A.

S. Bernard. Serm. in Cant. lxvii.

clusion. "*My God*, he says, *His mercy shall prevent me.*
And again, speaking to the LORD, he says, 'Let Thy tender Ps. lxxix. 8.
mercies speedily prevent us, for we are brought very low.'
Beautifully does the Bride later (if I err not) place these
same words not in the same order, but follows herself the
order of the Prophet, speaking in this wise: 'I am my Beloved's, and my Beloved is mine.' Why thus? Doubtless Cant. vi. 3.
that she may prove herself the more full of grace when she
attributes all to grace, ascribing the first and last parts
to it. Otherwise, how could she be full of grace, if she had
aught that is not of grace? For grace cannot enter in where
merit has already established itself. Therefore the full confession of grace denotes the fulness of grace itself in the soul
of the confessor." And so the greatest of Latin poets, in his
own lowly epitaph, acknowledges the sinfulness of man apart
from the grace of GOD:

> Hæres peccati, naturâ filius iræ,   Adam. Vic-
>   Exiliique reus nascitur omnis homo.   torin. Epi-
> Unde superbit homo, cujus conceptio culpa,   taphium.
>   Nasci pœna, labor vita, necesse mori?

And the words, *His mercy shall prevent me*, are especially D. C.
applied to the Manhood of CHRIST, united to Godhead from
the first instant of its creation, before the very possibility of
merit existed. *And God shall let me see my desire upon mine
enemies.* That desire is twofold—mercy and justice. Mercy
up to the last possible moment, "FATHER, forgive them, for S. Luke
they know not what they do;" justice for the finally impe- xxiii. 34.
nitent, "But those Mine enemies, which would not that I S. Luke xix.
should reign over them, bring hither, and slay them before 27.
Me." The LXX. and Vulgate are different. The former
has, *My God will show to me [His mercy] amongst mine enemies.* And this may be most fitly taken of the descent into
hell, when He came amongst His ghostly enemies in the
guise of a captive, but really as a conqueror. And so S.
Peter the Venerable:

> Mortis portis fractis, fortis   S. Petr.
>   Fortior vim sustulit,   Vener.
> Et per crucem regem trucem   Hymnus
>   Infernorum perculit.   Paschalis.
> Lumen clarum tenebrarum
>   Sedibus resplenduit.

The Vulgate is: *My God will show to me over* [or *concerning*]
mine enemies. And if we take the Chaldee Paraphrase as a
guide, we shall supply the word *vengeance.* But it is better
to explain it of the Divine foreknowledge of CHRIST, as to D. C.
the destiny of the Jews, revealed to Him by the FATHER, and
treated of in the following verse. But these are not the only
variants. The old Roman Psalter reads, *Show me good things
amongst mine enemies:* that is, Help me, while they perse-

Ep.lib.ii.13. cute. Or, with S. Peter Damiani, take it of the involuntary witness borne to CHRIST by the Jews by the very fact of their unbelief. The Gallican Psalter reads, *Show me amongst mine enemies.* And it may be taken of His being made a show of by Pilate, when he said, "Behold the Man;" or of His manifestation in the person of His martyrs, or of His appearing at the Last Day, when His enemies shall look on Him "Whom they pierced."

S. John xix. 5.

Zech. xii. 10.

11 Slay them not, lest my people forget it : but scatter them abroad among the people, and put them down, O LORD, our defence.

A.

Deut. xxviii. 64.

Gen. iv. 14, 15.

Ps. vi. 5.

Rom. xi. 20, 21.

A.

It is not surprising that almost all the commentators agree in explaining this verse of the dispersion of the Jews, and their mysterious preservation, distinct from all nations among whom they dwell, according to the saying of Moses, "And the LORD shall scatter thee among all people, from the one end of the earth unto the other." *Slay them not,* but drive them forth, to wander, as Cain, with the stain of righteous blood upon their hands. And yet not altogether in vengeance, but in mercy, "for in death no man remembereth Thee," that a remnant may be preserved which may return and believe. *Lest my people forget it.* And so the Apostle : "Because of unbelief they were broken off, and thou standest by faith. Be not highminded, but fear; for if GOD spared not the natural branches, take heed lest He also spare not thee." But the LXX. and Vulgate read, *Lest they forget Thy law.* And this is to be the especial sign of their separation. This is the mark which the Jews have : they hold fast by the remnant of their law; they are circumcised, they keep the Sabbaths, they sacrifice the Passover, they eat unleavened bread. These are therefore Jews; they have not been slain; they are necessary to believing nations. Why so? In order that He may show to us amongst our enemies His mercy. And there is yet another reason : "It is divinely appointed," observes S. Peter Damiani, "by the providential arrangement of our Redeemer, that the remnant of the Jews should be preserved, as it were, to keep the house of the Law; that they should be in a measure our librarians, and carry with them everywhere over the world the books of sacred speech in the same tongue as that in which they were composed, in order that they, who are our enemies, should take from us all doubt, if any doubtful scruple should appear." Wherefore it is said by the Psalmist, *My God, show me good among mine enemies ; slay them not, lest they forget Thy law.* And then follows : *Scatter them abroad among the people.* The LXX. and Vulgate are closer to the Hebrew, and read, *Scatter them in Thy might ;* or, as the Bible Version, *by Thy power.* Not merely by the power of the Romans, but with punishments dealt by the same mighty Arm which once brought

S. Pet. Damiani, Ep. lib. ii. 13.

2 Sam. xv. 16.

them out of the house of bondage. And so S. Gregory Na- S.Greg.Naz.
zianzen speaks: "Who of all those skilled in writing lamen- Orat. de
tations, and who could express suffering itself in speech, Pace, 1.
could lament their troubles fittingly? What books could
contain it? The whole world itself, throughout which they
are diversely scattered and dispersed, is the sole monument
of their calamity." But there is another way in which we
may take this verse. It is spoken also of the Apostles and
their converts. *Slay them not* by martyrdom till they have
preached the Word, teaching all nations; but *scatter them
in Thy might.* And so S. Paul answers the question, *For
who doth hear?* in this wise: "But I say, Have they not
heard? Yes, verily, their sound went into all the earth, and Rom. x. 18.
their words unto the ends of the world." *And put them
down,* from prosperity and temporal glory, from their king- D. C.
dom, from their priesthood, and all the honour of the law of
their fathers. But let it be as it was to one of themselves, C.
even Saul of Tarsus: bring them down in humility, that they
may arise again in faith. As the hymn runs:

> Quam bene, Saule, sterneris,   The Hymn
> Qui melius erigeris,   *Anni rotato*
> In te cadit supérbia,   *tempore.*
> Erigitur humilitas.

O Lord, our defence. Because, if they be not put down,—if
a rival temple and sacrifice, an Aaronic priesthood instead of G.
the order of Melchizedek, continue—the wheels of the Gospel
chariot will be stayed; therefore, *O Lord, My defence,* Fa- D. C.
ther of My Manhood, *put them down,* and hinder them from
working such a result.

12 For the sin of their mouth, and for the words
of their lips, they shall be taken in their pride: and
why? their preaching is of cursing and lies.

Here the Hebrew, LXX., and Roman Psalter all have—
The sin of their mouth is the word of their lips: that which
they spake, saying to Pilate, "If He were not a malefactor, S. John
we would not have delivered Him up unto thee." And xviii. 30.
again, "Sir, we remember that that Deceiver said, while He S. Matt.
was yet alive, After three days I will rise again." The Vul- xxvii. 63.
gate reads *sermonem labiorum* in the accusative, governed
either by the word *slay* or by *put down.* Therefore, *slay not
them, lest they forget Thy law;* but there is something in A.
them for Thee to slay, in order that Thou mayest fulfil that
which hath been said above, "Be not merciful unto them Ver. 5.
that offend of malicious wickedness." What, therefore, wilt
Thou slay? *The sins of their mouth, the word of their lips.*
What in them wilt Thou slay? The "Crucify, crucify" S. Matt.
which they cried out, not them that so cried out. For they xxvii. 23.
willed to blot out, cut off, destroy Christ; but Thou, by

raising to life CHRIST, Whom they willed to destroy, dost *slay the sins of their mouth, the word of their lips.* And further: *they shall be taken in their pride.* "A man is taken in his pride," observes the Master of the Sentences, "when, viewing the greatness of his sin, he perceives that he has dealt proudly, and that in vain." And S. Hilary takes it therefore of the compunction with which the remnant of the Jews will confess their sin when "there shall come out of Sion the Deliverer, and shall turn away ungodliness from Jacob." So the quasi-Jerome explains it: they shall be made humble. But it may also be spoken of the judgments upon them in despite of their boasting, "We are Abraham's children, and were never in bondage to any man," and their saying, "Who gave Thee this power?" whereon the LORD foretold, "The days shall come upon thee, that thine enemies shall cast a trench about thee, and compass thee round, and keep thee in on every side;" and "If ye believe not that I am He, ye shall die in your sins." *And why? their preaching is of cursing and lies.* Cursing, when they said, "He hath a devil, and is mad; why hear ye Him?" and "His blood be upon us." Lies, declaring, "Behold a man gluttonous and a wine-bibber;" and "He stirreth up the people;" and again, "His disciples came by night, and stole Him away." The LXX. and Vulgate render the passage differently. *They shall be declared of cursing and lying, in the consummation.* That is, at the Last Day their blasphemy and falsehood shall be judged. But it may also be taken of the remnant which shall return. *They shall have tidings brought to them* by preaching, concerning Him Who was made a *curse,* as it is written, "He that is hanged is accursed of GOD," and Who was the subject of their *lying.* Touching all these things *they shall be declared,* that is, *taught,* that they may learn not to curse the Name of CHRIST, may learn not to speak falsely of Him, that they may be *in the consummation*—that is, perfected in the number of the good. And with this agrees the reading of Cassiodorus, *They shall be torn away from cursing and lying.* And so, turned from impiety, *they shall be drawn from their cursing and lying,* and this *in the consummation,* because, when the fulness of the Gentiles enters in, then shall the remnant of Israel be saved.

13 Consume them in thy wrath, consume them, that they may perish : and know that it is GOD that ruleth in Jacob, and unto the ends of the world.

And so it is written in another place, "They shall know that I am the LORD, when I shall scatter them among the nations, and disperse them in the countries." And yet again a further reason is given, "I will consume the filthiness out of thee." But the LXX. and Vulgate read it differently. *In the consummation, in the wrath of consummation, and they shall not be.* That is, the final conversion of the Jews will be worked out by God's remedial punishments, in His wrath which maketh perfect; for there is a wrath of consummation wherewith God sometimes punishes that He may perfect, and a wrath of consummation which punisheth that it may destroy. Their sins, then, are forgiven them in the wrath of consummation, whoso are willing to be converted. And there follows, *And they shall not be :* doubtless because, thus perfected in the wrath of consummation, they shall no more be in their pride. For so the Scripture explains *not to be,* saying, " The wicked are overthrown, and are not." It is, however, also spoken of the finally impenitent, and thus sounds a note of warning as well as of hope. For they shall be convicted by Christ, their Judge, *in the consummation,* that is, in the end of the world and the Last Judgment. Touching which consummation Christ speaks in the Gospels, ".So shall it be in the consummation of the world." For then shall they look on Him Whom they pierced. Whence the Psalmist adds more plainly, *in the wrath of consummation,* that is, in the Divine vengeance and rebuke of the Day of Judgment, they shall be convicted by Christ; for He will then say to them, " Depart, ye cursed, into everlasting fire." *And they shall not be* in the number of the elect, nor in glory, according to that saying, " The wicked will not behold the Majesty of the Lord." *And know that it is God that ruleth in Jacob.* Whereas formerly, not made subject to the righteousness of God, but going about to establish their own, they were puffed up against the Gentiles, whom they counted unclean as dogs, and thought that God had no care save for the Jews, justified, as they deemed, by the righteousness of the Law ; now, purified by the wrath of consummation, and enlightened by grace, they will know that, as all have sinned, Jews and Gentiles, so all have come short of the glory and grace of God. For as He *ruleth in Jacob* by saving whom He will of the stock of Jacob, so also He ruleth *unto the ends of the world,* by saving whom He will, not only in all Judea and Samaria, but hearkening unto the voices of all that cry to Him from the *ends of the earth,* whether Jews or Gentiles, of all whom is formed that one Church, which is that Queen who came from the ends of the earth to hear the wisdom of Solomon. They did not know at first that He *ruleth in Jacob ;* for when Pilate wrote the title on the Cross, they said, " Write not, The King of the Jews ; but that He said, I am King of the Jews ;" and again, " We have no king but Cæsar." Nor did they remember His lordship over the *ends of the world,* according to the words of the Prophet, " Thy Redeemer, the Holy One of Israel ; the God of the whole earth shall He be called."

Ay.

Prov. xii. 7.

D. C.

S. Matt. xiii. 40.

S. Matt. xxv. 41.

Isa. xxvi. 10.

G.

Ay.

S. John xix. 21.

S. John xix. 15.

S. Albertus Magnus.

Isa. liv. 5.

14 And in the evening they will return : grin like a dog, and will go about the city.

M 3

15 They will run here and there for meat; and grudge if they be not satisfied.

This is the second part of the latter portion of the whole Psalm, wherein, after a first statement touching the conversion of the Jews, here the full conversion of the same Jews is added, and four things are spoken of: First, their conversion. Next, the affection of the converted, and their longing to convert others, *They shall hunger.* Thirdly, their anxiety to fulfil their longing, *And will go about.* Fourth and lastly, their compassion and distress for those whom they shall not be able to convert, *and grudge if they be not satisfied.* They will *hunger* to convert souls, accounting themselves *as dogs,* and not as sheep. So their humility is indicated, that they are not like the proud Pharisee, who counted himself a sheep, and not a dog. Or, *as dogs,* in the capacity of preachers eager to devour the fleshliness of others, "Come, that ye may eat the flesh of kings, and the flesh of captains." And hence it was said to Peter, "Kill, and eat." And note, that a good preacher is a good dog. First, because with his mouth he barks against tyrants and heretics, who are wolves and robbers; with his teeth he rends sins like flesh; with his tongue he heals the wounds left in the soul by sin, "And the dogs came and licked his sores;" with the sense of smell he follows his prey, ever pressing on the track. So the preacher follows CHRIST, keeping in His steps, "because CHRIST also suffered for us, leaving us an example, that ye should follow in His steps." Such a dog was blessed Job, "My foot hath held His steps." He dies for his Master: "For Thy sake also are we killed all the day long." He is born blind, and remains so till he have for awhile sucked his mother's teats; so the preacher, till he have sucked the breasts of his mother, the Church. For the Church has two breasts, which are the two Testaments.

They will run here and there for meat. The LXX. and Vulgate render it, *They shall be scattered, that they may eat.* S. Hilary takes it to mean the hungering of the Jews after the oblations and sacrifices of the Temple, and their murmuring against the Divine decrees which deprive them of this food of their souls. But others for the most part explain it of the dispersion of preachers seeking to make converts, and their regret when the harvest is small. Therefore they who have acquired the true learning, *are scattered, to eat,* to wit, spiritual food, that the Gentiles may be converted, coming to the Catholic faith, as was said to Peter the Apostle in his vision, "Kill, and eat." It is *meat* they long for, because, as natural eating is to incorporate in one's self food from without, and to assimilate it, so spiritual eating is to incorporate one's neighbour by means of love, and to convert him to that true faith which the preacher holds. There follows, *they will grudge if they be not satisfied.* Teachers are

Marginal notes:

S. Albertus Magnus.

Rev. xix. 18.

Acts x. 13.

S. Luke xvi. 21.

1 S. Pet. ii. 21.

Job xxiii. 11.

Ps. xliv. 22.

H.

C.

Acts x. 13.

Ay.

satisfied when they see the people eagerly accept their preaching. On the other hand, they hunger and *grudge* if they see their words failing to bear fruit in the minds of unbelievers.[1] So their *grudge* or *murmur* (as the Vulgate has it) is thus taken in a good sense, and means that they shall *grieve*, and show that grief by reproaching men, by imploring GOD, and by ascribing their unsuccess to their own sins.

G.

16 As for me, I will sing of thy power, and will praise thy mercy betimes in the morning : for thou hast been my defence and refuge in the day of my trouble.

The words mystically apply to CHRIST giving thanks to the FATHER for the conversion of the Jews and Gentiles. For the justification of the unrighteous is a work of vast *power* and *mercy*, exceeding the quickening of a dead body, or the creation of heaven and earth out of nothing. Dionysius will have it that CHRIST the SON here speaks of His Resurrection through the power of the FATHER, and because it was given Him to announce the tidings with joy and gladness on the first day of the week, when "joy cometh in the morning." And others prefer to attribute the words to each elect soul, when it comes to that morning which knows no evening of its blessedness, or of the glory of the Resurrection. And so speaks S. Augustine of the unending sabbath of heavenly rest. "The seventh day is without evening, and hath no sunset, because Thou hast hallowed it for everlasting continuance." And of this meaning the Cluniac sings :

L.

D. C.

Ps. xxx. 5.

S. Augustine, Confess. xiii. 36.

> Spe modo nitimur; ubere pascimur hic, ibi pane;
> Nox mala plurima dat, dabit intima gaudia Mane.

Bernard. Cluniacen. Rhythmus de Cœlest. Patr.

In the morning, when temptations have been overcome; in the morning, when the night of this world shall have passed away; in the morning, when no longer the lyings in wait of robbers and of the devil and of his angels we dread; in the morning, when no more by the lamp of prophecy we walk, but Himself, the WORD of GOD, as it were a sun, we contemplate. With reason in another Psalm is said, "Early in the morning will I direct my prayer unto Thee, and will look up." With reason also of the LORD Himself the Resurrection was at dawn, that there should be fulfilled that which hath been said in another Psalm, "Heaviness may endure for a night, but joy cometh in the morning."

A.

Ps. v. 3.

Ps. xxx. 5.

---

[1] S. Albertus Magnus drily observes, This verse may also be read against archdeacons, who are literally scattered through the episcopate, not to preach, but to eat, and who murmur if they are not provided for according to their fancy. Not like Eliezer, who says, (Gen. xxiv. 33,) "I will not eat till I have told mine errand." And when he had finished, he was content with a little; for it is found in the same place, "And there was bread set before him." (Gen. xxiv. 33, Vulg.)

D. C.

For Thou hast been my defence (Vulg. *lifter up*) *and refuge.
in the day of my trouble.* It is spoken of CHRIST in the mystery of His Passion, for then He took refuge with His FA-
THER, praying and saying, "FATHER, if Thou be willing, remove this cup from Me." And also, when dying, He cried,
"FATHER, into Thy Hands I commend My Spirit." And this befitted CHRIST, in so far as He was subject to passions, and in some wise a pilgrim. It also explains why humanity rejoices in CHRIST the LORD, because He *has been* its *lifter up.* For He Himself is *lifted up* when the whole Church is saved, according to that saying, "Inasmuch as ye have done it unto one of the least of these My brethren, ye have done it unto Me." He adds: *And My refuge in the day of My trouble.* O how pleasant is that refuge, when granted in the time of trouble! For all flesh is under suspicion until it hear, "Come, ye blessed of My FATHER." But when we arrive at that most longed for speech, our refuge becomes eternal: a refuge from the devil and his angels, from the whirlwind of Divine wrath, from everlasting burning, as it is written, "Thou hast been a refuge from the storm, a shadow from the heat, when the blast of the terrible ones is as a storm against the wall."

*S. Luke xxii.
42.*

*S. Luke
xxiii. 46.*

C.

*S. Matt.
xxv. 40.*

*S. Matt.
xxv. 34.*

Isa. xxv. 4.

17 Unto thee, O my strength, will I sing : for
thou, O GOD, art my refuge, and my merciful GOD.

Ay.

Here he gives thanks by works; for to *sing* is to praise by works. And observe that good men sing to GOD both in this life and in glory, because they have good works both here and there. *My strength,* or as the LXX. and Vulgate read, *my helper.* "What was I," exclaims S. Augustine, "unless Thou didst succour? How much despaired of was I, unless Thou didst heal? Where was I lying, unless Thou didst come to me? Later with a huge wound I was endangered, but that wound did call for an Almighty Physician." *For Thou, O God, art my refuge.* The Bible Version has it, *my defence,* coming nearer to the LXX. and Vulgate, *my lifter up.* Lifting up, first to grace, and then to glory. And that because *Thou art my merciful God.* For by Thy goodness I was created, by Thine Incarnation I was deified, by Thy conversation I was hallowed, by Thy Passion redeemed, by Thine Ascension glorified. And all this is of Thy mercy, "for the gift of GOD is eternal life;" and, moreover, "not by works of righteousness which we have done, but according to His mercy He saved us." S. Gregory the Great, commenting on the words of the Psalmist, observes, "Let us recall before our eyes the evils which we have done, and ponder how great is that goodness of GOD by which we are tolerated. Let us mark what are the bowels of His loving-kindness, that He does not merely pardon our faults, but promises the kingdom of heaven to penitents even after

A.

Lu.

D. C.

*S. Albertus
Magnus.*

Rom. vi. 23.

Tit. iii. 5.

*S. Greg.
Mag. Hom.
in Evang.
xviii.*

their faults; and let us say, from all the marrow of our hearts, *My merciful God.*"

Therefore:

Glory be to the FATHER, strong and merciful, Whose power and mercy I will sing; glory be to the SON, Who is the Power of the FATHER, Which I will sing; glory be to the HOLY GHOST, Who is the Mercy of the FATHER and the SON, which I set before me as the subject of my song.

As it was in the beginning, is now, and ever shall be: world without end. Amen.

COLLECTS.

O Almighty LORD, Whose power and mercy we laud in the morning season, we beseech Thee, our Strength, to guard us, that we, freed from all blackness of darkness, may be illumined by the morning light. (1.) — *Ludolph.*

O CHRIST the LORD, restrain by the might of Thy power the mighty men that are gathered against me; and as for them that laid wait for Thy soul in the Passion, let their offspring be brought under the yoke of Thy service, that Thou only, O LORD, mayest be confessed the Redeemer of the world, when Thou arisest to help Thy Church. (11.) — *Mozarabic. For the Jews.*

O CHRIST the LORD, the mighty men that laid wait for Thy soul gathered themselves fiercely against Thee, when at the time of Thy Passion the company of the proud rushed upon Thee; we therefore beseech Thee, hearken to the prayer of Thy Church, and take away the bloody sword from the hand of the enemy, that they may feel its edge blunted when they shall know that the doctrine of Thy Faith is preached by them who announce Thee. (11.) — *Mozarabic, Passiontide.*

Deliver us from our enemies, O LORD; and as Thou didst vouchsafe to lay down Thy life for us, save us evermore from them that rise up against us. (11.) — *Mozarabic, Passiontide.*

O CHRIST, SON of GOD, Who, without cause of sin, wast even delivered unto death, and caught in the snare of the hunters; grant that, through Thine unmerited death, the death which we merit may be overcome, that Thou, Who, though innocent, wast given up for us, mayest through the gift of innocency make us come at length in blessedness to Thee. Through Thy mercy. (11.) — *Mozarabic, Passiontide.*

O CHRIST, GOD of our salvation, Who by Thy Passion dost guard our passions, deliver us from the bloodthirsty men and from all our corruptions, that, shunning the deeds of flesh and blood, we may not share in the headlong ruin of the bloodthirsty men, but be added to the number of them that please Thee. Through Thy mercy. (11.) — *Mozarabic, Passiontide.*

The LORD vouchsafe to grant that we, protected by His help, aided by His mercy, glorified by His Resurrection, may with spotless minds lift up His praises in the holy Church. Amen. — *S. Jerome.*

PSALM LX.

TITLE: To the chief musician upon Shushan-eduth, Michtam [or, a golden *Psalm*] of David, to teach, when he strove with Aram-naharaim and with Aram-zobah, when Joab returned, and smote of Edom in the valley of salt twelve thousand. Or, to the Supreme, for the Lily of Testimony, [that is, a lily-shaped instrument of music] a golden Psalm of David, for instruction, when he strove with Aram of the two rivers, and Aram of Zobah, &c.

LXX. Vulgate: To the end, for them who shall be changed. In the inscription of the title, to David for instruction, when he wasted with fire Mesopotamia of Syria and Syria of Sobal, and Joab turned, and smote of Edom in the valley of salt-pits twelve thousand. Syriac Psalter: Which David put forth, saying, If I fall into the hands of Saul, I perish, and took to flight, and they that were with him. To us it expresses the conversion of the Gentiles, and the abolition of Judaism.

ARGUMENT.

ARG. THOMAS. That CHRIST is a convenient bulwark in trouble. The Voice of the Apostles in the Passion of CHRIST. The Voice of CHRIST to the FATHER touching the Jews, and that of every believer. Concerning the devil, and sins, and the evil man. CHRIST prays that the enemies may not prevail to hurt Him. The Voice of the Apostles, when CHRIST suffered. The Prophet, concerning the Person of CHRIST.

VEN. BEDE. *To the end.* He means that in CHRIST the SA-VIOUR. *For them that shall be changed,* doubtless in the manner of which the Apostle speaks, " Ye were sometime darkness, but now light in the LORD." And in what manner they can be changed to this end is explained in order. *In the inscription of the title,* denotes JESUS CHRIST the King. So then they shall be changed, that deserting the devil, they will put their necks under CHRIST the King. He adds, *for doctrine,* to wit, Christian, for it is not enough to believe that CHRIST is a King, unless His doctrine also be kept. *When he wasted with fire Mesopotamia of Syria and Syria of Sobal.* These victories of David imply the triumph of CHRIST over the Gentiles, whom, kindling them with the fire of His love, He delivered from the kingdom of the ancient enemy (which Hadarezer denotes,[1]) and made them tributary to His Faith. And inasmuch as Syria, which in Hebrew is called *Aram,* and is interpreted *Lofty,*[2] implies the pride of the Gentiles, He *burns up* two tribes of *Syria,* Who corrects at once the words and deeds of the Gentiles, that they may bring the tribute of faith and works to the One true King. *And Joab returned and smote of Edom in the valley of salt-pits, twelve thousand.* The Valley of Salt-pits, which in Hebrew is called Ge-mélach, denotes weak and earthly wisdom, wherewith Gentile philosophy and

---

[1] This is an error of Beda. Hadadezer or Hadarezer is "whose help is Hadad." Hadad is the name of a Syrian God, derived from עדד *to shout.* Lat. *Adodus.* Macrob. Saturn. i. 23.

[2] This is correct. אֲרָם *highlands,* from רום *to be high.*

Jewish obstinacy are armed against CHRIST. But by the turning again of Joab (who, by interpretation, is *He is a father*,)[1] both are smitten, as the teacher of the Faith presses more vigorously on them. Gc-melach, then, as it is a region of the Edomites, may denote the savour of Gentile knowledge; but it is better taken of the Jews who shall believe at the end of the world, either because of the twelve thousand, according to the number of the tribes of Israel, or because of the name of Edom, which often means the Jews, whence under its person is said of them, "The elder shall serve the younger." Therefore that people, which is changed from its old errors to the Faith, intreats in the first division that it may be restored by new benefits after the affliction which it has suffered by way of satisfaction: O GOD, Thou hast cast us out, &c. In the second place, after the Diapsalma, it asks that after the tribulation it has endured, it may be led by the LORD into the well-fenced city, seeking that help in trouble may be granted it, which is proved to be possible to GOD only, (That Thy beloved may be delivered,) and so forth.

ÉUSEBIUS OF CÆSAREA. The rejection of the Jewish people, and the calling of the Gentiles.

VARIOUS USES.

Gregorian. Wednesday. Nocturns.
Parisian. Saturday. Nones.
Ambrosian. Friday of First Week. III. Nocturn.
Monastic. Wednesday. I. Nocturn.
Quignon. Wednesday. Terce.
Lyons. Wednesday. Lauds.

ANTIPHONS.

Gregorian. As preceding.
Parisian. Let the poor and needy * give praise unto Thy Name, O LORD.
Ambrosian. As preceding.
Monastic. Be Thou our help, O LORD, * in trouble.
Lyons. The same.
Mozarabic. First verse of the Psalm.

1 O GOD, thou hast cast us out, and scattered us abroad : thou hast also been displeased; O turn thee unto us again.

The mournful character of this Psalm, contrary to what might be looked for from its title, has been noted by all the Fathers who have treated of it. The title itself has been dwelt upon and allegorized by S. Hilary, S. Augustine, Cassiodorus, and many others, but their happiest interpretations have been summed up as above by Beda. It is the key-note by which they pitched their explanation of the brief psalm which succeeds. And first then, let Lorinus tell us why this is not a triumphal chant, but rather a wail. David, looking back to the former times on the sins of the people, enume-

[1] Rather, *The LORD is Father*.

rates the punishments of old time which GoD inflicted upon
it, giving it over in His anger to its enemies, although He
freed it at length in mercy.   Thus the discourse seems not
to be touching the Egyptian captivity, nor that yet to come
in Babylon, but concerning the various wars with which the
Hebrews were harassed in the promised land by divers na-

D. C. tions, especially the Philistines.   *Thou hast cast us out* from
Thy protection, *and destroyed us* (Vulg.) by suffering our
foes to pass our borders, waste our cities, and slay our countrymen.   *Thou hast also been displeased with us,* because ot
our sins.   For the kingdom of Israel was much troubled in
the time of the Judges.   And it holds true of more than this;

B. for GoD, because of Adam's sin, hath *cast us out* of Paradise,
and destroyed us by subjecting us to heat and cold, hunger
and thirst, disease, sorrow, and death; and this not unjustly,
but in His righteous vengeance against those sins with which

**Pseudo-
Hieron.** *Thou art displeased.*   And as it is spoken firstly of the Jewish
people, so it applies to the Christian Church, when GoD tries
her by suffering.   For in no other sense does He cast her

Rom. xi. 2. out, for S. Paul says, "GoD hath not cast away His people
which He foreknew."   Whence also the Voice speaks to the

Jer. i. 10. Prophet Jeremy, "I have set thee to root out, and to pull
down, and to destroy, and to throw down, to build, and to
plant."   As though He had said, "Destroy vices and sins,
build up virtues."   He casts us out and destroys us when we
sin, He has mercy and builds us up when we return to Him

**S. Bonaven-
tura.** in penitence.   Where note, observes S. Bonaventure, that
GoD casts out the bad, by depriving them of grace, whence

Ps. xxxvi.12. it is said, "They are cast down, and shall not be able to
stand."   He will cast them out in time to come, when He

**S. Matt.
xxv. 41.** shall say, "Depart, ye cursed, into everlasting fire."   He
casts out the good, by exposing them to passions, delivered

Ps. cxxiv. 6. whence they say, "Our soul is escaped even as a bird."   By

Ps. xxii. 1. depriving them of temporal blessings, whence, "My GoD,
my GoD, why hast Thou forsaken me?"   He casts out the

Hosea iv. 6. bad from spiritual charges, whence it is written, "Because
thou hast rejected knowledge, I will also reject thee, that
thou shalt be no priest to Me."

O turn Thee unto us again.   This is the cry of the penitent

Prov.xvi.15. in all ages, knowing that only "in the light of the King's
countenance is life."   And He Who bore the weapons of our
warfare for us, and Who made Himself our servant, tells us
that it is we, and not He, that need to be turned.   Wherefore He speaks to each of us who longs to strike a blow for

**1 Sam. xiv.
7.** liberty, "Do all that is in thine heart; turn thee, behold I
am with thee according to thy heart."   But the LXX. and
Vulgate have here not a prayer, but a thankful confession of
His goodness.   They read, *Thou hast pitied us.*   Wherefore

**Deut. xxxii.
39.** that Eternal FATHER of all, Who hath said, "I kill, and I
make alive; I wound, and I heal," so *casts us out and
destroys* us, as yet to *pity us* in His anger.   For He destroyed

the temple of Jerusalem, but gave instead the Heavenly   H.
City to the Saints. He cast out from the working of the
law, but, justifying the ungodly by faith, gave him the justification of faith; He dissolved the earthly kingdom, but
made us kings in heaven. So mercy hath followed on displeasure, whilst an exceeding weight of eternal blessings com-
pensates for the loss of earthly things present. And so too
speaks Bernard of Morlaix :

> O retributio ! stat brevis actio, vita perennis :   Bernard.
Cluniac.
Rhythm.
> O retributio ! cœlica mansio stat lue plenis.

**2 Thou hast moved the land, and divided it : heal
the sores thereof, for it shaketh.**

It is spoken of the fiery trials of Christians, when GOD   P.
moved all the whole Church and *troubled* it by the fierce persecutions of tyrants, so that the cry of the faithful went up
that He would *heal its sores*, because it *shook* under the
storm, though it could not be overthrown, because founded
on the rock. And so the cry of the suffering Egyptian
Church is heard still in the words of her primeval Liturgy. Liturg. S.
Marci.
"Help them that are in prison, or in mines, or in courts of justice, or with sentence given against them, or in bitter slavery,
or tribute, have mercy on all, free all; for Thou art our GOD,
He that sets free the bound, He that raises those that are in
misery, the Hope of the hopeless, the succour of the defenceless, the Resurrection of the fallen, the harbour of the tem-
pest-tossed, the avenger of the afflicted." It is also spoken of
sinful man, who is of the earth, earthy. GOD *moves* and Ricard.
breaks up the hard soil of the heart by His husbandmen, the Hampol.
S. Albertus
preachers of the Gospel, convincing the guilty of sin, and Magnus.
making them *shake* with fear of judgment to come. And   Ay.
only He who has made us *sore* with that sword of the Spirit
which He wields, can heal us again with His grace.

**3 Thou hast showed thy people heavy things :
thou hast given us a drink of deadly wine.**

Or, *hard things.* For CHRIST, by His teachings and His   R.
sufferings, has shown His people an example which they find
hard and painful to follow so long as they are not conformed
to Him. Hard for His whole mystical Body, the Church, in
time of persecution, which "all that live godly in CHRIST   D. C.
JESUS shall suffer." Hard for the individual soul, which has 2 Tim. iii.12.
to learn that GOD "scourgeth every son whom He receiveth." Heb xii. 6.
Wherefore we read of the sinner crying out,

> Woe is me ! what is existence below,   The Hymn
O quam glo-
rificum.
> Trouble on trouble, and blow upon blow ;
> What is in this world save sorrowful years,
> Much tribulation, and plentiful tears ?

And the Master answers:

> Wouldst thou but ponder the promise I make,
> Willingly, joyfully, pain wouldst thou take;
> That in My kingdom the joys thou may'st see
> Of the Confessors who suffered for Me.

Thou hast given us a drink of deadly wine. Not so, for the "wine of the wrath of GOD, which is poured out without mixture into the cup of His indignation," is for the finally impenitent only. The Bible Version is nearer the Hebrew, and terms it "*wine of astonishment*," (יַיִן תַּרְעֵלָה) or *intoxication*. And then it may be taken of that Cup of the Passion promised to the sons of Zebedee, that which so numbs the sense of pain, that the Martyrs are ready to bear all so long as they may drink it, saying, "They have stricken me, and I was not sick: they have beaten me, and I felt it not; when shall I awake, I will seek it yet again." And so S. Bonaventure, singing of the sorrows of the Passion:

Rev. xiv. 10.

Prov. xxiii. 35.

The Hymn In passione Domini.

> Hæc omnia nos satient,
> Et dulciter inebrient.

A.

Or, if we take the LXX. and Vulgate, *wine of compunction* or of *goading*, we get another beautiful meaning. Of *goading* is what? Not of killing; for it was not a killing that destroyeth, but a medicine that smarteth. And more; we *goad* oxen that they may advance in the furrows; and the stimulant for Christians in their path is the wine of GOD, the wondrous chalice of the Holy Eucharist.

4 Thou hast given a token for such as fear thee : that they may triumph because of the truth.

And that Cup is the *token*, as it is written in another Psalm of the other species of the Sacrament, " He hath given meat to them that fear Him, He shall ever be mindful of His covenant." And so runs the hymn:

Ps. cxi. 5.

> Bread of the world, in mercy broken,
> Wine of the world, in mercy shed ;
> By Whom the words of life were spoken,
> And in Whose death our sins are dead ;
> Look on the heart by sorrow broken,
> Look on the tears by sinners shed,
> And be Thy feast to us the token,
> That by Thy grace our souls are fed.

Pseudo-Hieron.

The quasi-Jerome explains this *token* of Holy Baptism, the especial sign given to them who seek to serve the LORD. But the majority take it of the various warnings given to the Apostles of impending persecution. *That they may triumph because of the truth.* If we take this of the Holy Eucharist, it will denote the reward of them who believe CHRIST's words touching It, as the hymn runs :

The Hymn *Adoro Te devote.*

> Credo quidquid dixit Dei Filius,
> Nihil veritatis Verbo verius :

and who object not, " This is a hard saying ;. who can hear it ?" but hear the promise to the Church of Pergamus, " To him that overcometh, will I give to eat of the hidden manna." But if we follow the Bible Version and the Targum, we shall get a fresh idea. *Thou hast given a banner to them that fear Thee, that it may.be displayed because of the truth.* What that banner is, the Church proclaims in her hymn for Passion Sunday :

S. John vi. 60.
Rev. ii. 17.

> The Royal Banners forward go,
> The Cross shines forth in mystic glow.

The Hymn *Vexilla Regis prodeunt.*

And again, in another hymn :

> Crux cœlestis, signum victoriæ,
> Belli robur, et palma gloriæ.

The Hymn *Salve Crux.*

But the LXX. and Vulgate are totally different from the English in the latter clause of this verse ; they read : " Thou hast given a token to them that fear thee, *that they may flee from the face of the bow.*"[1] And that bow, observes S. Augustine, is the Judgment of GOD. " For the time is come that judgment must begin at the House of GOD, and if it first begin at us, what shall the end be of them that obey not the Gospel of GOD?" The bow is bended, still in menacing posture it is, not yet in aiming. And see what there is in the bow : is there not an arrow to be shot forward? The string, however, is stretched back in a contrary direction to that in which it is to be shot ; and the more the stretching thereof hath gone backward, with the greater swiftness it starteth forward. The more the judgment is deferred, with so much the greater swiftness it is to come. Therefore even for temporal tribulations let us give GOD thanks, because He hath given to.His people a sign, *that they should flee from the face of the bow.* And that too remembering, as Gerhohus aptly points out, that " Thy arrows are very sharp, and the people shall be subdued unto Thee, even in the midst among the king's enemies."

A.

1 S. Pet. iv. 17.

S. Greg.
Mag. Moral.
xix. 28.

G.

Ps. xlv. 6.

5 Therefore were thy beloved delivered : help me with thy right hand, and hear me.

Rather, with A. V., LXX.; and Vulgate, *That Thy beloved may be delivered,* which is the reason why the token is given, as declared in the vision of Ezekiel. " Go through the midst of the city, through the midst of Jerusalem, and set a mark

Z.

Ezek. ix. 4.

---

[1] Reading נֵסׄ instead of קֹשֶׁט.

upon the foreheads of the men that sigh and that cry for all the abominations that be done in the midst thereof. And to the others He said in my hearing, Go ye after him through the city, and smite; let not your eye spare, neither have ye pity. Slay utterly old and young, both maids, and little children, and women ; but come not near any man upon whom

Rupert.Tuit. is the mark." And the mark is the Thau, or Cross set on us not with ink, but with the Blood of CHRIST and with the

G.   HOLY GHOST. *Help me with Thy right hand.* Not with Thy left hand, says Gerhohus, wherein are riches and glory, but with Thy right hand, wherein is length of days. Give me then little or much, or nought, from Thy left hand, according to Thy will, as Thou knowest to be expedient for me. But open Thy right hand abundantly, and fill all things living with plenteousness of blessing, whereby Thy blessed elect and beloved may be set at Thy right hand in the ·Judgment.

R.   *And hearken unto me,* praying for perseverance in the right way.

6 GOD hath spoken in his holiness, I will rejoice, and divide Sichem : and mete out the valley of Succoth.

C.   He hath spoken in the Person of His Holy One, when
S. John i.   "the Word was made Flesh, and dwelt among us," and that
14.   by the truths of the Gospel. And the Incarnate Word says,
Heb. i. 2.
H.   *I will rejoice.* For two reasons, because His "delight is in
Ps. i. 2.   the law" of His FATHER, and therefore He "rejoiceth as a
Ps. xix. 5.   giant to run His course," and also because He rejoices as the
D. C.   Bridegroom in the triumphs of His Bride the Church, and in pouring His blessing on her children. And so it is written,
    "Yea, I will rejoice over them to do them good." *And*
Jer. xxxii.   *divide Sichem.* Where note that Shechem was the first rest-
41.   ing-place of Abraham in Canaan. Afterwards it was bought
Gen. xii. 6.   by Jacob with money, then further taken out of the hand of
Gen. xxxiii.   the Amorite with his sword and his bow. Lying between
19.   Mount Gerizim and Mount Ebal, it was the place where the
Gen. xlviii.   Israelites heard the second promulgation of the Law. It was
22.   the scene of the first schism and rebellion against the com-
Josh. viii. 33. monwealth of Israel, when Abimelech was made king there,
Judg. ix.   and also of the second, when Jeroboam I. revolted from Reho-
1 Kings xii.   boam. And it appears again in the Gospels as Sychar, the
16.   place of Jacob's Well, where the LORD talked with the
S. John iv.   woman of Samaria. In this last page in the Scripture history
    of the place many commentators have seen the fulfilment of
H.   the prediction. Others, with S. Hilary, take it to mean the division of the Judgment Day, fitly shadowed by the blessings and warnings of the Law pronounced from the two mountains which bordered the valley. And others again have found in the meaning of the word *Shechem*, which is

A.   "shoulder," a reference to the burden which CHRIST shares

with His people. It is, says Cassiodorus, the burden of **C.**
divine devotion, which is granted to all by heavenly division.
This is the burden, without which we fall, bearing which we
stand upright, of which it is written, "My yoke is easy, and **S. Matt. xi.**
My burden is light." *And mete out the valley of Succoth.* **30.**
As Shechem, given up from the time of the Captivity to an
alien and idolatrous race, typifies the Gentile Church, so the **Gen. xxxiii.**
valley of Succoth, where Jacob made "booths" (*Succoth*) for **17.**
his cattle, denotes the Hebrews subject to CHRIST. In the
mention of the *valley*, Cardinal Hugo finds a reference to **Hugo Card.**
the Christian grace of humility, and in that of the *booths* or
tabernacles, the tents of the great army of the Church militant, of which Balaam spoke in prophecy, "How goodly are **Num. xxiv.**
thy tents, O Jacob!" **5.**

7 Gilead is mine, and Manasses is mine : Ephraim
also is the strength of my head; Judah is my lawgiver;

And in those words *Gilead is mine*, the Church has always
set forth the glory of the Martyrs, for Gilead means the
"Heap of Witness." So then, taking it in close union with
the preceding verse, we may say with a poet of our own, as
he dilates on the bliss of the "cloud of witnesses:" **Heb. xii. 1.**

> Here may the band, that now in triumph shines, **Giles**
> And that (before they were invested thus) **Fletcher:**
> In earthly bodies carried heavenly minds, **Christ's**
> Pitch round about, in order glorious, **Victory.**
> Their sunny tents, and houses luminous;
> All their eternal days in songs employing,
> Joying their end, without end of their joying;
> While their Almighty Prince destruction is destroying.

And Manasses is mine. And as Manasseh ("forgetful-
ness") was so named by Joseph, because, said he, "GOD hath
made me forget all my toil," so this is spoken of CHRIST, Who **Gen. xli. 51.**
saith to the penitent sinner, "I will not remember thy sins," **Isa. xliii. 25.**
Who saith to the soul which He would win for Himself,
"Forget also thine own people, and thy father's house," Who **Ps. xlv. 11.**
saith to His Church purified by affliction, "Thou shalt forget **Isa. liv. 4.**
the shame of thy youth, and shalt not remember the reproach **Ric. Ham-**
of thy widowhood any more." And Manasses is His also, **pol.**
because His contemplative saints "press towards the mark **Philip. iii.13.**
of their high calling," forgetting those things which are be- **Jansen.**
hind. As also do the Confessors, who abandon wealth and **Gandav.**
home for the Gospel. *Ephraim also is the strength of my head.* **L.**
And that because the Gentiles, though the younger in the
Church, are its strength, as Ephraim was preferred to his
elder brother Manasses. Again, as Ephraim denotes "fruitfulness," it will imply the Saints of active life. So the Holy **Liturg. S.**
Eastern Church in her august Liturgy prays, "Remember, **Chrysost.**
LORD, them that bear fruit, and do good deeds in Thy holy

Church, and that remember the poor." Yet again, hear S.

A. Augustine: Ephraim is interpreted fruitfulness. Mine, he saith, is fruitfulness, and this fruitfulness is the strength of my Head. For my Head is CHRIST. And whence is fruitfulness the strength of Him? Because unless a grain were to fall into the earth it would not be multiplied, alone it would remain. Fall then to earth did CHRIST in His Passion, and there followed fruitbearing in the Resurrection. *Judah is my lawgiver. My king,* say the LXX. and Vulgate.

Heb. vii. 14.
S. Matt. xxvii. 37.
Numb. xxiv. 17.
Deut. xxxii. 12.
Gal. iii. 19.
S. Alb. Mag.
Judg. i. 2.

My sceptre, or else *my leading-staff* of battle, in stricter accordance with the Hebrew. However we take it, the reference is alike to the LORD, Who "sprang out of Judah," Who is alike "King of the Jews," the "Sceptre" which rose out of Israel, Who "alone did lead" His people, and Who is the Mediator, in Whose hand the Law was given. And so it is written of the Ascension of the LORD, "Judah shall go up: behold, I have delivered the land into his hand."

> 8 Moab is my wash-pot; over Edom will I cast out my shoe : Philistia, be thou glad of me.

Where note that the humbling of Moab follows immediately on the exaltation of Judah, as in Balaam's prophecy.

Numb. xxiv. 17.

D.C.
Jer. xiv. 8.

"A Sceptre shall rise out of Israel, and shall smite all the corners of Moab." But the LXX. and Vulgate both read here, *Moab is the pot of my hope.* Wherein Dionysius à Rykel sees a prophecy of the descent of CHRIST, the "Hope of Israel," from Ruth the Moabitess, a vessel elected of GOD. Nor let it be thought unfit, he adds, that CHRIST should be denoted by Moab. For Moab, by interpretation, is "from

S. John xvi. 28.

the father,"[1] by which CHRIST may be understood, Who said of Himself, "I came forth from the FATHER." If we take here the reading of the Syriac Psalter, *Moab is the washing of my feet,* we shall be reminded of the lowliness with which the LORD washed the feet of His Apostles. And

Deut. xxiii. 3.

whereas the Law declares, "A Moabite shall not enter into the congregation of the LORD," the Æthiopic Psalter here singularly reads, *Moab is my priest, my hope,* pointing to that prophecy of Isaiah concerning the Gentiles, "I will also

Isa. lxvi. 21.
B.
Jer. i. 13;
Ezek. xi. 3;
xxiv. 6; Joel
ii. 6, marg.

take of them for priests and Levites." But others also explain the *pot,* of those tried by the fire of suffering at the hands of the evil (of whom a pot is a frequent Scriptural type) till, when all the scum has been removed, only wholesome and refreshing food remains in the vessel. *Over Edom will I cast out my shoe.* And here the commentators have devised various reasons for this *casting out* of the *shoe.* Some interpret it as a sign of claiming the inheritance of the land, others conversely (with reference to Ruth iv. 7,) as a renunciation of such a claim. Again, it is explained as a token of

---

[1] מוֹאָב, literally, "seed of the father."

superiority, as though Edom were compelled to feel the shoe _{Josh. x. 24.}
of his conqueror on his neck, or, more peacefully, to become _{S. Matt. iii.}
the disciple of a Master "Whose shoes" he is "not worthy _{11.}
to bear." Mystically, it is explained by S. Gregory the _{S. Greg.}
Great: What is meant by Edom, save the Gentiles, what by _{Mag. Hom. in Evang.}
the shoe, save the taking of mortality? The LORD, there- _{i. 8.}
fore, declares that He casts His shoe over Edom, by making
Himself known in the flesh to the Gentiles. Where note, _{Ay.}
that by the shoe, which is made of the skins of dead animals,
our mortal nature is typified, which CHRIST took, the latchet
of which is that unspeakable union of the Word to human
nature, so great a mystery that the Baptist, unable to fathom
it, confesses, "Whose shoe's latchet I am not worthy to un- _{S. John i. 27.}
loose." And the holy author of the "Pricke of Conscience" _{Ric. Hamp.}
adds yet another interpretation, that CHRIST sends His mes-
sengers, "shod with the preparation of the Gospel of peace," _{Eph. vi. 15.}
into heathen lands. Wherefore is said, "How beautiful are _{Cant. vii. 1.}
thy feet with shoes, O prince's daughter." *Philistia, be thou
glad of me.* Here, as constantly, the LXX. and Vulgate
turn the proper name into a common one, and render it *the
aliens,* and further translate the remainder, *are subjected to
me.* And thus it speaks of the conversion of the Gentiles to
the Gospel, so that they should be "no longer strangers and _{Eph. ii. 19.}
foreigners, but fellow-citizens of the saints, and of the household of GOD."

9 Who will lead me into the strong city : who
will bring me into Edom?

S. Augustine, translating thus, *the city of standing round,* _{A.}
explains the verse of the great heathen population lying all
round the small Jewish people, and later, round the Christian
Church. The Carthusian sees a reference to the conversion _{D. C.}
of Rome, emphatically the *strong city,* by the preaching of
the Prince of the Apostles, and also to that text of Isaiah,
"The lofty city, He layeth it low." Others, as Cassiodorus, _{Isa. xxvi. 5.}
Ayguan, and Richard of Hampole, see in the *strong city* the
heavenly Jerusalem, the longing of pilgrims here on earth.

> Urbs cœlestis, Urbs beata,
> Supra Petram collocata,
> Urbs in portu satis tuto,
> De longinquo te saluto,
> Te saluto, te suspiro,
> Te affecto, te requiro.

_{Hildeb. Ven. The Hymn *Extra portam.*}

Who will bring us in? Let another sweet singer answer
the question :

> CHRISTE, Palma bellatorum, hoc in municipium,
> Introduc me, post solutum militare cingulum ;
> Fac consortem donativi beatorum civium.

_{S. Pet. Dam. The Hymn *Ad perennis vitæ fontem.*}

But why, after expressing a desire for the Celestial city, come back to *Edom*, which typifies earth? Because, observes Ayguan, the number of the Gentiles must be filled up, before the kingdom of GOD can come, and the Church prays that she may be brought into Edom, in order to hasten that blessed time.

Ay.

10 Hast not thou cast us out, O GOD : wilt not thou, O GOD, go out with our hosts?

A.

This is the cry of the Martyrs, who die without seeing the dominion of the Church widened by their valour, or any such results as came of the wars of Moses and Joshua, and David. Was He then by any means forsaking, because He was not marching forth with their hosts? By not marching forth with their hosts, did He not the more lead down the Church even unto Idumæa, lead down the Church into the city of standing round? For if the Church chose to war and to use the sword, she would seem to be fighting for life present; but because she was despising life present, therefore there was made a heap of witness for the life which shall be.

11 O be thou our help in trouble : for vain is the help of man.

B.

And therefore it is not for life, abundance, peace, or any such gifts which man can take away or leave with us, that the Church prays, but only that He will bring her safe through the water-floods, and bestow those blessings which are eternal, that our very tribulations may be the way of our salvation.

12 Through GOD will we do great acts : for it is he that shall tread down our enemies.

Wherefore the Holy Eastern Church speaks thus in her Great Compline that defiance of the infidel which she chants as a war-song in Lent alone.

Horolog.

GOD is with us, know it, ye nations, and be made weak.
For GOD is with us.
Hear ye, to the ends of the earth.
For GOD is with us.
Though ye were strong, ye were made weak.
For GOD is with us.
And if again ye shall strengthen yourselves, again shall ye be weakened.
For GOD is with us.
And if ye shall devise any counsel, the LORD will scatter it.
For GOD is with us.
And if ye speak any word, it shall not abide in you.
For GOD is with us.
And we will not be afraid of your fear, neither will we be troubled,
For GOD is with us.

And therefore:
Glory be to the FATHER, Who delivereth His beloved; and to the SON, Who is the Right Hand of the FATHER, wherewith He helps His people; and to the HOLY GHOST, Who is Himself the Love wherewith GOD loves His elect.

As it was in the beginning, is now, and ever shall be: world without end. Amen.

COLLECTS.

Most merciful GOD, save Thy suppliant people with the help of Thy right hand: that while in tribulation it is roused to good works, it may ever be comforted by Thy grace. (1.) *MSS. Thomas.*

Almighty and most merciful GOD, restorer and ruler of mankind, Who puttest down Thy faithful in order to raise them up, Who humblest them to bring them to the kingdom of heaven; keep with Thy loving mercy the ranks of them that believe in Thee; that flying to the remedy of confession of Thee, they may, when their sores are healed, attain, through Thy bounty, to the enjoyment of everlasting felicity. (1.) *Ludolph.*

Help us, O LORD, in trouble, and hear us to our salvation; that Thy beloved may be made anew by that same Hand which made them, so that by the fervour of that Arm, whereby they have been broken, they may attain the healing which they desire. (11.) *Mozarabic.*

Give us help, O LORD, in trouble, for vain is the help of man, in Thee we shall do great acts, Who strengthenest Thy servants and bringest the enemies to nought. (11.) *Mozarabic.*

Save Thy people, O LORD, with Thy right hand, and as Thou didst give the Cross as a token to them that fear Thee, so grant the fullest worthiness of faith, that Thou mayest convert and receive them whom Thou didst cast out in their sins, and do Thou, Who wast made the price of sinners, vouchsafe needful help in trouble; and Thyself bring to nought the enemy which troubleth. Thyself lead Thy redeemed into the strong city. (11.) *Mozarabic.*

PSALM LXI.

TITLE: To the Chief Musician upon Neginah, a Psalm of David. LXX. and Vulgate: To the end, in the hymns, a Psalm of David. Or, To the Supreme, for the stringed instruments of David. Mozarabic: To the end. A Psalm of David. A prayer with good grace. Syriac Psalter: Of David, when Jonathan revealed unto him the counsel of Saul plotting his death. Spiritually, it means prayer and thanksgiving. Arabic Psalter: Of David; in the praises, touching the last end.

ARGUMENT.

ARG. THOMAS. That CHRIST is a most strong tower set against the face of the enemy. The Voice of the Church. The Voice of Paul the Apostle to the LORD concerning CHRIST. The Voice of the whole Church, asking that it may be sheltered under the covering of CHRIST's wings. The Voice of CHRIST to the FATHER. The Prophet gives thanks. And information who they are that shall believe in CHRIST.

VEN. BEDE. *In the hymns*, is Greek, and is interpreted, *In the praises*, because the whole Psalm will sound the laudations of CHRIST. In the first part the faithful people makes its prayer from the ends of the earth, that its petition may be heard, in order that, persevering in the holy Church, it may be protected under the covering of His wings, *Hear my crying, O God.* In the second, it gives thanks, because He hath given His heritage to the righteous, and hallowed His Name for everlasting glory: whence it promises that it will ever give thanks to the LORD. *For Thou, O Lord, hast heard my desires.*

EUSEBIUS OF CÆSAREA. Prayer with thanksgiving.

S. ATHANASIUS. A Psalm of address, and prayer, and supplication.

VARIOUS USES.

Gregorian. Wednesday. Matins. [Common of Apostles, II. Nocturn. All Saints, III. Nocturn.]

Monastic. The same.

Parisian. Friday. Matins.

Lyons. Wednesday. Compline.

Ambrosian. Friday of First Week. Matins.

Quignon. Friday. Nones.

Eastern Church. Mesorion of Third Hour.

ANTIPHONS.

Gregorian. Ferial. As preceding. [Common of Apostles. Thou hast given an heritage * to them that fear Thy Name, O LORD. All Saints. O LORD, Hope of the Saints, and their strong tower, Thou hast given a heritage to them that fear Thy Name * and they shall dwell in Thy tabernacle for ever.]

Parisian. As Psalm lix.

Ambrosian. The same.

Mozarabic. From the ends of the earth have I cried unto Thee * O LORD.

1 Hear my crying, O GOD : give ear unto my prayer.

In the double petition of the first verse, the commentators find a reference to temporal and spiritual, to outer and inner needs. For *crying*, say they, may be addressed to man, while *prayer* belongs to GOD only. *Hear my crying* in such wise, that men may see that Thou deliverest me from

evil. *Give ear unto my prayer*, by storing within me Thy   G.
hidden treasure. *Hear my crying*, that without, there may
be lamps shining with clear light, unquenchable. *Give ear
unto my prayer*, that oil may secretly abound in the vessels
within till the coming of the Bridegroom. *Hear my prayer*,
that when seeking abroad for my Bridegroom, Thy Son, I   Cant. i. 7.
may not turn aside by the flocks of His companions. *Give
ear unto my prayer*, that when I find Him, I may hold Him   Cant. iii. 4.   ·
and not let Him go.

2 From the ends of the earth will I call upon
thee : when my heart is in heaviness.

Whether these words apply literally to David's wanderings   L.
around En-gedi, on the very frontier of the kingdom of Israel,
or, as the Greek Fathers prefer, to the Jews of the Captivity   Z.
in Babylon, the mystical interpretation is clear. Spoken of
the Church, she appears as that Queen who " came from the
uttermost parts of the earth to hear the wisdom of Solomon ;"   S. Matt. xii.
spoken of Saints, wherever they may be, they *call from the*   42.
ends of the earth, because of their communion in that Body   C.
which is spread everywhere ; spoken of penitents, it tells how
they turn again when they have come to the end of earthly
pleasure and vanity, and have found no peace. And fitly the   Ric. Hamp.
ends of the earth, for indulgence in earthly sin puts us far from
God. *When my heart is in heaviness.* And thus it is the
cry of the persecuted Church, when the Roman empire from
India to Spain, from Syria to Æthiopia, reeked with the   P.
blood of martyrs. Again, it is the cry of the soul in time of
temptation, for no one can be crowned unless he conquer,
nor conquer unless he fight, nor fight unless he have enemies   Pet. Lom-
and temptations.   bard.

3 O set me up upon the rock that is higher than
I : for thou hast been my hope, and a strong tower
for me against the enemy.

Here, as so often, the LXX. and Vulgate read the verse
in the past tense. *Thou hast set me up upon the Rock.* "And
that Rock," says the Apostle, " was Christ." *That is higher*   1 Cor. x. 4.
than I. For " God hath given Him a Name which is above   Phil. ii. 9.
every name." Now, therefore, remarks S. Augustine, we   A.
perceive who is crying from the ends of the earth. Let us   S. Matt.
call to mind the Gospel: "Upon this Rock I will build My   xvi. 18.
Church." Therefore she crieth from the ends of the earth
whom He hath willed to be builded upon a Rock. Here
in the LXX. and Vulgate, and Æthiopic, are the words,
Thou hast led me down because Thou hast been my hope.   C.
Down into that future rest which He hath promised to His   D. C.
Saints, out of this present exile, and that by the way of Thy
commandments. He leadeth down as being the Leader, and

N 2

A.
S. Albertus
Magnus.

Eccl. iv. 12.

Isa. v. 2.
Prov. xviii.
10.
G.

on Himself leadeth as being the Way, and to Himself leadeth home as being the Country. *For Thou hast been my hope.*
Because Thou leadest not any save those who hope in Thee.
Thou hast been my hope of pardon to release my sins, *my hope*
of grace to do good works henceforward, *my hope* of glory in
winning the prize. With this threefold hope, as a threefold
cord, Thou leadest me to Thyself, "And a threefold cord is
not quickly broken." *And a strong tower for me against the
enemy.* Because the FATHER hath built a tower, even His
SON, in the midst of His fruitful vineyard, and "the Name
of the LORD is a strong tower; the righteous runneth into it,
and is safe." And we are not merely safe there, adds Gerhohus, but we can hurl the darts of work and prayer from
its battlements to destroy our enemy.

4 I will dwell in thy tabernacle for ever : and my
trust shall be under the covering of thy wings.

B.

2 Sam. xi.
11.

H.
Rev. iii. 12.

S. Albertus
Magnus.

Mal. iv. 2.

S. Matt.
xxiii. 37.

If we take *for ever* to mean, as it often does, till the
end of this world, the promise is that of abiding in the camp
of Christian warfare till the battle is won. Not turning away
to the enjoyment of worldly pleasure, but saying with Uriah
the Hittite, "The ark, and Israel, and Judah, abide in tents,
and my lord Joab, and the servants of my lord, are encamped
in the open fields; shall I then go into mine house, to eat
and to drink, and to lie with my wife? as thou livest, and as
thy soul liveth, I will not do this thing." If *for ever* is to
be taken in the higher sense of eternity, the reference will
then be, as S. Hilary explains it, to the abiding of the Saints
in heaven, as it is written, "Him that overcometh will I make
a pillar in the temple of My GOD, and he shall go no more
out.". *And my trust shall be under the covering of Thy wings.*
The wings of the LORD, observes S. Albert the Great, are
justice and mercy. Under justice the righteous are sheltered,
that they may not presume, under mercy the sinners, that
they may not despair. And He, Who hath "healing in His
wings," desires to gather us under their protection, "even
as a hen gathereth her chickens under her wings." There is
heat in the world, touchingly says S. Augustine, but there
is great shade under the wings of GOD.

5 For thou, O LORD, hast heard my desires : and
hast given an heritage unto those that fear thy Name.

Ps. ii. 8.

Heb. i. 2.
Rom. viii.
17.

What was that desire? The prayer of CHRIST for the
salvation of the world. "Desire of Me, and I shall give Thee
the heathen for Thine inheritance, and the utmost parts of the
earth for Thy possession." Him then the FATHER "hath
appointed heir of all things." And because He has made us
joint-heirs with Him, these words are true of all those who
fear His Name. Especially the Western Church has de-

lighted to use them of the Apostles, who not only inherit with CHRIST the dominion over the Gentiles and the glories of heaven, but whose better heritage is CHRIST Himself. And so Santolius Victorinus, speaking of S. Barnabas:

> Quem propter, agro vendito,
> Opes caducas deseris,
> Magno rependens fœnore,
> En fundus ipse fit tuus.

The Hymn *Cœlo datur quiescere.*

6 Thou shalt grant the King a long life : that his years may endure throughout all generations.

The marginal reading of the Bible Version is here more exact, and agrees with the LXX. and Vulgate. *Thou shalt add days to the days of the King.* To the days of this world Thou shalt add the days of eternity. And they are rightly called *days of the King*, which shall be formed from His glory. Even here we walk in the light of the King's days, those which our King and Sun of Righteousness, shrouded in the cloud of mortality, has enlightened by His teaching and example. He will *add* yet brighter *days* to us, which that same Sun and King of Righteousness, now that the cloud of mortality is withdrawn, frames in the calm glory of His supreme Godhead, wherein "the light of the moon is as the light of the sun," because assumed Manhood shines in GOD the SON with that glory which He, the Sun of Righteousness, had in His Godhead, before the world was made. The children of night and darkness know not these days, because every one that doeth evil hateth the light. But the Saints long for them, knowing that, as it is written, "One day in Thy courts is better than a thousand," and desire that light of which the Cluniac sings:

Ay.

G.

Isa. xxx. 26.

Ps. lxxxiv. 10.

> Luce replebere jam sine vespere, jam sine lunâ,
> Lux nova, lux ea, lux erit aurea, lux erit una.

Bern. Clun. Rhythm.

That his years may endure throughout all generations. Because the Manhood of CHRIST, united to the Godhead of the WORD, shares by virtue of the Hypostatic union in the Divine attributes, and thus fulfils the prophecy of Micah. "Thou, Bethlehem Ephratah . . . . out of thee shall He come forth unto Me that is to be ruler in Israel; whose goings forth have been from of old, from everlasting."

Mic. v. 2.

7 He shall dwell before GOD for ever : O prepare thy loving mercy and faithfulness, that they may preserve him.

And this is spoken not only of CHRIST's throne in heaven, but also of every Saint who treads in His steps. Where note, remarks Ayguan, that three things are of the essence of formal blessedness, to wit, clear vision, true fruition, and

Ay.

firm or eternal hold. For who could be truly blessed, if he were not assured of the eternity of his blessedness? Since he would always dread a fall, and as such a dread is in itself a punishment, the blessed would be in a state of punishment, which is a contradiction. So they are made sure of that eternity, by looking on the divine essence in which it shines. That is the reason for adding *before God*, as though to say, Their inheritance is eternal, and they are sure of it, because they are before GOD, and their "eyes see the King in His beauty."

Isa. xxxiii.
17.

O prepare Thy loving mercy and faithfulness, that they may preserve him. So, it is a prayer for the grace of perseverance, lest any should "come short of the glory of GOD," through despair of His mercy, or distrust of His faithfulness. But the LXX. and Vulgate are different from this. They read, *Who shall seek His mercy and truth?* And the answer is, No one. For in the sight of GOD there will be no more sorrow, and therefore no more need of mercy, "for GOD shall wipe away all tears from their eyes." They will not seek for truth, because the Truth Himself will be present to them in open vision, and in that day they shall ask Him nothing. And thus S. Peter Damiani:

Rom. iii. 23.

S. Albertus
Magnus.

Rev. xxi. 4.

S. John xvi.
23.

The Hymn
Ad perennis
vitæ fontem.

To their first estate return they, freed from every mortal sore,
And the Truth, for ever present, ever lovely, they adore,
Drawing from that living fountain living sweetness evermore.

8 So will I alway sing praise unto thy Name : that I may daily perform my vows.

And while this verse has been truly interpreted of all Christians, performing their baptismal vows and praising GOD by daily holiness of life; and also of the Heavenly City, of which it is written, "Joy and gladness shall be found therein, thanksgiving, and the voice of melody;" and yet again of the Church on earth, which has daily, through the ages, sung praise to GOD in the words of David; it is not strange that others should have seen in it the pledge of due fulfilment of the duties of the Religious and priestly life. Wherefore, says the Master of the Sentences, at the end of the ecclesiastical offices is said, "Bless we the LORD," figuring this divine praise after the present life, because in that which is to come we shall ever praise GOD for all good works which we do here. And this duty of daily recitation of the Church's offices is a primary one, because, as S. Bernard observes, nothing which thou canst offer to GOD pleases Him, if that to which thou art bound be neglected. Therefore, teaches Arvisinet, Remember thou art doing the work of Angels; believe that thou art standing with them before My throne; and with them worship, praise, bless, love. Imagine that thou art praying with Me in the garden of olives, and if thy

Lu.

Ay.

Isa. li. 3.

L.

Pet. Lomb.
gloss. in loc.

S. Bernard.

Arvisinet,
Mem. Vit.
Sacerd.

mind be drawn to sleep, hear Me. Couldst not thou, my son,
watch with Me one hour? Watch and pray.
  And therefore:
  Glory be to the FATHER, Who hath set me upon the Rock;
and to the SON, Who is the Rock; and to the HOLY GHOST,
the LORD of loving-mercy and faithfulness.
  As it was in the beginning, is now, and ever shall be:
world without end. Amen.

COLLECTS.

  O GOD, most merciful Comforter of our heaviness, protect Ludolph.
Thy household from the face of the enemy, that guarded by MSS.
Thee, the strong tower, it may attain to inhabit the everlasting tabernacles. (1.)
  The LORD vouchsafe to grant us: that conformed to His S. Jerome.
glory, and delivered from the corruption of the second death,
we may sing to His Name in the presentation of our spiritual
vows. (1.)

PSALM LXII.

TITLE: To the Chief Musician, to Jeduthun.[1] A Psalm of David.
LXX. and Vulgate: To the end, for Idithun, a Psalm of David.
Mozarabic: To the Conqueror, for Idithun, a Psalm of David.

ARGUMENT.

  ARG. THOMAS. That CHRIST is the Helper, in Whom the assembly of the Church ought to hope. The Voice of the Church, or
of any one turned from evil to good. The Voice of CHRIST touching the Passion. The Prophet, concerning the Passion of CHRIST,
or concerning the Jews.
  VEN. BEDE. Idithun is interpreted *Leaping over* (*them*), that is,
the lovers of the world: for here is brought in the person of a
soldier of CHRIST, who hath abandoned the desires of the world,

[1] On this name Jeduthun, see
under Psalm xxxix. The interpretation "leaping over," though
a favourite one with mediæval
writers, is incorrect. The root is
יָדָה, *to praise*, and the word is
thus akin to Judah. The other
interpretation appears in S. Gregory the Great, (Hom. in Evang.
29:) "Veniendo ad redemp-
tionem nostram, quosdam ut ita
dicam saltus fecit. De cœlo
venit in uterum, de utero venit

in præsepe, de præsepe venit in
crucem, de cruce venit in sepul-
crum, de sepulcro rediit in cœlum." And so S. Notker, in a
sequence for Ascension:

Huic nomen extat conveniens
  Idithun.
Nam transilivit omnes strenue
  montes colliculosque Bethel.
Saltum de cœlo dedit in virgi-
  nalem ventrem; inde in pe-
  lagus sæculi, &c.

and abideth with firmest hope in the LORD. That leaper over sins, of whom we have been speaking, seeing the world very full of errors and sorrows, in the first part of the Psalm acknowledges that his soul is subject to GOD, because he hath obtained the gift of salvation through the Only-Begotten SON of GOD, blaming those who wish to be called Christians in name only. *Shall not my soul be subject to God?* In the second part he again says that his soul is subject to GOD the FATHER, because through His Word he hath gained wholesome patience; strengthening the people with his faithful confession, that it should ever hope in the LORD with all the affection of the heart: *My soul, wait thou still upon God.* In the third division he warns the erring people, that they should rather trust in the LORD than in the fading happiness of this world. *As for the children of men, they are but vanity; the children of men are deceitful upon the weights, &c.*

SYRIAC PSALTER. Named from Jeduthun the singer. The literal sense is said to be when the servants of Abner and the servants of David played, and slew one another, and one of those who belonged to Abner slew Joab's brother, the youngest son of Zeruiah. And this Joab kept for long, and slew Abner, a giant of the time of Saul. The spiritual sense offers a remedy for sin, if we use penance and confession.

EUSEBIUS OF CÆSAREA. The doctrine of duties, (or, touching observances and duties towards GOD.)

S. ATHANASIUS. A Psalm of glorying in GOD.

VARIOUS USES.

Gregorian. Wednesday. Matins.
Monastic. The same.
Parisian. Saturday. Matins.
Lyons. Saturday. Prime.
Ambrosian. Monday of Second Week. I. Nocturn.
Quignon. Tuesday. Sext.

ANTIPHONS.

Gregorian. Shall not my soul be subject to GOD?
Monastic. Bless, ye nations, * our GOD.
Parisian. Unto Thee, O GOD, * do we give thanks, and we will call upon Thy Name ; we will tell of Thy wondrous works.
Ambrosian. The GOD of my health, * and in GOD is my trust.

1 My soul truly waiteth still upon GOD : for of him cometh my salvation.

And so spake the dying patriarch, "I have waited for Thy salvation, O LORD." And that because it is sure to come, however our impatience may think it to linger. "Though it tarry, wait for it; because it will surely come, it will not tarry." And the reward for those who do so wait is set forth by Isaiah. "It shall be said in that day, Lo, this is our GOD ; we have waited for Him, and He will save us : this is the LORD, we have waited for Him ; we will be glad, and re-

Gen. xlix. 18.

Hab. ii. 3.

Isa. xxv. 9.

joice in His salvation." But the Hebrew is yet deeper. *My soul is silent to God:* implying the hushed and awful reverence which befits His servants, and which the holy Cardinal Bona declares to be more fitting than any hymns or antiphons at the moment of the elevation of the LORD's Body in the Mass. The LXX. and Vulgate, however, agree here in reading, *Shall not my soul be subject to God?* For, as S. Gregory the Great observes, humility is the mother and mistress of all virtues, and we must begin by humbling ourselves in the sight of GOD, that He may lift us up. And shalt thou not be subject unto Him, O my soul? "Is not He thy FATHER that hath bought thee? Hath He not made thee and established thee?" "Let others, then," saith Dionysius the Carthusian, "be subject to the desires of the flesh, others to the princes of the world, others again to the promptings of devils, and to divers sins: I and my soul will obey the LORD. For no man can serve two masters whose wills are opposed. Since, then, we cannot obey GOD and the world, I prefer to serve GOD rather than the world." Whence it is written in Jeremiah, concerning disobedience, "Thou saidst, I will not serve;" whereas CHRIST commandeth us, "Take My yoke upon you." And the Psalmist adds the reason of his obedience: *For of Him cometh my salvation,* because the SON, Who is my SAVIOUR, cometh from Him, since "GOD so loved the world, that He gave His Only-Begotten SON."

Bona. Card.
Rer. Liturg.
ii. xiii. 2.

S. Greg.
Mag. Mor.
xxiii. 13.
S. James iv.
10.
Deut. xxxii.
6.

D. C.

Jer. ii. 20.

S. Matt.
xi. 29..

S. John
iii. 16.

2 He verily is my strength and my salvation : he is my defence, so that I shall not greatly fall.

The ancient Versions here agree in departing from the Hebrew, and translate, *He is my God.* For my salvation, says Gerhohus, is GOD the SON, Who, like GOD the FATHER, is Most High and Incomprehensible. He is GOD of all by nature; He is *my* GOD by grace; and He is *my taker up,* when, leaping to Him,[1] I leave the vanities of the world behind my back. And since I have so great a Salvation and Defence, than Whom there is no stronger, I, leaping to Him, taken up by Him, *shall not be moved any more.*[2] And as the Manhood of CHRIST, united to Godhead, can no more be moved, so too the redeemed, when taken up by GOD to bliss, *shall not be moved any more,* because they cannot fall. And this is what the Schoolmen call *Beata necessitas non peccandi.*

G.

Ay.

3 How long will ye imagine mischief against every man : ye shall be slain, all the sort of you ; yea, as a tottering wall shall ye be, and like a broken hedge.

---

[1] Referring to the supposed meaning of Jeduthun.
[2] So the Vulgate, nearly agree-
ing with A. V. The LXX. is stronger: *I shall not be shaken any more.*

N 3

If we read it thus, the reference will be to the final overthrow of the wicked by the second death; while the comparison of them to a bowing wall will suggest those lines,

S. Paulin.
Nol. Nat. S.
Felicis,
Poëm. xvi.
147.

Sic ubi Christus adest nobis, et aranea muro est :
At cui Christus abest, et murus aranea fiet.

But the true meaning of the passage is lost here, and is but little clearer in the Bible Version. The Æthiopic reads correctly, *How long will ye attack a man, and slay him, all of you,* [falling upon him] *like a tottering wall, and an overthrown barrier?* And so too Apollinarius :

Μέχρι τεῦ ἀνδρὶ μάχεσθε, ὅμως τ' ἐναρίζετε πάντα
Τοίχῳ κεκλιμένῳ ἴκελοι φραγμῷ τε πεσόντι ;

The Syriac is nearly identical. The LXX. and Vulgate are almost the same up to the last clause, which they read in the dative, as meaning, [dealing with him] *as with a tottering wall and an overthrown barrier.* The Psalm seems spoken in the first instance of David, when he alone was aimed at by the counsel of Ahithophel : "All the people that are with him shall flee, and I will smite the king only." And it thus points to CHRIST, Who said to the attendants of Judas, "I have told you that I am He; if, therefore, ye seek Me, let these go their way : that the saying might be fulfilled, which He spake, Of them which Thou gavest Me have I lost none." *How long,* then, *do ye rush upon a man?* or, as He words it Himself elsewhere, "But now ye seek to kill Me, a man that hath told you the truth." I ask no partner in My Passion, I, Who need no helper to save all. I want no ambassador, I send before Me no herald. I am Myself the herald to them that sought Me not : I gave Myself up to them that seized Me not, that I might free them who were bound in the cords of death. And the words *how long* denote the continuance of persecution, since from the blood of righteous Abel they ceased not to rush on that Man. Not merely on the members, as in the persecution of the Prophets and of the Fathers, but on the Head Himself, which is CHRIST. *How long?* For wars will never fail CHRIST'S soldier, because the two cities are now mingled together, the one Jerusalem, the other Babylon, each at unity with itself. Here there is one king, there also but one; here there is one people, one there likewise; the one fights for righteousness, the other for unrighteousness; the one for truth, the other for error; the one that it may build up what is cast down, the other that it may cast down that which is built : and yet our City is gathered out of that other one. Wherefore the Cluniac says :

2 Sam. xvii. 2.

S. John xviii. 8.

S. John viii. 40.

S. Ambrose.

Ay.

R.

Bern. Clun. Rhythm.

And now we fight the battle,
But then shall wear the crown,
Of full, and everlasting,
And passionless renown.

And now we watch and struggle,
And now we live in hope,
And Syon, in her anguish,
With Babylon must cope.

Ye slay, all of you. And they explain it of the suicide of
their own souls which the persecutors commit when aiming
at the ruin of the Church. Of them Lactantius speaks: Lactant. De
They who wrestled against GOD lie low; they who overthrew mort. per-
His holy Temple have fallen in greater ruin; they who secut. i.
butchered the righteous breathed out· their guilty souls
amidst heaven-sent plagues and well-earned torments: tar-
dily, but terribly.

As though [I were] *a tottering wall and a falling barrier.* P.
In your ignorance, not knowing that I, Whom ye "esteem
stricken of GOD, smitten, and afflicted," am in truth a "de- Isa. liii. 4.
fenced city, and an iron pillar, and brazen walls against the Jer. i. 1b.
whole land;" that the Man on Whom ye are rushing is the
Eternal WORD of the FATHER. Others, referring the whole
passage to the spiritual enemies of mankind, compare the
soul of man, loosened by sin, and prone to evil, to a wall
which needs but a little to ruin it altogether. For the un- S. Pet.
happy flesh, observes S. Peter Chrysologus, can of itself Chrys. Serm.
bring about its own ruinous fall. Whereupon we may add 174.
that saying of S. Basil, that when, through sin, the wall of S. Basil.
human nature has bulged out, it must be taken down, and Mag. Hom.
built up again by GOD Himself. With living stones, adds H.
S. Hilary, in the House of GOD. S. Ambrose sees in the S. Ambrose.
tottering wall that middle wall of partition which CHRIST, Eph. ii. 14.
our Peace, hath broken down. But, as we have seen, the
whole figure is more truly interpreted of those persecutors
who are ready to overwhelm the righteous, even at the cost
of their own ruin.

4 Their device is only how to put him out whom
GOD will exalt : their delight is in lies ; they give good
words with their mouth, but curse with their heart.

The first clause of this verse differs alike from the Bible
Version, (which, adhering closely to the Hebrew, runs, *They
only consult to cast him down from his excellency;*) from the
Syriac and Æthiopic, which are nearly the same; and from
the LXX. and Vulgate, which agree in reading here, *They
have counselled to repel my price,* or *honour.* (LXX. τιμήν, S Ambrose.
Vulg. *precium.*) *My price.* For when the traitor Judas
brought back His price, the Jews refused to put it into the S. Matt.
treasury, saying, "It is not lawful for to put them into the xxvii. 6.
treasury, because it is the price of blood." *Mine honour,* S. Luke xix.
because "His citizens hated Him, saying, We will not have 14.
this man to reign over us," and yet again, "they sought S. John xv.
the more to kill Him, because He said that GOD was His 8.

FATHER, making Himself equal with GOD." *My price*, because the sinner who rejects the salvation offered to him "hath counted the blood of the covenant, wherewith he was sanctified, an unholy thing." Or, as Remigius will have it, applying the words to CHRIST's soldier, they endeavour to turn me from my crown, my reward, by declaring the way to be too difficult, the task impossible. Not unlike this is the explanation of Cardinal Hugo, who takes it of seducers leading men away from paying that price in good works which GOD asks from them who would buy Him. *Their delight is in lies.* So the Hebrew, followed by Symmachus and S. Jerome, and the Syriac Psalter. And it will then refer to the Jewish slanders against CHRIST, as also to the Pagan calumnies against His followers. Of these *lies*, such as the worship of an ass's head, the murder of children, nocturnal orgies, and the like, we may read in Minucius Felix. But the Vulgate and Æthiopic read, *I have run in thirst.* It is true, observes S. Ambrose, that our LORD JESUS thirsted. Blessed is that thirst of the LORD, because He thirsted for us, and chiefly in His Passion. And then it was that He at length said, "I thirst." For He thirsted at the moment when He was pouring from His Side streams of living water, to quench the thirst of all. And *I have run :* that is, I have hastened to take on Myself the thirst of all, that I might satisfy all with the abundance of My perennial fountain, for, as was said to the woman of Samaria, "Whosoever shall drink of the water which I shall give him, shall never thirst." And what is true of the Master is true also of His servants. For saints, too, run and thirst. They run, as S. Paul says, "I have finished my course, I have kept the faith." They thirst, as it is spoken, "Blessed are they which hunger and thirst after righteousness, for they shall be filled." It is also true, notes S. Ambrose, (following the LXX., *They ran in thirst*,) in another sense, of sinners. For "they have forsaken Me, the Fountain of living waters, and hewed them out cisterns, broken cisterns, that can hold no water." *They give good words with their mouth, but curse with their heart.* And this was fulfilled, says Cardinal Drogo, in the greeting of Judas. It had been so even before in that speech of the Pharisees, "Master, we know that Thou art true, and teachest the way of GOD in truth." The ungodly gave *good words with their mouth* to the martyrs,—flatteries, caresses, and promises of wealth, honour, and dignity, on condition of abandoning the faith of CHRIST; *but cursed with their heart*, because their object was simply evil and perverse. And so Adam of S. Victor :

Ad cruenta Datiani
Dei servus inhumani
 Rapitur prætoria.
Præses sanctum prece tentat,
Nunc exterret, nunc præsentat
 Mundana fastigia.

Marginal notes:
Heb. x. 29.

R.

Hugo Card.

Min. Fel. Octav. ix.

S. Ambrose.

S. John xix. 28.

S. John iv. 14.

S. Hieron.

2 Tim. iv. 7.

S. Matt. v. 6.

Jer. ii. 13.

Drogo Card. Serm. de Pass.
S. Matt. xxii. 16.

P.

Adam. Victorin. Sequ. de S. Vincent. *Triumphalis lux illusit.*

5 Nevertheless, my soul, wait thou still upon GoD : for my hope is in him.

6 He truly is my strength and my salvation : he is my defence, so that I shall not fall.

In this repetition of the opening thoughts of the Psalm the Fathers agree in seeing the inculcation of patience under affliction, of perseverance in the good way. And they dwell the more on this, because the LXX. and Vulgate both read, *My patience is from Him.* And there is another phrase wherein these versions agree. The words אל־אמוט, which they rendered in verse 2, *I shall not be moved,* they here translate, I shall not *emigrate*,[1] I shall not *change my city*.[2] Most fitly is it said of those who seek the one Country, who yearn for the freedom of the Heavenly Jerusalem, whence they shall never depart.

> In Urbe meâ, Jerusalem summâ,
> Sunt en tot luces, Quot insunt felices,
> Quas et illustro Jugiter me ipso
> Lumine vero.

7 In GoD is my health, and my glory : the rock of my might, and in GoD is my trust.

Saved I shall be in GoD, glorious I shall be in GoD; for not only saved, but also glorious : saved, because a just man have I been made out of an ungodly man, by Him justified ; but glorious, because not only justified, but also honoured. For "whom He did predestinate, them He also called." Calling them, what hath He done here? "Whom He hath called, them He also justified ; and whom He justified, them He also glorified." For *the rock of my might,* the LXX. and Vulgate read *the God of my help.* For, adds S. Augustine, He giveth help to men striving. To men striving against whom? "We wrestle not against flesh and blood, but against principalities, against powers." *God therefore is my help, and my trust is in God.* And because He saved me of His free grace, observes S. Bruno, and glorified me, and is also my helper to do good works, *my trust is in God,* Who hath already bestowed such blessings upon me ; and I have the hope of gaining those which are in GoD only—immortality and impassibility.

A.

Rom. viii. 30.

Eph. vi. 12.

B.

8 O put your trust in him alway, ye people : pour out your hearts before him, for GoD is our hope.

The LXX. and Vulgate strengthen the first clause by

---

[1] *Non emigrabo.*   [2] οὐ μὴ μεταναστεύσω.

278 A COMMENTARY ON THE PSALMS.

reading, *All the congregation of the people.* And it is explained of the assembly of the Church. The Psalmist speaks
thus, because "Whoso trusteth in the LORD, happy is he;"
and yet more when this trust is the joint action of a larger
number, for "where two or three are gathered together in
my name, there am I in the midst of them." The blessing did
come on them, as it is written, "The multitude of them that believed were of one heart and one soul." *Pour out your hearts
before Him.* He who puts on faith, comments S. Ambrose,
ought first to strip off unbelief, and empty his heart of every
pollution of sin, that his heart may be fit to contain spiritual
grace. Therefore the Apostle says, "Be ye renewed in the
spirit of your minds." For when the old wickedness is poured
out, the new grace is received, whereby each man is renewed.
Therefore the SON of GOD saith, *Pour out your hearts before
Him,* because He knew that the FATHER would say, "I will
pour out My Spirit upon all flesh." And S. Basil adds that
the counsel is that of a wise physician, who prescribes purging medicines to clear the system, before he gives restora-
tives; or like the housewife who washes a foul-smelling vase
carefully before attempting to put perfumed unguents into
it. And this must be thoroughly done, observes Cardinal
Hugo; for it is written, "Pour out thy heart like water
before the LORD," that there may be in external signs no
colour, in words no smell, in desire no taste, before the LORD,
in order that He may deal with it according to His will.
Like water, adds S. Albert, not like wine, which leaves a
smell in the vase; nor like honey, leaving a taste; nor milk,
leaving its colour. Yet, again, He *pours out his heart* before
the LORD, who confesses his sins with copious tears. For the
heart can no otherwise be poured out than by an abundant
shower of weeping, as is spoken in the 42nd Psalm, "My
tears have been my meat day and night: I pour out my
heart by myself." *For God is our hope.* Wherefore we
ought to make full confession to Him of our sins, knowing
that He will in no wise cast out any that cometh to Him on account of their past wickedness. Do not keep back your hearts
within your hearts: *Pour out your hearts before Him.* That
perisheth not which ye pour out. For He is my Taker up.
If He taketh up, why fear ye to pour out? "O cast thy
burden upon the LORD."

9 As for the children of men, they are but vanity:
the children of men are deceitful upon the weights,
they are altogether lighter than vanity itself.

Whence we learn by contrast the steadfastness of the children of GOD. If the children of men be vanity, if they be
deceitful, the sons of GOD may easily not be vain, since they
are "born, not of blood, nor of the will of the flesh, nor of the
will of man, but of GOD." For the children of men seem to

Margin notes: S. Albertus Magnus. Prov. xvi. 20. S. Matt. xviii. 20. Acts iv. 32. S. Ambrose. Eph. iv. 23. Joel ii. 28. S. Bas. Mag. Hom. Hugo Card. Lam. ii. 19. S. Albertus Magnus. C. Ps. xlii. 3, 4. A. Ps. lv. 23. S. Ambrose. S. John i. 13.

themselves to weigh equity, and to test justice by the accuracy of strict judgment, when they are hard to others and lax to themselves, unjust in their deeds, and censorious in their words. And note that the balance on which the sons of men are deceitful is threefold: to wit, the balance of redemption; the balance of buying and selling, and the balance of words or outward show. The first of these balances is CHRIST Himself, Who weighs all our merits and demerits, the one with rewards, the other with penalties. This is the balance of which Job speaks, "Oh that my grief were thoroughly weighed, and my calamity laid in the balances together." We are deceitful in this balance, notes S. Gregory, when we vainly hope that He is too merciful to punish sins, and therefore continue adding one fault to another. The second balance is that of merchants, by which is understood fair dealing in buying and selling. And of this is said, "Ye shall do, no unrighteousness in judgment, in meteyard, in weight, or in measure. Just balances and just weights shall ye have." And this is spoken against all tricks of trade; for he has not a just balance who sells a bad article as good, a small one as large, and who keeps one weight for selling and another for buying. Against such it is written, "A false balance is abomination to the LORD, but a just weight is His delight." The third is the balance of speech, or outward seeming. He has a true balance herein who deceives not by word or sign. Of this balance of words and deeds is written, "Weigh thy words in a balance, and make a door and bar for thy mouth." Flatterers are deceitful on it who say one thing with their heart and another with the mouth, because the balance is not true between heart and mouth. And so too of hypocrites, who make one kind of show outside, and are very different within. But in truth the Hebrew does not imply deceit, but lightness; and the passage means that the children of men, when weighed in GOD's balance, will mount rapidly in the scale. And so it is written, "Thou art weighed in the balances, and found wanting." And with this agrees the last clause, *They are altogether lighter than vanity itself*, where the LXX. and Vulgate read, *They deceive [going] from vanity unto the same;* that is, as the commentators note, from one vain act to another, not returning to better things.

Ay.
Job vi. 2.
S. Greg. Mag. Mor. vii. 1.
Lev. xix. 35.
Prov. xi. 1.
Ecclus. xxviii. 25.
Dan. v. 27.

10 O trust not in wrong and robbery, give not yourselves unto vanity : if riches increase, set not your heart upon them.

Vain is iniquity, naught is iniquity, mighty is nothing save righteousness. Truth may be hidden for a time; conquered it cannot be. Iniquity may flourish for a time; abide it cannot. Thou art not rich, and wilt thou rob? What findest thou? what losest thou?. O losing gain! thou findest money, thou losest righteousness. What thou robbest thou

A.

seest: by whom thou art robbed seest thou not? Knowest
thou not thine enemy goeth about "like a roaring lion, seeking whom he may devour?" That prey which thou desirest
to rob is in a trap: thou seizest, and art seized. For robbery, therefore, be not covetous, O poor man; but fix thy
desires upon GOD, "Who giveth us richly all things to
enjoy." He shall feed thee that hath made thee. Shall He
that feedeth a robber not feed an innocent man? He shall
feed thee that "maketh His sun to rise on the evil and on
the good, and sendeth rain upon the just and on the unjust."
Therefore for robbery be not covetous. This hath been said
to a poor man, that perchance will steal something out of
necessity. Let the rich man come forth: I have no necessity, he saith, to rob; to me nothing is wanting, all things
abound. And do thou, too, hear: *if riches flow, set not your
heart upon them.* Seest thou not that, if there the heart
thou shalt have set, thou also wilt flow? And the rich, too,
may rob, as S. Prosper observes; for he who gives not alms,
robs the poor. And the warning extends, wisely teaches
Gerhohus, to spiritual riches. Pour out your hearts before
GOD, so as to store up with Him your treasure of riches,
whether bodily or spiritual; and store up your heart also
therewith, because "where your treasure is, there will your
heart be also." Not well nor prudently did he pour out his
heart, who, counting up his riches, said, "GOD, I thank Thee
that I am not as other men are, extortioners, unjust, adulterers, or even as this publican." The thanksgiving was, as
it were, a channel which might have borne this Pharisee's
riches along with his heart into heaven, had it not been
gaping with the fissure of pride, whereby, in his contempt
for others, he so boasted, as to take more pleasure in the
shortcomings of others than in his own amendment.

11 GOD spake once, and twice I have also heard
the same: that power belongeth unto GOD.

He spake once, in that He begat His SON, Who is the
Eternal WORD. And He spake on this wise: "Thou art
MY SON; this day have I begotten Thee." I have heard it
once, because He spake in the Law; I have heard it twice,
because He "hath in these last days spoken unto us by His
SON," manifest in the flesh. But the LXX. and Vulgate
translate, *I have heard these two things,* namely, *that power
belongeth unto God*—

12 And that thou, LORD, art merciful: for thou
rewardest every man according to his work.

That is, that the power of GOD is His justice and mercy,
of which all the Scripture treats, because of which the Law
and the Prophets were given, because of which CHRIST Himself was sent, and the Apostles. Let His power, then, be

Margin notes:
1 S. Pet. v. 8.
1 Tim. vi. 17.
S. Matt. v. 45.
S. Prosper.
G.
S. Luke xii. 34.
S. Luke xviii. 11.
C.
Ps. ii. 7.
Heb. i. 2.
A.
Ay.
G.

feared; let His mercy be loved; nor let His power be contemned because of His mercy, nor His mercy despaired of
because of His power and justice. The Psalmist, therefore,
says of the Incarnate WORD, *I have heard these two things,*
that He is the Power of GOD, and also that He is the Justice
of GOD; according to that Psalm, "Give the King Thy judg- Ps. lxxii. 1.
ments, O GOD, and Thy righteousness unto the King's Son."
And because it is so, the Psalmist turns to the SON, beseeching Him, Who is Himself Mercy, not to suffer him to be 1 Cor. x. 13.
tempted above that he is able to bear; but to deliver him, S. John v.
knowing that "the FATHER judgeth no man, but hath com- 22.
mitted all judgment unto the SON," and that the Judge of all Gen. xviii.
the earth shall do right.   25.

And therefore:

Glory be to the FATHER, of Whom cometh my salvation;
and to the SON, Who is my Salvation, and the Rock of my
might; and to the HOLY GHOST, Who spake by the Prophets
of the power and mercy of GOD.

As it was in the beginning, is now, and ever shall be:
world without end. Amen.

COLLECTS.

Subdue our souls unto Thee, O LORD; for Thou art our Ludolph.
very patience: that we, rejecting the uncertainty of riches,
and despising all earthly vanity, may follow Thee only. (1.)

Thou, O LORD, Who art the Hope of all, hearken and Mozarabic.
have pity, as we pour out our hearts before Thee in prayer,
and subject us unto Thee, that we may serve Thee; and of
Thy loving-kindness help us when we are subject to sin; remove from us all wrong and robbery, bestow on us the jewels
of Thy riches, and grant that we may know Thee, desire
Thee, and have Thee for our GOD all the days of our
life. (11.)

Unto Thee alone, O LORD, Whom all nature acknowledges Mozarabic.
as its Creator, our soul is subject. From Thee we receive
the virtue of patience, that we be not moved by any stumbling-block; and to Thee we know that we owe all that we
are. Grant, therefore, that we never be sustained with unrighteous hope, nor set our hearts upon deceitful riches; that
we may be wont to rest in Thee only, and to the end that we
may attain our petitions, make our hearts contrite before
Thee. (11.)

O GOD, Might unbounded; let our soul and body be sub- Mozarabic.
dued unto Thee, and our life serve Thee most faithfully;
vouchsafe to the soul that longing by which it may attain to
Thee, and receive the prayer of our lips, so that the thousand-
formed one may not creep in. Overcome the hidden enemy
with Thy might; prevent us with Thy blessing, and lead us
by the way of life to joys everlasting. (11.)

PSALM LXIII.

TITLE: A Psalm of David, when he was in the wilderness of Judah. Vulgate: A Psalm of David, when he was in the wilderness of Idumea. Syriac: Of David, literally, when he said to the King of Moab, "My father and mother tarried with thee when they fled from the face of Saul, and I likewise fled to thee." By us now it is taken as the thanksgiving of a perfect man to GOD in the spirit.

ARGUMENT.

ARG. THOMAS. That CHRIST is He on Whom we should direct the brightness of the mind in the morning thoughts. The voice of the Church concerning CHRIST, or that of any one withdrawing from darkness, and longing for CHRIST.

VEN. BEDE. *Psalm* and *David* often denote CHRIST the LORD, often the Church, because CHRIST is in His members, and the members are contained in their Head. Wherefore words which signify the LORD the SAVIOUR are fitly ascribed to the Church, which is to speak in this Psalm. She therefore dwells in the desert of Idumea; that is, in the dryness of this world, where she thirsts and longs for CHRIST. Whence also *Idumea*, where David was in exile, is interpreted *earthly*. In the first part of the Psalm the Church longs after the power of the LORD, desiring to be filled with the fulness of all good things, that she may be found worthy of His praises: *O God, Thou art my God: early will I seek Thee.* In the second, she gives thanks, because, under the shadow of the LORD'S wings, she has escaped the storms of the world; and she declares that CHRIST the King will rejoice with His Saints in GOD the FATHER, when His enemies are condemned under the earth, *Have I not remembered*, and so forth.

EUSEBIUS OF CÆSAREA. A thanksgiving of him who is perfect according to GOD.

S. ATHANASIUS. A Psalm of thanksgiving.

VARIOUS USES.

Gregorian. Daily. Lauds.
Monastic. Sunday. Lauds.
Parisian. Sunday. Lauds.
Lyons. Sunday. Lauds.
Ambrosian. Monday of the Second Week. Matins. I. Nocturn.
Quignon. Saturday. Prime.
Eastern Church. Third Psalm of the Hexapsalmos. Matins and Compline.

ANTIPHONS.

The *Gregorian* Antiphons to this Psalm vary not only for every day in ordinary weeks, but for every festival, and are therefore too numerous to set down.
Monastic. Alleluia.

Parisian. GOD * my GOD, I wake to Thee from the light; my soul thirsteth for Thee.

Lyons. Thus will I bless Thee * while I live, I will lift up my hands in Thy Name.

Ambrosian. As preceding Psalm.

Mozarabic. In the wilderness, in the pathless, in the dry place, GOD, my GOD, I wake to Thee from the light.

1 O GOD, thou art my GOD : early will I seek thee.

Because of these opening words, this Psalm has been set apart from the infancy of the Church for morning use. Its daily recitation is enjoined in the Apostolical Constitutions, is urged by S. Athanasius and S. Chrysostom, and has never failed in either the East or the West in all the ages since. *My God.* The repetition of the Name of GOD, and the claiming Him for the Psalmist's very own, denotes, observes S. Chrysostom, deep love and eager pressing towards GOD, to the neglect of all earthly things. It is therefore taken chiefly of Him Who alone could with truth call GOD His own, as being One with Him, Consubstantial, Co-eternal. *Early will I seek Thee.* "In the beauty of holiness, from the womb of the morning," it is said of the SON, Who created the light, Who Himself rose from the dead very early in the morning. And it is spoken also of the faithful soul which turns eagerly to the first rays of the light, and opens its petals to the Sun. There is a sleep of the soul, says S. Augustine, there is a sleep of the body. Sleep of the body we all ought to have; but of this let us take heed, that our soul sleep not, for evil is the sleep of the soul. Good is the sleep of the body, whereby is recruited the health of the body; but the sleep of the soul is to forget her GOD. Therefore the Apostle saith, "Awake, thou that sleepest, and arise from the dead, and CHRIST shall give thee light." Was the Apostle waking up one sleeping in body? Nay, but he was waking a soul sleeping, in order that she might be enlightened by CHRIST. And therefore the Bride in the Canticles answers to this appeal, "I sleep, but my heart waketh." Sleep, free from all temporal anxiety, waketh to the contemplation of GOD.

S. Chrysost. Hom. in 1 Cor. ii.

Ps. cx. 3.

A.

Eph. v. 14.

Cant. v. 2.

S. Greg. Mor. v. 22.

2 My soul thirsteth for thee, my flesh also longeth after thee : in a barren and dry land, where no water is.

It is the cry of David, cut off in exile from the public rites of the Jewish Church, either (as the great majority of commentators prefer) when he was hiding from Saul in the wilderness of Ziph, which lay sufficiently near the borders of Edom to be called indifferently "of Judah" and "of Idu-

1 Sam. xxiii. 15.

Agellius.

2 Sam. xv.
28.

2 Sam. xv.
25.

R.

Job xix. 26.

S. Bernard.
Hom. in
Adv. vi.

Ay.

R.

A.

mea;" or, as Agellius, almost alone amongst the commentators, takes it, in the flight from Absalom, "in the plain of the wilderness." There are two reasons for adopting this view. First, the reference in the third verse to previous access to the sanctuary, which fits in with David's parting from the Ark, saying, "Carry back the Ark of GOD into the city: if I shall find favour in the sight of the LORD, He will bring me again, and show me both it and His habitation." Secondly, the title of king assumed by David in the last verse, which points to a time after the death of Saul. *My soul thirsteth for Thee*, the Fountain of living waters: it thirsts not for any gifts in this wilderness, but for everlasting rest, everlasting blessedness, which are nowhere save in Thee. *My flesh also longeth after Thee*. The LXX. and Vulgate here read, *In how many ways my flesh [thirsteth] for Thee*. Much more than even the soul; for the soul is immortal and impassible, the body mortal, and subject to passions, and therefore more in need. And its longing is for the Resurrection, that man may say, "In my flesh I shall see GOD." Wherefore S. Bernard observes, citing this Psalm, the soul of the Prophet desired the first Advent, whereby it knew that it should be redeemed; but much more did his flesh desire the second Advent, and its own glorification. *In a barren and dry land, where no water is*. For *dry* the LXX. and Vulgate read *pathless*. The world is *desert* because the saints dwell not therein, since they are not of it; it is *pathless*, because it knows not CHRIST, Who is the Way; it *hath no water*, because the Fountain of Grace for cleansing is not there. Evil is the desert, and horrible, and to be feared; and, nevertheless, GOD hath pitied us, and hath made a Way in the desert, Himself, our LORD JESUS CHRIST; and hath made to us a consolation in the desert, in sending to us preachers of His Word; and hath given unto us water in the desert, by fulfilling with His HOLY SPIRIT His preachers, in order that there might be created in them a well of water springing up unto life everlasting. And lo! we have here all things, but they are not of the desert.

3 Thus have I looked for thee in holiness : that I might behold thy power and glory.

The LXX. and Vulgate read, *Thus have I appeared to Thee in the Holy* [Place.] The Rabbins understand it of the Ark of the Covenant, and the splendour of the Hebrew ritual, from which David was now cut off. And they compare 1 Kings viii. 8, where "holy place" occurs, with 2 Chron. v. 9, where "ark" is the parallel word in the description of the dedication of Solomon's temple. And this agrees with the Authorized Version: *As I have seen Thee in the sanctuary*. It may then be taken of the LORD JESUS in the wilderness of this world, speaking of the glory which He had with His FATHER before the world began, and ere He emptied Himself of that glory, to take on Him the form of a servant. And, spoken of His servants, we may take it literally, as S. Athanasius does, of those compelled to fly to the desert because of their religion, and longing there for the solemn services of the Church. In this wise it is especially true of those early Confessors who were driven into the Thebaid under the persecuting reigns of Valerian and of Maximian. Mystically, it tells of the longing to depart and be with CHRIST, to be free from fleshly sin, to enjoy the vision of GOD, no more as in a glass darkly, but face to face. Where note, says the Carmelite, that we are taught in Exodus how we should appear before GOD. Thrice in a year should all males come unto Him; so we also, thrice in our year of mortal life, should do the same. In the past, by recalling with grief our former sins, and repenting of them; in the present by doing good works while there is yet time, according to that saying of the Apostle, "Behold, now is the accepted time;" in the future by a firm resolve to persevere in holiness, saying with Job, "Till I die, I will not remove mine integrity from me. My righteousness will I hold fast, and will not let it go." In these three periods of the year, then, every male,—that is, every perfect man,—ought to appear before GOD; which if he do, then GOD will appear to him, so that he will see GOD even as he is seen by GOD. And then he will say to GOD, *In holy* desire *I have appeared to Thee, that I might behold Thy honour and glory.*

margin notes: S. Athan. Ep. ad Marc. — Ay. — Exod. xxxiv. — 2 Cor. vi. 2. — Job xxvii. 5.

4 For thy loving-kindness is better than the life itself : my lips shall praise thee.

The LXX. and Vulgate here read, *better than lives.* Better than all the lives we men choose for ourselves, however various these may be; better than the active and contemplative lives, figured by Leah and Rachel, Martha and Mary; better than the four kinds of life typified in Ezekiel's vision, —the face of man, that of married persons; the face of a lion, the dweller in deserts, that of hermits; the face of an ox, which tilleth the earth, that of prelates; the face of an eagle, that of the cloistered, soaring in contemplation. And reading in the singular, with S. Hilary and Cassiodorus, we shall find a reference to the martyrs, who counted not their lives dear unto themselves, so that they might finish their course with joy; and of whom it is accordingly written, "Right dear in the sight of the LORD is the death of His saints." *My lips shall praise Thee.* So it proved to be when the language of praise and thanksgiving to CHRIST the Victor went up from the lips of the martyrs as their bodies suffered under the hands of torturers. Such is the triumphal prayer of S. Laurence in the Peristephanon, such the cheering words addressed to each other by the great forty martyrs

margin notes: A. — S. Albertus Magnus. — Ps. cxvi. 13. — Prudent. Peristeph. ii. 413.

on the frozen lake of Sebaste. And no fitter gloss can be
found than the dying words of S. Polycarp of Smyrna:
"God of Angels, God of Archangels, our Resurrection and
Deliverance from sin, Ruler of all the elements and the whole
habitable world, sheltering all the generation of the just
who live in Thy sight, I, Thy servant, bless Thee, Who hast
deemed me worthy of this passion, that I should receive the
lot and crown of martyrdom, the beginning of the Cup,
through Jesus Christ, in the unity of the Holy Ghost;
that when this day's sacrifice is ended, I may receive Thy true
promise. Wherefore I bless Thee in all things, and make
my boast in Thee, through the Eternal High Priest Almighty,
Jesus Christ, by Whom and with Whom, and with the
Holy Ghost, glory be to Thee now and henceforth to ages
of ages. Amen."

5 As long as I live will I magnify thee on this
manner : and lift up my hands in thy Name.

Rather with the Authorized Version, LXX., and Vulgate,
Thus will I bless Thee while I live. Not only by constant
praise and thanksgiving, as it is written, "Bless the Lord
thy God alway," but I will so live that my conversation
shall be a blessing of Thy Name, because I will rule my
whole life to the honour, praise, and glory of that Name.
For God is not less blessed by a righteous life than by a
clear voice. *And lift up my hands in Thy Name.* Firstly,
as Moses did during the battle with Amalek; as Jeremiah
counsels, "Let us lift up our heart with our hands unto God
in the heavens;" and as S. Paul directs, adding, that the hands
should be "holy." Next, in almsgiving through compassion,
"She stretcheth out her hand to the poor, yea, she reacheth
forth her hands to the needy." Lastly, by general zeal and
diligence in well-doing, "that ye study to work with your
own hands."

6 My soul shall be satisfied, even as it were with
marrow and fatness : when my mouth praiseth thee
with joyful lips.

It is true of that Heavenly Banquet of the Eucharist,
wherein the Church makes her glad offering to God, truly a
"feast of fat things, a feast of wines on the lees, of fat
things full of marrow, of wines on the lees well refined."
Wherefore in that hymn of thanksgiving it is said,

> Saturatus ferculis
> Et cibis sacrosanctis,
> Saginatus epulis
> Deliciisque tantis.

* * * *

Jam confectus macie,
   Hoc pane impinguatus,
Fortis sum in acie,
   Nam bene sum armatus.

So, too, in the Antiphon for Corpus Christi, taken from Gen. xlix.
Jacob's blessing of Asher, "The bread of CHRIST is fat, and 20.
He shall yield royal dainties." Again, it holds of those   Ay.
graces wherewith GOD cherishes the soul with warmth, and S. Greg.
especially those typified by chrism or unction, because fat Mag. Mor.
gives heat to the body; and therefore it is written in the 19.
Law, "All the fat is the LORD'S." Whereby we learn that Lev. iii. 16.
all good desires come from Him, and must return to Him.
And as the fat is parted from the flesh in sacrifice, so the
saints are severed from among sinners; as it is written, "As Ecclus.
is the fat taken away from the peace-offering, so was David xlvii. 2.
chosen out of the children of Israel." Finally, the verse
tells us of the endless rejoicing at the marriage-supper of the
Lamb, whereof S. Peter Damiani tells us,

Ever full, but hungry ever,   S. Pet. Dam.
   What they have, they still desire;   Hymn. de
Never suffer surfeit's loathing,   Gaud. Pa-
   Nor yet famine's torments dire: rad.
Hungering still, they eat, and eating,
   Still the Sacred Food require.

7 Have I not remembered thee in my bed : and
thought upon thee when I was waking?

Or, with the LXX. and Vulgate, *If I have remembered, &c.*
And so S. Bernard in that loveliest hymn:

Jesum quærens in lectulo,   S. Bern.
Clauso cordis cubiculo.   Rhythm.
                           Jubilus.

That is, as S. Bruno teaches, in the peaceful quiet of a pure   B.
conscience, and as Richard of Hampole wisely adds, also in Ricard.
the time and place of sickness and pain. Yet again, notes S. Hampol.
Albert, the ease and quiet of the bed denotes a time of tem- S. Alb. Mag.
poral prosperity, when it specially behoves the Christian to
think on his GOD. And rising from the servant to the
Master, let us hear the Carthusian, "On the Cross where I   D. C.
hung weak and dying, I remembered Thee, O MY FATHER,
saying, 'Why hast Thou forsaken Me?' and, 'FATHER,
forgive them;' and yet further, 'FATHER, into Thy Hands
I commend My Spirit.'" *And thought upon Thee when I was
waking* in the early morn of My Resurrection. The Hebrew,
however, does not speak of the morning, but of *watches,* to
wit, *of the night.* And then we are reminded of those words
of the Bride: "By night on my bed I sought Him whom my
soul loveth. I sought Him, but found Him not." It is not Cant. iii. 1.
thus He is to be found. Let the sentinels shake off their
slumbers, arise, and *watch,* and they shall be blessed when

the LORD cometh and findeth them so doing, for then (and note the bearing on the previous verse of the Psalm,) " He shall gird Himself, and make them to sit down.to meat, and will come forth and serve them."

S. Luke xii. 37.

8 Because thou hast been my helper : therefore under the shadow of thy wings will I rejoice.

A.

Here S. Augustine beautifully observes, that we are the chickens under the hen's wings, but whereas the young of a hen do not need her protection when they are full grown, we, the more we are grown, more need the shadow of CHRIST's wings. *I will rejoice.* So the Bride: " I sat down under His shadow with great delight, and His fruit was sweet to my taste."

Cant. ii. 3.

9 My soul hangeth upon thee : thy right hand hath upholden me.

So the Hebrew: The A. V. is different. My soul *followeth hard after Thee,* as it is written, " Draw me, we will run after Thee." The Vulgate has *adhæsit,* hath *clung after Thee;* the LXX., strongest of all, *ἐκολλήθη, hath been glued behind Thee.* What is that same glue? asks S. Augustine; the glue itself is love, which fastens us behind GOD, that we may follow Him. And S. Chrysostom compares this close and binding union to the nails of the Cross, to the hold which the roots of a tree have of the earth. But the Prayer Book Version in this place seems to be entitled to the preference, and we shall best come at its full meaning by comparing the prophecy of Isaiah concerning Eliakim, prefiguring CHRIST. " The key of the house of David will I lay upon his shoulder; so he shall open, and none shall shut; and he shall shut and none shall open. And I will fasten him as a nail in a sure place; and he shall be for a glorious throne to his father's house. And they shall hang upon him all the glory of his father's house, the offspring and the issue, all vessels of small quantity, from the vessels of cups even unto the vessels of flagons." So we hang on Him, because we are the jewels of His FATHER's House, and are used to deck the Heir in His majesty, deriving ourselves all our own honour from our place as His ornaments, those ornaments wherewith "the Bridegroom decketh Himself." *Thy right hand hath upholden me.* Of this the very heathen had a type. In the right hand of Jupiter's statue often stood a figure of a winged Victory, shadowing forth the victory of that Right Hand which hath the pre-eminence, a victory which enables man to soar above the sky. Wherefore the hymn fitly says:

Cant. i. 4.

A.

S. Chrysos. Hom. ix. in 2 Tim.

Isa. xxii. 22.

Isa. lxi. 10.

Salutatio aurea.

Ave dextra manus CHRISTI,
Perforata plagâ tristi,
Nos ad dextram jube sisti,
Quos per crucem redemisti.

10 These also that seek the hurt of my soul : they
shall go under the earth.

11 Let them fall upon the edge of the sword :
that they may be a portion for foxes.

The LXX. and Vulgate are slightly different from the first
of these verses. They read: *In vain have they sought after
my soul, they shall go into the lower* [LXX. *lowest*] *parts of
the earth.* Not merely falling *to* the ground, as they did in
Gethsemane, but going *under* it, into the grave of second Hugo Card.
death. It was fulfilled even in this life, remarks S. Augus- A.
tine. Earth they were unwilling to lose, when they crucified
CHRIST; they have gone into the lower places of the earth.
What are the lower places of the earth? Earthly lusts.
For every one that in prejudice of his salvation desireth
earthly things, is under the earth; because earth he hath put
before him, earth he hath put upon himself, and himself he
hath laid beneath. Fearing to lose earth, they said of the S. John xi.
LORD JESUS: "If we let Him thus alone, the Romans will 48.
come, and take away our place and nation." Behold, they
have lost at the hands of the Romans the place, because they
slew CHRIST.

Let them fall upon the edge of the sword. The sword Ay.
wielded in this life by Titus and by Hadrian, the more terrible two-edged sword of judgment to come, proceeding out
of the mouth of CHRIST. *That they may be a portion for
foxes.* They would not have the Lamb for their King, and
therefore they have been given up to the will of crafty and
worldly princes, like that Herod whom the LORD called a
"fox." Nay, more, they themselves have degenerated in S. Luke xiii.
character, and become wily and deceitful, and thus have had 32.
their portion with foxes. And it is written, "Foxes have C.
holes, and the birds of the air have nests, but the Son of Ay.
Man hath not where to lay His head," because the demons of S. Luke ix.
craft and of pride are freely allowed room in the heart of the 58.
sinner, while he closes it against CHRIST, and therefore "He L.
shall cut him asunder, and appoint him his portion with the S. Matt.
hypocrites." The Hebrew word שֻׁעָלִים however, more pro- xxiv. 51.
bably here means *jackals*, (which devour dead bodies, rather
than foxes, which rarely do so,) and thus warns us against
casting in our lot with the angels of him who goeth about as
a roaring lion, seeking whom he may devour. 1 S. Pet. v. 8:

12 But the King shall rejoice in GOD; all they
also that swear by him shall be commended : for the
mouth of them that speak lies shall be stopped.

That King, Whose kingdom, though it be not of this world, G.
is yet in this world, as it is in heaven, CHRIST the King; King
of the Jews, Who hath on His vesture and on His thigh a Rev. xix. 16.
II. O

name written, "King of kings, and Lord of lords," Who
S. Luke i. 33.   shall reign over the house of Jacob for ever, and of His kingdom there shall be no end; the King, I say, crowned with a
diadem of thorns, and sorrowful unto death in the desert of
Edom, now raised up from death, *shall rejoice* in GOD, for in
that He liveth, He liveth unto GOD, and is Himself GOD in
S. John xiv.   GOD, as He hath said, "I am in the FATHER, and the FATHER
10.   in Me." And whereas He also saith, "All power is given
S. Matt.   unto Me in heaven and in earth," He ever had that power
xxviii. 18.   in His Godhead, but in His Manhood the King hath received
it from GOD, and therefore rightly He *shall rejoice in God.*
Then follows the reward of loyalty, bestowed on those faithful
ones who followed their King into the desert, when His enemies held His city against Him : *All they that swear by Him*
P.   *shall be commended,* who shall pledge themselves to Him
in His Sacraments, the oaths of His military service, to be
His faithful soldiers and servants unto their lives' end. And
2 Chron. xv.   so it is written, "And all Judah rejoiced at the oath; for
15.   they had sworn with all their heart, and sought Him with all
their desire, and He was found of them, and the LORD gave
them rest round about." Nor are we at a loss to know what
are the words of commendation; they run : "Well done,
S. Matt.   good and faithful servant, enter thou into the joy of thy
xxv. 21.   LORD." *For the mouth of all them that speak lies shall be*
Ricard.   *stopped.* Even in this world, when they see the glory of the
Hampol.   faith of the Saints, they will have nothing to allege against
the truth of GOD, or the pure lives of His servants. But the
perfect silence of slanderous tongues will not be till evil is
Rev. xxii.   overcome in the final victory of CHRIST, when He bars out
15.   of the Heavenly City " whosoever loveth and maketh a lie."
Wherefore :

Glory be to the FATHER, Whom we seek early; and to the
SON, Who watcheth in Himself and in His members, and by
His watches intreats for His members mercy better than the
life itself; and to the HOLY GHOST, Himself the mercy in
judgment to be extolled above all life.

As it was in the beginning, is now, and ever shall be :
world without end. Amen.

COLLECTS.

Ludolph.   O GOD, Author of light eternal, bestow abundance of perpetual brightness on them who watch to Thee early, that our
lips may praise Thee, our life bless Thee, our morning meditation glorify Thee. (1.)

Mozarabic.   In the morning we think of Thee, O LORD, because Thou,
giving us Thy light, art our lifter up; for we confess that
Thou wast born for us, and under the shadow of Thy wings,
protected by Thy Cross, we praise Thee. Grant therefore
that we who preach Thy gifts in the Holy Mystery, may enjoy Thee in the best gift of all. (11.)

Mozarabic.   O LORD, unto Whom our soul watcheth from the light, grant that we may ever hasten from darkness unto light; that the mist of the mind may utterly pass away, and the fulness of Thy light abide in us. (11.)

We beseech Thee, O LORD, that watching for Thy light, and ever thirsting for Thee, we may, by Thy bounty, be fulfilled with good works. (1.) S. Jerome.

O GOD, our GOD, grant that we may watch unto Thee in prayer from the light of the SPIRIT, and thirst for Thee, that by the gift of Thy grace, our soul may be filled with the marrow and fatness of virtue, whereby, as it clings to Thee, Thy right hand may lift it up unto the heavenly places. (1.) D. C.

PSALM LXIV.

TITLE: To the Chief Musician; a Psalm and Song of David. Vulgate: To the end; a Psalm of David. Arabic Psalter: Of David, when Saul persecuted him.

ARGUMENT.

ARG. THOMAS. That CHRIST delivers innocent souls from the arrows of the ungodly. The Voice of Paul. Concerning the Passion of CHRIST. The Voice of the Prophet in the HOLY GHOST, touching the Jews, and CHRIST, and His members. The Voice of the Martyrs of CHRIST.

VEN. BEDE. The words of this title denote CHRIST, Who is to speak throughout the Psalm of His Passion. In the first part, the LORD prays that He may be delivered from the fear of the Jewish people, teaching that they were foiled in their snares, and that He hath risen again to glory. *Hear my voice, O God, in my prayer.* In the second place He mocks the cruelty of the Jews because they were sorely troubled by reason of their sins when, by the LORD'S rising, His might was declared unto them, for then the rejoicing of the righteous, and the virtue of true faith, appeared.

SYRIAC PSALTER. Put forth by David when the Prophet Gad warned him, saying, Tarry not in Masrot, for Saul seeketh thy death. To us, spiritually, the triumph of the athletes, the instruction of them that fear GOD, and victory in the struggle.

EUSEBIUS OF CÆSAREA. The doctrine of an athlete who serves GOD.

S. ATHANASIUS. A Psalm of address, prayer, and supplication.

VARIOUS USES.

Gregorian. Wednesday. Matins. [Common of Apostles, II. Nocturn.]
Monastic. Wednesday. Lauds. [Common of Apostles, II. Nocturn.]
Parisian. Saturday. Matins.
Lyons. Wednesday. Lauds.
Ambrosian. Monday of Second Week. Matins. I. Nocturn.
Quignon. Friday. Sext.

Gregorian. Ferial. As preceding Psalm. [Common of Apostles. They have declared the works of the LORD * and have understood His deeds.]

Monastic. Ferial. Preserve my life * O LORD, from fear of the enemy.

Parisian. As Psalm lxii.

Lyons. As Monastic.

Ambrosian. As Psalm lxii.

1 Hear my voice, O GOD, in my prayer : preserve my life from fear of the enemy.

L.

A.

C.

There is a Jewish tradition in the Midrash that this Psalm was prophetic of Daniel, and that it was recited by him in the den of lions. It unquestionably contains several passages peculiarly apposite to that event. The Church has always interpreted it of CHRIST, and of the Martyrs, especially the Apostles. Stress has thus been laid on the latter clause of the first verse: *Preserve my life from fear of the enemy.* Not from the enemy himself, but from *fear* of him. Let him do his worst with the body, but let the soul remain unterrified, yielding neither to his menaces nor to his torture.

S. Matt. x. 28.

So it is written, "Fear not them which kill the body, but are not able to kill the soul." And still more, let there be no fear of that worst enemy of all, whose suggestions urge the human foes of the Church to their evil task. Let him be accosted in the words of S. Aurelius Prudentius:

Prudent. Cathem. vi. 141.

O tortuose serpens,
Qui mille per meandros
Fraudesque flexuosas
Agitas quieta corda,

Discede, CHRISTUS hic est,
Hic CHRISTUS est, liquesce,
Signum, quod ipse nôsti,
Dampnat tuam catervam.

Isa. viii. 12.

Therefore, "Neither fear ye their fear, nor be afraid : sanctify the LORD of Hosts Himself; and let Him be your fear, and let Him be your dread."

2 Hide me from the gathering together of the froward : and from the insurrection of wicked doers.

This is an acknowledgment of past help, not a prayer, in the LXX. and Vulgate. *Thou hast protected me from the assembly of the evil.* The *gathering together,* when " assembled together the chief priests and the scribes, and the elders of the people, into the palace of the high priest, and consulted

that they might take JESUS by subtilty, and kill Him." The
insurrection (LXX. and Vulgate, the *multitude*,) when "the
whole multitude of them arose, and led Him to Pilate."
The comment of S. Augustine on this passage has been em-
bodied by the Western Church in the Office for Good Friday.
Thus he speaks : " Now upon Himself, our Head, let us look :
Like things many Martyrs have suffered ; but nothing doth
shine out so brightly as the Head of Martyrs, in Him let us
rather behold what they have gone through. Protected He
was from the multitude of malignants, GOD protecting Himself, the SON Himself and the Manhood He was carrying,
protecting His flesh ; because Son of Man He is, and SON
of GOD He is ; SON of GOD because of the form of GOD, Son
of Man because of the form of a servant ; having in His
power to lay down His life, and to take it again. To Him
what could enemies do ? They killed the body : the soul they
killed not. Observe ; too little therefore it were for the LORD
to exhort the Martyrs by word, unless He had enforced it
with example. Ye know what a gathering together there
was of malignant Jews, and what a multitude there was of
men working iniquity." And it was true also of the Church
in the ages of persecution, when the Christians were alike exposed to the formal inquisition of laws enacted by the Government, and to the savage attacks of infuriated mobs.

*3 Who have whet their tongue like a sword : and
shoot out their arrows, even bitter words.*

Let not the Jews say, We have not killed CHRIST. For to
this end they gave Him to Pilate the judge, in order that
they themselves might seem as it were guiltless of His Death.
For when Pilate had said unto them: "Take ye Him, and
judge Him according to your law;" they replied : "It is
not lawful for us to put any man to death." The iniquity of
their deed they wished to lay upon a human judge ; but did
they deceive GOD the Judge? O ye Jews, ye killed Him ;
Whence did ye kill Him? With the sword of the tongue,
for ye did whet your tongues. And when did ye smite, except when ye cried out, "Crucify, Crucify." And thus ye
crucified Him with your tongues at the third hour, as the
soldiers did with their hands at the sixth. *And shoot out
their arrows, even bitter words.* Of accusation, before Pilate,
of reviling, before the Cross. The LXX. and Vulgate render,
And bend their bow, a bitter thing. The Targum paraphrases thus : They have anointed their arrows with deadly
and bitter poison. The bow smites secretly, the sword openly.
They smote with the tongue as a sword openly, when they
cried " Crucify." But they smote with the bow when they
craftily plotted His death, and laid snares for Him, especially
that He should be betrayed by a Disciple, which is *a bitter
thing.*

Margin notes: S. Matt. xxvi. 3. S. Luke xxiii. 1. A. / A. / S. John xviii. 31. / S. Luke xxiii. 21. / Ay.

4 That they may privily shoot at him that is perfect : suddenly do they hit him, and fear not.

Yes, truly was it foretold of Him by His ancestor seventeen hundred years before : " The archers have sorely grieved Him, and shot at Him, and hated Him : but His bow abode in strength, and the arms of His hands were made strong by the hands of the mighty GOD of Jacob; (from thence is the shepherd, the stone of Israel.)" *Privily*, in their secret councils, in their bargain with Judas, in the irregular trial before Caiaphas. *At Him that is perfect*, or, with the Vulgate, *spotless*. Other targets for archers are marked with spots to direct the aim; this one, remarks S. Augustine, had not even so much of spot as could be pierced with an arrow. *Suddenly*, for His capture followed at once on the bargain of Judas. *And fear not.* Because they knew Him not, and thus had not the fear of GOD before their eyes. S. Hilary applies this passage to the attacks of ghostly enemies on the newly-baptized, who are washed from the spots of sin, but are not as yet steadfast in the faith, nor experienced in resisting temptations.

Margin: Gen. xlix. 23.

Margin: A.

Margin: D. C.

Margin: H.

5 They encourage themselves in mischief : and commune among themselves how they may lay snares, and say, that no man shall see them.

Here the older versions agree in rendering : *They have confirmed for themselves a wicked saying.* That saying was, " Crucify, Crucify," which they repeated again and again in their hate, as it is written, " They were instant with loud voices, requiring that He should be crucified." Further hear, adds S. Augustine, in what manner they confirmed malignant discourse. They said, " His Blood be on us and on our children." They confirmed to themselves malignant discourse, not to the LORD, but to themselves. Death killed not the LORD, but He death; but them iniquity killed, because they would not kill iniquity. And they have continued to confirm a wicked saying, by denying the LORD's Resurrection from the dead. *And commune among themselves how they may lay snares, and say, that no man shall see them.* Plotting that the capture should be the act of a disciple, the condemnation that of a Roman judge, and the Crucifixion the deed of foreign soldiers, so that they might be held guiltless of all participation in the matter.

Margin: A.

Margin: S. Luke xxiii. 23.

Margin: S. Matt. xxvii. 25.

Margin: S. Athanasius.

Margin: B.

6 They imagine wickedness, and practise it : that they keep secret among themselves, every man in the deep of his heart.

The A. V. is clearer, and shows that the passage means to point out the craftiness of all the plotters. The LXX. and Vulgate are widely unlike this, and read, *They have searched out iniquity, they have failed in searching out* [Vulg. *with*] *searchings.*

A man shall come, and [Vulg. *to*] *a deep heart.* The *searching*   **A.**
out is explained of their long plotting against the LORD, and
especially of their treasonable bribe to Judas. The *failure*
is the result of the Resurrection, and denotes the vain attempt
to spread a story of the theft of the LORD's Body by the Disciples. *They have failed* as Diocletian and his colleagues failed,   **L.**
when they raised the column to commemorate the total overthrow of the Christian Faith, beneath which, ten years later,
the empire bowed. *A man shall come, and a deep heart.*
So read the LXX., followed by many Latin Fathers. The
Psalmist speaks of The Man, Whose heart, S. Augustine re-   **A.**
marks, is *deep*, that is, *secret*, presenting before human faces
Man, keeping GOD within. *To a deep heart.* And it may
be spoken of that gradual perfecting of CHRIST's human nature, whereby He came at last, even as Man, to the full
knowledge of the deep things of GOD. But the reading of
the Syriac Psalter is the loveliest of all. It is this: *For the
searching out from within the Son of Man, and from His deep
heart.* We shall find no worthier comment here than the
language of S. Bernard, echoed by the voice of a singer of S. Bernard.
our Israel. " Since we have once for all come to the most Pass. Dom.
sweet Heart of JESUS, and as it is good for us to be here, let
us not readily suffer ourselves to be torn from Him of Whom
it is written, ' They that depart from Me shall be written in
the earth.' What of those who draw near? Thou Thyself Jer. xvii. 13.
teachest us. Thou hast said to them which drew near to
Thee, ' Rejoice, for your names are written in heaven.' S. Luke x. 20.
Let us then come to Thee, and rejoice, and be glad in Thee,
remembering Thy Heart. O how good, and how sweet to
dwell in this Heart! At this temple, at this Holy of holies,
at this Ark of the Covenant I will worship and praise the
Name of the LORD, saying with David, My heart hath found 1 Chron.
that I should pray before my GOD. I too have found the Heart xvii. 25.
of the loving JESUS, my King, my Brother, and my Friend.
Shall I not then worship? In this Thy Heart, therefore, O
most sweet JESU, and in my own, new found, I will worship
Thee, my GOD. Only suffer my prayers to enter into the
sanctuary where Thou hearest, nay, draw me altogether into
Thy Heart." So too the hymn :

> Cor tuum est apertum, ut intrem libere,   The Hymn
> Ut cordi cor insertum condatur intime,   *Cor meum*
> Ah JESU mi, amoris vi,   *tibi dedo.*
> Dedisti te, ut darem me,
> Ah amem te, ut amas me,
> JESU suavissime!
>
> Hic cordis firmamentum, hic tuta quies est,
> Amoris fulcimentum, hic certa salus est,
> In petræ hoc foramine,
> In cordis hac macerie;
> Hic muniar, hic uniar,
> JESU carissime!

7 But GOD shall suddenly shoot at them with a swift arrow : that they shall be wounded.

Here the LXX. and Vulgate depart completely from the English version. The first clause they render, *And God shall be exalted,* connecting it with the previous sentence, *A man shall come, and a deep heart.* GOD shall be exalted in the human heart of CHRIST, by the perfect subjection of His own will to His FATHER'S. GOD, in the Person of CHRIST, shall be exalted by all the faithful who come to that Heart for comfort and shelter. The second clause in LXX. and Vulgate runs : *Their smitings have become the arrows of*

A. *children.* That is, the Jewish weapons of attack were as idle

D. C. as the toys of a child. Or, as it has also been taken, *Their childish arrows have been their smitings,* the ruin of their city and the scattering of their nation being the fruit of their useless attempt to stay the Gospel. Yet again, it has been

H. interpreted of the preaching of the lowly Apostles, who, though they became as little children in docility and meekness, yet

S. Greg. sent the arrows of their preaching home to many a heart.
Mag. Moral. And with these arrows was the Church smitten when she
xxxiv. 5. said, I am wounded with love.
Cant. v. 8,
Vulg.

8 Yea, their own tongues shall make them fall : insomuch that whoso seeth them shall laugh them to scorn.

G. The LXX. (in some copies) and Vulgate read, *And their tongues became weak against them, all that saw them were troubled.* It may be taken of the silence of the chief priests and rulers after the Resurrection, when, no longer daring to speak as they had done before, they feebly had recourse to the falsehood of the watch at the sepulchre. Yet again, *their tongues became weak against themselves,* because whereas they said that it was expedient that one man should die for the people, lest the Romans should come and take away their place and

D. C. nation ; the death of that Man proved their utter overthrow. Or it may be, *their tongues became weak against* the Apostles, and *they were troubled* when they saw them, as it is written, "Now when they saw the boldness of Peter and John, and

Acts iv. 13. perceived that they were unlearned and ignorant men, they marvelled;" and again, "They were not able to resist the

Acts vi. 10. wisdom and the spirit with which" Stephen "spake." Moreover, because their own tongues have made them to fall ; *all that see them are troubled,* and take the punishment of the Jews as a warning to themselves against rejecting the truth. Where note, that the Hebrew of this last clause is rather, "*All that see them shall shake their heads,*" in fit requital of that day, when "they that passed by reviled Him, wagging

S. Matt. their heads." So the prophecy is fulfilled, "Because My
xxvii. 39. people have forgotten Me . . . . every one that passeth
Jer. xviii. thereby shall be astonished, and wag his head."
15, 16.

9 And all men that see it shall say, This hath
GOD done : for they shall perceive that it is his
work.

Here also the LXX. and Vulgate vary from the English
Version. They read: *And every man feared; they declared
the works of God, and understood His deeds.*. The Prayer
Book Version simply recognizes that the dispersion of the
Jews is an act of Divine vengeance; the A. V., somewhat
nearer to the Vulgate, brings in the idea of preaching. Because the Apostles feared GOD, observes S. Augustine, they
feared not man, but declared the works of GOD, declared
that a Man had come, and that GOD was exalted. *And understood His deeds*, by the illumination of the HOLY GHOST,
especially after the Day of Pentecost, when CHRIST fulfilled
His promise to them. What is, *And they understood His
deeds?* Was it, O LORD JESU CHRIST, that Thou wast silent,
and like a sheep for a victim wast being led, and didst not
open before the shearer Thy mouth, and we thought Thee to
be set in smiting and in grief, and knowing how to bear
weakness? Was it that Thou wast hiding Thy beauty, O
Thou beautiful in form before the sons of men? Was it that
Thou didst not seem to have beauty or grace? Thou didst
bear on the Cross men reviling and saying, "If He be the
Son of GOD, let Him come down from the Cross." What
servant of Thine and beloved of Thine, perchance knowing
Thy power, cried not out and said, O that now He would
come down, and all these that revile would be confounded!
But it was not so: He must needs have died for the sake of
men to die, and must rise again for the sake of men alway to
live. This thing, they that would have had Him come down
from the Cross, understood not; but when He rose again,
and, being glorified, ascended into Heaven, *they understood
the works* of GOD.

A.
D. C.
A.

S. Matt. xxvii. 40.

10 The righteous shall rejoice in the LORD, and
put his trust in him : and all they that are true of
heart shall be glad.

It is spoken firstly of that Just One Who rejoiced in doing
His FATHER's will, in the victory of His own Resurrection,
in the glory of His Ascension. And then it holds of every
faithful soul which is made glad by the Gospel tidings, and
still more by the presence of CHRIST, risen and appearing
bodily, as to the Apostles, invisibly in the hearts of Christians now. Thus the Church sings:

Omnis fidelis gaudeat,
Et grates Deo referat,
Quantum quit tantum audeat
Laudesque dignas offerat.

Brev. Misen.
Off. de Vultu
D. N. J. C.

o 3

JESUS in mundum veniens
Se manifestum præbuit,
Fines orbis pertransiens,
Consolari nos voluit.

P.

Shall be glad. LXX. and Vulgate, *Shall be praised.* It was fulfilled in this world when, by the victory of Constantine, the despised Nazarenes were uplifted, and the finger of scorn was no longer pointed against them, when the Confessors of the previous persecution were honoured most of all living men, and next to the Martyrs in whose steps they had trodden. It will be fulfilled yet more blessedly when the LORD comes: "Who both will bring to light the hidden things of darkness, and will make manifest the counsels of all hearts: and then shall every man have praise of GOD."

1 Cor. iv. 5.

Wherefore:

Glory be to GOD the FATHER, Who is the Deep Heart, and to the SON, Who cometh to that Deep Heart; and to the HOLY GHOST, Who is the Gladness wherewith the righteous shall rejoice in the LORD.

As it was in the beginning, is now, and ever shall be: world without end. Amen.

COLLECTS.

Ludolph.

O GOD, the Protection of all believers, keep Thy Church from the gathering together of the froward, who strive to assault it with secret arrows; that holding to Thee with a sound and right mind, it may always rejoice in the merits of the Saints. (1.)

Mozarabic.
Passiontide.

Protect us, O LORD, from the gathering together of our froward enemies, Thou Who didst bear the reproach of the Cross; that they who whetted their tongues as a sword against Thee, won over by the most healthful gift of Thy grace, may be swallowed up by the eating of the Church. (11.)

Mozarabic.
Passiontide.

Deliver my soul, O LORD, from fear of the enemy, and save it from the gathering together of the froward, that as it hath been brought out of the horrible pit by the wound of Thy Passion, it may, believing in Thee, be led to the freedom of everlasting glory. (11.)

S. Jerome.

GOD vouchsafe to grant us, that we, freed from the arrows of the enemy, delivered from the bow of falsehood, may be guarded by Him Who giveth all His Saints the glory of immortality for their hope of salvation. (2.)

PSALM LXV.

TITLE : To the Chief Musician, a Psalm and Song of David. Vulgate: To the end. A Psalm of David. A Song : of Jeremiah and Ezekiel, to the people of the emigration, when they began to go forth.

Syriac: Of David. Literally, when he brought up the Ark of GOD to Sion. To us, therefore, spiritually, it denotes the preaching of the Apostles. Arabic : Of David, concerning the emigration of the people.

ARGUMENT.

ARG. THOMAS. That CHRIST is the hope of all lands. The Voice of the Apostles with the praise of CHRIST. The Voice of the Prophet concerning the Apostles and the people. Truly the Voice of the Church. Of Baptism at length in the Passover. The Voice of the Church before Baptism.

VEN. BEDE. Since the first portions of the title are already remarked upon, we shall explain the latter in a few words. When the people of Israel had passed over into Chaldæa, the above-named Prophets foretold that they should return to their country after seventy years, and should restore, in a happier state, Jerusalem, which had been overthrown by the enemy. It does not follow that Jeremiah and Ezekiel composed the Psalm; but as it historically agrees with their date, it is prefaced with their names. Most authors assert that this was done by Ezra, saying that he fitted titles to all the Psalms, and collected them into one volume, as they had been unarranged and scattered, according to variety of authority and date, up to that time. Spiritually, the people which, leaving Babylon, hastened after the Captivity to Jerusalem, refers to them who, after past sin, and condemnation of the confusion of this world, emulously press into the Church of CHRIST. And to these the entire Psalm is, by the authority of the Fathers, to be adapted. That people which, abandoning the sins of the world, hath returned to the LORD, in the first opening of the Psalm, now free, acknowledging its Author, beseeches that its prayer may be heard, declaring the only happy man to be him that has succeeded in reaching His courts. *The hymn befits Thee, O God, in Sion.* In the second section it asserts the LORD to be the hope of all the ends of the earth, describing His power in varied praise by allegorical comparison, and saying that His Saints rejoice in Him with hymns of gladness. *Hear us, O God of our salvation.*

EUSEBIUS OF CÆSAREA. The Calling of the Gentiles.

S. ATHANASIUS. A Psalm with hymns.

VARIOUS USES.

Gregorian. Wednesday. Lauds. [Office of the Dead. Lauds.]
Monastic. The same.
Parisian. The same.
Lyons. Thursday. Lauds.

Ambrosian. Monday of the Second Week. Matins. I. Nocturn.
Quignon. Wednesday. Sext.
Eastern Church. Saturday. Nocturns.

ANTIPHONS.

Gregorian and *Monastic.* Ferial. Thee befits * the hymn, O GOD. [Office of Dead. Hear my prayer, and unto Thee shall all flesh come.]

Parisian. Ferial. Hear us, O GOD of our salvation, * the hope of all the ends of the earth.

Lyons. As Gregorian.

Ambrosian. As Psalm lxii.

Mozarabic. The outgoings of the morning, * and at evening Thou shalt be gladdened, O GOD.

1 Thou, O GOD, art praised in Sion : and unto thee shall the vow be performed in Jerusalem.

There is much contest amongst the expositors as to the intent and occasion of this Psalm. The title of the LXX. and Vulgate versions points to the beginning of the Captivity. Some readings bring it still lower, by adding the names of Haggai and Zechariah. S. Basil and Theodoret have objected to this view, as contradicting the language of Ps. cxxxvii., which implies that no Psalms were sung during the

L. Captivity. To this Lorinus replies that the title does not show that this Psalm was recited by the people, or in Assyria, and besides, that the refusal to sing denoted no more than the absence of any public ritual, and does not exclude private recitation. The great majority of ancient commentators take this view of the Psalm, some holding it to be a prophecy of David's, and others a Psalm of much later date, classed under his name. Herein they are followed by some modern critics, as Hupfeld and Ewald. Again, the Psalm has been ascribed, as by the Syriac Psalter, to the festival held by David on bringing up the Ark to Jerusalem. This is accepted by Jansen of Ghent. A third view is that it is a Psalm of thanksgiving for the Levites after the cessation of a drought. This is the theory adopted by Agellius amongst older commentators, and Delitzsch in the present day. There is, however, a greater unanimity amongst the Fathers as to the mystical interpretation. *Thou, O God, art praised in Sion,* or, as the LXX. and Vulgate, *The hymn befits Thee in Sion.* Not in Babylon,

A. the city of confusion, but in Sion, the place of expectation. But thou art yet in Babylon. There I am, doubtless, but in flesh, not in heart. With the latter I sing, not with the former; for not in flesh I sing, but in heart. The sounding of the flesh even the citizens of Babylon hear, but the heart's sound the Builder of Jerusalem heareth. And so the Cluniac:

Bern. Clun.
Rhythm.

Even now by faith I see thee,
Even here thy walls discern ;

To thee my thoughts are kindled,
And pant, and strive, and yearn :
* * *
And though my body may not,
My spirit seeks thee fain,
Till flesh and earth return me
To earth and flesh again.

And unto Thee shall the vow be performed in Jerusalem, the
Vision of Peace, the Heavenly City, that vow which was made
in the Church Militant below, made by pilgrims journeying
through a strange land, and hastening to fulfil their promise in
their own Country.[1] The saints *praise* GOD indeed in the Way,
but shall perfectly praise Him in their Country, when they
see Him face to face. The first vow which we make to GOD
in Baptism is to renounce the devil and all his works, and to
keep GOD's holy Will and Commandments; but this vow,
through the infirmity of the flesh, we cannot fully observe in
this present life, but we shall perfectly perform it in the Heavenly Jerusalem.

B.

Ay.

2 Thou that hearest the prayer : unto thee shall
all flesh come.

Because of the prophecy of the Resurrection of the Body
contained in this verse, the whole Psalm has been made part
of the Western Office for the Dead, and this forms its Antiphon. The Vulgate differs a little, beginning, *Hear my
prayer.* S. Augustine takes the verse to mean the prayer of
the Church for the ingathering of the Gentiles, that *all flesh,*
that is, men and women of all ages, ranks, capacities, and
nations may continue, as they have begun, coming to CHRIST.
Hear my prayer, now, in the Way, urges Gerhohus, which
if Thou hear,—rather, because Thou wilt hear—*all flesh shall
come to Thee.* For if the evil days were not shortened, as
Thou sayest, no flesh could be saved; but for the elect's
sake, as Thou promisest, and as I ask, trusting that promise,
the evil days will be shortened; and when they are so, *all
flesh will come to Thee.* That it may be fulfilled, "they
twain," the Bridegroom and Bride, "shall be one flesh,"
doubtless all flesh shall come to Thee, as well that of which
it is certain that it shall be saved, weak and frail though it
be, but also that which shall not be saved, will then come to
Thee, its Judge, when, as it is written, "Every valley shall
be filled, and every mountain and hill shall be brought low,
and all flesh shall see the salvation of GOD." And because
it is so, the Church makes her petition to Him Who heareth
the prayer, beseeching Him for all flesh, living and departed,
that He will have mercy on it in that day. "Further, we
offer to Thee for all the Saints, who have pleased Thee from

A.

G.

Gen. ii. 24.

S. Luke iii. 5.

[1] On the subject of the contrasted use of the words Sion
and Jerusalem, see Vol. I. pp.
397—405.

Liturg.
Clement.
Apost.
Const.

the beginning of the world; the patriarchs, prophets, righteous men, apostles, martyrs, confessors, bishops, priests, deacons, subdeacons, readers, singers, virgins, widows, laymen, and all whose names Thou knowest. We further offer to Thee for this people, that for the glory of Thy CHRIST Thou wilt make them a royal priesthood, a holy nation," &c.

3 My misdeeds prevail against me : O be thou merciful unto our sins.

B.

Rather, with the LXX. and Vulgate, (to which the A. V. is nearer,) *The words of the ungodly¹ have prevailed,* as the passage is not a confession of personal guilt, but a prayer for help. And they explain it variously. *To Thee,* says S. Bruno, *shall all flesh come,* to Thee from Whom it departed through the *words of the ungodly* Adam and Eve, when they thought in their hearts, "We shall be as gods,"—words which have *prevailed* against us to bring us all under death. But Thou, Who art GOD the WORD, *shalt be propitiated for our sins,* blotting them out by Thy Atonement, and thus bringing us

H. & A.

back to Thee, the True Life. And *the words of the ungodly have prevailed* in another sense, that of the spread of heathen errors over the face of the earth, which are yet to be swept away by the power of GOD. Yet again, it was true of the Church in many a persecution, when the very name of Christian seemed on the point of extinction; and most true when, in the great Arian trouble, the Catholics were as a flock of kids, while the Syrians (most literally, for the Patriarchate of Antioch was the Arian stronghold) filled the country.

4 Blessed is the man whom thou choosest, and receivest unto thee : he shall dwell in thy court, and shall be satisfied with the pleasures of thy house, even of thy holy temple.

G.

Blessed is that Man, elect from thousands, whom Thou, O GOD the FATHER, hast chosen, and made GOD, not of adoption, but very natural GOD, Thy SON; not by the taking away of manhood, but by the taking of Manhood into GOD. Blessed, likewise, after Him, in Him, and through Him, is that man whom

D. C.

Thou choosest out of the world, and receivest to some ministry of salvation for himself and others. And as the words are spoken literally of the happiness of those whom GOD should suffer to return from Babylon to Jerusalem, so they hold spiritually of all whom GOD elects out of a state of sin, and brings to the riches of His grace. *He shall dwell in Thy court,* (A. V., Vulg., &c., *courts.*) Not at first in the inner chambers, but in the outer vestibule, in the Church Militant

C.

here on earth. And this is even more forcibly expressed by the rendering of some ancient Psalters, *in Thy tabernacles,*

¹ More exactly, *words of wickednesses,* דְּבְרֵי עֲוֹנֹת

the tents of the great army of GOD. The plural number, moreover, denotes the wide extent of the House of GOD, whether on earth or in heaven. On earth, for it is written, "O Israel, how great is the house of GOD, and how vast the place of His possession!" In heaven, for "in My FATHER's house are many mansions." *And shall be satisfied with the pleasures of Thy house.* Not resting, like Lazarus, merely within the shelter of the gate, sore and hungering, but sitting at the Host's own table, clad in the purple of a king, in the fine linen of a priest, and faring sumptuously every day at the feast which the King makes for His SON. So, in the Church on earth, after Baptism in the outer court has given us a right to dwell therein, we are led on to the inner sanctuary, there to be filled with the good things from the Altar of GOD. True it is also of that House of GOD, the Shrine of Divinity, the Body of the LORD JESUS, whence, by the mystery of the Incarnation, His faithful people are filled with grace and strength.

> We taste Thee, O Thou Living Bread,
> And long to feast upon Thee still;
> We drink of Thee, the Fountain Head,
> And thirst for Thee our souls to fill.

Even of Thy holy temple. Thus we pass from glory to glory, till to the GOD of gods we appear. From the courts into the House, from the House into the Temple, He draws us, and we run after Him, because, as S. Bernard says, " our prize is to see GOD, to live with GOD, to live on GOD, to be with GOD, to be in GOD, Who will be all in all; to have GOD, Who is the highest good." But the LXX. and Vulgate read thus, joining the words to those which follow them: *Thy temple is holy, wonderful in righteousness.* What is more fitly styled the Temple of GOD than CHRIST Himself, in Whom dwelleth all the fulness of Godhead bodily? And it belongs to distributive justice to bestow rewards according to difference of merit. Wherefore the Temple of GOD, that is, CHRIST, is *holy,* and *wonderful in righteousness,* because, as righteousness directs, He bestows rewards on the just. And so it is said of Him, " He shall judge the world with righteousness." The Church Triumphant is also the Temple of GOD; *holy,* because there is no spot, or wrinkle, or imperfection there; *wonderful in righteousness,* unlike the righteousness of the Way, which is but filthy rags. And note, that it is not the structure of the building, its gold, its silver, nor its precious stones, to which the title *wonderful* is given, but its righteousness; for the holiness of CHRIST, not His majesty, is that which is set before His people to admire, love, and follow. Love ye righteousness, and ye are the Temple of GOD.

5 Thou shalt show us wonderful things in thy

Marginal notes: D. C.; Baruch iii. 24.; S. John xiv. 2.; S. Albertus Magnus.; S. Bern. Rhythm. Jubilus.; S. Bernard. de Præm. Pat. Cœlest.; Ay.; Ps. xcvi. 13.; D. C.; A.

righteousness, O GOD of our salvation : thou that art the hope of all the ends of the earth, and of them that remain in the broad sea.

The first clause of the verse is, as we have seen, construed differently, and with the preceding words, by the Vulgate. But as it stands above, it speaks of the marvels which followed the Crucifixion; not merely the rent veil, the torn rocks, the opened graves, and the Resurrection itself, but that crowning event which the Church calls the "Wonderful Ascension." *Wonderful things* again in the judgment on the guilty city ; wonders in the triumphs of the Church over her persecutors, and in the calling of the Gentiles ; and wonders yet to come in the awful portents which will herald the Second Coming of the LORD. And besides, our true Hezekiah, the "Strength of the LORD," will show us, who have come to Him from Babylon, all the house of His precious things,—the silver of His pure confessors, the gold of His martyrs, the spices of the incense of His perpetual intercession, the precious ointment of the HOLY GHOST, and all the house of His armour, the panoply of GOD, that they may be our very ówn, what time we take the Kingdom of Heaven by violence. *Hear us, O God of our salvation,* as we knock at the gate of Thy courts, as we call to Thee from afar. *Thou that art the Hope of all the ends of the earth.* Because all flesh shall come to Thee, not Jews alone, but Gentiles ; for the holy Church throughout the world is formed from "all nations, and kindreds, and people, and tongues." *And of them that remain in the broad sea.* Because "the isles shall wait for His law," so that they, His messengers, who go down to the sea with the tidings of salvation, "shall declare His praise in the islands." If He were not the *Hope* of them which *are in the sea afar,* He would nót have said to His disciples, "I will make you fishers of men." Now, in the sea, being taken by the nets of the faith, we rejoice that we there are swimming yet within the nets, because this sea is raging with storms, but the nets which have taken us will be drawn out to shore. The shore is the end of the sea; therefore the landing will be at the end of the world. So the Cluniac :

When the heavenly net is laden
 With fishes many and great;
So glorious in its fulness,
 · Yet so inviolate.

He is the *Hope of them who are in the broad sea,* perishing in their sins, even in the very jaws of the monsters of the deep. So cries the Holy Eastern Church to Him at Whitsuntide :

Sick with the tide of mortal cares,
Tossing on sin as on the wave,

Marginal notes:
2 Kings xx. 13.
G.
Rev. vii. 9.
Isa. xlii. 4.
Isa. xlii. 12.
A.
S. Matt. iv. 19.
S. Bern. Clun. Rhythmus.
Pentecostar. Dom. Pent. Od. vi.

Cast to the beast that never spares,
Like Jonah, LORD, I cry, O save
From the abyss which brings a grave.

He is the Hope of them whose faith and endurance fail for a **S. Matt. viii. 25.**
moment when they believe Him to be asleep during the
storm, and who, in their terror, cry, "LORD, save us, we **S. Matt. xiv. 30.**
perish;" and of those whose over-bold confidence leads them
to come to Him upon the water, and who become afraid, and **Ay.**
begin to sink, till He catches them, as He did His chief
Apostle. And He is the hope of them who are in the salt
sea of penitential tears, feeling themselves afar from Him.

6 Who in his strength setteth fast the mountains:
and is girded about with power.

For, observes S. Hilary, the mountains are whatsoever **H.**
powers lift themselves proudly against GOD, which He brings
low, and binds surely in their place of punishment. But **A.**
there are other mountains which are GOD's hills, humble in
themselves, and exalted in Him; and of them also it is
spoken. Especially of the Apostles, those holy hills on **S. Albertus Magnus.**
which Jerusalem is founded, those mountains of Israel which **Ps. lxxxvii. 1.**
shoot forth their branches, and yield their fruit to His people
of Israel. The Targum singularly reads here, *Who prepareth* **Ezek. xxxvi. 8.**
food for the wild goats of the mountains, which may be interpreted of GOD's providential care even for sinners. *And is*
girded about with power. They that put CHRIST in the **A.**
midst, *girded about,*—make Him, that is, on all sides begirt.
We all have Him in common, therefore He is in the midst:
all we gird Him about that believe in Him; and because our
faith is not of our strength, but of His power, therefore
He is girded about in His power, not in our strength.
Girded about with power, the power of His Godhead, by **Pet. Lomb.**
which, as with majesty, the Manhood of the WORD is girded.

7 Who stilleth the raging of the sea: and the
noise of his waves, and the madness of the people.

Here the LXX. and Vulgate read, *Who troublest the*
depth of the sea. And it is explained of the hearts of **A.**
ungodly men, which GOD searches to the very bottom,
and turns into dry land, reclaiming them, and making
them productive of the fruit of righteousness. The English Version tells us of the peace of the Church after the
fiercest of all the persecutions, when that great raging sea of
heathenism heard the voice of JESUS, saying, "Peace, be **S. Mark iv. 39.**
still; and there was a great calm." Of this, too, the *noise of*
his waves speaks, reminding us not only of the edicts sounding across the world, but the deep roar of the amphitheatre,
Christianos ad leones! Truly, the *madness of the people.*
These latter words, however, are rendered by the Vulgate,

The nations shall be troubled, and are joined on to the next verse:

8 They also that dwell in the uttermost parts of the earth shall be afraid at thy tokens : thou that makest the outgoings of the morning and evening to praise thee.

Troubled at first with that dim anticipation of a mighty change which Virgil expressed:

Virg. Eclog.
iv. 4.

Ultima Cumæi venit jam carminis ætas ;
Magnus ab integro sæclorum nascitur ordo,
Jam redit et Virgo, redeunt Saturnia regna:
Jam nova progenies cœlo demittitur alto.

Ay.

Troubled then at the actual coming of the Master, and at the miracles wrought by His Apostles ; fearing at first with that servile dread which begets sadness, learning to fear Him afterwards with the loving awe which is the parent of joy, because "the fear of the LORD is honour, and glory, and gladness, and a crown of rejoicing." The sea, the people, is troubled, but the mountains which GOD hath set fast are unmoved while the waves dash against them.

Ecclus. i. 11.
A.

Thou that makest the outgoings of the morning and evening to praise Thee. Or, with the Vulgate and LXX., *Thou that shalt delight the outgoings of the morning and evening.* By the morning he signifieth the prosperity of the world, by the evening he signifieth the trouble of the world. The morning signifieth prosperity, because the morning is glad, the sadness, as it were, of the night being overpast. But sad is the darkness when the evening cometh on ; therefore, when the evening, as it were, of the world came, He offered an evening Sacrifice. Let each one, therefore, not fear the enemy, neither in the morning let him be corrupted. And Thou wilt accept and make delightful to the angels alike the repentance and conversion of the young who flee from their sins, and of the old who turn again at the close of life. Moreover, the Psalmist tells of the joy of the whole earth, from east to west, at the Coming of the Redeemer. Thus the Christian poet:

A.

D. C.

P.

S. Cœl. Se-
dul. Hymn.
in Nativ.

A solis ortus cardine,
Ad usque terræ limitem,
CHRISTUM canamus principem,
Natum Mariâ Virgine.

Once again, it has been well taken to denote the ceaseless Daily Service throughout the world:

And, as each meridian line
Gains the travelled sun, that day,
Still begin those rites divine,
Still new priests begin to pray ;

Still are blessed the bread and wine,
Still one prayer salutes his ray:
Continent and ocean round
Rolls the tided wave of sound.

9 Thou visitest the earth and blessest it : thou makest it very plenteous.

By the earth is implied our human nature, because, though it be made up of an earthly body and a spiritual soul, yet, because we have more practical acquaintance with the earthly portion, GOD sometimes calls man by the name of earth. The LORD, then, *visited the earth* when He, by His Incarnation, united our manhood to the Person of the WORD. So spake Zacharias: "Blessed be the LORD GOD of Israel, for He hath visited and redeemed His people." *And blessest it.* Yet stronger are the LXX. and Vulgate, *Thou hast intoxicated it.*[1] With the Wine of His Passion, good wine kept until now, the Bridegroom hath gladdened His guests. *And madest it very plenteous* in the riches of good works and spiritual gifts wherewith the faithful abound. Cardinal Hugo takes the verse as prophetic of the LORD's visitation as Judge, when He shall make the earth to overflow by giving up its dead, now plenteously revived, so that the dry bones shall live, and stand upon their feet, "an exceeding great army."

Ay.

S. Luke i. 68.

Arnobius,

Ay.

Hugo Card.

Ezek.
xxxvii. 10.

10 The river of GOD is full of water : thou preparest their corn, for so thou providest. for the earth.

What, then, is this river of GOD? Let the Eastern Church answer: "As Thou art the Divine River of Mercy, and the abyss of much compassion, O merciful One, show the Divine streams of Thy mercy, and heal us all." *Full of water :* for with Him is the well of Life, flowing as a "pure river of water of Life, clear as crystal, proceeding out of the Throne of GOD and of the Lamb." And because this is so, the Body shares in the titles of the Head: "He that believeth on Me, out of his belly shall flow rivers of living water;" and therefore the first Hebrew believers, thus filled, were the river ("come out of the waters of Judah") which went forth to fertilize the earth. Yet again, the rivers of GOD are the Gospels, filled with the promises of GOD, set forth in the Beatitudes. And so Adam :

Eucholog.
Ord. Olei
Sanct.

Rev. xxii. 1.

A.

S. John vii.
38.

G.

Isa. xlviii. 1.

S. Athanas.

Paradisus his rigatur,
Viret, floret, fœcundatur;
His abundet, his lætatur,
Quatuor fluminibus,

Adam. Victorin. Hymn.
*Jucundare,
plebs fidelis.*

---

[1] And, most exactly, *Thou makest it overflow*, תְּשֹׁקְקֶהָ.

> Fons est Christus, hi sunt rivi,
> Fons est altus, hi proclivi,
> Ut saporem fontis vivi,
> Ministrant fidelibus.

D. C. The whole passage may also be interpreted of the visitation of Pentecost, when the LORD poured out His Spirit on all flesh, and when the fount of Holy Baptism was filled with the graces of cleansing and hallowing. *Thou preparest their* **Omn. Patr.** *corn.* First, and most truly, of that principal Sheaf, cut down, ground in the mill of the Passion, and in the oven of suffering made into that Bread which is the Life of the world.

> He chose one little sheaf, and said,
> O Food for man's salvation,
> No sweeter sheaf the winds have kissed,
> Elect of GOD for Eucharist,
> Thou shalt become the Living Bread,
> For mortals' adoration.

And, in the second place, the Psalm speaks to us of the Great Sower and Husbandman, Who puts the seed of His Word into our hearts, and cherisheth it till the day of His harvest; so providing for that new earth which shall stand when the old is passed away.

11 Thou waterest her furrows, thou sendest rain into the little valleys thereof : thou makest it soft with the drops of rain, and blessest the increase of it.

There is a good deal of variation from this in the LXX. and Vulgate. *Intoxicate its furrows, multiply its produce, let that which springeth up rejoice in the droppings thereof.* **Ay.** As the former verse speaks of the Holy Eucharist under the species of Bread, so here the Carmelite finds a reference to the Chalice. The *furrows,* observes he, are the Apostles, who first tasted that heavenly draught; the *produce* is that succession of Saints who have followed in their footsteps in the strength of that Sacrament; the *droppings* are those first **G.** instructions in the mystery of the Faith given to those babes which cannot yet receive the full flood of instruction, nor follow the counsels of perfection, as the Saints who are the true produce of Apostolic teaching, the offspring of that universal Motherhood bestowed from the Cross on the Blessed Virgin, are wont to do. The English Version will supply another train of thought. The *little valleys* of the soul are those more hidden thoughts and actions which are counted but little things, but which are as truly filled in Saints with the stream of Divine grace as the more boldly-marked furrows which denote the principal actions of their lives. The hard ground of worldliness and impenitence is softened by the gentle showers of GOD's love, and He blesseth the increase in sanctification, and that a hundred-fold even in this world, and in the world to come with everlasting life. *Thou sendest rain into the little valleys.* We may take it, as the hymn does, of the gift of tears to lowly hearts—

> JESU bone, CHRISTE mitis,
> Suscipe me, qui emittis
> Fontes in convallibus:
> Dona fontem lacrimarum,
> Ut fonte deliciarum
> Fruar in cœlestibus.

Psalterium
de Nomine
JESU.

12 Thou crownest the year with thy goodness ; and thy clouds drop fatness.

Or, with the Vulgate, *Bless the crown of the year of Thy goodness.* That year of His goodness was when " the kindness and love of GOD our SAVIOUR toward man appeared, not by works of righteousness which we have done, but according to His mercy He saved us, by the washing of regeneration, and renewing of the HOLY GHOST." The Saints are the crown of that year, the jewelled crown which JESUS wears as King of ransomed Israel. And note that He crowns the righteous in many ways. He crowns them eternally by election. So it is written, " Thou shalt also be a crown of glory in the hand of the LORD." In GOD's Hand, because no one is chosen to such a crown by his own antecedent merits. Next, He crowns by redemption. We lost our crown, as Jeremiah laments : " The crown is fallen from our head." CHRIST came to win it back by His death, when He wore the Crown of Thorns for us. Thirdly, He crowns in temptations, for a man "is not crowned, except he strive lawfully." Fourthly, He crowns by guarding us from being overcome of lust; and therefore the Virgins are diademed with gold, because of its purity. Of this it is said, " Having on His Head a golden crown." Fifthly, He crowns by giving the righteous wisdom and knowledge of the Scriptures. This crown, which is starry, belongs to the Doctors. For the star, by its brightness, denotes Scriptural wisdom, because as the star guides wanderers, so Holy Writ directs the erring. "And upon her head a crown of twelve stars ;" doubtless because Scripture is chiefly concerned with the twelve articles of the Faith. The sixth is clear : GOD strengthens His own under torments, that they fail not. This crown belongs chiefly to the Martyrs, and it is of stone, which, by its hardness, denotes firm patience in adversity. Of this crown it is said, "Thou hast set on his head, O LORD, a crown of precious stone." In all these ways GOD blesses the crown of the righteous. *And Thy clouds drop fatness.* Rather, with the Bible Version, *Thy paths drop fatness.* The footsteps of the Incarnate GOD bring health and blessing wherever they

(margin: G. Tit. iii. 5. Ay. Isa. lxii. 3. Lam. v. 16. 2 Tim. ii. 5. Rev. xiv. 14. Rev. xii. 1. Ps. xxi. 3, Vulg.)

tread, so that of Him we may reverently use the words of a heathen poet:

Lucret. i. 6.

> Te fugiunt venti, te nubila cœli,
> Adventumque tuum : tibi suaves dædala tellus
> Submittit flores ; tibi rident æquora ponti,
> Placatumque nitet diffuso lumine cœlum.

G.

The Vulgate, however, reads, *Thy plains shall be filled with abundance*, which, says Gerhohus, denotes that men who are just and plain dealers shall be filled with all good works.

13 They shall drop upon the dwellings of the wilderness : and the little hills shall rejoice on every side.

Ay.

Isa. xxxv. 1.

D. C.

S. Athan.
S. Bas. Mag.
S. Cyrill.
Theodoret.

H.

Dwellings is also the version of the Syriac Psalter, but the LXX. and Vulgate reading, the *beautiful places*, is nearer to the A. V., *pastures*, and to that which is most probably intended, the oases in the waste. It means, says Ayguan, the Gentile wilderness, which shall rejoice at the Coming of CHRIST, according to the prophecy, "The wilderness and the solitary place shall be glad for them, and the desert shall rejoice, and blossom as a rose." And the Carthusian extends the reference to all sinners, whose hearts have not yet been made the garden of GOD. Nor is it strange that many should be reminded of the solitaries of the Thebaid, who made the Egyptian desert resound with the praises of CHRIST. *And the little hills shall rejoice.* The Eastern Fathers note here, that as the deserted idol temples were hallowed by Christian prayers, so too the hills whereon heathen rites once had been celebrated were now thronged by men who had embraced the angelic life, and worshipped the true GOD in purity. Athos and Sinai still testify to their words. The hills are also mystically explained as the more eminent Saints, such as Apostles and Martyrs, rising above the plains of which the Psalm spoke before.

14 The folds shall be full of sheep : the valleys also shall stand so thick with corn, that they shall laugh and sing.

L.

The A. V. is here more exact, *The pastures are clothed with flocks*, but the LXX. and Vulgate agree in reading, *The rams of the sheep are clothed*, which the commentators unite in explaining to mean, that the leaders of GOD's flock are clothed in righteousness, the marriage garment of the Lamb. *The valleys*, the humble Christians, shall be so blessed by GOD, *that they shall laugh* (rather, with A. V., LXX., and Vulg., *shout*) in glad triumph of heart, and then burst out into a song of thanksgiving to GOD.

> O blesséd is that land of GOD,
> Where Saints abide for ever,

Where golden fields spread fair and broad,
Where flows the crystal river.
The strains of all its holy throng
With ours to-day are blending;
Thrice blessèd is that harvest song
Which never hath an ending.

And therefore:

Glory be to the FATHER, Whose temple is holy in righteousness; and to the SON, Who is that holy temple; and to the HOLY GHOST, Who is that fatness which drops upon the pastures of the wilderness.

As it was in the beginning, is now, and ever shall be: world without end. Amen.

COLLECTS.

O GOD, the Hope of all the ends of the earth, hearken to the humble prayer of Thy family, that while it praises Thee with tuneful harmony and the chanted hymn, it may, adorned by the inward flow of the Comforter, be enriched with abundant fruit. Through. (2.)   MSS. Thomas.

Vouchsafe, O heavenly King, that we, delivered from the dryness of sin, and plenteously watered with the river of Thy mercy, may be well filled, and join in the hymn sung by Thy Saints. (1.)   Ludolph.

Hear us, O GOD of our salvation, and gird us with Thy might; and while we desire steadfastness of faith, let us attain the quiet of hope, and reach the rest of love. (11.)   Mozarabic.

Hear us, O GOD of our Salvation, Who art the Hope of all the earth, and in Thy might make ready the mountains, which Thou makest bright with Thy power, and lofty with abundance of eminent virtues; for Thine it is to enrich us with higher graces, by which we may climb the steeps of a blessed life: that Thy Church, spread abroad in all the ends of the earth, may, while seeking loftiness of faith, attain the quiet of hope, and reach the summit of love. (11.)   Mozarabic. Week before Pentecost.

Bless, O LORD, the crown of the year of Thy goodness in the day of our great solemnity, that our minds may shine with the plenteousness of doctrine, and the plains of Thy gifts may be fat with abundance, that nourishment together with Thy grace may be granted us, so that our flesh may be made glad with corn, and our soul with Divine virtues. (11.)   Mozarabic.

We humbly beseech Thee, O GOD, that we may be united to the merits of Thine elect, that we may be joined in their rewards; and that, if we attain not to be graced with rewards, or decked with crowns, we may at last obtain pardon, and be saved from the pain of everlasting judgment. (1.)   S. Jerome.

O GOD, merciful FATHER, the Hope of all the ends of the earth, and of them in the broad sea, we beseech Thee to pardon our iniquities, and to the end that the words of the ungodly prevail not for ever against us, let Thine invincible protection never forsake us. (1.)   D. C.

PSALM LXVI.

TITLE: To the Chief Musician; A Song or Psalm. LXX. and Vulgate: To the end; a Song of a Psalm of Resurrection.

ARGUMENT.

ARG. THOMAS. That CHRIST is to be adored by all nations. The Voice of the Apostles. The Voice of Paul and of all Apostles for the edification of the people. Then, the Voice of the Martyrs. The Voice of the Apostles to the People. The Voice of the Church praising GOD.

VEN. BEDE. The title is distinct, implying the joy of the LORD's Resurrection, not only to the Jews, but also to the Gentiles. Contrary to the persuasion of the Jews, who alleged that they alone of all belonged to the life of blessedness; our Mother, the Church, joyously chants her hope of the General Resurrection, interposing three pauses. In the first portion she exhorts all men to rejoice together in the LORD's Resurrection, which should bring eternal rewards to all the faithful. *O be joyful in God, all ye lands.* In the second place, she invites all to come to the contemplation of GOD's works, that one belief may unite those whom one reward awaits. *O come hither, and behold the works of God.* Thirdly, she again warns the Gentiles to bless the LORD, Who, though He try us with divers troubles, will yet bring us to the rest of His mercy. *O praise our God, ye people.* In the fourth part, she again invites all, that advised by the example of her deliverance, they may trust the LORD more fully, blessing Him because He has vouchsafed to hear her prayer. *O come hither, and hearken, all ye that fear God, and I will tell you.*

SYRIAC PSALTER. Uncertain. Of Sacrifice, and burnt-offering, and incense of rams. Spiritually, the calling of the Gentiles, and preaching.

EUSEBIUS OF CÆSAREA. The calling of the Gentiles, and the preaching of the Apostles.

S. ATHANASIUS. A Psalm of rejoicing and of the Resurrection.

VARIOUS USES.

Gregorian. Wednesday. Matins.
Monastic. Wednesday. Matins. [Transfiguration. I. Nocturn.]
Parisian. Sunday. Matins. III. Nocturn.
Lyons. Thursday. Terce.
Ambrosian. Monday of Second Week. Matins. II. Nocturn.
Quignon. Sunday. Lauds.
Eastern Church. Saturday. Nocturns.

ANTIPHONS.

Gregorian. O bless * our GOD, ye people.
Monastic. [Transfiguration. The disciples, coming to the LORD JESUS, fearing the Voice of the FATHER, fell on their faces.]
Parisian. O come * hearken, and I will tell you what He hath done for my soul.
Ambrosian. First verse of the Psalm.
Mozarabic. Sing a Psalm to His Name, give glory to His praise, say unto GOD, O how terrible are Thy works.

The occasion of this Psalm, as of the preceding one, is the subject of much doubt. A few commentators ascribe it to the later years of David; the Greek Fathers generally to the return from Babylon, perhaps at the dedication of the Second Temple; others count it as a Maccabee thanksgiving; and others again, followed by some modern critics, assume it to speak of the deliverance of Jerusalem from Sennacherib. The words of the LXX. and Vulgate title, *Of the Resurrection*, are not in the Hebrew or Chaldee, and Leo Castro charges the Jews with erasing them. But although they are cited by various early Fathers, yet their absence from S. Hilary's Psalter and from the Hexapla seems to mark them as a late addition. They are, however, much commented on by the ancient and mediæval expositors, who interpret the whole Psalm by them as a key.

1 O be joyful in GOD, all ye lands : sing praises unto the honour of his Name, make his praise to be glorious.

S. Hilary, commenting on the word ἀλαλάξατε, with which **H.** the LXX. opens this Psalm, reminds us that it is a battle-cry, and calls on all the Christian world to do its duty manfully in the fight, that it may chant the song of victory at the end. And because it is CHRIST'S Resurrection which **Ay.** hath put the enemy to flight, let His Name be praised, and give the glory to His praise alone, and not to any works of man. But the praise must be the active praise of holy works, **D. C.** not merely the recitation of holy words.

2 Say unto GOD, O how wonderful art thou in thy works : through the greatness of thy power shall thine enemies be found liars unto thee.

For *wonderful*, the early versions read *terrible*. And fitly, however we regard those works. *Terrible* in the expulsion from Eden, *terrible* in the Flood, *terrible* in the overthrow **D. C.** of the Egyptians. More terrible still in the stupendous mystery of the Incarnation, whereby the Creator of Angels en- **S. Leo Mag.** dured to become a mortal, invisible in Himself, visible in our **Ep. x. ad** nature; Incomprehensible, Who willed to be comprehended; **cap. iv.** before all time, yet beginning to be in time. Terrible in the **P.** eclipse of the sun at His crucifixion, the three hours' darkness, and the rent rocks; terrible in the broken gates and bars of hell; terrible in His Resurrection. Not less so in **A.** the judgment by which He broke off the branches of His own olive-tree, that the wild Gentile boughs might be graffed in, an awful warning to us not to be high-minded, but to fear, and not to boast ourselves either against Jews, broken off of old, or against heretics, fallen later. We pray you to beware, says S. Augustine, whosoever ye are in the Church, do not revile them that are not within; but pray ye rather, that they too may be within; for GOD is able to graff them in

II.   P

D. C.

S. Matt.
xii. 24.

Ay.

S. Matt.
xxviii. 12.

again. *Thine enemies shall be found liars.* As when they ascribed the *greatness of* CHRIST'S *power* to diabolic agency, saying, "This fellow doth not cast out devils, but by Beelzebub, the prince of the devils." And yet again when they bribed the soldiers to spread a false report of the stealing of His Body from the sepulchre. Still more in our own day, when the very existence of CHRIST as a personage belonging to history has been denied, on the express ground of the miraculous acts ascribed to Him.

3 For all the world shall worship thee : sing of thee, and praise thy Name.

4 O come hither, and behold the works of GOD : how wonderful he is in his doing toward the children of men.

A.

D. C.

C.

A.

At the end of the third verse some copies of the LXX. and the Roman Psalter add, *O most Highest.* Vain have been the lies of the Jews; He Whom they branded as a deceiver is worshipped and praised over all the Gentile world, and not only there, but in the courts of heaven, because His Name is above every name. A little before, most lowly, now Most Highest; most lowly in the hands of lying enemies, Most Highest above the heads of praising Angels. *Come hither,* then, to hear the word of GOD : come to His Church, *and behold,* by truer contemplation, by the light of Faith, by the irradiation of the HOLY GHOST, *how wonderful He is in His doing* towards those Apostles whom He made the channels of His miracles; wonderful in His election to grace; wonderful in His judgment of sinners in the rejection of the Jews, in the call of the Gentiles.

5 He turned the sea into dry land : so that they went through the water on foot; there did we rejoice thereof.

A.

Ps. cxliii. 6.

Ay.

A.

Spoken first of the Red Sea triumph, it tells of a greater triumph of GOD'S power and grace. The world, notes S. Augustine, was a sea, bitter with saltness, troubled with tempest, raging with waves of persecution. Truly, the sea hath been turned into dry land, and now, the world that was filled with salt water thirsteth for water that is sweet, so that now the Gentile world cries: "My soul gaspeth unto Thee as a thirsty land." What He did for all the world He does for every soul flooded with the salt sea of penitential tears, drying it up, and making it able to bear fruit for Him. Next, the Vulgate reads, *They shall go through the river on foot.* And it is spoken of the courage with which the faithful shall pass through this life, not affected by the flood of worldliness, and yet on foot, because lowly, and not lifted up with pride, thus following more safely Him of Whom it is written in mystery: "With my staff I passed over this Jordan; and now I am become two bands." He went with His Cross *Gen. xxxii.* alone, and returned LORD of Jews and Gentiles, of the Church *10.* Militant and the Church Triumphant, of men and angels. *We did rejoice* at the exodus from Egypt, at the entrance into Canaan; *we shall rejoice*, as the Vulgate reads, far more *D. C.* truly in passing from the way to our Country, from the waters of sin to the haven of quiet and safety. For even if we are joyous now, in hope we are joyous, but then in Him shall *A.* we be joyous. Even now in Him, yet through hope, but then *1 Cor. xiii.* "face to face." *12.*

6 He ruleth with his power for ever; his eyes behold the people : and such as will not believe shall not be able to exalt themselves.

So He joins the two ideas Himself, "All power is given *H.* unto Me in heaven and in earth. Go ye therefore, and teach *S. Matt.* all nations, baptizing them in the Name of the FATHER, and *xxviii. 18.* of the SON, and of the HOLY GHOST." And thus His behold- ing is the look of compassion which He turns on His suffer- ing people. *Such as will not believe.* The LXX. and Vul- *D. C.* gate have, *They that embitter*, or that *exasperate*, the A. V. more exactly, the *rebellious*. They cannot exalt themselves, *Prov. xvi.* because a "haughty spirit goeth before a fall," and "the *18.* soul that doeth ought presumptuously, the same reproacheth *Numb. xv.* the LORD, and shall be cut off from among His people." But *30.* they may be exalted by Him Who beareth His people on His *Deut. xxxii.* wings. *12.*

7 O praise our GOD, ye people : and make the voice of his praise to be heard ;

Make it heard, by declaring it to others, that he who loves GOD may show his love to his neighbour also, by bringing *Pet. Lomb.* him profitable tidings. Wherefore the priests bless GOD in the churches with a loud voice. For which reason it is said, "Behold now, praise the LORD, all ye servants of the LORD, ye that by night stand in the house of the LORD." S. Augus- *Ps. cxxxiv.* tine reads, *Hear ye the voice of His praise*, listen to the glad *1.* news of His Gospel.

8 Who holdeth our soul in life : and suffereth not our feet to slip.

The Vulgate runs, *Who hath set my soul unto life.* And *Theodorus* that not only by breathing into man the breath of life, *Mopsuest.* but by giving him the natural law, which, had Adam kept it, would have preserved him alive. More than this, He *P.* set our soul unto the higher life of grace and glory, by means of faith. Nay, more than all, He has made us look to Himself, Who is emphatically the Life. *And suffereth not* *S. Albertus* *our feet to slip*, because He hath set those feet upon a Rock, *Magnus.*

P 2

Origen.

Gen. iv. 16.

Deut. v. 31.

Cant. v. 15.
firm and unshaken, and ordered our goings thereon. Not
like Cain, who "went out from the presence of the LORD,
and dwelt in the land of Nod," which means *wandering*, but
like Moses, to whom was said, "Stand thou here by Me,"
and of whom those words were then true, "His legs are as
pillars of marble, set upon sockets of fine gold."

9 For thou, O GOD, hast proved us : thou also hast
tried us, like as silver is tried.

With fire, first of persecutions and sufferings, and then
with the more searching fire of heavenly love. For the odour
of a saintly life needs the divine fire to make its perfume
S. Cyrill.
Alex. in Gen.
lib. x.
A.
known, as incense requires glowing coals to quicken its properties. *As silver*, which is purified by heat, not as stubble,
which is burnt up by it. And note, that the precise moment
when silver is truly refined, is that in which the finer can see
his face exactly mirrored in the molten surface. Whereby
we know that our purification is complete, when CHRIST can
see His Image reflected in our hearts. And as earthen ves-
R.
sels continue porous and friable till they are baked, so we,
who are earth in the hand of the potter, need fire to make us
fit to be the receptacles of grace. The early Fathers, holding
the doctrine of a purgatorial fire through which the very
S. Ambros.
in Ps. cxix.
H. 20.
1 Cor. iii. 13.
Saints, and even the Mother of GOD herself, must pass at
the Last Day, dwell on this verse, and compare it with that
saying of S. Paul, "The fire shall try every man's work."

10 Thou broughtest us into the snare : and laidest
trouble upon our loins.

Being crafty, He caught us with guile, and when He had
so taken us, He put His yoke on our shoulders, and His
burden on our backs, that in this world we might have tribu-
H., C.
lation. And literally, His martyrs were brought into the
snare of dungeons, chains, and strangulation, and had scourges,
heavy weights, and even plates of red-hot metal, laid upon
their sides as they were extended upon the rack.

11 Thou sufferedst men to ride over our heads :
we went through fire and water, and thou broughtest
us out into a wealthy place.

It is spoken of the persecuting Emperors, and of evil rulers,
L.
temporal and spiritual, in all ages. Lorinus, writing at a
time when the Turkish corsairs ravaged the Mediterranean
coasts, and even at times the shores of Northern Europe, applies the text to the hard lot of the Christian captives in
Algiers and Morocco. *Through fire and water.* Again we
are told of the sufferings of the martyrs, some winning their
crown in fire, like S. Polycarp; some in water, as S. Clement
of Rome. Or you may take it, as S. Ambrose does, of the

first purification of the soul in Baptism, and the second S. Ambros.
in Ps. cxix. cleansing by the fire of purgatory. Or it may be explained, Serm. 3. with S. Augustine, of the mingled sorrows and pleasures of A. this life. S. Bernard expands this idea, and observes of a S. Bernard. Saint lately departed, "He passed over right manfully, yea, Vit. S.
Malach. and happily; he passed over through fire and water, he whom sorrow could not break, nor ease delay. The knowledge of good and evil lies in this mean, and this is to make trial here of pleasure and of trouble. Happy is that soul, which passes through both alike, neither clinging to pleasure, nor failing in trouble." Once more, the *water* of penitential tears, and the *fire* of divine love, are the fit preparation for entrance into the wealthy place of unity with GOD. *A wealthy place.* The Vulgate reads, *a cool place.* And it will then tell us of that shelter with Him Who is a refuge from the heat, the shadow of a great rock in a weary land, of those cool waters and green pastures which wait for the Saints who have followed their Shepherd in this life. But if we take our English reading, *a wealthy place*, it will tell of that field of the Church wherein the treasure of grace is hidden, and of that more glorious Church where the treasure is no more hid, but open to all gazing eyes.

> About the Holy City rolls a flood
> Of molten crystal, like a sea of glass;
> On which bright stream a strong foundation stood,
> Of living diamonds the building was;
> That all things else it wholly did surpass,
> Her streets, the stars, instead of stones, did pave,
> And little pearls for dust it seemed to have,
> On which soft streaming manna like pure snow did wave.

Giles Fletcher, CHRIST'S Triumph.

The two preceding verses of the Psalm have been applied with much ingenuity to the vocation for the claustral life. *Thou hast brought us into the snare* of the cloister, binding us with the threefold cord of the monastic vow, and *laidest* Alvarez. *trouble*, the regular tasks and enforced duties of the convent, *upon our loins. Thou hast set men*, abbats and prelates, *over our heads*, whom we must obey: *we go through fire and water* in the various trials of that obedience, and then *Thou hast brought us into a cool place*, where we are free from the heat and anxiety of this world, and look forward to the coolness of the life to come.

12 I will go into thine house with burnt-offerings: and will pay thee my vows, which I promised with my lips, and spake with my mouth, when I was in trouble.

Into Thine house, either by withdrawing into myself for D. C. secret communion with Thee, remembering that my body is the temple of the HOLY GHOST, or into the place of Thy

A.

public worship, or at last into the heavenly City. *With burnt-offerings*, having consumed all that is mine, by victory over self, and leaving only what is God's. So the Paris Breviary, singing of Confessors:

Hymn. in
Comm. Just.

> Corpus subegit castitas,
> Et liberam mentem fides ;
> Amor supernis ignibus
> Totam litavit hostiam.

H.
P.

Genebrar-
dus.

Ay.

It is true of the Martyrs also, and chiefly of Him, their King, Who ascended into the Holy of holies with the whole burnt-offering of Himself. *My vows*, whether of baptism, of the religious or priestly life, or of self-dedication of any kind. And the word *pay* marks that such vows are debts, not mere voluntary offerings which need not be made. *Which I promised with my lips.* The Vulgate reads, *which my lips distinguished* (i.e. *articulated*.) Where note, says Ayguan, that he distinguishes his vows, who vows discreetly, but he who vows indiscreetly, does not distinguish, because distinguishing belongs to discretion, and he distinguishes his vows of God's praise, who says in his heart that he is nothing, and God is all, that he needs God, not God him. *And spake with my mouth*, implying a distinct contract made with God, not a mere passing resolution of the mind, but a positive action of the will, binding itself to future performance. *When I was in trouble.* So the Patriarch, "And Jacob vowed a vow, saying, If God will be with me, and will keep me in this way that I go, and will give me bread to eat, and raiment to put on, so that I come again to my father's house in peace ; then shall the Lord be my God." And to all this He answers, to the first request, "When thou passest through the waters I will be with thee;" to the second, "Behold, I send an Angel before thee, to keep thee in the way;" to the third He replies, "The bread that I will give is My flesh, which I will give for the life of the world." For raiment, He declares, "Behold, I have caused thine iniquity to pass from thee, and I will clothe thee with change of raiment," and will say to His servants, "Bring forth the best robe, and put it on him ;" and last of all, that we may come to our Father's House in peace, He says, "In My Father's house are many mansions. I go to prepare a place for you." Wherefore let us keep the vow, and have the Lord for our God.

Gen. xxviii.
20.

Isa. xliii. 2.

Exod. xxiii.
20.

S. John vi.
51.

Zech. iii. 4.

S. Luke xv.
22.

S. John xiv.
2.

13 I will offer unto thee fat burnt-sacrifices, with the incense of rams : I will offer bullocks and goats.

A.

The LXX. and Vulgate read here *marrowy burnt-offerings*. Within may I keep Thy love, comments S. Augustine, it shall not be on the surface, in my marrow it shall be that I love Thee. For there is nothing more inward than our marrow; the bones are more inward than the flesh, the marrow is more inward than those same bones. Whosoever therefore on the

surface loveth GOD, desireth rather to please men, but having
some other affection within, he offereth not holocausts of
marrow. The fat burnt-offerings are also explained of the   Theod. Mop-
Martyrs, as strong and resolute under torture. *With the*   suest.
incense of rams. The rams are the rulers of the Church;
the whole Body of CHRIST is speaking, this is what it offereth
to GOD. The incense of rams is therefore the prayer offered   Ay.
as incense before GOD by the rulers of the Church. Bullocks,
which labour in the LORD's field, signify doctors and preachers; while the goats are repentant sinners. Sinners, because
of the LORD's own distinction between sheep and goats; repentant ones, because goats were the victims used in sin-   Origen.
offerings.

14 O come hither, and hearken, all ye that fear
GOD : and I will tell you what he hath done for my
soul.

He calls not only the living, but the Patriarchs and Pro-   Theod. Mop-
phets of old time, who longed to see these things, to hearken   suest.
to the Gospel tidings, and to rejoice with us. The Gentiles   L.
who serve GOD by the law of nature, are also summoned in
these words to join the Church, that the law of grace may be
explained to them. The soul which has been healed is eager
to point out the Great Physician to those which are still suffering from disease.

15 I called unto him with my mouth : and gave
him praises with my tongue.

I, a man, was crying to a stone, I was crying to a deaf   A.
stock, to idols deaf and dumb I was speaking; now, the image
of GOD hath turned to the Creator thereof; I that was " saying to a stock, Thou art my father; and to a stone, Thou   Jer. ii. 27.
hast brought me forth," now say, " Our FATHER, Which art   S. Matt. vi.
in heaven." *I called unto Him with my mouth.* With *my*   9.
mouth now, not with the mouth of another. When I was
crying to stones in the "vain conversation received by tra-   1 S. Pet. i.
dition from the fathers," with the mouth of others I was cry-   18.
ing; when I have cried unto the LORD with that cry which
Himself hath given, which Himself hath inspired, I called
unto Him with my own mouth. *And gave Him praises with*
my tongue. The LXX. and Vulgate read, *And have exalted*   A.
Him under my tongue. That is, notes S. Augustine, confessed Him secretly in my heart, as well as preached Him
openly. Many Psalters, and the majority of mediæval expositors read, *I have exulted under my tongue.* And they explain it of spiritual joy within the heart. It is like the Bride,   G.
says one, "Honey and milk are under thy tongue;" so that
my tongue may be busied with the praise of GOD and with
holy prayers, and my spirit within rejoice in GOD my SA-
VIOUR. *I exulted under my tongue,* while that tongue was

the pen of a ready writer uttering good words without, and within my heart was inditing a good word wholly in harmony with those outer words. The Hebrew would be more closely rendered, *A song of praise was under my tongue*, and it will then imply the absolute certainty of GOD's answer to prayer, and that the believer has his thanksgiving ready even while he is uttering his cry of supplication.

16 If I incline unto wickedness with mine heart : the LORD will not hear me.

H.
Not merely, notes S. Hilary, if I have actually done an evil deed, but if I have thought on it with pleasure, and given the assent of my will. And the Vulgate puts this very forcibly, *If I have beheld iniquity in my heart.*

17 But GOD hath heard me : and considered the voice of my prayer.

18 Praised be GOD who hath not cast out my prayer : nor turned his mercy from me.

Lu.
1 S. John iii. 21.
Because I have not inclined to wickedness with my heart, for thus speaks the Apostle, "Beloved, if our heart condemn us not, then have we confidence towards GOD. And whatsoever we ask, we receive of Him;" and it therefore urges us to perseverance. Not to vain confidence, for GOD, notes

L.
1 S. John v. 16.
Lorinus, sometimes does cast out prayer. Moses was not heard for his sister, nor Samuel for Saul, nor Antiochus for himself, and there is a sin unto death, for which it is not said that we are to pray. *Praised be God.* Let all His

G.
Angels and Saints praise Him; heaven and earth, the sea and all that is therein. Praise the LORD, O my soul, and all that is within me, for He hath given me perseverance in crying unto Him, and turned not His mercy far from my prayer,

S. Matt. vii. 7.
and I have found it true, that, "Ask, and it shall be given you; seek, and ye shall find; knock, and it shall be opened unto you."
Wherefore:
Glory be to the FATHER, Who hath heard my prayer; and to the SON, my Resurrection and Life, through Whose mediation my prayer hath reached the FATHER; and to the HOLY GHOST, the Mercy of FATHER and SON, which hath not been turned from me as I prayed.
As it was in the beginning, is now, and ever shall be: world without end. Amen.

COLLECTS.

Ludolph.
Instil into my mind, O LORD, the glory of Thy praise, that while we shun the burnings of this world, we may, under Thy guidance, be carried into eternal refreshment. (1.)

Mozarabic.
Grant, O LORD, that we who, believing in Thee, go into

Thine house with burnt-offerings, may serve Thee with dedication of our works and sanctification of the body, that so Thou mayest not cast out our prayers, nor turn Thy mercy from us, whilst Thou dost inspire us to seek that which Thou knowest to be good for us. (11.)

Let all the earth worship Thee, O LORD, and sing to Thee, *Mozarabic.* being made partaker of incorrupt life; that as all things are framed by Thy handiwork, they may likewise be submitted to Thy sway. (11.)

O GOD, Who hast willed that Thy Saints should be tried *Mozarabic.* on earth by Thy wonted loving probation, but not that they *For the Saints.* should be tempted above the gift of endurance which Thou seest to be in them by Thy bounty, deliver us from all temptation, lest it overcome our mind; that serving Thee faithfully in well-pleasing obedience, Thou wouldst suffer us to be so tried, that temptation lead us not into the confusion of error, but bind us firmly in the embrace of truth. (11.)

O GOD, to Whom all the earth sings loud praise in rejoicing, *Mozarabic.* and Whose glory it proclaims with the tuneful voice of a psalm, Whose awful might in Thy works it confesses, grant that our voices may yield Thee acceptable praise, and our prayers give Thee a perfect psalm, and celebrate Thee, the Maker of all powers; and inasmuch as Thine eyes behold the nations, and invisibly search the inmost parts of all things; we beseech Thee so to look on us graciously with Thine eyes, and to correct us so in mercy, that Thou mayest not pour Thy wrath upon us, angered by our misdeeds, nor restrain Thy mercy when Thou art intreated. And grant, that our very fear of Thee for our sins may be our chastisement, and our belief and confession of Thy Godhead, the reward of our pardon. Set our souls then, O LORD, unto life, that we may weep here for our doings, and win that grace which we have lost through sin. (11.)

We humbly beseech Thee, O LORD, open Thine ears to *S. Jerome.* our prayers, and, granting us pardon of our sins, deliver us from our present troubles, and making us, by the death of our vices, a pure burnt-offering to Thee, unite us to the company of the Saints. (1.)

PSALM LXVII.

TITLE: To the Chief Musician on Neginoth; a Psalm or Song. LXX. and Vulgate: To the end, in the hymns, a Psalm of a song of David. Or, To the Supreme, on the stringed instruments; a Psalm of Song.

ARGUMENT.

ARG. THOMAS. That CHRIST is the Light of believers. The Prophet counsels believers. The Apostolic voice. The HOLY GHOST by the Prophet counsels believers. The voice of the Apostles. The Prophet, concerning the Advent of CHRIST and His Resurrection.

VEN. BEDE. *Hymn* and *Song* denote praise, and that it may be shown that these are given to CHRIST the LORD alone, *To the end* is prefixed. After the "Song of Resurrection," the Prophet supplicates that we may be blessed, and be led to the knowledge of GOD, to which our own merits cannot attain. For, in the first part, speaking to the faithful, he prays that he may with them attain to be blessed by the LORD, so that, enlightened in heart, they may know that CHRIST the LORD is to be preached among all nations. *God be merciful unto us.* Then, turning to the LORD, he says in the spirit of prophecy that He is to have thanks given Him by the peoples, because He judges the nations in equity. *Let the people praise Thee, O God,* &c. Thirdly, he repeats the same verse which he had uttered above; adding this in a mystery, that the earth had already brought forth her fruit: and therefore, iterating the phrase, he again asks that we may be blessed. *Let the people praise Thee, O God, . . . increase,* &c.

SYRIAC PSALTER. It is uncertain who composed it. The people which brought David over the River Jordan sang it. To us it signifies the prophecy touching the call of the Gentiles, the preaching of the Apostles, and the judgment of the LORD.

EUSEBIUS OF CÆSAREA. The calling of the Gentiles, and the preaching of the Apostles.

S. ATHANASIUS. A Psalm declaring things to come.

VARIOUS USES.

Gregorian and *Monastic.* Daily. Lauds.
Parisian. Thursday. Prime.
Lyons. Thursday. Lauds.
Ambrosian. Monday of Second Week. II. Nocturn.
Quignon. Saturday. Prime.
Eastern Church. Saturday. Nocturns.

ANTIPHONS.

Gregorian and *Monastic.* Vary with every day and festival.
Parisian. The LORD show us the light * of His Countenance, that we may know Thy way upon earth, O LORD.
Lyons. GOD * be merciful unto us, and bless us.
Ambrosian. As preceding Psalm.
Mozarabic. The LORD show us the light of His Countenance.

The use of this Psalm in the Gregorian and Monastic Psalters is peculiar. It is always said together with Ps. lxiii., under one Antiphon, and with but one Gloria, at the close. The custom is a very ancient one, and is mystically explained by Durandus, as follows: "It is asked, why the two foregoing Psalms, to wit, *O God, Thou art my God,* and *God be merciful unto us,* are united, and said under one *Gloria Patri* and one Antiphon. To which the reply is fourfold. First, because the Psalm, *O God, Thou art my God,* signifies thirst for GOD; in the Psalm, *God be merciful,* the Trinity is indicated. This is done therefore to signify thirst and continual longing for GOD. Secondly, to note that, before the persecution of Antichrist, the people of believing Gentiles, referred to by the Psalm, *O God, Thou art my God*, and the repentant people of the Jews, referred to by the Psalm, *God be merciful*, shall be one in faith; and after they are united, the tribulation of Antichrist will come. Thirdly, because the former Psalm signifies love of GOD; wherefore it is there said, *My soul thirsteth for Thee*. The latter Psalm signifies love of one's neighbour; wherefore it is said, *That we may know Thy saving health among all nations*, which two things are so joined together, that a Christian cannot have one without the other. Fourthly, because the grace of which the Church seems conscious in the former Psalm is evidently conferred in the latter; wherefore there is an invitation to thanksgiving, when it is said there, *Let the people praise Thee, O God*. Again, at the end of the Psalm, *O God*, the *Gloria Patri* is not said, because therein human sorrow is treated of; whence it is there said, *My soul thirsteth*. For it is not every Psalm treating of sorrows and other adversities which praises Him for them, though they should do so. But in the following Psalm the *Gloria Patri* is subjoined, because in it the mercy of GOD is treated of." Psalm lxvii. is also used in several benedictions, as in the churching of women, and the blessing of bells, and in the processions for fine weather.

1 GOD be merciful unto us, and bless us : and show us the light of his countenance, and be merciful unto us.

The words first rise to a climax, and then are further emphasized by repetition of the opening prayer. Mercy for past error and sin is first sought, and then blessing. But as GOD blesses in many ways, sometimes granting only temporal gifts, the special desire of the suppliant is added—enlightenment by Divine grace. The prayer for mercy is repeated, because GOD's mercy is as necessary for perseverance in grace as for the original call to it. And observe, remarks Eusebius, that there is a clear reference to the Levitical benediction under the Law: " Speak unto Aaron and unto his sons, saying, On this wise shall ye bless the children of Israel, saying unto them, The LORD bless thee, and keep thee: the LORD make His Face to shine upon thee, and be gracious unto thee: the LORD lift up His Countenance upon thee, and give thee peace. And they shall put My Name upon the children of Israel; and I will bless them." So that the Psalm must have a prophetic relation to the return from exile, when the priests should resume the interrupted custom of benediction. The whole Psalm is the prayer of the Vineyard to the Husbandman, of the Church to GOD the FATHER, praying Him to send His rain to increase the fruits which He has planted and tilled Himself. But though it is collectively the cry of the whole vineyard, yet each section belongs to a different part. *Be merciful* is the cry of penitents; *bless us*, that of advancing Christians; *show us the light of His Countenance*, of dying ones; asking severally

C.

Euseb. Cæsar.

Numb. vi. 23.

A.

Hugo Card.

Z.

for pardon, justification, wisdom, and glory. Observe the repetition of the words, *be merciful unto us.* Divine grace is as necessary for final perseverance, as for the first call to repentance. *And show us the light of His Countenance.* The Countenance or Face of the FATHER is the SON. For, saith

S. John xiv. 9.

He, " He that hath seen Me hath seen the FATHER." Therefore the Prophet saith, in the way of desire, Let His Countenance appear; that is, May the FATHER's Countenance, even the SON Himself, shine on us, here on earth, by His Incarnation.

2 That thy way may be known upon earth : thy saving health among all nations.

A.

Thy way is that which leadeth to Thee. What is it? We can learn it from the Gospel. The LORD saith, CHRIST saith,

S. John xiv. 6.

"I am the Way." But dost thou fear lest thou shouldst stray? He hath added, "I am the Truth." Who strayeth in the truth? He strayeth that hath departed from the truth. The Truth is CHRIST, the Way is CHRIST; walk therein. Dost thou fear lest thou die before thou attain unto Him? "I am the Life." "I am," He saith, "the Way, the Truth, and the Life." As if He were saying, What fearest thou? Through Me thou walkest, to Me thou walkest, in Me thou restest. And note, observes S. Albert,

S. Albertus Magnus.

that we may *know* His way in three manners here *on earth.* By natural understanding, which is wisdom; " for the invi-

Rom. i. 20.

sible things of Him are clearly seen, being understood by the things which are made." By grace, through faith, " for

1 Cor. xiii. 12.

now we see through a glass, darkly." And there is the glorious manner, by which it shall be known in our Country. " Then shall I know, even as I am known." And therefore rightly does the hymn address the Light of GOD's Countenance :

Brev. Misen. The Hymn *Omnis fidelis gaudeat.*

O Blessed Face, whose praise we sing!
Here in the way we worship Thee;
That in the Country of our King,
Filled with Thy glory we may be.

G.

Thy saving health among all nations. It is the doom of Jewish isolation and supremacy. Let us not, then, stand outside with the envious elder brother, angry with his brother who was lost; but let us enter in, and be gladdened with that harmony which that great choir sang. And that it may become greater day by day, and be multiplied unto the end, we pray and cry :

3 Let the people praise thee, O GOD : yea, let all the people praise thee.

A.

Walk ye in the Way together with all nations; walk ye in the Way together with all peoples, O sons of peace, sons of the One Catholic Church. Walk ye in the Way, singing as ye go. Wayfarers do this to beguile their toil. Sing ye in this Way, I implore you by that same Way, sing ye in this Way; a new song sing ye, let no one there sing old ones; sing ye the love-songs of your fatherland, let no one sing old ones. New Way, new wayfarer, new song.

4 O let the nations rejoice and be glad : for thou shalt judge the folk righteously, and govern the nations upon earth.

They shall be glad, and not in servile terror of the Judgment, because not only will it be just, and therefore merciful, instead of arbitrary and cruel, but Thou shalt *govern* and guide *the nations* in the right way, so that they shall be safe from all peril, because taught by Thee to avoid all sin. **G.**

5 Let the people praise thee, O God : let all the people praise thee.

6 Then shall the earth bring forth her increase : and God, even our own God, shall give us his blessing.

The LXX., Vulgate, Syriac, and Æthiopic all translate, more correctly, *The earth hath brought forth her fruit,* and join these words to the preceding ones. It is a fresh reason for the exultation of the people, more glorious and joyous than the former. For the earth is that holy soil, of which is written, "Drop down, ye heavens, from above, and let the skies pour down righteousness; let the earth open, and let them bring forth salvation." The earth hath brought forth her fruit; Mary hath born Jesus. **Ay.** **Isa. xlv. 8.**

ἀνήρωτος ἄρουρα ὡράθης, τὸν στάχυν τεκοῦσα τῆς ζωῆς. **Octoechus ἠχ. δ΄.**

So too the Western hymn:

Gaude Virgo gloriosa,
Verbum verbo concepisti,
Gaude tellus fructuosa,
Fructum vitæ protulisti.

7 God shall bless us : and all the ends of the world shall fear him.

The mystery of the Holy Trinity is shadowed out in the triple recitation of the Name of God. God the Father, Unbegotten, Underived, shall bless us. Our *own* God, our Brother, God the Son, made like unto us, shall bless us. God the Holy Ghost shall bless us. And the singular verb and pronoun which follow express the Unity. *All the ends of the world shall fear Him.* Not with the servile terror which the devils feel, but the filial awe of sons, the wholesome re- **Ay.** **G.** **D. C.**

verence of disciples, that by that fear we may be guarded from the wrath to come.

Wherefore:

Glory be to the FATHER, Who hath imprinted on us, His sons by adoption, His Countenance, that is, His SON by nature; and to the SON, Who is the FATHER'S Countenance; and to the HOLY GHOST, the mercy and light of the Countenance of GOD.

As it was in the beginning, is now, and ever shall be: world without end. Amen.

COLLECTS.

Ludolph. Show the light of Thy Countenance upon us, O LORD, and vouchsafe us Thy perpetual blessing; that giving thanks to Thee in holy fear, we may attain to win the fruit of righteousness before the face of Thy majesty. Through. (1.)

Mozarabic. Let all the people praise Thee, O GOD, Thy prizes which Thou hast redeemed; and let them who were subject to punishment for unbelief, rejoice in being saved by Thy free grace. (11.)

Mozarabic. Show the light of Thy Countenance upon us, O LORD, and pour Thy blessing abundantly into our breasts; that our hearts, bedewed with the gladness of Thy light, may know Thy way upon earth, and be glad in the full knowledge of the holy faith among all nations. (11.)

S. Alcuin. Knowing Thy way on earth, O LORD, and Thy saving health among all nations, we confess that CHRIST the LORD is both the Way and the Country, by Whom we pass on aright, and come to the fullest attainment. (2.)

D. C. O GOD, Who hast mercy on all; O GOD, Light of light and Fount of brightness; show the light of Thy merciful Countenance upon us, bless us, and make us to know Thy way on earth, that, walking therein without offence, rejoicing and being glad, we may reach the heavenly mansion. (9.)

PSALM LXVIII.

TITLE: To the Chief Musician; a Psalm or Song of David. Vulgate: To the end; a Psalm of a Song of David.

ARGUMENT.

ARG. THOMAS. That all the kingdoms of the earth sing to CHRIST alone. The Prophet announces the Advent of CHRIST, and His Assumption into heaven. The Apostolic voice, desiring that the LORD would rise from the dead, and ascend into heaven, and arise in the heart of each one. The Prophet announces the Resurrection of CHRIST, and subsequent glories.

VEN. BEDE. *David* denotes the LORD, Whom also the *End* denotes. The Psalm is long, and marked by five pauses, by which we have distinguished its divisions. The whole Psalm speaks through mystic parables; it is full of Gospel Sacraments, and is chiefly shown to be concerning the Ascension of CHRIST. At the beginning of the Psalm the Prophet says what things are to happen to the LORD's enemies, or to the faithful, in the judgment to come; *Let God arise, &c.* Next, it signifies the mighty gifts which He bestowed on the Jewish people, and then says how He perfected the Church with these. *The earth shook, and the heavens dropped at the presence of God.* Thirdly, under the form of a mountain it denotes the LORD the SAVIOUR, recites the benefits He has vouchsafed the Church, when He raised it by the gift of His Resurrection. *When the Almighty scattered.* Fourthly, it declares that the pride of the enemies shall be utterly shaken, and that conversions and martyrdoms will abound from both sexes and the worst of sinners, what time the Advent of the LORD the SAVIOUR shineth on the world. *God shall smite the head of His enemies.* Fifthly, it says that the LORD should be blessed in the Churches, where the Apostles and CHRIST Himself preached, intreating that He will preserve those gifts which He gave His faithful. It warns, further, that they who tarry in this world as in Egypt and Æthiopia, should come quickly to the LORD. *Give thanks unto God the Lord in the congregations.* In the sixth clause it counsels all men to sing to CHRIST the LORD, Who hath now disclosed the wonders of His Resurrection; and then endeth the Psalm with praise of the LORD. *O sing praises unto the Lord, Who sitteth above the heavens.*

SYRIAC PSALTER. Of David, when the kings made them ready to battle against him. Also, a prophecy of the dispensation of CHRIST, and the calling of the Gentiles to the Faith.

EUSEBIUS OF CÆSAREA. The Incarnation of CHRIST, and calling of the Gentiles.

S. ATHANASIUS. A Psalm in prayer.

VARIOUS USES.

Gregorian. Ferial. Wednesday. Matins. [Whitsunday. Matins.]
Monastic. Wednesday. Matins.
Parisian. Thursday. Matins.
Lyons. Wednesday. III. Nocturn. [Whitsunday. Matins.]
Ambrosian. Monday of Second Week. II. Nocturn.
Quignon. Thursday. Matins.
Eastern Church. Saturday. Nocturns.

ANTIPHONS.

Gregorian. Ferial. As preceding Psalm. [Whitsunday, (and *Lyons.*) Stablish the thing, O GOD, * which Thou hast wrought in us, from Thy holy temple, which is in Jerusalem. All. All.]
Monastic and *Lyons.* In the congregations * give thanks unto the LORD.
Parisian. The LORD * gave the word to the preachers. The GOD of Israel, He shall give power unto His people.
Ambrosian. As Psalm lxvi.
Mozarabic. First verse of the Psalm.

1 Let GOD arise, and let his enemies be scattered :
let them also that hate him flee before him.

Ay.

That is, let CHRIST arise from death, that by exalting us
He may scatter His enemies. Where note, that in the time
of Moses, when the Tabernacle and Ark of the LORD were
fashioned in the wilderness, at what time soever the Jews
were about to fight with their foes, in order that they might
triumph over them, the Ark of the LORD was uplifted by the
Numb. x. 35. Priests, and then Moses said, "Rise up, LORD, and let Thine
enemies be scattered ; and let them that hate Thee flee before
Thee." Wherein was prefigured, that when CHRIST should
rise from the dead, His visible enemies, the Jews, and His
invisible ones, the evil spirits, should alike be scattered ; the
Jews over the face of the earth, the prince of this world cast
out of the hearts where he once ruled. *Flee before Him.*
Pet. Lomb. Vulgate, *Before His Face.* Not as though they could escape
to any place where His Presence is not, but flee in terror,
though knowing escape impossible. It is the prayer of the
G. Church in times of coldness and backsliding, when the Truth
has been crucified afresh, and laid in a tomb with a great
stone rolled to its mouth, and when unfaithful priests, bishops,
and judges are encouraging falsehood. Then let CHRIST
arise in the holiness and constancy of His true saints and
penitents, that His enemies may be scattered.

> Cold, cold Church, in thy death-sleep lying,
> Thy Lent is past, thy Passion here, but not thine Easter-day.

2 Like as the smoke vanisheth, so shalt thou
drive them away : and like as wax melteth at the
fire, so let the ungodly perish at the presence of
GOD.

G.

Smoke vanisheth in two ways, either by rising up on high,
or being consumed by the intensity of flame. So the sinners
will vanish, either by their own vanity, unable to accomplish
their desire, or will be burnt up in the unending fire of the
wrath to come. Wherefore, let their smoky wickedness
vanish, either here by penitence, as we pray, or by punishment hereafter, as we foretell. *As wax melteth at the fire.*
Our GOD is a consuming fire, burning up sin. When by the
fire of His love He melts the hearts of sinners into penitential tears, they perish, so far as they are sinners, but they
Ay. live, as redeemed men. And the Carmelite dwells at much
length on the properties of wax, as symbolizing certain virtues. It denotes humility, because it is easily melted, and
when so melted, instead of sinking, rises up and floats above
other liquids. It signifies purity, because light is fed by it,
and only the pure in heart can see GOD, Who is Light. It
denotes love ; for waxed cloth protects all things round which

it is wrapped, and so a loving man guards his neighbour from
harm. The love is faithful, as a wax seal protects the secrets
of a letter. And we may add one point more, which Ayguan
omits, that wax signifies docility, as it receives readily, and
retains, the image impressed on it by its owner. The verse
has a warning in it also. It tells of the terrible vengeance   **A.**
which will fall on the wicked in the Judgment-day, when the
LORD appears in His glory.

**3 But let the righteous be glad and rejoice before
GOD : let them also be merry and joyful.**

The Vulgate reads, *Let the righteous feast,* and it is explained   **Ay.**
of the Holy Eucharist in the Church Militant, and of everlasting glory in the Church Triumphant. *And rejoice before*   **G.**
God, because they are His guests, and He hath said, "Eat,   Cant. v. 1.
O friends; drink, yea, drink abundantly, O beloved;" and
they fear not when He comes in to see them, because they
know that they have the wedding garment on, and therefore
will not be cast out. Rejoicing before GOD in this life means   **D. C.**
delighting in those things which please Him, and being glad,
in the calmness of a good conscience, of virtuous actions and
of His honour. In their Country, the Saints rejoice in the
vision of the Divine Essence, for they see Him as He is.

**4 O sing unto GOD, and sing praises unto his
Name : magnify him that rideth upon the heavens,
as it were upon an horse; praise him in his Name
JAH, and rejoice before him.**

The second clause of this verse here and in the Authorized
Version differs widely from the LXX. and Vulgate, which   **H.**
read, *Make a road for Him Who ascendeth above the sunset.*   S. Greg.
That sunset was His own death, over which He rose by His   Mag. Moral.
Resurrection.   xix. 3.

> Love's redeeming work is done,   Charles
> Fought the fight, the battle won;   Wesley,
> Lo! our Sun's eclipse is o'er,   Easter
> Lo! He sets in blood no more.   Hymn.

And because He comes also to ascend over the darkness of   **Ay.**
our hearts, and to lighten it with His rays, we are to make
a road for Him, and to "prepare the way of the LORD," by
correcting our evil habits. The words are addressed to
Angels as well as to men. For the Jewish Holy of holies was
towards the west, and the text signifies the rising of the
LORD above the place of human worship, to that of heavenly
adoration; and the angelic hosts are called on to lift up the
everlasting doors, that the King of Glory may come in. The
Hebrew בָּעֲרָבוֹת, which the Vulgate renders *above the sunset,* and the English Versions, *upon the heavens,* (following

the Targum and Talmud,) is explained by Symmachus, S. Jerome, and by modern critics, to mean *in the wilderness;* and
the whole passage will thus be a parallel to the prophecy,
Isa. xl. 3. "Make straight in the desert a highway for our GOD." The
words *as on a horse* are peculiar to the Prayer Book Version,
and are not added by any others. They may, however, serve to
remind us of the Rider on the white horse, Whose Name is
Rev. xix. 11. "Faithful and True, and in righteousness He doth judge
and make war." *Praise Him in His Name JAH,* because
He is Very GOD of Very GOD, and all power is given unto
Him in heaven and earth.

5 He is a Father of the fatherless, and defendeth
the cause of the widows : even GOD in his holy habitation.

H.

The LXX. and Vulgate here prefix, *They shall be troubled
by the face of Him* Who is a FATHER, &c. Because they
have oppressed His suppliants. Who, then, are the orphans
G. and widows whom He thus protects? The orphans are those
who, born of their father the devil and of worldly desire, are
now orphaned by abandoning their evil parents, and seeking
a better FATHER, even GOD, and a tenderer Mother, His
S. Athana- Church. The widows are they who, once wedded to sins,
sius. now dead, have not yet the WORD for their Bridegroom, but
who have come, like Ruth, to Bethlehem to seek for Him.
A. The text has a more literal application, especially true of the
early times of the Christian Church, when the sword which
the LORD sent on earth cut asunder the ties of so many
families, and when children were cast out by parents, and
wives by husbands, for clinging to the Nazarene. *Even God
in His holy habitation.* For out of these orphans and widows,
that is, persons destitute of partnership in this world's hope,
the LORD for Himself doth build a temple, whereof in continuation He saith, The LORD is in His holy place.

6 He is the GOD that maketh men to be of one
mind in an house, and bringeth the prisoners out of
captivity : but letteth the runagates continue in
scarceness.

C. For by His inspiration the Prophets, and Evangelists, and
Apostles all teach the same great truth, all tend to the one
Ay. goal, and His will it is that His Church on earth should be
at one, undivided by schisms and heresies, as it is written,
Acts iv. 32. "The multitude of them that believed were of one heart and
one soul." But as human pride and weakness mar that unity
here, the words are most truly interpreted of the perfect har-
mony of heaven, where
S. Pet. Dam. Unum volunt, unum nolunt,
Rhythmus. Unitas est mentium.

Or we may take it, *Who setteth the lonely in homes*, and we
shall see a reference to that great Christian family which
gives new ties of kindred and affection to the desolate; and,
with many Greek Fathers, to that Religious Life, where virgin
souls are united. One old Greek reading is very beautiful,
men of one belt, which may be taken of the belt of warfare,
(*militare cingulum*,) worn by CHRIST'S chosen soldiers,
wherewith the loins are girt. The Targum interprets the
passage thus: "GOD it is Who maketh one marriage union for
a lawful son;" wherein we may read of the mystical union
between CHRIST and the Church. *And bringeth the pri-*
soners out of captivity. The Vulgate differs slightly: *Who*
hath brought out the prisoners in might. It is spoken
first of the deliverance of Israel from Egypt; then of
the miracles of JESUS, by healing those whom Satan had
bound by disease or by possession; and next of His accom-
plishment of Zechariah's prophecy, "As for thee also, by
the blood of thy Covenant, I have sent forth thy prisoners
out of the pit wherein is no water," what time He spoiled
hell, and freed the Fathers of the elder Covenant from bon-
dage. Fourthly, it denotes His deliverance of men who
are bound and tied with the chains of their sins, and that
in might, which before His gift of grace they had not.
Wherefore the soul cries to Him:

> Lux mea, pande fores, inamœnaque claustra resolve,
> Et sine sidereas ætheris ire vias.

And letteth the runagates continue in scarceness. This is not
the meaning of the passage. The Authorized Version, with
S. Jerome, rightly translates, *The rebellious dwell in a dry*
land. And it may well be taken of the Israelites who pe-
rished in the wilderness during the forty years' wandering,
and thence of those members of the visible Church who do
not persevere, and therefore attain not to the Land of Pro-
mise. But the LXX. and Vulgate read, *Likewise they who*
rebel [*exasperate* or *embitter*,] *who dwell in sepulchres.* That
is, observes S. Augustine, every way dead, taken up with dead
works. For these men provoke Him to anger by withstand-
ing righteousness; for those fettered men perchance would
walk, and are not able, and are praying to GOD that they
may be able, and are saying to Him, "O bring Thou me out
of my troubles." It appears, then, that CHRIST draws His
Church from three sources: from Jews, bound under the
Law, whom He looses in His might; rebellious Gentile
heathens, who persecute His followers; and those who, like
S. Matthew and S. Mary Magdalene, were dead and buried
in their sins. These He makes of one mind, to dwell in His
house, under the Gospel law of grace.

7 O GOD, when thou wentest forth before the
people : when thou wentest through the wilderness,

Marginal notes:

Cd.

D. C.

Zech. ix. 11.

A.

Herm.
Hugo,
Pia Desid.

A.

Ps. xxv. 16.

P.

8 The earth shook, and the heavens dropped at
the presence of GOD : even as Sinai also was moved
at the presence of GOD, who is the GOD of Israel.

Before the people. Visibly in a pillar of cloud by day, and
a pillar of fire by night, during the forty years' journey ;
visibly too in that Manhood which was a pillar of cloud,
veiling from the eyes of man the fiery pillar of hidden Godhead, when He walked in the desert of this world, and when
the earth shook at the tidings of His Coming, and at the
preaching of His Apostles. *The heavens also dropped.* They
dropped manna for the bodily wants of the people, and holy
laws and precepts to be the food of their souls. Regarding
the manna, a Jewish legend asserts that its fall was preceded
by one dew, and succeeded by another, so that it lay enclosed
between the two till sunrise, when the upper veil of dew dis-
appeared, leaving the manna exposed ; a shadow, doubtless,
of CHRIST, the True Manna, under the forms of bread and
wine, so that when the sun of faith arises on the soul, the
dew of mere human reason vanishes, and leaves His Presence
clear to the believing heart. *Even as Sinai also was moved
at the Presence of God, Who is the God of Israel.* The
LXX. and Vulgate more briefly : *From the Face of the God of
Sinai, from the Face of the God of Israel.* And they explain
it thus : The heavens are the Apostles, dropping the gospel
dews on the hard earth of sinful and heathen souls, taught
by the same GOD Who gave the Law on Sinai, Who is the
King of Israel, and Who gave the Gospel to His disciples ; thus
showing the perfect conformity between the Old and New
Covenants. And as Mount Sinai is chief of its range of hills,
so S. Augustine takes it as a type of that Hebrew of the Hebrews, after the Law a Pharisee, who laboured more than
they all, after that he, in his journey to Damascus, had seen
the Face of the GOD of Israel, and dropped upon the ground.

9 Thou, O GOD, sentest a gracious rain upon thine
inheritance : and refreshedst it when it was weary.

The Targum declares that this means the peace and calm
which GOD sent on Israel when it was faint and affrighted at
the terrors which attended the giving of the Law. It is
more usually taken of the manna, and the shower of quails.
The LXX. and Vulgate read, *Thou shalt separate a voluntary rain for Thine inheritance, and it was made weak : but
Thou hast perfected it.* It is the rain of GOD's free grace,
sent upon His Church, feeble without that grace, but strengthened and made perfect by it. It is also spoken of the free
offer of the Gospel to the Gentiles, whom the FATHER hath
given to the SON for His inheritance, who were once weak
through idolatry and sin, but now have been perfected in
faith.

Margin notes (left column):
A.
S. Athanas.
Eusebius.
Genebrar-
dus.
Cd.
Ay.
A.
Cajetanus.
D. C.
Z.

10 Thy congregation shall dwell therein : for thou, O God, hast of thy goodness prepared for the poor.

The LXX. and Vulgate read, more literally, *Thine ani-* **L.**
mals dwell therein. And of this there are many explanations. One ingenious idea is that it means the twelve tribes,
distinguished by their standards ; as the lion of Judah, the
hind of Naphtali, the wolf of Benjamin, and so forth. An- **Ay.**
other view is, that the living creatures seen by Ezekiel and
by S. John, and therefore the Evangelists, are intended.
But as the primary reference doubtless is to the flocks and **Lu.**
herds, which had pasture secured to them by the seasonable
rain in the wilderness, we shall best interpret it of those
meek and lowly ones to whom Christ's yoke is easy and
His burden light, and who are nourished in His Church with
the Word of Holy Writ and the Sacrament of the Eucharist,
who are truly the "sheep of His pasture," and follow the **Ps. c. 3.**
Shepherd, because they know His voice. *For Thou, O God,*
hast of Thy goodness [Vulg., *sweetness*] *prepared for the*
poor. And we therefore may say, with the Angelic Doctor, **S. Thom.**
"I approach, as a sick man, to the Physician of Life ; un- **Aquin.**
clean, to the fount of mercy ; blind, to the light of eternal
glory ; poor and needy, to the Lord of heaven and earth."
He hath *prepared for the poor* in another sense, nay, gone to
prepare a place for them ; for He hath said, "Blessed are **S. Matt. v. 3.**
the poor in spirit, for theirs is the kingdom of heaven."

11 The Lord gave the word : great was the company of the preachers.

He did indeed give the Word ; for He "so loved the **S. John iii.**
world, that He gave His Only-begotten Son," and spared **16.**
Him not. *Great was the company of the preachers.* How
great shall never be known until the graves open, and the
sea gives up its dead ; when the martyrs in the ten great persecutions of the Early Church take their stand with those
who died in the middle ages by Danish, Arab, Turkish
swords, and with those who, yet later, lay down to rest on
the crosses of Japan ; and when the confessors of every
nation, every rank and age, who published the Gospel by
word or by life, will offer their spiritual children before the
throne of God. But the LXX. and Vulgate read, *The* **G.**
Lord shall give the Word to them that preach the Gospel,
with great might. It was soon to be fulfilled when He said,
"I will give you a mouth and wisdom, which all your adver- **S. Luke xxi.**
saries shall not be able to gainsay nor resist." And there- **15.**
fore, after "they were filled with the Holy Ghost, they **Acts iv. 31.**
spake the Word with boldness." And the *great might* expresses the miracles which the Apostles were empowered to **Ay.**
work as proofs of their Divine mission ; while, as S. Gregory

S. Greg.
Mag. Mor.
xxvii. 14.

S. Albertus
Magnus.

the Great observes, the spiritual miracles of overcoming sin,
still worked by the Church in our own day, are equally marvellous, though not alike patent to the senses. S. Albert
lays stress on the word *give*, and points out that GOD's gift
should not be sold, but imparted as freely as He has bestowed it. And so the old rime of counsel to priests:

Rhythmus
*Viri Venera-
biles.*

Gratis Eucharistiam plebi ministrate,
Gratis et absolvite, gratis baptizate,
Vobis gratis coelitus data gratis dato,
Salutemque omnium sedulo curate.

It is to be noted, however, that the Hebrew הַמְבַשְׂרוֹת
is a feminine noun, and the passage ought to run, *Great shall
be the company of the women, messengers of victory.* No
longer a single Miriam, Deborah, Huldah, Anna, marking
generations far distant from one another, but that great
army of Virgin martyrs which, with constancy and valour
more than manlike, followed the standard of the King into
the thickest battle, and taught the astonished heathen that
His strength was made perfect in weakness.

Mone,
Hymn. Lat.
754.

Gaude, coelestis curia,
Quæ Virginum tot millia
Laureata suscepisti,
Et Regi regum junxisti.

Cujus ingressæ thalamum
Per cruorem purpureum,
Ut castitatis lilia
Pingunt, serenant omnia.

12 Kings with their armies did flee, and were dis-
comfited : and they of the household divided the
spoil.

Kings fled, when Maxentius turned before the troops of
Constantine, when Eugenius, the last hope of Paganism, was
routed by Theodosius at Aquileia, when Penda and his power
fell at Winwidfield by the hands of Oswy, and *they of the
household,* or, more literally, with the A. V., *she* of the household, *she that tarried at home,* in prayer and watching, the
Church of GOD, shared the spoils of the victory He had won
for her by other hands than her own. The LXX. and
Vulgate read quite differently, *The King of the powers of
the beloved of the beloved, and [gives] to the beauty of the*

S. Athanas.
Theod. Mop-
suest.

house to divide the spoils. The Greek Fathers explain it
in two ways. It may mean that the King of the armies
of the beloved people, Who is Himself the Power of that
people, gives them the spoils of His enemies. Or, He is
Himself the Beloved, as being the Only-begotten of His
FATHER, and then the *powers* or *virtues* of the Beloved will

mean the heavenly graces with which He enables His army on earth to divide the spoils for the purpose of beautifying His house therewith. It is no wonder, says Gerhohus, that the LORD gives the Word with much power. For He is able to do so, Who is *King of the virtues of the Beloved, of the Beloved.* He is twice called *Beloved,* just as in the Song of Songs He is twice styled *fair* by the Bride, who saith, " Behold, thou art fair, my love; behold, thou art fair." For she is not content to call Him but once fair, but repeats it, either to denote His pre-eminent loveliness, or that His beauty in each of His natures is worthy of all admiration, in one that of His glorious Divinity, in the other that of His glorified humanity. By reason of which double beauty He is now twice called Beloved, or else because the FATHER loves Him according to both natures, and gave Him, already sharing all with Himself eternally, in His Divine nature, to be, in His assumed Manhood, King of all powers, not only earthly, but heavenly. And CHRIST, says another, hath made His house, that is, the Church, beautiful, by dividing to her spoils, stripped from conquered foes. What this is the Gospel adviseth us in the passage where we read, " How can one enter into a strong man's house, and spoil his vessels [Vulg.] except he first bind the strong man?" CHRIST therefore hath bound the devil with spiritual bonds, and from him so bound He took away his vessels as spoils. These vessels the LORD cleansing by the remission of sins; sanctifying these spoils wrested from the foe laid prostrate and bound; these He hath divided to the beauty of His house: making " some Apostles, some prophets, some pastors, and teachers, for the work of the ministry, for the edifying of the body of CHRIST." And such is the beauty of the house whereto the spoils are divided, that a lover thereof with this fairness being enkindled, crieth out, " LORD, I have loved the beauty of Thy house."

Euseb. Cæsar.

G.

Cant. i. 15.

A.

S, Matt. xii. 29.

Eph. iv. 1

Ps. xxvi. 8, Vulg.

13 Though ye have lien among the pots, yet shall ye be as the wings of a dove : that is covered with silver wings, and her feathers like gold.

This difficult verse is otherwise turned by the LXX. and Vulgate. They read: *If ye sleep in the midst of the lots* (κλήρων), *the wings of a dove are silvered, and the hinder parts of her back are in the paleness* (LXX. *greenness*) *of gold.* Modern critics, agreeing with the Chaldee Targum, instead of *pots* or *lots*, read *sheepfolds.* The obscurity of the passage has given birth to a great variety of interpretations. S. Augustine says that the *lots* probably mean the two Testaments, and that sleeping in the midst of them implies resting on their authority. And the reason he gives for this interpretation is, that inheritances are given by testament, and the Greek word for inheritance is κληρονομία, derived from κλῆρος,

A.

Bellarmine De Verbo Dei. 13.

the word of the LXX. in this passage. Another says that the *lots* are the contemplative and active lives, and that by observing a due medium between these, the beauty of the Church will be raised to the highest point. S. Jerome, *S Hieron.* agreeing with S. Augustine in the explanation of the *lots*, differs in his reason. He points out that the Holy Dove appears in both Testaments, silver-winged in the outer letter, golden in the mystical sense. S. Gregory the Great explains *Ap. S. Pate-* *sleeping* to be quiescence from all evil, the silver wings of the *rium de Ex-* Church to be the clear preaching of the Gospel, while the *pos. V.N.T.* golden back denotes the prize, yet richer and more glorious *xi. 139.* than even the promises, which awaits believers. Gerhohus, *G.* keeping to the idea of the two Testaments, blended with that of the two great commandments, compares this passage with *Cant. iii. 9,* the description of Solomon's chariot or bed, whose pillars *10.* were silver, whose bottom was gold, and whose midst was paved with love, and sees in both a picture of the Church adorned *Ay.* and glorified by the loving deeds of her children. The Carmelite sees here a type of the Mother of God, the Undefiled Dove whom the HOLY SPIRIT made His Spouse. Her wings are lowliness and purity, silvered in that she was the Mother of the Incarnate WORD; golden in her perfect and spotless virginity; silver in grace and knowledge; golden, bright and yet pale, in wisdom and patience. Again; the whole passage may mean that no temporary repose, no abasement nor persecution, can stay the upward flight or mar the beauty of GOD's Church. So the heathen poet, uttering more than he knew, sings,

Tibull. Eleg. i. 7.

Volitet crebras intacta per urbes
Alba Palæstino sancta columba Syro.

14 When the Almighty scattered kings for their sake : then were they as white as snow in Salmon.

The words recall that famous "Alleluia Battle," when the Pictish hosts fled before the shout uplifted by the British army, as it stood upon the hills, clad in the white chrisom-robe of baptism, no unfit type of those armies in heaven, which, on white horses, and clothed in fine linen, white and *Rev. xix. 14.* clean, follow Him Who is called Faithful and True. The Vulgate reading, however, but little different from that of the LXX. is, *When the Heavenly One parteth* (discernit) *Kings over her, they shall be white with snow in Salmon.* *Ay.* That is, when GOD distributes His Apostles and their successors over the Church, then the Gentiles who were in Salmon, the mount of *shade* or *darkness*, shall be made whiter than snow by remission of sins and faith received in *A.* Baptism. S. Augustine, while accepting part of this explanation, differs in his comment on the words *in Salmon.* He says that *shade* denotes the grace of GOD, as distinguished from human merit, the shadow of our Beloved which protects

us from all carnal heat and from the flame of spiritual sins.
As shade comes from light and a body, so grace comes from
the WORD, Who is the Light, and from His human Body.
And as He shelters His faithful, He is rightly called *Salmon*.

15 As the hill of Basan, so is GOD's hill : even an
high hill, as the hill of Basan.

The LXX. and Vulgate translate *Bashan* ("fertile") as an
adjective, and read, *The mountain of God is a fat mountain,
a mountain curdled, a fat mountain.* What mountain ought **A.**
we to understand by the *mountain of God, a mountain fruitful, a mountain full of curds,* but the same LORD CHRIST, of
Whom also another Prophet saith, "In the last days, the Isa. ii. 2.
mountain of the LORD's house shall be established in the top
of the mountains?" He is Himself the Mountain full of
curds, because of the babes to be fed with grace as though
it were with milk, a mountain rich to strengthen and enrich
them by the excellence of the gifts. For even the milk itself,
of which curd is made, in a wonderful manner signifieth grace,
for it floweth out of the overflowing of the mother's bowels,
and of a sweet compassion unto babes it is freely poured
forth. The Greek Fathers, whom Ayguan follows, interpret
the mountain as the Church, and dwell on the word *curdled*
as denoting the firmness of Christian dogma, which does not
remain in a state of flux, but forms solid food for the soul. **Z.**
Modern critics translate a *mountain of many heights,* not
having one summit only, and thus, if taken of CHRIST, it implies the perfection of all the Divine attributes in Him ; if of
the Church, it expresses the various forms of saintliness,
penitential, active, contemplative, and the like.

16 Why hop ye so, ye high hills? this is GOD's
hill, in the which it pleaseth Him to dwell : yea, the
LORD will abide in it for ever.

It should rather be, *Why look ye askance?* And it will
naturally refer first to the rejection of CHRIST by the chief
priests, by Herod, and by Pilate, and then to the contempt
poured on the Christian Church by Jews, confident in their
own spiritual supremacy, and by Pagans, trusting, if Romans,
to their temporal dominion, if Greeks, to their intellectual
gifts. But the Vulgate reads, *Why do ye imagine curdled
hills [to be God's hills?]* That is, observes S. Augustine,
why should ye compare any of the Saints, however illustrious, to their Master, any hill to that Mountain which is
established on the tops of the mountains? Or, again, why
should you suppose that there are other *mountains of curds,*
other Churches besides the one Catholic Church, in which
the abundance of divine grace can be found? *This is God's
hill, in the which it pleaseth Him to dwell, yea, the Lord will*

II.   Q

abide in it for ever. If we take the hill of CHRIST, then we are taught that the FATHER abideth in Him, and that "in Him dwelleth the fulness of the Godhead bodily." If of the Church, we recall CHRIST's promise, "Lo, I am with you alway, even unto the end of the world," and the continual presence of the HOLY SPIRIT in the Christian body.

C.
Coloss. ii. 9.
S. Matt. xxviii. 20.

17 The chariots of GOD are twenty thousand, even thousands of angels : and the LORD is among them, as in the holy place of Sinai.

S. Athanasius.
2 Kings ii. 12.
Ezek. i.
Dan. vii. 10.

It is taken first of the glorious hosts which surround the Heavenly King, as He sits on the throne, "the chariot of Israel, and the horsemen thereof;" Ezekiel saw the chariot, the four mystic living creatures, advancing on the wheels which the Spirit moved; Daniel counted the horsemen, "Thousand thousands ministered unto Him, and ten thousand times ten thousand stood before Him."

Paradise Lost, vii.196.

About His chariot numberless were poured,
Cherub and Seraph, Potentates, and Thrones,
And Virtues, wingéd Spirits, and Chariots winged,
From the armoury of GOD, where stand of old
Myriads.

A.
Z.
G.

And the chariots of GOD are also His Saints on earth; those who are fastened to the easy yoke of CHRIST, and have Him as their charioteer, guiding them with the reins of faith. Especially it is true of those who preach the Word, and thus carry GOD Himself into the hearts of their converts. *Twenty thousand.* The LXX. and Vulgate do not express this precisely. They say *ten thousand multiplied* (μυριοπλάσιον, *decem millibus multiplex,*) and thus there is no exact mystical signification of the number given by the old commentators. The following interpretation, however, is according to the rule of such explanations. Because the number *five* denotes the five bodily senses; *ten,* as its double, implies the two sexes, men and women. A *thousand* is the accepted sign of universality, and therefore the number *ten thousand* would denote the Catholic Church of mankind. But it has been held by many Fathers that the number of redeemed men will exactly fill up the gaps in the heavenly ranks left by the fall of the rebel Angels, of whose chief, the great dragon, it is written, "His tail drew the third part of the stars of heaven, and did cast them to the earth." Ten thousand, then, represents also the number of the fallen Angels, and thus the faithful two-thirds are denoted by *twenty thousand,* leaving the full total of the Church triumphant thirty thousand, the factor *three* signifying the mystery of the Holy Trinity; *ten* the redeemed of both sexes endowed with spiritual bodies; and a *thousand* implying the perfection and immortality of the Communion of Saints. The Vulgate, instead of "thou-

S. Greg. Mag. Hom. in Evang. xii.

Rev. xii. 4.

sands of Angels," reads, *thousands of rejoicing ones*, because what they do is done not sorrowfully or on compulsion, but with ready and devout cheerfulness, because, rejoicing in hope, and patient in tribulation, though they be sometimes sorrowful, yet they are always glad in Him Whose chariot they are. *And the Lord is among them, as in the holy place of Sinai.* That is, the invisible Presence of GOD in His Church is as real and majestic as the vision on Sinai during the giving of the Law. And this comes out more forcibly in the Vulgate, *in Sinai in the holy place*, which means, either that GOD has come from Sinai to Sion, (an interpretation accordant with Heb. xii. 22,) or that Sinai itself has, in a figure, been transferred into the sanctuary.   L.

18 Thou art gone up on high, thou hast led captivity captive, and received gifts for men : yea, even for thine enemies, that the LORD GOD might dwell among them.

On high, first on the Cross, and then into Heaven; nay,   Z.
adds another, to the highest of the seven heavens, that of the Holy Trinity, leaving behind Him the heavens of air, of æther,   Ay.
of fire, of stars, of crystal, and the empyrean itself. *Thou hast led captivity captive*, overcoming the devil and his angels on the Cross, drawing to Thyself, there uplifted, the nations   Z.
erewhile bound and chained in their sins, and bringing with Thee, at Thy Resurrection, the Patriarchs and Fathers who   Ay. .
waited in Hades. *And received gifts for men*, the sevenfold gifts of the HOLY SPIRIT, sent down on the Apostles at Pentecost. *For Thine enemies.* Vulgate, *for unbelievers.* Because the gifts were not confined to the twelve on whom the fiery tongues came at first, but were poured out on those Jews who had before rejected CHRIST, and even on the Gentiles of the heathen world; and this in order *that the Lord God*, the HOLY SPIRIT, *might dwell among them*, and make their bodies His temple. Wherefore, S. Paul, when citing this verse, reads, "He gave gifts to men," showing that all which Eph. iv. 8. CHRIST received *in the Man*, in His human nature, He accepted in order to give it to us, for "of His fulness have all we received, and grace for grace."   S. John i. 16.

19 Praised be the LORD daily : even the GOD who helpeth us, and poureth his benefits upon us.

The Vulgate reads in the second clause, *The God of our salvation shall make our journey prosperous*, that is, observes   D. C.
the Carthusian, He will show us the safe and happy road to eternal life, by enlightening our hearts, and directing our works towards our last end, as He Himself speaks, "I will cause you to walk in My statutes, and ye shall keep My judg- Ezek. xxxvi. ments, and do them." For man cannot walk in the right way 27.

unless grace be his leader. S. Jerome translates, more exactly, *The God of our salvation shall carry us.* It comes to the same thing, remarks Cardinal Bellarmine, for he goes on prosperously whom God carries.

Bellarmine.

20 He is our God, even the God of whom cometh salvation : God is the Lord, by whom we escape death.

In this triple ascription of praise is shadowed the mystery of the Holy Trinity. God the Father is our God, by eternal right; God the Son is our God Who brought us salvation; God the Holy Ghost is the Lord and Giver of Life. The Vulgate reads in the last clause, *The issues of death are of the Lord, the Lord,* that is, of Jehovah Adonai. As though he were saying, Why art thou indignant, O lot of humanity, that thou hast the outgoing of death? Even thy Lord's outgoing was no other than that of death. Rather, therefore, be comforted than indignant; patiently, therefore, let us suffer even death, by the example of Him, Who, though by no sin was He debtor to death, and was the Lord, from Whom no one could take away life, but Himself laid it down, yet had Himself the outgoing of death. And the true outgoing of death, that by which we pass from it, and not unto it, is His too, namely, His Resurrection.

A.

G.

21 God shall wound the head of his enemies : and the hairy scalp of such a one as goeth on still in his wickedness.

S. Athanasius.

It is spoken, observes S. Athanasius, of the crushing of serpents, and therefore tells of Him Who bruised the serpent's head, and Who also punished that generation of vipers, the Jewish priests and rulers, by bringing on them the destruction of Jerusalem, which, remarks Ayguan, was the *hairy scalp,* the adorned and fortified head of their kingdom. Again; God wounds the head of His enemies by bringing them to repentance. Once more; some read, *God shall wound the head of His enemies which walk upon the hairy scalp in their sins,* which is explained of the evil spirits trampling upon men whom they have made their slaves. The *hairy scalp* has also been explained of subtil questions, as minute and subdivided as hairs, the investigation of which leads often unto sin, or of the little sins themselves to which men give way, as thinking them to have no binding power.

Ay.

G.

Z.

22 The Lord hath said, I will bring my people again, as I did from Basan : mine own will I bring again, as I did sometime from the deep of the sea.

The Vulgate reading is, *I will turn from Basan,* and that of SS. Hilary and Augustine, with the Ambrosian Psalter, *I*

shall be turned from Basan. They explain Basan variously S. Hieron.
as meaning *confusion*, that of this world, from which CHRIST
delivered us on the Cross, or the confusion of idolatry and   Z.
sin; or *thirst*, from which, as S. Augustine notes, the LORD   A.
turns them who hunger and thirst after righteousness. And
with this latter interpretation, some take the succeeding words,
I will turn into the depths of the sea, that is, I will send the   G.
plenteous rain so abundantly on Mine inheritance, as to make
a sea of the dry land. It may be also spoken of GOD's mercy
to sinners drowning in the depth of their sins, or dissolved
into an ocean of penitential tears. The interpretation given
by S. Athanasius enables us to use the true meaning of S. Athana-
Basan ("fertile,") though he was unaware of it. He takes sius.
Basan to be the Cross, that truly fertile Tree of which Venantius Fortunatus sings:

> Faithful Cross! above all other,   The Hymn
> One and only noble Tree!   *Pange lin-*
> None in foliage, none in blossom,   *gua.*
> None in fruit thy peers may be :

and interprets the passage of CHRIST's descent from the
Cross down into the depths of hell to spoil it, and lead it captive. S. Hilary, also interpreting it of CHRIST, says that the   H.
depth of the sea denotes the sorrows which He bore in His
life of Passion, when He brought His people out of the Basan
of confusion into the Land of Promise.

23 That thy foot may be dipped in the blood of
thine enemies : and that the tongue of thy dogs may
be red through the same.

When He trod the winepress alone, and trampled His S. Hieron.
ghostly foes in His fury, then their blood was sprinkled on Isa. lxiii. 3.
His garments. When He loosed the armies of Vespasian and
Hadrian against the rebellious nation, His foot was dipped   H.
in the blood of His human enemies. And He avenged Himself again, when the Roman Empire, which had so long per-   L.
secuted the Saints, fell before the barbarian invaders. The
LXX. and Vulgate, however, read only *That Thy foot may be
dipped in blood*. And they say *Thy foot* means the preachers
of the Gospel, who became as it were the feet of CHRIST,   A.
by carrying Him into all lands, and who, sealing their wit- G.
ness with martyrdom, are dipped in their own blood. *That
the tongue of Thy dogs may be red through the same*. Here too
the Vulgate reading is different; it is, *That the tongue of
Thy dogs from enemies [may be dipped] in the same*. They
take it of CHRIST's enemies, such as S. Paul, who have be- S. Greg.
come His faithful dogs, to guard the flock they once harassed, Mag. Mor.
and to preach His Name. S. Augustine reminds us of Gideon's xx. 5.
three hundred, who lapped like dogs, and who overthrew the   A.
army of Midian, and he points out that the letter T, which,

S. Ambros.
in S. Lucam.
lib. v. c. 7. in the Greek alphabet, is the symbol of the number three hundred, is also the sign of the Cross. And as CHRIST dipped His foot in the Blood of His own Passion, so all Christians should dip their feet, the goings of their souls, in that same tide, by confession of the LORD's Cross, and by washing away their sins, carrying about in their bodies His dying. Their tongues also, by drinking the Chalice of His most precious Blood, and by open acknowledgment of His redeeming love.

24 It is well seen, O GOD, how thou goest : how thou, my GOD and King, goest in the sanctuary.

Ay.

More exactly, with the A. V. and Vulgate, *They have seen Thy goings.* They saw them when the Angels brought the glad tidings of great joy at His Nativity, when the Wise Men presented their gifts at the Epiphany, when He passed through the land preaching, and working miracles. They saw His goings along the Way of Sorrows, His elevation on the Cross, His passage to the tomb, His Resurrection, His Ascension into heaven, and they will see His terrible coming again to judgment. *Thy goings, my God and King, Who art in the holy place.* So the LXX. and Vulgate. And it is David's confession of CHRIST, Who, Very GOD, and King of Israel, is exalted to the FATHER's right hand in heaven. He is also in His holy place on earth, that Church of which He is the Head, where His goings may be seen in the tokens of holiness exhibited by those who follow His steps, as the march of a general may be known even by those who merely watch the advance of the rear-guard.

H.
A.

Z.

25 The singers go before, the minstrels follow after : in the midst are the damsels playing with the timbrels.

If we take the first half of the verse as it stands in our version, and explain it by the usual rules of mystical interpretation, it will denote the preaching of the Word in the first place, and, following on that, the union of praise and active works in the lives of Christians who hearken to such preaching. But the LXX. and Vulgate read, *The princes went before, joined with the minstrels, in the midst of the damsels who play on timbrels.* If we take the words of the triumphal

S. Hieron.
S. Bernard.
Serm. in
Cant. 7.
Ps. xxiv. 7. Ascension of CHRIST, then the Princes will be the Angels who formed His court, the minstrels the train of ransomed Fathers, saying, "Lift up your heads, O ye gates." *The damsels playing on the timbrels* are explained to be Saints who have attained the grace of spiritual beauty by mortifying the

B. deeds of the body. For the timbrel or drum is formed of the skin of a dead animal, tightly strained, and then giving out a musical sound when struck, and thus typifies the harmony which comes after the death of carnal sin. The text also applies to the Church on earth, and the Princes then are the Apostles, who went first, joined with those whom they had won to CHRIST, and who praised Him thenceforth by word and action, while the damsels denote the Virgins of the Religious Life, who continually celebrate the praises of GOD. And as Miriam led the songs of the Hebrew maidens at the Red Sea triumph, so the chant of Christian Virgins is led by that other Miriam whom S. Augustine calls "our timbrel-player," whose song of praise still resounds daily throughout the earth, and of whom it is said that in Paradise,

D. C.

S. August.
Serm. de
Sanct. 18.

> Our Lady sings *Magnificat*
> With tones surpassing sweet,
> And all the Virgins bear their part,
> Sitting about her feet.

26 Give thanks, O Israel, unto GOD the LORD in the congregations : from the ground of the heart.

The A. V. is here to be followed, *Bless ye God in the congregations, even the Lord, from the fountains of Israel.* He says, *in the Churches*, notes S. Augustine, lest any should suppose that choral bands of revellers are meant. Rather Churches are intended by the damsels, decked with new graces, playing on timbrels with spiritual tunefulness. And the fountains of Israel are the Apostles, according to that saying, "Whosoever drinketh of the water that I shall give him shall never thirst; but the water that I shall give him shall be in him a well of water springing up into everlasting life." Wherefore also it is written that when Israel camped in Elim, there were in that place, "twelve wells of water."

A.

S. John iv.
14.

Exod. xv. 27.

27 There is little Benjamin their ruler, and the princes of Judah their counsel : the princes of Zabulon, and the princes of Nephthali.

He who is a Prince of the Apostles, though he calls himself the least, the Israelite of the tribe of Benjamin, is here indicated. The LXX. and Vulgate read, *Benjamin the younger in a trance. Younger*, because S. Paul was called later than the other Apostles ; *in a trance*, because of that vision which he saw on the journey to Damascus, or the unspeakable things he beheld when caught up to the third heaven. The names of the other tribes occurring in this verse are said by S. Athanasius (with whom S. Augustine agrees) to refer to various Apostles. SS. Peter, Andrew, James, and John being of Zebulun and Naphtali; S. Matthew, and the other Apostles, of the tribe of Judah. S. Jerome reads here, *The princes of Judah in their purple*, and it is taken of their resisting unto blood,

A.

Ay.

S. Athanasius.

> They who nobly died believing :
> Martyrs purpled in their gore.

The Hymn
Sponsa
CHRISTI.

Mystically, Benjamin, the Son of God's Right Hand, is their Ruler. Judah, denoting *praise*, comes next, as confession of God's Name is the truest counsel for Christians ; then follows (by seniority) Naphtali, *wrestling* with God in prayer, wrestling against the world, the flesh, and the devil for victory ; and last, Zebulun, *dwelling*, denotes the final rest of the people of God, when the Bride shall say, " Now will my Husband dwell with me." Princes, says S. Augustine, of confession, of strength, of breadth, princes of faith, of hope, of love. And thus, remarks another, they may be taken of the Apostles, by whom the praise and confession of Christ was spread abroad, of the Martyrs who contended for the faith unto torture and death, and of the Doctors who, dwelling in the peaceful days of the Church, kept the flock safe from the assaults of heresy.

Gen. xxx. 20.

A.

G.

28 Thy God hath sent forth strength for thee : stablish the thing, O God, that thou hast wrought in us.

29 For thy temple's sake at Jerusalem : so shall kings bring presents unto thee.

The Vulgate reads, *Command, O God, Thy might.* It is, says Gerhohus, a prayer to the Father to send His Might, His Only-begotten, to save us, knowing assuredly that " He that spared not His own Son, but delivered Him up for us all, how shall He not with Him also freely give us all things ?" And we then turn to God the Holy Ghost, to confirm and stablish what the Son, as commanded by the Father, hath wrought in us. Where note, that God confirms His elect in many ways. By endurance of suffering. "The God of all grace, after that ye have suffered a while, make you perfect, stablish, strengthen, settle you." He confirms by Apostolic preaching, for the Apostles and their fellows " exhorted the brethren with many words, and confirmed them." He confirms by the Catholic Faith, as S. Paul says, " For I long to see you, that I may impart unto you some spiritual gift, to the end you may be established, that is, that I may be comforted together with you by the mutual faith both of you and me." He confirms, by the operation of the Holy Eucharist, "Wine that maketh glad the heart of man, and bread to strengthen man's heart." By the grace of the Holy Ghost, "Stablish me with Thy free Spirit." And by true repentance, as the Lord spake to S. Peter, " When thou art converted, strengthen thy brethren." The Carthusian takes the *Might of God* to be the help of Angels, and if we do so interpret it, we shall take it chiefly of the errand of Gabriel, (the " Strength of God,") to Nazareth.

G.

Rom. viii. 32.

Ay.

1 S. Pet. v. 10.

Acts xv. 32.

Rom. i. 12.

Ps. civ. 15.

Ps. li. 12.

S. Luke xxii. 32.

D.C.

Pet. Abelard. Hymn. in Annunc.

Mittit ad Virginem
Non quemvis angelum,
Sed fortitudinem
Suam, Archangelum
Amator hominis.

From Thy temple, which is in Jerusalem, is the Vulgate reading, that is, from heaven, send Thy Might, CHRIST, or His Angels, to us. Or, let the waters of salvation pass, as in Ezekiel's vision, from the earthly Jerusalem over the face of the world. *So shall kings bring presents unto thee.* Temporal kings will do it by becoming nursing fathers of the Church; spiritual rulers by offering spiritual gifts, which must, in order to be acceptable, come first from GOD's temple in Jerusalem, the vision of peace, before they can be presented in His temple of expectation in Sion. And this is most true of the Holy Eucharist, which derives its sacrificial value not from the earthly species of Bread and Wine, but from the heavenly substance of the Body and Blood of CHRIST, sent down by the power of the HOLY GHOST.

G.

G.

30 When the company of the spearmen, and multitude of the mighty are scattered abroad among the beasts of the people, so that they humbly bring pieces of silver : and when he hath scattered the people that delight in war.

The first clause of this difficult verse stands nowhere else as above. The LXX., the Vulgate, and the margin of the A. V. agree with modern criticism in translating it, *Rebuke the beasts of the reed.* The reference is in the first place to the Egyptian King, typified by the crocodile dwelling in the reedy banks of the Nile, and thence we may apply it, as S. Hilary does, to the evil spirits, to whose chief an Angel said, "The LORD rebuke thee." S. Augustine, playing on the meaning of *reed,* used as a *pen,* declares that the *beasts of the reed* are heretics who pervert the Scriptures by their writings, and "wrest them to their own destruction." Gerhohus gives another reason for accepting this interpretation, namely, that heretics are as a reed shaken by every wind of doctrine. The next clause runs in the LXX. and Vulgate, *The assembly of the bulls amongst the cows of the peoples :* or, as S. Jerome, the A. V., and modern critics, read, *the calves of the peoples.* S. Augustine, carrying on his reference to heretics, sees in the bulls a type of the obstinate and determined enemies of the truth: and in the cows the weaker souls which are content to follow their lead. "For of this sort are they which creep into houses, and lead captive silly women laden with sins, led away with divers lusts, ever learning. and never able to come to the knowledge of the truth." The Carmelite, who sees in the *beasts of the reed* the persecuting Roman Empire, refers the bulls who mix with the cows to those tempters who endeavoured to make the Christians give up their faith by means of rewards and fair promises rather than by open violence. And Euthymius explains it of the Jewish priests and rulers urging on the multitude at their will. *So that they humbly bring pieces of silver ;* that is, by way of tribute, submitting themselves to the kingdom of CHRIST. This is the

H.

S. Jude 9.
A.

2 S. Pet. iii. 16.

G.

A.

2 Tim. iii. 6.

Ay.

Z.

346   A COMMENTARY ON THE PSALMS.

been most variously rendered. The LXX. reads: *That
they who are tried with silver may not be shut out;* and the
Vulgate, conversely, *That they may shut out those who, &c.* S.
Augustine's explanation of the words is singularly far-fetched.
Those *proved with silver* are such as have been tested with
the sayings of GOD, for "The words of the LORD are pure
words, even as the silver, which from the earth is tried, and
purified seven times in the fire." *May be excluded* means,
may appear, may stand forth. Whence also in the silver-
smith's art, they are called *exclusores,* who out of a shapeless
lump are skilled to mould the form of a vessel. This power
of showing the beauty which lies hid in Scripture belongs
only to a few, and they are forced to their work by the reed
of opposing heretics, the beasts of the reed, the bulls of the
people. Others, as S. Hilary, are content with the simpler
explanation that the enemies of the faith desire to exclude
those who have been purified, like silver, from the dross of
earthly vices. S. Jerome translates, *who kick against the
silver wheels;* others, *who walk proudly in silver ornaments;*
others again, *who strike silver cymbals;* but the true meaning
is, as noted above, that of bringing tribute. In the last clause
the LXX. and Vulgate read, *Scatter the people that desire
war.* It holds of the Jews, who delighted to war against
CHRIST; of His spiritual enemies; of the Romans, pre-eminently
the warlike people, at last converted to the faith they had opposed, and becoming its missionaries; and finally, of all oppressors and heretics, who disturb the peace of the Church.

Ps. xii. 7.

H.

*S. Athana-
sius.*

Ay.

D. C.

31 Then shall the princes come out of Egypt : the
Morians' land shall soon stretch out her hands unto
GOD.

The Vulgate reads, *Ambassadors shall come.* They tell a
legend, how that Philo of Alexandria, sent on a mission
to the Court of the Emperor Caius, met S. Peter in Rome,
and learnt from him the Faith, which he then followed in
his country, under the guidance of S. Mark, thus fulfilling
the prophecy. It needs not, however, to dwell on a mere
tradition such as this, for the long array of Christian nobles
who came out of Egypt is enough, and more than enough, to
bear out the prediction. Martyrs, such as SS. Mark, Ani-
anus, Peter, Leonidas, Plutarch, and Potamiæna; Doctors,
as SS. Pantænus, Clement, Athanasius, Cyril; Confessors, as
SS. Antony, Pachomius, Hilarion, Pambo, and other Fathers
of the Desert, adorn the roll-call of the Saints. *The Morians'
land,* or, as the Vulgate, *Æthiopia,* stretched out her hands to
GOD when the treasurer of Queen Candace took S. Philip up
into his chariot, and asked him of Isaiah's prophecy, and thus
learnt the Gospel sooner than they of Egypt. And still,
even in her degradation, the ancient Church of Æthiopia
loves to recall these words. Four times in the pre-anaphoral

Ay.

Acts viii. 31.

portion of her Liturgy she prays to CHRIST to "Stretch forth His Hand," to hallow the paten, the chalice, the Communion spoon, and the ark. And, mystically, the ambassadors coming out of Egypt denote the Apostles passing from the bondage of the Synagogue, while Æthiopia tells of those who were black with sin, but now are made white as snow in Salmon.

Renaudot. Lit. Orient.

G.

32 Sing unto GOD, O ye kingdoms of the earth : O sing praises unto the LORD.

33 Who sitteth in the heavens over all from the beginning : lo, he doth send out his voice, yea, and that a mighty voice.

The LXX. and Vulgate read, *Who hath ascended over the heaven of heaven to the East.* That is, to the right hand of His FATHER, for He Who visited us as the Day-spring from on high, hath returned to the throne of His glory. And so S. Ambrose in the great Christmas hymn:

A.

> From GOD the FATHER He proceeds,
> To GOD the FATHER back He speeds;
> Proceeds,—as far as very hell,
> Speeds back,—to light ineffable.

The Hymn Veni Redemptor Gentium.

Or, as some read, *from the East,* that is, from the Mount of Olives, on the East of Jerusalem, or from Jerusalem itself. And it may be taken of the far more wide and rapid spread of Christianity towards the West than in the Eastern parts of the world. *He shall send out His voice, yea, and that a mighty voice.* He that like a lamb before his shearer was dumb, *shall send out His voice,* and not the voice of weakness, as though to be judged, but the voice of power, as about to be Judge. "Our GOD shall come, and shall not keep silence." And the might of His Voice may be known by its effects, for it will raise the dead.

Ay. C.

Genebrardus.

A.

Ps. l. 3.
S. Athanasius.
Pet. Lomb.

34 Ascribe ye the power to GOD over Israel : his worship, and strength is in the clouds.

Glorify Him, Christian Saints, more than His own people Israel did when He came to them. Glorify Him because of His bounties to Israel, to His chosen Apostles and servants. Or, construing the words in a different order, *Over Israel is His magnificence,* as He shall be throned in glory above the true Israelites, His faithful disciples. *In the clouds.* They who did "fly as a cloud," bearing the gracious rain of the Gospel to the dry places of the earth, shall shine above others with the brightness of the sun, and glow with many colours, yea, with the seven splendours of the HOLY GHOST.

Ay.
D. C.
A.
G.

Isa. lx. 8.

35 O GOD, wonderful art thou in thy holy places : even the GOD of Israel; he will give strength and power unto his people; blessed be GOD.

They all take it to be *Wonderful in His Saints,* wonderful in them before the Law, in Enoch, whom He translated, in Noah, whom He saved in the Ark, in Abraham, whom He called. Wonderful in His people whom He brought out of Egypt: to whom He appeared in terror and majesty on Sinai; in Joshua, at whose bidding the sun and moon stood still; in Elijah, Elisha, and others under the Law. But most wonderful in the time of grace, in His incomprehensible working and abiding in Christians, and especially in the Sacrament of the Altar. *He will give strength and power unto His people.* In this life He gives strength to resist sin, to endure shame, torture, and death, power to attain to righteousness by grace, to work mighty works, to declare the Gospel fully. He gave strength and power in the fiery tongues of Pentecost, when the Apostles were endued with power from on high. And He will give the power of His Resurrection to us at His Second coming, that this mortal may put on immortality.

And therefore: because of all these His wondrous works, *blessed be God.*

Glory be to the FATHER, Who gave the WORD to the company of the preachers; and to the SON, the WORD Who is preached; and to the HOLY GHOST, the Power of Both, given in gifts to men.

As it was in the beginning, is now, and ever shall be: world without end. Amen.

COLLECTS.

O LORD our Governor, Who, vouchsafing a spiritual banquet to the righteous, makest them joyful in gladness: grant that Thy flock may understand Thy death, and confess Thee, the Victor over death, sitting at the right hand of the FATHER. Who livest.

O LORD JESU CHRIST, Who didst ascend over the Heaven of heavens to the East, conquering the West, perfect in Thyself them whom Thou didst undertake to redeem, that they may be raised on high, that where Thou, the Head, hast gone before, thither Thou mayest draw Thy whole glorified body to receive honour, and leave not in the sunset of the world those whom Thou, in Thy triumph, exaltest towards the everlasting East. (11.)

O LORD, Who ascendedst up on high, leading captivity captive, deliver us by the triumph of Thy victory from the captivity of the devil, that whilst Thou givest Thy gifts to men, Thou mayest make men themselves altogether partakers of Thy gifts. (11.)

O LORD GOD of hosts, wonderful in Thy Saints, we earnestly beseech Thee to grant us strength to drive away adversities. Thou Who didst bestow on Thy Saints the honour of attaining to heavenly ways; grant Thy people also power, we pray Thee, at their intercession whom Thou vouchsafest in Thy divine goodness to unite in friendship with Thee. (11.)

Margin notes:
D. C.
Z.
A.
S. Hieron.
Ludolph.
Mozarabic.
Mozarabic. Ascension.
Mozarabic For the Saints.

God vouchsafe to change us from death unto life, from corruption into incorruption, that made partakers with His Saints, we may rejoice in Him with everlasting gladness. Through. (1.)   *S. Jerome.*

O Lord, King of virtues, set apart for us of Thine inherit-   *D. C.* ance the gracious rain of compunction, that as we are weak through sins, we may receive from Thee the strength of holy resolve, and advance to that life which is pleasing unto Thee. Through. (1.)

PSALM LXIX.

Title: To the Chief Musician upon Shoshannim, a Psalm of David. LXX. and Vulgate: To the end, for them who shall be changed, a Psalm of David. Chaldee Targum: For praise; of the Captivity of the Sanhedrim, by the hands of David. Or, To the Supreme, for the Lilies, a Psalm of David.

Argument.

Arg. Thomas. That Christ was given bitter gall and sharp vinegar to drink for our salvation. The Voice of Christ at the time of the Passion. This Psalm is to be read at the reading of the Prophet Jonah, and at the Gospel of S. John. The Voice of Christ to the Father, when He was suffering. Of the Passion of Christ, and the rejection of the Jews. A prayer for the Church.

Ven. Bede. *To the end,* every one knows, refers to Christ, Who, by the very testimony of the Gospel, is about in this Psalm to narrate His Passion, by which believers *shall be changed,* putting off the old man, and putting on the new.

Throughout the Psalm Christ speaks in the form of a servant. In the first section He intreats that He may be saved by the Father, seeing that He is hated by the Jews without a cause. *Save Me, O God, &c.* In the second He asks, on behalf of His members, that the hope of the faithful trusting in His Resurrection be not baulked, saying that He hath patiently borne whatever the ungodly laid on Him. *God, Thou knowest My simpleness, &c.* In the third place, He intreats that His prayer may be heard, so that His spot-less conversation may be delivered from the mire of this world, saying that the Lord knoweth by what snares of the enemies He is beset, that He may arrive at the issue of His Passion, having over-come the peril. *But, Lord, I make My prayer unto Thee.* In the fourth place, through the power of His foreknowledge, He declares things to come, which may happen to His enemies. *Let their table be made a snare to take themselves withal, &c.* Fifthly, in the form of a servant He calls Himself poor, whence He says that He will give thanks to His Father's mercy, encouraging the faithful to trust in the Lord, Who hath delivered His Church from the ad-versity of this world, and hath provided therein for the eternal happiness of His Saints. *When I am poor and in heaviness, Thy help, O God, shall lift Me up.*

SYRIAC PSALTER. Of David. Literally, when Sheba son of Bichri sounded with a trumpet, and the people refrained from going after David. And it is said to be a prophecy of CHRIST's sufferings, and the reprobation of the Jews.

EUSEBIUS OF CÆSAREA. The sufferings of CHRIST, and the rejection of the Jews.

S. ATHANASIUS. A Psalm in address alone.

VARIOUS USES.

Gregorian. Ferial. Thursday. Matins. [Maundy Thursday. I. Nocturn.]

Monastic. Ferial. Wednesday. Matins. [Maundy Thursday. I. Nocturn.]

Parisian. Friday. Matins.

Lyons. As *Gregorian.*

Ambrosian. Ferial. Monday of the Second Week. III. Nocturn. [Maundy Thursday. Matins.]

Quignon. Friday. Matins.

Eastern Church. Saturday. Nocturns.

ANTIPHONS.

Gregorian. Ferial. O LORD GOD, * haste Thee to deliver me. [Maundy Thursday. The zeal of Thine house hath even eaten me, * and the rebukes of them that rebuked Thee are fallen upon me.]

Monastic. Ferial. Alleluia. [Septuag. Seek ye after GOD, * and your soul shall live. Maundy Thursday. As *Gregorian.*]

Parisian. In Thy sight * are all mine adversaries : my heart hath waited for reproach, and misery.

Lyons. Ferial. Seek ye after GOD, * and your soul shall live. [Maundy Thursday. As *Gregorian.*]

Ambrosian. Ferial. Draw nigh unto my soul, * and save it. [Maundy Thursday. I am become a stranger * unto my brethren, even an alien unto my mother's children.]

1 Save me, O GOD : for the waters are come in, even unto my soul.

2 I stick fast in the deep mire, where no ground is : I am come into deep waters, so that the floods run over me.

C.

A.

D. C.

P.

This Psalm, observes Cassiodorus, is the fourth of those which speak at length of the LORD's Passion and Resurrection. And the fact of its being thrice cited in the New Testament in this sense, by the Apostles Peter, John, and Paul, does not permit us to doubt that its primary intention was Messianic prophecy. *Save Me, O God.* When CHRIST utters these words to His FATHER, He does not pray, as we must, to be delivered from sin, but from the sufferings of body and soul endured in His Passion. *The waters are come in.* And they may come in three ways: as a river torrent swollen

with rains, as in a deep and muddy pool, or as in a storm at
sea. The first will denote the Jewish people, lashed into Hugo Card.
sudden fury by the secret instigations of the priests; the
second the still, deadly hypocrisy of the Scribes and Pharisees; the third, the fierce wrath of kings and rulers. Applied to the servants instead of to the Master, these waters
denote temptations and persecutions threatening the very life
of the Church, or of single members thereof. *Even unto my*
soul. Of the Church, as when a ship has sprung a leak, or   L.
been filled by waves, and is sinking; of a man, when the
waters have risen to his lips, and threaten suffocation. *I*
stick fast in the deep mire. Yes; for if He had not taken
upon Him the nature of man, a creature of clay, He would   G.
have been free from danger and pain; but because He had
stuck fast therein, joining His Godhead for ever to it, therefore He endured suffering. And He came into the mire in
another sense when, laid in the tomb, He gave His Body to   D. C.
the earth. *Where no ground is.* The Vulgate has it, *where*
there is no substance. And they take it variously. It may
be the poverty of CHRIST in His human life, when He
stripped Himself of His glory; or it tells us of His death,   A.
when His soul was parted for a time from the substance of
His Body; or, again, it may refer to the utter exhaustion of   G.
His wounded Form as He hung dying on the Cross. Spoken
in the person of sinners, the *deep mire* most fitly denotes the   D. C.
slough of carnal sin into which men sink ever deeper by mere   Cd.
continuance, without any fresh volition on their own part,
where there is no *ground,* no certain point of stoppage, and
no real or lasting pleasure. *I am come into deep waters.*   A.
Like Jonah, He suffered Himself to be cast into the sea, for
the salvation of those in His ship, and after three days came
forth again, after the *floods ran over* Him. And He says
deep waters, as contrasting with the height from which He   D. C.
descended into them, when He came down from heaven; nay,
denoting that He penetrated down to hell itself. This peril   Ay.
of deep waters, wisely observes the Carthusian, may well be   D. C.
that of high rank and office, so that the storm and noise of
worldly cares and duties, overwhelm peace of mind, clearness of devotion, and guard over the heart. And when the
ship of any human soul is in peril through the waves and
storm, if CHRIST be there, the terrified mariner has but to
call on Him; if He be not there, then let the waters be baled
out with holy fear and confession of sin, lightened with alms- Hugo Card.
giving, and steadied with the anchor of hope, till He come to   L.
save.

3 I am weary of crying; my throat is dry : my
sight faileth me for waiting so long upon my GOD.

Or, with the LXX. and Vulgate, *I have toiled in crying.*   G.
Not only in the Seven Words from the Cross, but in the

Cd.

long and thankless labour of preaching the kingdom of heaven to a gainsaying people; and in the prayer of His Agony, whereof the Apostle says, "Who, in the days of His flesh, when He had offered up prayers and supplications with

Heb. v. 7.

strong crying and tears unto Him that was able to save Him from death, and was heard in that He feared." *My throat is dry.* We nowhere read that this prophecy was literally fulfilled, though the Carthusian says that it must have been,

D. C.

from the toil, pain, and loss of blood which CHRIST endured, drying up the natural moisture of His Body; but we may

A.

well take it with S. Augustine, and those who follow him, that as the voice of one that is hoarse is scarcely audible or intelligible, so the Voice of CHRIST was unheard and misunderstood by the Jews. Ayguan, comparing that passage

Ay.

of the Apocalypse wherein it is said that a mighty angel

Rev. x. 3.

"cried with a loud voice, as when a lion roareth," explains this crying as that of the Lion of the tribe of Judah, and dwells at length on the ideas prevalent in his day touching the king of beasts, to find lessons of CHRIST in them. *My sight faileth Me for waiting so long upon My God.* The Vulgate: *While I hope in My God.* That is, as we may best

L.

take it, My bodily powers are weakened by the near approach of death, while my soul remains steadfast in its trust.

Faber.

> How fast His hands and feet are nailed,
> His blessèd tongue with thirst is tied,
> His failing eyes are blind with blood,
> JESUS, our Love, is crucified!

A.

The LXX. reading, followed in some Latin Psalters, is, *from hoping in My God.* And this, observes S. Augustine, cannot be spoken by the Head of Himself, but in the person of His members only, of those Apostles whose faith and courage

D. C.

failed. So too the Body *toils in crying* when lamenting its own sins, when eagerly preaching the Gospel to others, when calling on GOD for pardon, for grace, for illumination, for amendment. And the Church becomes hoarse when her preaching, like her LORD's, is unheeded, or when she is exhausted by toil or suffering; or again, when GOD tires her, by remaining long without giving an answer to her prayers.

4 They that hate me without a cause are more than the hairs of my head : they that are mine enemies, and would destroy me guiltless, are mighty.

Ay.

Which teaches that the enemies of the Saints are ever more numerous than the Saints themselves, who are, as it were, the hairs adorning the great Head of the Church, Who, like Sam-

Hugo Card.

son, placed His strength therein, and like Absalom, His beauty. And when these hairs were plucked out and shorn away by the martyrdoms of countless athletes, then the mocking Jews

2 Kings ii. 23.

and heathen said, as the children to Elisha, "Go up, thou bald head," and were speedily punished for their sin. Of the

latter clause in the verse 8. Augustine observes that it is the   A.
very voice of martyrs, not in the punishment, but in the
cause ; for the mere suffering of persecution or death is not
in itself praiseworthy, but to endure such things for a good
cause. CHRIST's enemies were *mighty*, for there were united   D. C.
against Him the religious influence wielded by the chief
priests, and the civil power in the hands of Herod and Pilate.
Mighty, too, are the enemies of the Church,—heathen emperors and persecutors in time past; unbelievers, heretics,
schismatics, and false brethren in the present. *Mighty* are
the enemies of our souls ; " for we wrestle not against flesh
and blood, but against principalities and against powers, and
against the rulers of the darkness of this world, against spi-   Eph. vi. 12.
ritual wickedness in high places."

5 I paid them the things that I never took : GOD,
thou knowest my simpleness, and my faults are not
hid from thee.

Or, with the Vulgate, *that I never robbed*. For He paid   A.
the penalty of sin by His Death upon the Cross, being Himself without sin. And yet more, whereas the devil's power
is the produce of robbery, and Adam's knowledge of good
and evil came from robbery too, the power and wisdom of
CHRIST are His own by Divine right, for "all power is given   S. Matt.
unto Him in heaven and earth;" so that He, "being in the   xxviii. 18.
form of GOD, thought it not robbery to be equal with GOD."   Phil. ii. 6.
And He shares His glory with His members, as it is written,
"To him that overcometh will I grant to sit with Me in My   Rev. iii. 21.
throne, even as I also overcame, and am set down with My FA-
THER in His throne." *My simpleness*. Rather, with the LXX.,
Vulgate. and A. V., *My foolishness*. It is the Eternal Wisdom Who speaks. But "the foolishness of GOD is wiser than
men." What was so much like foolishness as, when He had   1 Cor. i. 25.
it in His power with one word to lay low the persecutors, to   A.
suffer Himself to be held, scourged, spit upon, buffeted, to
be crowned with thorns, to be nailed to the Tree? It is like
foolishness, but this foolish thing excelleth all wise men.
And it is true of every Saint who has given up all for CHRIST,
of whom the wicked shall one day exclaim, "This was he   Wisd. v. 4.
whom we had some time in derision, and a proverb of reproach : we fools accounted his life madness, and his end to
be without honour: how is he numbered among the children
of GOD, and his lot is among the Saints!" But the words   D. C.
also are true of sinners, who are wise in their own conceits,
with that wisdom which is foolishness with GOD, disobeying
His commandments, serving the vices of the body, neglecting
the salvation of their souls. *My faults are not hid from Thee.*
It is the Most Holy Who speaks. He speaks as He was   R.
judged by man : "This Man is not of GOD, because He   S. John ix.
keepeth not the Sabbath day ;" "We know that this Man is   16, 24.

S. Luke v. 21.

Ay.

a sinner;" and again, "Who is this which speaketh blasphemies?" It is spoken of Saints also, who do not attempt to hide their sins from GOD, but confess them openly with hearty repentance and humility. Of sinners, moreover, because their refusal to confess and amend cannot shelter them from the all-seeing eyes of GOD.

6 Let not them that trust in thee, O LORD GOD of hosts, be ashamed for my cause : let not those that seek thee be confounded through me, O LORD GOD of Israel.

Eusebius.

Herein CHRIST prays against that which was the great peril of weak souls in the first days of the Church, the offence of the Cross, the scorn heaped upon those who worshipped the Crucified; to the Jews a stumbling-block, to the Greeks foolishness. The Vulgate, however, reads, *them that wait for Thee.* And they take it of the Fathers waiting in Hades till CHRIST should come to set them free, on whose behalf He prays that He may rise again from death, that they may not be disappointed of their hope. And as in the first part of the verse He intreats that His people may not fail from weakness within, so, in the latter clause, His petition is that they may not be overcome by revilings and persecutions from without, but that, when they look for Him with prayer and holiness, it may be said to them as to the women at the sepulchre, "Fear not, for I know that ye seek JESUS."

Ay.

G.

S. Matt. xxviii. 5.

7 And why? for thy sake have I suffered reproof: shame hath covered my face.

Ay.

S. Matt. xi. 19.
S. John viii. 48.

G.

For Thy sake. Where note, that all CHRIST'S words and works were to the end of increasing the honour of His FATHER in the hearts of men; wherefore He reproved sin, preached holiness, and worked miracles, that they might believe His sayings. And He indeed *suffered reproof,* for they said of Him, "Behold a man gluttonous and a wine-bibber," and "Thou art a Samaritan, and hast a devil." *Shame covered His Face* when He was buffeted, and blindfolded, and spit upon, and at last dragged to the most ignominious of deaths. And this is the cry of the Bride also. For His sake the Martyrs contended to the death; for His sake the Confessors bore not only spoiling of their goods, chains, and torture, but what was harder, the reproach of worshipping with foul and sanguinary orgies, rather than reveal to the mockery of the heathen the mystery of the Holy Eucharist; for His sake the Virgins bore to be dragged to dens of infamy, to stand, stripped of their garments, a mark for the insulting and cruel stare of eighty thousand spectators.

8 I am become a stranger unto my brethren : even an alien unto my mother's children.

It was bitterly true when the chief of His brethren, the **B.** Prince of His Apostles, "began to curse and to swear, saying, S. Mark xiv. I know not this Man of whom ye speak." It was true also 71. on the way to Emmaus, when the eyes of His two disciples S. Hieron. were holden, and Cleopas said, "Art Thou only a stranger S. Luke in Jerusalem?" *An alien unto My mother's children.* As xxiv. 18. Joseph's brethren sold him into Egypt, and knew him not when he became ruler of the land, so the children of the · **G.** Synagogue rejected CHRIST, giving Him over to the Gentiles, and confessed Him not when He became Head of the Church gathered from the heathen. And the Jews did not even admit His Hebrew descent. They said to Him, "Say we S. John viii. not well that Thou art a Samaritan?" They said of Him, S. John ix. "As for this fellow, we know not from whence He is." More 29. literally still, we read, "Neither did His brethren believe in S. John vii. Him." 5.

9 For the zeal of thine house hath even eaten me: and the rebukes of them that rebuked thee are fallen upon me.

We have the comment of the Apostles themselves on the first part of this verse; for we read, that when JESUS drove the sellers of oxen, sheep, and doves, and the money-changers out of the temple with a scourge of small cords, then "His S. John ii. disciples remembered that it was written, The zeal of Thine 17. house hath eaten Me up." And therefore it was that He be- **Ay.** came an alien to His Mother's children, because they would not endure His severity, but rejected Him for interfering with their gains, as did also the Gergesenes, when He suf- S. Matt. viii. fered the devils to destroy their swine. The latter clause has 34. also an inspired gloss, for S. Paul says, "For even CHRIST pleased not Himself; but, as it is written, The reproaches of Rom. xv. 3. them that reproached Thee fell on Me." And that, because **A.** whoso knoweth CHRIST knoweth the FATHER also; because **G.** whoso insults an ambassador, dishonours also the King from whom he comes: a King, moreover, Who hath said, "They S. Matt. xxi. will reverence My SON." There is another sense in which it 37. may be truly said that CHRIST is eaten up with zeal for His **L.** FATHER's House. For in His great love for the Church He desires to edify it in all ways, and especially by giving Him- self in the Holy Eucharist to be the Food of believers, so that He is therein eaten up. The whole verse may well be **D. C.** applied, as by the Carthusian, to those who have been raised up at different times as reformers of abuses in the Church, and especially in the Religious Life, and who, like S. Gregory VII.,—and in far later days S. Teresa, and the not less holy Mère Angelique of Port Royal,—have been subjected to all manner of hostility and slander in consequence.

10 I wept, and chastened myself with fasting: and that was turned to my reproof.

S. Paulin.
Ep. x. ad
Sever.

S. Ambros.
de Eliâ. 4.

L.

Ay.

Hugo Card.

B.

R.

D. C.

S. Luke
xxiii. 35.

The LXX. (in some copies) and Vulgate here read, *I covered my soul with fasting.* David did so, observes a Saint, that he might clothe it with true abundance; for in this wise we learn that such fasting, as is abstinence from sin, is a garment of the soul. Gluttony, observes another, makes men naked; fastings clothe even the stripped, and that is a good covering which shelters the soul from the tempter. Where note, that it is not spoken of mere bodily or external abstinence, for that does not cover the soul. Our Blessed LORD covered His soul with fasting, when His continual abstinence of forty days caused the devil to doubt if He were Very Man Who could so endure. And He covered His Godhead from men, by abstaining from putting out His strength to punish His enemies, and that for the purpose of giving an example of patience. And He had a yet sorer fast than either of these, —His unappeased hunger and thirst for the salvation of sinners, whom He yet found to reject His offers, and even to deliver Him over to death. And His fasting was *turned to His reproof,* when it encouraged the devil, seeing Him so destitute of all succour, to tempt Him to vain confidence and idolatry; and when His human enemies cried out, "He saved others, let Him save Himself, if He be CHRIST, the Chosen of GOD."

11 I put on sackcloth also : and they jested upon me.

A.

C.

Ven. Bede.

Ay.

P.

D. C.

Agellius.

C.

That sackcloth was the form of a servant, the Manhood of poverty and suffering, which men scorned and derided. And as sackcloth is the garb of mourning, it tells also of His sorrows Who wept over Jerusalem and at the grave of Lazarus. Beda, following the Vulgate reading, *haircloth,* observes that goats, of whose hair such texture is made, are the symbol of guilt; and that CHRIST, by taking sinners close to His side, and joining them in one body, does, as it were, clothe Himself with them. And many recount a legend that the seamless coat was of haircloth, and the customary garb of CHRIST. Agellius declares that it was customary to wrap a piece of coarse sackcloth round the loins of those about to be crucified, that they might be fastened more securely, and that this passage is thus a prophecy of the last stage of the Passion. *They jested upon Me.* LXX. and Vulgate, *I became a parable unto them;* or better, as A. V., a *proverb.* Whereupon some take occasion to point out, that as the LORD taught chiefly by parables, so He may be said to have been Himself a parable to His disciples. But the plainer sense, an object of ridicule, is more generally followed.

12 They that sit in the gate speak against me : and the drunkards make songs upon me.

The sitters in the gate, according to primeval Eastern

usage, are the elders and rulers of the city, and here, as all the commentators agree, it is used of the chief priests. The *drunkards* are variously explained. Some apply it to those Jews who, having just been quaffing the Paschal wine-cups on the night of Maundy Thursday, hastened from their feast to the house of Annas, to join in reviling CHRIST. Again, it is said by another, following literally the Vulgate, *they who drank the wine*, to refer to a brutal jest of the soldiers employed at the Crucifixion, swallowing themselves the spiced wine prepared for the sufferers to deaden their sense of pain, and substituting vinegar in its stead. The prophecy was true in another sense at a later day, when not only was the Arian heresy encouraged by the chiefs of the State, but the ribald songs of the heresiarch's own *Thalia*, directed against the Consubstantial, were trolled in the wine-shops of Alexandria.

G.

Ay.

13 But, LORD, I make my prayer unto thee : in an acceptable time.

14 Hear me, O GOD, in the multitude of thy mercy : even in the truth of thy salvation.

That *acceptable time* was when the good seed which had fallen into the ground, and was lying buried, should spring up again in the new life of the Resurrection. Or it may be taken of CHRIST'S prayer in His Passion, because in that Passion were three things well pleasing to GOD: first, the absolution of sinners, in CHRIST'S Blood, for " to depart from wickedness is a thing pleasing unto the LORD;" secondly, union and love between neighbours, also brought about by the Cross, for " in three things was I beautified—the unity of brethren, the love of neighbours, a man and his wife that agree together;" thirdly, the faith of the devout, which He in His Passion prayed might not fail; for " faith and meekness are His delight." And the Carthusian will not limit it even thus, but declares that the acceptable time, the day of salvation, was the whole period of CHRIST'S sojourn upon earth. *In the multitude of Thy mercy*, whereby Thou hast sent Me into the world to save it, hear Me in the promised *truth of Thy salvation*, that My Atonement may redeem mankind, and My Resurrection justify all believers, and the sayings of the prophets thus be fulfilled.

A.
G.

Ay.
Ecclus.
xxxv. 3.

Ecclus.
xxiv. 1.

Ecclus. i. 27.

D. C.

Ay.

15 Take me out of the mire, that I sink not : O let me be delivered from them that hate me, and out of the deep waters.

Out of the mire. That is, deliver Me from the ungodly and treacherous Jews, from the sorrows and cares of My weary life, from the corruptibility of My human Body, from the depth of the grave. *Out of the deep waters*, from the troubles and persecutions which encompass Me. When the sin-

G.

D. C.

ner utters these same words, his prayer is to be delivered
from carnal sin and worldly greed within his own soul, and
from outward troubles and sufferings which may shake his
faith.   He saith this, because of the infirmity of His mem-
A.   bers.   Whenever thou art seized by one that urgeth thee to
iniquity, thou art in body fixed in the deep clay ; but so long
as thou consentest not, thou hast not stuck.

16 Let not the water-flood drown me, neither let
the deep swallow me up : and let not the pit shut
her mouth upon me.

A.   He had said already in the beginning of the Psalm that
the *floods run over* Him.   It hath drowned after the flesh,
let it not drown after the spirit.   And it is thus throughout a
prayer for the Resurrection.   *Let not the water-flood drown
Me*, but rather be a wall to Me on each side as I pass over
Jordan with the staff of My Cross.   Neither *let the deep*
swallow Me up, by My Body lying to moulder in the grave
Ay.   unto corruption ; and *let not the pit shut her mouth upon Me*,
to hold Me prisoned in Hades ; but open before Me as I return in triumph, leading the ransomed Fathers back with Me
to light and glory.   The sinner may use these words, too, of
A.   a spiritual resurrection from the grave of iniquity, and he
will find that, so long as he is willing to confess his guilt, the
S. Pet. Dam. mouth of the pit will not close over him ; but when he at-
Opusc. 24. tempts to excuse himself, then it shuts.

17 Hear me, O Lord, for thy loving-kindness is
comfortable : turn thee unto me according to the
multitude of thy mercies.

C.   The Head herein teaches His members how to pray,
namely, that they are to plead with God His loving-kind-
A.   ness, and not their own merits ; to deal with them according to
the multitude of His mercies, not according to that of their
Joel ii. 13. sins.   And it is the reason given by the prophet Joel, " Turn
unto the Lord your God, for He is gracious and merciful,
slow to anger, and of great kindness, and repenteth Him of
the evil."   Ayguan, not unwilling to show his learning, cites
Ay.   here various examples from Roman history, as parables of
God's loving-kindness in Christ.   The aptest of them is the
story of Panopion's slave, who, learning that his master was
proscribed, and the soldiers come to find him, changed clothes
Val. Max.   with him, let him out by a private door, lay down on Pano-
vi. 8.   pion's bed, and was stabbed in his place.   Who, asks Ayguan,
is that proscribed Panopion, but man exiled from Paradise
by the sin of our first parents?   Who is that faithful and
loving slave, but the Son of God, Who emptied Himself of
His glory, and took on Him the form of a servant?   That
He might save us from the pains of hell, He changed His

garb with us, and was found in fashion as a man, and suffered Himself to be slain for us.

18 And hide not thy face from thy servant, for I am in trouble : O haste thee and hear me.

The word in the LXX. and Vulgate may be rendered not only *servant*, but *child*. And it thus points at once to Him Who is the Only-begotten of His FATHER, and Who is also pure and meek as a little child. Most truly a servant also, not only by His having taken on Him the nature of man, and being, so far, inferior to the FATHER, but by His perfect obedience. He then, Who only can look on the Face of GOD, before which even the Seraphim must veil theirs, prays that it may not be hidden from Him, Who merits to be heard because of His unstained holiness. And every penitent who has become as a little child in humility may use these words too, for though "GOD resisteth the proud, He giveth grace to the humble." **D. C.** **C.** **G.** **A.** S. James iv. 6.

19 Draw nigh unto my soul, and save it : O deliver me, because of mine enemies.

These words form the Versicle and Response prefixed to the Lauds of Passiontide in the Sarum Breviary. It is not for Himself that He asks to be delivered, but for His enemies; for the thief who reviled Him, for the soldier who pierced Him, for the nation that rejected Him, that by His being delivered from the grave, they may be converted and believe in Him. And for those who harden themselves also, that they may be weakened and confounded when they find all their plottings vain. And observe, that whereas the priests were His chief enemies, yet after the day of Pentecost we read that a great company of them became obedient unto the Faith. GOD, however, delivers in two ways : sometimes He delivers the soul alone from the peril of sin, allowing the body to perish, as with the Seven Maccabees and the Christian martyrs—this is hidden deliverance; sometimes He delivers from bodily dangers also, as the three children from the fiery furnace,—and this is open deliverance. And both these deliverances are for the sake of the enemies as well as for that of the faithful, that they may see, like Antiochus, that the constancy of the saints cannot be overcome; that they may worship, like Nebuchadnezzar, the GOD Who can save to the uttermost. **A.** **G.** **D. C.** **A.**

20 Thou hast known my reproof, my shame, and my dishonour : mine adversaries are all in thy sight.

My reproof, in the words of insult addressed to Me by the Jews, calling Me a demoniac, a glutton, and a winebibber. *My shame*, outer, indeed, and before men only, not **Ay.**

of the soul before GOD, in that I have been bound, scourged, condemned, and crucified as a robber. *My dishonour,* the stripes and spitting. Or, with the Vulgate rendering, *My reverence,* the mock coronation, and jeering homage of the soldiery. *Mine adversaries are all in Thy sight.* And unless Thou deliver Me openly, they will not know why I suffer these things, and will neither be confounded nor corrected; though they have increased their sin by committing it before Thee.

G.

A.

21 Thy rebuke hath broken my heart; I am full of heaviness : I looked for some to have pity on me, but there was no man, neither found I any to comfort me.

There is no authority whatsoever for the word *Thy* in the Prayer Book Version here. It is not in the Hebrew, nor in any other translation, and is quite out of keeping with all the context. In the true reading, that of the A. V., *Reproach hath broken My heart.* we may well see a reference to that notion, so often upheld by Saints, that the immediate cause of the Redeemer's death was not the Crucifixion, but a heart broken by man's ingratitude; whence it was that the soldiers marvelled at finding Him dead before His fellow-sufferers. And at the least we may take it, with the old Dutch poet, of the spear-wound in His side:

The Hymn, *O JESU CRISTE, geminde Here.*

Doe gî ane t-cruce gestorven waert,
Quam daer een ridder ongespaert,
Die u met ênen spere stac
Ene wonde, dat u t-herte brac
In uwe sîde, ende ût-en steke
Ran bloet ende water als een beke.

G.

S. Luke xxii. 15.

D. C.

A.

The Vulgate, however, reads, *My heart hath expected rebuke and misery.* Not only did that loving Heart foresee and expect its coming sorrows, but longed for them, saying, "With desire I have desired to eat this Passover," although the weakness of our human nature was such as to make the expectation bring on the Agony and Bloody Sweat. The Syriac Psalter here reads, beautifully, if inexactly, *Heal the breaking of My heart, and bind it up.* And we may take it either as a prayer of CHRIST to His FATHER, intreating for the joy of the Resurrection, or of the sinner seeking refuge with the SAVIOUR. *I looked for some one to have pity on Me, but there was no man.* The Hebrew, followed by the Vulgate, goes deeper than this, and reads, *to be sorrowful with Me.* That is, it was not merely pity, but sympathy, for which the SAVIOUR looked in vain. Sorrow there was, and that abundantly, amongst His disciples, but not the closer bond of fellow-feeling. They mourned for His death, whereas their mourning should have been, as His was, for His murderers slaying their Healer. Even His Mother, though the sword of grief passed through her heart, and His Apostles, whose sorrow, because true and praiseworthy, was soon to be turned into joy, did not rise to this height, nor attain to the likeness of His sorrow. *Neither found I any to comfort me.* By repenting at the sight of My patient suffering, and coming to Me, the Physician, to be healed. Nay, observes another, His very Godhead, because impassible, was no help to His Manhood in the Passion, and did not comfort It nor suffer with It, any more than the sunshine suffers when a piece of wood on which its rays are falling is chopped up.

G.

Arnobius.

22 They gave me gall to eat : and when I was thirsty, they gave me vinegar to drink.

The literal fulfilment of this double prediction in the successive acts of the soldiers who, before the Crucifixion, "gave Him vinegar to drink mingled with gall, and when He had tasted thereof, He would not drink ;" and again when He, upon the Cross, said, " I thirst," " filled a sponge with vinegar, and put it upon hyssop, and put it to His mouth," has been most justly dwelt on by all commentators. But they find spiritual mysteries underlying the letter. In the refusal of the mingled cup first offered, they see His rejection of the double-minded, whose good is corrupted by evil. Such were Judas, whose confession, " I have sinned, in that I have betrayed the innocent blood," though wine, was mingled with the gall of bitterness and despair ; and Simon Magus, whose request for the prayers of the Apostles was also uttered in the " gall of bitterness." But in His acceptance of the vinegar offered on the sponge is discerned His welcome to the bitter penitence of a contrite heart, like that of Peter weeping for his fall : where note, that one who drinks from a sponge, does not drain it like a cup, but leaves some of the contents behind. And so CHRIST, in accepting a sinner's penitence, does not drain his heart of it, but takes only so much as He knows to be profitable. Why it should be said, *They gave Me gall to eat,* rather than to *drink,* (seeing that no solid food was offered to the LORD,) is a question which the early commentators discuss at length. They accept, for the most part, the explanation of S. Augustine, who, translating literally, *They gave gall into My food,* glosses thus : Because already the LORD GOD had taken food, and into it there had been thrown gall. But He Himself had taken pleasant food when He ate the Passover with His disciples : therein He showed the Sacrament of His Body. Unto this Food, so pleasant, so sweet, of the Unity of CHRIST, of which the Apostle makes mention, saying, " For we being many, are one bread, and one body,"—unto this pleasant Food who is there that addeth gall, except the gainsayers of the Gospel, like those persecutors of CHRIST? For the Jews sinned less in crucifying

S. Matt. xxvii. 34.

S. John xix. 29.

G.

S. Matt. xxvii. 4.

Acts viii. 23.

A.

1 Cor. x. 17.

II.   R

Him Who walked on earth, than they that despise Him seated in heaven. That which the Jews did there, in giving above the food which He had already taken that bitter draught to drink, the same do they that by evil living bring scandal upon the Church,—the same do embittered heretics. They give gall after such pleasant meat.

23 Let their table be made a snare to take themselves withal : and let the things that should have been for their wealth be unto them an occasion of falling.

And they note, that as CHRIST'S table was made a snare for Him by those who bribed one of them who dipped with Him in the dish at the Paschal Supper, so the horrors of the siege of Jerusalem by Titus were mainly due to the blockade beginning just as the city was thronged for the Passover, so that not only the ordinary population, but crowds of Jews from all parts of the Empire, were taken as in a snare. The words hold good also of the spiritual table of Holy Writ, which proved a snare to the Jews by their misinterpretation of its Messianic prophecies. Where observe further that every chastisement which fell on the Jews corresponded exactly to some one of their outrages against CHRIST. They rebelled against Him, the promised King and Messiah, saying, "We have no King but Cæsar." It was the harsh rule of Cæsar's soldiers which drove them into the rebellion which was their destruction. They betrayed CHRIST at the Passover: it was at the Passover they were besieged. They crucified CHRIST at Paschaltide itself, and gave Him vinegar and gall : they suffered all the tortures of famine themselves, and ate their Passover in bitterness. They blindfolded CHRIST, smote Him, and bade Him prophesy: they were blinded themselves in ignorance, and unable to behold the mysteries of Scripture. They laid the Cross on His shoulders: on their own was laid the yoke of slavery. And as they raged against CHRIST, crying, "Crucify, crucify," so almost every year the people are excited against them, rob and murder them.[1] They cast CHRIST out of the city to crucify Him, and were cast out of their own city themselves, and scattered over the world. We may add, as Josephus says, that such of them as attempted to escape from the city were crucified in such numbers, that room was wanting for the crosses, and crosses for the bodies.

Marginal notes: G. Ay. | Joseph. Bell. Jud. v. 3. | L. | P. | S. John xix. 15. | Joseph. Bell. Jud. v. 11.

24 Let their eyes be blinded, that they see not : and ever bow thou down their backs.

L. *Blinded* to the true meaning of Scripture, *bowed down*

---

[1] Parez writes of Spain towards the close of the fifteenth century, when and where this statement was only too true.

under the weight of the Law. And S. Augustine compares **s. Aug.**
the attitude of Jews and Christians towards the truth to the **Serm. de**
spies carrying the grapes on the pole. The Jews go first, **Temp. 100.**
counting themselves to have the pre-eminence, but not seeing
the precious freight, and even turning their backs upon it;
while the Christian, coming behind, beholds and worships.

> They who were grace-expectant, they who lived and died in grace,
> They who saw CHRIST far off, and they who see, though veiled,
>   His Face—
> Those went before: these follow, they are all one brotherhood,
> And in the midst the True Vine hangs upon the Holy Rood.

Like the men of Sodom, whom the angels smote with blindness when they endeavoured to break into the house of Lot, **G.**
the Jews, under the curse, were unable to find CHRIST, Who
is the Door. We see the prayer fulfilled in mercy when
Saul was blinded on his way to Damascus, and that stiff neck
was bowed beneath the yoke of his Conqueror.

25 Pour out thine indignation upon them : and let
thy wrathful displeasure take hold of them.

26 Let their habitation be void : and no man to
dwell in their tents.

Pour out, not drop by drop, but in a flood of vengeance.
And they note the difference between *indignation, (ira,)* which **G.**
GOD always shows against sin, when He corrects the offender
with His chastisements, and *wrathful displeasure, (furor* **Ay.**
iræ,) which is the punishment dealt out to hardened impenitence. *Let their habitation be void.* It is taken first by S.
Peter of the traitor Judas, in whose person the prophecy was
first accomplished, since the field bought with the price of **Acts i. 20.**
blood was inhabited only by the dead. For a yet wider ful- **L.**
filment we must look not merely to the utter destruction of
Jerusalem, and the raising of Ælia Capitolina on another **Euseb. Hist.**
site, but to the decree of Hadrian, after the suppression of **Eccl. iv. 6.**
Bar-Cochab's revolt, forbidding all Jews to approach near
enough to Jerusalem even to behold its former site from any
neighbouring hill. *In their tents.* Not only so far as they
are a community is ruin to fall on them, but even solitary **G.**
dwellings are to share the fate of the city, that the vengeance may be at once universal and particular. Or the
habitation may well refer to the Temple, left void when the
mysterious sound of an unseen departing multitude was
heard, saying, "Let us go hence." And as the Feast of
Tabernacles, when *tents* or booths were erected by the Jews, **Joseph.**
was no more to be kept in the Holy City, it is well said that **Bell. Jud.**
no man should dwell in their tents. Ayguan, interpreting **vi. 5.**
the *tents* or tabernacles of the souls of the unbelieving Jews,
well says, that as the Man was not suffered to dwell therein, **Ay.**

they were given over to evil spirits of darkness and sin.

Isa. xiii. 21. "Owls shall dwell there, and satyrs shall dance there."

27 For they persecute him whom thou hast smitten : and they talk how they may vex them whom thou hast wounded.

A.

Pet. Lomb. Sent. iii. 21.

B.

Isa. liii. 10.

Zech. xiii. 7.

Isa. liii. 4.

Lu.

S. Albertus Magnus.

S. Matt. xxv. 40.

Mal. iii. 8.

Heb. vi. 6.

Gal. iii. 1.

What then was their sin, asks S. Augustine, if they did but carry on, as it were, GOD's work? The Master of the Sentences answers the question well : CHRIST was delivered up by the FATHER, delivered up by Himself, by Judas, and by the Jews. What then is the difference between the cases? It is that the FATHER and SON acted out of love, Judas from treachery, the Jews from hate. And it is truly said, *Whom Thou hast smitten,* for GOD smote the SAVIOUR first in giving Him a mortal and passible Body, and then by giving Him up as a Sacrifice for us; as it is written, "Yet it pleased the LORD to bruise Him : He hath put Him to grief;" and again, "Smite the shepherd, and the sheep shall be scattered." *They talk how they may vex them whom Thou hast wounded.* The Hebrew is rather, *They talk of the grief of Thy wounded.* That is, they gloat over the details of the sufferings of Him Whom they "did esteem stricken, smitten of GOD, and afflicted," and of those inflicted on the martyrs who trod in His steps. But the LXX. and Vulgate have, *They added unto the pain of My wounds,* (doubtless reading חַלְלֵי יִסְפֹּרוּ instead of חַלְלֶיךָ יְסַפֵּרוּ,) and this by blasphemy and the insults of the soldiery in My own Person, and by afflicting the faithful of My Church, so that I suffer in My members also. And note, observes S. Albert, that we may crucify the SAVIOUR afresh in four ways. First, by afflicting His poor, according to His own saying in S. Peter's vision, "I go to Rome to be crucified again," because "inasmuch as ye have done it unto one of the least of these My brethren, ye have done it unto Me." Next, by depriving His ministers of their due assistance. "Ye have robbed [Vulg., *ye pierce*] Me, even this whole nation. But ye say, Wherein have we robbed [Vulg., *do we pierce*] Thee? In tithes and offerings." Thirdly, by making light of the Sacrament, "seeing they crucify to themselves the SON of GOD afresh, and put Him to an open shame." Fourthly, by apostatizing from the right way, and especially from the promise, "before whose eyes JESUS CHRIST hath been evidently set forth, crucified among you."

28 Let them fall from one wickedness to another : and not come into thy righteousness.

29 Let them be wiped out of the book of the living : and not be written among the righteous.

From the wickedness of slaying the messengers of the LORD A.
of the vineyard to that of killing His SON; from the wickedness
of killing that SON, counting Him a mere man, to that of out-
raging the SON of GOD. *And not come into Thy righteousness,* D. C.
because the only door into that is faith, from which in their
perversity they turn away to their sins. *Let them be wiped* A.
out of the book of the living. Had they ever been written
therein? Brethren, we must not so take it as that GOD writeth
any one in the Book of Life, and blotteth him out. If a
man said, "What I have written, I have written," concerning S.John xix.
the title where it had been written "King of the Jews," doth 22.
GOD write any one, and blot him out? He foreknoweth,
He hath predestined all before the foundation of the world
that are to reign with His SON in life everlasting. These He
hath written down; these same the Book of Life doth contain. Lastly, in the Apocalypse, what saith the Spirit of
GOD, when the Scripture is speaking of Antichrist's oppres-
sions? "All shall worship him whose names are not written Rev. xiii. 8.
in the Book of Life." So then, doubtless, they who are
written will not do so. How, then, are these men blotted
out of that book wherein they were never written? It hath
been said of their hopes, because they thought themselves to
be written. Let it be plain even to themselves that they are
not therein. And then to be *written among the righteous*
will mean to be numbered amongst the citizens of the kingdom of heaven. Others refer the verse to temporal chastisements, so that the *book of the living* means simply the muster-
roll of those yet upon earth, out of which death blots each H.
man in his turn; and the *number of the righteous* such a ca- Pseudo-
talogue of illustrious men as that contained in the Book of Hieron.
Ecclesiasticus. Bellarmine, objecting to S. Augustine's view
as merely evading the difficulty of reconciling the blotting Bellarmine.
out with eternal predestination, and to the merely temporal
explanation as involving a contradiction between the members
of the verse, explains it of the Book of the people of GOD,
wherein His true worshippers are enrolled; once filled with
the name of the Jewish nation, but now, on its erasure, containing the Gentiles instead. And he aptly cites Ezekiel's
prophecy, "They shall not be in the assembly of My people, Ezek. xiii. 9.
neither shall they be written in the writing of the house of
Israel."

30 As for me, when I am poor and in heaviness :
thy help, O GOD, shall lift me up.

Poor, in taking on Himself our human nature, thus empty- S. Cyrill.
ing Himself of His glory, *in heaviness,* (or with the LXX. and Alex.
Vulgate, *suffering,*) upon the Cross. *Shall lift Me up,* in the Z.
might of My Resurrection, in the glory of My Ascension.
And not in My own Person alone, but lifting up with Me G.
the members whose Head I am.

31 I will praise the Name of GOD with a song :
and magnify it with thanksgiving.

32 This also shall please the LORD : better than a
bullock that hath horns and hoofs.

A.

G.

A.

G.

B.

Ay.

They see in these words the joy of the Resurrection, and
the greater pleasure felt by GOD in the voluntary praise of a
rational being, than in the sacrifice of a brute animal, incapable
of self-dedication. The Vulgate reading in the latter clause
is, *A young steer, putting forth its horns and hoofs;* that is,
not yet fully ready for the yoke of CHRIST, but going on in
obedience, and having horns for His violent enemies, and
hoofs to tread under those who grovel in earthly desires.
Gerhohus dwells at length on this simile, and instances
Moses in his early efforts in favour of his countrymen in
Egypt; Peter, in his smiting of Malchus; Saul, in his first
persecuting zeal; and even our LORD Himself, while yet increasing in wisdom and stature, and in favour with GOD and
man, as when He sat in the midst of the doctors, and again,
when He purged the temple at the beginning of His ministry. S. Bruno the Carthusian adopts this last view for another reason. In the *steer* he sees the Victim for the Sacrifice; in the epithet *young* or *new* (*novellus*) he recognises the
New Man, the Second Adam. Ayguan, going yet deeper,
sees in this sacrifice of thanksgiving, attended with song, and
preferable to animal victims, the Oblation of the Gospel, the
most Holy Eucharist, dearer to GOD than all sacrifice besides. And because this is so—

The Hymn,
*Pange
lingua.*

Tantum ergo Sacramentum
  Veneremur cernui,
Et antiquum documentum
  Novo cedat ritui;
Præstet fides supplementum,
  Sensuum defectui.

33 The humble shall consider this, and be glad :
seek ye after GOD, and your soul shall live.

Ay.

The *humble*, that is, in the first place, the Apostles, and
then all that are poor in station and lowly in heart since
their day; and they will *be glad,* because the abolition of the
old sacrifices, and the acceptance of a spiritual service in
their stead, has removed one advantage which the rich had
over the poor under the Law. They can *seek God* directly
in the Eucharist, and feeding there on Him, their *soul shall
live.* Wherefore we cry to Him—

O panis dulcissime,
O fidelis animæ
  Vitalis refectio!

O Paschalis Victimæ
Agne mansuetissime,
Legalis oblatio.

34 For the LORD heareth the poor : and despiseth
not his prisoners.

And as He had pity on the children of Israel, and brought
them out of the bondage of Egypt, so He looks on sinners
even now, and looses them from the chains of their sins.
Those who are willing so to be freed by Him are His prisoners, because they are held captive by the devil against
their will. And all Saints who submit themselves to His
commandments, keeping them strictly, are, in another sense,
His prisoners also. Yet, again, we may take it of all men
who are tied down on earth by their bodies. Or it may be
fitly taken of the Fathers who waited in Hades for the
Coming of CHRIST, whom Zechariah styles by this same
title. We may extend the application of the verse, and its
connection with the two preceding ones, yet further, and explain it of the Holy Eucharist, as a propitiation for the living
and the dead. And so the Missal of Liege :

G.

Ay.

Zech. ix. 11.

> King of Glory, hear our voices,
> Grant Thy faithful rest, we pray ;
> We have sinned, and may not bide it,
> If Thou mark our steps astray ;
> Yet we plead that saving Victim
> Which for them we bring to-day.

The Se-
quence, *De
profundis
exclamantes*,
for All Souls.

So far, the confession of sin is a prayer to the LORD, Who
heareth the poor. Then follows :

> That which Thou Thyself hast offered
> To the FATHER, offer we ;
> Let it win for them a blessing,
> Bless them, JESU, set them free :
> They are Thine, they wait in patience,
> Merciful and gracious be.

That is, *He despiseth not His prisoners.*

35 Let heaven and earth praise him : the sea, and
all that moveth therein.

The *heaven*, because the ranks of the angelic hierarchies,
left incomplete by the fall of the rebels, have been filled up ;
the *earth*, because man is ransomed ; the *sea*, because the
glad tidings of salvation have spread to the islands afar. Let
the *heaven* of His chief Saints, Apostles, Martyrs, Confessors,
praise Him ; let the *earth* of believing Jews, less exalted, do
the like : let the *sea* of Gentiles, coming from the ends of
the earth, and compassing the Jews round as a sea, join in
the hymn. *All creeping things therein*, is the Vulgate read-

P.

B.

G.

Arnobius.

ing; and they take it of weak and imperfect Christians, who, nevertheless, are encouraged to add their voices to swell the praises of GOD. Let heaven praise CHRIST, for He ascended; let earth praise Him, for He rose again; let the sea praise Him, for He walked upon its surface.

36 For GOD will save Sion, and build the cities of Judah : that men may dwell there, and have it in possession.

37 The posterity also of his servants shall inherit it : and they that love his Name shall dwell therein.

C.

Ay.

It is spoken first of the Church Militant, saved by its Founder, so that the gates of hell cannot prevail against it; and of the various local Churches forming parts of that one, (as the branching chapels of a great cathedral are portions of one harmonious whole,) and fitly styled *cities of Judah*, as springing out of the Hebrew dispensation. Men shall *dwell* there, as not being mere sojourners or temporary worshippers, and *have it for a possession*, enjoying full membership as their very own, instead of the imperfect position allowed to proselytes of Gentile race by the Jews. *The posterity of His servants*, not necessarily their literal offspring, but those spiritually begotten in the Gospel, and continuing in the same belief and zeal as the first Fathers of the infant Church.

And we may also take the verses of the Church Triumphant, saved by the constant addition of new names to its roll-call, new stones to its buildings. Then the cities of Judah will denote those orders of angels who serve the Lion of the tribe of Judah, whose ranks, thinned by the fall of Lucifer and his hosts, will be filled up with redeemed mortals; and thus the cities shall be built, the waste places repaired, while the eternal tenure of blessedness in heaven is expressed by the words, *They shall have it for a possession*.

Wherefore :

Glory be to the FATHER, to Whom the GOD-Man cried, *Save Me, O God;* and to the SON, JESUS CHRIST, praying for Himself and His members to be saved and delivered from the floods; and to the HOLY GHOST, Who is that love and salvation wherewith GOD shall save Sion, and whereby all that love His Name shall dwell therein.

As it was in the beginning, is now, and ever shall be; world without end. Amen.

COLLECTS.

Ludolph.

O most merciful LORD, hear us in the truth of Thy salvation, that, delivered from the filth of sin, we may be written in the Book of Life by Thy heavenly finger. Through. (1.)

Bestow Thyself, O LORD, as the life of our soul, upon us who seek Thee; hearken to Thy poor, who have nothing because of their own righteousness, but are filled with Thy gift, and are nourished with Thy substance, that they may be defended by Thy grace. Despise not Thy prisoners, whose longings sigh for Thee, whose souls shall be present with Thee, and which ever follow after the desires of Thy Saints. Through. (11.)

O LORD GOD of Hosts, let not those who look for Thee to *Mozarabic.* sit in judgment on the doings of men be ashamed for our cause, that the power of Thy Cross may make us workmen of salvation, acceptable unto Thee, and not suffer the court of the heavenly army to sorrow because of our doings. Through Thy mercy. (11.)

O LORD GOD, with Whom our offences are not hidden, *Mozarabic.* Whose eyes behold not only outward things, but with invisible gaze pierce the secrets of the heart; grant us the medicine of penitence as a raiment of sackcloth; grant us open confession for the gain of pardon; grant that our eyes may pour forth floods of tears for our sins; grant that our voice may with sighings intreat a hearing for our prayers. And Thou, O LORD, hearken to our petition, for Thy lovingkindness is comfortable; let not the deep of hell swallow us up, nor our miry deeds overwhelm us; let the multitude of Thy mercies look upon us. Through Thy mercy. (11.)

CHRIST our GOD, Sole-Begotten SON of the Unbegotten *Mozarabic.* FATHER, draw nigh unto my soul, and save it, because of Thine enemies, who war against Thy Church; for Thou art our Redemption: and let us, who have waited for Thee in Thy gift, obtain Thee in everlasting glory. Through Thy mercy. (11.)

JESU, our GOD, Who, making a whip of small cords, *Mozarabic.* dravest out those who buy and sell in Thy temple; grant to us in Thy Church not to be taken with the gain of temporal things, nor to dwell within it in filthy conversation; but that the zeal of Thy House may so eat us up, that Thou wouldst make of us examples for the brethren, pleasing unto Thee. Through Thy mercy.

O CHRIST, SON of GOD, Whom zeal for GOD's House, even *Mozarabic.* Thy FATHER'S Church, eateth up; whilst Thou dost boldly drive from it with a cord those who do unrighteously, loose us from the cord of all our sins, and grant that we may dwell worthily in the midst of Thy House, that we ourselves, made a spiritual house for Thee, may receive from Thee the crown of heavenly laurel. Through Thy mercy. (11.)

Remember, O JESU, the wormwood and the gall, which *Mozarabic.* bitter cup Thou wast given to drink for sinners; and there- *Passiontide.* fore let Thy bitterness, we pray Thee, be our everlasting sweetness, so that wherein Thou wast willing to be made bitter for us, therein we may both here and evermore rejoice in blessedness. Through Thy mercy. (11.)

Mozarabic. Passiontide. CHRIST our King, Who didst bear reproach for sinners, whilst all the crowd of the unbelievers in the gate, drunken with the wine of malice, spake against Thee; do Thou with Thine unfailing pity both cleanse us from the contagion of our sins, and glorify us by working in us with the might of holy doing, that at the end of our life we may not be ashamed to speak with our enemies in the gate; but, met by Thy holy Angels, may be lifted up in everlasting gladness. Through Thy mercy. (11.)

Mozarabic. Passiontide. O CHRIST, SON of GOD, Who, in the last issue of Thy Passion, wast given gall and vinegar to drink by the Jews; grant that, by that bitterness which Thou wast given, Thou mayest inebriate us with the draught of Thy bitternesses, and that the bitterness of Thy death may increase the flame of love within us, and the power of Thy Resurrection may set before us the perfect glory of Thy promised Face. Through Thy mercy. (11.)

Mozarabic. Passiontide. Wherefore, O LORD, should the creature Thou hast made resist Thee, for which Thou didst bear the reproaches of the mockers, and didst sit alone to be filled with threatenings? We pray, therefore, that Thou wouldst not permit that they, for whom Thou didst bear such wounds of sufferings, should be cast down by the passion of the flesh, or be drowned in the deep of hell. Through Thy mercy. (11.)

Mozarabic. S. Clement. O GOD, Who didst not suffer the body of Thy most blessed Martyr Clement to be held in the deep mire by any waves of the sea, so that no depth of waters could drown it; deliver us from all our temptations by the intercession of Thy Martyr, who, in Thy Name, overcame the bands of the enemies rising up against him, and, saving us from the deep of wickedness, lift us up in the calm light of dwelling in Thee, that by Thy help we may be free from sin and abound in virtues. Through Thy mercy. (11.)

Mozarabic. S. Vincent. O GOD, Who didst crown Vincent, conquering marvellously in manifold sufferings, delivering him from all destructive. torments, so that his steps, which stuck not fast in the mire of sin, marvellously trampled under foot all his cruel punishment, that he who, treading in soul upon the world, was now next heir of heaven, should not be swallowed up in the deep waters; Grant to us, by the prayer of so great a Martyr, not to be reached by the mire of sin, not to be drowned in the deep whirlpool of despair, but that we may be set before Thee in the day of judgment, adorned with spotless liberty of conscience. Through Thy mercy. (11.)

Mozarabic. For the Jews. Pour forth Thy wrath, O LORD, upon mine enemies, that their habitation may remain void, but let them at length understand the place of their fury and unrighteousness, that there may be access unto Thee by conversion in Thy Church for them who have lost the help of the earthly city Jerusalem. Through Thy mercy. (11.)

S. Jerome. We pray Thee, O LORD, that Thou wouldst build us, turned from heathendom, in the cities of Judah, and loosing us from the yoke of the devil, love us as Thine own children, that as Thou didst redeem us by the bitter gall, the sharp vinegar, the painful cross, the wounding nails, and the shameful death, Thou wouldst so vouchsafe and keep us in this world by the glory of Thy Resurrection, that Thou mayest make us partakers with the Saints in Thy kingdom. Who livest.

O GOD, to Whom every thought is open, and from Whom our sins are not hid, look upon us in the multitude of Thy mercy, and wash away from us the stains which offend Thee, draw nigh unto our soul, and save it from reproof and eternal shame. Through. (1.)

D. C.

PSALM LXX.

TITLE: To the Chief Musician, A Psalm of David, to bring to remembrance. LXX. and Vulgate: To the end, of David, in remembrance that the LORD saved me. Or: To the Supreme, of David, for the memorial [i.e., the meat-offering.]

ARGUMENT.

ARG. THOMAS. That CHRIST is the helper and redeemer of believers. The voice of CHRIST set on the Cross. Or the voice of the Church to the LORD in a fast. The voice of martyrs and confessors intreating to be delivered from the dangers of persecutors. The voice of the Church crying in the Advent of the LORD.

VEN. BEDE. *The end* and *David*, as has been often observed, denote the LORD the SAVIOUR, to whom these words of the faithful are addressed, since the whole Psalm is spoken in the person of the martyrs, *in remembrance* either of their deliverance or of the future reward. For it was suitable, inasmuch as the LORD had in the previous Psalm set forth His Passion and Resurrection, that the members also should speak after the Head, declaring their sufferings and the glories to follow. The nation of martyrs and confessors, which endured manifold yet happy slaughter, in the first place beseeches the LORD that it may be delivered from the danger of its persecutors, and that He may make their mockings vain, so that, converted, they may be profitably ashamed of their words: *Haste thee, O God, to deliver me.* In the second part it supplicates, that the assembly of the faithful magnifying the LORD may rejoice, because He vouchsafes to help and deliver His poor and needy. *Let all those that seek Thee be joyful and glad in Thee.*

SYRIAC PSALTER. Of David. Literally when he sent Joab to take Sheba, who had rebelled. Then also the supplication of the just, and even of CHRIST Himself.

EUSEBIUS OF CÆSAREA. The supplication of the just, or even of CHRIST Himself.

S. ATHANASIUS. A Psalm in single address.

VARIOUS USES.

Gregorian. Ferial. Thursday. Matins. [Fridays in Lent. Litany. Maundy Thursday. I. Nocturn.]

Monastic. Wednesday. Matins. [Fridays in Lent. Litany. Maundy Thursday. I. Nocturn.]

Parisian. Sunday. Lauds.

Lyons. Friday. Lauds.

Ambrosian. Monday of Second Week. III. Nocturn.

Quignon. Friday. Nones.

Eastern Church. Saturday. Nocturns. Mesorion of Sexts.

ANTIPHONS.

Gregorian. Ferial. O LORD GOD * make speed to save me. [Maundy Thursday. Let them be turned back and put to confusion * that wish me evil.]

Monastic. The same.

Lyons. The same.

Parisian. Let them be joyful * and glad in Thee, who delight in Thy salvation, O LORD.

Ambrosian. As preceding Psalm.

Mozarabic. First verse.

1 Haste thee, O GOD, to deliver me : make haste to help me, O LORD.

This Psalm is, with but very slight variations, merely a repetition of Psalm xl. 16, to the end. But the first verse is noticeable as being more often recited in the Western Church than any other part of the Old Testament. The Versicle and Response, ℣. *O God, make speed to save us.* ℟. *O Lord, make haste to help us,* which are prefixed to the offices of all the Canonical Hours, and which are retained in the Anglican Matins and Evensong, are taken from it. On this usage, let us hear the Carthusian : "Great and wonderful is the virtue of the first verse of the present Psalm, wherefore rightly hath our Mother the Church, instructed by the HOLY GHOST, appointed that this verse should be recited at the beginning, or near the beginning, of each of the Hours, so that, protected by the shield of Divine assistance, we may escape all the snares of the enemy, who plots against us more determinedly, and opposes us more wickedly, when we are engaged in beginning divine service. Moreover, our most eminent Father, Cassian, in the first Book of his Collations, beautifully sets forth the praise of the verse, setting down what he heard from the mouth of the holy anchoret, the Abbat Isaac. That we may have, says he, continual remembrance of GOD, this verse is to be set inseparably before the mind, for it receives all the attacks which can be directed against man's nature, and is thoroughly and suitably fitted to all conditions and every assault. It contains invocation of GOD against peril, the lowliness of devout confession, the vigilance of constant anxiety and fear, thought of frailty, trust in being heard, and in a safeguard ever standing by." As the corresponding

D. C.

verses of the earlier Psalm were passed over in their place, the comments which follow have been drawn from glosses on both, combined as appeared most suitable. The opening words then, spoken in the Person of CHRIST, are primarily a prayer for His own Resurrection, and deliverance from the depth of hell; and then a petition for His mystical Body, the Church, to be preserved from the peril of false brethren and of open enemies. It is the prayer of the members too, penitent, in pain, crying out under the steel of the physician, but yet hoping.

B.
Ay.
G.
A.

2. Let them be ashamed and confounded that seek after my soul : let them be turned backward and put to confusion that wish me evil.

Observe, says the Carthusian, that these words may be taken either in a good sense or a bad one, for there are two kinds of confusion mentioned in Scripture, according to that saying, "There is a shame that bringeth sin; and there is a shame which is glory and grace." And so it was with Saul, who was *ashamed and confounded*, and laid low, and then raised up again to preach what he had before persecuted. This confounding is necessary for the salvation of persecutors, that they may fear, instead of boasting and glorying in their cruel deeds. And it also speaks of the woe and terror which GOD sends on the impenitent, such as the awful death of Maximin Daïa and other persecutors, or the more terrible doom of the Last Day. *That seek after My soul to destroy it.* There is another seeking after the soul of CHRIST, which is that of the Bride, or even of those sinners who pursue the LORD's soul, that they may imitate it, as a robber chases a man to take his cloak to warm himself, but here only the intent of murder is spoken of. *Let them be turned backward.* That they may follow Me. And so S. Peter, when he attempted to go before JESUS, by counselling Him, was met with the rebuke, "Get thee behind Me, Satan," that he might no longer be his LORD's adversary, but His follower. All who censure the Christian religion and suggest amendments in it, or who count themselves wiser than the martyrs, do as S. Peter did in his error, and need the same rebuke. And we may take it also of all who would parley or offer to make terms of peace when our true Jehu ("the LORD is He,") newly crowned, is riding to war against the house of Ahab. To each of them is said, when he advances, "What hast thou to do with peace? turn thee behind Me." There is another way in which those who will not turn backward in this wise, must do so at length, at the Judgment, before Him at Whose sight the soldiers fell back in the garden.

D. C.

Ecclus. iv. 21.
A.

A.

S. Matt. xvi. 23.

2 Kings ix. 19.

G.

Retro ruent tum injusti ignes in perpetuos,
Vermis quorum non morietur, flamma nec restinguitur.

The Hymn
Apparebit repentina.

G.

B.

R.

But the Saints *turn backward* in yet another fashion, as Mary Magdalene turned, saying, "Master," when JESUS called her by name. *Who wish me evil.* Not only those who *seek after my soul* with open violence, but those who nourish secret ill-will, are to meet with the same check and punishment. And it is most aptly pointed out that the two clauses mark the successive perils of the Church, first from the open violence of heathen kings and people, seeking the utter abolition of Christianity by the slaughter of its adherents, and then the risk from false teachers and heretics. Heathen kings have been baptized, quaintly observes S. Remigius, but the devil is not baptized.

3 Let them for their reward be soon brought to shame : that cry over me, There, there.

G.

They dwell on the word *soon* (not, by-the-by, in the Hebrew text,) as showing the greater guilt of the flatterers and mockers, whose punishment is to be speedier than even that of those who seek after the life of CHRIST. For *There, there,* all the old versions read, *Well, well,* or, in modern phrase, *Bravo.* And they take it first of those who hypocritically praised CHRIST, saying, "Master, we know that Thou art true, and teachest the way of GOD in truth," or who openly mocked Him with words of feigned homage, "Hail, King of the Jews." And then it is spoken of those who attribute the good works of the Saints to human merit, and give praise to them for such works, instead of ascribing the fertility of the branches to the Vine, which bears and nourishes them. And so, the tongue of the flatterer harms more than the hand of the persecutor. Or it applies to those enemies of the soul, whether visible or invisible, who encourage a man in sin, by praising him for persevering in it.

S. Matt.
xxii. 16;
xxvii. 29.

A.

4 But let all those that seek thee be joyful and glad in thee : and let all such as delight in thy salvation say alway, The LORD be praised.

A.

D. C.

Ric. Hamp.

2 Cor. x. 17.

G.

That seek Thee. Not in the first instance, for He sought out the lost sheep Himself, and brought it back, on His shoulders when it knew Him not, but now, knowing His voice, it goes after Him and only with Him can find joy. *Be joyful and glad.* With outward tokens of rejoicing, but also with the deeper inward gladness of the soul. *In Thee.* Not in themselves, lest they should fall through trust in their own strength, but, as it is written, "He that glorieth, let him glory in the LORD." *Thy salvation.* Not alone in the blessedness of heaven, but in Him whose countenance makes heaven blessed, the LORD JESUS, Who is the Salvation which the FATHER hath sent. *Say alway, the Lord be praised.* The Latin Fathers construe the sentence a little differently. *The Lord be magnified alway.* Magnified now

in the Resurrection and glorifying of CHRIST, magnified from
generation to generation unto the end of the world in con-   **B.**
tinually granting pardon to sinners and grace to Saints. Or,
if we construe the sentence as in the Prayer Book, we may
take it of the perpetual canticle of heaven, and join in the   Brev. Moz.
words of the Mozarabic Breviary, "Alleluia in heaven and in   Dom. i.
earth; in heaven it is perpetuated, on earth it is sung. There   Quad.
it sounds unceasingly; here faithfully. There everlastingly,
here sweetly. There happily, here harmoniously. There
unspeakably, here earnestly. There, unsyllabled; here in
measured strain. There, by the Angels; here, by the people."

5 As for me, I am poor and in misery : haste thee
unto me, O GOD.

It is most truly spoken of Him Who had not where to lay   **H.**
His head, Who was a Man of sorrows and acquainted with
grief. *But*, it is added in the fortieth Psalm, *the Lord careth
for me*, with the care of a FATHER for His Only-begotten
and beloved SON, the care of the Divinity of the WORD for
that Manhood which He assumed, the care of the HOLY
GHOST for Him on Whom He descended in Jordan. And
because it is so, I may cry, sure of being heard, *Haste Thee*   **B.**
unto me, O God, and raise me up in the joy of the Resurrection. It is the cry of all those who have hearkened to the
warning voice of CHRIST, and who no longer say, "I am rich,
and increased with goods, and have need of nothing," but   Rev. iii. 17.
have learnt that they are "wretched, and miserable, and poor,
and blind, and naked;" and who therefore desire to buy of
the LORD gold tried in the fire, and white raiment. Many
of the Saints have dwelt on these words, spoken in the   **Ay.**
Person of CHRIST, as teaching the counsel of perfection in
voluntary poverty, as a state well-pleasing to GOD. And ob-   **G.**
serve, that all beings save GOD are always *needy*, because
they require His aid, while He alone is "without need," and   Theoph.
they are *poor* besides, when they have not got the things   ad Autol.
which they require. How true it is of mankind, let a great
Saint tell us; Man is a beggar and poor, for though he once   S. Chrysost.
was rich and noble, (enriched by GOD's law, and joined in
kinship with Him by the royal image,) yet he was reduced to
such want that his poverty passed on to many generations, so
that at last, brought up in that poverty, he was named poor.
What art thou to do then, poor and needy one? Beg before   **A.**
the gate of GOD, knock, and it shall be opened to thee. And
what are the alms? Let the Beatitude answer, "Blessed are   S. Matt. v. 3.
the poor in spirit, for theirs is the kingdom of heaven."

6 Thou art my helper, and my redeemer : O LORD,
make no long tarrying.

Helper, in all good works—*Redeemer* from all evil ones.
Make no long tarrying. It is the cry of the individual sinner,   **D. C.**

G.
A.

asking for instant help in trouble. It is the cry of the
Church in days of persecution and affliction, and yet more,
it is the prayer of all who long for the speedy coming of
CHRIST, of the Martyrs under the golden Altar in heaven,
who cry, "How long, O LORD, how long," and of Confessors
on earth uttering the petition, "Thy kingdom come." And
the answer is alike for all:

The Hymn
Heu, heu,
mundi vita.

Ecce Rex desideratus
Et a justis expectatus,
Jam festinat exoratus,
Ad salvandum præparatus!
Apparebit, non tardabit;
Veniet et demonstrabit
Gloriam quam mereantur
Qui pro fide tribulantur.

Wherefore:
Glory be to the FATHER, Who maketh speed to save me;
and to the SON, Who maketh haste to help me; and to the
HOLY GHOST, my Helper and Redeemer, for the SPIRIT helpeth our infirmities, and where the SPIRIT of the LORD is,
there is liberty.

As it was in the beginning, is now, and ever shall be:
world without end. Amen.

COLLECTS.

Ludolph.
O Everlasting GOD, Whose help is inexhaustible, make
haste to help Thy humble servants, that overcoming the reproaches of the ungodly, we may ever be guarded by Thine
aid. Through. (1.)

Mozarabic.
O LORD, make speed to save us, and advance in haste to
help us, give us strength to fulfil what we know, and count
as perfect that we desire to do, that when by Thy working
in us Thou shalt have made us perfect in Thy statutes, Thou
mayest count it as Thy praise; by Thy effectual operation
let us be exalted in reward; let right work magnify Thee,
and Thy repayment lift us up. Through Thy mercy. (11.)

Mozarabic.
O LORD, make speed to save us; and make haste to help
us, for our efforts in good works are of no avail if Thou cease,
for Thou, from Whom all goings are directed, art He, through
Whom our frailty is strengthened. Through Thy mercy. (11.)

Mozarabic.
O GOD, make speed to save us, that we who pant with most
hearty desires to share in Thy Passion, may find Thee our
helper in our very efforts. Through Thy mercy. (11.)

Mozarabic.
O GOD, make haste to help us: lest temptation prevail
whilst Thou delayest assistance, or despair succeed, whilst
Thou keepest back aid. Set Thy succour against both, and
grant us, and all Christians, holy prudence, that we, who
put all our trust in Thy might, may ever be guarded by Thy
Divinity. Through Thy mercy. (11.)

He Who was wounded for our transgressions and rose S. Jerome.
again for our justification, Himself with His wonted mercy
bestow on us help now in our time of trouble, that, rejoicing
with His Saints, we may be able to praise and magnify Him.
Who liveth.

O GOD, Who art the author of man's salvation, make speed   D. C.
to save us from them that seek after our soul, that by Thee
their assault may cease from us, and we may evermore praise
Thee, our Helper and Protector. Through. (1.)

PSALM LXXI.

TITLE : LXX. and Vulgate : A Psalm of David, of the sons of
Jonadab, and of the first captives. Without title in the Hebrew.

ARGUMENT.

ARG. THOMAS. That CHRIST opens our lips to declare the glory
of His Name. The Voice of CHRIST to the FATHER. The Voice of
CHRIST to the FATHER against the Jews, concerning the Resurrection. The Prophet concerning the Passion and Advent of
CHRIST.

VEN. BEDE. The Prophet Jeremiah mentions that Jonadab was
a priest of GOD, who had commanded his *sons* not to drink wine,
and not to dwell in houses, but in tents, and that they found great
favour with the LORD for their obedience in these respects; and
they are now put for faithful and devout persons. Whence *Jonadab*
is interpreted *The voluntary one of the Lord*, who can say, *An
offering of a free heart will I give Thee.* With whom the *former
captives* also shed tears, that is, they who were first made captives
and then ransomed, who, made captive by sinning, but ransomed by
repenting, say, *And Thou broughtest me from the deep of the earth
again.* A representative person is introduced, who, freed from the
captivity of sins, remained firm in the Divine commands, preaching
to us the mighty love of CHRIST the LORD, which is always freely
bestowed on us, with no previous merits of our own. In the first
part of the Psalm this person intreats that he may always be delivered from human iniquities, that he may give thanks unto the
LORD. *O God, in Thee have I trusted.* In the second place, he
prays that he may not be deprived in old age of His bounties, by
Whose help he was guarded in his youth, *Cast me not away in the
time of age.* Thirdly; numbering His gifts, he promises ever to
give thanks. *Thy righteousness, O God, is very high, &c.*

SYRIAC PSALTER. Composed by David, when Saul warred against
the house of David. Also a prophecy of the Passion and Resurrection of CHRIST.

EUSEBIUS OF CÆSAREA. CHRIST'S Sufferings and Resurrection.

S. ATHANASIUS. A Psalm in solitary address.

VARIOUS USES.

Gregorian. Thursday. Matins. [Maundy Thursday. I. Nocturn.]
Monastic. Wednesday. Matins. [Maundy Thursday. I. Nocturn.]
Parisian. Friday. Lauds.
Lyons. Thursday. Compline.
Ambrosian. Monday of Second Week. III. Nocturn.
Quignon. Friday. Matins.
Eastern Church. [vv. 1—8.] Prime.

ANTIPHONS.

Gregorian. Ferial. Be Thou * my protecting GOD. [Maundy Thursday. O my GOD * deliver me out of the hand of the ungodly.]
Monastic. Ferial. Thou art my helper and redeemer * O LORD, make no long tarrying. [Maundy Thursday. As Gregorian.]
Parisian. O my GOD * deliver me out of the hand of the ungodly, for Thou art my patience.
Ambrosian. As Psalm lxix.

1 In thee, O LORD, have I put my trust, let me never be put to confusion : but rid me, and deliver me, in thy righteousness; incline thine ear unto me, and save me.

This Psalm of David belongs to the close of his life and reign, and it may be noted that it is, in great part, a cento from previous Psalms, as 22, 25, 31, 35, 38, 40, although the noble passage vv. 14—21 is new. It has been also frequently grouped with the preceding Psalm, and counted as part of it. They see in it the pilgrimage of the Church from the days of Adam to those of Antichrist, counting the seven ages of man's estate in this wise. From the Fall to the Incarnation are three periods,—infancy, childhood, and youth, typified by exile, the patriarchal dispensation, and the Law. From the first to the second Advent are four stages : early manhood, from the Ascension, through the ten persecutions to the accession of Constantine the Great; the prime of life, through the Arian troubles, till Justinian; middle age, during which the yet unended power of Mohammedanism sprang up; and that eld during which the Church still waits in dread for the coming of Antichrist; and the Psalm contains petitions apt for each of these troubles in turn. *In thee, O Lord, have I trusted.* Once I trusted in myself, and then I was confounded; now I have turned to Thee, and I shall never be confounded again. And that because, as the Apostle tells us, "Hope maketh not ashamed," following therein the saying of another wise man: "Look at the generations of old, and see; did ever any trust in the LORD, and was confounded?" Rightly so, since in trusting Him, we are not merely relying on Almighty power, but on infinite love, on purest bounty, on the merit of CHRIST's Passion. *Let me*

never be confounded. That in this world, however I may
seem to be brought low and despised, I may feel myself
strong in Thee at all times. Or, if we take the Vulgate, *confounded eternally,* it will be a prayer against condemnation
in the doom. In the mouth of CHRIST, the words are but
another way of putting what Isaiah prophesied: "I gave My Isa. l. 6.
back to the smiters, and My cheeks to them that plucked off
the hair; I hid not My face from shame and spitting; for the
LORD GOD will help Me, therefore shall I not be confounded;
therefore have I set My face like a flint, and I know that I
shall not be ashamed." The insults of the soldiers, of Herod,
of the Jews, may fall on the Man of Sorrows, but they cannot
touch the Eternal WORD, and therefore, observes S. Bruno, B.
Our LORD trusts in the immortality and impassibility of His
Godhead, derived from that FATHER in Whom He trusted.
Deliver me in Thy righteousness. When the sinner utters
this prayer, he beseeches GOD to deliver him by Him Whom
He hath made Judge of all the world, because He is the Jus- S. Augus-
tice of GOD, the King Who reigneth in righteousness, and tine.
executes judgment and justice in the earth. And our claim
on GOD's justice is based on our trust in His promise, which G.
He binds Himself to fulfil, that He may be justified in His
sayings. What we say by reason of our sin, CHRIST speaks
by reason of His innocence. His claim for deliverance is
that in Him His enemies find no fault at all, and therefore
justice demands that He should go free. *Incline Thine ear
unto me, and save me.* It is the cry, says Gerhohus, of one
lying sick and wounded, unable to rise, and asking the Physician to bend over him to listen to his account of his suffer- G.
ings, asking the good Samaritan to stoop down and save him,
by pouring oil and wine into his wounds.

2 Be thou my strong hold, whereunto I may alway
resort : thou hast promised to help me, for thou art
my house of defence, and my castle.

In the LXX. and Vulgate the first part of this verse reads
differently; *Be Thou to me for a protecting* [LXX. *shield-
bearing*] *God,* and for a *strong place to save me.* And we
may see in it the prayer of the Church under two circumstances, when she goes out to aggressive battle against error
and sin; and again, when she is compelled by pressure from
without to act chiefly on the defensive, as in days of persecution. And thus, as the Carmelite observes, because the Ay.
Martyrs were so fortified by the grace of GOD, that the darts
of the persecutors could not pierce their hearts, they are
mystically called "fenced cities," as was Jeremiah. Or, if Jer. i. 8.
we look at it from another point of view, the Church intreats
for her active and her contemplative members, of whom the
former are in the open battles; the latter within the strong-

hold of the religious life, which Hugh of S. Cher likens to a
fortress, for twelve reasons, thus summed up:

Hugo Card.

> Murus, dentales, turris, vigiles, tuba, scuta,
> Mons, aqua, saxa, cibi, machina, fossa, viri.

Thou art my house of defence, and my castle. The first title
belongs to GOD as our *Protector;* the second as our *strong
place.* And the *house of defence* will then be His help against
peril in this world ; the *castle,* or with the Vulgate, *refuge,*
C.   the eternal habitation whither no danger can come.

3 Deliver me, O my GOD, out of the hand of the
ungodly : out of the hand of the unrighteous and
cruel man.

The words are first those of CHRIST, enduring the contra-
Ay.   diction of sinners. And note, that two kinds of sinners are
set before us. *The unrighteous* (Vulg. *transgressor of the
law*) evil Jews or Christians, who know GOD's will, but
refuse to do it, and the *cruel* (or *unjust*) the heathen who sin
through comparative ignorance. And as CHRIST thus prays
for Himself against Caiaphas and Pilate, so He prays for
G.   His Church to be delivered from false brethren and from
Pagan oppressors. The Carthusian will have the *ungodly*
D. C.   to be our ghostly enemy, and yet more, the whole three
clauses to apply to the pleading sinner, who makes his
Ay.   prayer to be delivered from himself, his own ungodliness,
his own transgressions. And GOD does save, notes Ayguan,
2 S. Pet. ii. triply. From the temptation of the flesh, "The LORD know-
9.   eth how to deliver the godly out of temptation." From the
Col. i. 13.   snares of the devil, "Who hath delivered us from the power
of darkness." From the lures of the world, "Who gave
Gal. i. 4.   Himself for our sins, that He might deliver us from the present evil world."

4 For thou, O LORD GOD, art the thing that I long
for : thou art my hope, even from my youth.

My patience, is the Vulgate reading in the first clause.
Pet. Lomb. And they explain it, rather frigidly, *the cause of my patience.*
Let us look deeper, and take it with S. Ambrose. Doubtless
S. Amb. in CHRIST Himself is slain in the Martyrs, and in them who
iv. cap. 2, ad suffer death, or bonds, or stripes, for the faith, the sufferings
Corinth.   are CHRIST's, that His life may be manifest in their body.
He then Who endures in them is truly their *patience,* since
it is not their own powers that hold out. *From my youth,*
since I was generated in grace, and not merely from my
bodily childhood. And the mediæval writers, looking to the
R.   usage of their time, see here the candidate for Christian chi-
G.   valry, already following his liege lord to battle, armed with
Ay.   faith, hope, and charity, but not yet more than an esquire

who has still to win his spurs, and to be trained in the pure-
ness of chastity, the prudence of truth, the obedience of humility. And so the prophet speaks, "It is good for a man Lam. iii. 27.
that he bear the yoke in his youth."

5 Through thee have I been holden up ever since
I was born : thou art he that took me out of my
mother's womb; my praise shall be always of thee.

They see in the first clause here the mystery of predesti- Ay.
nation, and the Angelic Doctor adds, that the task of guar- S. Thomas
dian Angels is intrusted to them even before the birth of the Aquin.
children whose keepers they are to be. *My mother's womb.*
Literally, says Gerhohus, because of infant baptism, whereby G.
children of but a few days or hours old, are received in the
arms of GOD. Ayguan, pointing to the same rite, explains Ay.
the words of our Mother the Church, who bears us to GOD
in the Sacraments. And, applied to CHRIST, the words may
be taken of His Incarnation, and also bear reference to the
pious opinion of the Church that the pains of childbirth took
no hold on His Virgin-Mother.

> Gaude, sine partu tristi   Conrad v.
> Virgo partum edidisti,   Gaming.
> Immo gaudens protulisti   The Hymn
> Prolem mater filia.   *Gaude Virgo,*
> *dico gau-*
> *dens.*

Others again give long lists of Saints, who from early child- Le Blanc.
hood persevered in holiness, as fulfilling this prediction, P.
while Parez and S. Bonaventure explain it of the infancy of S. Bonaven-
the Church in Abel's days. *My praise shall be always of* tura.
Thee. It is more in the Vulgate, *My singing,* implying not B.
only praise, but rejoicing for victory. And they take it of Haimo.
Church song, as contrasted with heathen or secular ballads.

6 I am become as it were a monster unto many :
but my sure trust is in thee.

If we take the Prayer Book Version literally as it stands,
we may well think on that *graffito* scrawled by a Pagan hand,
and lately discovered, wherein a Christian is seen worshipping
a crucified figure, having a man's body, but an ass's head, a
notion once widely spread, and a serious bar to the reception
of the Faith by the Empire. But the word hardly notes so
much. It is rather, with the Vulgate and A. V., *a wonder,*
yet still referring to the offence of the Cross, to the astonish- C.
ment with which the world looked on the life and sufferings
of CHRIST and His Apostles, regarding even their miracles S. Alb. Mag.
rather as something to stare at than as proof of a new revelation. And as Isaiah, walking naked and barefoot for three
years was "a sign and wonder," so the Apostles, who left all Isa. xx. 3.
their earthly possessions, and followed CHRIST during the

three years of His earthly ministry, and all Christians who spiritually did the like in the three stages of holiness, the purgative, illuminative, and unitive ways, were made, as S. Paul says, "a spectacle unto the world, and angels, and men." But we may take the words in another sense of our LORD, Whose Incarnation, Passion, and Resurrection have made Him indeed a *wonder* and a glory to His people, as well as even to those Jews and heathens who rejected Him.

1 Cor. iv. 9.

Eusebius.

7 O let my mouth be filled with thy praise : that I may sing of thy glory and honour all the day long.

Ay.

It is the song of our country, notes the Carmelite, a song ever accompanied with joy. And that joy is threefold, the inner gladness of the heart, the vocal sound of the lips, the tokens of external actions. The words, *that I may sing of Thy glory,* (from the LXX. and Vulgate,) are not found in the Hebrew, but are none the less dwelt on by the commentators. One, with a quaint literalness of interpretation, explaining the words of the Song of the Church, takes *glory* to refer to the recitation of the Doxology, *honour,* or as the Vulgate reads, *magnitude,* to that of the Magnificat, which seems to accord with the remark of Cassiodorus that *all the day long* means the whole twenty-four hours, as otherwise Vespers and Nocturns would be shut out. Parez, more happily, takes *glory* to refer to the Resurrection : *honour* to the Ascension of CHRIST.

Hugo Card.

C.

P.

8 Cast me not away in the time of age : forsake me not when my strength faileth me.

In the time of age. They question in what sense CHRIST, Who never knew eld of body or soul, can use these words of Himself, and they explain them differently. They take it either of the physical and mental exhaustion of the Passion, like in its wasting effects to old age, or, with yet deeper meaning, of His crucifying our old man in His own Person. Again; it is the prayer of the Church, looking forward to the great apostasy of the latter days, and dreading lest her love, waxing cold, should expose her to yet more terrible losses than she sustained when so many Eastern Communions fell before the advance of Islam, or when the mighty Nestorian Church, once vaster than Greek and Latin together, and ranging from the Yellow Sea to the steppes of Eastern Russia, from Siberia to Ceylon, vanished like a dream before Gengiz-Khan and his successors. It is also the cry of each member of the Church for himself. For, just as we have seen two kinds of youth spoken of above, so there are two kinds of age, decrepitude of body and of soul. The latter exists when the spiritual heat of love waxes cold, and the soul is not renewed by increase of grace, but either grows old in negligence and sin, is bowed down by weary persecutions, or becomes less

A.

D. C.

G.

P.

D. C.

active in good works. Well may we, with S. Thomas Aquinas, recite this verse with tears of contrition and hope; well
may we, with a holy man of a later day, cry, " O fire ever
burning, and never waxing low : behold, I am chill and cold,
kindle my veins and my heart, that they may burn with love
of Thee. For Thou hast come to send fire upon the earth, *Arvisinet: Mem. Vit. Sac.*
and what wilt Thou, save that it be kindled ?" So praying,
He will hear us, and will give us, even in extreme age, strength
to say with His Martyr, S. Polycarp, " Eighty and six years *Act. Mart. S. Polycarp. ix.*
have I served Him, and He never did me wrong; how then
can I blaspheme my King and my SAVIOUR ?"

9 For mine enemies speak against me, and they
that lay wait for my soul take their counsel together,
saying : GOD hath forsaken him; persecute him, and
take him, for there is none to deliver him.

They take it first of the Passion, of that Council of the Pha- *A.*
risees gathered after the raising of Lazarus, and of the mock- *Ay.*
ings suffered by CHRIST upon the Cross, when His cry was, *S. Matt.*
" My GOD, My GOD, why hast Thou forsaken Me ?" and *xxvii. 46, 43.*
theirs was, " He trusted in GOD that He would deliver Him,
let Him deliver Him now if He will have Him." It is the
cry of the Church under the three greatest trials, the Pagan *P.*
persecutions, the Mohammedan successes, the rise of the *L.*
sects, which last in especial say, *God hath forsaken her,* " with
our tongue will we prevail; we are they that ought to speak; *Ps. xii. 4.*
who is lord over us ?"

10 Go not far from me, O GOD : my GOD, haste
thee to help me.

11 Let them be confounded and perish that are
against my soul : let them be covered with shame
and dishonour that seek to do me evil.

Again; the words are both of CHRIST and of the Church.
The LORD asks for His members rather than for Himself,
that for the elect's sake the days may be shortened. And
note, that whereas type and prophecy both foretold that the
SAVIOUR should be three days and three nights in the grave,
yet the time was too long for the infant Church to bear, and
therefore the FATHER hasted to help the SON, and raised Him
up just after the midnight of Easter Eve, Who had given up
the ghost at the ninth hour of Good Friday. Thus the *con-*
fusion will refer to the alarm caused by the signs at the Cru- *D. C.*
cifixion, the darkness, the earthquake, the rending of the
rocks, and still more to the dismay on hearing the news that
the sepulchre was void, while the *perishing* denotes the overthrow of the Jewish nation. The Church, fallen on evil days,
intreats for help also. And we may note again, as so often

before, the warnings against the persecutors, how they were
confounded and *perished*, as Nero, Julian, Valens; how they
were put to *shame and dishonour*, as Valerian, whom the
Persian Sapor made his footstool, and as Eugenius, who was
the last to raise the standard of ancient Paganism against

G. the Cross. Once more, the words are those of the penitent
sinner, to whom GOD is always near, but who feels that he

D. C. has been departing from GOD, and going afar off in his wickedness. And the prayer will then be chiefly directed against
ghostly enemies, though also against human tempters.

12 As for me, I will patiently abide alway : and
will praise thee more and more.

13 My mouth shall daily speak of thy righteousness and salvation : for I know no end thereof.

Rather, with the A. V., LXX. and Vulgate, *I will hope
continually*, and that not merely when I am afflicted by the

G. devil, with poverty, disease, or lust, but when even the hand
of GOD is heavy against me, I will say with holy Job, " Though

Job xiii. 15. He slay me, yet will I trust in Him." *And will praise Thee
more and more.* The LXX. and Vulgate here read, *And
will add above all Thy praise.* How can this be? ask they
all. They answer it diversely. Literally, it may tell us how
David was the first to set forth the praises of CHRIST's Incarnation, Resurrection, Ascension, and Kingdom, for the instruction of the people, whereas the Saints who praised GOD

Ay. in former times told far less of these mysteries. And the

D. C. Carthusian sees in it a promise to persevere in the compositions of fresh songs of praise. Or we may reflect how the
Synagogue praised GOD for temporal blessings, while the

G. Church, not forgetting such thanksgiving, lauds Him yet more
for spiritual gifts. Yet again ; S. Augustine remarks that
GOD's justice deserves all praise, even were He to condemn

A. all mankind, but seeing that He has shown us mercy, we add
that praise to the glory of His Name. When I confess
that the WORD of GOD created the heaven and the earth and

C. all that is therein, observes another, I have praised the LORD
with perfect devotion. But when I add that He became incarnate for the salvation of men, I have added to His praise.
Once more—and the lesson is a practical one—I will not

Z. merely praise Thee in speech and words, but with my works
also, because the LORD is praised in this wise too, and therefore the SAVIOUR said, " That they may see your good works,

S. Matt. v. and glorify your FATHER which is in heaven." *My mouth
16. shall daily speak of Thy righteousness and salvation.* It is

Ay. the voice of the Bride. The *righteousness and salvation* is
He of whom Paul says that " CHRIST JESUS of GOD is made

1 Cor. i. 30. unto us wisdom, and righteousness, and sanctification, and

S. Luke ii. redemption ;" of whom Simeon said, " Mine eyes have seen
30. Thy salvation." *Daily.* The LXX. and Vulgate read, *All*

the day. That is, adds Ayguan, both in the day of prosperity and the night of sorrow. Or with the Gloss, *All the day* means the day with the night, because night serves day, not day night. The night is our flesh, and the day is righteousness, and whatever is done in the flesh is of the night, while deeds of righteousness belong to the day. And there is yet another meaning, that of the everlasting praise of CHRIST in the land where is no darkness at all.

Pet. Lomb.

G.

> Dies sine vesperâ, nocte non sepultus,
> Quem non sol per aëra sed divini vultûs
> Illustrat serenitas.

The Hymn,
*Redeundo
per gyrum.*

I know no end thereof. More exactly, with the A. V., *I know not the numbers.* The word סְפֹרוֹת (closely connected as it is with סֵפֶר a *book* or *writing*) has been rendered by some copies of the LXX. and by the Vulgate similarly, *I know not letters.* And they take it first of CHRIST, concerning Whom the Jews said, "How knoweth this man letters, having never learned?" answering the question by saying that He indeed knew not the letter that killeth, but the Spirit that giveth life. And again they say that the letter means the old Law, which they compare to the staff of Elisha, sent by the hand of a servant to recover the dead child, but vainly, so that Elisha needed to come and lay himself down on the child, that is, our true Elisha ("GOD of salvation") needed to humble Himself and become as a servant, nay, as one dead, to do what Moses failed to accomplish. Or again, the Five Books of Moses are the porches of Bethesda, where men lie waiting and sick. It needed the Angel of the Covenant to come down into the water of the Jewish nation that the sick might be healed. And then they take it of the Church, or of single Christians, saying the like of that which the LORD had said. For there are three kinds of letters, those which puff up, those which make man a servant, and those which make him a son. They are the secular learning of philosophers, the Jewish law, and the New Testament, the last of which only is needful for the soul to know. The Carthusian adds that the words may be a confession of the utter ignorance of man contrasted with the infinite wisdom of GOD, or that it may be used of inspired Saints like SS. Peter and John, of whom it was said, truly in one sense, that "they were unlearned and ignorant men." S. Augustine, who probably had the reading πραγματείας instead of γραμματείας before him, gives a various translation, *negotiationes, tradings,* and dwells on the spiritual dangers which attend on all commerce; and Cassiodorus follows him, limiting his censure carefully to avarice and fraud. The various reading is said by another to apply to the Church of the last days, resisting the wiles of Antichrist, who will bring to bear all worldly learning, and even a bare literal rendering of Holy Writ, to aid his cause. And Hugh

S. John vii. 15.

Ay.

A.

S. Bonaventura.

D. C.

A. Acts iv. 13.

A.

C.

P.

II. 8

of S. Victor, taking both readings, sums up the matter by saying that whoso reads the Scripture for mere curiosity and not for edification, knows indeed its letter and its tradings, but has not the true weight granted to the man who studies it for the savour of godliness.

Hugo Vic. torin.

14 I will go forth in the strength of the LORD GOD : and will make mention of thy righteousness only.

The LXX. and Vulgate, for *go forth* read *enter in*, and more correctly, as the first sense is that of proceeding to the temple to praise GOD because of His mighty deeds. Euthymius connects the words with those of the preceding verse. *I know not letters*, that is, observes he, the Scribes lay down a rule in their writings that all Jews must enter the temple of Jerusalem thrice a year, but I will go for a better reason, the strength of the LORD. Ayguan, more deeply says, I will go from the mere letter of the Old Testament into its spiritual meaning, the power of CHRIST. I will not look, adds Gerhohus, to the mere outward rite of even the Gospel Sacraments, but will enter further into them to find there the saving might of JESUS, Who gives me faith, endurance, and power to fulfil His commands, a triple cord to draw me and bind me to Him. *And will make mention of Thy righteousness only.* Not of my own, but ascribing all that is good in me, all virtue, and all grace, to Thee ; all evil, defective, or sinful, to myself, saying with the Apostle, " By the grace of GOD, I am what I am;" and again, " If a man think himself to be something when he is nothing, he deceiveth himself." Since, as the same Apostle says, such persons " being ignorant of GOD's righteousness, and going about to establish their own righteousness, have not submitted themselves unto the righteousness of GOD." And he says *only*, because when the soul has left human weakness behind, and entered into the spiritual power of GOD, it will think no more of the flesh, but will ponder on GOD alone.

Z.

Ay.

G.

D. C.

1 Cor. xv. 10. Gal. vi. 3. Rom. x. 3.

S. Bernard. Ep. xi. ad Carthus.

15 Thou, O GOD, hast taught me from my youth up until now : therefore will I tell of thy wondrous works.

16 Forsake me not, O GOD, in mine old age, when I am gray-headed : until I have showed thy strength unto this generation, and thy power to all them that are yet for to come.

Here, as so often, the words may apply to CHRIST or to the Church. *Thou hast taught Me*, is the LORD's address to His FATHER, even according to that saying, " My doctrine is not Mine, but His that sent Me." And again, " As My

S. John vii. 16.

FATHER hath taught Me, I speak these things." *From my* S. John viii.
youth up, because the human soul of CHRIST "increased in ²⁸.
wisdom and stature, and in favour with GOD and man." It S. Luke ii.52.
is also the voice of the Church. *Thou hast taught me;* re-   Ay.
ferring all her gifts to Him as her Teacher, Who said, "Nei- S. Matt.
ther be ye called masters, for one is your Master, even xxiii. 10.
CHRIST." And that from the *youth* of the Church, from the
time when the Apostles drew their lessons from His lips
during His three years' ministry, when He opened the Scriptures to them after His Resurrection, when He sent the HOLY
GHOST on them at Pentecost. *Therefore will I tell of Thy*
wondrous works. How Thou rulest me, how Thou hast set
me in the way of salvation, how Thou makest me to live
whom Thou hast wonderfully quickened in soul. For what
greater marvel is there than to quicken those dead in soul?
A quickened body lives even when its quickener is absent,
as Lazarus did in the corporal absence of CHRIST, because
the life of the body is in the soul. But the quickened soul
cannot live thus without GOD, Who is its life. This then is
wondrous grace, which can quicken the dead, and abide with
us afterwards, that we die not. *Wondrous* too are those
works whereof the Church tells, the Incarnation of the WORD,
the Passion and Resurrection of CHRIST, and that GOD so
loved us that He gave His Only-begotten SON unto death
for us. *Forsake me not, O God, in mine old age, when I am*
gray-headed. They take it of the coming of Antichrist in the
last times, when the faith of the Church has become weak,
and from Augustine in the fifth century to Parez in the fifteenth, each accounts his own days as near the end, and finds
all the marks of decrepitude in the belief and lives of Christians, all the signs of growing strength and insolence in the
powers of evil. *Until I have showed Thy strength unto this*
generation, and Thy power unto all that are yet for to come.
The LXX. and Vulgate translate, *Until I declare Thine arm*   Ay.
to every generation that is to come, and couple the word *power*
with the next verse. *Thine arm* is the Incarnate WORD, and
the phrase *until* notes that the preaching of Him will not be
carried beyond this life, because the vision of GOD in the life
to come will thus supply all spiritual knowledge to the Saints, and
there will thus be no preaching in heaven; nor yet in hell,
because the time for conversion has gone by. *To every gene-*   R.
ration, as against the teaching of certain heretics, that the
Church was to endure for a time, as the Jewish dispensation
did, and then be supplanted by a more perfect revelation.

17 Thy righteousness, O GOD, is very high : and
great things are they that thou hast done; O GOD,
who is like unto thee?

The LXX. and Vulgate couple the first words with the
preceding, so that the clause runs [*I will declare*] *Thy power*

Ay.
R.
Cd.

B.
A.
C.

A.

L.

A.

Gen. iii. 5.

Heb 1. 3.

1 S. John
iii. 2.

and righteousness, O God, unto the highest, great things which Thou hast done. That is, I will declare the power of Thy justifying grace from its first beginnings in the soul up to its highest achievement in turning sinners into perfect Saints; or again, I will tell of Thy marvels, not only to Thy humbler creature, man, but I will call on Thy highest works, the Thrones, Dominations, and Princedoms of the heavenly host to join in the praise which is Thy due. Higher yet, observes Cassiodorus, even to that right hand of the FATHER where the Man of Sorrows is throned. Again; GOD'S *power* is shown in His setting man free, His *righteousness* in causing His SON to die for us. His *power* gives man strength to do good works, His *righteousness* justifies man. His *power* is seen in the valiant endurance of the Martyrs, His *righteousness* in the holy lives of the Confessors. *O God, who is like unto Thee?* It is the cry of Adam, after he had sinned by tasting of the fruit, whereof the serpent told him, "In the day that ye eat thereof, then your eyes shall be opened, and ye shall be as gods, knowing good and evil," and had thereby lost the likeness which he had before, as being made in the image and likeness of GOD. And none can answer it, save the Second Adam, because He is the "brightness of GOD'S glory, and the express image of His Person;" and He can change our vile body, making it like to His glorious Body, and so "we know that when He shall appear, we shall be like Him, for we shall see Him as He is."

18 O what great troubles and adversities hast thou showed me! and yet didst thou turn and refresh me : yea, and broughtest me from the deep of the earth again.

D. C.

A.
G.
R.

C.

Ay.

All the bitter sorrows of My Passion, the Agony, the Betrayal, the mocking, scourging, crucifixion, the yet sharper pangs of man's sin and thanklessness. *And refresh me.* The LXX., Vulgate, and A. V. more truly, *revive* Me, raising Me from the grave, where I lay in *the deep of the earth.* And we may take it next, with S. Augustine and all who follow him, of the wretchedness of mankind after the Fall, and the bounty of GOD in lifting it up from the depth of sin by the message of salvation, and giving it new life in CHRIST. And observe, says Cassiodorus, that there are seven ways in which GOD gives us remission of our sins. Firstly, in baptism ; secondly, by martyrdom ; thirdly, by almsgiving; fourthly, by our forgiveness to our debtors ; fifthly, by our conversion of our brethren; sixthly, by abundant charity ; seventhly, by penance. Again; it is the voice of the Church, thanking GOD for all her early sufferings and persecutions, when the blood of the Martyrs was the seed of the faithful, and the Gentiles, attracted by their valiant constancy, were turned by GOD, and brought to life, and out of the abyss of earthly sin.

We may see too a literal meaning here which seems to have escaped the commentators, that is, the public recognition of Christian worship after the edict of Constantine, when the Church emerged from the deep of the catacombs into the light **D. C.** of day. Lastly; it is the grateful acknowledgment of every elect soul which GOD has brought through great tribulation **Z.** into the kingdom of grace. And so Ezekiel says, "O My **Ezek.** people, I will open your graves, and cause you to come up out **xxxvii 12.** of your graves, and bring you into the land of Israel."

19 Thou hast brought me to great honour : and comforted me on every side.

Again it is the voice of CHRIST, speaking of His own Re- **D. C.** surrection, Ascension, and of His deliverance from all the liability to suffering which had belonged to His humanity. And this is brought out strongly by the Vulgate reading, *Thou hast multiplied Thy magnificence upon me. Mul-* **Ay.** *tiplied*, observes another, because CHRIST, Who is the *magnificence* of GOD, was multiplied, not in person, but in nature, by His Incarnation, where GOD was made Man, and thus was built up of Godhead, body, and soul. It is the voice of the Church, raised to high dignity of grace, and to the earthly honour of having kings and queens at her feet, and stored with all the gifts of the Comforter. And, lastly, it is the thanksgiving of sinners whom GOD has first scourged **G.** with fatherly chastisement, and then made kings and priests, clothing them with the garment of salvation, and comforted, as He is the GOD of Consolation, in all their trouble. For *comforted on every side*, the Vulgate reads, *Thou hast turned and comforted me. Turned*, because by CHRIST's Incarnation the sternness of the law was turned into the loving tenderness **Ay.** of the Gospel, so that He whom we called LORD in fear, we now call in love, "FATHER of mercies, and the GOD of all **2 Cor. i. 3.** comfort, who comforteth us in all our tribulation."

20 Therefore will I praise thee and thy faithfulness, O GOD, playing upon an instrument of music : unto thee will I sing upon the harp, O thou Holy One of Israel.

On an instrument of music, LXX. and Vulgate, *On the vessels of psalm,* which most of them take, as does the A. V., to be the psaltery. And S. Augustine points out that the chief difference between the psaltery and harp is that the former has the hollow sounding-board placed above the strings, and the latter has it below. And because the Spirit is from above, flesh from the earth; there seemeth to be signified by the *psaltery* the Spirit, by the *harp* the flesh. And men who are appointed to sing GOD's praises with psalmody may be aptly called *vessels of psalm;* in particular the clergy, some of whom are vessels to honour, and some to dishonour. Yet again, our bodies, within which the truth dwells, are its vessels, and the Psalms themselves are vessels holding the truth, as a pure and fragrant wine. Truth, in three ways, of life, of righteousness, and of doctrine. *O Thou Holy One of Israel.* Because all nations will become a part of the true Israel when the fulness of the Gentiles is gathered in. Note too, that this is the only Psalm of David's writing which contains this title of GOD, and as it is the very last of his songs, it looks forward in this wise to the universal kingdom of CHRIST, as the sea into which all the streams flowing from the vessels of song shall one day empty themselves. That is a poor house, says Gerhohus, where there are vessels for oil and wine, and nought to put in them, but what is the wretchedness of a house which has not even vessels fit to hold them!

21 My lips will be fain when I sing unto thee : and so will my soul whom thou hast delivered.

They all agree in seeing here the union of bodily and spiritual praise of GOD, the harmony of will and deed, of heart and life, when the body is subdued to the spirit, and obeys its rule with gladness. It is the idea which has been expressed by a poet of our own day:

> Let knowledge grow from more to more,
> But more of reverence in us dwell,
> That mind and soul, according well,
> May make one music as before,
> But vaster.

Gal. v. 17. Not here, however, where "the flesh lusteth against the Spirit, and the Spirit against the flesh," can this harmony be perfectly free from discord. We must look forward to the time of which the next verse tells us.

22 My tongue also shall talk of thy righteousness all the day long : for they are confounded and brought unto shame that seek to do me evil.

In the Land of beauty there will be no false notes to mar the sweet song of praise, because—

S. Pet. Dam. The Hymn, *Ad perennis vitæ fontem.*
Fleshly wars they know no longer, since with blemish stained is none,
For the spiritual body and the soul at last are one ;
Dwell they now in peace eternal, with all stumbling they have done.

D. C.
G.
All the day long. The unending day of eternity, during which the song of the redeemed shall ever ascend before the throne of GOD, when the ghostly enemies of our souls have been brought to everlasting shame.

Pectora plausibus atque canoribus ora parabit,
Cum sua crimina, lapsaque pristina stans memorabit,
Quo fuit amplior error, iniquior actio mentis,
Laus erit amplior, hymnus et altior, hanc abolentis.

Bern. Clun. Rhythm.

And therefore:

Glory be to the FATHER, from Whom cometh soberness; and to the SON, of Whom is righteousness; and to the HOLY GHOST, Whose is loving-kindness.

As it was in the beginning, is now, and ever shall be: world without end. Amen.

COLLECTS.

Incomprehensible Ruler of the throne on high, Who sufferest not them that trust in Thee to be condemned to everlasting confusion, fill our lips, we beseech Thee, with Thy praise, and ever inspire us with thoughts of holy things. Through. (1.)

Ludolph.

Deliver us, O our GOD, out of the hand of the ungodly, Who didst vouchsafe to bear for us the pain of the Cross, that Thou only mayest be our patience, Who for us didst endure the grave. Through Thy mercy. (11.)

Mozarabic. Passiontide.

Let our tongue, O LORD, be talking of Thy righteousness, that Thy praise may proceed from our lips all the day long, that inasmuch as the glory of Thy Passion hath been set forth by us, so we may now and ever without end praise Thee in that righteousness whereby we live through faith. Through Thy mercy. (11.)

Mozarabic. Passiontide.

We beseech Thee, O Crucified LORD, to be our house of defence and our castle, that delivering us from the hand of the enemy, Thou mayest place us in a stronghold, to receive our crown. Through Thy mercy. (11.)

Mozarabic. Passiontide.

O GOD of might, Who, though Thou wast GOD, didst willingly suffer Thyself to be seized at the time of Thy Passion, when they took their counsel against Thee, saying, "Let Him deliver Him, if He will have Him;" forsake us not in our trouble, and go not far from us, that Thou only mayest look on us and help us, Who on Thy Cross triumphest over the powers of this world. Through Thy mercy. (11.)

Mozarabic. Passiontide.

O JESU, SON of GOD, Whom the multitude of Thine enemies vainly persecuted, and drove from themselves the bounty of Thy loving-kindness while taking counsel together against Thee to seize Thee, and sought to take Thy life from Thee, a willing victim, Whom they knew not to be the author of life; Grant that we may with holy devotion in good works follow after Thee, Whom they pursued with ill will, so that wherein Thine enemies shall for ever mourn, therein we may have everlasting joy. Through Thy mercy. (11.)

Mozarabic. Passiontide.

Let our lips be firm in Thee, O LORD, with the tidings of truth, that they never be loosed in the vain speech of error, and may ever speak Thy glory and never cry aloud in the unseemly disputes of quarrelling, that our soul which Thou

Mozarabic. S. John Baptist.

hast redeemed, may, when praising the triumph of Thy Martyr and Forerunner, John Baptist, obtain Thy favour through his intercession. Through Thy mercy. (11.)

S. Jerome.

We beseech Thee, O LORD, that our human mouth being filled with Thy praise, we may ever think in our hearts of that which we offer Thee with acceptable voices. Through. (1.)

D. C.

O GOD, unspeakable mercy, go not far from us, make haste to help us, and forsake us not in our old age when we are gray-headed, quicken us, and comfort us in Thy love, and grant that we may ever worthily sing the majesty of Thy glory. Through. (1.)

PSALM LXXII.

TITLE: A Psalm for [or of] Solomon. LXX. and Vulgate: For Solomon; a Psalm of David. Chaldee Targum: By the hand of Solomon, uttered prophetically.

ARGUMENT.

ARG. THOMAS. That CHRIST, having brought the slanderer low, is to be adored by all kings of the earth. The Voice of the Church concerning CHRIST. The Voice of the Church concerning CHRIST to the FATHER.

VEN. BEDE. *Solomon* is interpreted *Peaceful*, signifying CHRIST the LORD, of Whom it is said, *Of His dominion and peace there shall be no end.* Throughout the Psalm the Prophet speaks, foretelling the Advent of CHRIST. In the first part he addresses the FATHER, asking for the SON judgment to judge the nations, which thing, however, he knew to be predestined before the world. *Give the King Thy judgments, O God.* In the second place, he declares that the children of the poor shall be saved in the judgment of the LORD, and the pride of the devil be humbled; and also explains in parables the child-bearing of the Virgin. *He shall keep the simple folk by their right.* Thirdly, he narrates the blessings which are to come when CHRIST the LORD is born of the HOLY GHOST and the Virgin Mary. *In His time shall the righteous flourish.* Fourthly, he says He is to be worshipped by all kings, because He hath redeemed mankind from the power of the devil. *All kings shall fall down before Him.* In the fifth place he declares that CHRIST, made visible to human eyes, hath been the defence of believers, and without doubt the profit of the righteous. *He shall live, and unto Him shall be given of the gold of Arabia.* Sixthly, he affirms that praise is to be given by the assent of the whole world to the everlasting LORD. *His Name shall remain under the sun.* In the seventh place, he offers, with purest devotion, a hymn to CHRIST. *Blessed be the Lord God, even the God of Israel : which only doeth wondrous things.*

SYRIAC PSALTER. Of David, when he made Solomon king, and a prophecy of the Coming of CHRIST and the calling of the Gentiles,

EUSEBIUS OF CÆSAREA. A prophecy of the kingdom of CHRIST and the calling of the Gentiles.

S. ATHANASIUS. A psalm of prophecy. Hortatory to endurance.

VARIOUS USES.

Gregorian. Ferial. Thursday. Matins. [Christmas-day. II. Nocturn. Epiphany. II. Nocturn. Maundy Thursday. II. Nocturn. Trinity Sunday. II. Nocturn.]

Monastic. Ferial. Wednesday. Matins. [Christmas-day. I. Nocturn. Epiphany. I. Nocturn. Maundy Thursday. II. Nocturn. Trinity Sunday. II. Nocturn.]

Parisian. Tuesday. Matins.

Lyons. Thursday. Terce.

Ambrosian. Tuesday of Second Week. I. Nocturn.

Quignon. Tuesday. Sext.

ANTIPHONS.

Gregorian. Ferial. As preceding Psalm. [Christmas-Day. In the days of the LORD shall arise abundance of peace,* and He shall have dominion. Epiphany. The kings of Tharsis and of the isles shall give presents. Maundy Thursday. The LORD hath delivered the poor from the mighty, and the needy also, and him that hath no helper. Trinity Sunday. Deliver us, save us, quicken us, O Blessed Trinity.]

Monastic. Ferial. Truly GOD is loving unto Israel. [Christmas, Epiphany, and Maundy Thursday, as Gregorian. Trinity Sunday. Therefore the FATHER, the WORD, and the Comforter is one Substance, O Blessed Trinity.]

Parisian. I have not set before Mine eyes an unjust king.* Whoso privily slandereth his neighbour, him will I destroy.

Ambrosian. Spare, O LORD, the simple and needy.

Mozarabic. The mountains also shall bring peace : and the little hills righteousness unto the people.

This Psalm, one of the most conspicuously Messianic canticles of Scripture, is of disputed authorship. The majority of ancient commentators ascribe it to David, and often attribute it to the occasion of Solomon's coronation. The greater number of later critics assign it to Solomon himself. But it is agreed on both sides that the Psalm contains many prophecies which never found their fulfilment in Solomon, and that it must refer to another and greater than he, that Prince of Peace, of Whom the wise king was but a type.

1 Give the king thy judgments, O GOD : and thy righteousness unto the king's son.

The Psalmist, observes S. Augustine, does but foreshow that saying of the LORD in the Gospel, " The FATHER judgeth no man, but hath committed all judgment unto the SON." And note that CHRIST is styled both *King*, and *King's Son.* He is King, in that He is Very GOD from all eternity ; He is the King's SON, in that His Godhead is derived from the FATHER, Whose Only-begotten He is. And He is the *King's Son* in another sense, in that by His Manhood He is of the house and lineage of David. The two members of

A.

S. John v. 22.

Z.

L.

D. C.

s 3

A.
Ay.
G.

the verse are, according to some commentators, only the same idea, restated for the sake of emphasis and variety, as in Ps. ii. 4, and Ps. xix. 1. Rather let us say, with Gerhohus, that it is a prayer to Him Who sometimes suffers unrighteous men to bear rule, and Who permits a Pilate to condemn the innocent, that He will make His Son judge in equity, and with righteous judgment. That He should do so was typified by the names of those who set the crown on Solomon's head—Zadok, the "righteous," and Nathan, "the giver,"—telling us of that righteousness which is not of the works of the Law, but of faith, given freely through grace from above.

2 Then shall he judge thy people according unto right ; and defend the poor.

G.

The Bible Version is here more in accord with the LXX. and Vulgate, and it runs, *He shall judge Thy people with righteousness, and Thy poor with judgment. Thy people*, he says, *Thy poor*, as he has already said *Thy judgment* and *Thy righteousness*, that he may dwell on the perfect harmony of will, the co-equal majesty of the Son with the FATHER, even

S. John xvii. 10.

as He Himself hath said, "All Mine are Thine, and Thine are Mine." They have been His from all eternity as GOD ; they are to be given to Him anew as Man. And whereas the Psalmist expresses CHRIST'S jurisdiction in two ways, so there is a double judgment, that of separation, whereby He parts the lowly from the proud ; His people from aliens, even in this world ; and that of doom, finally determining the lot of each according to his works. *Thy poor.* That is, the poor in spirit, who are blessed ; for theirs is the kingdom of heaven. The world and the devil have their poor too—the miser, the arrogant, the thief, the covetous, poor against his will. *Thy poor.* And we may take it of all Christians, but especially of the Apostles, who left all to follow CHRIST, and who shall sit on thrones, judging the twelve tribes of Israel. Thus *Thy people* and *Thy poor* will in truth mean the same Church Militant, but distinguished into the general body of the faithful *people*, and those voluntary *poor* who follow counsels of perfection. Wisely they, knowing how Holy Scripture again and again dwells on their blessedness, and on the danger of riches. Wherefore S. Peter Chrysologus says very well : "In heaven the first harvest is that of the hungry, the first payments in heaven are to the poor, the dole of the needy is the first entry in the daily books of GOD." Yet another interpretation explains the *people* of the Jewish, the *poor* of the Gentile Church.

Ay.

D.C.
S. Matt. v. 3.

Hugo Card.

P.

A.

Ric. Hampol.

L.

S. Pet. Chrysol. Serm. 14.

Z.

3 The mountains also shall bring peace : and the little hills righteousness unto the people.

C.

By the *mountains*, observes Cassiodorus, are denoted the

Apostles and Prophets, who preach the gospel of *peace*, that is, of CHRIST, the Prince of Peace, to the nations ; and the *hills* denote the lesser saints, who have not attained the same heights of Divine grace, but who yet declare *righteousness*, by announcing the precepts of the LORD to the earth. Others interpret the *mountains* of the Angels, who brought, at the Nativity, the tidings of *peace* on earth, to men of good will ; and explain the *hills* of earthly teachers. Or, with Theodoret, we may take the *mountains* to denote the religious who withdrew from the world to such shelters. Yet, again, the *mountains* denote the authorities of the Church, to whom is committed the ministry of reconciliation, to establish *peace* between GOD and man ; while the *hills* are the flock, who are bound to show righteousness by holy obedience to the Divine commands. And thus it will be the especial duty of the rulers, who have charge of *peace*, to prevent all schisms in the Church, that it may be One; and that of the hearers to be zealous in good works of righteousness, that it may be Holy. And these two things cannot be parted in CHRIST'S kingdom, for it is written, " Righteousness and peace have kissed each other."

Ay.

S. Luke ii. 14.

Cd.

A.

R.

C.

Ps. lxxxv. 10.

4 He shall keep the simple folk by their right : defend the children of the poor, and punish the wrong-doer.

Rather, with A. V., LXX., and Vulgate, *He shall judge the poor of the people.* The greater number of the commentators take this as little more than a restatement of the second verse, and they explain the words *the poor of the people* as denoting all truly humble Christians. And they carry on this interpretation to the next clause. For, observes S. Augustine, the *poor* and the *children of the poor* mean the same persons, just as the same city is called Sion, and the daughter of Sion. Gerhohus, more happily, applies the varying language to the altered state of the Church. GOD, he says, protects and defends His people now, as He did in the days of the Apostles, His true *poor.* We, their spiritual *children*, are inferior to them in all saintliness ; but He does not therefore cast us out. JESUS took His chosen, perfect disciples unto a high mountain apart, and there disclosed to them the deepest mysteries of grace; but He did not the less descend into the plain, to give there His instruction to the people. Euthymius, on the other hand, explains the *poor of the people* to be those Jews who, clinging to the letter of the Law, rejected the rich Gospel message, and were judged accordingly. But the *children* of those poor, whom GOD *defends* (or, as the Vulgate, *will save*,) are such as have sought the Christian fold, and gained therein wealth, which their fathers, poor in faith and piety, and in the knowledge of GOD, never enjoyed. *And punish the wrong-doer.* The LXX. and Vulgate read,

A.

G.

Z.

A.

C.

And humble the slanderer. They agree, for the most part, in explaining it of the devil, whom CHRIST humbled once when He made him fall as lightning from heaven; yet again, when He overcame him in the Temptation; most gloriously when, by His Resurrection, He bore from him the keys of death and hell. He will humble him again in the Judg-

G.

ment, by acquitting the saints from his accusations, and casting him down for ever. But the words have a further ap-

D. C.

plication, which comes out more fully in the A. V., *And shall break in pieces the oppressor.* Every tyrant, every perse-cutor of the righteous, every tempter of the Church, shall partake of the punishment of Antichrist, according to that

Isa. xi. 4.

saying, "He shall smite the earth with the rod of His mouth, and with the breath of His lips shall He slay the wicked."

5 They shall fear thee as long as the sun and moon endureth : from one generation to another.

It cannot be spoken of Solomon, remarks R. Kimchi, but must refer to the Messiah. How it refers to Him we may see in divers ways. The version before us, which is also that of S. Jerome and of the A. V., tells us of CHRIST as wor-shipped in the Church on earth, where "the fear of the LORD is the beginning of wisdom." But it looks also forward to the manner in which He shall be served in heaven, when

Rev. xxi. 23.
1 S. John iv. 18.

sun and moon have passed away, because "there is no fear in love," and His saints will then know the "perfect love which casteth out fear." S. Peter Damiani sings :

S. Pet. Dam.
The Hymn,
Ad perennis vitæ fontem.

There nor waxing moon, nor waning;
   Sun, nor stars in courses bright;
For the Lamb to that glad City
   Is the everlasting light:
There the daylight shines for ever,
   And unknown are time and night.

Ay.

The LXX. and Vulgate, however, read somewhat differ-ently: *And He shall abide with the sun, and before the moon.* Where note, observes the Carmelite, that in CHRIST there is a twofold nature, Divine and human. He is simply eternal in that He is GOD; He is relatively eternal as Man. More-over, the sun denotes all time, the moon all temporal things. And accordingly the sense is, *He shall abide with the sun :* that is, He shall abide, according to His Manhood, so long as He will; to wit, in the Church by the Sacrament of His

S. Matt.
xxviii. 20.

Body, as it is written, "I am with you alway, even unto the end of the world." This He says to confute those who allege that the Church or the Christian religion will ever cease to be. As respects His Godhead, it says *before the moon.* By the moon, which never abides in the same phase, we understand all creation, which is changeful. If then CHRIST *abide before the moon,* it follows that He abides before all

creation, and thus is eternal, "JESUS CHRIST, the same yes- Heb. xiii. 8.
terday, to-day, and for ever." Again, by the sun we may understand GOD the FATHER, because He, as the Sun, hath
glory coeval with Himself; and so too has the SON, Who is
the "brightness of His glory, and the express image of His Heb. i. 3.
Person," and therefore *abides with the sun*, because He is
coeternal with the FATHER as touching His Godhead. He
also abides *before the moon*, by which we understand the
Church, which shall pass through phases from mortal generations to the immortal one. And as He stands in sight of
His Church, guarding it, so He abides *before the moon*. Once G.
more, the words imply that the Church, tried by the prosperity of day and the adversity of night, will never be deserted by her LORD, Whose glory is her sun, Whose mild
and pure life on earth is her moon. In that our Solomon dwelt
among us in mortal and passible flesh, amidst many sorrows,
He hath shown us the ways of patience, that we should "not be Ps. xci. 5, 6.
afraid for any terror by night, nor for the thing that walketh
in darkness." And His Transfiguration on the Mount, when
His Face shone as the sun, or rather His glory on the exalted throne of the FATHER'S Majesty, makes this world's
show and pomp mean in our eyes in the day of prosperity,
that we be not hurt by "the arrow that flieth by day, nor Ps. xci. 5, 6.
for the sickness that destroyeth in the noon-day," so long as
the bright and gladsome vision of faith and hope is present
to our sight.

6 He shall come down like the rain into a fleece
of wool : even as the drops that water the earth.

The earliest commentators, as Tertullian and Lactantius, Tertull. c.
explain these words of the silence and secrecy of the Advent. Marcion. 9.
It is spoken, observes S. Augustine, of CHRIST'S First Lactant. de
Coming. For as Gideon laid a fleece on the ground, which Verâ Sap.
alone received the dew, whilst the ground remained dry, so 16.
Israel was that fleece, alone bedewed in the midst of a parched A.
world; as He said, "I am not sent, but unto the lost sheep S. Matt. xv.
of the house of Israel;" and again, speaking to His dis- 24.
ciples, "Go not into the way of the Gentiles, and into any
city of the Samaritans enter ye not: but go rather to the S. Matt. x. 5.
lost sheep of the house of Israel." And as the sign was reversed, when the ground was wet and the fleece dry, so
here is added, *even as the drops that water the earth*, because
the Jewish people remains dry of the grace of CHRIST, and
the whole round world throughout all nations is being rained
on by clouds full of Christian grace. So too Ruffinus, more
tersely: "CHRIST is the *rain*, Judea the *fleece*, the multi- Ruffin.
tude of the nations the *earth*." With him agree some others
also. But the majority of commentators explain the words
of the mystery of CHRIST'S Incarnation. "What is so silent
and noiseless," asks S. Ambrose, "as rain pouring on a fleece

S. Ambros. Hom. 13 in Nativ. Dom. of wool? It strikes no ears with sound, it sprinkles nobody with spray; but, unnoticed by man, it draws into its whole substance all the rain which is diffused through its many parts. It knows not any severance, because of the firm passage, permitting, as it does, many passages through its softness; and that which seemed closed by reason of its density is open because of its tenuity. Rightly, I say, is Mary compared to a fleece, who conceived the LORD in such wise as to drink Him in with all her body, and yet suffer no rending of that body; but showed herself soft in obedience, firm in holiness. Rightly, I say, is Mary compared to a fleece, since from her fruit the garments of salvation are woven for the peoples. Mary is truly a fleece, since from her soft bosom the Lamb came forth, Who Himself wearing His Mother's wool, that is, the flesh, covers the wounds of all nations with soft fleece. For the wound of every sin is bandaged with CHRIST'S wool, is fomented with CHRIST'S Blood; and, that **Serm. sup. Missus. 2.** it may recover health, is covered with CHRIST'S raiment." And S. Bernard speaks in similar language of this mystery. He came therein, observes Ayguan, not in His mighty **Ay.** power, but in the gentleness of deep humility, as was fore**Zech. ix. 9.** told: "Behold, thy King cometh unto thee, lowly." Noting which, the Psalmist says, *He shall come down like the rain into a fleece*—that is, gently and imperceptibly He will come down into the Virgin, because He shall come with all low**Pet. Lomb. in loc.** liness and meekness. And the simile is apt, as the Gloss notes; for as wool is not hurt by receiving or yielding water, **L.** so in the glorious Virgin Mary virginity abode inviolate before, during, and after her childbearing. So too S. Peter **S. Pet. Chrysol. Serm. 143.** Chrysologus: The fleece, though it is of the body, yet knows not the body's passions; and so, when there is virginity in the flesh, it knows not the sins of the flesh. Wherefore that heavenly rain came with gentle descent into the virgin fleece, and the whole tide of Godhead hid itself in the thirsty fleece of our flesh, till, wrung out upon the Cross, it poured forth in the rain of salvation over all the lands. And thus the Western Church, in the Antiphons for Lauds of the Circumcision and First Vespers of the Purification includes this, which Sarum carries through the year as a Me**Brev. Rom. et Sarisbur.** morial: "When Thou wast born of a Virgin ineffably, then were the Scriptures fulfilled; as the dew upon the fleece didst Thou descend to save mankind, we praise Thee, O our GOD." So, too, in many a hymn, as thus:

Adam. Victorin. The Hymn, *Splendor Patris*.

Frondem, florem, nucem sicca
Virga profert, et pudica
   Virgo Dei Filium.
Fert cœlestem vellus rorem,
Creatura Creatorem,
   Creaturæ pretium.

Ric. Hamp. And as the rain on the fleece stains not, but purifies, violates not, but beautifies, so CHRIST, born of the Virgin, left her brighter, fairer, more perfect than before. There is, however, another interpretation of the word גז, here, and in all the old versions, translated *fleece*. It literally means, "that which is shorn or clipped;" and the A. V., with most later critics, explains it, *mown grass*. It is then, remarks Cardinal de Vio, spoken of the Second Advent, when CHRIST comes after the hope and bud of this life has been cut down by the scythe of death, that He may cause it to spring up again in the aftermath of the Resurrection. And whereas most other commentators follow S. Augustine in explaining the *drops that water the earth* of the spread of the Gospel amongst the nations, Cajetan takes this also of the renewal of the earth after the Judgment. Parez is another exception. He explains the ground wetted when the fleece was dry, of the Church, empurpled with the Blood drained from CHRIST'S Body on the Cross. Cajetanus, in loc. P.

7 In his time shall the righteous flourish : yea, and abundance of peace, so long as the moon endureth.

The LXX. and Vulgate read as the first clause, *In His days shall righteousness arise*. It is, says Ayguan, a prophecy of that first true preaching of perfect righteousness, when He spoke the Sermon on the Mount to His disciples. It is more, according to Gerhohus—even the righteousness which is of faith, whereby the righteous lives, and is reconciled to GOD. *And abundance of peace*. Not of temporal peace, for He hath not come to send it on earth, but a sword. It is the peace of GOD which passeth all understanding, peace between GOD and man, between spirit and flesh, between the Church Triumphant of Angels and the spirits of just men made perfect in the LORD, and the Church Militant in its sojourn amongst mortals. And of this peace the Easter hymn sings: Ay. G.

> Triumphat ille splendide,
> Qui dignus amplitudine
> Soli polique patriam
> Unam facit rempublicam.

S. Fulbert. The Hymn, *Chorus novæ Hierusalem.*

"Rightly is it called *abundance of peace*," exclaims Gilbert of Hoyland, "which is given without measure. How should it not be abundant which did away the offence, and heaped up the former grace? The first man in Paradise had peace, so that he could not be led away against his will; but he had no strength to will his return. He had grace that he need not go out; he had it not to come back at a wish. But now is peace more plenteous in the grace of CHRIST, which is freely offered after repeated transgressions, and rejects not, but recalls the penitents. Well is it named *abundance* Serm. in Cantic. 16.

Cd.

of peace, which no wrong-doing can exhaust, which is ever more ready for pardon than for vengeance." And therefore the first greeting He gave His disciples as He returned in triumph and glory from death was, " Peace be unto you ;" denoting that, after He had laid the enemies of mankind low, had overcome death and harrowed hell, peace was the wage of His toils, the fruit of His Passion, the trophy of His Cross, the common gain of all. So an unknown poet sings :

Aelredi Opp.

> Virgam pacis CHRISTUS portat,
> Qui nos regit et confortat
>   Manu sapientiæ ;
> Qui per virgam creat pacem,
> Frangens virgam contumacem
>   Per virgam justitiæ.

> Pax concordat malos bonis,
> Per quam regnum Salomonis
>   Eleganter floruit ;
> De caminis Babylonis
> Tres Hebræos cum coronis
>   Liberos eripuit.

So long as the moon endureth. More exactly, as in the margin of A. V., *till there be no moon,* with which agree the LXX. and Vulgate, *till the moon be taken away.* The *moon* is interpreted of the Church, which has no light save from the Sun of Righteousness, and is subject to incessant change and vicissitude here below. When the earthly Church shall

Didymus.

vanish in the full light of the reappearing Sun, then GOD shall be all in all. The Roman Psalter, S. Ambrose, Cassio-

A.

dorus, and others read, *till the moon be lifted up.* That is, observes S. Augustine, till the Church be exalted, through the glory of the Resurrection, to reign with Him, the First-

G.

born from the dead, Who went before her in this glory, to sit at the right hand of the FATHER. Then she who is now

Cant. vi. 10.

"fair as the moon" shall be "clear as the sun." S. Chry-sostom, somewhat differently, explains it to mean till the

Hom. in loc.

preaching of the Church be ended ; the Church which is crescent in the good, waning in the bad, but which at last shall be full in the saints, when the number of the predestined is filled up. There remains one very singular interpretation :

C.

the *moon,* as ruling the night, is explained by Procopius of

L.

Satan, the prince of the darkness of this world, whose light is cold and deceptive. And he notes that CHRIST suffered on the fourteenth day of the moon, when her brightness begins to wane, and is near to disappearing.

8 His dominion shall be also from the one sea to the other : and from the flood unto the world's end.

The literal sense is from the Red Sea to the Mediterranean, from the Euphrates to the Desert, denoting the wide scope of Solomon's rule. It is next taken by all the commentators to denote the spread of CHRIST's kingdom on earth. Then they come to the mystical sense. And first, *from one sea to the other* is explained of CHRIST's coming forth from the hallowed womb of the Virgin Mary, who is the sea of glass, like unto crystal for purity and clearness, before the throne of GOD, a sea into which all the rivers of grace empty themselves. Thence He comes to all penitent hearts, which are seas of bitter tears. And so Lope de Vega :

Ay.

> Ya, JESUS, mi corazon
> No sabe mas de llorar,
> Que le ha convertido en mar
> El mar de vuestra pasion.

Soliloquio vi.

This gives us another and finer idea for the first sea than that of Ayguan, while agreeing with him as to the second. Yet a third grouping may be found, by explaining the words of our LORD's double sovereignty over earth and heaven; from the troublesome waves of this world, whereon His disciples are tossed in the ship of the Church, to that haven where

> in the ocean of Thy love
> We lose ourselves in heaven above.

Keble, Christian Year.

And from the flood unto the world's end. They take the *flood* to be the River Jordan, where CHRIST's ministry and preaching of the Gospel began, thence to spread over the whole earth. And it further denotes CHRIST's especial rule over the baptized, whose spiritual life begins with the cleansing flood, and perseveres to the end of the world, because He is with them always till then.

A.

9 They that dwell in the wilderness shall kneel before him : his enemies shall lick the dust.

The LXX., Vulgate, and Æthiopic Psalters read, *The Ethiopians shall fall down before Him.* The *Ethiopians,* says one, as clothed in coarse leathern garments, denote sinners laden with iniquity. Or, as another suggests, those who are dark and black with sin. Others take it with equal literalness of the Queen of Sheba coming to Solomon, and of the conversion of Queen Candace at the preaching of her eunuch, followed by that of the king and a great part of the nation through the labours of S. Matthew. There is yet another explanation: the *Ethiopians* are said to be the devils, made subject to CHRIST by His victory on the Cross. *His enemies shall lick the dust.* S. Clement of Alexandria aptly cites here the curse pronounced upon the serpent which deceived Eve, and warns his readers against imitating the crafty being who, as he grovels, seeks to bruise the heel of the just. Not dissimilar is the explanation that the words

C.
S. Cyril.
Alex.
Ay.
Z.
Clem. Alex.
Gen. iii. 14.

G.

A.

Ay.

Isa. lx. 14.

Hugo Card.

Lyranus.

Z.

denote the low and earthly desires and aims of the ungodly. S. Augustine will have it to refer to heretics, loving mere human teachers, who are but dust, and not willing to hear the divine wisdom of the Church. It may, however, remarks Ayguan, be taken in a good sense also, that they who at first resisted CHRIST, shall at last become His true servants; as it is written, "The sons also of them that afflicted Thee shall come bending before Thee, and all they that despised Thee shall bow themselves down at the soles of Thy feet." Yet again, several take it of the Jews, literally because of the extremity of the famine in the siege under Titus, when they were forced to devour all manner of filth; and allegorically by reason of their mere earthly wisdom. Euthymius, with a quaint exactness, interprets it of converts kissing the floors of churches, after the Eastern fashion.

10 The kings of Tharsis and of the isles shall give presents : the kings of Arabia and Saba shall bring gifts.

A.

The words denote the universality of CHRIST's Kingdom. And the first fulfilment of the prophecy must be sought in the adoration of the Magi, whose triple offering of gold, frankincense, and myrrh denotes the Godhead, Kingship, and Manhood of CHRIST. So Adam of S. Victor :

The Sequence *Virgo, Mater Salvatoris.*

> Tria dona reges ferunt :
> Stella duce regem quærunt,
> Per quam semper certi erunt
>   De superno lumine,
> Auro regem venerantes,
> Thure Deum designantes,
> Myrrhâ mortem memorantes,
>   Sacro docti flamine.

And as *Arabia and Saba* denote the far Eastern regions, so *Tarshish and the isles* point to the West, if we identify Tarshish with the Spanish Tartessus, as the isles most probably refer to the Archipelago. What rich treasures Spain and Saba (if Saba be Africa) shall bring to the feet of their King let Prudentius tell us :

Peristeph. iv. 13.

> Orbe de magno caput excitata,
> Obviam CHRISTO properanter ibit
> Civitas quæque, pretiosa portans
>   Dona canistris.
> Afra Carthago tua promet ossa,
> Ore facundo Cypriane doctor :
> Corduba Acisclum dabit et Zoellum
>   Tresque coronas.
> Tu tribus gemmis diadema pulchrum
> Offeres CHRISTO, genetrix piorum
> Tarraco, intexit cui Fructuosus
>   Sutile vinclum.

And with this presentation of sacred relics agrees that remark of S. Augustine, that the kings are said to *lead gifts*,
that is, to bring living victims, following them readily, to be
offered to CHRIST. Cassiodorus, followed by many others,
finds a mystical sense in the word *Tharsis*, which he interprets *contemplation*,[1] and its *kings* will then be contemplative Saints; while the *kings of the isles* are those engaged
in active life, surrounded by the sea of worldly cares, but
rising above it firmly. He carries on the allegory to *Arabia*
and *Saba*, which, as the lands of spices and perfumes, denote
the temptations of the flesh; and their *kings* are the Saints
who subdue them. **A.** **C.**

11 All kings shall fall down before him : all nations shall do him service.

We see not yet this prophecy fulfilled on earth, but in the
Apocalyptic vision it has come to pass already in heaven.
Kings shall fall down before Him, for it is written, "The four
and twenty elders fall down before Him that sat on the
throne, and worship Him that liveth for ever and ever, and
cast their crowns before the throne." *All nations do Him
service;* for again it is written, "I beheld, and lo, a great
multitude, which no man could number, of all nations, and
kindreds, and people, and tongues, stood before the throne,
and before the Lamb, clothed with white robes, and palms
in their hands; and cried with a loud voice, saying, Salvation to our GOD which sitteth upon the throne, and unto the
Lamb." But the LXX. and Vulgate read, *All kings of the
earth.* And we may take it literally of the subjection of the
Roman Empire to the Faith by the conversion of Constantine, or of the royalty of Christians drawn into the Catholic
Church from all nations, and now made kings by ruling over
their passions and desires, and serving CHRIST with body,
mind, and will. Rev. iv. 10. Rev. vii. 9. **Ay.** Ric. Ham-pol.

12 For he shall deliver the poor when he crieth :
the needy also, and him that hath no helper.
13 He shall be favourable to the simple and
needy : and shall preserve the souls of the poor.

The LXX. and Vulgate read, *He shall deliver the poor
from the mighty one.* Thus it tells of Him that spoiled the
strong man armed who kept the souls of men as his goods in
the palace of this world. *And him that hath no helper.* For
neither angel nor righteous man, neither law nor free-will,
could help mankind, but only the Lion of the tribe of Judah.
No helper. For man, like him who went down from Jeru- **G.** Pet. Lomb. **G.**

[1] This is S. Jerome's notion. | seems to be "stony ground,"
But the true meaning of קשׁשׁ | from קשׁ "to be hard."

salem to Jericho, and fell among thieves, hath fallen from
Paradise into the power of Satan, who hath stripped and
wounded him, leaving him half dead. Neither Priest nor
Levite, no help from the old Law, availed him, till the Great
Physician came that way, poured oil and wine into his
wounds, and placed him in the Church to recover. And because CHRIST is a skilful Physician, it is said that *He is favourable* (*He spares*, Vulg.) the simple and needy, but He
does not spare their sins. He makes war on the disease, He
Ay. cuts away the proud flesh, but He *preserves the souls of the
poor* from their triple danger—slavery to the devil, pollution
by sin, liability to punishment. And therefore, as the Master
Pet. Lomb. of the Sentences points out, CHRIST'S mercy and justice appear in His double gift of grace, in that *He spares* first, in-
S. Albertus stead of avenging Himself; then *preserves the souls of His
Magnus.** *poor*, blotting out past sins, bestowing grace to guard against
relapses, remitting the penalty due.

14 He shall deliver their souls from falsehood
and wrong : and dear shall their blood be in his
sight.

From falsehood, because He saves them from him who is
the " father of lies," and from the worship of false gods,"
Acts xiv. 15. turning them " from these vanities unto the living GOD."
From wrong, because He hath " broken the rod of the op-
Isa. ix. 4. pressor." But the LXX. and Vulgate read, *He shall redeem their souls from usury[1] and from iniquity.* What are
A. these usuries but sins, which are also called debts? They
seem to be called *usury*, because the punishments are more
grievous than the sins. For instance : a homicide slays only
the body of a man, but can in no wise hurt his soul; while
G. his own soul and body perish together in hell. Again, eternal punishment is called *usury*, because it so far surpasses
any pleasure or advantage which sin can give us here, just as
heavy compound interest soon exceeds the principal of a
A. debt. *From iniquity* is added because GOD is not content
with remitting punishment, but desires that sinners should
turn from their wickedness and live, He bestows grace upon
them, whereby justified, they may become holy, and not
merely escape hell, but be fitted for heaven. But S. Chrysostom reminds us that, while GOD exacts no usury for our
sins, He will, according to the parable of the ten pounds, demand usury for the divine gifts He has bestowed on us. *And
dear shall their blood be in His sight.* It is spoken of His
martyrs, whom He delivered from the *falsehood* of heathenism, from the violent *wrong* of persecution; and of whom it
is said in another Psalm, " Right dear in the sight of the

---

[1] Apparently because the | rived from הרמ, which, however,
LXX. supposed τόκος to be de- | means "fraud."

LORD is the death of His Saints." Wherefore the Paris Ps. cxvi. 13.
Breviary:

> Quem lictor insanus sitit,   Santol. Vic-
> Quem cæcus effundit furor,   torin. The
> Amor sacerdos prodigum   Hymn,
> Christo cruorem consecrat.   Fortes ca-
>   dendo Mar-
>   tyres.
> Et ille, mixtus sanguini
> Quem fudit in ligno Deus,
> Fundentibus placabilem
> Orare non cessat Deum.

The LXX. and Vulgate, however, for *blood* read *name*. So A.
then *their name is honourable in His sight*, for it is His own.
They have left behind them the Pagan names they once bore, D. C.
derived from Gentile superstition, or from their own defects
and misdeeds; and now they are called Christians, the sons
of the Eternal FATHER. And therefore GOD foretold His
will to the unbelieving Jews, " Ye shall leave your name for Isa. lxv. 15.
a curse unto My chosen; for the LORD GOD shall slay thee,
and call His servants by another name, that he who blesseth
himself in the earth shall bless himself in the GOD of Truth."
There is another reading: *His Name shall be honourable in* Z.
their sight. How honourable, how precious, let the hymn
tell us:

> Nomen dulce, nomen gratum, nomen ineffabile,   The Hymn,
> Dulcis JESUS appellatum, nomen delectabile,   Gloriosi Sal-
> Laxat pœnas et reatum, nomen est amabile.   vatoris.
>
> Hoc est nomen adorandum, nomen summæ gloriæ,
> Nomen semper meditandum in valle miseriæ,
> Nomen digne venerandum supernorum curiæ.

15 He shall live, and unto him shall be given of
the gold of Arabia : prayer shall be made ever unto
him, and daily shall he be praised.

He shall live. And first let us take it of Him of Whom Prov. i. 11.
they said, " Let us lay wait for blood, let us lurk privily for
the innocent without cause ;" and again, " Let us condemn Wisd. ii. 20.
Him with a shameful death." To Him alone can those words L.
of Eastern reverence be addressed with truth, " O King, live
for ever !" for He only can say, " I am He that liveth, and Dan. ii. 4.
was dead; and, behold, I am alive for evermore, Amen; and Rev. i. 18.
have the keys of hell and of death." And next, it is spoken Pseudo-
of Him as He lives in His Saints, according to that saying Hieron.
of the Apostle, " I am crucified with CHRIST ; nevertheless I
live, yet not I, but CHRIST liveth in me." And with this Gal. ii. 20.
nearly agrees that other interpretation, that He shall live in Ric. Ham-
the hearts of His poor. *And unto Him shall be given of the* pol.
gold of Arabia. Literally we may take it, with Cassiodorus, C.
of the gifts brought by the Eastern wise men ; mystically

A.

with S. Augustine, and most of those who follow him, of the intellectual wisdom of the Gentiles laid at the feet of CHRIST, as when Justin and Cyprian, Gregory Thaumaturgus, and Augustine himself devoted their powers to His service.

Z.

Euthymius explains it of the Arab converts whom he supposes S. Paul to have made during his three years' sojourn in their country. *Prayer shall be made ever unto Him.* This, though true in fact, is not the meaning of the passage. The A. V. reads, *Prayer also shall be made for him continually.* The LXX. and Vulgate are nearly the same, *concerning Him;* the Ambrosian Psalter, as A. V., *for Him.* It is said, observes Euthymius, of the Prophets, who desired to see His day. It is said of Christians, remarks S. Augustine, who utter daily the petition, "Thy kingdom come." They who are *of Him,* (*de ipso,* Vulg.,) notes the Carmelite, even members of His Body, ever make their prayer to Him. They pray (*de ipso*) in His own words, says another, when they recite the Our FATHER. They shall pray (*de ipso*) in His strength, having none of their own. If it be further asked how we can be said to pray *for* CHRIST, we may answer with S. Augustine and S. Remigius, that we pray for His Body the Church, that it may be filled up with His elect; or, with a later commentator, that we may fitly, when desiring the spread of His kingdom, cry with the children in the temple, "Hosanna to the Son of David." *And daily shall He be praised.* The LXX. and Vulgate read, *All the day.* Either way it denotes the perpetual worship paid to Him in earth and heaven, all the day of our toil here, before "the night cometh when no man can work;" all the endless day of heaven, which hath no night. *All the day.* So a poet of our own:

Gal. 1. 17.

Z.
A.
Ay.
G.
Ric. Hampol.
Lu.
A.
R.
De Muis.
S. Matt. xxi. 15.

> The night becomes as day
> When from the heart we say,
>   May JESUS CHRIST be praised.
>
> In heaven's eternal bliss
> The loveliest strain is this,
>   May JESUS CHRIST be praised.
>
> To GOD the WORD on high
> The hosts of Angels cry,
>   May JESUS CHRIST be praised.
>
> Be this while life is mine
> My canticle divine,
>   May JESUS CHRIST be praised.
>
> Be this the eternal song
> Through all the ages on,
>   May JESUS CHRIST be praised.

16 There shall be an heap of corn in the earth, high upon the hills : his fruit shall shake like Li-

banus, and shall be green in the city like grass upon
the earth.

There has been much doubt as to the precise meaning of
the first clause in this verse. The word פִסַּת here translated *heap*, occurs nowhere else, and a variety of renderings
have been suggested. The A. V. reads *handful*. The LXX.
στήριγμα, the Vulgate, similarly, *firmamentum* (both omitting
the word *corn*) the Syriac Psalter *multitude*. Gesenius, somewhat alike, *diffusion* or *abundance*, with which Olshausen and
Hupfeld agree. Delitzsch explains it a *level surface*, i.e.,
either a threshing-floor, or an artificial terrace for cultivation.
The Chaldee Targum paraphrases פִסַּת־בַּר as *substance-
making bread*. And S. Jerome turns it *a memorial of corn*.
According to the LXX. and Vulgate reading, the words of
the Psalmist are but another form of the prophecy of Isaiah
and Micah. "It shall come to pass in the last days, that the Isa. ii. 2.
mountain of the LORD's house shall be established in the tops Mic. iv. 1.
of the mountains, and shall be exalted above the hills; and C.
all nations shall flow unto it." CHRIST the LORD is the *firmament*, or strong foundation of those Prophets and Apostles
who are called mountains, and yet He is also lifted up over
them. "We read," observes Gerhohus, "that there was G.
made 'a firmament in the midst of the waters,' when as yet Gen. i. 6.
'the earth was without form and void.' We see the heaven
adorned with stars, a beauteous and wondrous work, performed by the WORD, not yet Incarnate. But a far more
wonderful and awful thing is that the WORD should become
Flesh, and be a *firmament* on the earth, hitherto void and
formless. *There shall be a firmament upon the earth*, for man
did eat angels' food, and this bread which strengthens man's
heart shall be a *firmament upon the earth*, as much fairer
than that heavenly firmament as He hath by inheritance obtained a more excellent name than it. For He Who called
that ethereal heaven the *firmament* because by firm division
it parted the waters from the waters, He, setting a *firmament
on earth*, 'hath given Him a Name which is above every Phil. ii. 9.
name' and hath bestowed on Him power and judgment to
divide the waters from the waters: His people from them
who are not His people. For the 'waters are peoples, and Rev. xvii. 15.
multitudes, and nations, and tongues.'" *There shall be a
firmament upon the earth*, remarks another, because they who
rest on Him shall be firm and steadfast in faith and charity, Ric. Hamp.
even amongst the cares and troubles of this life. Another,
(though unauthoritative) reading in some Latin Psalters, however, *frumentum* instead of *firmamentum*, has brought back
several of the expositors to the word *corn*, which is the promi-
nent one in the Hebrew text. And they all take it then of
the Holy Eucharist. A cloud of Rabbinical tradition hovers
round the passage, and helps to frame it that we may see it

L.
Cd.
Genebrar-
dus.

in this aspect. Besides the rendering of the Targum given above, the following may be cited. In the Midrash Cohe-leth, a comment on Ecclesiastes, it is said that as Moses caused manna to come down from heaven, so Messiah shall be *a cake of corn upon the earth.* Rabbi Jonathan in his Targum reads, *There shall be a sacrifice of bread upon the earth, on the head of the mountains of the Church.* And this is further explained in the Sepher-Kibucim to the effect that in the days of Messiah there shall be a cake of corn lifted in sacrifice over the heads of the priests in the temple.

Ay.

Herein, most naturally, the commentators see the Elevation of the Host, that primeval rite of the Divine Liturgy wherein He Who is the substantiating Bread, the Memorial Sacrifice, the Corn of mighty men, is uplifted in oblation to the FA-THER, Himself the Victim and Himself the Priest. Where-fore Hildebert of Tours:

Hildeb. Ven.
Versus de
Myst. Miss.

Sub cruce, sub verbo natura novatur, et aram
    Panis honorificat carne, cruore calix.
Presbyter idcirco, cum verba venitur ad illa,
    In quibus altari gratia tanta datur,
Tollit utrumque, notans quod sit communibus escis
    Altior, et quiddam majus utrumque gerat.

Again, we may find a more literal fulfilment of the prophecy in the events of the Gospel history, wherein He Who is the Bread of Life is seen so often "like a young hart upon the mountains." In the temple on Moriah, in the place of His first preaching, in the scene of many an hour of prayer, in the Transfiguration, the Crucifixion, the Ascension, again and again His feet are beautiful on the mountains.

Cant. ii. 17.

Thrice for us the Word Incarnate high on holy hills was set,
Once on Tabor, once on Calvary, and again on Olivet;
Once to shine, and once to suffer, and once more, as King of kings,
With a merry noise ascending, borne by cherubs on their wings.

If, however, we explain the words of His husbandry, the Church, we shall still not lose our grasp of mystical interpre-tation. The *heap* or *handful of corn* will then denote the Christian body, the "city set on a hill that cannot be hid." *High upon the hills,* either because raised on the "founda-tion of the Apostles and Prophets," those mountains of GOD's house, or because of its own prominence in the world. Again, if we take the interpretation a *floor* or *level spot* covered with corn; this may denote one of two things. The *corn,* even after being parted from tares, has yet to be separated from its own husk and chaff on GOD's lofty threshing-floor, and the words will thus denote the purifying of His people through afflictions in this world, and through the cleansing of purga-tory in the intermediate state. Once more, Delitzsch's inter-

Eph. ii. 20.

pretation, a *terrace* planted with *corn*, gives a very beautiful meaning. Till the Gospel came, only the plains and lower slopes of the life of holiness were cultivated. The higher ground soared rugged and barren far above, showing, indeed, peaks kissed by the first sunbeams, but difficult of ascent, and almost untrodden by man's foot. Terrace after terrace now rises up the mountain side, and earth, borne slowly and laboriously from below, covers the bare rock, until the whole height is scaled, and the golden corn waves on the very summits of the spiritual life, to wit, the practice of those counsels of perfection which were once deemed too hard for men to follow. *His fruit shall shake like Libanus.* That is, the waving of the cornfield which the LORD hath blessed, shall be like that of the cedar-forest of Lebanon bending before the wind. And in this prophecy we may see shadowed the height to which the Gospel rises above the Law. For the stateliest forest-king known to the Hebrews is here compared to the single ear of corn, undistinguishable by human eyes from any other in the harvest. So even the humble and hidden Christian Saints of GOD in daily acts of holiness rise higher than the very mightiest seers of the elder dispensation, because the Church is exalted above the Synagogue. And with this agrees the Æthiopic Psalter: *His fruit shall be loftier than the cedar.* The LXX. and Vulgate read a little differently: *His fruit shall be lifted up above Lebanon.* Lebanon, observes S. Augustine, we are wont to take as this world's dignity, for Lebanon is a mountain bearing tall trees, and the name itself is interpreted 'whiteness.' What wonder is it then, if the fruit of CHRIST be exalted over every splendid position of this world, since the lovers of that fruit despise all worldly dignities? But if we take the words in a good sense, because of the "cedars of Libanus which He hath planted;" what other fruit can be understood, as being exalted over this Libanus, save that whereof the Apostle speaketh when about to speak of charity, "and yet show I unto you a more excellent way?" For this is put in the front place of divine gifts, in that passage where he saith, "But the fruit of the Spirit is love." Again; it may be taken of the effects of the Passion of CHRIST, lifting up His Saints above all the glory and temptations of the world. Or if we continue to take it of the Holy Eucharist, the words denote its pre-eminence over all other means of grace given by GOD to His Church. Euthymius sees here a reference to the idol-worship anciently practised in Lebanon, and the victory of the Gospel over it and all other idolatry. *And shall be green in the city like grass upon the earth.* The LXX. and Vulgate have: *They shall flourish out of the city like grass* (or *hay* Vulg.) *of the earth.* From the Church, GOD's city, notes S. Augustine, and as grass beareth fruit, like wheat, which is called grass in Holy Scripture. There are two cities, adds Gerhohus, of either of which these words may be spoken, Jerusalem

Margin notes:
Euseb.
Cæsar.

A.

Ps. civ. 16.

1 Cor. xii. 31.
Gal. v. 22.

D. C.

Ay.
P.
Cd.

Z.

A.

Gen. i. 11.

G.

II.   T

and Babylon. If we take it of the former, GOD's city, then
S. Augustine's explanation holds, if of the latter, the city of
the world and the devil, it warns us that all flesh is grass, and
that all the goodliness of that city is as the flower of the field.
So they who seek an abiding city here shall quickly perish in
the judgment, for as soon as the sun ariseth, straightway the
grass shall be dried up. It is of this world we must understand the words, aptly remarks Cassiodorus, because it is
written, *out of the city*, not *in the city*, that CHRIST's fruit
will flourish. They will rise out of the earthly state in which
they are planted into the bright sun and pure air of His presence. And they are compared to grass, because of its fresh-
ness and beauty, not with any thought of its brief life, because theirs is immortal. The Carthusian, laying stress also
on the words *out of the city*, draws a very different corollary
from them. They are spoken, says he, of those who having
approached to the Communion of CHRIST's Body in the Eucharist, return from church strengthened and refreshed, and
flourishing in grace. S. Antony of Padua, also referring to
the Holy Eucharist, explains the text of the Angels winging
their flight down from the heavenly city to gaze on the mysteries of the altar. Lastly; the *city* is taken to mean, as so
often, the earthly Jerusalem, whence the Gospel began, so
that the preachers who went forth from it *flourished*, while
those who remained behind perished quickly as the grass of
the field.

Isa. xi. 6.
Ric. Hamp.

C.

D. C.

L.

Z.

17 His Name shall endure for ever; his Name
shall remain under the sun among the posterities :
which shall be blessed through him; and all the
heathen shall praise him.

A very beautiful meaning of the second clause in this verse
is lost as well in the Bible version as in this one, nor does it
appear in LXX., Vulgate, or Syriac. For *His Name shall
remain*, we shall read, (having regard to the word יִנִּין)[1]
His Name shall burgeon, shall *put forth fresh shoots*. And
we shall thus find a reference to the perpetual vitality of the
Gospel, the way in which it continually renews its youth and
vigour when men deem it most effete, and also to the incessant additions of Christian names to the roll-call of GOD's
army, made in the Sacrament of Baptism. The LXX. and
Vulgate read, *His Name abideth before the sun. Before the
sun*, because the sun is the measure of time, and the Eternal
WORD is before all time. *Before the sun*, because CHRIST
existed before the angels, who are compared to the sun, were
created. And there is a Rabbinical saying that there were
seven things existing before the world was made, of which
one was the Name of Messiah. With this agrees the Targum,

A.

Ay.
De Muis.

---

[1] The *Keri* reading here is יִנּ.

Before the sun His Name was prepared. The reading of the
margin in the A. V. is : *His Name shall be as a son to continue
his father's name for ever*, which is nearly that of R. Kimchi.
Others take it : *His Name shall be the Son.* Either way it
speaks of Him Who came down to reveal His FATHER unto
us, Who is that Holy Thing born of the Virgin Mary, and
" called the SON of GOD." *Among the posterities which shall* S. Luke i.
be blessed through Him. The LXX. and Vulgate, somewhat ³⁵.
differently : *In Him shall all the tribes of the earth be
blessed.* It is the renewal of the promise made to Abraham. D. C.
"In thy seed shall all the nations of the earth be blessed," Gen. xxii.
on which we have the inspired comment of the Apostle, ¹⁸·
" Now to Abraham and his seed were the promises made.
He saith not, And to seeds, as of many ; but as of one, And Gal. iii. 16.
to thy seed, which is CHRIST." They explain also *all the
tribes of the earth* of all elect souls, according to their varying Lu.
merits, because it is written, " In My FATHER's house are S. John xiv.
many mansions." ².

> Ye know the many mansions
> For many a glorious name,
> And divers retributions,
> That divers merits claim ;
> For midst the constellations
> That deck our earthly sky,
> This star than that is brighter,—
> And so it is on high.

18 Blessed be the LORD GOD, even the GOD of
Israel : which only doeth wondrous things ;
19 And blessed be the Name of his Majesty for
ever : and all the earth shall be filled with his Majesty. Amén, Amen.

The triple utterance of the Divine Name, found in the He- Ricard.
brew, but not in the LXX. and Vulgate, denotes, remarks Cenoman.
S. Jerome, the mystery of the Holy Trinity. Observe, that Ep. ad Su-
in the four last verses of this Psalm four reasons are given niam et Fra-
why worship and praise are due to CHRIST. First, because tellam.
of His Eternity, *before His Name endureth before the sun ;* P.
secondly, because of His infinite goodness and mercy, for *all
nations are* to be *blessed* and redeemed through Him ; thirdly,
by reason of His omnipotence, for *He only doeth wondrous
things ;* fourthly, because of His supreme Majesty. *Which* G.
only doeth wondrous things. For He alone does them by His
own might, whether He work of Himself or through agents,
which is true of no one else, since none worketh them without
Him. And though He saith : " The FATHER that dwelleth in S. John xiv.
Me, He doeth the works ;" yet without Him, Who is the hand, ¹⁰·
arm, might, and wisdom of the FATHER, the FATHER doeth
nought, nor yet the SPIRIT of the FATHER, Who is His SPIRIT
T 2

too, because the operation of the Most High Trinity is undivided. Thus *He only doeth wondrous things*, yet He is not
alone, for it is Man, assumed into the WORD, of one essence
with the FATHER and the HOLY GHOST, Who worketh in the
might and power, or majesty of the whole Trinity. And so
it is written, "All things were made by Him;" and again,
"LORD, Thou also hast wrought all our works in us." And
therefore He says of His Saints, "He that believeth on Me,
the works that I do shall he do also." *For ever.* It can be
no prophecy for Solomon, observes Tertullian, since he fell
into idolatry, and lost that glory he had in GOD beforetime.
It can only be of Him Who is the Name of GOD's Majesty,
the Eternal SON. *And all the earth shall be filled with His
Majesty.* And that in divers ways, as first by the Incarnation, whereby His Infinite Majesty is united to all human
nature, for man is called by the Fathers the "second world."
Secondly, by the preaching of the Gospel, for "the earth
shall be filled with the knowledge of the LORD, as the waters
cover the sea." Thirdly, by the glory of the Resurrection.
So S. Bernard: "All the earth, I say, shall be filled with
the Majesty of the LORD, when it shall be clad in the glory
of the Resurrection. Why then murmurest thou still, O
hapless flesh? why resistest thou still, and strivest against
the Spirit? If He humble thee, if He scourge thee, if He
bring thee into bondage, it is for thy sake, doubtless, in thy
generation, not less than for His own." *Amen. Amen.*
Rabbi Jehudah the Holy said, "He that said *Amen* in this
world, is worthy to say it in the world to come. David,
therefore, utters *Amen* twice in this Psalm, to show that one
Amen belongs to this world, the other to that which is to
come. He who saith Amen devoutly, is greater than he who
uttereth the prayers, for the prayers are but the letter, and
the Amen is the seal. The scribe writeth the letters, the
Prince alone seals them." *Amen,* (*Be it so,* Vulg.) now, particularly, *Amen* then, universally. *Amen* now, for we need
it as comfort in our journey. *Amen* then will befit the full
joy of our heavenly country. Let us then all say *Amen, Amen,*
with eager longing to behold the King Solomon, not only
with that crown of thorns wherewith His mother crowned
Him, denoting thereby the Church formed of sinners and
set upon CHRIST as a crown, but also with that diadem wherewith His FATHER crowned Him, because of His death and
passion, with honour and glory, setting Him on the throne
of everlasting brightness. From which throne we pray that
He may rule all that is not yet under Him, that the *whole
earth may be filled with His Majesty.*

And therefore:

Glory be to the FATHER, the King Eternal, Who giveth
His judgment unto the King His SON; glory be to the SON,
the true King Solomon, Who maketh peace in all His
kingdom; glory be to the HOLY GHOST, Who is the Peace

Ay.
S. John i. 3.
Isa. xxvi. 12.
D. C.
S. John xiv.
12.
Tert. in
Marc. 9.
L.

S. Greg.
Naz. Orat.
3.
Isa. xi. 9.
Cd.
S. Bern.
Serm. in
Isa. 2.

Bakius.
Buxtorf.
Synag. 8.

G.

of all them who fight for Solomon, and serve Him here below, and Who will be yet more fully the peace of them that reign with Him in heaven.

As it was in the beginning, is now, and ever shall be: world without end. Amen.

COLLECTS.

Almighty God, we pray Thee, calling on Thy Name, Ludolph. blessed before all worlds, that, humbling the slanderer, Thou wouldst vouchsafe to bestow peace and righteousness upon Thy people. Through. (1.)

O Lord, by the indulgence of Thy bounty, let us receive D. C. peace and righteousness, and alway possess them through Thine aid, that our slanderers may be brought low, and we may praise Thy blessed Name for evermore. (1.)

O Lord, be favourable unto the poor, and heal the souls Mozarabic. of the needy, that we, who trust not in our own strength, and hopefully intreat Thy mercy, may, through poverty of spirit, obtain the fulness of heavenly blessing. (11.)

Let the mountains, enlightened with the earliest ray of Mozarabic. faith, bring peace unto Thy people, that the righteousness of the hills may come down from the height of the Saints, and small and great together attain the summit of perfect deserving. (11.)

O God, Son of God, Whose Name abideth for ever, and Mozarabic. Who, making Thyself known as only God and Lord, camest, Christmas. through the mystery of the Incarnation Thou tookest on Thee, to be a King, to redeem the world; grant us such warmth in this mystery of love, that we may escape the snare of the deceiver, so that, as we proclaim with loud voice the joys of Thine Advent, we may exult in our salvation when Thou, our Judge, comest to judgment. (11.)

O Lord, to Whom the kings and the isles bring gifts, Who Mozarabic. with Thine unconquered power, and through Thy heavenly pity, camest to save the poor from the mighty, and frail mankind from the sway of the ancient enemy; seeing that we are far from Thee, and in need of Thy mercies, that we are subject to his unrighteousness, tied and bound with the chains of our sins, let Thy lovingkindness deliver us now from his service, restore us to Thee, and keep us safely to abide with Thee, that we, who confess ourselves redeemed by Thy mercy, may hereafter glory in the gifts attained by Thy bounty. (11.)

PSALM LXXIII.

TITLE: A Psalm of Asaph. LXX. and Vulgate: The praises of
David, son of Jesse, are ended. A Psalm of Asaph.

ARGUMENT.

ARG. THOMAS. That CHRIST repays evil to the ungodly for their
craft. The voice of the Prophet to GOD touching the Jews. The
voice of CHRIST to the FATHER touching the Jews. Or, the voice
of the Apostles touching the present judgment or the future one, to
the FATHER. Compline prayers. For greater works.

VEN. BEDE. Whereas in the former titles *David* only appears in
the inscription; here he has added *Son of Jesse*, doubtless that we
may understand that *David* who was Solomon's father. Therefore
the temporal *Praises* offered to the LORD under the Law by animal
sacrifices and musical instrumentation, *are ended* and changed;
because now the Catholic Church accomplishes her sacred psalmody
in the immolation of the Body and Blood of CHRIST. The Synagogue did indeed worship the LORD, but had fallen into most evil
thoughts through seeing the ungodly flourish. In its person *Asaph*
himself speaks in this *Psalm*, who in his name contains the meaning
Synagogue;[1] for he is about to speak many things of the Gentile
people and of those who have received the Law of the LORD, which
are uttered profitably for our correction, lest we be defiled with such
thoughts. Otherwise: That *The Praises of David, son of Jesse,
are ended*, belongs to the close of Psalm LXXI. (lxxii.); and *Psalm*,
which follows, is the beginning of the next one. *Asaph*, as we have
said, speaks throughout the Psalm in type of the Synagogue. In
the first part he declares that he was jealous of this world's happiness, beholding the peace of sinners, marvelling why such prosperity
fell to the lot of GOD's enemies and heathens, that they seemed to
stretch forth their mouth unto the heaven: *Truly God is loving
unto Israel!* In the second part, he says that his people would return to wholesome counsel, and be ashamed of the wickedness of
their former thought, till it should attain to understand and behold
the last end of the ungodly: *Therefore His people return hither*,
(A. V.) and so on. Thirdly; he witnesseth that evil shall befall the
ungodly because of their deceits, because they shall be seen to cause
scandals to holy men by their happiness; yet he declares that by
GOD's goodness he hath been delivered from these evils: *Truly because of their deceits.* (Vulg.) Fourthly; he states how, by GOD's
mercy, he attained perfect understanding: *Whom have I in heaven
but Thee? and there is none upon earth that I desire in comparison
of Thee.*

SYRIAC PSALTER. Composed by Asaph the recorder, on the death
of Absalom. Moreover, a confession of human weakness, and of
the prosperity of the ungodly, and the longsuffering of GOD.

EUSEBIUS OF CÆSAREA. A prophecy of the kingdom and longsuffering of GOD. A confession of human weakness at the prosperity
of the ungodly, and of GOD's longsuffering.

S. ATHANASIUS. A Psalm in narration.

---

[1] אסף *collector*, from אסף συναγωγεῖν, *to gather together.*

VARIOUS USES.

Gregorian. Thursday. Matins. [Maundy Thursday. II. Nocturn.]
Parisian. Monday. Nones.
Ambrosian. Tuesday of Second Week. I. Nocturn.
Monastic. Wednesday. II. Nocturn [Maundy Thursday. II. Nocturn.]
Quignon. Thursday. Matins.
Lyons. Wednesday. Nones.

ANTIPHONS.

Gregorian. Thou hast redeemed the rod * of Thine inheritance. [Maundy Thursday. They have pondered, and spoken wickedness * they have spoken unrighteousness in the high place.]
Parisian. In Thy will * Thou hast guided me, O LORD, and hast received me with glory.
Ambrosian. As preceding Psalm.
Monastic. As preceding. [Maundy Thursday. As Gregorian.]
Lyons. Alleluia.
Mozarabic. First verse of the Psalm.

As the patristic and mediæval commentators on this, the first Psalm of the third book of the Psalter, agree in attaching to it the words which properly form the colophon of the preceding Psalm, *The prayers of David, the son of Jesse, are ended;* it will be more convenient to take them here than in the critical order. And first let us hear S. Augustine: "What means, *There have failed the hymns of David, son of Jesse?* Hymns are praises of GOD accompanied with singing; hymns are songs containing the praise of GOD. If there be praise, and not of GOD, it is no hymn; if there be praise, and GOD's praise, and it be not sung, it is no hymn. It must needs then, if it be a hymn, have these three things, praise, that of GOD, and singing. What is then, *there have failed the hymns?* The praises which are sung unto GOD have failed. He seemeth to tell of a painful and, so to speak, deplorable thing. For he that singeth praise, not only praiseth, but also praiseth with gladness; he that singeth praise, not only singeth, but also loveth Him of whom he singeth. In praise, there is the utterance of one giving thanks; in singing, the affection of one loving. He saith then, *The hymns of David have failed,* and he hath added, *the son of Jesse.* For David was King of Israel, son of Jesse, at a certain time of the Old Testament, at which time the New Testament was therein hidden, like fruit in a root. For if thou seek fruit in a root, thou wilt not find it, and yet thou findest no fruit in the branches, save that which hath issued from the root. In like manner CHRIST Himself, yet to be born after the flesh, was hidden in the root, that is, in the seed of the Patriarchs, to be revealed at the set time, as it is written, 'There shall come forth a rod from the stem of Jesse.' In the time of the Old Testament the promises of GOD to that carnal people were earthly and temporal. All that course of temporal promises was a figure and prophecy of things to come. Accordingly, when that kingdom where David, son of Jesse, reigned, was failing, the carnal people were praising GOD only for things which were passing away, and therefore the *hymns of David*—not the SON of GOD, but the

A.

Isa. xi. 1.

son of *Jesse, failed.*" With this view, which is also that cited in Beda's argument drawn from Cassiodorus, the great body of the commentators agree, and thus we may pass to the Psalm itself.

1 Truly GOD is loving unto Israel : even unto such as are of a clean heart.

G.

"*Israel*," observes Gerhohus, following in the track of S. Augustine, "is the man who seeth GOD, or the Prince with GOD, who, having clear and pure eyes, rejoices in gazing on the eternal light of truth, righteousness, wisdom, and goodness, for that light which is torture to diseased eyes, is pleasant to pure and healthy ones. Wherefore he adds, *unto such as are of a clean heart,* because they, with gladness of the inner man delighting in the law of the LORD, recognize the goodness of GOD even in those things, which the evil, judging all, censure as done unjustly and out of due order."

A.
Ps. xviii. 26

And so it is written, "With the clean thou shalt be clean : and with the froward thou shalt learn frowardness." Not that GOD changes, but that we do, and we see Him as we are.

2 Nevertheless, my feet were almost gone : my treadings had well-nigh slipt.

D. C.

My feet, that is, my affections, or else my intellect and will, whereby I should attain towards GOD in contemplation and love. *My treadings,* the acts resulting from my will, and leading me out of the path of righteousness. *Well-nigh,* because GOD's grace was sufficient for me to rise again when I stumbled, that I might go on my way once more. And so S. John Climacus :

G

Cd.

> The prize, the prize secure !
> The athlete nearly fell :
> Bare all he could endure,
> And bare not always well :
> But he may smile at troubles gone,
> Who sets the victor-garland on !

B.

Slipt. The LXX. and Vulgate have *poured out.* As fluid spilt on the ground from a vessel, notes S. Bruno, which is wasted and comes to nothing, so are our acts without the grace of perseverance.

3 And why? I was grieved at the wicked : I do also see the ungodly in such prosperity.

Z.

I was grieved. The A. V., more truly, *I was envious.* And so the LXX., ἐζήλωσα, and the Vulgate, *zelavi.* We may take it, observes Euthymius, of that anger and indignation, which, starting from a good reason, proceeds to attack something unreasonably. It was no true and good zeal, adds

Cd.

Corderius, but rather that which Ezekiel calls the "image of jealousy," whereby the holiest minds are often tempted, but *Ezek. viii. 3.* which is pardonable, because it does not prove a man guilty, nor make him so, as neither the will nor the reason assent to it. Wherefore David says only, *My feet were almost gone.* He adds the cause of his jealousy, the *prosperity* of the *ungodly.* The LXX. and Vulgate, more close to the Hebrew, read *the peace of sinners.* What *peace?* Earthly peace, **R.** changeful peace, peace not of grace, but of doom. They cannot be in peace, for it is written, "There is no peace, saith *Isa. lvii. 21.* my GOD, to the wicked." But there is an inward peace, that *S. John xiv.* calmness of mind whereof it is said, "Peace I leave with *27.* you." And there is outward peace, security in sin and in worldly vanity, of which it is written. "Their houses are *Job xxi. 9,* peace from fear." This is that miserable peace of which is *marg.* said, "I came not to send peace, but a sword." This peace *34.* causes manifold troubling within, as Cassiodorus observes, for **C.** it is ever contending with conscience, is quarrelling within, and having no exterior foe, wars with itself. And observe, **Ay.** that sinners have three sorts of peace: the peace of impure association, which is that of carnal sinners; the peace of brotherhood in slander, which is that of worldly accomplices;. the peace of slothful impunity; which belongs to negligent bishops. Of the first, Rome was an example, giving itself up to vice and luxury after peace came by the overthrow of Carthage. The second, that of men who plot together for evil to resist the good, of which the alliance of Herod and Pilate was a type. And so we may see that there is closer connection between barren thorns than between fruitful trees, as there is readier union between the bad for gangs and disputes, than amongst the good for good ends. So too Judas made peace with the Jews to betray CHRIST. Thirdly comes slothful peace. This is nothing but negligence in correction. For when a Bishop sees that an offence ought to be punished, yet takes no notice, and does not punish, then his dependents call him peaceable. So too when GOD sometimes does not punish the wicked, they say that they are at peace with GOD. And it is of this peace that the Psalmist speaks here. But let them take heed that it is written, "When they shall say, *1 Thess. v. 3.* Peace and safety; then sudden destruction cometh upon them." Not till the SAVIOUR came was the good war begun, **G.** that such an evil peace should be broken.

4 For they are in no peril of death; but are lusty and strong.

This rendering is incorrect, and without authority. The A. V. is the true one. *There are no bands in their death,* *De Muis.* i.e., they die easily, and without bodily pain. So it is in the version of Aquila, οὐκ εἰσὶ δυσπάθειαι τῷ θανάτῳ αὐτῶν. Compare that other saying concerning the wicked, "They spend *Job xxi. 13.* their days in wealth, and in a moment go down to the grave."

T 3

D. C. We may take it of many of those who persecuted the Martyrs, of their long lives and quiet deaths amidst all household tendance and alleviation, compared with the fiery passage of their victims. In this wise also some of the commentators explain

Ay. the Vulgate reading, *There is no regard (respectus) to their death.* That is, they feel no pain or alarm, they abound in wealth, and can obtain every resource of medicine and other

Ric. Hamp. help in their sickness. Or, as others take it, they never think about death, nor prepare for their latter end. There is, however, a yet more terrible interpretation of the words. The

G. mercy of GOD regards them not as they hasten to death,

S. Matt. viii. 22. since it is of such that the saying is, "Let the dead bury their dead." The LXX. reading, ἀνάνευσις, is very obscure, and probably corrupt. It is diversely explained. Some, as

Cd. Theodore of Mopsuestia and Hesychius, take it, *There is no refusal of death* on their part, for they have no idea of its peril to them. And with this agrees a reading *declinatio*, found in the Roman and Gallican Psalters, and similarly explained by some. The more general view, however, is that

A. of S. Augustine, that there is no *avoidance* of death for them, They may keep it at bay by all measures, and may drive it from their thoughts, but it is inevitable. The Arabic Psalter

L. reads, *There is no rest in their death,* (like the reading of S. Ambrose, *reclinatio,*) words which have an awful significance when compared with those of our LORD, "The rich man died,

S. Luke xvi. 22. and was buried; and in hell he lift up his eyes, being in torments." *But are lusty and strong.* The LXX. and Vulgate here are very unlike this version: *There is a strengthening in*

A. *their scourge* (καὶ στερέωμα ἐν μάστιγι αὐτῶν, et firmamentum in plagâ eorum.) There is a *firmament in their scourge*, be-

G. cause their scourge is not temporal, but firm for everlasting. Their wounds, observes another, which have gangrened in their peace and prosperity, need to be cut away with vigorous surgery. But *there is no firmament in their plague.*

Ay. Their sin is old and deep, but the knife has not gone far enough to reach the depths of the sore. The Carmelite, continuing to explain the words of the false security of the wicked, interprets it, *There is no endurance in their plague,*

D. C. their earthly sufferings are short, and easily cured. Or, with the Carthusian, we may take it to mean that the wicked do not become firm and steadfast by accepting GOD's chastisements as warnings to repentance, a sense in which he has

Cd. been anticipated by Theodore of Mopsuestia.

5 They come in no misfortune like other folk : neither are they plagued like other men.

This verse also is read differently by the LXX. and Vulgate. They run: *In the labours of men they are not, and*

A. *they shall not be scourged with men.* S. Augustine's comment on these words is brief and pregnant : "Doth not the devil

himself, for whom an eternal punishment is prepared, escape
scourging with men ?" They are not punished for their cor- **G.**
rection and profit, they have no share in the toils and labours **Ay.**
of the righteous, they have no part in the lot of Lazarus and **D. C.**
Paul. Toils of their own they have, doubtless, seeking this
world's riches, seizing them when found, guarding them carefully when seized. In toils such as these the righteous have **S. Greg.**
no share, for they love not passing things, and therefore **Mag. Mor.**
labour not in such heavy cares. So too the evil are not in **vi. 5.**
the labours of the righteous, for they care not for celestial
things, and do not subdue the flesh for the sake of such
things. They keep no vigils, they offer no pure devotions, **D. C.**
they regard not fitting discipline, they reject fasts, they do **R.**
not remember that "whom the LORD loveth He chasteneth, **Heb. xii. 6.**
and scourgeth every son whom He receiveth." And that
too, remembering that man is born to labour, and does not
answer the end of his being if he shun it. Labour he must, **S. Bern.**
and suffer too, but if he shrink from that which is appointed, **Serm. de**
heavier toils await him. " I hold," adds S. Bernard in an- **Divers. 2.**
other place, " that the words apply best to the clergy of our **Serm.**
time. Every class of men has some labour and some pleasure. But note the cleverness of these, and marvel how with
modern ingenuity they make a division, taking everything
that is pleasant, shunning and refusing all that is troublesome. Like knights, they keep up great households, costly
furniture, caparisons, hawks, dice, and the like, and borrow
from women all their show and effeminacy. But they take
excellent care to avoid the heavy corslet, the sleepless nights
in camp, the doubtful issues of battle. They have none of
woman's modesty, discipline, and whatever else of toil belongs to that sex. Husbandmen sweat, and vine-dressers
prune and dig ; the clergy are sunk in sloth all the time.
When the time of fruit comes round, they require new barns
and have their cellars filled. Would that it were not more
than the toilers have, or that it were shared with them."
And he goes on to draw a similar contrast with merchants
and others who labour to get their living. All men, he con-
cludes, will reject such drones, who will have all the profit
and none of the trouble. *They are not in the labour of men.*
Whither can they go, save to the place of unending dread ?

6 And this is the cause that they are so holden
with pride : and overwhelmed with cruelty.

More literally, *pride is their collar, violence covers them as*
a garment. They are like a bull intended for sacrifice, notes
S. Augustine, untamed, undisciplined, allowed to feed and **A.**
wanton at their pleasure, only because slaughter awaits them.
They are not merely proud, adds Gerhohus, sinful as that is, **G.**
but they are the captive slaves of pride. They are not merely
guilty of *iniquity*, but are so *covered* with it as a cloak of

double folds, that they can neither see nor be seen. Their eyes are not opened, like those of our first parents, to see their nakedness, and to be ashamed, their prosperity hides their inner misery from the eyes of others.   That garment of iniquity is bad itself, and comes from a bad loom, remarks S. Albert: It gives no real covering nor warmth, as it is written, "They weave the spider's web, their webs shall not become garments, neither shall they cover themselves with their works."   It is doomed to destruction, for "He will destroy in this mountain the face of the covering cast over all people." It is no easy thing to get rid of it, adds Gilbert of Hoyland, for the habit of sin becomes a very skin, so that to remove it is not to strip, but to flay. And another aptly compares it to the *tunica molesta,* the garment smeared with pitch in which Nero caused his victims to be clad, because, like it, the flames are its destiny.

S. Albertus Magnus.
Isa. lix. 5, 6.

Isa. xxv. 7.

Serm. in Cant. 9.

Cd.

7 Their eyes swell with fatness : and they do even what they lust.

Cd.

L.

Abundance of temporal prosperity has, as it were, closed up their eyes and darkened their understanding, so that they can no longer see God's will, but hurry after their own enjoyment. Lorinus aptly cites the heathen poet:

Horat. Sat. ii. 2, 77.

Nam corpus onustum
Hesternis vitiis animum quoque praegravat ipsum,
Atque affigit humo divinæ particulam auræ.

A.

The Vulgate reads : *Their iniquity hath come forth as though from fat.* That is, inexcusably, because without the pressure of need. A beggar steals, but his hunger palliates his sin, but when a rich man plunders the goods of others, there is no excuse for him. The good deeds of the self-indulgent grow slowly and scantily out of a barren soil ; the crop of their vices grows fast and rank from the rich ground, with no help from spades or harrows, and destined to be fatal to the owner. *They have passed over unto the desire of their heart.* Away from God's will to their own, as one Father observes. They have gone from the true faith to idolatry or to avarice, as another remarks. They have passed the limits of our common humanity, more pointedly says a third : and count themselves as of different clay from ordinary mortals. They have gone from sin to sin, from one vice unto another, till they fulfil all their desires, is the explanation of a fourth.

Cd.

S. Hieron.

C.

A.

S. Albertus Magnus.

8 They corrupt other, and speak of wicked blasphemy : their talking is against the most High.

The words at once suggest the Chief Priests, bribing Judas with the thirty pieces of silver, giving money to the guard at the sepulchre, and saying of Him Whose throne is for ever and ever, "He hath a devil and is mad." But this is not the

S. John x. 20.

true meaning of the passage, nor yet the Vulgate reading.
The A. V. is closer to the original, but not exact. The translation ought to run: *They scoff, they speak proudly of oppression,* De Muis.
they talk from a high place. And the Jewish commenta- Exod. v. 2.
tors cite the examples of Pharaoh, Sennacherib, and Nebu- 2 Kings
chadnezzar as instances in point. The Christian may add Isa. xiv. 14.
those of Diocletian and Maximian, when they erected the
pillar to commemorate the annihilation of the Nazarene creed.
But the Vulgate reads: *They have meditated and spoken
wickedness, they have spoken unrighteousness in the lofty place,*
(or with the LXX. *to the height.*) The words, as Gerhohus G.
observes, rise to a climax. It was sin enough to have admitted the evil thoughts, it was yet worse to give them utterance, and the guilt is completed by the publicity and
boastfulness of speech. "They declare their sin as Sodom, Isa. iii. 9.
they hide it not."

9 For they stretch forth their mouth unto the
heaven : and their tongue goeth through the world.

"The sheep," quaintly comments an unknown writer, Cd.
"bleats with its head downwards, but the wolf lifts his head Auct. Op.
in the air, turning it to the sky, and so howls. Thus he who Incert.
according to GOD's will utters the voice of lowliness and confession, is a sheep, while he who howls against the truth of
GOD with shameful blasphemy, is a wolf." The Yorkshire Ric. Hamp.
hermit puts it tersely: "They think and speak, in their pride
and deceit, high things of themselves, as though with the
authority of heaven, and yet all their thoughts and language
aim only at wandering after the acquisition and enjoyment
of earthly gain." Cardinal Hugo boldly applies the words in Hugo Card.
a good sense to the priesthood: *They stretch forth their mouth
unto the heaven,* in prayer to GOD; *their tongue goeth through
the world,* in preaching to sinners. Another, returning to
the sterner interpretation, explains it, that the wicked spare Flaminius.
neither GOD nor man in their reviling. And, finally, Euthy- Z.
mius quaintly takes it of astrologers uttering foolish predictions.

10 Therefore fall the people unto them : and
thereout suck they no small advantage.

The words, so read, tell of the temporal success of the ungodly, drawing away the multitude for their own private
interest, not for any general good, as Absalom first "stole 2 Sam. xv. 6.
the hearts of the men of Israel," and then made himself
king: and as, in a later day, Jesus who is called Barabbas,
after he had made insurrection, was delivered from death by
the voices of the people instead of JESUS Who is called
CHRIST. But the reading is incorrect, and varies widely
from Hebrew, LXX., Vulgate, and A. V. The rendering of
the last is, *Therefore His people return hither, and waters of*

a full cup are wrung out to them; a version practically accepted, with minute variations, by later critics. The LXX. and Vulgate have, *Therefore my people shall return [be converted,* Vulg.] *hither, and full days shall be found amongst them.* That is, "when the fulness of the time was come, GOD sent forth His SON," to teach men to despise temporal things, to be the Way, to recall us to inward thought, to convert us to Himself. *Hither,* because it is in this life our conversion must take place, where our FATHER chasteneth us as sons; whereas they who continue in sin *shall not be scourged with men,* but shall go thither where the evil spirits dwell. Or, *hither,* to the same estimate as mine of the prosperity of the wicked, learning to count it vain and unprofitable. They will do more than ponder on the instability of worldly gain, for they will turn to meditating on the sweetness of adversity to the Saints, as being the path which has led them through temptations to the love of GOD. *Full days.* Truly is it said *full,* for the life of Saints hath fulness, but the days of the evil are empty. And in Holy Writ *fulness of days* is always taken in a good sense, as in speaking of the death of holy men, and of the births of the Forerunner and of Him of Whom he prophesied. On the other hand, empty or half days are of evil import, as it is written, "The bloodthirsty and deceitful men shall not live out half their days;" and again, "In the half of my days I shall go to the gates of hell." Thus, as we call that a "long day" in which we have accomplished, by steady labour, the work of two or three days, so length or fulness of true life is not to be computed by years and days, but by good works done for the love of GOD; whereas a life of many years spent in sin and idleness is short and empty, and leads to the gates of hell. Wherefore the Wise Man says, "For honourable age is not that which standeth in length of time, nor that is measured by number of years. But wisdom is the grey hair unto men, and an unspotted life is old age. . . . He, being made perfect in a short time, fulfilled a long time." . The later commentators, however, take the whole passage in a bad sense, and interpret it 'of the falling away of GOD's people to the sinners, and partaking of their abundance. The *waters of a full cup wrung out* are diversely explained. One takes it of the cup of bitterness which the prosperity of the wicked is to the just. Another, yet more strongly, sees here the tears which are thus forced from righteous eyes. A third finds a reference to high living and copious drinking. And we may, perhaps, taking this last view, dwell on the word *wrung,* as denoting the suffering of the many poor from which the luxury of the few rich is derived. The cup of the wealthy noble may have been filled by rackrenting his tenants, that of the yet richer trader by overworking or underpaying his operatives; the costly dress of the delicate lady may be paid for with the life of the seamstress.

Marginal notes (left column):

A.
Gal. iv. 4.

G.
S. Alb. Mag.

Ay.

S. Ambrose.
G.
Gen. xxv. 8;
xxxv. 29;
1 Chron.
xxiii. 1; Job
xlii. 17; S.
Luke i. 57;
ii. 6.
Ps. lv. 25.
Isa. xxxviii.
10, Vulg.
Cd.

Wisd. iv. 8,
13.

L.

•

Campensis.
Genebrardus.
Pineda.

Half ignorant, they turned an easy wheel,
That set sharp racks at work, to pinch and peel.

11 Tush, say they, how should GOD perceive it :
is there knowledge in the most High?

The commentators agree in taking these words as uttered
by GOD's people in their perplexity at the prosperity of the
wicked, not by the wicked as the reason of their evil deeds.
So in that most pathetic "Cry of the Children" we read :

C.
D. C.
L.

"'Our FATHER!' If He heard us, He would surely
(For they call Him good and mild)
Answer, smiling down the steep world very purely,
' Come and rest with Me, My child.'
' But no!' say the children, weeping faster,
' He is speechless as a stone ;
And they tell us, of His image is the master
Who commands us to work on.
Go to!' say the children ; 'up in heaven,
Dark, wheel-like, turning clouds are all we find.
Do not mock us ; grief has made us unbelieving—
We look up for GOD, but tears have made us blind.'
Do you hear the children weeping and disproving,
O my brothers, what ye preach?
For GOD's possible is taught by His world's loving—
And the children doubt of each."

12 Lo, these are the ungodly, these prosper in
the world, and these have riches in possession : and
I said, Then have I cleansed my heart in vain, and
washed my hands in innocency.

13 All the day long have I been punished : and
chastened every morning.

The enigma is well explained by S. Gregory the Great,
commenting on the very similar language of Job : "How
much such things are to be contemned, the righteous man
considers, which Almighty GOD bestows, even on the froward. For if they were of primary importance, the Creator
would by no means give them to His enemies ; whence the
righteous thinks it unworthy of him to crave after those ad-
vantages which he sees abounding for the evil, but turns his
mind to the acquisition of heavenly things, which cannot be
common to him and to the reprobate." But he who has not
yet learnt this truth argues at first as the Psalmist, complaining that he not only suffers passively by missing the
wealth which others win, but actively, by enduring direct
persecution. It was the argument applied again and again
to the confessors in Pagan days, never with such fatal effect
as in the persecution of Decius. *Cleansed my heart*, by

S. Greg.
Mag. Mor.
xiii. 14.
Job xxi. 7.

Ay.

G.
R.
L.
Beda.
B.

S. Ambrose.
Hugo Card.

S. Greg.
Mag. Mor.
iv. 6.

Ay.

2 Macc. vi.
13.

2 Cor. xii. 7.

Ps. lxxviii.
31.

keeping it free from evil thoughts, or by confessing my sins. The Vulgate reading is *justified my heart*, whence Lorinus takes occasion to point out men's co-operation with GOD in the work of their own salvation. *Washed my hands.* As the *heart* refers to thoughts, so the *hands* imply actions, which need to be kept pure also. They note, however, that the words lay no claim to perfect sinlessness. They represent the steady desire, not the complete innocence of the Psalmist, observes S. Ambrose. And another points out that they denote no more than freedom from grosser sins. Lesser sins of desire or act, resembling the soiling of the feet, are not denied. *All the day long.* In this world, because the righteous is shaken by adversity throughout all his life, or at least a great part of it. *Every morning.* The punishment has come early and swiftly. For when the elect fall into sin, GOD delays not their chastisement, but in His great mercy inflicts it soon. And so it is written: "It is a token of His great goodness, when wicked doers are not suffered any long time, but forthwith punished." And observe, that chastisement sometimes precedes sin, because GOD sometimes sends scourges, that sin may be shunned. So the Apostle said: "Lest I should be exalted above measure through the abundance of the revelations, there was given me a thorn in the flesh." Sometimes it accompanies sin: "While the meat was yet in their mouths, the heavy wrath of GOD came upon them." Sometimes it follows on the sin, as was the case when the Jewish people was led into captivity.

14 Yea, and I had almost said even as they : but lo, then I should have condemned the generation of thy children.

G.
S. Albertus
Magnus.

Mal. iii. 14.
Ay.

More exactly, with A. V. and Vulgate, *If I say, I will speak thus :* that is, that GOD does not know, that there is not knowledge in the Most High ; and hold with the wicked, that "it is vain to serve GOD : and what profit is it that we have kept His ordinance?" then I slander all the Saints of old, the Patriarchs and Prophets who have passed through tribulation for the love of GOD, by denying the truth of their teaching, the wisdom of their acts.

15 Then thought I to understand this : but it was too hard for me,

16 Until I went into the sanctuary of GOD : then understood I the end of these men.

C.

It is the first step in knowledge, when we begin to think that we know less than we supposed. At first Asaph persuaded himself that GOD took no care of human affairs; now he begins to doubt this hasty conclusion, and applies himself to the task of inquiry,—a most difficult one for the toiler, to learn contempt of riches, to praise the wise providence of GOD. And so is added, *This labour is before me.* Yes, *before me,* standing like a wall in my way; but "with the help of my GOD I shall leap over the wall." And though it be *labour before me,* yet it is no labour in GOD's sight. So, then, as He only opens, and none can shut, shuts, and none can open, that Sanctuary where all that now is dark shall be clearly seen, I add, *Until I go into the sanctuary of God.* That is, as Hugh of S. Cher tells us, until I, Adam's descendant, turn from that unprofitable knowledge of good and evil acquired by sin, to meditate on the Passion of JESUS, to know nothing save Him crucified. In Him are hidden all the treasures of the wisdom and knowledge of GOD, and we may enter into that Sanctuary by being incorporated amongst His members, being quickened and illuminated by His SPIRIT, may enter, in conforming to His sufferings, into His wounded Side, and there learn all we need to know. Well may we cry with the old poet—

A.

Ps. xviii. 29.

G.

Hugo Card.

> O pleasant spot! O place of rest!
> O royal rift! O worthy wound!
> Come harbour me, a weary guest,
> That in the world no ease have found!

Robert
Southwell.

Or, in a sense lower than this, and than this only, we may take it of entrance into the hidden places of Holy Writ by pious contemplation. The Greek Fathers mostly interpret it in the far inferior sense of the return of the Jews to the Holy City from the Captivity, and would teach thereby that it was not in vain that they had at last turned from idolatry. S. Athanasius, however, explains it of the Day of Judgment, when the secrets of all hearts shall be revealed, and every man shall be rewarded according to his works. And some of the later commentators will have it that the Church is intended, whose children learn a wisdom superior to that of this world. However we may take it, the words of the most Scriptural of commentators will profit us. The first step into this sanctuary is lowly confession of sin: "O go your way into His gates with confession." Then we advance further by baptismal purity: "I went on in my innocence." We come up to the sanctuary itself in communion: "I will go unto the Altar of GOD." Then into His very presence by contemplation, even while here: "Come before His Presence with a song." And at last, when the glory is won, we go into the very innermost shrine: "Enter thou into the joy of thy LORD." And again: "They that were ready went in with Him to the marriage." *The end of these men. Their last things,* says a variant of the LXX., as does the Vulgate. And we know what the *last things* are for all men—death, judgment, heaven, hell.

G.

D. C.

S. Basil.

Z.

S. Athanasius.

L.

S. Albertus Magnus.

Ps. c. 3, Vulg.

Ps. xxvi. 11, Vulg.

Ps. xliii. 4.

Ps. c. 1.

S. Matt. xxv. 23. 19.

17 Namely, how thou dost set them in slippery places, and castest them down, and destroyest them.

D. C.
Jer. xxxviii. 22.

Dionysius à Rykel, commenting on the similar language in Jeremiah, "Thy friends have set thee on, and have prevailed against thee: thy feet are sunk in the mire, [slippery places, Vulg.,] and they are turned away back," expounds it thus: "They have led thee on to ruin and tottering. And it may be explained morally of all those who, made ductile by the flattery, promises, or instigation of others, oppose themselves to righteousness, fall and perish, because they plunge into the mire of the vilest iniquity, and set their affections in a slippery place, that is, in shifting and earthly things, not in the supreme and unchangeable good." But the Vulgate reads, *Truly, because of deceits Thou hast set for them,* to which the Complutensian LXX. adds *evils,* to fill up the sense; while S. Augustine repeats the word *deceits.* Because they

Ric. Hampol.

are crafty and deceitful, and thereby harm their neighbours, not only does eternal death await them, but *Thou hast set for them* the gnawings of conscience, to afflict them even in this life. *Thou hast set for them* a speedy end, observes another,

D. C.

a bound which they cannot pass; a death sudden to man's eyes, but coming only when their iniquities are full. *And castest them down, and destroyest them.* The Vulgate reading is, *Thou didst cast them down when they were being lifted up.*

A.
G.

Not because they were lifted up, nor after they were lifted up, but in the very act itself, since such exaltation is itself a fall. They are as a wheel whose revolutions bring one part down just as the other rises; and as their temporal prosperity is lifted up, so their hopes for the world to come sink

D. C.

into the pit of desolation. And that because of their pride, as it is written, "Though thou exalt thyself as the eagle, and though thou set thy nest amongst the stars, thence will

Obad. 4.

I bring thee down, saith the LORD." And so He dealt with Nebuchadnezzar, driving him from the intercourse of men;

Ay.

with Holofernes, slaying him by the hand of a woman; with Antiochus Epiphanes, hurling him from his chariot, to die of a loathsome disease; with Herod, giving him to be food for worms.

18 O how suddenly do they consume: perish, and come to a fearful end!

19 Yea, even like as a dream when one awaketh: so shalt thou make their image to vanish out of the city.

G.

Consume. The LXX. and Vulgate have, *Are made a desolation,* (ἐρήμωσιν.) And the words are spoken in wonder, not as a question. So the Prophet speaks, "How doth the

Lam. i. 1.

city sit solitary, that was full of people!" They are desolate, stripped by death of all that pomp and service which

once awaited them. "Where," cries the Eastern Church in
her Burial Office, "where are the world's affections, where
the vain dreams of passing delights, where gold and silver,
where the crowd and noise of attendants? All are dust, all
ashes, all but a shadow that fleeteth away." *Come to a fearful
end.* Not that which causes fear in others, but rather, as
the A. V. runs, *they are utterly consumed with terrors.* For
"it is a fearful thing to fall into the hands of the living
GOD." And so S. Peter Damiani, in his awful hymn, the
Dies Iræ of individual life, cries out—

C.

S. Johan.
Damasc.
Eucholog.

Ric. Ceno-
man.

Heb. x. 31.

> O what terror in thy forethought,
> Ending scene of mortal life!
> Heart is sickened, reins are loosened,
> Thrills each nerve with terror rife,
> When the anxious heart depicteth
> All the anguish of the strife!

The Hymn
*Gravi me
terrore
pulsas.*

The LXX. and Vulgate, less strikingly, read, *They have perished, by reason of their iniquity.* And yet even these few
words are so terrible, that we may well leave them, as S. Augustine does, to be their own comment. "Except ye repent,
ye shall all likewise perish." *Like as a dream when one
awaketh.* That is, as they diversely take it, either the wicked
themselves shall vanish as completely as a dream, or all
their prosperity shall disappear, as do the night visions of a
beggar who fancies himself a king. And note, that there is
another arousing from sleep, far unlike to this, of which it is
said, "When I awake up after Thy likeness, I shall be satisfied with it." *So shalt Thou make their image to vanish out
of the city.* They who brought to nothing the image of
GOD in their earthly city, shall have their image brought to
nothing in His city. And it is true whether we take it of
them who slew Him, Who is the Image of GOD, once in
Sion, or of those evil Christians who, in the spiritual Sion,
"crucify to themselves the SON of GOD afresh, and put Him
to an open shame." They take this *image* of theirs to be
temporal glory, which, as well as earthly enjoyment of all
kinds, cannot pass beyond this world. Then they who have
degraded their human nature, and turned GOD's image into
that of a lion, by yielding to anger; into that of a swine, by
coarse indulgence; into that of an ass, by sloth and obstinacy; shall vanish out of the City; for it is written, "There
shall in no wise enter into it anything that defileth, neither
whatsoever worketh abomination, or maketh a lie; but they
which are written in the Lamb's Book of Life." And for
these happy ones the words hold good likewise, though in a
blessed sense; for, leaving their old sins, and walking in
newness of life, they shall become conformed to the Image of
GOD, because, being made like unto CHRIST, they are the
adopted children of the FATHER. "For whom He did fore-
know, He also did predestinate to be conformed to the image

S. Luke
xiii. 3.

Ay.

Ps. xvii. 16.

A.

Heb. vi. 6.

G.

Rev. xxi. 27.

Rom. viii.
29.

of His Son, that He might be the first-born among many
brethren." And as metal, melted in the fire, loses its former
shape, and is interpenetrated with the fire itself, so we, delivered from our pilgrimage here, and brought to Jerusalem
G. which is free, shall be filled with the heat and glow of that
Divine Love, which is a consuming fire, burning up all our
rust and dross, and leaving only pure gold, perfected by the
Son, Who is the fire, splendour, and glory of the FATHER,
with Whom He is Consubstantial. And therefore he who
loved Him best says, "Now are we the sons of GOD, and it
1 S. John iii. doth not yet appear what we shall be; but we know that,
2. when He shall appear, we shall be like Him; for we shall
see Him as He is."

Hildeb. Ven.
The Hymn,
*Extra por-
tam.*

> Non est ibi corruptela,
> Non defectus, non querela;
> Non minuti, non deformes,
> Omnes CHRISTO sunt conformes.

The Bible Version, however, with most modern critics, instead of *out of the city*, translates *when Thou awakest*, (sc. to
judgment,) reading בְהָעִיר instead of בָּעִיר.

20 Thus my heart was grieved : and it went even through my reins.

The LXX. and Vulgate differ here from the English Version, and from one another. The former usually reads, *My
heart was delighted*, which also appears in the Roman Psalter,
and is adopted by SS. Ambrose and Augustine. The common
Vulgate rendering, and that of some Greek texts, however, is
was inflamed, and they agree in rendering the last clause, *My
reins were changed*. When I *delighted* in GOD, explains the
Doctor of Grace, my lusts were changed, and I became
A. wholly chaste. Those who read *inflamed*, take it in various
S. Ambrose. ways. With spiritual joy, says one. With the love of GOD,
Arnobius. others maintain. With heavenly wisdom, observes S. Bruno.
Ay. With holy zeal for righteousness, as his spiritual descendant
B. and others take it. However we may explain the words, the
G. cry of S. Augustine will suit all. " What fire is this that so
warmeth my heart? What light is this that so enlighteneth
D. C. my soul? O Fire, that always burnest, and never goest out,
S. August. kindle me! O Light, which ever shinest and art never dark-
Solil. 34. ened, illumine me! O that I had my heat from thee, most
holy Fire! How sweetly dost thou burn! how secretly dost
thou shine! how desirably dost thou inflame me!" And as
the disciple can only follow afar off in the Master's steps,
S. Jerome wisely tells us to find here the longing of
Beda. CHRIST to do His FATHER's will. There are not wanting
S. Albertus some who tell us to take the words of the ungodly, rather
Magnus. than of Saints, and to understand the *inflaming* of envy and
Hugo Card.

jealousy through a desire of worldly prosperity, and then the *reins are changed* from steadfastness to vacillation.

21 So foolish was I, and ignorant : even as it were a beast before thee.

The Vulgate reads, in the first clause, *And I was brought*   G.
to nothing, and knew not. Brought to nothing, so long as I 1 Cor. xiii.
was envious; because, while I have not charity, which en- 3, 4.
vieth not, I am nothing : *ignorant*, because I knew not my
sin. *Brought to nothing*, as being tried by adversity, to
bring me to the love of GOD, till *I knew not ;* till I confessed
my ignorance, and counted myself as nought. *Brought to*   Ay.
nothing, by having the old man wholly stripped off, that I
might no longer glory in earthly things, and be *ignorant* of Ric. Hamp.
my wants and guiltiness. *As a beast before Thee.* The quasi
Jerome, continuing to explain the whole passage of CHRIST, Pseudo-
Who made Himself nothing for us, and submitted, though Hieron.
the Eternal Wisdom, to take on Him human imperfection,
reminds us that He bore the load of our sins, as though He   Lu.
were a beast of burden. And there are some who take the   Ay.
words accordingly in a good sense, of all who are ready to
bear whatever GOD lays on them, obediently and without S. Greg.
                                                                                Mag. Mor.
complaint, moving in the harness of His precepts, and ad- x. 15.
vancing steadily on the road at His signal. Others, however,   C.
interpret them of the sinner continuing in his animal desires, Hesychius.
and letting evil passions ride upon him at their pleasure, so S. Albertus
that he is counted in GOD's sight "like to horse and mule, Magnus.
                                                                                Ps. xxxii.
which have no understanding."   10.

22 Nevertheless, I am alway by thee : for thou
hast holden me by my right hand.

If we continue, with the quasi Jerome, to take the words of Pseudo-
our dear LORD, we shall understand them of His continued Hieron.
Presence in heaven in the midst of His pilgrimage on earth,
His throne at the Right Hand of the FATHER, even while He
was hanging on the Cross of Calvary ; of His being upheld
in His descent into hell, His Resurrection, and Ascension.
Cassiodorus takes it of the human nature of CHRIST, sup-   C.
ported and uplifted by His Godhead. S. Athanasius sees S. Athana-
here the doctrine of His Consubstantial nature ; and Arno- sius.
bius, still taking it of CHRIST, tells us how He took dead Arnobius.
mankind by the right hand, as He did Jairus' daughter, and
lifted it up to glory. Gerhohus, most singularly, explains it
that the *right hand* is CHRIST's Godhead, the *left hand* His   G.
Manhood, and that the FATHER *held the right hand* bound
by the duty of filial obedience, that it might not put forth its
power to defend the left in all its bitter troubles. The Car-   Ay.
melite, adopting the common mystical explanation of the
right hand, explains the passage of GOD's delaying the re-

ward of good works, prosperity, in this life; so that, instead of bidding His Saints stretch forth their right hands to receive the prize, He holds back these hands for the present, and leads us by them instead of filling them. Wherefore it follows :

23 Thou shalt guide me with thy counsel : and after that receive me with glory.

As the Angel of GOD's Presence was sent before Israel, to keep it in the way, and to bring it into the place which He had prepared, so now the Spirit of Counsel, dwelling in the Church, leads the pilgrims of JESUS on to the Land of Promise.

(margin: Exod. xxiii. 20.)

(margin: Hild. Ven. Carm. de Spir. Sanct.)

Consolator piorum, inspirator bonorum, consiliator mœstorum,
Purificator errorum, eruditor ignotorum, declarator perplexorum,
Debilem erigens, devium colligens, errantem corrigens,
Sustines labantem, promoves conantem, perficis amantem ;
Perfectum educis de lacu fæcis et miseriæ,
Deducis per semitam pacis et lætitiæ,
Inducis sub nube in aulam sapientiæ.

*   *   *   *   *   *   *

Dirigens rectum, formans affectum, firmans provectum,
Et ad portas Paradisi coronans dilectum.

(margin: G.)

The Vulgate reading is, *Thou hast led me in Thy will.* Me, Who am ever with Thee, Consubstantial, Co-eternal, Thou *hast led* down from heaven into the Virgin's womb, from the womb into the world, from the world into hell, from hell back into the world, and from the world *hast received Me with glory* into heaven, there to reign with Thee henceforth in My glorified Manhood, as I reigned with Thee from all eternity in the everlasting glory of My Godhead. It is true of the servants too, as well as of the Master. "What is *in Thy will?* Not in my merits. Hear the Apostle, who was at first a beast longing for earthly things, and living according to the Old Testament : 'I was before a blasphemer, and a persecutor, and injurious; but I obtained mercy.' What means, *in Thy will?* 'By the grace of GOD, I am what I am.' *And hast received Me with glory.* To what glory He was received, and in what glory, what man can explain, or who can say? Let us wait for it, since it will appear in the Resurrection." "Thanks be to Thee, O LORD," exclaims Gerhohus, "Who, bridling me with curb and rein, hast made me, from being a dull and untamed beast, so docile; that I am ever *before Thee;* since *Thou hast held my right hand,* even my good works, which belong to the right, as evil ones do to the sinister hand. Thou heldest me by my right hand, lest I should sink altogether, as I began to do when walking to Thee upon the sea, where my footing would have been perilous, hadst Thou not held my right hand, and led me to

(margin: A.)

(margin: 1 Tim. i. 13.)

(margin: 1 Cor. xv. 10.)

(margin: G.)

a haven of safety, and from the haven to that firm shore, where peril is never henceforth to be feared. This I foretell by the Spirit of truth. *Thou shalt guide me with Thy counsel, and after that receive me with glory.* The counsel of GOD is a desirable bower for those fleeing from this vast and open sea. Virginity, voluntary poverty, and holy obedience in all things and through all things, which our fathers practised, and other like rules of the higher life, are the haven for those who fly from the billowy storms of the world, and early reach the shore of eternal steadfastness, where is glory everlasting." And note, observes the Carmelite, that GOD receives the righteous in more ways than one. He receives them, preserving their innocence by His grace: "As for me, Thou upholdest [hast received, Vulg.] me in mine integrity, and settest me before Thy face for ever." He receives penitents by restorative grace: "Return again unto Me, saith the LORD, [and I will receive thee," Vulg.] He receives to crowning glory those who bear tribulation; as it is written, "LORD JESUS, receive my spirit."

Ay.

Ps. xli. 12, A.V.

Acts vii. 59.

24 Whom have I in heaven but thee : and there is none upon earth that I desire in comparison of thee.

"In having nothing," says a Saint of old, "I have all things, because I have CHRIST. Having, therefore, all things in Him, I seek no other prize, for He is the universal prize Himself." So, too, our own poet, treading in the steps of S. Augustine:

S. Chrysost. Hom. v. in Rom.

Serm. in S. Joan. xix.

> CHRIST is a path, if any be misled ;
> He is a robe, if any naked be ;
> If any chance to hunger, He is Bread ;
> If any be a bondman, He is free ;
> If any be but weak, how strong is He !
> To dead men life He is, to sick men, health ;
> To blind men, sight ; and to the needy, wealth ;
> A pleasure without loss ; a treasure without stealth.

Giles Fletcher, CHRIST'S *Victory.*

None else *in heaven;* for "He that descended is the same also that ascended up far above all heavens, that He might fill all things." None *upon earth* to be desired in comparison ; for He is "fairer than the children of men," "the chiefest among ten thousand." Well then does S. Anselm exclaim, "O how good and sweet art Thou, LORD JESU, to the soul which seeks Thee! JESU, Redeemer of the captives, SAVIOUR of the lost, Hope of the exiles, Strength of the toiling, Ease of the unquiet spirit, sweet Consolation and pleasant Coolness of the tearful soul running after Thee in sweat, Crown of the victors, sole Reward and Gladness of the heavenly citizens, most abundant Fountain of all grace, glorious offspring of GOD most High, Thyself most High GOD, let

Eph. iv. 10.

Ps. xlv. 3.

Cant. v. 10.

S. Anselm, Medit. ix.

all things which are in heaven above, and in the earth beneath, bless Thee; for Thou art great, and holy is Thy Name."

Far lower than this, the true meaning of the Hebrew, is the Vulgate: *What have I in heaven, or what have I desired of Thee on earth?* And they take it, for the most part, of the contrast between the glory which awaits the victor, and the poor earthly things which are all the sinner has yet asked GOD to grant. *What?* That is, how great, how priceless is that reward prepared for me *in heaven*, if I love GOD, for He will give Himself to them that love. Him. This, O GOD, Thou hast prepared for them that love Thee, and I, in my folly, have desired somewhat else instead of Thee. A miserable barter! mire for gold, earth for heaven, a short-lived creature for the Creator Himself! *What have I in heaven?* That great *What* cannot be set down in words: it may be gained, it cannot be priced.

G.

25 My flesh and my heart faileth : but GOD is the strength of my heart, and my portion for ever.

G.

My flesh faileth, because chastened with penance, to weaken it from doing evil. *My heart faileth* to pursue its former vain and idle thoughts. Others, remembering that it is written, "Eye hath not seen, nor ear heard, neither have entered into the heart of man, the things which GOD hath prepared for them that love Him," interpret the words of the overpowering might of the thought of heavenly glory. So the Cluniac :

Ay.
1 Cor. ii. 9.

Bernard.
Cluniacen.
Rhythmus.

Urbs Sion aurea, Patria lactea, cive decora,
Omne cor obruis, omnibus obstruis et cor et ora.
Nescio, nescio, quæ jubilatio, lux tibi qualis,
Quam socialia gaudia, gloria quam specialis.
Laude studens ea tollere, mens mea victa fatiscit,
O bona gloria, vincor; in omnia laus tua vicit.

But God is the strength of my heart, and my portion for ever. "Thee, not Thine," as two great Saints have said. The Carmelite here gives a quaint illustration, borrowed from the sport of falconry, at its height in his day. We see, he observes, when a bird of race takes flight from its master's hand, and seizes the enemy, it expects to get the heart as its prey. So CHRIST, that noble Bird, Who flew from the FATHER's hand into the Virgin's womb, to the world, to the Cross, and who seized mankind as His prey out of hell, demands man's heart as His share. Wherefore the Psalm taketh thought for this, and saith, "Pour out your hearts before Him." And He speaks Himself to each of us: "My son, give Me thine heart." "Thou art the GOD of my heart," cries S. Albert, heaping up all loving epithets, "Who art Salvation, Praise, Glory, Brightness, Prince, Light, Joy,

Ps. lxii. 8.

Prov. xxiii. 26.

S. Albertus agnus.

Prize, Bridegroom, Rejoicing, Truth, Love, Sweetness, Reward, and Life." If He is to have our hearts, we too ask to be close to His. So the Bride: "Set me as a seal upon Thine heart;" and we, like her, may say,

Cant. viii. 6.
L.

> Cor meum tibi dedo, JESU dulcissime!
> En cor pro corde cedo, JESU suavissime!
> Tu sola corda expetis,
> Tu sola corda diligis,
> Ah amem te, ut amas me,
> JESU suavissime!

S. Augustine aptly points out that whereas both flesh and heart are said in one clause of the verse to fail, yet in the second member GOD is said to be the GOD of our heart alone, and that because the heart, when purified, cleanses all the body. And if my heart be like His, seeing that GOD holds all His blessedness without need of heaven or earth, so I can enjoy mine without any earthly thing, or heavenly thing. He, because He eternally holds His felicity entirely in Himself; I, because I shall eternally hold all mine in Him, for *God is my portion for ever.* De Civ. Dei, x. 25.
Vieyra, Serm. on David's Sling.

26 For lo, they that forsake thee shall perish : thou hast destroyed all them that commit fornication against thee.

Observe, with Hugh of S. Cher, it is not said "those whom GOD forsakes," but they that forsake Him. S. Chrysostom compares sinners who rebel against GOD's chastisements to froward children who run away from the school where their parents have placed them, to avoid tasks or stripes, and who thus expose themselves to worse perils amongst strangers—hunger, sickness, and hard service. It is sin that puts us away, as it is written, "Your iniquities have separated between you and your GOD;" and again, "The LORD is far from the wicked." Not because of His will, but of theirs ; for "they say unto GOD, Depart from us; for we desire not the knowledge of Thy ways." The Vulgate is, *They that put themselves far from Thee,* as did the Prodigal by going from his father into a far country. "What is further," asks S. Ambrose, "than to depart from oneself; to be separated by habits, not by countries ; to be divided by desires, not by lands ; and to have a divorce between one's actions, as though the tide of worldly luxury flowed between? He who divides himself from CHRIST is an exile from his country, a citizen of the world." The same Saint takes the words before us as spoken of those who shun partaking of the Holy Eucharist. "Of this Bread it is written, *All they who go far from Thee shall perish.* If thou goest from It, thou shalt perish; if thou drawest near to It, thou shalt live. This is the Bread of Life. He that eateth Life, cannot die." *Fornication.* It L.
Hugo Card.
S. Albertus Magnus.
Isa. lix. 2.
Prov. xv. 29.
Job xxi. 14.
Theophylact.
Expos. in S. Luc. xv. 13.
Comm. in Ps. cxix.

II.   U

is idolatry, say most of the commentators, citing the many texts of Scripture which bear out this sense. The Carthusian, following S. Thomas Aquinas, takes it in a wider sense. There is, he says, a spiritual fornication, whereby a soul, marked with the image of the Most High Trinity, and which ought to be the daughter of GOD and the spouse of CHRIST, becomes unfaithful to her GOD, leaning on, delighting in, and enjoying creatures rather than the Creator.

27 But it is good for me to hold me fast by GOD, to put my trust in the LORD GOD : and to speak of all thy works in the gates of the daughter of Sion.

To hold me fast. We cannot *hold fast* to Him directly, but we may be joined to Him by some means. There are three bonds by which, and by which alone, all things are fastened to one another, and by which we may be united to Him. They are cords, nails of wood or metal, and glue. The first binds strongly and hardly, the second more strongly and hardly, the third gently and firmly. A man is bound with a cord to his SAVIOUR, if, when sorely tried by temptation, he sets before him the insight into what is honourable, and the memory of the promise; and he for the time holds himself by this cord, lest his resolution should be utterly broken. But hard and unpleasant as that bond is, it is precarious, and cannot last long. For the cords decay, and we forget, or break, the bond of shame. Another is fastened by the nails of the LORD's majesty, as the fear of GOD binds him who fears not the looks of men, but the thought of hell torments; and it is not sin, but desire, which he fears. Yet he is more sternly and strongly impressed than the former, seeing that he does not lose his resolution, whereas the other wavers in it. A third is cemented with glue, that is, with love, who, holding fast to GOD, as bound sweetly and surely to Him, is one spirit with Him. That last union, however, cannot be perfected here, and therefore the truest *holding fast* to GOD will be seeing Him face to face. That we may do so, it is good for us to put our trust in Him.

"For Thou, O LORD," exclaims one of His great Saints, "art my hope, whatever I have to refuse, whatever to endure, whatever to desire. Thou, O LORD, art my hope; this is for me the one cause of the promises, the whole reason of my expectation. Let another set forth his merit, let him boast of his abstinence, his bearing the burden and heat of the day; let him say that he fasts twice in the week; let him glory that he is not as other men are. *But it is good for me to hold me fast by God, to put my trust in the Lord God.*" There follows then : *And to speak of all Thy works in the gates of the daughter of Sion.* The reading of the old Latin Psalters and of S. Augustine is *Thy praises,* that of the Vulgate *Thy preachings.* All point to the same Gospel which

preaches CHRIST and His works, and shows forth His praise.
The last clause, *in the gates, &c.*, is not in the Hebrew, and
seems to have been interpolated from Psalm ix. 14. They
agree in explaining it, as does S. Augustine, that GOD, to be **A.**
praised rightly, must be praised in the unity of the Church
militant here in earth, the Sion of expectation and watching, **G.**
whence we pass to Jerusalem, which is free. And the *gates,* Ric. Hamp.
notes our English hermit-saint, are faith, hope, and charity.
The *daughter* only as yet, soon the City which is above, the
Mother of us all.

Wherefore:

Glory be to the FATHER, the GOD of Israel, Who is loving
unto such as are of a clean heart; glory be to GOD the SON,
Whose right hand the FATHER hath holden, Whom He hath
guided in His will, and received with glory; glory be to the
HOLY GHOST, Who is that Will of the FATHER, whereby He
led His SON, willingly obedient in His Manhood, for the salvation of mankind.

As it was in the beginning, is now, and ever shall be:
world without end. Amen.

COLLECTS.

O LORD, make us ever hold fast by Thee, and fix in Thee Ludolph.
all the might of our hope, that we may tell of Thy praises in
the everlasting gates. Through. (1.)

O LORD, it is good to hold fast by Thee; it is hurtful to Mozarabic.
withdraw from Thee; to be far from Thee is destruction; to
be joined to Thee fulness of life. Grant, therefore, that we
who put our trust in Thee, may attain the perfect blessedness of life, and sing Thy praises in the gates of the daughter
of Sion, as we are passing into Thy kingdom. Amen.
Through. (11.)

It is good for us, O LORD, to hold fast by Thee; but do Mozarabic.
Thou so heap up the desire of good in us, that the hope
which joins us unto Thee may not waver through any stumbling of faith, but abide in the firmness of love. Amen.
Through. (11.)

O LORD GOD of Israel, we beseech Thee, we intreat Thee, Mozarabic.
that Thou wouldst not refuse us sinners, because of our con- For the
versation, Thy goodness, which Thou bestowest freely on lapsed.
them that are true of heart, that Thou mayest make them
who are their own slaves rebel by that same grace whereby
Thou rulest the lowly; and that the same goodness, wherewith Thou ever crownest the righteous, may continually in-
terpose for us; that Thou mayest spare us sinners, that, rejoicing in the goodness wherein the Saints are glad, they
may delight in being restored by it to Thee from their wanderings; and that sincere confession may make them to hold
fast by Thee, whom worldly lures have drawn from Thee
through the contagion of divers things, and that with humble

devotion of soul they may pay their vows unto Thee, crying together in Thy praise. Amen. Through. (11.)

Mozarabic. For the Jews. O LORD, the sinners spake against Thee in the high place, when with loud voices they uttered the hidden pride of their hearts. Let them, then, who are fain to stretch forth their mouth unto the heaven against Thee, return to earth, to be dashed down by repentance, that, humbly acknowledging with us that Thou art the SON of GOD, they may not be high-minded, but ever submit to Thy precepts. Amen. Through. (11.)

D. C. O GOD of our heart, GOD our portion for ever, let not our heart and flesh fail. With Thee to strengthen us in good works, make us ever hold fast by Thee, and put our trust in Thee, our LORD GOD, till, with Thee going as our Leader before us, we enter into Thy heavenly sanctuary, Who, Trine and One GOD, livest and reignest for ever and ever. Amen.

S. Jerome. CHRIST the LORD, not looking unto our merits, but granting freely His pardon, bring us into the fellowship of His elect. Amen.

PSALM LXXIV.

TITLE: Maschil of Asaph. LXX. and Vulgate: Of understanding, for Asaph.

ARGUMENT.

ARG. THOMAS. That CHRIST created all the elements which we see. The Voice of CHRIST touching the Jews. The Voice of CHRIST, or of the Church, to the FATHER. Of teaching, and of Judgment.

VEN. BEDE. *Understanding* is prefixed in the title for this reason: because a two-fold captivity follows, one spiritual, the other carnal; one which led into Babylon when the Temple was destroyed, the other which subdued by faith, when the confusion of errors was overthrown. Jerome believes this Psalm to have been sung against the Chaldees; Cassiodorus, against the Romans; Arnobius against the Philistines, when, after the slaughter of Hophni and Phinehas, the Ark of GOD was taken. The Synagogue speaks throughout the Psalm. In the first place, it laments the reason why they were delivered to the Gentiles, so that the boldness of her foes profaned the LORD's Sanctuary, stating that the impenitent heart of certain Jews had provoked GOD's chastisement; yet it prophesies that some of them shall be converted at the end of the world. *O God, wherefore hast Thou cast us off unto the end?* In the second part it says that the superstitions and iniquities of men were destroyed by the coming of CHRIST, counting up the divers great works He hath done, amongst which it beseeches Him to help the erring Jews. *For God is my King of old.* Thirdly; it asks, that mindful of His promise, He may deliver the seed of Abraham from destruction, and that the pride of the enemies, who extol themselves vainly, may go up before Him. *Deliver not the soul that confesseth Thee to the beasts.*

SYRIAC PSALTER. Of Asaph, when David saw the Angel destroying the people, and wept, and said, Upon me and mine offspring,

and not on these guiltless sheep. Moreover, a prophecy of the
siege of the city Jerusalem forty years after the Ascension, by Vespasian the aged, and Titus his son, who slew tens of thousands of
Jews, and destroyed Jerusalem; thence, unto the present day, Jews
are despised.

EUSEBIUS OF CÆSAREA. A Proclamation of the final siege of
Jerusalem under Vespasian and Titus.

S. ATHANASIUS. A Psalm in solitary address. A Psalm of
thanksgiving.

VARIOUS USES.

Gregorian. Thursday. Matins. [Maundy Thursday. II. Nocturn.]

Parisian. Saturday. Nones.

Ambrosian. Tuesday of Second Week. I. Nocturn.

Monastic. Thursday. I. Nocturn. [Maundy Thursday. II.
Nocturn.]

Quignon. Friday. Nones.

Lyons. Monday. Nones.

ANTIPHONS.

Gregorian. As preceding Psalm. [Maundy Thursday. Arise,
O LORD, and judge my cause.]

Parisian. The poor * and needy shall give praise unto Thy
Name, O LORD.

Ambrosian. As Psalm lxxii.

Monastic. As Gregorian. [Maundy Thursday. As Gregorian.]

Mozarabic. Remember Thy congregation, O LORD * which
Thou hast created from the beginning.

There has been much discussion, ever since the time of Theodoret,
as to the date and occasion of this Psalm. The views are practically
four: (1) that it refers to some of the earlier spoilings of Jerusalem
by Egyptians or Chaldeans, in the time of Rehoboam or of Ahaz;
(2) that it speaks of the destruction of the first Temple by Nebuchadnezzar; (3) that it is Maccabean, and refers to the cruelties of
Antiochus Epiphanes,—a view adopted by most modern critics; or
(4) that it is simply prophetic of the final overthrow under the
Romans. The last view is universally given up now. The objection to the second is, that the Psalm does not speak of the utter
destruction of the Temple (as Psalm lxxix. does) but only of its
spoiling and profanation. The third opinion is difficult to reconcile
either with the history of the Canon, or with the language in verse
10, which implies a recent cessation of prophecy. But the order of
Prophets had died out two centuries before the date of Antiochus
Epiphanes, and we may therefore most probably adopt the second
conjecture. The name of Asaph does not help to fix the date, as it
appears certain that it was attached to Psalms of his descendants
and successors in the office of choirmaster.

1 O GOD, wherefore art thou absent from us so
long : why is thy wrath so hot against the sheep of
thy pasture ?

It is no murmuring or rebellion that prompts this question,
nothing but a deep sense of desolation, and of inability to

C.
G.
fathom God's hidden purpose. *Absent from us.* It is far more. That would be painful enough, but the A. V. more truly reads, *Wherefore hast Thou cast us off?* and the Vulgate, *Ut quid repulisti nos,* is nearly the same. Yet the

Rom. xi. 2.
Apostle tells us that "God hath not cast away His people which He foreknew." It is in truth we who have gone from Him, for as the soul never quits the body till the body fails

Ay.
it, so God never leaves those who are willing to abide by Him. *So long.* Not for a brief time of trial and chastisement, as in

G.
former days, followed by the advent of a deliverer, Gideon, Samson, Samuel, David, but utterly, or, with the Vulgate, *to*

Ay.
the end, sparing neither age, nor sex, nor holy place, and de-

P.
laying help till the end of the world. Whether we take it in its first sense, of the Jewish people, harassed by Assyrian or

D. C.
Roman foes, or of the Christian Church, beset by heretics, schismatics, unbelievers, and false brethren; or again, of each soul which thinks itself bereft of God's help, we may

A.
find the answer in the question. *To-the end.* He drives us

Rom. x. 4.
to Him Who is the "end of the law for righteousness to them which believe," even to His Son Jesus.Christ. O blessed casting off, which leads us to take refuge in those everlasting

B.
arms of infinite mercy! *The sheep of Thy pasture.* It is spoken of the Jews, whom He led as sheep by the hands of Moses and Aaron in the pastures of the Law, but far more deeply and truly of them who follow the Good Shepherd,

Ric. Ham-
pol.
and are nourished with His pasture, His own precious Body and Blood.

2 O think upon thy congregation : whom thou hast purchased, and redeemed of old.

3 Think upon the tribe of thine inheritance : and mount Sion, wherein thou hast dwelt.

Ay.
Thy congregation, or, with the LXX. *Thy synagogue,* not merely as the specific name of the Jewish Church, but as showing how God began the work of deliverance, by gathering together in Rameses the people previously scattered throughout the land of Egypt. *Whom Thou hast purchased.* Or, with LXX. and Vulgate, *possessed.* He Who is Lord of all, is more especially said to *possess* those who have freely bound themselves to obey Him. The word *redeemed,* which follows here in the Prayer Book version, properly belongs to the first clause of the next verse. *Of old.* Or, as the Vulgate, *from the beginning.* It cannot be the voice of the

A.
Gentiles, notes S. Augustine, but must refer to the seed of Abraham, the people of Israel, born of the Patriarchs, whose

G.
seed we are, in faith though not in flesh. The great German commentator goes further back, and reminds us of the distinction put ages before Abraham's day between the descendants of Cain and the righteous progeny of Seth. *O think*

upon the tribe of Thine inheritance. Here we should read, with the Vulgate, *Remember the rod of Thine inheritance, which Thou hast redeemed.* S. Augustine reminds us of that rod of Moses, wherewith the miracles of the Exodus were wrought. It thus comes to typify the Jewish people, whom GOD used as His rod to scourge the seven nations of Canaan. And they add, aptly enough, that so long as that rod was in the hand of Moses, so long as the Hebrew people obeyed the Law·and the Prophets, the rod was straight, and waited for the promise of CHRIST. But when it left the hand of Moses, it became a serpent, from which Moses himself fled. And then, in a deeper and lovelier sense, the *rod* of GOD's *inherit-ance* is "the Man Whose Name is the Branch," the "Rod out of the stem of Jesse," Whom also "He hath appointed heir of all things." He is the rod of Moses, because He is the sceptre of Israel, and yet more, because He is the brazen serpent lifted up in the wilderness, that those bitten by the fiery serpents might look on Him and live.

marginal notes: A. Jer. x. 16. G· Zech. vi. 12. Isa. xi. 1. Heb. i. 2. Gen. xlix. 10. Numb. xxiv. 17. G.

> Porque
> Para sanar las dolencias
> Del que mordido del aspid,
> Al pecador se semeja,
> No siendo èl el pecador,
> Convendrà que lo paresca.

marginal note: Calderon, *La Serpiente de Metal.*

And even as Moses fled from his rod, when it took the ser-pent form, so when the "beautiful Rod" was lifted up to draw all men unto Him, His disciples forsook Him and fled. Again; because the words denote the Head, they include the mem-bers, and tell of that Church which GOD chose to be His in-heritance, the rod which has budded and brought forth leaves, flowers, and fruit, while those of the twelve tribes remain barren. And with this sense the dearest meaning of the words which follow agrees : *Which Thou hast redeemed* with Thy most precious Blood. Redeemed from the spiritual Egypt, from worldly conversation, from sin and darkness, from many an error, from all its sins, and from the pains of hell. He has not redeemed it as one may buy the possession of some place or thing he has never seen, for there follows : *And Mount Sion, wherein Thou hast dwelt.* The primary meaning is of that Temple where the uncreated WORD dwelt in the Shechinah between the Cherubim, and next of that whole city where He, when Incarnate, went in and out before all the people, and then more fully of that Church Militant of " expectation," wherein He condescends to tabernacle sa-cramentally. There He is indeed lifted on the tree of life in the midst of the garden, that rood to which we look for all our help. There too, as He gives His inner grace to each hungering and fainting soul, He is the Rod dipped in honey wherewith Jonathan, when he put it to his mouth, found his eyes enlightened.

marginal notes: Jer. xlviii. 17. D. C. Ay. 1 Sam. xiv. 27.

4 Lift up thy feet, that thou mayest utterly destroy every enemy : which hath done evil in thy sanctuary.

Taking the words in this wise, we shall see Him invoked Who hath said of Himself: "I have trodden the wine-press alone ; and of the people there was none with Me : for I will tread them in Mine anger, and trample them in My fury," and will remember how He sent His chastisements on all those nations whom He permitted to scourge Jerusalem for her sins, and last and most terribly on the Jews themselves, who *did evil in His sanctuary*, when the chief priests and Pharisees gathered a council against Him. But the A. V. gives the true sense : *Lift up Thy feet unto the perpetual desolations*, that is, Come down, and behold the utter destruction which the enemy hath wrought in Thy holy place. Not so the LXX., Vulgate, and the Æthiopic. They read, *Lift up Thine hands upon their insolences unto the end.* That is, Put forth Thy might to punish. *Their insolences*, as well those of the heathen who have wasted Thy holy places, as of the people of Israel, whose sins have deserved such judgments. So say they all, most strangely passing over the deeper meaning of the words, which tell us how He did deal with the pride of His enemies, nailing it to His Cross, when He stretched out His hands thereupon all the day unto a disobedient and gainsaying people. Yes, and *unto the end*, for He said, "It is finished." The Syriac Psalter reads in this place, *Lift up Thy servants above them who are raised over us in might*, foreshadowing the conquest of the Empire by the Cross. And this is the meaning which S. Augustine, though following a reading scarcely differing from the Vulgate, attaches to the passage. "Whose pride?" he asks; "Theirs by whom Jerusalem was overthrown, the Kings of the Gentiles. Well was His hand lifted up on their pride at the end, for they too have now known CHRIST. Now on the brows of monarchs the sign of the Cross is more precious than the jewels of a crown." *What mischief the enemy hath wrought in Thy holy place.* They take it variously of the successive profanations of the Temple, by Nebuchadnezzar, Antiochus, and Titus, and thence transfer the reference to the Christian Church, vexed first by heathen persecutors and then by Arian and other heretics. Lastly ; it is explained tropologically of every friend of this world, who is therefore GOD's enemy, defiling with sin the heart which He had made His sanctuary by the waters of Baptism.

Isa. lxiii. 3.

Ay.

Rom. x. 21.

S. John xix. 30.

A.

P.
L.
D. C.

Ric. Hampol.

5 Thine adversaries roar in the midst of thy congregations : and set up their banners for tokens.

This is the true rendering of this difficult verse, and R. Kimchi aptly compares its first clause with the words of Je-

De Muis.

remiah : "The LORD hath cast off His altar, He hath abhorred Lam. ii. 7.
His sanctuary, He hath given up into the hand of the enemy
the walls of her palaces; they have made a noise in the house
of the LORD, as in the day of a solemn feast." And the obvious meaning is to contrast the tumult of a profane soldiery,
heard in the sacred shrine, with the voice of priestly chant
and supplication, which alone befits it. Again and again it
has been true of times of suffering in the Church, when Roman
soldiers rushed in on the worshippers in the catacombs, when
Syrianus invaded the church of S. Theonas at Alexandria, Theodoret.
to seize S. Athanasius; worst of all, at that terrible Whitsuntide of 1453, when the armies of the false prophet burst
into S. Sophia. But the LXX. and Vulgate, with the Syriac
and Æthiopic, read, *They which hate Thee have boasted in the
midst of Thy festival.* They remind us that it was in the
midst of the Passover that Jerusalem was compassed with A.
the armies of Titus, a fit punishment for the city which at
that same time had crucified its King. S. Albert the Great S. Albertus
applies the words to careless and indevout clerics, who, when Magnus.
the restraint of Lent is over, jest and revel in the midst of
the Paschal Festival, betwixt Mass and Vespers. They have
not only boasted, but have *set up their banners for tokens.*
The LXX. and Vulgate, with little difference of wording,
read, *have set their signs as signs.* The Jewish commentators De Muis.
explain this to mean that the Eastern conquerors of Jerusalem, seeing the event correspond with their divinations and
oracles, asserted the truth of those signs given to Nebuchadnezzar when "he consulted with images, he looked in the Ezek. xxi.
21.
liver, [and] at his right hand was the divination for Jerusa- P.
lem." Others take it of the erection of idols in the place of G.
the holy symbols, but most agree in seeing here the military Ay.
standards, bearing the images of various animals on their
tops, and planted by the invaders in the courts of the temple.
And with this accords S. Jerome's translation : *They have set
up their ensigns for a trophy.* The Carthusian does not fail to D. C.
remind us of the Arian processions with music and banners,
and of that which was nearer to his own time, the military
show of the Bohemian fanatics under the terrible John Ziska,
that blind leader of the blind. They are not slow to mark S. Hieron.
how, on the other hand, the Christian warriors can in their
turn, *set up their banners,* those royal banners of their King— Cd.
for tokens. And they quote the well-known words of Tertullian : "At every advance and movement, at all goings out Tertull. de
and comings in, when dressing and putting on the shoes, Cor. Mil. 5.
when washing, at meals, on lighting of lamps, at bed-time, on
sitting down, whatever act of our lives we are engaged in, we
mark our forehead with the sign of the Cross."

6 He that hewed timber afore out of the thick
trees : was known to bring it to an excellent work.

7 But now they break down all the carved work thereof : with axes and hammers.

As we read these words, the first meaning suggested is the contrast between the skilful labour of the Sidonian timberers whom Solomon employed to hew the cedars of Lebanon for his excellent work, and the mere savage destructiveness of the heathen enemy. But this is certainly not the sense of the passage, nor is the A. V. nearer to it. The words imply that the strokes of the invaders fell thick and fast, like those of a woodman hewing down a stately tree. And so the Chaldee Targum runs : He bruises it with a hammer, *like a man who lifts up his hand on the thickness of trees, that he may cut it down with axes.* But the reading of the LXX. and Vulgate is at once utterly unlike either of these, obscure, and corrupt. In the first place, instead of being a new member of the Psalm, it belongs to the preceding verse, and runs thus : *And they have not known, as at the going forth over the top* (LXX. ὡς εἰς τὴν ἔξοδον (*al.* δσοδον) ὑπεράνω. Vulg. *Sicut in exitu super summum.*) *They have not known* that it was GOD's work, not their own, when they set up their banners *at the going forth* of the gates of the conquered city, and *over the top* of her towers and fortifications, nay, of the very temple itself. A holy writer explains this whole passage of the harsh judgments of distrustful and censorious men. *They have set up their signs, and have not known :* they set up what they do not find, they set up what they afterwards explain in a bad sense. He says, *their signs ;* for it is themselves they set up for a sign, when they measure others by the rule of their own faultiness. He says, *signs* as meaning only signs, and not truth, signs not of certainty, but of suspicion. *And they know not.* Then follows : *As in a copse of wood they have cut down with axes her doors there together, with hatchet and mattock they have cast her down.* The first words recall those sayings, "Now is the ax laid unto the root of the trees, therefore every tree which bringeth not forth good fruit is hewn down, and cast into the fire ;" and "If GOD spared not the natural branches, take heed lest He spare not thee." *As in a copse of wood,* as recklessly as a wood-cutter, or, by hewing down the doors, leaving the entrance into the city as undefended and open to every step as the paths of a forest. The reference to the *doors,*[1] ornate and costly as they were, and overlaid with plates of gold, implies the destruction of the remainder, while *there together* (ἐπιτοαυτό, *in idipsum*) shows the deliberate hostility and combined attack of the enemy. *With hatchet and mattock.* The Latin Fathers dwell on the completeness of the destruction denoted by these words, saying, that the former tool is used to cut down large masses of timber, and the latter for

Marginal notes:
1 Kings v. 6.
Ay.
R.
Gillebert. Serm. xiv. in Cantic.
Rupert.
S. Matt. iii. 10.
Rom. xi. 21.
Ay.
S. Alb. Mag.
B.
C.

---

[1] Reading דלתים *doors,* instead of פתוחיה *carved work.*

further and more minute subdivision. The Greeks, with the   Z.
same general meaning, refer the first instrument to hewing
down wood; the second to defacing stone.   There is an unusual vein of literalism in all the commentators in dealing
with this whole passage; and little is to be drawn from any
save the Carmelite, who bids us note, that by the *doors* of the   Ay.
city we may understand the approaches to the heavenly
kingdom.   There are three such: the upper, the inner, and
the outer.   The first is opened by the free bounty of GOD.   Ps. lxxviii.
"He opened the doors of heaven—He rained down manna   24.
also upon them for to eat."   The second is opened by preparation of the soul; "Behold, I stand at the door, and   Rev. iii. 20.
knock; if any man hear My voice, and open the door, I will
come in to him."   The third is opened by the condemnation
of the proud; "I will loose the loins of kings, to open before   Isa. xlv. 1.
him the two-leaved gates."   But the first of these gates, that
is, the heavenly one, is done away by thanklessness for the
divine gifts, so that it is no longer open for the ungrateful, as
it is written, "And Ahaz gathered together the vessels of the   2 Chron.
house of GOD, and cut in pieces the vessels of the house of   xxviii. 24.
GOD, and shut up the doors of the house of the LORD."
Wherefore it is now said of the ungrateful, *They have cut
down her doors*, and that *with hatchet and mattock*.   By the
hatchet, which hews great logs, understand thanklessness for
spiritual gifts, but by the *mattock*, which cuts in small pieces,
understand thanklessness for corporal benefits, which are
small in comparison with spiritual ones.

8 They have set fire upon thy holy places : and
have defiled the dwelling-place of thy Name, even
unto the ground.

Unto the ground, or, as the Vulgate reads, *Thy sanctuary
on the earth*.   And they delight in pointing out to us, those   G.
old commentators, that we have a sanctuary in heaven, which   Ay.
no evil can defile or draw near.   They tell us, too, that GOD
has three earthly tabernacles: His Virgin Mother, the Church,
and every faithful soul; that the first is insulted by heretics,
who deny her perpetual virginity; the second by sinners, who
prefer to dwell in the tents of ungodliness to abiding humbly in the House of GOD; the third by those who deny the
Resurrection and the Life everlasting.   There is another   P.
sanctuary of GOD yet more holy than these, which was defiled with spitting and insult, which was smitten with hammers, which was cast to the ground, even the LORD JESUS
Himself.   And S. Albert reminds us that there is no pollu-   S. Alb. Mag.
tion so deep as that of sin, so that prelates and priests, who
ought to be GOD's sanctuaries, are *defiled unto the ground*
when they pass from the contemplation of divine things down
to mere earthly passions and desires.

9 Yea, they said in their hearts, Let us make havock of them altogether : thus have they burnt up all the houses of GOD in the land.

The LXX. and Vulgate read this verse very differently : *The kindred of them[1] said together in their heart, Come, and let us make all the feasts of God to cease from the land.* The first question they ask here is, Who are they who said this in their hearts ? Is it to be taken of the invading heathen, or of the Jews ? And the answer they give, for the most part, is the latter. Parez aptly states the reason, by referring to the arguments of the apostate Jews in the Maccabean era, who urged that the superior prosperity and cultivation of the Greeks was a sufficient ground for adopting Pagan customs, and abandoning the Law of Moses. Others, however, see herein the policy of the invaders, who, unable to discover the object of Jewish worship, and seeing their own deities despised, determined to destroy every trace of the Hebrew religion, as being at the root of the national resistance. *The houses of God.* This rendering is in accord with that of Symmachus, which is *synagogues,* but the LXX. and Vulgate reading, *festivals,* which is also that of the Syriac and Æthiopic, appears to represent better the meaning of מוֹעֲדֵי (*assemblies*) which nowhere else in the Bible (unless perhaps in Lam. ii. 6,) denotes a building. And we are taught by it of the perpetual striving of the world to break in upon the Sabbath rest of the Church, a rest never unquiet, never unbroken, till we reach that Land where the true Sabbath remaineth to the people of GOD. So Adam of S. Victor :

The Sequence, Superna Matris gaudia.

The world, the flesh, and Satan's rage,
Their differing wars against us wage ;
And when their phantom hosts come on,
The Sabbath of the heart is gone.

This triple league, with fierce dislike,
At holy festivals would strike ;
And set the battle in array
To drive their peace from earth away.[2]

[margin notes: A. C. Pet. Lomb. P. B. Heb. iv. 9.]

[1] The word יָנָם which the English takes as the Kal future from יָנָה *he did violence,* is explained in the Chaldee Targum by בְּנֵיהֶן *their sons* (as from יִן *sobolescere.*) Hence the variant.

[2] It is probable that the great majority of educated people who read vv. 5—9 of this Psalm, instinctively apply them to iconoclasm, and have in mind the ruined abbeys of Great Britain and the defaced shrines of many foreign lands. Yet there is almost total silence on this subject in the commentators, early or late. Cassiodorus, who lived when the memory of Attila and Genseric was still fresh, Remigius, the contemporary of the worst inroads of the Northmen, the Greek Office for Orthodoxy Sunday, composed against the de-

S. Albert remarks that our ghostly enemies strive to abolish all S. Alb. Mag.
the festivals of our souls, the Nativity of Baptism, or of penitence, the Resurrection from earthly things to seek things on
high, the Ascension from one grade of holiness to another, the
Pentecost of spiritual illumination and burning love of GOD.

10 We see not our tokens, there is not one prophet more : no, not one is there among us, that understandeth any more.

These words may be taken in various ways. In their most
obvious sense, they are a lamentation on the part of the Jews   L.
that their case appears utterly helpless, that they have no
celestial aid, no inspired teaching, and then this is a piteous
cry for relief, such as had been granted by Divine miraculous
interposition many times before. The *tokens* or *signs* will   G.
then denote such chastisements as those which fell on Pharaoh, Sennacherib, and Heliodorus. Again; the *signs* may
refer to the symbolical Hebrew ritual of priesthood and sacrifice, the type of better things to come, but now itself vanished
before the appearance of those better things. Or the words   P.
may denote unbelief, not sorrow, and be uttered by apostate
Jews as a reason for ceasing their accustomed worship. GOD
had ceased to favour them, and had begun to show preference
for the Gentiles, and therefore it was better to adopt Pagan
usages. Some do not fail to point out, moreover, that the   G. ·
Jews did *see*, but did not understand, the *tokens* which GOD
sent by His SON, that there was no need of a Prophet after
He of whom the seers spoke had come. And the failure of   L.
the Temple miracles, acknowledged by the Rabbins, is set
down by them to the time of Simeon the Just, who is said
to be he·that uttered the *Nunc dimittis*. The Greek Fathers point out that the chief aggravation of the final over-   S. Basil.
throw of Jerusalem, is that no series of prophets, such as   Theodoret.
comforted the exiles of the Babylonian captivity, has been
granted to the Jews. S. Albert reminds us that we, of the
modern Church, may truly say, *We see not our tokens*, the
poverty, the stern self-denial, the humility of the early Christians. Nor miracles, nor prophecies either, such as were   S. Alb. Mag.
vouchsafed to our fathers, adds the Carthusian, wherefore   D. C.
our chiefest need is patience with steadfast faith, and we must
say, as did the Maccabees, "We are ready to die, rather than   2 Macc. vii.
·to transgress the laws of our fathers," remembering that it is   2, 9.
added in the same place, "The king of the world shall raise

stroyers of icons, and even the | stadt, and a lament of De Muis
Jesuit Lorinus, who lived during | over Orleans cathedral, are all I
much of the Thirty Years' War, | have found. Even the great
have not a word on the subject. | controversialist Bellarmine him-
A brief allusion in Corderius, a | self is silent; and I will follow
fuller one in a Lutheran com- | his example,
mentator, directed against Carol-

us up, who have died for His laws, into everlasting life."
Hugo Card. There are yet other signs more important still which we lack,
the Tau, or Cross, and the marks of the LORD JESUS, and
therefore we have no true prophet to declare by word and
deed the vileness of this world, the loveliness of that to come,
so that we have reason to fear that GOD *will not know us any*
S. Matt. *more* (LXX. and Vulgate,) but will say to us in the Doom,
XXV. 12. "Verily, I say unto you, I know you not."

11 O GOD, how long shall the adversary do this
dishonour : how long shall the enemy blaspheme
thy Name, for ever?

B. The cry goes up because the faithful and the unbelieving
alike suffer in the persecution ; the grain is beaten as well as
D. C. the chaff, and so long as the righteous suffer, GOD's Name is
blasphemed by His enemies, who declare that He has either
not the power or not the will to deliver His people; and,
S. Luke x. moreover, it is written, "He that heareth you heareth Me ;
16. and he that despiseth you, despiseth Me ; and he that despiseth Me, despiseth Him that sent Me." *How long* then,
G. *for ever?* Yes, answers Gerhohus, not so far as the grain is
concerned, but as far as the chaff.

12 Why withdrawest thou thy hand : why pluckest
thou not thy right hand out of thy bosom to consume the enemy?

The last words of the verse as here read are not in the
Hebrew, the A. V., nor in any of the old Versions. Nor
does the negative occur. The true meaning is that of the
A. V.: *Pluck Thy right hand out of Thy bosom.* But the
LXX. and Vulgate read the latter clause thus: *And Thy*
right hand out of the midst of Thy bosom unto the end. Many
A. Latin Fathers see in these words the rejection of the Jewish
G. people, who, till their final sin, were GOD's right hand. And
Rupert. they remind us how the hand of Moses, when he took it out
Exod. iv. 7. of his bosom, became leprous as snow, and did not become
clean till he had put it in again. So the Jewish Synagogue,
when it refused and slew its King, plucked its hand out of the
bosom of GOD, and became outcast and leprous. Accordingly,
the prayer goes up to GOD to put that polluted hand back
into the bosom of His love, and to make it clean once more,
Z. washed in the Blood of CHRIST. The Greek Fathers understand the passage differently : The *bosom,* they say, is the
treasure of GOD's bounty, the *right hand* the operation of
His Providence, whereby He distributes His gifts, and it is
Ps. cxlv.16. then a prayer to Him to open His hand and fill all things
living with plenteousness. Another interpretation, which has
found favour with the Jews, is, *Why pluckest Thou not the*
R. Kimchi. *enemies out of Thy sanctuary,* that holy land which they pollute with their presence?

18 For God is my King of old : the help that is done upon earth he doeth it himself.

Here is the triumphal answer to all the complaint in the earlier part of the Psalm. While I am crying as if forsaken, *God, my King before the worlds, hath wrought salvation in the midst of the earth.* While we Jews are sleeping, and looking for signs in the night, the Gentiles are awake, and rejoicing in that salvation. · CHRIST is *my King,* not merely since He appeared on earth, but from everlasting, because He is consubstantial with the FATHER, and is begotten by Him *before the worlds. In the midst of the earth.* They take it in three ways. By His Incarnation in the womb of the Blessed Virgin. So the hymn :

Tota descendit deitas
In templum tui pectoris,
De terrâ tui corporis
Nobis est orta veritas,
Et æterna divinitas
Incepit esse temporis.

By His Passion at Jerusalem, once believed to be the very centre of the world. Thus we read :

Golgotha locus est, capitis Calvaria quondam,
Lingua paterna prior sic illum nomine dixit,
Hic medium terræ est, hic est victoria signum.

By His descent into hell, to deliver the captives there. Only once, warns S. Bernard, was that visitation made. It can never be again. In hell there is no more offering for sin, for it was CHRIST's soul, not His Blood, which descended thither. His Blood hath watered the dry earth, and made it glad, and established peace between it and heaven ; and therefore it is here we must be reconciled to GOD.

14 Thou didst divide the sea through thy power : thou brakest the heads of the dragons in the waters.

15 Thou smotest the heads of Leviathan in pieces : and gavest him to be meat for the people in the wilderness.

The primary reference is, of course, to the passage of the Red Sea, and the overthrow of the Egyptian power ; typified here, as in other places, by the crocodile or Leviathan. But the reading of the LXX. and Vulgate in the first clause of verse 14 is a little different. It runs, *Thou hast strengthened the sea in thy power,* and implies, no doubt, the miracle whereby "the waters were a wall unto them on their right hand and on their left." S. Augustine explains it mystically

Marginal notes:

A.

G.

Ay.

Guido v.
Baroches.
The Hymn,
Laudes ca-
namus Vir-
ginis.

Tertull. c.
Marcion.

S. Bernard.

G.

Exod. xiv.
20.

A.

that the Jews were the dry land; and the Gentiles, in the bitterness of unbelief, the sea. Now that sea has been confined by God's power, and the pride of demons, the *heads of the dragons*, whereby the Gentiles were once possessed, He hath now *broken in the waters* of Baptism. Another Saint, of a much later age, interprets the *heads of the dragons* as sins, *broken in the waters* of penitential tears. S. Gregory, amplifying the first part of S. Augustine's explanation, teaches that the *sea* denotes this present world, wherein men's hearts are tossed on the billows of care, of pride, and of adversity. But now those seas are stablished by God's power; for, since the Incarnation of the Lord, the hearts of those of this world, once at discord, now believe in concord, and Peter walks upon the waters, since Christ is preached, and the people hear in meekness. Others, while interpreting the *waters* as those of Baptism, dwell on the word *strengthened* as denoting the certainty of that Sacrament, whoever and whatever the minister of it may be, provided the true matter and form be used. The properties of the *dragons*, by which they become fit emblems of evil spirits, are thus summed up by Cardinal Hugo:

Sibilat, ignivomus, eremi Babylonis, arenæ ;
Et maris incubitor, cristatus, edax, volat, ingens ;
Os breve, cauda ligans elephantem, pervigil, astu
Aspiciens, pugnans, sensus petit, est capitosus.

Thou smotest the heads of Leviathan in pieces. Here, for *Leviathan*, the LXX. and Vulgate read *the dragon*, that is, the chief of all evil spirits, the beginning of sin; and these words denote the fulfilment of the prophecy, that the Seed of the woman should bruise the serpent's head. *And gavest him to be meat for the people in the wilderness.* The Talmudists have interpreted this text with a literalism more extravagant than any allegory. According to them, Leviathan is a huge sea-serpent, which encompasses the earth, (exactly like the Eddaic Jormungandr,) and strives to swallow the sun. At the last day, it, and Behemoth, and the huge bird Barjuchna, are to be killed, and served up as a banquet for the children of Israel. The interpretation at other hands is widely different. With some, the *people of the wilderness* mean the Hebrews, who are said to have spoiled the corpses of the Egyptian warriors as they lay upon the shore. Others, and most modern critics, explain it of birds and beasts of prey, comparing texts where the word *people* is applied to the lower animals. The LXX., Vulgate, and Æthiopic, however, read, *to the peoples of the Æthiopians.* The literal interpretation, that the loss of the Egyptian army made the nation an easy prey to the neighbouring powers, may be briefly mentioned. The mystical explanations are full. The *Æthiopians* are they who were once black and defiled with sin; who "were sometimes darkness, but now light in the

Marginal notes:
S. Brun. Ast.

S. Bern.
Senen.
Moral. xvii.
15.

L.

A.

Gen. iii. 15.

L.

* Lyranus.
De Muis.
Prov. xxx.
25, 26.
Joel i. 6.

Theodoret.

A.

Eph. v. 8.

LORD." And Leviathan has been given them for meat, because GOD has given power over the devil into the hands of His faithful, and especially to the martyrs, so that they should not only devour him up, but by drawing away his members from him by conversion, actually incorporate them into the body of the Church, which thus grows by feeding on Leviathan. This mystery was foreshadowed under the Law by Moses grinding the golden calf into powder, and compelling the children of Israel to swallow it; and again under the Gospel, when S. Peter in his vision was told to "kill and eat." And in this wise Aaron's rod hath swallowed up those of the magicians.

C.

B.

A.

Exod. xxxii. 20.

Acts x. 13.

Exod. vii. 12.

16 Thou broughtest out fountains and waters out of the hard rocks : thou driedst up mighty waters.

The words *out of the hard rocks* are not in the Hebrew, nor in any of the other versions; but they represent accurately enough the meaning of the verb בָּקַעְתָּ, which implies splitting or rending something hard. The commentators dwell for a little on the events of Horeb, Kadesh, and Jordan, and on the contrasted exhibition of Almighty power, softening that which is hard, and solidifying that which is fluid; and then turn to the hidden sense. *Fountains and torrents* are both produced by GOD in men's hearts. The *fountain* is the "well of water springing up into everlasting life," the Word of GOD in holy and steadfast souls; while the *torrent*, impetuous in winter, but dry in summer, denotes those who are eager in words and preaching, but who lack perseverance and sanctity. *Thou driedst up mighty waters.* Or, as the LXX. and Vulgate, the *waters of Ethan.*[1] And they take it diversely of the power of the devil, of idolatry, and of Gentile philosophy and learning, all subdued and dried up before the advance of the hosts of the LORD.

Ay.

A.

S. John iv. 14.

A.

B.

Ric. Hamp.

17 The day is thine, and the night is thine : thou hast prepared the light and the sun.

18 Thou hast set all the borders of the earth : thou hast made summer and winter.

They pass at once from the natural to the spiritual creation, and tell us how GOD rules alike over the spiritual, who are the *day,* and the carnal, who are the *night,* over the unwise and imperfect Christians, who are but the *dawn* of light, and over those perfected in the wisdom and faith of CHRIST, who are like the *sun.* Another reading, instead of *light* or *dawn,* is *moon,* which Cassiodorus follows, and reminds us of that saying of the Wise Man, "A fool changeth as the

A.

Ay.

C.

[1] אֵיתָן, *firmness, strength,* from יתן, *to be constant.*

moon." *Thou hast set all the borders of the earth*, by appointing Apostles and Prelates, as boundaries, to mark the limits of our obligations, lest we should transgress. Or, set all *the borders of the earth*, by giving each man his special talent to use for the service of GOD. *Summer and winter*. The first tells of those who are ardent and zealous in faith, from whom Confessors and Martyrs come. *Winter*, or with the LXX. and Vulgate, *spring*, denotes those of a colder and less devotional temperament, who are yet servants of GOD. And others contrast here the active and contemplative lives, giving the higher place to the latter. The Carthusian has yet another explanation. The *sun* is the glorified Manhood of CHRIST, the *dawn* His Virgin Mother, of whom is written, "Who is she that looketh forth as the morning?" the *borders of the earth* are GOD's elect in this world; *spring*, with its leafy promise, denotes the merit of good works; *summer*, with its fruits, the everlasting reward awaiting them.

19 Remember this, O LORD, how the enemy hath rebuked : and how the foolish people hath blasphemed thy Name.

The word *how* is not in the Hebrew, nor in the old versions; and the verse thus seems made up of two separate members. They ask, accordingly, What is *this* which GOD is called on to *remember?* The Roman Psalter, the Æthiopic, Arabic, and some recensions of the LXX. add the words *Thy creation* or *creature*, and it is explained by some to mean the Jewish nation; while others, as the Greek Fathers, refer it to the *congregation* spoken of in a former verse. Again, it is taken of the works of GOD's power or bounty, which He is asked to *remember;* that is, to exhibit once more in the time of need. And lastly, there are some who explain it in the same sense as the Prayer Book Version. The latter clauses are taken first of the heathen raging against the worship of the GOD of Israel, and then of the Jewish people itself, become the enemy of its King, and blaspheming His Name with slander and reproaches.

20 O deliver not the soul of thy turtle-dove unto the multitude of the enemies : and forget not the congregation of the poor for ever.

Here we have the cry of the afflicted Church; of her whom her Bridegroom calls, "My sister, My love, My dove, My undefiled," imploring to be delivered from all her foes, ghostly and earthly. She is His sister, as has well been said, because she is of His Blood; His love, because reconciled by His death; His dove, because dowered with the HOLY GHOST; His undefiled, as washed in the Sacrament of Baptism. It is rightly said, *the soul of Thy turtle-dove.* For

Margin notes:
Ecclus. xxvii. 11.
C.
G.
C.
Hugo Card.
D. C.
Cant. vi. 10.
Ay.
G.
Z.
S. Basil. Mag.
L.
Ay.
Cant. v. 2.
Just. Orgel.

God gives no promise that He will not give the *body* of His Church, or of His individual Saints, up to those who can kill, or, at least, sorely hurt it; but the *soul* is His darling, and He will rescue it. So we read in the passion of a Virgin Martyr:

> Eager for peace, she breathed the fire,
>   And so she went to rest:
> Forth from her lips, most pure and white,
>   There sprang a snowy dove,
> And shooting on its heavenward flight,
>   It sought the realms above;
> So swift, so pure, so innocent,
> It was Eulalia's soul that went
> To seek its native firmament,
>   The dwelling-place of Love.

Prudent.
Peristeph.
iii. 159.

Yet, again, as the Dove implies the HOLY GHOST Himself, this may well be a prayer that we "quench not the SPIRIT" by those works of the flesh which lust against Him, and are at enmity with Him. But this, the preferable sense of the Hebrew, is lost in the old versions, and they read in the first clause, *Deliver not to the beasts the souls which confess Thee.* Lorinus mentions that this text was twisted by various Gnostic heretics, as Manichæans and Albigenses, to imply the transmigration of human souls into the forms of brutes. The majority of commentators here follow S. Augustine, and interpret the passage as a prayer to be delivered from the evil spirits. *Forget not the congregation of the poor for ever.* They take it diversely of the poor in spirit, trodden down in this world, but looking humbly to GOD in hope; and of the Jewish nation, poor indeed, as having rejected the true riches, but not utterly cast away from its FATHER's love. As a prayer for the departing Christian soul, fleeing away as a dove to be at rest, this verse forms the Versicle and Response after the Psalms of the Third Nocturn of the Office for the Dead.

1 Thess. v. 19.

Gal. v. 17, 19.

L.

A.

Ay.

21 Look upon the covenant : for all the earth is full of darkness, and cruel habitations.

Have regard, not to the Old *Covenant* or *Testament,* but to the New; not to the promise of the earthly Canaan, but to the gift of salvation in the kingdom of heaven. The second clause should run, as in the A. V., *The dark places of the earth are full of the habitations of cruelty.* The mystical reference will then be to the secret machinations of the devil and his ministers, ghostly or human, to destroy the souls which CHRIST came to save; and He is implored, therefore, by the Blood of His Covenant, to "send forth His prisoners out of the pit where is no water:" truly a dark place of the earth, where afflicted souls are cruelly tortured. But the LXX. and Vulgate read, *They that are darkened have been*

A.

G.

Zech. ix. 11.

filled with the houses of the iniquities of the earth. They are

Rom. i. 21.

G.

Z.

darkened, because, "when they knew GOD, they glorified Him not as GOD, neither were thankful; but became vain in their imaginations, and their foolish heart was darkened." *Darkened,* moreover, with earthly desires and possessions, while their *houses of iniquity* are those foolish hearts, given up to sin, wherein their thoughts ever dwell. Euthymius refers the whole passage more especially to the Jews, whom he calls the *dark ones of the earth,* now filled, nay, more than filled, with their own iniquity.

22 O let not the simple go away ashamed : but let the poor and needy give praise unto thy Name.

A.

Ay.

C.

They take it differently, of those who are humble and poor, knowing themselves to be such, and make their prayer to GOD, as devout Christians; and of those who do not know themselves to be in utter poverty, as the Jews. It is thus a prayer for the fuller acceptance of the former, and for the conversion of the latter. Let us see how glorious is that poverty, exclaims Cassiodorus, how happy is that neediness to be accounted, which even in silence praises the LORD, and celebrates Him with the might of its patience. If the proud man make music, he is silent; but the poor and needy praise the LORD, even when they seem to be still. O priceless good! if we ponder it within. The *poor* is GOD's, the rich belongs to this world; the one is the possession of the Everlasting King, the other that of passing time.

23 Arise, O GOD, maintain thine own cause : remember how the foolish man blasphemeth thee daily.

24 Forget not the voice of thine enemies : the presumption of them that hate thee increaseth ever more and more.

L.

P.

G.

They read, some of them, *my cause;* others, *our cause :* it is all one. The cause of GOD is that of every soul which trusts in Him, that of the whole company of the faithful. *Arise,* and come in the flesh to help us ; or, *arise,* not merely sitting on Thy throne in heaven, but lifting Thyself up in might, to help Thy people. So the hymn,

Adam. Victorin. The Sequence, *Herimundus exultavit.*

En a dextris DEI stantem
JESUM pro te dimicantem,
Stephane, considera.

Z.

L.

The foolish man. The Greeks, with singular baldness, take this to mean Titus, or any boastful Roman soldier, exulting in the victory of his gods. The Latins, more deeply, take it of the unbelieving Jewish people, here represented as one person. *Thine enemies.* There are several variants here. *Thy suppliants* is the Gallican reading; *them that pray to Thee*, the Italic, the Illyrian, and S. Augustine; the Roman and Cassiodorus, *them that seek Thee*, which is retained in the introit of the Roman Missal for the thirteenth Sunday after Pentecost. *Of them that hate Thee.* Here the School- Pet. Lomb. men raise the question, How can God, Who is the Supreme Good, and altogether lovely, be the object of hate? And Ay. they answer that He cannot be so in His Essence; but that certain results of His justice and holiness, taking the form of prohibition, prevention, and punishment of sin, are hateful to evil-doers, and that He is said, in this secondary sense, to be hated. *Increaseth.* The Vulgate reads, *ascendeth*. That S. Albertus is, goeth up unto Thee, into Thine ears, that Thou mayest Magnus. note and punish it; or ascendeth up higher and higher, that Ric Hamp. it may be cast down more terribly in the Doom. With this last meaning we may compare those terrible words of the Apocalypse, " And the smoke of their torment ascendeth up for ever; and they have no rest day or night who worship Rev. xiv. 11. the beast and his image, and whosoever receiveth the mark of his name."

Wherefore:

Glory be to the FATHER, Who hath given His judgment to the SON; glory be to the SON, Who hath judged the city of Jerusalem, and Who will yet judge the whole Church; glory be to the HOLY GHOST, Who in His just judgment shall protect those poor in spirit, of whom it is said, *The poor and needy shall give praise unto Thy Name.*

As it was in the beginning, is now, and ever shall be: world without end. Amen.

COLLECTS.

O GOD, Creator of all the elements, King Everlasting be- Ludolph. fore the worlds, remember Thy flock which Thou hast re- deemed by the shedding of Thine own Blood, and graciously hear the voices of all them that seek Thee, O SAVIOUR of the world. Who livest.

. Remember, O LORD, Thy congregation, which Thou hast Mozarabic. created from the beginning; and forget not Thy Church, which Thou hast predestined in CHRIST from all time; and, mindful of Thy mercy, look upon Thy Covenant, and ever embrace us with Thy promised freedom. Through Thy mercy. (11.)

O LORD, deliver not into the hands of the persecutors the Mozarabic. souls of the peoples which confess Thee; that Thou, Who Passiontide. didst endure the slanders of false witnesses, mayest be glori- fied by the voices of the redeemed which worship Thee. Through Thy mercy. (11.)

Remember, O LORD, Thy congregation, which Thou hast Mozarabic. created from the beginning, and which Thou hast wondrously and mercifully redeemed at the price of Thy Blood, and chosen it as Thy possession from out of the nations. Deliver, then, the rod of Thine inheritance from the attacks of the supplanter, and so rule it in this present world by justifying, that it may inherit in the world to come; and that it which prays, as divinely taught, for Thy kingdom to come, may, after pardon freely given, attain by hereditary succession, to the same Thy kingdom. Through Thy mercy. (11.)

Forget not, O LORD, the voice of them that seek Thee, and the pride of them that hate Thee, ascending for evermore; that these, who by formal registration are received into the bosom of Mother Church, may attain to the grace of Holy Baptism; that, inasmuch as they desire such things, the Sacrament of washing enjoined amongst us may not be denied them, and that they may, with us, possess everlasting gladness. Through Thy mercy. (11.)

D. C.

O CHRIST, our GOD and King before the worlds, Who at the end of the world hast wrought salvation in the redemption of Thy Church, which Thou hast possessed from the beginning through predestination, look upon the covenant confirmed in Thy Blood, by making the same Thy Church to abide in devotion, and to stand evermore in safety. Who livest.

PSALM LXXV.

TITLE: To the Chief Musician, Al-taschith, [or Destroy not,] A Psalm or Song of Asaph. LXX. and Vulgate: To the end, Destroy not, a Psalm of a Song of Asaph. Chaldee Targum: For the Praises, what time David said, Destroy not Thy people. A Hymn and Song by the hand of Asaph.

ARGUMENT.

ARG. THOMAS. That CHRIST, for the redemption of man, drank the Cup of the Passion. The Voice of CHRIST touching judgment to come.

VEN. BEDE. *Asaph*, as we have often said, is interpreted *Synagogue;* to wit, that which believed, not that which remained obstinate; for we read that many thousands of the Jews confessed after the LORD's Resurrection, whom this *Asaph* now warns that they should *not destroy* their faith, that is, in the LORD their SAVIOUR, *unto the end.*

At the outset the faithful Jews profess themselves about to speak of all His wondrous works. In the second part, CHRIST the King Himself speaks, promising to judge according to right when the time of the General Resurrection hath come; and, moreover, warns them that none should presume in aught against the Divine commands, lest eternal punishment should torture him. *When I receive the time*, (Vulg.,) *I shall judge according unto right.*

EUSEBIUS OF CÆSAREA. A discourse of the Divinity of CHRIST, and a warning of the judicial tribunal of GOD.

S. ATHANASIUS. A Psalm in thanksgiving.

VARIOUS USES.

Gregorian. Thursday. Matins. [Maundy Thursday. III. Nocturn. Common of Apostles. III. Nocturn.]
Parisian. Saturday. Matins.
Ambrosian. Tuesday of Second Week. I. Nocturn.
Monastic. Thursday. I. Nocturn. [Maundy Thursday. III. Nocturn. Common of Apostles. II. Nocturn.]
Quignon. Monday. Terce.
Lyons. Monday. None.

ANTIPHONS.

Gregorian. Ferial. And we shall call * upon Thy Name, O LORD. [Maundy Thursday. I said unto the unrighteous, Speak not unrighteousness against GOD. Common of Apostles. The horns of the righteous shall be exalted. Alleluia.]
Parisian. Unto Thee, O GOD, * will we give thanks, and will call upon Thy Name : we will tell of Thy wondrous works.
Ambrosian. As Psalm lxxii.
Monastic. Ferial. As Psalm lxxiii. [Maundy Thursday. As Gregorian. Common of Apostles. As Gregorian.]
Mozarabic. First verse of the Psalm.

1 Unto thee, O GOD, do we give thanks : yea, unto thee do we give thanks.

2 Thy Name also is so nigh : and that do thy wondrous works declare.

The Vulgate reads these two verses as one, and translates   **A.**
the whole, *We will confess to Thee, O God, we will confess to Thee. We will invoke Thy Name, and tell of Thy wondrous works.* Do not *invoke* before thou *confess.* Confess first, and then invoke. For thou art calling Him to thee Whom thou invokest. To whom, then, doth He draw near? Not to a proud man. It is written, "The LORD is nigh unto   Ps. xxxiv. them that are of a contrite heart." And the words *We will*   18. *confess* are repeated, to show that we do not repent of having done so once. It is written in another Psalm, "Confess to   Ps. cvi. 1. the LORD, for He is good." Why, then, do ye fear to confess? Fear to confess to a human judge, lest he punish thee after confession ; fear not to do so to GOD, but make Him by confession merciful, Whom thou canst not make ignorant by denial. *We will confess to Thee, O God,* and now, being safe, *we will invoke Thy Name.* We have emptied our heart by confession ; come to us in our lowliness. And the sense is, besides, strengthened by repetition ; as when the LORD

S. John i. 51.
Ps. lxxii. 19;
lxxxix. 52.

saith, "Verily, verily, I say unto you;" or when in the Psalms we read, "Amen, Amen;" or when Pharaoh's dream was doubled. There are, says the Carmelite, three kinds of confession: that of the tribunals, condemning the guilty; that of penitence, cleansing sin; that of praise, giving thanks. The first has no place here, and thus *we will confess* is said twice; first of repentance, and then of giving glory to GOD after absolution: wherefore is added, *we will invoke Thy Name.* For if any one invoke that Name indevoutly, he would seem to call for judgment, not for pardon. But the English Version is the true one, *Thy Name is nigh.* How can that be *nigh,* which is Most Highest, and "above every name?" Because the Psalmist is looking forward to the Incarnation, when only it can be truly said to Israel, "The WORD is very nigh thee, in thy mouth, and in thy heart."

Ay.

C.

Phil. ii. 9.

Deut. xxx. 14.

S. Bern.
Rhyth. Ju-
bilus.

> JESUS decus angelicum,
> In aure dulce canticum,
> In ore mel mirificum,
> In corde nectar cœlicum.

In mouth and heart alike, that does *His wondrous work declare,* even the great Sacrament of His Love, whereof is written, "O taste and see how gracious the LORD is!"

But the Vulgate reading is, *We will tell of Thy wondrous works.* That is, when we ourselves have come near to Thee in confession and lowliness, then, and not till then, we can go forth as preachers of Thy Word. Not till then; for we are warned in another Psalm, "Unto the ungodly said GOD, Why dost thou preach My laws, and takest My Covenant in thy mouth?" and again, "Praise is not seemly in the mouth of a sinner, for it was not sent him of the LORD." *Thy* works, not our own; for we preach not ourselves, nor seek our own glory, but that of Thy Name; and so let our good works be seen, that men may glorify, not us, but Thee. *Thy wondrous* works—Thine Incarnation, Nativity, Passion, Death, Resurrection, and Ascension, which Thou hast wrought for man's salvation. And this not only to gladden our own hearts, but to warn and alarm sinners; because there follows:

Ps. xxxiv. 8.

S. Albertus
Magnus.

Ps. l. 16.

Ecclus. xv. 9.

G.

P.

Ay.

3 When I receive the congregation: I shall judge according unto right.

It is no longer the voice of the Psalmist, but of CHRIST, telling us of judgment to come. When the mighty *congregation,* "the dead, small and great, stand before GOD," then shall He, Who was Himself judged unrighteously, judge righteous judgment, and reward every man according to his works. The Vulgate, instead of *congregation,* reads *time,* the set time appointed by the FATHER. It is the same word מוֹעֵד, which in Ps. lxxiv. 9 is translated in the Prayer

Rev. xx. 12.

G.

Book *houses*, and in the Vulgate *festivals*. Its true meaning
is, " a fixed time of assembly," and hence it.is often taken for
the assembly itself. There is an evident reference here to
the previous Psalm, implying that, whereas the ungodly have   A.
made GOD's festival times to cease, He will requite them
when His time of vengeance is at hand. Again, it is spoken   Ay.
of the Incarnation, when He, Who is before all time, began,
as Man, to be in time, and subject to its laws. " O the Menæa,
marvel !" exclaims the Holy Eastern Church, " GOD amongst March 25.
men, the Incomprehensible in the womb, the Timeless One
in time !" Then indeed did He *judge according unto right*,
as it was foretold : " A bruised reed shall He not break, and Isa. xlii. 3.
the smoking flax shall He not quench : He shall bring forth
judgment unto truth."

4 The earth is weak, and all the inhabiters
thereof : I bear up the pillars of it.

Is weak. Better with the A. V., *is dissolved*, nearly the
same as the Vulgate, *liquefacta*. The *earth*. All the human   A.
race, sunk in sin, as S. Augustine will have it ; the Jewish
Church, melting and sliding down as a glacier from the   R.
Mount of the Law, as another takes it. In a good sense we
may take the *earth* of the Church, once frozen hard in cold-   G.
ness, but now softened by the south wind breathing upon it,
to make it the LORD's garden, that it may bear fruits and
flowers for Him. Then we may explain *dissolved* as mean- Ric. Hamp.
ing melted by the fire of GOD's love, so that *all the inhabiters* of the Church glide away from this world's affections,
and flow into the Heart of CHRIST. *I bear up the pillars of
it.* More precisely, *I have poised*, or, with the Vulgate, *I*   Ay.
have strengthened. The *pillars* are the Apostles, and all
other elect, whom, once weak, CHRIST hath *strengthened* by
His Resurrection, *strengthened* in love, *strengthened* by the
seven gifts of the HOLY GHOST; whence it is written, "Wisdom Prov. ix. 1.
hath builded her house, she hath hewn out her seven pillars."
And on these pillars a copious rain of allegory is poured.
"The Saints," observes one of themselves, " are fitly com- S. Albertus
pared to pillars. For a pillar is tall, wherein is longsuffer- Magnus.
ing ; it is slender, denoting humility ; it is 'level, without
projecting, implying poverty ; it is round, signifying eternity, which they desire." We should be strong as a pillar, Ric. Victor.
in faith, remarks another ; as straight, in equity ; as erect, in Cant. 3.
in intention ; as lofty, in contemplation ; as ready to bear
up others, by words of comfort, by intercession of prayer, by
example of action. And the Carmelite tells us that the   Ay.
seven columns are fear, piety, knowledge, fortitude, counsel,
understanding, and wisdom, which he compares to pillars of
cloud, gold, silver, iron, smoke, marble, and peace, supporting
his similes by Scriptural references.

II.   X

5 I said unto the fools, Deal not so madly : and
to the ungodly, Set not up your horn.

6 Set not up your horn on high : and speak not
with a stiff neck.

G.
A.
Ay.

I said, speaking Myself in Paradise before the Fall, and
since by My Prophets and Apostles through the HOLY
GHOST, *unto the fools*, (Vulg., the *unrighteous*,) but they
would neither hear while they stood, so as not to fall. nor yet
when fallen, so as to rise again. *Set not up your horn*, by
continuance in sin, resisting GOD. *On high*, not merely sinning, but boasting of the sin, or, at any rate, excusing it.
And speak not with a stiff neck. So the Hebrew and Syriac ;
but the LXX. and Vulgate read, *And speak not unrighteousness against God*, which is, in fact, a gloss, rather than
the text.

7 For promotion cometh neither from the east,
nor from the west : nor yet from the south.

De Muis.
Z.

Cd.

Rupert.

L.

The word הָרִים, here rightly translated *promotion*, or
elevation, coming in the Hebrew at the close of the verse, is
translated by the LXX. and Vulgate as *hills*, and joined with
מִמִּדְבָּר, rendered in the Prayer Book and A. V. as *south*,
less exactly than in the margin of the latter, which reads
desert. The whole verse runs thus, then, in the Vulgate :
*For neither from the east, nor from the west, nor from the
desert hills ;* i. e., the chain of mountains lying to the south
of Palestine. Almost the oldest gloss on this passage is that
of Rabbi Ezra, followed by Euthymius, that it is a protest
against the falsehoods of astrology and demonology, and a
vindication of GOD's Providence as the sole Power which
disposes of our destiny. Others, more happily, see here a
prophecy of the Catholic Church, not to be bounded, like
the Jewish, by limits of country or race. Again, taking it
with reference to the Judgment, mentioned just before, it
may well point out the impossibility of escaping in any direction from the hand of GOD. Of the sinner who strives to do
so, we may well say with the heathen poet :

Soph. Œd.
Col. 1237.

τόνδε κατάκρας
δειναὶ κυματοαγεῖς
ἆται κλονέουσιν ἀεὶ συνοῦσαι,
αἱ μὲν ἀπ' ἀελίου δυσμᾶν,
αἱ δ' ἀνατέλλοντος,
αἱ δ' ἀνὰ μέσσαν ἀκτῖν',
αἱ δὲ νυχίαν ἀπὸ Ῥιπᾶν.

A.

There is no place, says S: Augustine, whither thou mayest
flee from GOD angry, save to GOD reconciled. Flee to Him.
Again, they take the *east* of the elect, on whom the Sun of

Righteousness arises in His glory ; the *west*, of the evil, in whom His rays are quenched ; and the *desert hills* of evil spirits, mountains, in their obstinate pride, desert, in being unvisited by the grace of GOD. And we may also take the *desert hills* of those preachers who, set on high in the Church, are unfruitful in their lives. Gerhohus, in his burning zeal against the simoniacs of his day, turns the text against them, and compares them to those mountains of Gilboa, cursed by withholding of rain and dew, because there the shield of the mighty was vilely cast away. All these, good and bad alike, must stand at the tribunal of CHRIST.

G.

Ric. Hamp.

Ay.

G.

2 Sam. i. 20.

8 And why ? GOD is the Judge : he putteth down one, and setteth up another.

He putteth down one, as He did the Pharisee, who exalted himself, and was showing the Physician his whole members, not his wounds. *He lifteth up another*, who humbleth himself as did the Publican. He putteth down the Jew, and lifteth up the Gentile. Very aptly another heathen bard may here be cited :

A.

S. Luke
xviii. 10.

Ay.

ῥέα μὲν γὰρ βριάει, ῥέα δὲ βριάοντα χαλέπτει,
ῥεῖα δ᾽ ἀρίζηλον μινύθει καὶ ἄδηλον ἀέξει,
ῥεῖα δέ τ᾽ ἰθύνει σκολιὸν καὶ ἀγήνορα κάρφει
Ζεὺς ὑψιβρεμέτης, ὃς ὑπέρτατα δώματα ναίει.

Hesiod. Opp.
et Dies. 5.

9 For in the hand of the LORD there is a cup, and the wine is red : it is full mixed, and he poureth out of the same.

10 As for the dregs thereof, all the ungodly of the earth shall drink them, and suck them out.

The Cup in the hand of the LORD is understood in the first place of His Law in Holy Scripture, full of good wine, which maketh glad the heart of man. *The wine is red.* These words we may well take in their deepest meaning, when the mysteries hidden in that Cup were poured forth in the blood-shedding of the Passion.

S. Albertus
Magnus.

Cuspis arundinea
Cum coronâ spineâ·
Sacra membra forat,
Fundatori vinea
Vina dat sanguinea,
Naturaque plorat,
Dum JESUS laborat.

The Hymn
*Plange Sion
filia.*

But this is not the Hebrew, which is, *The wine foams*, nor yet the LXX. and Vulgate reading, *Full of pure wine*, (LXX. οἴνου ἀκράτου, Vulg. *vini meri*) *with mixture.* This *pure wine*, continues S. Albert, is the spiritual meaning of Holy Writ, which GOD *hath inclined from this* [vessel] *into that*, (Vulg.,)

S. Albertus
Magnus.

S. Matt.
xxi. 43.

C.

Ay.

Z.

Theod.
Heracl.

B.

Vieyra.

D. C.

Hugo Card.

Vieyra.

to wit, taken from the Jews, and given to the Gentiles, as it is written, "The kingdom of GOD shall be taken from you, and given to a nation bringing forth the fruits thereof." This spiritual sense is *full of mixture*, because the Old and New Testament are joined in the teaching of the Christian Church; unlike the Jews, who have only the Old, and the Manicheans, who admit but the New. *As for the dregs thereof.* The LXX. and Vulgate read here, *The dregs thereof truly are not exhausted.*[1] That is, the mere carnal sense has not been poured out for the Church, but is left behind in the bottom of the cup, for sinners who refuse the good wine. And this holds especially of the Jews, clinging to mere typical and shadowy sacraments, while rejecting the substance. Again, the cup is explained of the judgments of GOD. Euthymius says that we must understand two cups here, one of *pure wine*, of the unmingled wrath of GOD; the other *full of mixture*, wherein the water of mercy tempers the draught. Both are in the hands of GOD, and He pours from one into the other, according as His judgments are to be lighter or heavier. But the *dregs* are never mingled. They are kept in their full strength for the finally impenitent. Again, the *mixed cup* may well refer to the Last Judgment, with its mingled retribution of lifting up and casting down for the elect and the reprobate, to the former of whom it will be *pure wine*, sweet, though terrible, but to the latter *dregs* never to be emptied. Vieyra, in one of his noblest sermons, explains the *cup* of the terrors of hell. All sinners of the earth must drink of this cup; yet those who fear hell, not slavishly, nor because of its pains, but because GOD is blasphemed there, will drink only the pure and clear part of the cup; while those who dread the punishment, although loving the sin, must swallow the dregs. The Carthusian, after citing some of the previous explanations, gives yet another, following Hugh of S. Cher. He takes the *pure wine* of the unmingled gladness of the Saints in their country; the *mixture*, of their blended sorrow and comfort in their journey here, where they are scourged by the rod of GOD, even when supported by His staff. And, returning to that former explanation of the Passion, Vieyra, in another sermon, reminds us that the cup was *pure wine*, because of the perfect holiness of CHRIST; and it was *full of mixture* from our sins, which He took on Himself.

11 But I will talk of the GOD of Jacob: and praise him for ever.

The Vulgate differs a little: *But I will announce for evermore: I will sing unto the God of Jacob.* They take the

[1] Probably reading וְמָצָה, *shall be found*, instead of וּמָצָה, *shall suck out.*

first clause diversely, as meaning, I will continue to warn-   **Ay.**
men of GOD's judgments, or else, I will declare the doctrine
of CHRIST. *And sing unto the God of Jacob,* to the GOD of   **D. C.**
the *supplanter,* who wrestles against his sins till he overthrows them. Yes, and to the GOD of the younger son,
Who gave him the inheritance which the elder brother de-   **G.**
spised.

12 All the horns of the ungodly also will I
break : and the horns of the righteous shall be exalted.

They take it first, as is natural, of the pride and obstinacy
of sinners, but pass on to more hidden meanings. Thus we
are told that there were ten horns of the Jewish dispensa-   **Galatinus.**
tion, to wit, the Patriarchs, Prophets, Judges, Kings, Priests,   **L.**
Levites, the Law, the Temple, Jerusalem, and the Messiah,
all taken from them, and made over to the Gentile Church   **Cd.**
at the Coming of CHRIST. Again, *the horns of the ungodly*
are the soul, body, wealth, power, knowledge, pleasure, and
worldly wisdom of sinners, all of them vain to resist GOD.
The horns of the righteous shall be exalted. Because, "in   **L.**
the midst of the throne, and of the four beasts, and in the
midst of the elders, stood a Lamb as it had been slain, having
seven horns and seven eyes, which are the seven Spirits of   **Rev. v. 6.**
GOD sent forth into all the earth." He Who is highly ex-
alted is the "horn of salvation for us in the house of His
servant David." Or, we may take the *horns of the righteous*   **S. Luke i. 69.**
to be faith, exalted to open vision ; hope, to comprehension ;   **S. Albertus**
charity, to full fruition. Again, the Carmelite understands   **Magnus.**
the words of humility, typified by the bending of a beast's   **Ay.**
horns towards the earth ; of gentleness and mercy, from the
horns of oil wherewith kings were anointed ; and of purity,
because the horn, though derived, like the bone, from the
flesh, is, unlike the bone, uncovered by flesh, and thus denotes those who while in the body live as though out of it.
And we may find yet another explanation in the four corners
or horns of the Cross, which, S. Bernard tells us, are pa-   **S. Bern.**
tience, continence, prudence, and lowliness, all of them once   **Serm. 2, de**
lifted up on Calvary in the person of CHRIST, all to be lifted   **S. Andreâ.**
up to eternal glory in the persons of His Saints.

And therefore :

Glory be to the FATHER, to Whom we say, *Unto Thee, O*
God, do we give thanks ; and to the SON, Who saith, *When*
I receive the congregation, I shall judge according unto right,
and *all the horns of the ungodly will I break ;* and to the
HOLY GHOST, by Whose gift the horns of the righteous shall
be exalted for evermore.

As it was in the beginning, is now, and ever shall be :
world without end. Amen.

COLLECTS.

Ludolph. O Good Shepherd, Who, for the ransom of Thy mortal sheep, hast drunk the cup of the Passion; we humbly call upon Thy Name, that, stablishing us upon the pillars of wisdom, Thou wouldst strengthen us with the hallowing of Thy sevenfold SPIRIT. Through.

Mozarabic. O LORD, look mercifully on us who confess to Thee, that as the fear of punishment makes us contrite, so the love of pardon and the fulness of remission may gladden us. Through Thy mercy. (11.)

Mozarabic. Unto Thee, O LORD, will we confess, yea, unto Thee will we confess our sins and offences, which are better known to Thee than disclosed by our acknowledgment. We therefore call upon Thy Name, that Thou mayest pardon our open misdeeds against Thee, and not be swift to execute vengeance upon our secret sins; but that, as Thou art appeased by the confession of the lowly, Thou mayest grant us remission of all our offences. Through Thy mercy. (11.)

D. C. We confess to Thee, O GOD, we confess to Thee, with hearty repentance. Be gracious unto our sins, that, granting us pardon, Thou mayest make us worthy to call upon Thy holy Name, that we may, in thanksgiving for our salvation, sing to Thee, O GOD of Jacob, for evermore. (1.)

PSALM LXXVI.

TITLE. To the Chief Musician on Neginoth. A Psalm or Song of Asaph. LXX. and Vulgate: To the end, in the praises, A Psalm of Asaph, a Song to the Assyrians. Chaldee Targum: For praising with praise, a Psalm and Song by the hand of Asaph. Arabic Psalter: A Song of Asaph for the Beloved. Or: To the Supreme, on the stringed instruments, a Psalm of Asaph, a Song.

ARGUMENT.

ARG. THOMAS. That CHRIST was published by the preaching of the Apostles, not in Judea alone, but also in all the ends of the earth. The Voice of the Church to CHRIST. The Voice of the Church to CHRIST, or the Voice of the Prophets concerning the Nativity of CHRIST. Through the fast.

VEN. BEDE. The *Assyrians* are interpreted the *directing*, since, taught by the rules of faith, they strive to walk in the right ways. These *Asaph* addresses, *singing* GOD's *praises* with wonderful variety. Some copies have *A song against the Assyrians*, where it is understood that this *psalm* is *sung* against the devil, under the person of Sennacherib, King of the *Assyrians*, for against him the GOD of Israel was made *known in Jewry*, in CHRIST reconciling the world to Himself.

Asaph in the first part addresses the *directing*, that is, the faithful Jews, stating where GOD's Name is best made known by the declaration of His might. *In Jewry is God known.* In the second part, he tells the wondrous things which He hath wrought, *Thou shining wondrously*, (Vulg.) Thirdly, he warns all the devout that they should not cease to bring presents to GOD, Who ought to be feared, . Who purifies the spirit of, princes with His wholesome amendment. *For the thought of man shall confess unto Thee,* (Vulg.) And these sections are divided by Diapsalms.

SYRIAC PSALTER. Of Asaph, when Rabbath of the children of Ammon was wasted. Further, it denotes the vengeance of CHRIST's judgment against the ungodly.

S. ATHANASIUS. A Psalm of glorying in the LORD.

VARIOUS USES.

Gregorian. Thursday. Matins. [Maundy Thursday. III. Nocturn. Transfiguration. II. Nocturn.]

Parisian. Saturday. Matins.

Ambrosian. Tuesday of Second Week. I. Nocturn.

Monastic. Friday. Lauds. [Maundy Thursday. III. Nocturn.]

Lyons. Friday. Terce.

Quignon. Saturday. Sext.

ANTIPHONS.

Gregorian. As preceding Psalm. [Maundy Thursday. The earth trembled and was still, * when GOD arose to judgment. Transfiguration : Thou shining wondrously from the everlasting hills,* all the foolish of heart were troubled.

Parisian. As preceding Psalm.

Monastic. In Israel * His Name is great. [Maundy Thursday. As Gregorian.]

Ambrosian. As Psalm lxxii.

Mozarabic. Thou shining wondrously * from the everlasting hills.

1 In Jewry is GOD known : his Name is great in Israel.

2 At Salem is his tabernacle : and his dwelling in Sion.

The first words of this Psalm, observes S. Augustine, form a favourite boast of the Jews, as denoting not only that *God is known in Judea*, but that He is unknown elsewhere. And the boast is true, only not in their sense. For it holds good only of the spiritual Judah, not of that which is merely in circumcision and in the letter. For the very name of Jew is derived from the royal house of Judah, and when the Jewish people rebelled against the Son of David, and declared, "We

A.

G.

have no king but Cæsar," the sceptre and the knowledge of GOD passed from them to another people. It is, then, of the Christian Church we must understand the words, where GOD the SON is known with that knowledge which comes not of flesh and blood, but is revealed by our Heavenly FATHER. GOD is *known*, then, in His Apostles and Martyrs, *known* in His Confessors, *known* in all true Christians. For them who deny GOD by word or deed, though GOD may be known *to* them, yet He is not known *in* them. *His Name is great in Israel.* Israel, continues S. Augustine, is "he that sees

A.

GOD;" wherefore we cannot take it of those who took Him to be only a Man, when He walked in the flesh amongst them, and so slew Him, but must apply to those who see Him with the eye of faith. He is a true Israelite, adds

G.

Gerhohus, who wrestles with GOD, ever saying to Him, "I

Gen. xxxii. 26.

will not let Thee go, except Thou bless me." And this wrestling must be that of prayers and tears, struggling against the law of sin in our members, till we win the victory through assisting grace.

Z.

The Christian Church is called *Judah* first, say they, because Judah means "confession," and thus denotes the acknowledgment of sin, and the commencement of the active life ; and then *Israel*, as seeing GOD, because purified from sin, and therefore rising to the contemplative life of meditation and praise. *At Salem is His tabernacle, and His dwelling in Sion.* All the old versions, as well as the two English ones, have missed one especial force of this passage. There is no direct reference in words to any human habita-

De Muis.

tion, but to the lair of the Lion of Judah. The word סֻכּוֹ does not only mean *his tabernacle*, but *his covert*, and is so translated in another place, " He hath forsaken his covert, as

Jer. xxv. 38.

the lion ;" and the vaguer word מְעוֹנָתוֹ which succeeds may well be translated by "den," or some equivalent phrase. The

Ps. x. 9.

LXX. and Vulgate, reading, truly enough, *His place was in peace*, have yet lost sight of two noteworthy points : first, the parallel between *Salem* and *Sion*, answering to that of the previous verse, *Judah* and *Israel ;* and next, that the word *Salem* instead of Jerusalem occurs but twice elsewhere in all

Gen. xiv. 18. Heb. vii. 1, 2.

Holy Writ—once where Melchizedek is named as its king, and again when the Apostle is referring to that history. We are brought thus at once to the contemplation of that Lion of His people, Who is also the High Priest for ever after the order of Melchisedek, King of Salem, Prince of Peace. His

Cant. iv. 16; vi. 3.

leafy covert is indeed only in Salem, the Land of Peace, where in His garden He eats His pleasant fruits, and feedeth

B.

among the lilies ; but yet He dwells in Sion, the place of expectation, by His Sacramental Presence with His Church on

G.

earth. Gerhohus (as well as S. Bruno) has dwelt on this contrasted meaning, and, translating *His shade* (umbraculum) *is in Salem*, tells us of that shadow of the Most Highest which hovers over the peaceful soul, that it may rest there. Then he quotes as a parallel passage the words, "The LORD, Whose fire is in Zion, and His furnace in Jerusalem;" that is, as he explains it, the full vision of peace will be a furnace of perfect love, admitting no check, no waning; but as to the fire of our love in the earthly Sion, it is well with us if it be not actually quenched, but can be kept alive day by day, according to that precept of the Law, "The fire upon the altar shall be burning in it; it shall not be put out; and the priest shall burn wood on it every morning." *His place is in peace.* And that it may be with us, we must be at war with the world, with the devil, and with ourselves. So, warring externally and internally, we shall yet be at peace with GOD, in that peace which passeth all understanding; which begins with confession, and with abandonment of that quarrel of ours against Him which lasts so long as we seek to please ourselves. *And His dwelling in Sion.* Because He abides with those who look for Him, and dwells in their hearts. They add a touching explanation of this verse, taking it of CHRIST'S burial at Jerusalem. He was persecuted from the cradle to the grave, and there only was the malice of His enemies baffled; so that He was left in peace in Sion, in that new tomb of Joseph of Arimathea, where His rest was glorious.

Isa. xxxi. 9.

Lev. vi. 12.

A.

Ay.

3 There brake he the arrows of the bow : the shield, the sword, and the battle.

There. He had four resting-places, in each of which He destroyed some weapon of the enemy. In the Virgin's womb He cast down pride; in the manger, riches; in the Cross, the power of the prince of this world; in the grave, death. *There,* in that perfect peace where He now dwells, where there is no more sound of strife.

S. Albertus Magnus.

A.

> Summe pacatis,
> Semper feriatis
> In thronis vera
> Requies est mea.

The Hymn, In urbe med.

The arrows of the bow. The Vulgate has the *powers* of the bow; Cassiodorus, the *horns.* All fall short of the Hebrew, which is, *the lightnings of the bow,* a metaphor derived either from the swiftness of the arrow, or from the flashing of its point in flight. The literal sense of the whole passage appears to refer to the overthrow of Sennacherib's army, and it is most significant to read in the old Greek historian how that monarch's forces were routed by mice devouring by night their quivers, their bow-strings, and their shield-straps, leaving them defenceless and weaponless.

Herod. ii. 141.

Mystically, there are many explanations given. The *horns of the bow,* comments Cassiodorus, denote the malice

C.

S. Alb. Mag.

Jer. ix. 3.

Isa. ii. 4.

D. C.

of the proud, whereby they inflict wounds and hurt on others: the *shield* implies evil plottings and combinations, the *sword* open and violent wrong-doing, the *battle* all that makes against GOD's peace. Again, the *arrows of the bow*, striking from a distance, signify craft; as it is written, "They bend their tongues like their bow, for lies." The *shield* is excuse or defence of sin; the *sword*, evil suggestions, piercing even to the heart; and *war*, the struggle against holiness, which will end when men submit to be taught by the Saints, and to be subject to GOD. Wherefore is written, "Neither shall they learn war any more." Once more: the *arrows* denote sudden pleasure in an unexpected sin, often slaying the soul; the *shield* a perverse will, arming itself to defend its vices; the *sword* is sinful act; the *battle*, the habit of evil-doing.

4 Thou art of more honour and might : than the hills of the robbers.

A.

G.

S. Greg.
Mag. Mor.
xxvii. 10.

Didymus.

D. C.

Z.

This rendering, as well as that of the A. V., is incorrect. The true meaning of the passage is, *Thou art shining mightily from the mountains of prey*. It is still the Lion of Judah, leaping with a terrible bound from the mountains upon His enemies, and returning to His lair with His booty. The LXX. and Vulgate are nearer: they read, *Thou art enlightening wondrously from the everlasting mountains*. And they take it first of Him Who is the Light of the world, *shining* in it *wondrously* by the preaching of His *mountains*, the Apostles, whence the rays descend to the lowlier valleys of mankind. S. Gregory the Great carries us back further, and sets before us in long array the holy lives of the Fathers of the elder dispensation, receding from our view like a great mountain chain. Or it may be taken of the Angels whom GOD has appointed as ministering spirits, and especially those whom He sends as guardians to each human soul. And, finally, some take the *everlasting hills* to denote the heavens, whence GOD shines by His sending gladness and succour to darkened souls on earth.

5 The proud are robbed, they have slept their sleep : and all the men whose hands were mighty have found nothing.

P.

The mystical reference at once suggested by these words is to the Resurrection of CHRIST, when the proud Roman legionaries who watched at the sepulchre were spoiled, and the chief priests and scribes, those men whose hands were mighty to do evil, found nothing but the empty tomb : for He Whom they guarded was even then *shining wondrously* in the glory of His risen Body. But though this sense may fairly be got out of the Hebrew, which is, more exactly, as in the A. V., *The stouthearted are spoiled ; they have slept their sleep, and none of the men of might have found their hands,* (still referring to the nocturnal overthrow and disarming of Sennacherib's host,) it is not to be drawn from the LXX. and Vulgate, which read, *All the foolish in heart were troubled : they have slept their sleep, and all the men of wealth have found nothing in their hands.* They were *troubled* at the preaching of the Gospel, with its warnings of temperance, righteousness, and judgment to come ; *troubled* as the Athenians were when Paul preached on Mars' Hill ; but they continued to *sleep* in the pleasures of this life, wherein only they took delight ; and when the waking came for them, the vain show of their wealth vanished, *they found nothing in their hands,* because they had put nothing into the hands of CHRIST, had not given alms to the poor, nor laid up treasure in heaven like Zaccheus the Publican. They have slept *their* sleep, even when waking ; for, sleeping or waking, in all their life they sought their own gain, and glory, and pleasure, not the things of JESUS CHRIST. The Saints sleep their sleep too, slumbering to sin and to the world, as it is written, " I sleep, but my heart waketh." *Men of wealth.* Wealth which is gathered here, and left here ; which we, therefore, call a dream, not an inheritance. Wealth which we sum up in the old distich :

A.

S. Greg. Mag. Mor. xviii. 18.

G.

Cant. v. 2.

S. Ambros Lib. de Nab. 6.

> Somnus, bulla, vitrum, glacies, flos, fabula, fœnum,
> Umbra, cinis, punctum, vox, sonus, aura, nihil.

Cd.

6 At thy rebuke, O GOD of Jacob : both the chariot and horse are fallen.

The A. V., agreeing with the version of S. Jerome, completes the sentence with the words, *into a dead sleep.* The other old versions read, *They who mounted on horses have slept.* The primary reference is to the death-sleep of Sennacherib's warriors :

> For the Angel of Death spread his wings on the blast,
> And breathed in the face of the foe as he passed ;
> And the eyes of the sleepers waxed deadly and chill,
> And their hearts but once heaved, and for ever grew still.
>
> And there lay the steed with his nostril all wide,
> But through it there rolled not the breath of his pride ;
> And the foam of his gasping lay white on the turf,
> And cold as the spray of the rock-beating surf.
>
> And there lay the rider distorted and pale,
> With the dew on his brow and the rust on his mail ;
> And the tents were all silent, the banners alone,
> The lances unlifted, the trumpet unblown.

Who are they that *mount on horses?* They who will not be humble. It is no sin to ride, but it is a sin to be stiff-necked

A.

against GOD, and to count oneself as honourable. Because
thou art rich, thou hast mounted; GOD rebukes, and thou
sleepest. Terrible is the wrath of that rebuker, yea, terrible
is His wrath. Mark the awful truth. Rebuke involves
sound, and sound is wont to rouse men. But such is the
weight of GOD's rebuke, that the Psalmist says, *At Thy rebuke, O God of Jacob, they who mounted on horses have slept.*
Behold what Pharaoh's sleep was, when he mounted. For
his heart watched not, but was hardened at rebuke. Hardness of heart is sleep. I pray you, brethren, consider how
they sleep who still refuse to condemn their old life, and
wake to the new, when the Gospel, and Amen, and Alleluia
are sounding through the whole world. GOD's Scripture
was once in Jewry; now it is chanted through the whole
world. In that one nation it was said that there is One GOD,
Who made all things to be adored and worshipped. Now
where is He unnamed? CHRIST hath risen. He Who was
mocked on the Cross hath now set that very Cross whereon
He was mocked on the brows of kings, and yet men sleep.
GOD's wrath, my brethren, is great. Better for us who have
heard Him Who saith, "Awake, thou that sleepest, and
arise from the dead, and CHRIST shall give thee light." The
spiritual Assyrians, under their king Antichrist, riding on
the black horses of lying and the pale ones of envy, shall be
cast into the deep sleep of the second death at the last day.
But there are other riders who go out under that Captain,
Whose Name is "Faithful and True," on the white steeds of
chastity and the red ones of Martyrdom; who, when vexed
by scorn and torture in this world, yet have their rest in Him;
"for so He giveth His beloved sleep."

Margin notes:
Eph. v. 14.

G.

Rev. xix. 11.

Ps. cxxvii. 3.

Adam. Vic-
torin. The
Sequence,
*Heri mundus
exultavit.*

> In CHRISTO sic obdormivit,
> Qui CHRISTO sic obedivit,
> Et cum CHRISTO semper vivit,
> Martyrum primitiæ.

7 Thou, even thou art to be feared : and who may
stand in thy sight when thou art angry?

Margin notes:
Ay.

Acts vii. 51.

S. Greg.
Mag. Mor.
in Job ix.

The answer at first is, No one. For those sinners who, as
S. Stephen said, "do always resist the HOLY GHOST," can
make no effectual struggle against Him. But His Saints do
stand in His sight when He is *angry.* So Moses stood,
pleading for sinful Israel; so Aaron stood, with his censer
between the living and the dead; so Phinehas, when in his
zeal he executed judgment with his spear; so David, when
he offered himself to the destroying angel; so Elijah, when
he called down the rain. But they do it not in their own
strength. He supplies the weapons against Himself, by His
merciful grace infused into their souls. *When Thou art
angry.* The words have a special meaning, explained by the
following verses :

8 Thou didst cause thy judgment to be heard from heaven : the earth trembled, and was still,

9 When God arose to judgment : and to help all the meek upon earth.

They take it, for the most part, of the Last Day. *To be heard from heaven,* by the trumpet of the Archangel, sounding to the doom. The *earth,* all earthly and unholy souls, must then indeed *tremble,* and, utterly put to silence, unable to plead, must *be still,* when God the Son in His Majesty shall *arise to judgment.* There is no comment on these words so deep as the awful stanzas of Thomas of Celano : **R.**

> Quantus tremor est futurus,
> Quando Judex est venturus,
> Cuncta stricte discussurus.
>
> Tuba mirum spargens sonum,
> Per sepulcra regionum,
> Coget omnes ante thronum.
>
> Quid sum miser tunc dicturus,
> Quem patronum rogaturus,
> Cum vix justus sit securus?

The Sequence, *Dies Iræ.*

There are other ways also of looking at the passage, besides that literal one which sees here some fresh detail of the Assyrian overthrow. They remind us how, when the Judge ascended the tribunal of the Cross, and spoke His decision in the words, "It is finished," there was the stillness of the three hours' darkness, the trembling of the great earthquake, when the rocks were rent, and many bodies of the Saints arose. They tell us, too, of the time when He arose, yet more gloriously, from the tomb; "and behold, there was a great earthquake, for the Angel of the Lord descended from heaven, and came and rolled back the stone from the door, and sat upon it." And observe the reason given for the Lord's so arising to judgment, whether we take it of the Passion, the Resurrection, or the Last Day. It is not to show His power, not for the sake of vengeance, but *to help all the meek upon earth,* because the especial office of Christ is to be the Redeemer of mankind, whence also He is called Jesus. When He appears again, "Blessed are the meek, for they shall inherit the earth." Lorinus aptly cites lines meant for a very different monarch : **L.**

Hugo Card.

S. Matt. xxvii. 52.

D. C.

S. Matt. xxviii. 2.

Hugo Card.
S. Matt. v. 5.
L.

> Est piger ad pœnas Princeps, ad præmia velox,
> Quique dolet quoties cogitur esse ferox.

Ovid. Ep. ex Pont. 1, iii. 55.

And he stops there. Better had he carried on the quotation :

> Qui vincit semper, victis ut parcere possit,
> Clausit et æternâ civica bella serâ.

Multa metu pœnæ, pœnâ qui pauca, coërcet ;
Et jacit invitâ fulmina rara manu.

**10 The fierceness of man shall turn to thy praise :
and the fierceness of them shalt thou refrain.**

A.

The latter clause of the verse is rather, *with the remainder
of wrath Thou shalt gird Thyself.* And the whole meaning
of the verse is then that the display of GOD's might humbles
His enemies, till they are compelled to praise Him, and that
He binds all their power, so that they can only move at His
will. It is the history of S. Paul's conversion, and of many
a sinner since, turned from fierceness and wrath, to be
CHRIST's true servant, bound closely to Him for ever. But
the LXX. and Vulgate read, *For the thought of man shall
confess to Thee, and the remainder of* [*his*] *thought shall keep
festival unto Thee.* The interpretation, however, is not dissimilar, as many will have it that the words refer to GOD's
enemies, first led to confession of His Name and their sins,
and then devoting themselves to His service and glory.
Many, however, especially of the Greek Fathers, explain it
of the Last Judgment, when every secret thought of man's
heart must be disclosed to the Judge. The show and pomp
of that Great Day make it a *festival,* and the *remainder* of
our thoughts are here specified, because all will then come
out, even those suggestions and temptations of the evil one
which had no effect, but were cast aside. S. Bernard, following up a hint of S. Augustine, takes it of David, and then
of any preacher of righteousness, giving out from his stores
of learning all that the people can take in to make them confess GOD, and turning all his other acquirements, which are
too abstruse for them, to his own use, that he may rejoice
and praise the LORD. And, to omit many other explanations
of this most difficult passage, we may end with Vieyra's
quaint comment : that the *thought* refers to the conscious
mental acts of waking life, the *remainder of thought* to the
visions of gladness which GOD sometimes grants to His
chosen servants in their sleep.

Jansen.
Gandav.

Z.

Eusebius.

Serm. 62
in Cant.

Vieyra,
Serm. da S.
Franc. Xav.
dormido.

**11 Promise unto the LORD your GOD, and keep it,
all ye that are round about him : bring presents unto
him that ought to be feared.**

A.

Arnobius.

C.

S. Alb. Mag.

Innocent
III.

The Vulgate begins this verse with the word *Vow.* And
the Latin Fathers take it accordingly of all the solemn religious engagements into which Christians enter, as the Baptismal vow, and the marriage bond, of chastity, poverty, obedience, almsgiving, and the like, distinguishing them into
two classes, those necessary for all, and those profitable for
some. And they dwell at length on the obligation of such
promises. The matter is tersely stated by one who acted up

to the vows he had made : " To vow, is matter of choice, to   Ric. Hamp.
keep the vow, matter of necessity." *All ye that are round*
about Him. Not Pagans nor heretics, observes Cassiodorus,   C.
but only those who have the right to be round about His
Altar when they *bring presents unto Him.* All holy men are   Z.
round about Him, says the Greek monk, " for where two   S. Matt.
or three are gathered together in My Name, there am I in   xviii. 20.
the midst of them." The Carmelite adds that we must here   Ay.
include the Angels also, who stand " round about the throne,"   Rev. vii. 11.
and that the truest *present* we can bring is that of which
the Apostle tells us, " I beseech you therefore,.brethren, by   Rom. xii.1.
the mercies of GOD, that ye present your bodies a living sacrifice, holy, acceptable unto GOD, which is your reasonable
service."

12 He shall refrain the spirit of princes : and is
wonderful among the kings of the earth.

For *shall refrain,* the Vulgate reads *takes away.* They
explain it first of GOD's dealings with rulers like Pharaoh,   D. C.
Sennacherib, and Nebuchadnezzar, and indeed any who are
proud in heart, and presume to set their wills against Him.   A.
Or, in a good sense, He refrains and checks the *spirit* of His
princes, those saintly men whom He makes captains in His   B.
army, *He is wonderful* or *terrible* amongst those *kings of the*
earth who have conquered their own earthly bodies and keep
them in subjection for His dear sake. To them indeed those
words of another Psalm apply, " Be wise now therefore, O   Ps. ii. 10.
ye kings; be learned, ye that are judges of the earth," because in His Saints, kings to be crowned with gold in their
Master's kingdom, judges to be His co-assessors on the
throne of heaven, He is *wonderful* and *terrible* too : for " if   1 S. Pet. iv.
the righteous scarcely be saved, where shall the ungodly and   18.
the sinner appear ?"

ὦ βασιλεῖς, ὑμεῖς δὲ καταφράζεσθε καὶ αὐτοὶ   Hesiod.Opp.
τήνδε δίκην· ἐγγὺς γὰρ ἐν ἀνθρώποισιν ἐόντες   et Dies, 248.
ἀθάνατοι φράζονται ὅσοι σκολιῇσι δίκῃσι
ἀλλήλους τρίβουσι θεῶν ὄπιν οὐκ ἀλέγοντες.

Wherefore :
Glory be to the FATHER, known in the carnal Jewry ; glory
be to the SON, known in the spiritual Jewry, Whose Name is
great in Israel ; glory be to the HOLY GHOST, Who is that
Light wherewith Thou, O GOD, shinest wondrously from the
everlasting hills.
As it was in the beginning, is now, and ever shall be :
world without end. Amen.

COLLECTS.

Grant, O awful GOD, effectual working to the thoughts   Ludolph.
which confess Thee, that we, enlightened from the everlasting

hills, may, while we look for the glory of Thy Resurrection, be free from shame in the Judgment to come. Who livest.

Mozarabic. Lent. To Thee, O GOD the FATHER, the thought of Thine Only-begotten maketh confession; while His Manhood, by lowly obedience, brings back to Thee that which Adam lost through pride. Therefore vouchsafe to bruise our hearts, that by Thy training we may keep this solemn season fitly unto Thee. Amen. Through. (11.)

Mozarabic. Passiontide. O CHRIST, SON of GOD, Whose dwelling is mighty in Sion, turn our hearts unto Thee, that set on its watch-tower, we may in faith confess that Thou wast beaten, scourged, and condemned to death for us; that Thou, Who in time didst suffer for the ungodly, mayest be praised throughout eternity by the faithful. Amen. Through. (11.)

D. C. O GOD, the Searcher of deeds and hearts, to Whom every thought of man maketh confession, strengthen the weakness of our minds by the might of Thy blessing, that we may think such things as be just and holy, and by a good life pay our faithful vows to Thee, our LORD GOD. Through.

PSALM LXXVII.

TITLE: To the Chief Musician, to Jeduthun, A Psalm of Asaph. LXX. and Vulgate: To the end, for Idithun, A Psalm of Asaph. Chaldee Targum: For praise, by the hand of Jeduthun, a Psalm of Asaph.

ARGUMENT.

ARG. THOMAS. That CHRIST alone worketh great marvels. The Voice of CHRIST to the FATHER.

VEN. BEDE. *Asaph* denotes the *congregation* of the good. *Idithun*, the *leaper over* secular things; *the end*, that of them who advance in CHRIST. All this *Psalm* is sung by the faithful *congregation* which, *leaping over* the sins of this world with glorious steps, comes to that *end;* nought like which can be found. But it should be known that in the Hebrew it is *By Jeduthun*, not *For Jeduthun*, that it may signify that the Psalm, was not sung *for* him, but *by* him, and that which follows, *A Psalm of Asaph*, is not found in the true copies. This *Asaph*, whom we have said to be the *leaper over* sins, in the first statement of the Psalm testifies that he cried unto the LORD, and that he was taught by his troubles. *I cried unto the Lord with my voice.* In the second place, he counts up the thoughts which throb in hearts labouring in this world. *Thou holdest mine eyes waking.* In the third part he alleges that by the Divine goodness he was changed to a better tone of thought, so as to ponder steadfastly on the works and power of GOD, by constant attention to which things it is known that he profited. *And I said.* Fourthly; he proceeds to tell how divine wonders were wrought among the people by the LORD the SAVIOUR. *The waters saw Thee, O God.*

SYRIAC PSALTER. Of Asaph, concerning the longsuffering and wonders of GOD, and how David overcame the LORD's enemies.

VARIOUS USES.

Gregorian. Thursday. Matins. [Maundy Thursday. III. Nocturn.]
Parisian. Monday. Prime.
Ambrosian. Tuesday of Second Week. II. Nocturn.
Monastic. Thursday. Matins. [Maundy Thursday. III. Nocturn.]
Lyons. Friday. Matins.
Quignon. Monday. Vespers.

ANTIPHONS.

Gregorian. Thou art the GOD * that doest wonders. [Maundy Thursday. In the day of my trouble I sought the LORD with my hands.]
Monastic. The same.
Parisian. What is man, O LORD, that Thou art mindful of him ; or the son of man, that Thou visitest him ?
Ambrosian. I remembered GOD * and was glad.
Lyons. Be merciful * to our sins, O LORD.
Mozarabic. In the time of my trouble I sought the LORD * with my hands by night before Him, and I was not deceived.

1 I will cry unto GOD with my voice : even unto GOD will I cry with my voice, and he shall hearken unto me.

It matters little whether we read the verse thus, or, with the Vulgate, in the past tense throughout. Either way it represents to us the sure hope of a faithful soul in the promises of GOD. *With my voice.* And they note the stress on *my* voice. They who pray must do it for themselves, must do it with the articulate, intelligent voice of a man, not with the inarticulate sound of a beast, must direct their petition to GOD Himself. And hence it is laid down by all Canonists that a cleric or religious who is bound to the recitation of certain offices does not satisfy his obligation by being merely present while another is reciting them, without taking any more direct share himself, nor yet by silently reading the service, nor even by hasty and muttered recitation. He must cry to GOD with his *voice*, for "with the mouth confession is made unto salvation." Hence the words are repeated in the verse, because in all true prayer there is first a silent cry of the heart, which later finds utterance in sound. So it is written that "the LORD said to Moses, Wherefore criest thou unto Me?" though Moses had spoken no word. Who is the *I* that *cried?* It is spoken, they answer, of the mystical Adam, the type of mankind, crying from the creation till David, from David to CHRIST, and always *to the*

[margin notes:] Hugo Card. · Van Espen. · Rom. x. 10. · Ay. · Exod. xiv. 15. · P.

Ric. Ham-
pol.

Lord, as asking nothing save Himself, that He should be our
GOD and Master. *And He heard me.* How?

The Hymn
Te Christe
Patris Fi-
lium.

In fine namque sæculi
Constituit incarnari
Suum natum unicum
Lumen de lumine verum.

Qui hominem redimeret
Et paradiso redderet,
Unde est ejectus
A serpente quum deceptus.

2 In the time of my trouble I sought the LORD :
my sore ran, and ceased not in the night season;
my soul refused comfort.

Ay.
C.

That *time of trouble* is the whole of our earthly life, but
the Saints, instead of wasting it in vain complaints and angry
murmurs, turn at once to GOD from their sorrows, and cast
their burden on Him. The Vulgate has *the day of trouble.*

Ay.

And they point out how it is the *day,* as being the time for
work, and because sorrow clears and enlightens the soul.

S. Alb. Mag.

My sore ran. This is certainly not the meaning of the passage. The Hebrew literally is : *My hand was poured out :* a
metaphor denoting the act of stretching out. The LXX. and
Vulgate therefore give the sense, though not in its fulness,
by reading, *I sought the Lord with my hands before Him in*
the night, as it were groping eagerly for Him in the dark. S.

S. Hieron.
Orig. Hexap.

Jerome and Symmachus agree in reading *my hand was*
stretched out. It is the action of prayer that is implied, but
they add that good works also are here signified, and es-

D. C.
S. August.
Ep. cxxi. 13.
A.
S. John xx.
28.

pecially those of almsgiving. And they remind us how the
doubting Apostle stretched out his hands to CHRIST when he
was yet in the night of unbelief, and, touching Him, said,
"My LORD and my GOD." *In the night season.* We call

Ay.
A.

this life *night,* to distinguish it from the brightness of the
heavenly day. It is night till the day shines in the glorious
coming of our LORD JESUS CHRIST. Would you see that it is
night? If we had not a lantern here, we should have been
in darkness. For Peter saith: "We have also a more sure
word of prophecy; whereunto ye do well that ye take heed,

2 S. Pet. i.
19:

as unto a light shining in a dark place, until the day dawn,
and the day star arise in your hearts."

Hugo, Pia
Desid. i. 1.

Et dixi tam sæpe, Nitesce, nitesce, meus Sol!
Sol mihi tam longos obtenebrare dies.
Exorere, exorere, et medios saltem exere vultus,
Vel scintilla tui sola sat esse potest?
Quin etiam tanti si luminis abnuis usum,
Sufficiet radios expetiisse tuos.

Ceased not. The LXX. and Vulgate read, *And I was not*
deceived. By whom? By GOD, they reply for the most

part, "for He is faithful that promised," and He answered my Heb. x. 23.
prayer. By any snare or deceit of the devil, trying to dis- B.
tract my attention from prayer, is the wise comment of one
Saint. *My soul refused comfort.* That is, earthly comfort, Pet. Lomb.
for he estranges himself from the kingdom of heaven who Gl. in loc.
seeks comfort here. And that because, as S. Bernard ob- S. Bern.
serves, heavenly consolation is fastidious, and will not be
granted to those who accept any other. And therefore, Gerhohus is at some pains to dwell here on fasting as an element G.
of the spiritual life, and the fit preparation for all the great
Christian festivals.

3 When I am in heaviness, I will think upon
GOD : when my heart is vexed, I will complain.

This rendering does not agree either with the Hebrew or
the Vulgate. The literal sense is: *I will think upon God,
and will groan, I will ponder, and my spirit fainteth.* The
Vulgate reads: *I remembered the Lord, and was glad : I was
exercised,* [sc. in prayer] *and my spirit failed.* Having R.
turned from all earthly comfort, finding no help there, I
fixed my thoughts on GOD only, and found true pleasure
there. The LXX. reading, for *I was exercised,* is ἠδολίσχησα,
which in classical Greek, is used in a bad sense, *I prated.*
And so S. Augustine translates it *garrivi.* The spiritual A.
joy of GOD's presence has been too much for the newly-con-
verted sinner, he speaks too fluently and eagerly of holy
things, and thus exhausts his feelings, so that his spirit faints.
Others, keeping to the truer sense of meditation, explain this Ric. Ham-
fainting of the spirit to denote the utter failure of man's pol.
powers to penetrate the deep things of GOD. Or it may be
taken of the sudden collapse of the soul when it turns even for
an instant from the contemplation of divine things to indulge Ay.
any earthly thought. And so, one writing on the Song of
Songs cites this passage, adding, "Does not the Bride seem Gilb. de Hoyl.
to tell thee this, when she draws her Beloved to the secret Serm. xi. in
chamber? 'I held Him, and would not let Him go, until I Cant.
had brought Him into my mother's house.' She knew that Cant. iii. 4.
she could not keep her Beloved abroad, either surely or
wholly. And how hard it is for one that loves to halve the
mind between CHRIST and the world! How hard it is, I say,
to admit alien cares to the privileges of love, and to trouble
the heavenly secret with worldly strife."

4 Thou holdest mine eyes waking : I am so feeble,
that I cannot speak.

This verse also differs from the Vulgate, which is, *Mine
eyes have prevented the watches, I was troubled and spake
not.* Others may be content with taking their single turn of Z.
duty, I know the peril too well, and must myself see every L.

S. Mark xiii. 35.   guard relieved, "at even, or at midnight, or at the cock-crowing, or in the morning." And that is the best watch which
S. Alb. Mag.   is joined with fasting, as it is written, "Watching for riches
Ecclus.   consumeth the flesh." There is another reading here. *Mine*
xxxi. 1.   *enemies have prevented the watches*, warning us of the cease-
A.   less vigilance of our spiritual foes. *I was troubled* at the
  thought of my sins, and *spake not*, for very shame in the pre-
D. C.   sence of GOD, even to pray, far less to excuse myself, or
  to lay the blame on others, or, again, to seek for any human
  consoler.

5 I have considered the days of old : and the years that are past.

G.   *The days of old*, say they, refer to the time gone by in
S. Alb. Mag.   this world from Adam's fall, during which all things become
  old and frail, and the *years that are past*, or, as the Vulgate
  reads, the *eternal years*, to the unchangeable life for which
  man was created, where youth is perennial, and to that other
  awful existence, which is not life, but death for evermore.
D. C.   The literal sense, referring to the history of GOD's dealings
  with His people, as profitable for study, because showing that
Z.   He ever helped His Saints, is adopted by the Greek Fathers.
  But best and dearest of all is that interpretation which leads
  us to see here the contemplation of Him Who is the Ancient
L.   of Days, Whose years shall not fail.

> My GOD! how wonderful Thou art,
> Thy Majesty how bright,
> How beautiful Thy Mercy-seat
> In depths of burning light!
>
> How dread are Thine eternal years,
> O everlasting LORD!
> By prostrate spirits, day and night,
> Incessantly adored!
>
> How beautiful, how beautiful,
> The sight of Thee must be,
> Thine endless wisdom, boundless power,
> And awful purity!

6 I call to remembrance my song : and in the night I commune with mine own heart, and search out my spirits.

L.   They take the *song* literally, as denoting some psalm which
  Asaph had once composed, and now recalled for his own consolation. It would be better to explain it of meditation on
Exod. xv. 2.   Him of whom it is written, "The LORD is my strength and
  song." The word is entirely omitted by the LXX. and Vulgate, which read merely *I remembered*, construed with the
Ay.   previous verse, and then, *I meditated in the night with my*

heart, and pondered. Where, note, that the meditations of
righteous and unrighteous men differ in this, that the unrighteous think of all the good they have done, and forget
the evil, whereas the righteous remember and weep over their
past sins, and do not think of the good works they have done,
but of those which remain for them to do. And they observe how the verse marks the thoroughness of this meditation. It is *in the night*, with no disturbance or distraction,
with my heart, not with any companion, nor yet with the
powers of the head alone. *And pondered*, denoting that
time was taken over the task. Then, after all this self-ex-
amination, comes the practical result. *I hoed out my spirit*
(ἔσκαλλον) i.e., its weeds, say the LXX. *I swept out my spirit*
(*scopebam*) as with a broom, as the Vulgate takes it. And
that broom, say they, is sincere confession of sin. That is
the sweeping of the house which must precede its garnishing.
Cardinal Hugo points out the resemblance between a broom
and confession in the following lines, after urging that the
passage relates only to venial sins, like the dust of the pavement, not to such deeper ones as have to be dug out of the
soul :—

R.
G.

S. Alb. Mag.

S. Luke xi.
25.
Hugo Card.

> De virgis pannis, loca plana, noti vice verrit,
> Dum purgat, fœdat, pellit pulices, et arachnem,
> Scopa juvatur aquis, sonat, ferit, et lavat aras.

But all this is insufficient to content the soul which longs for
the coming of CHRIST, whether it be looking forward, like
Asaph, to His manifestation in the flesh, or desiring His
closer union with itself, as all that love Him do. And thus
there follows :

7 Will the LORD absent himself for ever : and will
he be no more intreated?

8 Is his mercy clean gone for ever : and is his
promise come utterly to an end for evermore?

9 Hath GOD forgotten to be gracious : and will
he shut up his loving-kindness in displeasure?

Will the Lord absent Himself? For *absent*, the A.V. more
correctly reads with the Vulgate, *cast off*. That is, observes
the Gloss, let man go, when man has cast himself off by his
sins. Or, reject the prayers of the penitent, by refusing him
the grace necessary to draw him back. And if He do it for
a time, will He also do it *for ever?* He has done it for a
time, in that He said, "Dust thou art, and unto dust shalt
thou return." He does it for a time still, in that He does
not give us such a measure of grace as that we cannot fall.
But He will not cast off *for ever*, because the time comes
when He will be intreated, or, as the Vulgate reads, *He will
yet add to be more pleased.* That will be, continues the Car-

Pet. Lomb.

D. C.

G.
Gen. iii. 19.

Ay.

G.

melite, in our country, when He will so stablish us that we can fall no more. That is already, more deeply says the Abbat of Reichensperg, for He Who in His just wrath cast off Adam for disobedience, hath recalled us to life by the obedience of one Man, and promising that He would be appeased by one of the seed of Abraham He fulfilled His pledge when He

S. Matt. iii. 17.
said, "This is My Beloved Son, in Whom I am well pleased."
Is His mercy clean gone for ever? That mercy is the Incar-

C.
nation, promised by the voice of the Prophets, but still un-revealed when the Psalmist spake. This is the *promise*, or, as the Syriac reads, the *Word*, which cannot fail. The Vulgate omits this phrase, and instead of *evermore*, reads

G.
with the A. V. thus: *from generation to generation*. The Mother of God will answer the question so put: "His mercy

S. Luke i. 50.
is on them that fear Him from generation to generation,"

L.
upon the elder Hebrew son and the younger Gentile one alike.

Forgotten. The word teaches us that God has begun *to be gracious*, so that our prayer is not that He should now first

B.
show Himself thus, but that He should carry on and complete His *mercy*, not *shutting up* its riches from mankind *in*

Hugo Vict. S. Bonaven-tura.
His displeasure at the guilt of original sin. They answer readily that God's mercy is greater than His anger, that He sends four blessings to counteract the three evils which befall man. Two outward troubles come on man, loss of goods or sickness of body. One inner sorrow, the worm of conscience, is added to them. But God's four consolations surpass them, quiet enjoyment of temporal blessings, health of body, peace of conscience, and the sweetness of everlasting joy, so that He gives more in His graciousness than in His displeasure.

10 And I said, It is mine own infirmity: but I will remember the years of the right hand of the most Highest.

O true medicine for the weakness of doubt! How better can we learn that it is only our *own infirmity* which makes us question the perfect love of God towards us, than by remembering the long and sorrowful three-and-thirty years which He, Who is the Right Hand of the Most Highest, spent in the form of a servant, that He might seek and save that which was lost? Not descending but for a moment, like His angelic messengers, but abiding Himself in His patience to help our infirmity.

The Hymn, *Apparuit benignitas.*

He sent no Angel to our race,
Of higher or of lower place,
But wore the robe of human frame,
And He Himself to this world came.

Nor willed He only to appear;
His pleasure was to tarry here;
And God and Man with us would be
The space of thirty years and three.

But this meaning, beautiful as it is, cannot be extracted from the Hebrew, nor from the old Versions. The passage is of extreme difficulty, and stands thus, literally, according to one reading: *It is my suffering, the changing of the right hand of the Most High:* and according to another, *the years of the right hand of the Most High.* The former is the sense De Muis. adopted by the Targum and by the Syriac Psalter, and the Z. intention there is to say, " It is for my sin, and in order to convert me, that the Hand of God is changed from working great marvels to deliver me from my enemies, as of old, to the chastisement of my offence." If the word שְׁנוֹת be taken to mean *years,* instead of *change,* the intention will be nearly the same, as the passage will then run, " My sorrow comes from meditating on the years of God's right hand, those years of old when He helped Israel whom He now chastises." The LXX. and Vulgate read thus : *And I said, Now have I begun, this is the change of the right hand of the Most High.* He says, *I have begun* my course towards God, and this is A. the *changing of His right hand,* because He has begun to G. change me, and to bring me into a secure place, where no enemy need be feared. *I have begun* to understand that which was too deep for me before, how God's mercy is greater than His anger, and that by the *changing* of the Eternal WORD, Ay. the *Right Hand of the Most Highest,* into the likeness of sinful man, and yet more, His *changing* me by washing me from my sins. Now, indeed, *I have begun* for the first time to live a spiritual life, to understand wisely, to know truly, going on the way of perfection, and beginning as it were D. C. afresh each day : *changed* from darkness to light, from sin to holiness, from carnal and animal to spiritual things, by the loving help and merciful presence of the Most High God.

11 I will remember the works of the LORD : and call to mind thy wonders of old time.

12 I will think also of all thy works : and my talking shall be of thy doings.

They take it of all GOD's works, of seeing His goodness S. Albertus and beauty in the whole creation, and then, more particularly, Magnus. of His dealings with the Patriarchs and the children of Israel. G. The Carmelite limits it yet further, explaining it chiefly of those signs which were types of the Incarnation, as the Ay. burning bush, Aaron's rod, and Gideon's fleece, and then of D. C. the wondrous mysteries of grace disclosed in the Passion and Death of the Redeemer.

13 Thy way, O God, is holy : who is so great a God as our God ?

The Prayer Book version weakens the first clause, which the A. V. renders better, *Thy way is in the sanctuary.* Of this way we have already spoken under Ps. lxviii. 24. We may refer it further to the visions of the Revelation, showing the Lamb of GOD at one time close to the golden altar before the throne, and at another in the mystic procession on Mount Sion, followed by the white-robed Virgin escort. That is His way, as He moves, Priest at once and Victim, in the ritual of heaven.

Rev. v. 6; xiv. 1.

Tibull. 2. i. 15.

> Cernite fulgentes ut eat sacer Agnus ad aras,
> Vinctaque post oleâ candida turba comas.

A.

But the interpretation of the present passage by the Fathers is somewhat different. They take it, *Thy way is in the Holy One*, in Him Who said, "I am the Way, the Truth, and the Life: no man cometh unto the FATHER but by Me." Then, His way will be in every holy soul which is conformed to CHRIST, which goes in the paths of righteousness opened by His example. CHRIST the Man is the Way, CHRIST the GOD is our Country. CHRIST is the Way in His lowliness, the Country in His Divinity. The Way, by which we come; the Country, to which we go. *Who is so great a God*, in all nobleness, wisdom, beauty, majesty, blessedness, holiness, sweetness, *as our God*, Who is Three in Persons, One in substance? None, most surely, for GOD, Most High and Blessed, excels all else incomparably, infinitely. "To whom then will ye liken Me, or shall I be equal? saith the Holy One."

S. John xiv. 6.

S. Hieron.

D. C.

Ay.

S. Bonaventura.

D. C.

Isa. xl. 25.

Bianco da Siena.

> Alfa e Omega, principio, mezzo, e fine,
> Altissimo creator di ciascuno,
> Amore immenso, le due divine
> Persone leghi tu, trino sol uno;
> A te, per te, gloria senza fine,
> O infinito sommo ben comuno
> Da tutti gloriosi triunfanti
> E dagli eletti quaggiù militanti.
>
> Bontà eterna, bontà infinita,
> Bontà increata, o bontà perfetta,
> Bellezza somma, bellezza inaudita,
> Bellezza immensa, a la qual suggetta,
> Ogni bellezza e bontà finita,
> Solo in te si ripos' e diletta,
> Bontà superna, bellezza divina,
> A te, per te, gloria senza fina.

14 Thou art the GOD that doeth wonders: and hast declared thy power among the people.

D. C.

Ex. ix. 16.

A.

Wonders in the land of Egypt, by overcoming Pharaoh, as it is written, "For this cause have I raised thee up, for to show in thee My power; and that My Name may be declared throughout all the earth:" greater *wonders* under the Gospel

by restoring sight to the blind, hearing to the deaf, health
to the sick; and marvels yet stranger than these wrought on
men's souls, making the drunken sober, idolaters believing,
plunderers charitable to the poor. And all this by His *power*,
to wit, " CHRIST the power of GOD, and the wisdom of GOD," 1 Cor. i. 24.
preached and *declared amongst the people* which are called,
Jews and Greeks alike. And to all lowly hearers since, who Hugo Card.
are not of the great ones, but are of the *people*, and among
them, yet are none the less capable of receiving the Word.

15 Thou hast mightily delivered thy people : even
the sons of Jacob and Joseph.

The A. V. more correctly reads, as does the Vulgate, *Thou* S. Albertus
hast with Thine arm redeemed Thy people. That arm is the Magnus.
Only-begotten SON, the " Arm of the LORD revealed" to all Isa. liii. 1.
the faithful, the arm stretched out once over Egypt to destroy, stretched out later upon the Cross to save. And it is   A.
well said, *the sons of Jacob and Joseph*, teaching us that He
saved two peoples, distinct, though sprung from the same
stock. *Jacob* denotes the believing children of Israel, *Joseph*
the Gentile Church, hated, rejected, sold into bondage by its
elder brethren, humbled, imprisoned, and then exalted and
throned, a fitting type of Him Who is the Head of that
Church, Who, suffering again in His Martyrs, is crowned
anew in their victory. And they take it mystically also, of Hugo Card.
the active Saints who wrestle with GOD, and of the contem- Ric. Hamp.
plative ones, who see visions of Him, both of whom He
redeems.

16 The waters saw thee, O GOD, the waters saw
thee, and were afraid: the depths also were troubled.

These words, applying in the first instance to the parting
of the Red Sea, have been referred since to the mysteries
of which that was a type. Thus they occur in the Baptismal
Offices of the Church of Edessa, as drawn up by the great Assem. Cod.
Mar Jacob, and in those of the Maronite Use. S. Augustine Liturg. i.
tells us, as is his wont, that the *waters* mean the nations of 247; ii, 349.
the earth, citing the Apocalypse in proof, and adds that the   A.
depths that are *troubled* are the consciences of sinners moved Rev. xvii. 15.
to confession. Others explain the *depths* to be the rulers   G.
and chief priests, Herod, Pilate, and Annas, Caiaphas, and
the like, who were *troubled* at the preaching of CHRIST, and S. Brun. Ast.
then carry on the reference to the Gentile monarchs who
received the Faith. And whereas the *waters* are mentioned Hugo Card.
first, they do not forget to remind us that fishermen were the
earliest believers in CHRIST. S. Ambrose tells us that the S. Ambrose.
waters which see GOD and fear Him are the good qualities
of the soul, which are calmed, not disturbed, by knowledge
of the Word; but that the *depths* which are *troubled*, denote

II.   Y

the evil qualities, which see Him not, and therefore have no
rest, according to that saying, "The wicked are like the
troubled sea, when it cannot rest, whose waters cast up mire
and dirt. There is no peace, saith my GOD, to the wicked."

Isa. lvii. 20. (margin)

17 The clouds poured out water, the air thundered : and thine arrows went abroad.

A.

If we take the *clouds* here, as so often, to denote the
Apostles, then the *water* will denote the gracious rain of the
Gospel, poured out by them over all the earth ; and the
second clause will also tell of the boldness of their preaching
who are called sons of thunder. And so the Paris Breviary,
in the Common of Apostles :

Santol. Vict.
The Hymn
Supreme
quales Ar-
biter. (margin)

> Totum per orbem nuntii,
> Nubes velut, citi volant :
> Verbo graves, Verbo DEO,
> Tonant, coruscant, perpluunt.

The *arrows* will then denote the words of the Evangelists,
which *went abroad* over the world. The LXX. and Vulgate
read here *pass through.* That is, the Gospel message does
not stop short in the ears, but pierces the heart. The first
clause of this verse reads thus in the LXX. and Vulgate,
The multitude of the sound of waters. It is, says S. Augustine, the mingled noise of confessions, hymns, and prayers
going up unceasingly from the Church. It is the multitude
of the nations themselves, converted to CHRIST, adds the
Carmelite. S. Bruno of Asti, connecting the words with the
previous verse, singularly explains it of CHRIST'S Passion,
saying, that when the depths, that is, the chief priests, had
been troubled, they stirred up the multitude, so that the cry
went up, as of the sound of many waters, "Crucify Him,
crucify Him." But the other interpretation accords better
with that verse of the Revelation : "And I heard as it were
the voice of a great multitude, and as the voice of many
waters, and as the voice of mighty thunderings, saying,
Alleluia, for the LORD GOD omnipotent reigneth."

A.
Ay.

S. Brun. Ast. (margin)

Rev. xix. 6. (margin)

18 The voice of thy thunder was heard round
about : the lightnings shone upon the ground ; the
earth was moved, and shook withal.

The first clause of this verse is of great difficulty, and the
Prayer Book rendering differs from all the other versions
except that of Hesychius, who reads ἐν κύκλῳ. The A. V.
reads *in heaven* instead of *round about;* the LXX., Syriac,
and Vulgate translate, *in the wheel.* The Æthiopic rendering
is *in the chariots.* The Hebrew is בַּגַּלְגַּל, which means a
sphere, wheel, or anything that revolves. It is explained by

Gesenius and Delitzsch of the whirlwind, and by Hupfeld of the rolling wheels of GOD's chariot, herein agreeing with the Carthusian, and with the Æthiopic Psalter, though the reference may rather be to the overthrow of Pharaoh's chariots. The interpretation *heaven*, as the sphere we behold, is that of Origen, as also of R. Ezra and R. Kimchi. S. Augustine, ridiculing the notion of a chariot in the sky, explains the *wheel* to be the round world, through which the Gospel was sent. Olympiodorus takes it of human life in general. S. Albert, citing that verse, "O my GOD, make them like unto a wheel," explains the words of the terrors of GOD's judgments amongst the multitude of the wicked. I am not sure that Parez is not the happiest in his explanation, referring, as he does, to the vision of Ezekiel, and reminding us of the Gospel chariot, borne by the four holy Evangelists.

D. C.
De Muis.
Z.
Origen.
A.
Cd.
S. Albertus Magnus.
Ps. lxxxiii. 13.
P.
Ezek. i. 15, 26.

> Hi sunt enim, CHRISTE,
> Quadrigæ tuæ, salvatio
> Quadrifidâ cruce,
> Quam rotæ dant evangelicæ.
>
> Auriga tui currus
> Super hos equos
> Scandens, Domine,
>
> Viam fac equis tuis
> In luto multo
> Nostri pectoris.
>
> Ut subvecti
> Hoc in curru
> Maris de tumultu,
> Portum perpetuæ
> Contingamus patriæ.

The Sequence *Regnum tuum*.

Thy lightnings. They explain it diversely, of the Apostles, of the miracles of CHRIST, of the mingled promises and threats of the Gospel, and of the rays of the Sun of Righteousness, visible to the world. *The earth was moved.* They take it first of the Jewish nation; occupied with the thought of a mere earthly deliverer, and then extend it to the stir and alarm of the whole Gentile world, beginning with Herod, and spreading over the Roman empire, at the advent of the new King. And it is also explained of each man's body, trembling at the terrors of judgment to come. *And shook withal.* So that the idols fell from their altars, and were destroyed, like the Egyptians in the Red Sea.

A.
Ay.
L.
G.
C.
P.

19 Thy way is in the sea, and thy paths in the great waters : and thy footsteps are not known.

Let us hear Prudentius, singing of Him Who trod the lake of Galilee in human form, as He trod the Red Sea ages before invisibly :

The Hymn
Da puer
plectrum.
Cath. ix. 49.
Ambulat per stagna ponti, summa calcat fluctuum,
Mobilis liquor profundi pendulam præstat viam,
Nec fatiscit unda sanctis pressa sub vestigiis.

G.

"And as Thou didst walk visibly upon the sea," exclaims
Gerhohus, "and gavest unto Peter the Apostle to do the
like, so now Thou walkest invisibly, and makest Thy ministers
also to walk upon the troubled hearts of the nations, which
yield themselves to Thee, to be trodden by Thy feet, beautiful with the preparation of the Gospel, that the *footsteps* of
Truth may be stamped on them in the *ways* of Thy commandments, and the *paths* of Thy counsels." It is in the
sea of bitter penitential tears, that His way to man's heart

Ay.
S. Albertus
Magnus.
Isa. xliii. 2.

lies; it is in the *mighty waters* of deep affliction and troubles
that He comes to the trembling soul, because He went
through the floods of sorrow Himself, and thus knows our
need, according to that which is written: "When thou
passest through the waters, I will be with thee; and through
the rivers, they shall not overflow thee." *Thy footsteps are*

Lu.

not known. Because, wisely says Ludolph, the lowly wisdom
of CHRIST is hidden from the wise and prudent of this world.

D. C.

And that especially is the case of them to whom He first
came, and who received Him not.

20 Thou leddest thy people like sheep : by the
hand of Moses and Aaron.

G.

They remind us how both Moses and Aaron were types of
CHRIST, our Lawgiver and High Priest, Who is alone the
Good Shepherd, and they dwell, as is their wont, on the supposed meaning of the names, taking Moses to be "Lifted up,"
and Aaron to be the "Mount of Strength." The true interpretations, telling us of Him Who was "drawn out" of
the grave, Who was the "Shining Light" to lighten the
Gentiles, bring us to the same thought. On the whole verse

Origen.
Comm. in
Num. 27.

there is no better comment than Origen's. "The hand of
Moses alone is not enough to draw out of Egypt. Aaron's
hand is needed also. Moses denotes knowledge of the Law,
Aaron familiarity with sacrifices and oblations to GOD. We
need then, when going out of Egypt, not only to have knowledge of the Law and the Faith, but also the fruit of works
pleasing to GOD. For if, departing from Egypt, and converted to GOD, I cast away pride, then I have sacrificed a
bullock to GOD by the hands of Aaron : if I overcome wan-
tonness and uncleanness, I will believe that I have offered a
goat to the LORD by Aaron's hands : if I conquer lust, a
calf ; if foolishness, then I shall appear to have sacrificed a
sheep. When these sins of the soul are being purged, the
hand of Aaron works in us ; and the hand of Moses is with
us, when we are enlightened by the Law to understand these
things, and therefore each hand is necessary for them that

come out of Egypt, that not only perfect faith and knowledge may be found in them, but perfect acts and deeds too."

And so:

Glory be to the FATHER, the Most Highest; and to the SON, the Right Hand of the Most Highest; and to the HOLY GHOST, the Gladness wherewith I thought upon GOD, and was glad.

As it was in the beginning, is now, and ever shall be: world without end. Amen.

COLLECTS.

O GOD incomprehensible, Who doest great wonders, Who Ludolph. changedst the waters, which once stood still in Thy sight, at later time into wine, we humbly beseech Thee to hear the voice of our crying, to bestow on us such remembrance that we may never forget Thee. Who livest.

O LORD, hear the prayer which we pour forth in the time Mozarabic. of our trouble, attend to our desire when we stretch out our Passiontide. hands in the night, hasten, as the best of Comforters, to our souls, and be our Redeemer by Thy pardoning grace: and as Thou didst purchase us by Thy voluntary Passion, so deliver us by Thine unconquered power from the snare of the hunter. (11.)

Almighty and wonderful GOD, Who alone doest great Mozarabic. marvels, and Who reignest for ever, forget us not, nor let us be lowered to the utterance of human praise, but grant us to be glad in thinking on Thee, in Whom is our fullest glorying. (11.)

We pray Thee, O LORD, cast us not away from favour with Mozarabic. Thee, but grant us yet time to win Thy mercy, that the Right Hand which punished our sins may be our everlasting remedy in our contrition. (11.)

O merciful GOD, of unspeakable lovingkindness to thou- D. C. sands, take not away from us Thy mercy for evermore in wrath at our sins, forget not to have pity on us, but by Thy compassion vouchsafe us to be counted worthy of everlasting salvation. Through. (1.)

PSALM LXXVIII.

TITLE: Maschil of Asaph. LXX. and Vulgate: Of understanding, for Asaph. Chaldee Targum: The understanding of the HOLY GHOST, by the hand of Asaph. Arabic Psalter: Of Asaph, an address to the people.

ARGUMENT.

ARG. THOMAS. That CHRIST feeds His people with the spiritual food of manna. The Voice of the Prophet to the Jews. The Voice of CHRIST touching the impiety of the Jews, and of Christians, eating the LORD's Flesh, murmuring against Him. The Voice of CHRIST touching the Jews, when GOD showed them many wonders by Moses, and they believed him not.

VEN. BEDE. *Asaph*, as we have said before, is to be explained as the *synagogue*, that is, *gathering together*, but as *Understanding* is prefixed, he shows that the faithful synagogue is here meant. In the first part of the Psalm only two verses are ascribed to the person of the LORD, to increase respect for the utterances whose opening the King Himself hath appointed. *Hear My law, O My people.* In the second part Asaph speaks more fully, charging the Jews with ingratitude for the LORD's bounties, and with despising His commands through their wicked heart. *Which we have heard and known.* Thirdly, he sums up the gifts which GOD bestowed on Israel, who, nevertheless, ceased not to murmur. *Marvellous things did He in the sight of our forefathers.* Fourthly, he tells what punishment came upon them, and how the sentence was mitigated by the LORD's mercy: *When the Lord heard this He was wroth.* Fifthly, they were punished for their murmurings, but they returned again to entreat the LORD, acknowledging His wondrous works. *While the meat was yet in their mouths.* In the sixth place, they spake again deceitfully and followed their wonted errors, yet the mercy of GOD destroyed them not as they deserved. *They did but flatter Him with their mouth.* Seventhly, he tells how they provoked the LORD in the wilderness, though Egypt had been afflicted for their sakes. *Many a time did they provoke Him in the wilderness.* Eighthly, the sin of Jewish obstinacy is joined to the narrative of the LORD's bounties. *But as for His own people, He led them forth like sheep.* Ninthly, a terrible vengeance follows, so that He forsook the tabernacle in Silo, and delivered His people into captivity, and afterwards chose the Mount Sion, and David for king, of whose seed CHRIST, the Physician of salvation, should come. *When God heard this, He was wroth.*

SYRIAC PSALTER. Of Asaph. He implies in it that they ought to keep GOD's commandments, and not be as their forefathers.

EUSEBIUS OF CÆSAREA. A plain statement of CHRIST to the Church concerning the transgression of the former people.

VARIOUS USES.

Gregorian. Thursday. Matins.
Monastic. The same.
Parisian. Wednesday. Matins.
Ambrosian. Tuesday of Second Week. II. Nocturn.
Lyons. Thursday. Matins.
Quignon. Tuesday. Matins.

ANTIPHONS.

Gregorian. As preceding.
Parisian. First portion : The children * which were yet unborn ; to the intent that when they came up, they might teach their children the same ; that they might put their trust in GOD. Second portion : He took away * His people like sheep, and brought them out in hope.
Monastic. Incline * your ear to the words of My mouth.

Ambrosian. As preceding Psalm.
Lyons. First portion: As Monastic. Second portion: He chose the tribe of Judah, even the hill of Sion, which He loved.
Mozarabic. Incline your ear to the words of My mouth, * My people, hear My law.

This long Psalm is unquestionably a religious protest from the Temple of Jerusalem against the schism of the Northern kingdom headed by the powerful tribe of Ephraim, at some period after the reign of Solomon. There are two occasions which seem to fit in with its language more than any others, to either of which it may be ascribed. The first is the outbreak of war between Abijah and Jeroboam I., and perhaps just after the great battle in which the latter was defeated. (2 Chron. xiii.) The second is the proclamation of Hezekiah, summoning all Israel and Judah to keep the Passover together at Jerusalem for the first time since the revolt from Rehoboam. (2 Chron. xxx.) The former of these opinions is that preferred by most critics; but the mention of Asaph in the title does not interfere with either view, as the name undoubtedly denotes a family, and not a single person.

1 Hear my law, O my people : incline your ears unto the words of my mouth.

They begin by asking who is the speaker here. And the answers vary. Some, of whom the greatest are S. Augustine, Cassiodorus, and Dionysius the Carthusian, take it of the FATHER; S. Athanasius, S. Jerome, and Beda, with several others, of CHRIST; S. Bruno of the Church, the mystical synagogue; and others of Asaph himself, or David. *My people,* whom I have made Mine own by separating thee from the nations, and by delivering thee from Pharaoh's power. *Hear My law,* not only that given on Sinai, especially the ten moral precepts, but the higher law (of which the earlier dispensation was but a figure) given after your rescue from the darkness of the spiritual Egypt by the offering of the true Paschal Lamb. *Hear,* ye on whom I have not laid the burden of the old Law, but to whom I have given a new law, written not on tables of stone, but on the tables of your hearts by My finger, in giving you the HOLY GHOST, to teach you all truth and to declare to you things to come. *Incline your ears* in faith *to the words of My mouth,* not going back, because they are hard to be understood, but saying with the Apostle, "LORD, to whom shall we go? Thou hast the words of eternal life." *S. John vi. 68.*

G.

D. C.

G.

2 I will open my mouth in a parable : I will declare hard sentences of old;

We have an inspired commentary on these words in that chapter of the Gospels which itself contains seven parables. "All these things spake JESUS unto the multitude in parables; and without a parable spake He not unto them : that it might *S. Matt. xiii. 34.*

be fulfilled which was spoken by the Prophet, saying, I will open My mouth in parables ; I will utter things which hav

S. Isidor. Hispal.

been kept secret from the foundation of the world." The

S. Clem. Alex. Strom. 2.

passage is thus fatal to the bare literal interpretation of Holy Writ, as it teaches us that all the events recorded therein have a deeper mystical intent underlying the narrative, a truth on

1 Cor. x. 1— 11.

which S. Paul dwells more than once. *I will open My mouth.* This form of speech occurs but rarely in Scripture,

Gal. iv. 24.

and always marks some important utterance to follow. Thus

Cd.

begins the account of Job's words: "Then Job opened his

S. Matt. v. 2.

mouth." It is spoken again of CHRIST's Sermon on the

Acts viii. 35.

Mount, of S. Philip's instruction to the eunuch, and of S.

Acts x. 34.

Peter's recognition of the Gentiles. *Hard sentences of old.*

L.

The Gospel gloss receives a supercommentary from the

Rom. xvi. 25.

Apostle, exhaustive of the meaning: "The preaching of JESUS CHRIST, according to the revelation of the mystery, which was kept secret since the world began, but now is made manifest, and by the Scriptures of the Prophets, according to the commandment of the everlasting GOD, made known to all nations for the obedience of the faith." *Of old.* The

S. Bonaventura.

Vulgate reads *from the beginning.* Where note that CHRIST is the beginning and the end; because the beginning is infinite, so must be the end. Wherefore, He is ever beginning, whether He begin or end. He ever beginneth, for He can lack no perfection, and therefore cometh to no defect, and He is thus perfect, because He is the Alpha and Omega.

3 Which we have heard and known : and such as our fathers have told us ;

4 That we should not hide them from the children of the generations to come :. but to show the honour of the LORD, his mighty and wonderful works that he hath done.

C.

We have *heard* from the Prophets of the Old Testament,

S. Albertus Magnus.

we have *known* by the revelation of CHRIST the WORD, as it

1 S. John i. 1.

is written, "That which was from the beginning, which we have heard, which we have seen with our eyes, which we have

Ay.

looked upon, and our hands have handled, of the WORD of

Deut. vi. 20.

Life." *Our fathers have told us.* According to the Commandment in the Law, which bade them explain to their sons the testimonies, statutes, and judgments which the LORD enjoined them. *That we should not hide them.* The Vulgate reads, *They have not been hidden from their sons in the other generation.*

C.

They explain it, their *sons* by succession of teaching, not of race, the spiritual *generation* of the Christian Church. *An-*

A.

other generation, notes S. Augustine, because regenerate. *The honour of the Lord* (where the Vulgate reads *praises*)

S. Albertus Magnus.

denotes, according to S. Albert, the increase and preservation of the children of Israel, and belongs to GOD's attribute of goodness. The *mighty works* refer to the deliverance from Egypt, and belong to His power. The *wonderful works* to the miraculous feeding, expressive of His wisdom.

5 He made a covenant with Jacob, and gave Israel a law : which he commanded our forefathers to teach their children ;

6 That their posterity might know it : and the children which were yet unborn ;

7 To the intent that when they came up : they might show their children the same ;

He made a covenant. The LXX. and Vulgate, a little more S. Athana-
forcibly, *He raised up a covenant,* or *testimony.* The earlier sius.
commentators agree in seeing here a reference to the Ark of A.
the Covenant or testimony, which was the visible witness to the Hesychius.
Law, which had been witnessed before by Angels. Gerhohus, P.
in a beautiful passage too long to extract, tells us that all the G.
early Hebrew story, from the visions of Bethel and Peniel,
was only the *testimony* borne by halting *Jacob* to the coming
Lawgiver ; and when He, the true *Israel,* the Prince with
GOD, appeared, then mere testimony ceased, and the *Law*
went forth from Sion, written with His finger on the hearts
of His Apostles and elect. *When they came up,* out of their R.
sins, to be born anew in the laver of baptism, then they were Ric. Hamp.
to be taught fully the mysteries of GOD theretofore hidden D. C.
from them. These are they of whom the Apostle speaks :
" My little children, of whom I travail in birth again, until Gal. iv. 19.
CHRIST be formed in you."

8 That they might put their trust in GOD : and not to forget the works of GOD, but to keep his commandments ;

9 And not to be as their forefathers, a faithless and stubborn generation : a generation that set not their heart aright, and whose spirit cleaveth not steadfastly unto GOD ;

Cardinal Hugo tells us that the three theological virtues Hugo Card.
are summed up in the former of these verses. Hope is expressly named ; Faith keeps GOD's doings in remembrance ;
Love seeks to obey Him for His own sake. The union and
growth of these virtues in the soul is, then, the end proposed
by the whole teaching of this psalm. They note the epithets L.
of the ninth verse, and point out that all unbelievers against
knowledge are included under them ; Jews, being *faithless
and stubborn ;* heretics, choosing error, *that set not their
heart aright ;* and bad Christians, *whose spirit cleaveth not
steadfastly unto God.*

10 Like as the children of Ephraim : who being harnessed, and carrying bows, turned themselves back in the day of battle.

Ay.

The Targum here mentions a Jewish legend that the Ephraimites sallied out of Egypt thirty years before the Exodus, and after a severe defeat from the first enemies they encountered, returned to their bondage. Other literalist interpretations take the words of the pressure put on Aaron to make the golden calf; of the defeat by the Amalekites, at Hormah; of the slaughter of Ephraim's sons by the Gittites; and of the more fatal rout by the Philistines, when the Ark was taken, so that the Israelites, in that sense, *kept not the covenant* of the LORD; and of the alliance of Ephraim and Syria against Jerusalem, in the days of Ahaz. The mystical explanations are not less various. The Doctor of Grace tells us that the words are spoken of them who live by works, and not by faith, that the *bows* denote outward acts and that shooting with the bow, and then turning back in the battle, implies heeding and purposing in the day of hearing, and deserting in the day of temptation. S. Gregory the Great explains the passage of Doctors of the Church, whom *Ephraim,* "fruitfulness," denotes, shooting their arrows of rebuke with the elastic cord of the New Testament from the stiff bow of the Old, but often shrinking from the toil of resolute struggle against the sins and vices of the day. Again, as Ephraim was set above his elder brother, Manasseh, so the Jewish people was chosen in preference to the Gentile nations, but fell away in its time of probation, despite the arrows of boastful promise to keep the statutes of the LORD. Or we may take it of the rich of this world, abounding in temporal fruitfulness, uttering crafty words of feigned religion, but turning back, and getting behind Satan, in the *day of battle,* that is, in the very first approach of a struggle against sin, being too cowardly to await the actual conflict.

C.
Ex. xxxii. 1.
D. C.
Numb. xiv. 44.
De Muis.
1 Chron. vii. 21.
P.
1 Sam. iv. 10.
S. Brun. Ast.
Isa. vii. 2.
A.

S.Greg.Mag.
apud S.
Paterium.
B.
Hugo Card.
Ay.

Ric. Hampol.

Cd.

11 They kept not the covenant of GOD : and would not walk in his law;

12 But forgat what he had done : and the wonderful works that he had showed for them.

Lu.
Deut. v. 27.

They kept not the covenant as they had promised, saying, "Speak thou unto us all that the LORD our GOD shall speak unto thee, and we will hear it, and do it." *And would not walk in His law,* by making progress and persevering therein. It is not their actions that are here blamed, but their will, since even when they did so walk, it was not heartily. Wherefore they are said not to have done it, because they did it not of good will and love, for there are men who do right, but would cease doing so if they dared. Fear, not love; necessity, not will; the fear of punishment, not the desire of righteousness, compels them. Thus they go on from falling away and turning back, which may be mere weakness, into *forgetting* what GOD has done, which is black ingratitude and sin, especially as the works were *wonderful* and *for them*. So when CHRIST came, not to destroy the Law, but to fulfil it, by making its moral precepts more stringent, the Jews hated Him, forgat all His wondrous works of healing and mercy, would not walk in His law, and slew Him. S. Alb. Mag.

G.

13 Marvellous things did he in the sight of our forefathers, in the land of Egypt : even in the field of Zoan.

Our forefathers. They raise the question here why the forefathers, but just blamed for unbelief, should be cited here as authorities. The Targum explains it of Abraham, Isaac, and Jacob, to which S. Augustine objects that they were dead before the miracles in Egypt were wrought, though they may have been still present in spirit; and he prefers to understand it of Moses and Aaron. *In the land of Egypt.* That is, as they for the most part agree, in the spiritual darkness of this world, of which Egypt is a common type in the Bible. *In the field of Zoan.* The name in the LXX. and Vulgate here is *Tanis,* a mere linguistic corruption. The word means " low country," and the expositors, understanding it as "lowly command," allegorize it freely. S. Augustine takes it of the lesson of humility given us in the dark world, that we may be exalted in the world to come. Cassiodorus points the remark by citing the words of CHRIST, "Take My yoke upon you, and learn of Me; for I am meek and lowly of heart, and ye shall find rest for your souls." And this law He gave to our fathers His first disciples, when He wrought His miracles in their sight. He who is the GOD of Abraham, Isaac, and Jacob, is the LORD of Apostles, Martyrs, Confessors, of whom they were the types. Apostles, because as He told Abraham to go forth from his own country, so He sent His Apostles throughout the world, wherefore S. Peter said, " Lo, we have left all, and followed Thee." Martyrs, because they devoted themselves freely to death as His Sacrifice, like Isaac. Confessors, because Leah and Rachel, Jacob's two wives, denote the active and the contemplative life. S. Albert explains Tanis or Zoan of the Blessed Virgin, compared to a plain or *field,* because it is healthy, smooth, wide, and fruitful, while she was sinless, gentle, loving, the Mother of the Divine Food; and that field *Zoan,* the "lowly command," because she said, "Be it unto me according to thy word;" and again, "He hath regarded the lowliness of His handmaiden." A.

A.

C.

S. Matt. xi.
29.

G.

S. Alb. Mag.

S. Luke i.
38, 48.

14 He divided the sea, and let them go through :
he made the waters to stand on an heap.

A.
G.

He not only brought the children of Israel through the
Red Sea, but brought His spiritual Israel through the waters
of Baptism, reddened with His own Blood, making the flowing and ebbing tides of carnal desire stand still. *On a heap,*

Ay.

The LXX. and Vulgate read, *As in a leathern bottle,* because
on the one hand these desires are swollen, and on the other,
they are so restrained by GOD's grace as to be unable to flow
out and drown the soul.

15 In the day-time also he led them with a cloud :
and all the night through with a light of fire.

A.

G.

Heb. xii. 29.

C.

Ay.

S. Albertus
Magnus.
Isa. xxv. 4.
Cant. ii. 3.
D. C.

S. Cyril.
Alex.

The *cloud* is the Incarnation of CHRIST, whereby He led
His people, during the *day-time* of the world, visible to them
in the lowliness of His Flesh. But in the *night*, when no
man can work, that terrible night of the Judgment, He will
appear as "a consuming fire" in the awful might of His
Godhead. Or, the cloud of the day-time is the shadowy type
of the earlier dispensation, the *fire* of the *night*, the revelation
of the antitype, CHRIST Himself, in the evening of the world.
Again, the *cloud* may denote the Sacramental veils under
which He is now hidden, the *fire*, the open vision yet to come.
Once more, the cloud typified Him of Whom it is written,
"Thou hast been a shadow from the heat," and Who, that
He might bestow that shadow, was willing to be planted as a
tree in this world, so that the Bride cries : "I sat down under
His shadow with great delight." And then the first words
tell us of the cool refreshment of His divine grace ; and the
latter, speaking of the Light of Light, express the glory of
wisdom, the enlightenment of the inner man by CHRIST in
all trouble and distress, seeing that He is ever near the afflicted. S. Cyril of Alexandria inverts one of the foregoing
explanations, saying that CHRIST led the Jews in the darkness by fire, that is, by a law of threatenings and punishment,
but that He leads Christians in the light by the watery clouds
of Baptism.

16 He clave the hard rocks in the wilderness : and
gave them drink thereof, as it had been out of the
great depth.

17 He brought waters out of the stony rock : so
that it gushed out like the rivers.

G.

"Wherever they went," observes Gerhohus, "He brought
waters for them out of the Rock, which followed them. Not
that the rock moved from its place, but the water which
flowed therefrom followed them. And one has expressed
this wondrous mystery very well in verse, saying:

Bis silicem virgâ Dux percuiit atque Propheta,
Ictio bina Ducis sunt duo ligna Crucis,
Fons est de petrâ populo datus absque metretâ,
Larga salus homini corpore de Domini.

For the smitten *Rock* is CHRIST crucified, from Whose right side flowed pure and living water, of which whoso drinks, it shall be in him a well of water springing up into everlasting life. This we say of the SPIRIT, Whom they that believe in Him receive. And this SPIRIT was certainly typified in that visible water which flowed from the right side of the Temple, to wit, of CHRIST's Body. For CHRIST had as it were two sides: the left, according to time, of His weakness and mortality; the right, according to time, of His glorified Humanity. From the left side water did not issue, so long as JESUS was not yet glorified; but His right side poured out water for the salvation of His people, because He, crowned with the glory and honour of the Resurrection, on the very day of His Resurrection and glory breathed on the Apostles, saying, 'Receive ye the HOLY GHOST: whosesoever sins ye remit, they are remitted unto them; and whosesoever sins ye retain, they are retained.' Also, when crowned with the diadem of the Ascension, He poured forth the water of the HOLY GHOST in such abundance that the Apostles and Disciples, drinking thereof, were accounted drunken, and said to be full of new wine." *In the wilderness.* In Judea, forsaken of GOD for its sins, as one will have it; on the Cross, where He was desolate and unfriended, as the Carthusian more touchingly explains it. But the majority keep to the usual allegory of the world, as opposed to the Land of Promise. *He brought waters out of the stony rock.* Smiting our hard hearts with His Cross, He caused floods of penitential tears to burst forth. So runs that ancient Western collect: "Almighty and most merciful GOD, Who broughtest a well of living water out of the rock for Thy thirsting people; bring forth tears of compunction from our hard hearts, that we may lament our sins, and of Thy pity, obtain pardon thereof." *Like the rivers:*

S. John iv. 14; vii. 39.

Ezek. xlvii. 1.

S. John xx. 22.

D. C.

Ay.

Sacram. Greg.

Prestad me, fuentes e rios,
Vuestras eternas corrientes,
Aunque en estas cinco fuentes
Las hallan los ojos mios.

Lope de Vega.

18 Yet for all this they sinned more against him : and provoked the most Highest in the wilderness.

Their additional sin, observes S. Augustine, was unbelief, wherefore it is said that they *provoked* GOD *in drought*,[1] because, though their bodies drank of the water from the

A.

---

[1] LXX. ἐν ἀνύδρῳ, Vulg. *in inaquoso.*

G.

Numb. xx. 10.

Ps. xcv. 11.

Hugo Card.

rock, their minds remained parched and dry of all spiritual grace. And as even Moses failed in belief at this time and place, saying, "Must we fetch you water out of this rock?" so the Scribes and Pharisees, smiting the true Rock with the two beams of the Cross, believed not that living water would flow out. The punishment of Moses and Aaron for their sin was exclusion from the Promised Land; "unto whom I sware in My wrath: that they should not enter into My rest," and the punishment of the unbelieving Jews is exclusion from the Paradise of GOD. And they too provoke GOD *in the dry place* who through hardness of heart refuse to weep for their sins.

19 They tempted GOD in their hearts : and required meat for their lust.

R.

Lyranus.

D.C.

S. Matt. vi. 31, 33.

Ay. L.

Note, observes Remigius, that the tempting consisted in asking with their lips for that which they thought beyond GOD's power to give them, and thus the Psalmist condemns all untrustful prayer. One mediæval commentator applies this text to monks seeking mitigation of their fasts and rules of diet from their superiors, without adequate cause. The Carthusian, more deeply, extends it to all Christians who neglect the SAVIOUR's counsel: "Seek ye first the kingdom of GOD and His righteousness;" and, "Take no thought, saying, What shall we eat? or, What shall we drink? or, Wherewithal shall we be clothed?" but are anxiously disquieted about mere temporal things. They remind us, as to tempting, that the act is ascribed to GOD, to man, and to the devil, and in all cases it implies making trial of the person tempted. It is never taken in a good sense when man is said to tempt GOD, by making unnecessary trial of His power, goodness, or wisdom, it is never in a bad sense when GOD is said to tempt man, it may be good or bad when one man tempts another, and it is always evil when the devil tempts man.

20 They spake against GOD also, saying : Shall GOD prepare a table in the wilderness?

21 He smote the stony rock indeed, that the water gushed out, and the streams flowed withal : but can he give bread also, or provide flesh for his people?

G.

C.

Haymo.

S. John vi. 52.

Gerhohus acutely remarks that the form their unbelief took was ascribing the miracle of the water to natural causes. They admitted the fact, but denied its true character, and now demanded a test from Moses; and he thus pierces more deeply into the nature of their sin than those who see here a denial of GOD's omnipotence. The words have been also most aptly applied to those unbelievers who said, "How can this Man give us His Flesh to eat?" and then to the heretics of

a later day, acknowledging one Baptism for the remission of   Rupert.
sins, but denying the Real Presence in the Holy Eucharist.   Ric. Hamp.
Another acute criticism of Gerhohus deserves citation.   He   G.
observes that two objections have been brought against the
order of events in this Psalm; first, that the literal manna
preceded the striking of the rock; and next, that the institution of the Holy Eucharist preceded the issue of water from
CHRIST'S side.   He replies that the Prophet has done it
rightly, because the Passion, whose power and virtue under-
lie the Sacrament, and give it efficacy, began before the
Last Supper, because the Betrayal had taken place, and the
horror of the Agony was drawing near; and Christians now
must be baptized into the Passion and Death of CHRIST before they can approach to feed on His Flesh and Blood at
the Holy Altar, the Table which He has prepared for His
people in the wilderness of this world.   Yet another interpretation may be added, taking the words of those who disbe-
lieve in the full remission of sins.   They allow that GOD can
touch a hard heart, and dissolve it into tears of remorse; they
doubt His power to strengthen the penitent in perseverance,
and to feed his soul with divine grace unto the end.

22 When the LORD heard this, he was wroth : so
the fire was kindled in Jacob, and there came up
heavy displeasure against Israel.

23 Because they believed not in GOD : and put not
their trust in his help.

For *He was wroth*, the Vulgate reads *He delayed*.   And   C.
they explain it that in His longsuffering He deferred the
punishment deserved, nay, even *heard* their petition.   And
this longsuffering of the LORD is most plainly evident, ob-   D. C.
serves the Carthusian, under the New Law.   Heathen philosophers knew somewhat of GOD's majesty; Jews knew His
righteousness, but only Christians know His patience.   *So*   L.
the fire was kindled in Jacob.   They take it literally of the   Numb. xi. 1.
burning at Taberah when the people complained, and then of
avenging wrath in general.   But Remigius and Richard of   R.
Hampole agree in seeing here the fire of appetite kindled in   Ric. Hamp.
the hearts of the murmurers by their own act, on account of
which *displeasure came up*, so as to reach the very chief of
the people.   The English hermit continues his explanation
by pointing out that when *Jacob* (that is, all Christians bound
to wrestle against sin,) is *kindled* with earthly passion, then
wrath ascends upon Israel, on those priests and prelates whose
duty it is to warn and correct by precept and example.   *In*
His help.   The A. V. more correctly, agreeing with the LXX.
and Vulgate, *In His salvation:* and thus the words tell us
of that day when the firebrand of the Roman soldier caught   Joseph. Bell.
the golden window of the Temple, and the doom of Israel   Jud. vi. 4, 5.

Hugo Card.

D. C.

was accomplished because it believed not in GOD's Salvation, the Crucified Son of David. Cardinal Hugo explains this whole passage, like the previous verses, as referring to the impugners of the Holy Eucharist; and the Carthusian takes it of all sinful Christians, unrepentant even when the Church has been scourged by infidels, heretics, and tyrants, for their sins.

24 So he commanded the clouds above : and opened the doors of heaven.

C.

This, observes Cassiodorus, is one of the parables and hard sentences of the Psalm, and denotes the command given to the *clouds*, His preachers, to declare, through the Holy Scriptures, which are the *doors of heaven*, the advent of the SAVIOUR, Who comes to be received as the Manna of our souls, in the mystery of Communion. They take the *clouds* also of

D. C.

the Angels, employed as messengers of the Incarnation, as when S. Gabriel came to Nazareth, and the heavenly host appeared to the shepherds of Bethlehem, and the *doors of heaven* are then explained as the mouth of the Apostles, opened to preach Wisdom, or, more literally, as denoting the everlasting doors lifted up to allow the egress of the angelic

Rupert. in
S. Matt. i.

herald. And Rupert beautifully explains these doors of the body and soul of the Virgin Mother of GOD. The LORD opened her soul to receive His command in faith, and her womb that His Only-begotten might come forth :

Venantius
Fortunatus.
The Hymn
O gloriosa
femina.

> Tu Regis alti janua
> Et porta lucis fulgida;
> Vitam datam per Virginem
> Gentes redemptæ plaudite!

25 He rained down manna also upon them for to eat : and gave them bread from heaven.

26 So man did eat angels' food : for he sent them meat enough.

Theodoret.

Z.

The Greek Fathers remind us that the literal manna is said by CHRIST not to have come from heaven, when the Jews quoted this very text: "Verily, verily, I say unto you, Moses gave you not that bread from heaven, but My FATHER giveth you the true bread from heaven," and that manna is called *Angels' food*, not because the Angels eat of it, but because they ministered it. And the Chaldee Targum, paraphrasing thus, "*food which came down from the dwelling-*

S. Ambros.

S. Alb. Mag.

D. C.

place of Angels," partly supports this teaching. The Latin Fathers, however, seasonably remind us that CHRIST, the true Manna, is rightly called *Angels' food*, because the heavenly powers derive their life and vigour from contemplating Him in open vision. So S. Peter Damiani:

Where the Sacred Body lieth, eagle souls together speed, The Hymn
There the Saints and there the Angels find refreshment in their *Ad perennis*
vitæ fontem.
   need,
And the sons of earth and heaven on that One Bread ever feed.

How CHRIST is fitly compared to Manna, we may read in
the eloquent words of the Carmelite. "As the manna came **Ay.**
down like dew or rain, so CHRIST descended upon earth into
the Virgin like the rain into a fleece of wool. As the manna
was like coriander seed, a fragrant herb, so CHRIST was the
fruit of the Blessed Virgin, a sweet and fruitful plant, as she
herself rightly speaks, 'As the vine brought I forth pleasant Ecclus. xxiv.
savour.' It is said to have been white, because of His pu- 17.
rity, which He ever retained, for 'He did no sin, neither
was guile found in His mouth.' It is said to have been
beaten in a mortar, because of the pains which He endured.
Its taste was like honey, because of His spiritual sweetness.
And it is particularly stated that the children of Israel gathered it every day except on the Sabbath. Where note,
that the six days wherein it was gathered denote our toil-
some life in this world, and by the Sabbath we understand
that blessed life which is free from labour. So long as we
live in this world, then, we need this spiritual food of CHRIST's
Body. Therefore It is daily sacrificed in the Church, and is
received for the support of devout believers. Wherefore It
is that daily bread for which we daily ask, saying, 'Give us
this day our daily bread.' But in the life of blessedness,
there will be no need of this Sacrament, because we shall see
Him as He is. Therefore it is said, that the manna was not
gathered on the Sabbath, but that a double portion was gathered on the sixth day, to signify that this food, given to
the righteous at their end, not merely increases their merit,
but leads them to the kingdom. And it seems wonderful
that all meted the same measure, so that he who gathered
much had no more, and he who gathered little, no less;
which figured that in the Sacrament whole CHRIST is contained in the whole, and the whole in each part, so that he
who receives an entire Host, receives just as much as he who
takes a part, and conversely. It is said to have been collected to the amount of an omer, which is a measure of three
pints, to denote that we have to take account of three things
in that Sacrament, to wit, the Body, Soul, and Divinity,
which are united. And observe, that the children of Israel
said, when they saw that food, *Man hu*, which is, being interpreted, What is this? For if we ponder on what this Sacrament contains, we shall find many wonders, surpassing all **A.**
natural thought." To set down here all that Saints of old S. Ambrose.
have loved to say on this great mystery, in hymn, and liturgy, S. John
Chrysos.
and comment, would be impossible. Enough, if we cite a S. Cæsarius.
very few. Thus, in accordance with that belief expressed S. Sedulius.
by so many Saints, that the Angels throng round the Altar Lanfranc.
Rupert, &c.

Liturg.
S. Jacobi.
when the Holy Sacrifice is being offered, we have the Prayer of the Cherubic Hymn from the ancient Church of Jerusalem :

Cf. Miss.
Mozarab.
Dom. 1 post
Oct. Epiph.
King of Kings, yet born of Mary, as of old on earth He stood,
Lord of Lords, in human vesture,—in the Body and the Blood,—
He will give to all the faithful His own self for heavenly food.

Rank on rank the host of heaven spreads its vanguard on the way,
As the Light of Light descendeth from the realms of endless day,
That the powers of hell may vanish as the darkness clears away.

At His feet the six-winged Seraph, Cherubim with sleepless eye,
Veil their faces to the Presence, as with ceaseless voice they cry,
Alleluia, Alleluia, Alleluia, Lord Most High !

Cd.
They tell us, too, of the purity and holiness, like that of Angels, which befits those who would receive that Food, even Him Who feedeth among the lilies. Thomas à
Kempis.
Imit. Christi.
iv. 5. 1. "Hadst thou the purity of Angels, and the holiness of S. John the Baptist," says one whose golden words have strengthened countless devout souls, "thou wouldest not be worthy to receive or handle this Sacrament. For it is due to no human merits that man may hallow and touch the Sacrament of Christ, and take the Bread of Angels for his food." The word which all the old Versions agree in rendering *Angels* is, more literally, *mighty ones*. Fitly is that meat called " the food of mighty men" which strengthened so many athletes in the arena of martyrdom, which gave women and children the valour of heroes, so that of their last struggle they might say,

> O that Bread! that Bread of Angels!
> O that Corn of mighty men !
> Never, never had we tasted
> Of its mightiness as then!

He sent them meat enough. The LXX. agreeing with modern critics, translate by ἐπισιτισμόν, *food for the journey*, a fitting name for the mystic food, whether as the cake baken on the coals of bitter suffering, in the strength of which Elijah went 1 Kings xix.
6. through the wilderness forty days and forty nights unto the mount of God, typifying the pilgrimage of all Christian souls, or as the viaticum in that yet more awful journey when the soul goes forth alone. The Vulgate reads *cibaria*, in the plural, and Rupert. Rupert reminds us, that though Christ be the One Bread, yet as He gives Himself freely like the rain, in all lands and nations and countless churches, we may well D. C.
B. say *foods*, multiplied as He is unspeakably to be the nourishment of His people.

> O esca viatorum,
> O panis Angelorum,
> O Manna cœlitum,

> Esurientes ciba,
> Dulcedine non priva
> Cor te quærentium.

Enough, for all, and that to the end of the world.

**27 He caused the east wind to blow under heaven :
and through his power he brought in the south-west
wind.**

In the first clause S. Jerome's version reads, *He took* **Ay.**
away the east wind, that is, made it cease to blow, in order
that the westerly wind from the Red Sea might bring over **Numb. xi. 31.**
the quails from Africa. And it is explained mystically of
GOD sometimes punishing man by taking from him the **Cd.**
wholesome but painful wind of discipline, and giving him the
softer but dangerous airs of temporal prosperity. Another **S. Greg. Mag. Mor. xxvii. 26.**
interpretation sees here the rejection of the Jewish people,
and the bringing in the Gentiles in their room. The Vulgate **D. C.**
reading, *transtulit,* is explained by the Carthusian to denote
the sending forth preachers, whom the winds typify, through
the world; the *south wind* (Vulg. *Auster*) denoting the most
saintly and lofty teachers of the Gospel, and the *south-west
wind* a lower and less mystical class. Cardinal Hugo, keep- **Hugo Card.**
ing still the Eucharistic Sacrifice in view, understands here
the breath of the HOLY SPIRIT effecting the consecration,
and the attendant ranks of angels which accompany the
rite.

**28 He rained flesh upon them as thick as dust :
and feathered fowls like as the sand of the sea.**

Flesh, in that He taught them the doctrine of the Incar- **B.**
nate WORD; and that like *dust,* either because He was light
in arising, because of His holiness, and free from all the
waters of sin, or because He was humbled even to the dust
for our sakes. *Feathered fowls.* Cardinal Hugo explains it **Hugo Card.**
of the Angels who bore the soul of CHRIST from heaven to
earth at the Incarnation. Gerhohus takes it of the winged **G.**
words of doctrine, clean or unclean, according as they are
Catholic or heretical. Ayguan, interpreting the *flesh* as **Ay.**
bodily troubles, takes the *fowls* to be spiritual consolations,
arising up from those very troubles, and bearing our souls
upwards towards GOD. Another will have it that both
clauses denote earthly pleasures : the flesh which brings us **Drogo Card. Serm. 3, de Passione.**
to the dust; the frivolous enjoyment, which, uplifting us for
a brief moment, brings at last to barrenness and bitterness,
denoted by the *sand of the sea.* Once more, the *feathered
fowls* have been explained in a good sense, as contemplative
Saints, friends of GOD, whom He rains upon the Church to **D. C.**
be the pastors of souls.

29 He let it fall among their tents : even round
about their habitation.

Z.

Their tents, implying the general diffusion of the gift
throughout the host of Israel; *their habitation*, showing that
each person in the camp had his own private share.   Thus it
tells us of the Flesh of CHRIST given to the Churches at
large, and also to be the food of individual Christians.   Their

D. C.

tents, again, as so often, denoting the militant Saints of active
life; their *habitation* the stiller retreat of the contemplative,
both filled alike with the bounty of GOD.

30 So they did eat, and were well filled; for he
gave them their own desire : they were not disappointed of their lust.

Ric. Hamp.

They remind us that in the eagerness of the Jews for
earthly food, and the full contentment of their longing, we
may see the Christian desire for spiritual delights, and especially for Communion with CHRIST in His own Sacrament.
He gives them Himself, the Desire of all nations; He does
not disappoint them, for He is more than they can imagine
or hope.

31 But while the meat was yet in their mouths,
the heavy wrath of GOD came upon them, and slew
the wealthiest of them : yea, and smote down the
chosen men that were in Israel.

D. C.

1 Cor. xi. 27.

Not in the mouths of the elect, but of them who eat unworthily, into whom Satan enters, as he did into the traitor
Judas, and of whom the Apostle says, "Whosoever shall eat
this bread or drink this cup of the LORD unworthily, shall be
guilty of the Body and Blood of the LORD."   *And slew the
wealthiest of them.*   The A. V. more exactly reads, as does
the Vulgate, *the fattest of them.*   That is, continues the Carthusian, He slays spiritually them who receive CHRIST car-
nally, by taking from them charity and grace.   For, as the

1 Cor. xi. 29.

Apostle says, "He that eateth and drinketh unworthily,
eateth and drinketh damnation to himself, not discerning the
LORD's Body."   *And smote down* (Vulg., *hindered*) *the chosen
men that were in Israel.*   He excluded those who seemed to
be eminent in the Church from entering the heavenly kingdom, because of unworthy communion; for the word *chosen*
does not always in Holy Writ imply election to everlasting

Ric. Ham-
pol.

life.   The slaying applies sometimes even to temporal chastisements, since the Apostle adds to the previous sayings,

1 Cor. xi. 30.

"For this cause many are weak and sickly amongst you, and
many sleep."

32 But for all this they sinned yet more : and believed not his wondrous works.

33 Therefore their days did he consume in vanity : and their years in trouble.

They refer the words in the first place to the evil report Ay.
brought back by the spies, and to the consequent reluctance P.
of the Israelites to attempt the conquest of Canaan ; followed
as it was by the punishment of the forced wandering in the
desert, till all the adults save Caleb and Joshua were *consumed
in vanity*, that is, cut off in the vain and endless toil of the
wilderness ; thus losing, as Parez adds, the hope revealed to
Abraham, Isaac, and Jacob, of being buried in the land
where Messiah should make His grave, that they might share Gen. i. 25.
in His Resurrection ; a hope which induced Joseph to command the removal of his bones from Egypt. *In trouble.* So R. Ezra.
The LXX., Syriac, and Vulgate read *with speed.* And they
explain it of the sudden judgments which fell on them, as in
the matter of Korah, and of the fiery serpents, Exactly like Ay.
this was the unbelief of the Jews in the time of CHRIST, refusing to believe, though they saw so many signs and wonders wrought by Him. Wherefore it is said, " But though S. John xii.
He had done so many miracles before them, yet they believed 37.
not on Him : that the saying of Esaias the Prophet might be
fulfilled, which he spake, LORD, who hath believed our re- Isa. liii. 1.
port? and to whom hath the arm of the LORD been re-
vealed?" They preferred to go back into the Egypt of the P.
carnal and ceremonial law, and their doom is to perish in the
spiritual wilderness, finding no entrance into the rest of the
people of GOD. *Vanity* and *speed* are rightly conjoined here, Z.
remarks Euthymius, because all who live easy and frivolous
lives find the years pass swiftly by them ; while those who
labour intently in the paths of virtue find their time long by
reason of their toil.

**34 When he slew them, they sought him : and
turned them early, and inquired after GOD.**

" GOD," observes Lactantius, rebuking the heathen, " passes Div. Instit.
away most readily from men's recollection, just when they ii. 1.
ought to give honour to Divine mercy, as enjoying His bounties. But if any heavy trouble come upon them—if the terrors of war resound—if deadly pestilence brood over them—
if long drought deny sustenance to the corn—if wild storms
or hail come upon them—they have recourse to GOD ; they
ask His aid ; GOD is besought to help. . . . They never remember GOD save when they are in distress ; but when fear
is over and perils are gone, then they hurry eagerly to the
temples of the gods. To these they make libations and sacrifices, and offer crowns. But GOD, Whom they besought
in their need, they do not thank by so much as a word."
Here, too, a false repentance is set before us. They sought Ay.
Him, not for the sake of eternal life, but fearing to end the A.

G.

vapour too soon. It was not they whom He slew that sought Him, but those who feared to be slain in like manner. But the Scripture speaks thus because they were one people, and it is spoken as of one body. *Early*, like hirelings obliged to come at a fixed hour, but not like men ready to endure the burden and heat of the day, far less to persevere until the evening, like that true labourer of GOD of whom it is written,

Ps. civ. 23.

"Man goeth forth to his work, and to his labour, until the evening." *And inquired after God.* The Vulgate reads, *came unto Him.* How may this be? asks Gerhohus. Is He, Who is everywhere, to be approached on foot, in chariots or on horses, in ships, or any like means? Nay, only by the movements of the heart can we come to GOD or depart from Him.

35 And they remembered that GOD was their strength : and that the high GOD was their Redeemer.

S. Brun. Ast.

It would not be said here, tersely remarks a Saint, that they *remembered*, if they had not first forgotten. Their

P.

strength, or, as LXX. and Vulgate, their *helper*, against Amalek, their *redeemer* from Pharaoh. Where note that the

C.

title *Redeemer* is here given to the FATHER, as it is also in

S. John viii. 36.

another place to the SON, "If the SON therefore shall make you free, ye shall be free indeed;" and in a third passage to

Rom. viii. 2.

the HOLY GHOST, "for the law of the SPIRIT of life in CHRIST JESUS hath made me free from the law of sin and death;" wherefore the attributes of power and redemption are common to the Holy Trinity. Moreover, the SON is our

B.

Helper, by co-operating with our good works, as He was our *Redeemer* on the Cross.

36 Nevertheless, they did but flatter him with their mouth : and dissembled with him in their tongue.

37 For their heart was not whole with him : neither continued they steadfast in his covenant.

Ay.

The old Versions, yet more forcibly, read, *They loved Him in their mouth.* This false love, offered to Him before Whom all the secrets of the heart are bare, endured till the

S. Matt. xv. 7.

time of CHRIST. Wherefore He Himself saith, "Ye hypocrites, well did Esaias prophesy of you, saying, This people

Isa. xxix. 13.

draweth nigh unto Me with their mouth, and honoureth Me with their lips; but their heart is far from Me." Isaiah fore-

S. Hraban. Maur.

saw, comments S. Hrabanus, the deceits wherewith the Jews should craftily war against the Gospel, and he speaks in the

S. Matt. xxii. 16.

person of the LORD. For they honoured CHRIST with their lips when they said, "Master, we know that Thou art true, and

teachest the way of GOD in truth;" but their heart was far
from Him, when they "sent forth spies, which should feign
themselves just men, that they might take hold of His words."   S. Luke xx.
20.
And if we take the passage to refer to false Christians, especially to the traitor Apostle, we may dwell on the reading of
the Illyrian Psalter, *They kissed Him with their lips. Their
heart was not right*, remarks Gerhohus, precisely because it   G.
was not *with Him*. And they were not *steadfast in His cove-*
nant, because they failed to keep the precepts of the Law,   P.
even under the terrible sanctions of the blessings and curses.   Deut. xxviii.
Nor were they faithful in the inheritance of the New Testa-   A.
ment, faith in which, though veiled, was found amongst the
elect even then; and now that it is revealed, it is not found
in many of the called. A German commentator sums up
this verse with a quaint old Teutonic saw:

> Lieben ohne Treu,   Bakius.
> Beichten ohne Reu,
> Und beten ohne Innigkeit,
> Die drei Ding sind verlohrne Arbeit.[1]

38 But he was so merciful, that he forgave their
misdeeds : and destroyed them not.

39 Yea, many a time turned he his wrath away :
and would not suffer his whole displeasure to arise.

GOD is *merciful* to both good and bad, "for He maketh   Ay.
His sun to rise upon the evil and the good, and sendeth rain   S. Matt. v.
on the just and on the unjust;" and this as regards temporal   45.
blessings. But this is the mercy of His left hand, not of His
right; temporal, not spiritual; since it is common to good
and bad. In this wise GOD was merciful to that nation,
in that He did not root it out from the earth, as it deserved.
The spiritual mercy, that of His right hand, whereby sins
are remitted and eternal blessings are conferred, is quite
other. That He did not bestow on that evil generation,
for the greater part of them perished in the wilderness, for
murmuring and rebelling against GOD. Therefore, when it
is said that *He forgave their misdeeds*, it is not to be understood of their evil fathers, but of the children who succeeded
them, such as David, Hezekiah, Josiah, and Daniel, and
other righteous men, to whose misdeeds GOD was merciful
when they sinned, as clearly appears in the case of David.
And destroyed them not. It is well said, *many a time.* Once   L.
He spared them at the intreaty of Moses, after the sin of the   Exod. xxxii.
Golden Calf; a second time at Taberah; thirdly, when Aaron   31.
stood with his censer between the living and the dead;   Numb. xi. 2;
  xvi. 48;
fourthly, by means of the brazen serpent; fifthly, by suffering   xxi. 9.

---

[1] Those who are interested in | seventh verse to be the middle
such details may like to know | one of the Psalter.
that the Jews count this thirty-

G.

B.

R.

the younger generation to enter Canaan. And even when the sins continued, He reserved the root of the tree whose branches He lopped, from which shot forth the Apostles and the first company of believers, *not suffering His whole displeasure to arise.* Even still He holds to His pledge, keeping a remnant of the Jews undestroyed, that they may turn at the last to CHRIST.

A.

The Doctor of Grace warns us that this text has been abused by those who, desirous of continuing in sin, exalt GOD's mercy at the expense of His justice. But, rejoins he, if, to speak in their own words, GOD will perhaps not destroy even bad men, He will certainly not destroy good men. Why then do we not rather choose that wherein there is no doubt? For they that lie to Him in their tongue, while their heart holds somewhat else, think and wish even GOD to be a liar, when He threatens them with everlasting punishment. But as they do not deceive Him with their lie, so He does not deceive them with His truth.

40 For he considered that they were but flesh : and that they were even a wind that passeth away, and cometh not again.

S. Bonaventura.

S. Alb. Mag.

Prov. ii. 19.

A.

G.

S. Greg. Mag. Mor. iv. 9.

S. Matt. iv. 10.

Cant. vi. 13.

Ay.

Two things are set before us here : GOD's clemency, *for He considered ;* and man's wretchedness. The latter is twofold. He is *but flesh,* and therefore liable to sin. He is a *spirit that passeth away* from GOD and holiness, and has no power to *come again ;* as it is written, "None that go unto her return again, neither take they hold of the paths of life." No power of himself, doubtless, adds S. Augustine, but he can be called back by grace. And that fitly; for man, who fell at another's tempting, may well be restored by another's help. But he who fell by his own pride may rise again, if he can, with no helper; but because he cannot, he may be styled as truly as man is (nay, more truly) *a spirit that passeth away, and cometh not again,* even as the Truth said unto him, "Get thee hence, Satan." It was not said to him, as in the Song of Songs to the faithful soul, the Bride of GOD, "Return, return, O Shulamite ; return, return, that we may look upon thee." And the words are also a terse definition of death, telling us how the *spirit passeth away* from this world, and *cometh not again,* but leaves the flesh here behind.

Francis Quarles, *Emblems,* iii. 13.

And what's a life? a weary pilgrimage,
Whose glory in one day doth fill thy stage
With childhood, manhood, and decrepit age.

And what's a life? the flourishing array
Of the proud summer meadow, which to-day
Wears her green blush, and is to-morrow hay.

And what's a life? a blast sustained with clothing,
Maintained with food, retained with vile self-loathing,
Then, weary of itself, again to nothing.

41 Many a time did they provoke him in the wilderness : and grieved him in the desert.

Already, when they were but in the second year of their wanderings, GOD complained that they had tempted Him "ten times ;" and it may thence be gathered how often they did so during the eight and thirty years which followed. The ten occasions were—(1) Murmuring at the three days' thirst, after the passage of the Red Sea; (2) Complaining for lack of food ; (3) The second demand for water, at Rephidim ; (4) The Golden Calf; (5) The demand for flesh-meat; (6) The attempt to return into Egypt after the report of the spies ; (7) The mutiny after the death of Korah; (8) The complaint because of the judgment of the mutineers ; (9) The third demand for water, at Kadesh ; (10) The revolt at Mount Hor, punished with fiery serpents. The place where they committed their sin was an aggravation of it, because it was precisely in the *wilderness*, with no human help near, that they ought to have felt most dependence on and trust in GOD. The words hold true still of all who are far from the spiritual Church, wandering in the *wilderness* of their sins, in the *dry place* unwatered by the streams of grace.

Ay.
Lyranus.
Numb. xiv. 22.
Exod. xv.
24 ;
xvi. 2;
xvii. 2;
xxxii. 1;
Numb. xi. 4;
xiv. 4;
xvi. 41;
xvii. 12;
xx. 2;
xxi. 5.

G.
S. Brun. Ast.
Ric. Hampol.
S. Brun. Ast.

42 They turned back, and tempted GOD : and moved the Holy One in Israel.

Turned. Whence and whither? From good to evil. *Moved.* The LXX. and Vulgate read *exasperated.* But the A. V. reads *limited*, that is, set bounds to His omnipotence. The Hebrew is הִתְווּ, the Hiphil of תָּוָה, which is properly "to mark with a Thau," the sign of the Cross. Hence the Targum explains the passage *signed Him with a sign,* which Delitzsch adopts in the sense of *casting a stigma* on Him. Most of the old Versions and of modern critics agree with the Vulgate, taking תָּוָה in the sense of the Syriac ܝܒ݂ܐ; but Gerhohus, keeping to the hint given by the Chaldee, boldly paraphrases, *They crucified the Holy One in Israel ;* and thus *limited* Him, the Omnipresent, to the narrow bounds of the Rood.

Delitzsch.
Gesenius.
Genebrardus.
G.
L.

43 They thought not of his hand : and of the day when he delivered them from the hand of the enemy.

44 How he had wrought his miracles in Egypt : and his wonders in the field of Zoan.

Lu.

So, too, bad Christians have *thought not of His hand,* nailed for them on the Cross, *that day when He delivered them,* after having *wrought His miracles* in the darkness of this world,

R.

of which *Egypt* is the type, and shown *His wonders* in *Zoan,* the " low estate" of His humble Manhood, the "lowliness" of His Maiden Mother, the mean origin of His princes, the

Hugo Card.

Apostles. Hereupon there follows a list of plagues sent on the Egyptians, agreeing in number with those recorded in

A.

Exodus, but differing in details and order. The three omissions are the lice, the boils, and the darkness; the additions are the caterpillar or "blight," (Vulg. *ærugo,*) the frost, and the hot thunderbolts—a special agent of destruction, and not

L.

a mere accompaniment of the storms. Lorinus applies here the canon of S. Jerome, that when in Holy Writ the topic is the praise of GOD, the historical order is frequently departed from, and a rhetorical one adopted instead, inverting the sequence of events. The actual order of the ten plagues

Hugo Card.

may be recalled by Cardinal Hugo's mnemonic verses:

Sanguis, rana, cyniph, muscæ, pecus, ulcera, grando,
Bruchus, caligo, mors, invaluere necando.

45 He turned their waters into blood : so that they might not drink of the rivers.

The especial appropriateness of the plagues which fell on the Egyptians to the circumstances and the religion of the country, has often been dwelt on. Their mystical import

A.

has not been less discussed. The first plague, of blood, is thus interpreted as the punishment for breach of the first Commandment, denoting, as it does, the change of men's

Ricard. Vict.

thoughts from pure and lofty ideas of GOD to carnal and animal ones, leading to debased idolatry. Again, it is taken

Ay.

as the token of Divine anger for the decree enjoining the drowning of the Hebrew infants. Rupert combines these

Rupert. in Exod.

two ideas, explaining the passage of idolatrous persecutors, who shed the blood of the Saints, and whose punishment is to be blood-drinking, not for one or two days, but a whole

Hugo Card.

week, that is, through eternity. Cardinal Hugo takes it in two ways : first, of those who give themselves up to flesh and blood, so that all things turn into condemnation for them; and secondly, of the tasteless water of the old Law, changed into the Blood of the New Covenant, ruddy from the veins of

Balduinus.

CHRIST. Once more, another mediæval writer speaks thus : " There is a conversion of water into blood, but that is confined to the Egyptians. There is another conversion of water into wine, but that is at a marriage. And there is a third conversion, of wine into blood, but that is in the LORD's Supper. The first conversion, of water into blood, is said to mean that the water of deadly wisdom, the wisdom of this world, the prudence of the flesh, turns into blood; that is, into death for them who walk according to the flesh. For the prudence of the flesh is death, and the wisdom of the flesh is at enmity with GOD. The Prophet, censuring men of this stamp, saith, ' What hast thou to do in the way of Egypt, to drink muddy water?'[1] or what hast thou to do in the way of Assyria, to drink the waters of the river?' For all earthly wisdom, whereof the Egyptians (the friends of this world, GOD's enemies) drink, is hateful to GOD. Therefore the water of Egypt is that which is turned into blood, because its blood is on them who drink it. The second change is of water into wine, and this seems to denote conversion, to wit, of fear into the love of righteousness. This change takes place at a marriage, because the Church is betrothed to GOD in faith and righteousness, that righteousness which is of faith in JESUS CHRIST. The third change, of wine into blood, is when righteousness so delights the soul, that one is ready to contend for it unto blood and death; and this is the perfection of righteousness." *Jer. ii. 18.*

> What is this silent might,
> Making our darkness light,
> New wine our waters, heavenly Blood our wine?
> CHRIST, with His Mother dear,
> And all His Saints, is here,
> And where they dwell is Heaven, and what they touch, divine.

Keble.
Lyr. Innoc.

46 He sent lice among them, and devoured them up : and frogs to destroy them.

The A. V. here, instead of *lice*, reads *divers sorts of flies*, which represents a reading suggested by S. Jerome in the LXX., κοινόμυιαν, instead of the usual one, κυνόμυιαν, or *dog-fly*. The Hebrew word is עָרֹב, *a mixture;* and the very ancient tradition mentioned in the Book of Wisdom, and accepted by Josephus, R. Jonathan, R. Aben Ezra, and R. Ishaki, alleges the plague to have been not of flies, but of wild beasts. Gesenius, however, giving the sense of *to suck* to the radical עָרַב, follows Bochart in accepting the LXX. interpretation, which is also that of the Roman, Gallican, Arabic, and Illyrian Psalters. S. Isidore, holding this view, urges that the fly, as a restless insect, was the fit punishment for restless and unquiet minds; and the Carmelite adds, that the *dog-fly* aptly denotes the animal passions and pursuits of the Egyptians. So far back as Origen's time the text was applied in this sense against the Cynics. S. Augustine notes the fact that dogs are born blind, so that they cannot see their parents; and Rupert, therefore, takes this, the fourth plague, as punishment for breach of the fourth Commandment, (according to the Latin reckoning,) which extends, the Gloss tells us, to those who despise the prelates of the Church. *S. Hieron. Ep. ad Suniam et Fratellam.*

Wisd. xvi. 3.

Antiq. Jud. ii. xiv. 3.

Hieroz. iii. 427.

S. Isid. Hispal. in Exod.

Ay.

Origenes in Exod.

A.

Rupert. in Exod.

Pet. Lomb.

---

[1] Vulgate. The A. V. reads, "waters of Sihor," i.e. the *black* | river, from שׁחר, to be black, denoting the turbidity of the Nile.

Origen.
B.
S. Pet. Dam.
D. C.
Hugo Card.
Ric. Hamp.
De Vitâ
Mosis.

Frogs denote talkative vanity, especially, as some will have it, the idle fables of heathen poetry and philosophy; and thus the peril of sins of the tongue is pointed out, in particular those committed by heretics in their resistance to the Gospel, by the word *destroy*. S. Gregory Nyssen, however, takes the *frogs*, as denizens of the mud, to denote persons of voluptuous and self-indulgent life, whom the very waters do not cleanse. Ayguan expands this idea, taking the frogs

Ay.

to mean the three chief sins of the modern world, pride, luxury, and avarice. The frog dwells in foul and muddy waters, which denote luxury. Next, the belly of the frog is far larger than any other part of its body, and keeps close to the ground; thus signifying those who are greedy of earthly riches. Thirdly, the frog advances by leaps; and this is a type of those who attempt to lift themselves to high position by a sudden bound, unwilling to pass by the true mean of the middle space, whereby honour is won. Wherefore of

Rev. xvi. 13.

these three sins it is said, " I saw three unclean spirits like frogs come out of the mouth of the dragon."

47 He gave their fruit unto the caterpillar : and their labour unto the grasshopper.

A.

The LXX. reads ἐρυσίβη, or *blight*, with which the Vulgate *ærugo* agrees. Aquila and S. Jerome have *bruchus*, and the probable meaning of חָסִיל is the *wingless locust*, or the larva

S. Albertus
Magnus.

of the locust. The blight, says a Saint, is hidden sin, and particularly the sin of self-sufficiency, which kills the soul when it seems to be healthiest. The *grasshopper*, or rather the *locust*, observes S. Augustine, is malice hurting with

Rupert in
Exod.

the mouth, that is, with false witness. And Rupert, taking the same view, teaches that it especially denotes the false witness of heretics, saying, that as the locusts were carried into Egypt, not by their own flight, but by a wind, so those who quote Scripture against the truth are not borne, as they suppose, on the wings of knowledge, but by the wind of spiritual pride, to the subversion of their hearers, and

C.
Hugo Card.
D. C.

their own destruction. And others refer the term chiefly to envious detractors.

48 He destroyed their vines with hailstones : and their mulberry-trees with the frost.

Ay.

" By this plague is shown," says the Carmelite, " how GOD alarms the life of the evil by the words of His preachers, and calls them back to grace. Wherefore Gregory saith, By hail

S. Greg.
Mag. Mor.
xxix. 11.

or snow, cold and hard, we understand the hearts of the evil. But since Almighty GOD chooses His Saints from such, and knows well how many elect He possesses who are as yet exposed amidst the life of the evil, He fittingly describes Himself as having His treasures in snow and hail. These elect

He brings out at His command, and by heavenly grace makes them white with the purity of righteousness. Saul was hail and snow at first by his cold insensibility; but he was made to be snow and hail against the breasts of his adversaries, by the whiteness of his righteousness and by the smiting of his vigorous speech. O what a treasure GOD had then in snow and hail, when the LORD saw him, His secretly elect, living in the life of evil! O what hail was that He took in His hand to smite full many a breast of the adversaries, hail wherewith He laid low so many hearts that resisted Him! Let no man, then, be uplifted because of his own works, nor despair of them whom he sees to be still cold, because he does not see the treasures in the snow and hail." The LORD *destroys vines with hailstones* when He strikes at carnal pleasures with the wise sayings of preachers. Others, following S. Augustine, take the verse in a bad sense, of the sins of violence and coldness. So the tyrannical and rapacious, while oppressing others, slay their own souls, and destroy their own former good works with the frost of hatred and ill-will, which is iciness of the soul. The Vulgate for *vines* reads *vineyards,* and then we may take the *vineyard* to be the Church, and the *mulberry-trees* its Priests; for they should bear fruit, at first white in purity of life; then red, in fervour of charity; and lastly black, in mortification of the flesh. Of these it is written, "To the end they might provoke the elephants to fight, they showed them the blood of grapes and mulberries." *Frost,* arising from the waters, is the love of riches, which is fatal to the priesthood; and *hail* denotes their quarrels and dissensions.

A.

D. C.

S. Albertus Magnus.

1 Macc. vi. 34.

49 He smote their cattle also with hailstones : and their flocks with hot thunderbolts.

"By the death of beasts," remarks S. Augustine, "was typified, so far as I can judge, the loss of chastity. For concupiscence, whereby offspring ariseth, we have in common with beasts. To have this, therefore, tamed and ordered, is the virtue of chastity." By the death of irrational cattle, consequently, the fate of those is denoted who live like beasts, not restraining their unlawful passions with the bridle of continence. *Their flocks.* The LXX. and Vulgate read, *their possession.* And this *possession,* say they, is the orderly condition of the mind or soul, which is wasted with *fire,* (Vulg.) when delivered over to the flames of passion or luxury. S. Augustine, noting that this plague is not specified in Exodus, suggests that it denotes fierce anger, which may lead even to homicide.

A.

Ay.

S. Albertus Magnus.
Ric. Hampol.

A.

50 He cast upon them the furiousness of his wrath, anger, displeasure, and trouble : and sent evil angels among them.

A.

S. Augustine comments at much length on this passage, touching the punitive ministry of good and evil angels, pointing out that both have great sway over the powers of nature, and that evil spirits are sometimes permitted by GOD to exhibit this influence of theirs. They may tempt also, as in the cases of Job and Ahab; and may, as well as good angels, be employed as the executioners of GOD's wrath. And he decides that evil angels were the instruments of the slaughter of the beasts and the first-born in Egypt, and also of the hardening of the Egyptian hearts, inasmuch as they were suffered to suggest sin to those whom GOD had forsaken because of their unbelief. But when GOD punishes the righteous with temporal penalties, He does it by the

Hesychius.
Z.

hands of His good angels. The Greek Fathers, however, say that the angels are here called *evil*, not by reason of their nature, but merely as bringing evils on the heads of sinners.

51 He made a way to his indignation, and spared not their soul from death : but gave their life over to the pestilence;

52 And smote all the first-born in Egypt : the most principal and mightiest in the dwellings of Ham.

C.
Pet. Lomb.

G.

The words *He made a way* denote that there could have been no approach made even to punish sinners, unless they were first deprived of the protection of GOD, so that the enemy had power to hurt them. And that *way* was GOD's hidden justice, whereby He might have chastised the Egyptians for the sin of their will; but He made that way broad and conspicuous, by permitting them to commit sins of act, drawing down fearful vengeance. Wherefore it is said that He *spared not their souls from death*, because He allowed those souls to sink into the death of sin even before He smote their bodies, giving *their life over to the pestilence*. The LXX. and Vulgate read this clause, *And shut up their cattle*

B.
D. C.

in death. Literally, by the hail and murrain; spiritually, by slaying their virtues of meekness and obedience, and by eternal condemnation of their carnal desires and works. *And*

Origen.
A.
S. Hieron.
S. Prosper.

smote all the first-born in Egypt. They refer it to a mightier overthrow than that in the Book of Exodus—to the victory of the Incarnate SAVIOUR over the devil and his angels, and over the false teachers who are their allies. And He has made us partakers of this victory by causing us also to renounce the devil, his pomps, and his angels. That, too, adds

Rupert. in Exod.

Rupert, by slaying original sin, the parent of so many offences, after the immolation of the true Paschal Lamb. They point out also that the words denote the spiritual chastisement of unfaithful Christians, when GOD deprives them of His grace. For the *first-born* mean those things which claim the highest

love and reverence, such as the two great commandments of   C.
love of God and love of one's neighbour, or as faith and righteousness.   Faith when formed is, as it were, the first-born   R.
of the soul, and God slays it when men persist in abiding in
Egypt, the darkness of this world. The Carmelite is even   D. C.
more mystical in his view. Taking this plague as vengeance
for breach of the tenth commandment, he says that they who   Ay.
covet, wish to be the heirs of those whose goods they desire,
and therefore wish them to have no other heirs, no first-born.
This is, in its degree, a sin like the slaughter of the Hebrew
children: and God punishes it by slaying faith, the first-
born of spiritual works, in the souls of the covetous. *The
most principal and the mightiest in the dwellings of Ham.*
The LXX. and Vulgate read, *The first-fruits of all their
labour in the tabernacles of Ham.* There is a contest be-   L.
tween the commentators as to whether these words refer
to children, to the fruits of the earth, or to the first-born of   Lu.
cattle. There is more agreement as to the mystical significa-   Ric. Hamp.
tion, which is, that God slays the fervour of charity and the   D. C.
principal virtues in souls which persist in dwelling amongst
the ungodly.

53 But as for his own people, he led them forth
like sheep : and carried them in the wilderness like
a flock.

54 He brought them out safely, that they should
not fear : and overwhelmed their enemies with the
sea.

He led them forth. The LXX. and Vulgate, more empha-   G.
tically, *He took them away.* That is, away from the jaws of the   P.
lion and the wolf, from the power of the devil, from worldly
conversation, from evil companionship, as He saith by Hosea,   D. C.
"I will ransom them from the power of the grave, I will redeem   Hos. xiii. 14.
them from death." And He hath elsewhere spoken of the elect,   S. John xv.
"Ye are not of the world, but I have chosen you out of the   19.
world." This the Saviour doth whenever He pours the grace
of conversion into man. There is a wild Jewish legend that a   L.
sheep appeared of a sudden to the people of the Exodus,
spoke with human voice, and pointed out the way; and that
these words of the Psalmist refer to that event, true enough
in a higher sense. Ayguan's gloss, that they recall the sacri-   Ay.
fice of the Paschal lamb, which opened the road from Egypt,
may be mentioned, but will hardly be adopted. *And carried*   D. C.
them. The A. V., better, *guided them,* as the Good Shepherd,
in the wilderness, of this world's exile, whereof the forty   Ric. Hamp.
years' wandering was a type, *like a flock,* because of the
unity of that Church which He founded, and that flock one   Ay.
of *sheep,* because the sheep, by their inoffensiveness, their
patience, their silence, and their usefulness to man, aptly   D. C.

signify devout and faithful souls, which their Shepherd feeds
with the priceless food of His own precious Body and Blood.
Safely. The LXX. and Vulgate read, *In hope.* Rightly, for
hope is the chariot whereon GOD brings His elect to Himself
across the wilderness of penitence, as Joseph sent for Jacob.
The *hope* of the Israelites was the Land of Promise, ours is
the better Country. We are being led home in hope, " for
by hope we are saved." *That they should not fear.* It is
written in the Book of Exodus, that when Pharaoh pursued
the children of Israel, "they were sore afraid." R. Kimchi
answers that their fear lasted but a moment, and was calmed
by the words of Moses, " Fear ye not ; stand still, and see
the salvation of the LORD." Ayguan's reply is, that there
are two kinds of fear : one which causes abandonment of a
plan, and the other which is less effective ; and that only this
slighter fear affected the Israelites. And then it is taken of
the constancy of Martyrs and Confessors in resisting suffering, losses, and temptations, because of the hope within them.

S. Alb. Mag.

A.

Rom. viii. 24.

Exod. xiv. 10.
De Muis.
Exod. xiv. 13.

Ay.

D. C.

The Se-
quence,
Hic est dies
celebrandus.

> Fides spe corroborata,
> Caritate radicata,
>   Fulget in martyribus,
> Corda DEO præparata,
> Passione sociata,
>   Præstant sacris legibus.

C.
R.

And overwhelmed their enemies with the sea, by destroying
our ghostly foes, and blotting out our sins in the cleansing
waters of Baptism.

55 And brought them within the borders of his
sanctuary : even to his mountain which he purchased with his right hand.

L.

The borders. So the Hebrew and S. Jerome. But the
LXX. and Vulgate read, *The mountain of His sanctification,*
not improbably from the copyists of the former confounding
ὄρος and ὅρος. The words imply first the entrance into Canaan generally, and then the special conquest of Jerusalem
itself. And the mountainous character of Palestine, especially on its Lebanon border, enables some of the commentators, though following the Vulgate text, to give this true
explanation. Others apply the first clause to Jerusalem,
whose "foundation is upon the holy hills," and the latter to
Mount Sion, or Moriah, whereon the Temple stood. The
mystical interpretation presents no difficulty. The Church
into which GOD leads His elect is mountainous, because He
hallows them by confession, praise, contemplation, and employment about heavenly things. The arrival at the *borders*
denotes the life of less perfect Christians, the ascent of the
mountain the victory of the Saints, of whom is written,
"LORD, who shall dwell in Thy tabernacle, and who shall

C.
Hugo Card.
Lyranus.
Ps. lxxxvii. 1.
Origen.

Ps. lxxxiv. 7.

Ps. xv. 1.

rest upon Thy holy hill?" And this mountain He *purchased*   S. Alb. Mag.
with His right hand, when He stretched that hand out to be
nailed upon the Cross. Wherefore He says of this especial
glory vouchsafed to His dearest ones, "Moreover, I have   Gen. xlviii.
given to thee one portion above thy brethren, which I took   22.
out of the hand of the Amorite with My sword and with
My bow."

56 He cast out the heathen also before them :
caused their land to be divided among them for an
heritage, and made the tribes of Israel to dwell in
their tents.

Here, as so often, they dwell on the seven Canaanitish   S. Chrysost. / S. Greg.
nations as typical of the seven deadly sins, assigning them,   Mag.
however, somewhat variously; and show how every peni-   S. Anton. / Pad.
tent soul is like Mary Magdalene, out of whom CHRIST cast   Pet. Lomb.
seven devils. Less mystical, though not less true, is the gloss   Hugo Card.
of Cassiodorus, that the words tell us of the disappearance   R.
of barbarous Pagan customs before the civilizing advance of
the Gospel, whereby, as another points out, Christians now   C.
dwell in lands formerly occupied by idolaters. *Caused their*   D. C.
land to be divided. This clause is more fully expressed by
the LXX. and Vulgate, *He divided by lot to them in the line*
of distribution. Cassiodorus, agreeing herein with a sugges-   C.
tion of the Pseudo-Dionysius, that *lot* sometimes means a   Pseudo-Dionys.
splendour or appointment of the SPIRIT, takes these words to   Ric. Hamp.
denote the various degrees of gift, reward, and beatitude in
the kingdom of heaven.

> In domo PATRIS
> Summæ majestatis
> Ecce sunt pulchræ
> Mansiones multæ,
> Quæ sunt certantum
> Pro virtute tantum
> Ac triumphantum.

By lot, because it is not of man's judgment, but by the elec-   Haymo.
tion of GOD; by *lot,* because it is a free gift of the SPIRIT,
and not of man's purchasing, and *in the line of distribution,*   B.
that the exact limits of each virtue may be marked out, so   Ricard. Vic-torin.
that frugality may not narrow itself into covetousness, nor
liberality expand into waste. Or, again, the *line* may denote   Ay.
the varying amount of grace and power given to each be-   B.
liever, "according to the measure of the gift of CHRIST."   Eph. iv. 7.
Once more, the passage has been explained of the partition
of the mission-field of the world amongst the Apostles, an   D. C.
event formerly celebrated in the Western Church by a
special festival. *And made the tribes of Israel to dwell in*
their tents. S. Augustine, who explains the *heathen* to be   A.

z 3

evil spirits, takes these words to mean the exaltation of ransomed men to the thrones left vacant by the fall of the rebel angels ; while others are content with seeing here, as in the earlier clause, the victory of Christianity over Paganism. And it is also taken of heavenly virtues dwelling in souls once the habitation of evil thoughts, because "where sin abounded, grace did much more abound."

57 So they tempted, and displeased the most high GOD : and kept not his testimonies ;

58 But turned their backs, and fell away like their forefathers : starting aside like a broken bow.

59 For they grieved him with their hill-altars : and provoked him to displeasure with their images.

There are six distinct sins here enumerated. Deceit, in *tempting* GOD ; infidelity, in *displeasing* Him ; omission of duty, in *keeping not* His testimonies ; apostasy, in *falling away ;* breach of promised vows, in likeness to a *broken bow ;* idolatry, in the *hill-altars* and *images.* They all agree that the *broken bow* refers to faultiness of will, as the bow is the intention, of which the practical issue is the arrow. The A. V. reading, a *deceitful bow,* is the true rendering ; and the meaning is therefore that of feebleness and laxity in spiritual things, when there is no real elasticity in the soul, sufficient to project a prayer or a good work as far as the mark, and therefore failing in the time of need. Euthymius, dwelling on the LXX. word στρεβλόν, *crooked* or *twisted,* explains it of a will which is not straight and honest, and which therefore cannot send the arrow in the right line, though it may do so with sufficient force. The Latin Fathers, for the most part reading *a perverse bow,* explain it of a weapon turned against its owner, rather than against his enemies. And it is thus taken especially of evil-living preachers, whose denunciations of sin recoil on their own heads. So it is written, "They return, but not to the Most High : they are like a deceitful bow." And the *hill-altars* imply spiritual pride, which gives not GOD the glory, but exalts human merit ; while the *images* are any objects of love and admiration which are not given us by GOD, but framed by ourselves in our hearts, even if not endued with bodily form.

60 When GOD heard this, he was wroth : and took sore displeasure at Israel.

61 So that he forsook the tabernacle in Silo : even the tent that he had pitched among men.

He *heard* it, as He heard the voice of Abel's blood crying out, as He heard the voices of Sodom and Gomorrah. For sins cry out before GOD, and disclose their authors. *And*

took sore displeasure at Israel. The LXX. and Vulgate,
even more forcibly, *And brought Israel exceedingly to nothing.* Literally, in the first instance, by the successive overthrows and bondage He permitted them to endure; and
later, spiritually, by the transfer of their privileges to the
Gentiles. *He forsook the tabernacle in Silo,* when the Ark
was captured in the days of Eli, and the tabernacle left A.
empty. The Ark never returned to Shiloh again, and thus
the vengeance which fell on that guilty city is cited as a
warning to Jerusalem: "Go ye now to My place which was Jer. vii. 12.
in Shiloh, where I set My Name at the first, and see what I
did to it for the wickedness of My people Israel." Mysti- Ric. Hamp.
cally, they take it first of the rejection of the whole Jewish D. C.
nation; then of the Christian Church, when punished for its
sins; and finally of our bodies, which are the temples of the
HOLY GHOST, forsaken by GOD when He leaves the soul, in 1 Cor. vi. 19.
displeasure at a carnal life. Wherefore is added, *Even the
tent that He had pitched amongst men.* It is not said, observes G.
Gerhohus, that *He dwelt in walls,* but in *men.* For GOD,
Who is a Spirit, dwells not in habitations made with hands,
but in rational spirits; for which reason, they who worship
Him must worship in spirit. But He chooses to have temples or tabernacles made with hands, wherein He may be
served by men, whose minds He inhabits by faith working
through love. And if this faith and love be quenched in
men, He cares little for the mere walls of temples, however
beautiful and costly. Thus He abandons heretics, who break
away from the unity of the Church, in whose bodies and
souls He had once dwelt through faith. Wherefore, adds R.
another commentator, it is needful to bear in mind that saying, "Trust ye not in lying words, saying, The temple of the Jer. vii. 4.
LORD, the temple of the LORD, the temple of the LORD, are
these." There remains one mystical sense, yet more pro-
found, which is strangely omitted by all the commentators.
It is the reference to Him of Whom the dying patriarch
spake by the name of Shiloh, Who was sent forth from the Gen. xlix.
FATHER when "the WORD was made flesh, and *tabernacled* 10.
among us." Because of our sins, which He bore in His ἐσκήνωσεν.
own Body on the tree, He was forsaken in His last trial by
His FATHER, so that He cried, "Eloi, Eloi, lama sabach-
thani?" Then, far more truly than when the Ark was taken,
or the Temple spoiled, was that fulfilled which follows:

62 He delivered their power into captivity : and
their beauty into the enemy's hand.

Into captivity, in the garden, and in the grave; *into the
enemy's hand,* when Judas betrayed, and Pilate condemned,
and death seized Him; their *Power,* because " the Arm of the Isa. liii. 1.
LORD;" their *Beauty,* because He is "fairer than the children of men." They take the passage otherwise, and va- Ps. xlv. 2.

A.
G.
S. Alb. Mag.
Ay.
Hugo Card.
1 Sam. iv. 2.
S. Greg.
Mag. Cur.
Past. 4.

D. C.
Hugo Card.
S. Alb. Mag.

R.

riously. Some explain it of the Ark, the *power* in which the Jews trusted for victory, the *beauty* which they had adorned with cost and skill. Others understand here the bravest and goodliest of the youth, slain in the battle with the Philistines at Aphek; and again in the slaughter and captivity of a far later age, under Titus and Hadrian. Mystically, it is interpreted of those who, by boasting of their own good works, suffer the enemy to rule over their souls, and thus deliver up that holiness which was their power and beauty into his hands. Or it may denote the soldiers of the Church, especially bishops and priests, giving their bodies, which are their *power*, up to sin, while their souls, their true *beauty*, also become the slaves of their ghostly foes. Our *power* and *beauty*, observes another, are our baptism and other divine graces, which we lose when we think we can be saved by faith alone, without good works as its fruit.

63 He gave his people over also unto the sword : and was wroth with his inheritance.

Ay.

1 Sam. xiii.
19.

Judg. v. 8.

1 Sam. xiii.
22.

Ay.

S. Greg.
Mag. Mor.
vi. 16.
Job xx. 25,
Vulg.

D. C.

The LXX. and Vulgate read, yet more strongly, *He shut up His people in the sword.* And they point out how complete was this chastisement; for not only was there a terrible slaughter at the time, but "there was no smith found throughout all the land of Israel: for the Philistines said, Lest the Hebrews make them swords or spears: but all the Israelites went down to the Philistines, to sharpen every man his share, and his coulter, and his axe, and his mattock." An earlier book tells us how vigilantly this mode of repression was carried out. "Was there a shield or spear seen among forty thousand in Israel?" Nor was it less strict later; for "there was neither sword nor spear found in the hand of any of the people that were with Saul and Jonathan; but with Saul and with Jonathan his son was there found." Mystically, adds the Carmelite, GOD *shuts up His people with the sword* whenever He suffers any to be overcome by the temptation of the devil. For the sword denotes evil counsel. But note, that this cannot be without our own consent. Wherefore Gregory shows in that saying in Job, "The sword drawn, and coming out of the sheath," the devil lays his snares for the righteous, but while he is plotting evil in his thoughts, the sword is in its sheath; and while he is carrying out his wicked scheme, then the sword is being drawn from the sheath, because the evil deed discloses the hidden thought. And observe that it says, "drawn and coming out of the sheath;" drawn by the seducer, but coming forth by our own will. The Carthusian, writing when the recovery of the Holy Sepulchre was still a lingering hope of Western chivalry and religion, takes the passage to denote the slaughter of Christians in the Holy Land by the Saracens, permitted for their sins, because GOD was *wroth with His inheritance.*

64 The fire consumed their young men : and their
maidens were not given to marriage.

65 Their priests were slain with the sword : and
there were no widows to make lamentation.

They take the *fire* mystically of carnal passions, working
more fatal results than the sword and brands of the Philistines. *Given to marriage.* This, though a paraphrase, is
the most probable meaning of the Hebrew הוּלָּלוּ, *were
praised*, to wit, in the bridal songs. The LXX. and Vulgate, however, refer it to the funeral ode, and translate, *were
not lamented.* And they explain it that sin had grown to
such a height, that there was no compassion felt for those
who had forfeited their purity, but rather admiration for
such as showed most openly their want of it. Others, more
literally, refer the words to the number and frequency of
the slaughters, which left neither time for solemn rites, nor
persons to perform them. Philip de la Grève explains the
young men to mean constancy of mind, and the *maidens*
purity, which are most abundant when the soul is guarded
with devout prayer, and is kept apart from bodily pleasures,
which two conditions are typified by the *priests* and the
widows of the latter verse. But when prayer and continence
disappear, then constancy and purity fail also. *Their priests
were slain with the sword.* The words refer first to the death
of Hophni and Phinehas, and then, mystically, to all clerks
and religious persons who fail either in soundness of doctrine or holiness of life. They are *slain with the sword* of
God's Word, proceeding out of their own mouths as they
preach. *And there were no widows to make lamentation.* Literally, the text refers to the death of Phinehas' wife in childbirth. *Widows* and *maidens* are taken of Religious women.
The Vulgate reads, *were not lamented.* Gerhohus, very
boldly, explains it that devout persons, in times of great spiritual coldness, are slow to lament over the loss of mere physical purity on the part even of Religious, because there is a
possibility of such a terrible fall rousing them to true repentance and zeal; while, if they possess that one merit, and no
other, they may trust in it to their destruction, and be
counted amongst the foolish virgins, who took no oil in their
lamps. The Carthusian, conversely, takes these latter words
to mean that coldness had spread so widely, that no one was
found to weep for those living in carnal sin, of whom the
Apostle says, "She that liveth in pleasure is dead while she
liveth."

Ay.
D. C.

Ay.
D. C.
A.
C.

Serm. clxix.
in Psalt.

1 Sam. iv. 11.
G.
D. C.

1 Sam. iv. 19.

G.

D. C.

1 Tim. v. 6.

66 So the LORD awaked as one out of sleep : and
like a giant refreshed with wine.

First, and most truly, it is spoken of that LORD Who

Hugo Card. *awaked*—what time His priests of the elder Law had spiritually died by their sin against Him—*out of His sleep* of three days in the grave, *refreshed with* the strong *wine* of the Cup of His Passion, which He had drunk to the very dregs. *Giant* He, as the noble old hymn calls Him:

S Ambrose, The Hymn, Vrni Redemptor gentium.

Geminæ Gigas substantiæ,
Alacris ut currat viam.

G.

He *awaked*, then, at the cry of Samuel and His other faithful servants lamenting that the Ark was carried captive into idol temples. He awakes in anger still when His priests, through neglect of godly discipline, give His Sacred Body, the Ark of the New Covenant, to unworthy communicants, the shrine of whose hearts is full of earthly idols.

67 He smote his enemies in the hinder parts : and put them to a perpetual shame.

1 Sam. v. 6, 9, 12.

Conc. Nic. Act. vii. Ep. ii. Text. Latin.

A.

Ric. Hamp. S. Luke ix. 62.

C.

G.

S. Alb. Mag.

Ay.

Literally, the text refers us to the diseases which He sent on the Philistines so long as they retained the Ark. Mystically, the Fathers of Nicæa explain it of the evil powers, behind whom the LORD came in the might of His Resurrection, and gave them over to everlasting reproach. He still *smites His enemies in the hinder parts* when they look back on things behind, and that after putting their hands to the plough, either by giving them up to their sins in the latter part of their life here, and suffering all those little suggestions of the evil spirits, which are like mice, to devour them, or by final condemnation in the end of the world, which is, in fearful truth, *perpetual shame.* Ayguan discusses at much length, and with illustrations borrowed from his classical lore, the three motives which cause men to smite—corrective love, hostile anger, and judicial punishment, of which the first and third alone can be predicated of GOD.

68 He refused the tabernacle of Joseph : and chose not the tribe of Ephraim ;

69 But chose the tribe of Judah : even the hill of Sion which he loved.

A.

He does not say that He refused the tabernacle of Reuben, nor the others of Judah's elders; for it might be replied that they deserved such rejection, as they were rebuked by their dying father for their sins. Nor does He speak of rejecting Benjamin, whence a king had already sprung; but those are named who seemed to excel in merit. For Joseph fed his father and brethren in Egypt, and after being wickedly sold, was justly exalted, because of his piety, chastity, and wisdom; and Ephraim was preferred before his elder brother by his grandfather Jacob's blessing : and yet GOD *refused the*

Z.

tabernacle of Joseph, (for Shiloh lay in the territory of

Ephraim,) *and chose not the tribe of Ephraim.* We learn
herein the rejection of the whole Jewish people, which looked
for mere earthly rewards, and the election of the Gentiles in
their stead; not because of merit, but of grace. And as
Joseph denotes *increase,* and *Ephraim* means *fruitfulness,* so
these words teach us that GOD does not choose the powerful
and wealthy of this world, as it is written, "For ye see your
calling, brethren, how that not many wise men after the
flesh, not many mighty, not many noble." He chooses
Judah, which means *praise,* or as the old commentators take
it, *confession,* denoting those sinners who acknowledge their
own weakness, and give Him the glory. So Peter attained
to the blessing of Judah, when he confessed CHRIST. As to
the one was said, "Judah, thou art he whom thy brethren
shall praise," so to the other was spoken, "I have prayed for
thee that thy faith fail not, and when thou art converted,
strengthen thy brethren." Of Judah was said, "Judah is a
lion's whelp; he stooped down, he couched as a lion." And
to Peter was signified by what death he should glorify GOD,
that is, girt by another, and with hands extended on the
Cross, dying as CHRIST the Lion, and Lion's whelp died, to
whom Peter was made like in death. But one thing which is
said of Judah far surpasses the person of Peter, "Thy father's
children shall bow down before thee," which saying pertains
especially to CHRIST, the only Man to be worshipped amongst
men. The name *Judah* befits not Peter only, who confessed
the Rock, but all GOD's elect, who believe with the heart
unto righteousness, and make confession with the mouth unto
salvation. So the LORD chooses the tribe of Judah out of the
mass of the ungodly. The more obvious references, to the
Davidic descent of CHRIST, and to the chief manifestations of
His miracles in Jerusalem, are not forgotten by the expositors. The Carmelite mentions a Hebrew legend to account
for the preference of Judah, that when Moses began the
passage of the Red Sea, the Israelites all hung back in fear,
till Amminadab, Prince of the house of Judah, set them the
example of boldly entering the waters. *Mount Sion,* "expectation," is the Church Militant which *He loved,* as it is
written by the Apostle, "CHRIST also loved the Church, and
gave Himself for it, that He might sanctify and cleanse it."

Marginal notes: S. Alb. Mag. G. 1 Cor. i. 26. Gen. xlix. 8. S. Luke xxii. 32. Gen. xlix. 9. Gen. xlix. 8. S. Hieron. Arnobius. Ay. D. C. Eph. v. 25.

70 And there he built his temple on high : and
laid the foundation of it like the ground which he
hath made continually.

The LXX. and Vulgate read, *He built His holy thing as
of a unicorn[1] upon the earth, which He founded for evermore.*
The words *as of a unicorn* denote that Christians uplift the
strong horn of their faith to the One GOD, the Undivided

Marginal note: S. Basil. Magn. C.

[1] Reading םימר *unicorns,* instead of םימר *high places.*

Trinity. *Holy thing* (ἁγίασμα, *sanctificium,*) they take diversely. First of that "holy thing" born from the earth of
Virgin flesh, but set up above the heavens for evermore.
Then it is taken of the Body of the Head, of that Church, the
Sanctuary of GOD stablished on the earth in the hearts of the
faithful and bound together in the unity of the SPIRIT, so as
to have "One LORD, one faith, one baptism." They dwell
also on some of the supposed characteristics of the unicorn,
such as his solitary habits, and repulse of all other beasts
from his den, which they explain of the law forbidding a
stranger to minister in the Temple, and of Solomon's peaceful
rule over the neighbouring peoples. The love of the unicorn
for chastity, so that he can be captured only as he sleeps
in the lap of a virgin, is a myth of which another commentator here avails himself; and a third sees in the strength of
the single horn the firm union of faith and charity, based on
belief and worship of One GOD, and growing up towards
heaven. The Æthiopic Psalter, nearly agreeing with modern
critics in reading, *He built His tabernacle in heaven on
high and founded it on the earth for evermore,* gives a far
truer and deeper meaning than these quaint fancies. For
that Sanctuary which is alike in *heaven* above and on *earth*
beneath, is the Only-begotten SON, GOD and Man at once,
and that for *evermore,* because of the indissoluble hypostatic
union of the Two Natures in His Person.

71 He chose David also his servant : and took
him away from the sheep-folds.

Though the words are spoken of CHRIST, yet He is called
here *servant,* and not *Son.* And that because the nature
which was taken of David was not that Substance which is
co-eternal with the FATHER, but the "form of a servant."
And took Him away from the sheep-folds, exalting Him to the
throne of glory, after He had fulfilled His office, as the Good
Shepherd upon earth. Or, as others will have it, taking Him
from the Jewish nation, the "few sheep in the wilderness,"
lost ones of the house of Israel, to whom He was first sent,
and giving Him the wider and more glorious rule over the
Gentile Church.

72 As he was following the ewes great with young
ones he took him : that he might feed Jacob his
people, and Israel his inheritance.

Great with young, because CHRIST did not ascend until
His Church began to be fruitful in faith and good works ;
great with young, even under the Jewish Law, for many
zealous and just ones were found in it ready to bear fruit,
of whom three thousand on one day and five thousand on
another, shorn of their fleeces by abandoning their old habits
and possessions, came up from the waters of Baptism at the

Marginal notes:
S. Luke i. 35.
G.

C.
G.
Eph. iv. 5.

Ay.
Numb. iii. 10.
Lyranus.
1 Kings iv. 24.

Beda.

B.

A.

Phil. ii. 7.

C.

1 Sam. xvii. 28.

G.

R.

G.

call of Peter. *That He might feed Jacob His people*, mili-   C.
tant here on earth, and *Israel His inheritance*, the Church
Triumphant in heaven, looking ever on His Face. Others   R.
see in *Jacob* a type of the Jewish Church, in *Israel* of the
Christian ; and yet another interpretation is that *Jacob* is the
faithful, but yet imperfect Christian, engaged in wrestling
with his sins and overthrowing them, while *Israel* is he   Ric. Ham-
who has attained to the peaceful contemplation of GOD. The   pol.
Carmelite, eagerly searching out every point that may sug-   Ay.
gest his LORD, tells us that there are eight marks of a good
shepherd. He must have bread in a wallet, a dog in a string,
a staff with a rod, a horn and a pipe. The *bread* is the Word
of GOD. The *wallet* is remembrance of that Word. The
dog signifies zeal, which the shepherd should have for the
LORD's house, that he may drive wolves thence with the holy
barkings of sound preaching and unwearied prayer. The
string which leads the dog, is moderation and discretion in
zeal. The *staff* is comfortable exhortation, to support the
weak, and console them lest they fall in time of trouble.
The *rod* is lawful power, to correct the restless. The *horn*,
by whose alarming sound warriors are roused to battle, is the
awful threat of hell, at which CHRIST's soldiers gird themselves with the spirit of might to war against soft sins. The
pipe, with its sweet notes, denotes the pleasantness of everlasting bliss, which the faithful Shepherd sweetly and oft-
times chants in the ears of His flock. It is thus that GOD
chose David *to feed Jacob His servant.*

73 So he fed them with a faithful and true heart :
and ruled them prudently with all his power.

The A. V., nearer at once to the Hebrew and to the Vulgate, reads, *So He fed them according to the integrity of His
heart; and guided them by the skilfulness of His hands.*
Truly in the *innocency* of His heart, for in Him was no spot   A.
of sin, He *fed* them with the WORD, even with Himself,   C.
and in the *skilfulness* of His hands, because He wrought in   Ric. Hamp.
wisdom all the works whereby He taught His people what to   L.
choose and what to shun. Or, more touchingly, when He,
in His dying hour, like His ancestor, "guiding His hands   Gen. xlviii.
wittingly," suffered them to be nailed upon the Cross, it was   14.
that He might guide us, according to that lovely reading, *in*   Arnob us.
the glory of His hands. Thus He leads His people from passive *innocency* of heart, which He gives them by purifying   B.
their souls, on by *skilfulness of* hands in every good work, till   Ric. Hamp.
He brings them into the eternal pastures :

Bone Pastor, Panis vere,   •   S. Thomas
JESU nostri miserere,   Aquin.
Tu nos pasce, nos tuêre,   The Se-
Tu nos bona fac videre   quence
In terrâ viventium :   *Lauda Syon.*

Tu qui cuncta scis et vales,
Qui nos pascis hic mortales,
Tuos ibi commensales
Coheredes et sodales,
    Fac sanctorum civium!

Wherefore:

Glory be to the FATHER of David; glory be to the SON, Who is David; glory be to the HOLY GHOST, Who is the abundance of the pastures of David the Shepherd.

As it was in the beginning, is now, and ever shall be: world without end. Amen.

COLLECTS.

Ludolph. Almighty GOD, most bountiful provider, refresh us with the food of spiritual manna; that guided by the skilfulness of Thine hands, we may glory at Thy right hand in the mountain Thou hast purchased. Through. (1.)

Mozarabic. Almighty, Incomprehensible, and Merciful LORD, Who destroyest not sinners so often as they grieve Thee by their offences, set mercy before Thy wrath; and as often as we provoke Thee to smite, so often let Thy loving-kindness cause Thee to forgive. Feed us, then, with the Bread of Angels; that receiving its might, we may overcome the wily craft of the evil one, and through Thine aid enter through the open gates of heaven into the number of its citizens. (11.)

Mozarabic. O LORD Most High, be Thou our Helper, that by the abundance of Thy might, we may be filled with comfortable strength, and by the overflowing bounties of Thy grace, may be enriched with the gifts of freedom. (11.)

Mozarabic. O GOD, Who givest the Bread of Heaven to the sons of men; and feedest an earthly being with the fatness of Angels, grant us the abundant corn of Thy Word, and refresh us with that spiritual food wherewith Thou didst nourish our fathers in the wilderness. (11.)

Mozarabic. O LORD, we who set our hope in Thee, forget not Thy works, for Thou art wonderful in Thy Saints with righteousness and mercy, and terrible amongst the ungodly, in that Thou bestowest seasonable remedies upon the righteous, and repayest the wicked the chastisements due to them. We therefore beseech Thee, most merciful GOD, that Thou wouldest enlighten with the light of Thy commandments them whom Thou savest from their cruel enemies, removing from them the waves of temptations, showing to them a path of safety, and refreshing them in this world's wilderness with the Body of Thy CHRIST as their heavenly Bread. (11.)

D. C. O GOD, Who hast pity upon all, and ceasest not to receive with fatherly kindness them who return unto Thee; remember, we beseech Thee, that we are but flesh; and be ready to turn Thy wrath away, nor kindle all that wrath against us, but soften it, and vouchsafe us Thine unfailing grace. Through. (1.)

CHRIST the LORD, Who was elected for our redemption s. Jerome. by the FATHER's counsel; taking flesh from the flock of mortals, feeding the Christian people, whether it be the Supplanter of its sins, or with the soul the Beholder of GOD; in the goodness of His heart vouchsafe to feed His Church, abiding in His will, and set it in the heavenly Jerusalem. To Him be glory with the eternal FATHER, and the HOLY GHOST, for ever and ever. Amen.

PSALM LXXIX.

TITLE: A Psalm of Asaph. Chaldee Targum: A Song by the hands of Asaph, of the destruction of the House of the Sanctuary. He spake it by the spirit of prophecy.

ARGUMENT.

ARG. THOMAS. That CHRIST avenges the blood of the slain, shed for the glory of His Name. The Voice of the Martyrs, concerning their own bloodshedding. The Voice of the Apostles, for any trouble, or of the Martyrs for bloodshedding. The Voice of the Apostles after the Passion of CHRIST. The Voice of the Martyrs for their own bloodshedding for the Name of the LORD JESUS CHRIST. A penitent soul makes prayer to GOD against its most evil neighbours, the devils. In any trouble.

VEN. BEDE. This Psalm, like the seventy-third [lxxiv.] is full of lamentation. It weeps over times to come as though past, and beseeches CHRIST, of His dear loving-kindness, to help the people sorely afflicted because of the hardness of its heart. *Asaph*, under the figure of the faithful people, speaks throughout the Psalm: relating in the first part, what sufferings the Jewish people bore at Jerusalem in the days of Antiochus, as the Book of Maccabees records. *O God, the heathen are come in.* Secondly; he prays the LORD to pour out His indignation on the mighty enemies, and to be graciously merciful to the sins of His servants. *Lord, how long wilt Thou be angry?* Thirdly; in the spirit of prophecy, he demands vengeance on them, not through desire for their destruction, but in eagerness for their correction. *O let the vengeance.*

ARNOBIUS. The seventy-eighth Psalm [lxxix.] following the close of its predecessor, pours out lamentation and prayer together unto GOD. While its historical sense details the past slaughter by Philistines, it relates in prophecy that yet to come from Nebuchadnezzar.

SYRIAC PSALTER. Spoken by Asaph, of the destruction of Jerusalem.

EUSEBIUS OF CÆSAREA. A prophecy of those things which befell the Jews through Antiochus. The history is in the Maccabees.

S. ATHANASIUS. A Psalm in solitary address.

VARIOUS USES.

Gregorian. Thursday. Matins.
Monastic. The same.
Parisian. Tuesday. Compline.
Lyons. Friday. Matins.
Ambrosian. Tuesday of Second Week. II. Nocturn.
Quignon. Saturday. Sext.

ANTIPHONS.

Gregorian. Be merciful * unto our sins, O LORD.
Monastic. For Thy Name's sake * be merciful unto our sins, O
. LORD.
Parisian. Thou forgavest * the wickedness of my sin; for this
shall every one that is godly make his prayer unto Thee.
Lyons. As *Gregorian.*
Ambrosian. As Psalm lxxvii.
Mozarabic. Have mercy upon us, and that soon.

The date and occasion of this Psalm are much disputed by modern
critics, who are divided as to the particular destruction of Jerusalem
referred to, some holding it to be the Chaldee inroad, and others
the spoiling of the Temple by Antiochus Epiphanes. From at least
the time of Cassiodorus the parallelisms between Psalm lxxiv. and
this one have been the subject of notice and comment, but the present Psalm depicts a still worse condition of things than the earlier
one. A few clues may be obtained to guide us. Thus verse 4 is
borrowed directly from verse 14 of the earlier Korhite Psalm xliv.
On the other hand, verses 6 and 7 are borrowed in turn by Jeremiah, x. 25, just as he borrows in the preceding verse from the Penitential Psalms. This composition, therefore, must date before the
final Captivity and after Psalm xliv. and it is certainly not a Maccabee Psalm, because it is actually quoted as part of Scripture in
1 Macc. vii. 17, a distinction which would not have been accorded
while it was still a new poem. Further, verse 6 seems to imply
invasion by confederate nations, or by an army recruited from various
peoples, which will not hold of the Seleucid forces. It has been ingeniously suggested that the defilement of the Temple and the
slaughter of the Saints refer to the idolatrous and tyrannical reign
of Manasseh, but it seems very difficult to reconcile this view with
the language implying the destruction of the holy city. It is possible that the true date lies between the dethronement of Jehoiakim
and the last capture of Jerusalem.

1 O GOD, the heathen are come into thine inheritance : thy holy temple have they defiled, and made
Jerusalem an heap of stones.

L.

A.

O God. The abruptness of this opening is, R. Kimchi re-
marks, a pathetic appeal. How can it be, seeing Thou art
GOD and Judge, that Thou sufferest the heathen to waste
Thine inheritance? We may not apply this as a prophecy
of the final destruction of the city and temple by Titus and
Hadrian, because the Jewish nation, by rejecting CHRIST, had

ceased to be any longer GOD's *inheritance.* The words must
therefore be taken of an earlier time, and of those faithful
ones who were the true heritage of the LORD, as were the
Apostles later. But S. Bonaventure takes them, deeply and   S. Bonaven-
beautifully, of the Person of CHRIST, outraged and crucified   tura.
by Gentile soldiers. *An heap of stones.* So the Hebrew and
S. Jerome. The LXX. and Vulgate read *a fruit shed,*
ὀπωροφυλάκιον, *pomorum custodiam,* that is, either a place for
temporary storage, or the hut erected by the gardener to
shelter himself during the harvest, and abandoned when that
immediate occasion ended. So the Prophet, "And the   Isa. i. 8.
daughter of Sion is left as a cottage in a vineyard, as a lodge
in a garden of cucumbers." They take it mystically of the   Arnobius.
inroad of evil thoughts and passions on the soul, making it
which should be GOD's temple, a polluted thing, and deserted
by the living principle of faith, or even by GOD Himself.
Again, it may be explained of those who discredit the Church   S. Hieron.
by their secular lives, who show no result of baptismal grace,
who care only for temporal, not for spiritual things, who,—   G.
to imitate the quaint language of a Saint,—"study in the   Ric. Hamp.
market, not in Mark, delight in scrip, not in Scripture."[1] It
is especially true of worldly prelates and priests, who *come*   S. Alb. Mag.
into God's inheritance, the Church, without being called or   Hugo Card.
drawn by Him, and who abandon it as soon as they have
made gain by it, just as the gardener or vintager leaves his
hut after harvest. Others again, applying it to times of persecution, interpret the *defiling* as forced apostasy ; the *fruit-*   A.
shed as the Church, falling into decay when the Martyrs,
the rich fruits once stored there, are carried into GOD's   Ven. Bede.
garners.[2]

2 The dead bodies of thy servants have they given
to be meat unto the fowls of the air : and the flesh
of thy saints unto the beasts of the land.

Once more they point out that the words cannot refer to   Ay.
the conquest of Titus, because the Christians escaped safely
from Jerusalem during a lull in the siege. They prefer to
dwell on the sufferings of the Martyrs in the ten great persecutions, noting that the poor vengeance of the heathen not   A.
only could not touch the soul, but that the Resurrection
makes even their attempts against the body vain. No fitter
comment can be made on this sense of these two verses,
than the words of S. Basil the Great, describing the results   Hom. de
of Diocletian's edict. "The private houses of Christians   Gordio M.

---

[1] "Student in marcâ, non in
Marco, gaudent in librâ, non in
libro."
[2] At this point the Golden
Commentary of Gerhohus ceases.
That portion of his great work

which he completed first, by no
means equal to the latter, begins
with Psalm cxix. His place in
this book will, for the present,
be occupied, not filled, by Honorius of Autun.

were laid waste, the goods of the innocent were plundered, the bodies of faithful and virtuous persons were rent by the hands of executioners; matrons were dragged through the streets . . . . Besides all this, the houses of prayer were desolated by profane hands; the most holy altars were overthrown; nor was there any oblation, any incense, any place for offering the Sacrifice left. Deep sorrow, like a spreading

Ay. mist, reigned everywhere." Mystically, they take the words as showing that our bodies may be, and are, exposed to the

Hugo Card. power of evil spirits, or human tyrants and slanderers, typified by *fowls* and *beasts*, but that our souls are not given into their power. Or, taking the *Saints* to mean all baptized Christians, their *dead bodies* will denote those of them who

Ric. Hamp. have allowed their souls to become dead in sin, and who are

Eph. ii. 2. thus given over to the "powers of the air," and their *flesh* will signify carnal passions and appetites, which end in becoming the prey of the devouring lion.

3 Their blood have they shed like water on every side of Jerusalem : and there was no man to bury them.

L. They try here to give some guess at the number of Christian Martyrs who resisted unto blood in the early days of the Church, and find only the rough calculation that the various Martyrologies, specifying only the more eminent cases, commemorate an average of five hundred Martyrs for each day of the year, whence they suggest the vast number of those

A. not so mentioned. *Like water*, that is, abundantly and wan-

Ric. Hamp. tonly, *on every side of Jerusalem*, that is, since Jerusalem denotes the Church, throughout the whole world. It holds of those who *shed* their own *blood*, that is, their spiritual life, by publishing their open and reckless sin committed in the

Hugo Card. Church. *And there was no man to bury them.* It may be taken of that height of disorder in the Church, when wickedness, instead of being buried in the grave of repentance, of confession, of restraint, or of a cairn of good works heaped over it so as to hide its evil savour, is openly preached and encouraged. The properties of a grave are thus summed up to enforce this sense :

> Terra, cadaver, hians, premit, et tumet, arcet odorem,
> Ossa negat, vermi dat carnem, vivida reddit.

Arnobius. *There was no man to bury them,* by hiding them from death with the example of life. Observe that in these two verses there is an apparent violation of the normal law of mystical language, whereby in Holy Scripture *Jerusalem* usually denotes the Church triumphant, and *Sion* the Church militant. They may, however, be very readily explained in accordance with that law. The words, *on every side of Jerusalem*, imply that the slaughter did not reach the inner city, but only its suburbs and outworks ; and the expression *made Jerusalem an heap of stones* will then denote the manner in which the great immigration of Martyrs thronged the City above, for the *heap of stones* will signify that Gilead, or "mound of witness," whereof is written, "Gilead is mine."[1] Ps. lx. 7.

4 We are become an open shame to our enemies : a very scorn and derision unto them that are round about us.

It is the cry of the Martyrs, whether in Pagan, Arian, P.
Vandal, or Saracen days, and yet not altogether a cry of sorrow, but of rejoicing in sharing in the Passion of Him Who was mocked, spit on, buffeted, blindfolded, and blas-
phemously reviled. Yet again, it is the confession of guilt S. Alb. Mag.
on the part of unworthy prelates and clergy, who have caused unbelievers and even many of the well-disposed laity to con- Ric. Hamp.
demn the Church on their account.

5 Lord, how long wilt thou be angry : shall thy jealousy burn like fire for ever?

The anger and jealousy of God are not emotions of God ; A.
as some charge against those Scriptures which they under-
stand not ; but by the name of anger is to be understood the avenging of iniquity ; under the name of jealousy, the ex-
action of chastity, that the soul may not despise the law of her Lord, and perish by departing in fornication from the Lord. *Like fire.* For God's anger and jealousy do burn S. Alcuin.
like fire till the gold, that is, perfect holiness, be purified, and the wood be reduced to ashes. Note too, that God's *anger*
may be aroused by any sin, but His *jealousy*, as well as that S. Bonaven-
of His servants, is usually spoken of in Scripture as directed tura.
against spiritual adultery, that is, idolatry. Thus Moses Honor Aug.
says, "They provoked Him to jealousy with strange gods." Deut. xxxii.
And Phinehas, slaying Zimri and Cozbi, is said to be " zealous Numb. xxv.
for his God ;" and Elijah complains, " I have been very 13.
jealous for the Lord God of Hosts." . 1 Kings xix.
10.

6 Pour out thine indignation upon the heathen that have not known thee : and upon the kingdoms that have not called upon thy Name.

7 For they have devoured Jacob : and laid waste his dwelling-place.

It is a prophecy, not a wish. S. Augustine queries how A.
this passage can be reconciled with the words of the Gospel,

[1] It will be seen, on reference to Vol. I. p. 401, that I have ventured to differ from the opi- | nion of this passage expressed by Dr. Neale.—R. F. L.

"That servant, which knew his lord's will, and prepared not, neither did according to his will, shall be beaten with many stripes. But he that knew not, and did commit things worthy of stripes, shall be beaten with few stripes." And the answer is, that even the worse of these two is at least his LORD's servant, calling upon His Name, whereas the heathen spoken of in the Psalm refuse to do so, not through mere ignorance, but through perversity of will. They call on other names in the three kingdoms of the devil, the world, and the flesh. The proud invoke Baal; the covetous, Mammon; the luxurious, Baal-Peor. *They have devoured Jacob.* That is, they have compelled apostasy, and thus caused Christians to pass into their body or society, *and laid waste his dwelling-place,* by preventing others from coming to the faith, and thus filling up the vacancies left by those who fall away. Taking the whole scope of the Psalm, with the Carthusian and Parez, to be the fall of the Latin kingdom of Jerusalem, and the capture of the Holy Places by the Saracens, we may cite the lament of a contemporary poet:

Margin notes: S. Luke xii. 47. / Hugo Card. / A. / Honorius. / D. C. / P.

> Eheu! terra inclyta, terra vere bona,
> Sola digna perfrui floridâ coronâ!
> Terra cui dederat DEUS tanta dona,
> Eheu! quantum impia te nunc cingit zona!
>
> Eheu! eheu! DOMINE, gloria justorum,
> Angelorum bonitas, salus peccatorum!
> Ecce canes comedunt panes filiorum,
> Velut aqua funditur sanguis nunc sanctorum!
>
> Flete, omnes populi, flete, et non parum!
> Graves luctus facite, planctum et amarum!
> Flumina effundite, undas lacrymarum!
> Sic ruinam plangite urbium sanctarum.

Margin note: Du Meril. Poes. Pop. Lat.

8 O remember not our old sins, but have mercy upon us, and that soon : for we are come to great misery.

Old sins: whether those of our fathers, entailing evils on their descendants, or those of original sin, committed before baptism, and remitted therein, but partially resumed, or else post-baptismal sins, repented of, and left behind. *Soon.* How soon, let the A. V. tell us, herein agreeing with the Vulgate: *Let Thy tender mercies speedily prevent us;* let Thy grace anticipate our fall, and not merely lift us up from it; let Thy mercy anticipate Thy judgment, that we be not condemned at the last. *We are come to great misery.* The LXX. and Vulgate read, *We have become exceeding poor,* having lost the gold of purity and the silver of a good conscience, and being destitute of all good works. Where note, that he is *poor,* who has none of this world's goods; he is *very* poor, who has not himself; he is *exceeding* poor, who not only has not him-

Margin notes: B. / Ric. Hamp. / A. / Arnobius. / C. / S. Albertus Magnus.

self, but is in another's power. "O how great is the might   D. C.
of this verse and of the two which follow! Their power out-
strips all human understanding; the tongue fails in uttering
their praise; but how good it is to confess our own poverty,
and thus to cry ceaselessly in the LORD's Prayer, 'Give us this S. Matt. vi.
day our daily bread.' Wonderful is the might of prayer in 11.
these verses, and most wholesome is it to use these holy words,
with loving soul, with steadfast attention, with hearty zest,
for it were easier for heaven and earth to perish, than for
such a prayer to be in vain!"

9 Help us, O GOD of our salvation, for the glory
of thy Name: O deliver us, and be merciful unto our
sins, for thy Name's sake.

Help us. While the Psalmist would have us to be helped,   A.
he is neither ungrateful to grace, nor doth he take away free-
will. For he that is *helped*, does something for his own part,   Ay.
wherefore S. Chrysostom saith, that grace is the help of hu- S. Chrysost.
man weakness. Help is not given to sleepers, but to them in S. Matt.
that bestir themselves. So when S. Antony warred against S. Hieron.
evil spirits, and was sore wounded in the conflict, he recog- Vit. Patr.
nized with gladness, as a sunbeam shone down on him and
put the demons to flight, that CHRIST had come to him, and
he said, "Where wast Thou, O good JESU: where wast
Thou?" And a voice came to him, saying, "Antony, I was
here; I was watching thy conflict. Now that thou hast not
ceased battling manfully, I will ever help thee." Whence
it is said, "The SPIRIT helpeth our infirmities." He does Rom. viii. 26.
not say "our negligence." *O God of our salvation, for the* Hesychius.
glory of Thy Name, which is JESUS, the SAVIOUR, not for any D. C.
merits of our own, *deliver us.*

> JESU, salva me, Salvator,   Psalterium
> Esto meus liberator   de Nomine
> De mortis voragine,   JESU.
> JESU, laudem tibi dico,
> Nomen tuum benedico,
> Manum mihi porrige.

Be merciful to our sins. As pardon was asked in a former   B.
verse for *old* sins, so here the remission of those which we
continue to commit is asked from the LORD. Do more than
pardon, grant that the sufferings which we deserve, but which,
as Christians, we bear *for Thy Name's sake,* may not cause Honorius.
us to fall away into the sins of the ungodly around us, but   R.
help to purge us, and fit to praise Thy holy Name with Ric. Hamp.
honour and thanksgiving.

10 Wherefore do the heathen say: Where is now
their GOD?

II.   A A

11 O let the vengeance of thy servants' blood that is shed : be openly showed upon the heathen in our sight.

The order of the clauses of the eleventh verse in the LXX. and Vulgate is the reverse of this, and the Vulgate adds one of them to the tenth, thus : *Where is now their God ? and be it known in the nations, &c.* That is, not merely that they should deny either GOD's power to save, or His knowledge of the distress of His people, but that this blasphemy, confined at first to a few, should spread abroad amongst the unbelieving nations around, as did the mockery of those who reviled Him when He hung upon the Cross. *The vengeance of Thy servants' blood.* There is a double comment on these words in the New Testament, the cry of the souls of the Martyrs under the Altar in heaven : " How long, O LORD, holy and true, dost Thou not avenge our blood on them that dwell on the earth?" and the promise given by their King Himself : " Shall not GOD avenge His own elect, which cry day and night unto Him, though He bear long with them? I tell you, that He will avenge them speedily." S. Augustine dwells at much length on this prayer, and shows that it is an intreaty in true charity for the correction of the wicked in this life, that they may be saved at last, (seeing that their sin must be punished somehow and some time,) rather than have it deferred to the world to come, and therefore it is said, *in our sight.*

Bellarmine.

L.

D. C.

Rev. vi. 10.

S. Luke xviii. 7.

A.

12 O let the sorrowful sighing of the prisoners come before thee : according to the greatness of thy power, preserve thou those that are appointed to die.

Prisoners, either in the bonds of the flesh, which they only feel heavy who " desire to depart and to be with CHRIST," or in the bonds of GOD's commandments, which, fitly worn, become ornaments, as it is written, " Put thy feet into her fetters, and thy neck into her chain," because, as is said further, " then shall her fetters be a strong defence for thee, and her chains a robe of glory." Or *prisoners* in the bonds of charity and brotherly love, who are constrained to make perpetual intercession on behalf of sinners, as Moses did for guilty Israel, and who thus bind the LORD Himself. Or, yet again, *prisoners* under the bondage of the old Law, not yet admitted into " the glorious liberty of the children of GOD." Lastly ; they take it of literal chains, wherewith the heathen bound the Martyrs and Confessors of CHRIST. And with this they take *those that are appointed to die.* The Hebrew literally is, *the sons of death,* and the LXX. and Vulgate turn the words, *acquire for Thy possession the sons of the slaughtered,* which is, that in accordance with the prayer of the Apostles and Martyrs, whose spiritual children we are, their blood-

A.
Pet. Lomb.
Phil. 1. 23.

Ecclus. vi.
24, 29.

D. C.

Hugo Card.
Rom. viii.
21.

C.

A.

shedding might not be fruitless, but enrich the field of the
Church with a rich harvest. And so it has been a proverb
for sixteen hundred years, "The blood of the Martyrs is the
seed of the Church." Another reminds us that when GOD
delivers us from any great peril of death, bodily or spiritual,
He thereby purchases us as His especial property, and we
are more than ever bound to His service. They are to be
acquired or *preserved* by the *greatness of God's power*, or, as
the Hebrew and the versions generally, of His *Arm*, that is,
of His Only-begotten SON, that Arm which is most potent to
deliver, most ample to embrace, most tenacious to hold; of
which it is written, "He shall gather the lambs with His
arm, and carry them in His bosom, and shall gently lead
those that are with young."

D. C.

Ric. Ceno-
man.

S. Albertus
Magnus.

Isa. xl. 11.

13 And for the blasphemy wherewith our neighbours have blasphemed thee : reward thou them, O
LORD, sevenfold into their bosom.

Sevenfold, as doing it perfectly, *into their bosoms*, as doing
it secretly. They take it, for the most part, of severe chastisements at GOD's hand, in vengeance on the seven deadly
sins, marked by seven deprivations of grace in this world,
and seven woes in the world to come. Far deeper and lovelier is the gloss of Cassiodorus, followed by many others,
that it is a prayer for the conversion of sinners by sending
into their hearts the sevenfold gifts of the HOLY GHOST;
the first effect of which will be to cover them with confusion,
so that they shall hide their faces in the bosom of GOD, and
there reproach themselves seven times as much as they once
did the Name of GOD.

A.

Ay.
S. Albertus
Magnus.

C.
Ven. Bede.
R.

B.

14 So we, that are thy people, and sheep of thy
pasture, shall give thee thanks for ever : and will
alway be showing forth thy praise from generation
to generation.

Cardinal Hugo, according to his wont, sums up in mnemonic verse the mystical properties of pasture :

Hugo Card.

> Pascua sponte virent ; pascunt inculta licenter
> Alta pecus, sed aquosa boves, dant fœna per imbres.

They remind us that the Jewish people were the first sheep
of GOD's pasture in this world, and that as sheep assemble
together in summer, and part in winter, so the Jews were
ready to give thanks to GOD in prosperity, but in time of
affliction they always fell away. But of His own elect, He,
the Good Shepherd, Who has given Himself to be their
Food, saith, "I will seek out My sheep, and will bring them
to their own land, and feed them upon the mountains of
Israel by the rivers, and in all the inhabited places of the

Ay.

S. Albertus
Magnus.

Ezek. xxxiv.
12—14.

A A 2

country. I will feed them in a good pasture, and upon the high mountains of Israel shall their fold be : there shall they lie in a good fold." How good that fold is, let us hear one tell us whose soul thirsted to be there :

S. Pet. Dam. Winters snowing, summers glowing, never thither pain may bring,
The Hymn, Everlasting roses blowing make an everlasting spring,
Ad perennis Lily blanching, crocus blushing, and the balsam perfuming.
vitæ fontem.

Pasture groweth, flowret bloweth, honey drops from combs of bees,
Liquid odours, fragrant spices, shed their perfume on the breeze,
Never-falling fruits are hanging from the ever-leafy trees.

Theod. *From generation to generation.* From the generation of cir-
Mopsuest. cumcision to that of baptism, from the generation of nature to that of grace, from the generation of this world to that of heaven, *we shall praise Thy Name* in the most blessed psal-
C. mody of the world to come, which the choir of Saints shall chant unceasingly, not to teach others, for none there will be untaught, but that, offering honour where it is due, they may be fed with the very sweetness of their own song. And so once more the holy Bishop of Ostia :

S. Pet. Dam. In new harmonies unceasing they with voice melodious sing,
ubi sup. While their listening ears are gladdened with the harps' exultant ring,
And, for He hath made them victors, praises chant they to their King.

Wherefore :
Glory be to the FATHER, the GOD of our Salvation ; and to the SON, the Greatness of His Arm ; and to the HOLY GHOST, Who giveth His sevenfold grace into our bosom.
As it was in the beginning, is now, and ever shall be : world without end. Amen.

COLLECTS.

Ludolph. Prevent us, O LORD, with Thy mercy, before the jealousy of Thine anger be kindled, that helped by the prayers of the Blessed, whose blood was shed for Thy sake, we may obtain Thy mercy and remission of our sins. Through. (1.)

Mozarabic. Be merciful to our sins, O LORD, and, for the glory of Thy Name, refresh us with perfect freedom. Let us not become a rebuke unto the heathen whilst we are oppressed with the record of our sins. Wash away, then, the source of our offences, that Thou punish us not with severe chastisement, and let the sighing of the prisoners enter in unto Thee, that Thy bountiful grace may come manifestly unto us from Thy hid treasures. Through. (11.)

Mozarabic. O LORD, let Thy mercy speedily prevent us, for there is neither comforting hope, nor trust in merit, nor helpful assistance to support us ; but the guilt and trouble of our life, the conscience of our sins, or the vengeance on our offences rebukes us in our unrest. Deliver us for the glory of Thy Name, and be merciful unto our sins for Thy Name's sake, that when Thou hast done both for Thyself, and hast looked on Thy people with Thy wonted loving-kindness, we may give Thee glory for our deliverance, and obtain propitiation through Thy Name. Through. (11.)

O LORD Most High, be Thou our Helper; and make haste Mozarabic. with speed to deliver Thy people, that by Thine abundant power we may be filled with mighty help, and be enriched with gifts from the bounty of Thine abundant grace, that our tongue may not become slow through falsehood when we profess love to Thee with our mouth, but let that profession of our mouth denote purity of mind, and let Thy praise ever sound on our lips from the organ of the heart. Through. (11.)

Remember not, O LORD, our old sins, nor let original guilt Mozarabic. bring sorrow on us, whom a second birth in CHRIST regenerates. Let Thy mercy, therefore, O LORD, take hold upon us; for the Creator of man is born in man, and man is assumed into GOD, Who is to be glorified. Through. (11.)

We beseech Thee, O LORD, mercifully to hear our prayers, D. C. and for Thy praiseworthy and glorious Name's sake, remember not our old sins, that, by Thy help, delivered from all our offences, we may ever watch unto the works of righteousness. Through. (1.)

PSALM LXXX.

TITLE. To the Chief Musician upon Shoshannim-Eduth. A Psalm of Asaph. LXX. and Vulgate: To the end, for them who shall be changed, a Testimony of Asaph, a Psalm, [because of the Assyrian, LXX.] Or: To the Supreme, for the Lilies, a Testimony of Asaph, a Psalm.

ARGUMENT.

ARG. THOMAS. That CHRIST, sitting upon the Cherubim, extends and protects the Vineyard of the Church. The Voice of the Priests of GOD for the Church and CHRIST. The Voice of the Apostles to the FATHER concerning CHRIST and the Church. Then, the Voice of the Priests of GOD concerning the Church and CHRIST. The Voice of the Prophets concerning the Advent of CHRIST, and the extension of the Vineyard, that is, the Church.

VEN. BEDE. As the first words of the title are already explained, it remains for us to inquire what the *Testimony of Asaph* means. This *Asaph*, aforetime fearful and disquieted, who in the previous Psalm made prayer for the offences of the *synagogue*, is now filled with such confidence, that, *changed* for the better, he gives *testi-*

mony of his change. For he speaks of the first Advent of the SA-VIOUR, Who brought back corrupted man to the gifts of salvation, and stablished with the root of His power the *vine* which He *brought out of Egypt.* This is what he means by saying, *A testimony for them who shall be changed.*

This *Asaph,* of whom the title sings as *changed,* in the first section, prays for the Coming of the LORD : Hear, *O Thou Shepherd of Israel.* Secondly, he testifies how that *Vine,* which is the Church, is spread over the whole world. *Thou hast brought a vine out of Egypt.* Thirdly, He prays Him to visit His Church, under the parable of a Vine, with the bounty of His Incarnation, and beseeches that he may cling to the LORD. *Turn Thee again, O God of hosts, &c.*

CHALDEE TARGUM. For Praise, for the ordinary sitting Judges, who apply themselves to the testimony of the Law.

EUSEBIUS OF CÆSAREA. A prophecy of the siege by the Assyrians, and a prayer for the appearance of CHRIST.

VARIOUS USES.

Gregorian. Thursday. Matins.
Monastic. Thursday. II. Nocturn.
Parisian. Thursday. None.
Lyons. Tuesday. None.
Ambrosian. Tuesday of Second Week. III. Nocturn.
Quignon. Monday. None.

ANTIPHONS.

Gregorian. As preceding Psalm.
Monastic. Exult unto GOD, * our Helper.
Parisian. Thy testimonies, * O LORD, are very sure.
Ambrosian. As preceding Psalm.
Mozarabic. First verse of the Psalm.

The most satisfactory explanation amongst the many which have been given as to the date and occasion of this Psalm, is that which represents it as composed after the captivity of the Northern Kingdom of Israel, and before that of the Kingdom of Judah. It will thus be a prayer for use in the Temple of Jerusalem for the release of the ten tribes from bondage, for their reunion under the sceptre of the House of David, and for the restoration of the limits reached by the Jewish monarchy in the time of Solomon. The mystical parallel thus afforded is abundantly clear.

. 1 Hear, O thou Shepherd of Israel, thou that leadest Joseph like a sheep : show thyself also, thou that sittest upon the cherubims.

Shepherd of Israel. So the LXX., Syriac, and S. Jerome. The Vulgate, less happily, reads, *Thou who rulest Israel.* He is the *Shepherd* of His people, because He pitches their tents as in a green pasture, and feeds them by the waters of comfort; because He is their leader, and champion against

S. Greg. Naz. Or. 4 de Filio.

wild beasts; because He turns back those which are going
astray, recovers the lost sheep, binds up the broken, protects
the whole, and gathers them into the heavenly fold. He is
Shepherd of *Israel*, as King of the Jews, *ruling* His people   **Z.**
in many ways, as a monarch does his realm, as a pilot steers
his ship, as a general marshals a battle, as a father governs Hugo Card.
his household, as a teacher directs his pupils, as a guide con-
ducts the blind, as a shepherd leads his sheep, as an abbat
rules a cloister, as the soul sways the body, as reason does
the heart, as a priest governs his church, or a bishop his dio-
cese. He rules and feeds *Joseph* also, the "increase" of the   **B.**
Gentiles, bringing him into the one fold with Israel, and
leading him on from strength to strength. And as He led   **L.**
the patriarch Joseph *like a sheep* in his innocence, simplicity,
purity, meekness, and patience, from prison to a throne; so
He led CHRIST, the antitype of Joseph, the Lamb of GOD,
from the grave to His own right hand in glory. He leads Ric. Ham-
still all pure and patient souls by the same path to His own pol.
fold. And not only the pure; for here we may see that hun-
dredth sheep which the Good Shepherd brings back on His Drogo Card.
shoulders to rejoin the ninety and nine. Our Pastor goes de Pass.
before His flock, for He is the guide into all truth, and He Dom.
leads the way to Paradise and Heaven. He goes behind His S. Chrysost.
flock, lest the weary one should halt, or be separated from its Hom. 58 in
companions. And so it is written, "Thy Righteousness shall S. Joan.
go before thee: the glory of the LORD shall be thy rere- Isa. lviii. 8.
ward."

Show Thyself. By Thine Advent and Thine Incarnation, S. Bern.
showing not Thy majesty alone, but Thy lowliness. *That* Serm. 2, de
sittest upon the Cherubims. "Cherubim is the seat of the Epiph.
glory of GOD, and is interpreted 'the fulness of knowledge.'   **A.**
There GOD sitteth in the fulness of knowledge. Though we
understand the Cherubim to be the exalted powers and virtues of heavens; yet, if thou desirest, thou wilt be cherubim.
For if cherubim be the seat of GOD, the soul of a righteous
man is the seat of wisdom. How shall I, thou sayest, be
the fulness of knowledge? Who shall fulfil this? Thou
hast the means of doing so; 'Love is the fulfilling of the Rom. xiii.10.
Law.' Run not after many things, nor strain thyself. The
spreading size of the branches alarms thee: hold by the
Root, and reck not of the greatness of the tree. Let Love
be in thee, and the fulness of knowledge must needs follow.
For 'GOD is Love.'" The primary reference is to the cloud 1 S. John iv.
hovering over the Ark in the journey in the wilderness, and 8.
later to the Shechinah in the Holy of holies in the Temple.
And of this passage we have an exceedingly early mystical
application to the Four Gospels. S. Irenæus writes: "The S. Irenæus,
WORD, the Framer of all things, Who sitteth upon the Che- Adv. Hæres.
rubim, and containeth all things, He Who was manifested to 3, xi. 8.
men, has given us the Gospel under four aspects, but bound
together by one Spirit. As also David says, when praying

Rev. iv. 7.

for His manifestation, *Thou that sittest upon the cherubims, show Thyself.* For ' the first living creature was like a lion,' typifying His effectual working, His leadership, and royal power; ' the second was like a calf,' signifying sacrificial and priestly order; but ' the third had, as it were, the face as of a man,' a clear description of His Advent as a human being; 'the fourth like a flying eagle,' denoting the gift of the SPIRIT hovering with His wings over the Church."

Adam. Vic-
torin. The
Sequence,
*Jucundare,
plebs fidelis.*

Ecce forma bestialis,
Quam scriptura prophetalis
Notat, sed materialis
  Hæc est impositio.
Currunt rotis, volant alis,
Visus sensus spiritalis ;
Rota, gressus est æqualis,
  Ala, contemplatio.

Quatuor describunt isti
Quadriformes actus CHRISTI ;
Et figurant, ut audisti,
  Quisque suâ formulâ.
Natus Homo declaratur,
Vitulus sacrificatur,
Leo mortem deprædatur,
  Et ascendit Aquila.

And taking the Ark, as they so often do, to represent her who was the shrine of Godhead, the Greek Fathers delight in describing the Holy Child lying on her bosom as on a throne, borne up by angels.

S. Andr.
Cretens.

Παρθένος καθέζεται, τὰ χερουβὶμ μιμουμένη.
βαστάζουσα ἐν κόλποις, Θεὸν Λόγον σαρκωθέντα.

Ay.

Till then, He was *sitting* upon the Angels, and, in respect of us men, He was, as it were, sleeping and lying down. Then, He arose in His power, and stood up to help us in the battle.

2 Before Ephraim, Benjamin, and Manasses : stir up thy strength, and come, and help us.

Numb. ii. 18,
20, 22.

These three tribes were marshalled together on the west side of the Tabernacle, and therefore nearest to the Holy of holies. This circumstance, and the meaning of their names, have given rise to a copious stream of mystical interpretation.

C.

And first they take all three as types of CHRIST, the " fruit-ful" Tree, which, buried first in the earth, shot up to the highest heavens; the " SON of the Right Hand" of the Almighty FATHER ; the " forgetting" One, Who pardoned the sins committed against Himself, and prayed upon the Cross for His murderers. Again, they interpret Ephraim of the

laity, who ought to be fruitful in good works, as they are Ven. Bede.
rich in worldly goods; Benjamin, of the clergy, who should Hugo Card.
be valiant, and do battle for the Church, caring nothing for
the heritage of the left hand, mere temporal prosperity; and **B.**
Manasseh, of Religious, who leave behind and forget worldly
matters, "reaching forth unto those things which are before." Phil. iii. 13.
The Carthusian, not dissimilarly, takes the first to mean **D.C.**
those who bring forth worthy fruits of repentance, the second
to be the workers of righteousness, the third those who forget the world. They remind us that Benjamin was the tribe Honor. Au-
whence S. Paul, the teacher of the Gentiles, sprang, and gustod.
that it thus denotes the missionary Jewish Church; that
Ephraim, the younger and more fruitful child of Joseph, **P.**
signifies the Gentiles, later called, but more numerous than
the Hebrew believers; and that Manasseh, meaning "forget-
fulness," and dwelling half in Bashan and half in Canaan, is
the Jewish nation, forgetting Christ, but having a remnant
which will not abide in unbelief, but will enter into the promises. Ayguan begins here, but does not finish, a long alle- **Ay.**
gory on the marshalling of the twelve tribes, comparing them
to twelve virtues encamped round the tabernacle of the
Christian's body: on the east, its new birth; on the south,
its time of wealth; on the north, its season of adversity; and
on the west, its setting or death. He does not reach the
west; but we may readily fill the blank by noting what he says
of the others. The dying Christian, then, should have "fruitfulness," because his Master has come looking for harvest;
he should have trust in his Saviour, for it is written, "Thou Ps. lxxiii. 22.
hast holden me by my right hand;" he should forget the
things now lying behind him, reaching forth unto those things **A.**
which are before. *Stir up Thy strength,* for Thou wast weak
when they said, "If He be the Son of God, let Him come S. Matt.
down from the Cross." Thou didst seem to have no strength, xxvii. 40.
the persecutor had power over Thee; and Thou didst show
this of old, for Jacob himself prevailed in wrestling, a man
with an Angel. Could he ever have done so, had not the
Angel been willing? And man prevailed, and the Angel was
conquered; and victorious man holdeth the Angel, and saith,
"I will not let Thee go, except Thou bless me." A great Gen. xxxii.
mystery! He both standeth conquered, and blesseth the 26.
conqueror. Conquered, because He willed it; weak in flesh,
strong in majesty. *Stir up,* therefore, *Thy strength.* How
long dost Thou seem weak? Having been "crucified 2 Cor. xiii. 4.
through weakness," arise in power, *and come.* No longer **Ay.**
send, as before, by the hand of Thy Prophets, but *come,* in Pet. Lomb.
Thine own Person, by the mighty power of Thine Incarna-
tion. *And help us.* The A. V. and Vulgate, more truly, S. Alb. Mag.
save us. First, by delivering us from error; then, by gathering us into unity; finally, by rescuing us from misery. *And* **D.C.**
save us from the guilt of original sin, from mortal and venial
offences, and from the power of the evil one.

A A 3

3 Turn us, again, O God : show the light of thy countenance, and we shall be whole.

L.

A.

Ay.

Zech. i. 3.

Cd.

S. Luke xxii. 61.

Pet. Lomb.

Heb. i. 3.

A.

Arnobius.

S. Alb. Mag.

D. C.

Prov. xvi. 15.

Turn us, as the Targum explains it, back from our captivity to our country, or, with other Rabbinical authorities, *revive us* from our faintness, bringing us to ourselves again. Either way it holds good of sinners, turning away first from God, and then by His grace, not by their own power, turned back, converted to Him in penitence, because He first turns to us. Wherefore He saith, "Turn ye unto Me, saith the Lord of Hosts, and I will turn unto you, saith the Lord of Hosts." And again it is written, "And the Lord turned, and looked upon Peter. And Peter remembered the Word of the Lord." *Show the light of Thy Countenance.* It is a prayer to the Father to make His Son, "the brightness of His glory, and the express Image of His Person," manifest in the flesh by His Incarnation; it is a prayer to the Son, Whose radiance was hid under the cloud of flesh, to show His light by arising from the grave, and by ascending into heaven. *And we shall be saved*, (A. V. and Vulg.,) as they are, who, on the point of perishing in the icy chill of winter, see and feel the bright and genial rays of the sun. *Turn us*, then, by pouring Thy grace upon us; *show us the light of Thy Countenance*, by illuming us inwardly with wisdom; and *save us*, by granting us perseverance in the right way. *Show us the light of Thy Countenance* after this life in our Country, *and we shall be whole* from all pain and sorrow; for "in the light of the King's Countenance is life."

4 O Lord God of hosts : how long wilt thou be angry with thy people that prayeth?

Isa. lvii. 16.

Bellarmine.

L.

A.

Ps. cix. 6.

Ecclus. ii. 1.

How long? Let Him answer Himself: "I will not contend for ever, neither will I be always wroth: for the spirit should fail before Me, and the souls which I have made." *Thy people.* The LXX., Syriac, and Vulgate read, *Thy servant.* And they contrast the might ascribed to God by the invocation in this verse with this lowliness of His suppliant Prophet, speaking in the name of the people, and fitly calling on the Lord of good angels to save Him from evil ones, on the Lord of armies to deliver from the enemy's hand. S. Augustine appears to have read here, *Thou wast angry at the prayer of Thine enemy ; wilt Thou still be angry at the prayer of Thy servant?* Till we turned from our wickedness, we were Thine enemies, and our very prayer was turned into sin; but now that Thou hast converted us, we know Thee, and wilt Thou still be angry with the prayer of Thy servant? Thou wilt, most plainly, but as a Father correcting, not as a Judge condemning. Thus Thou wilt clearly be angry, because it is written, "My son, if thou come to serve the Lord, prepare thy soul for temptation." Think not that God's wrath hath now passed away, because thou art converted. It hath passed away, but only so as not to condemn for ever. But He scourgeth, He spareth not; because He "scourgeth Heb. xii. 6. every son whom He receiveth." If thou refusest to be scourged, why dost thou desire to be received? He scourgeth every son whom He receiveth. He scourgeth every one, Who did not spare even His Only Son. But *how long?* Hear Him again: "For a small moment have I forsaken Isa. liv. 7, 8. thee; but with great mercies will I gather thee. In a little wrath I hid My Face from thee for a moment; but with everlasting kindness will I have mercy on thee, saith the LORD thy Redeemer."

5 Thou feedest them with the bread of tears : and givest them plenteousness of tears to drink.

The LXX. and Vulgate read, *Thou wilt feed us with the bread of tears, and give us drink of tears in measure.* Again we ask, How long? And there is an answer, "Thus saith 1 Kings xxii. the King: Put this fellow in the prison, and feed him with 27. bread of affliction, and with water of affliction, until I come again in peace." Till CHRIST comes in peace to the soul, it must mourn in bondage; till CHRIST comes again to the children of the bride-chamber, they must fast and weep in penitence for their sins. *The bread of tears* is a life of sor- C. rows, and GOD *feeds* us therewith when He teaches us, not destroys us, with affliction; for these tears are for our amend-ment and perfection, not for our destruction. With meat Pet. Lomb. and drink of this kind the sinful woman fed her LORD, when S. Greg. He sat in the house of the Pharisee; for CHRIST hungers Mag. Hom. 33 in Evang. after the groans of sinners, and thirsts for their tears, so that S. Pet. Chry- Mary, not Simon, truly banqueted Him. So He fed S. Peter sol. Serm. in daily, when the crowing of the cock reminded the Prince of S. Luc. vii. the Apostles of his denial. And as the Most Holy Eucharist is a memorial of His Death, Who strove for us here with strong crying and tears, It, as uniting us to His Passion, is the Bread and Water of tears. Cry we then to Him:

> JESU Victor, JESU vita,
> JESU, vitæ via trita,
> Cujus morte mors sopita,
> Ad Paschalem nos invita
> Mensam cum fiduciâ!
> Vive Panis, verax Unda,
> Vera vitis et fœcunda,
> Tu nos pasce, tu nos munda,
> Ut a morte nos secundâ
> Tua salvet gratia!

Adam Vic-torin. The Sequence, *Zyma vetus expurgetur.*

In measure, however, it is that He gives us tears to drink, S. Alcuin. according to the degree of our sinfulness; and yet merci- Haymo. fully even so, "for GOD is faithful, Who will not suffer you A. 1 Cor. x. 13. to be tempted above that ye are able, but will with the

0

temptation also make a way to escape, that ye may be able to bear it." *In measure*, for observe that there were six times appointed for this feeding of men. First, of rebuke, as when it was said to our first parents, "In the day that thou eatest thereof, thou shalt surely die." Secondly, of chastisement, when mankind was reduced to eight souls in the Ark. Thirdly, of sacrifice, when circumcision was given to Abraham for a sign. Fourthly, of prohibition, when GOD gave the Law. Fifthly, of declaration, when the Prophets announced the Advent of CHRIST, bringing His reward with Him. Sixthly, of reconciliation, when He came in the flesh. And He says *bread*, because it is made up of three things: flour, which is good works, whereof is written, "Labour not for the meat which perisheth, but for that meat which endureth unto everlasting life;" water, denoting tears of repentance, of which is said, "Pour out thine heart like water before the face of the LORD;" and fire, which is of love, and of which CHRIST has spoken, "I am come to send fire upon the earth; and what will I, if it be already kindled?" This alone consolidates and unites the flour and the water into nourishment of the soul.

S. Bonaventura.

Gen. ii. 17.

S. John vi. 27.

Lam. ii. 19.

S. Luke xii. 49.

6 Thou hast made us a very strife unto our neighbours : and our enemies laugh us to scorn.

A.

Strife. The LXX. and Vulgate read, *contradiction*, or *gainsaying*. This plainly came to pass; for out of Asaph were chosen they that should go to the Gentiles, and preach CHRIST, and should have it said of them, Who is this "setter forth of strange gods?" For a *contradiction*; for they were preaching Him Who was the subject of the contradiction. What did they preach? That CHRIST, after He was dead, rose again. Who would acknowledge this? It was a new thing. But signs followed, and miracles gave credibility to an incredible thing. He was contradicted, but the gainsayer was overcome, and from a contradictor became a believer. Our *neighbours* are the Jews, the "gainsaying people;" but we are further exposed to the heathen, our *enemies*, who *laugh us to scorn* as worshipping a crucified malefactor. Even still, our *neighbours*, heretical Christians, near the Church, but not of it, *contradict;* and unbelievers, whether Jews or Pagans, *scorn* the Catholic Faith.

Acts xvii. 18.

Rom. x. 21.

Honorius.

Ay.

7 Turn us again, thou GOD of hosts : show the light of thy countenance, and we shall be whole.

L.

In the former invocation, CHRIST was besought to come in the flesh, in human weakness; wherefore He is there called GOD simply. Now, He is besought to come in the might of His Resurrection to eternal life, and is therefore given the title of power, *God of Hosts.*

8 Thou hast brought a vine out of Egypt : thou hast cast out the heathen, and planted it.

First, let us take it of the True Vine Himself, of Whom it was written in mystery, "Out of Egypt have I called My Son." And so it has been explained by some Rabbis. Next, of the branches collectively, springing from that one Root, and forming the Christian Church. They delight in heaping up similes to show the fitness of this parable. A Saint, writing in the days of martyrdom, allegorizes thus, with a copiousness of mystical allusion very rare at so early a date : "There is first of all a trench to receive the plant; that is the sacramental font of Baptism. Next, there is a pole to support the tendrils, denoting the Cross. The vines are trained up on terraces, signifying the steep ascent of the heavenly way and life. They are bound with cords, which are the answers and vows made when the questions of renunciation of the world are put at the font. The too luxuriant branches are pruned away with a knife, typifying the work of the HOLY SPIRIT in purging our sins. As the vine, so pruned, weeps happily, so from the baptized man more happily stream rills of heavenly wisdom. When the buds of the vine burst open, and fruit follows the leaves, this denotes the Christian, guarded and nourished alike by obedience to those holy precepts whence comes the fruit of everlasting life. The vine climbs to the top of its pole, and so the Christian, who gives all his goods to the poor, and carries his cross, thus fulfilling all righteousness, follows CHRIST with more alacrity. Tempests, heat, and rain bring the vine to maturity ; trial and persecution lead the Christian to his crown. In the time of harvest rough hands pluck off the grapes, and bear them to the wine-press, to be trodden under foot by the vintagers, as martyrs are dragged to the place of execution, and slain with insult and cruelty. And as the grape-juice is squeezed out between two boards, with all the weight of the press ; so, at the Last Judgment, vengeance for the blood of the martyrs will be exacted, according to the two tables of the Law, to the last farthing from their persecutors." S. Ambrose, dwelling on the same topic, tells us that the Vine of the Church is planted with the root of faith, pruned by humility, hedged about with heavenly precepts and angel guards; that a tower in the vineyard is built up of Apostles, Prophets, and Doctors; that the earth is dug round about the vine, that the care of worldly things may lie less heavily on it; and that the orderly rows signify the equality of rich and poor, gentle and simple, in the Church.

Cardinal Hugo reminds us that the wood of the vine, once cut away from its root, is good only for burning ; that the tree needs severe treatment to be fruitful ; that it is the only source of true wine ; that it grows lush and rank in rich soil, but then produces weak and poor wine ; that it flou-

Galatinus.
S. Matt. ii. 15.
Hos. xi. 1.

S. Zeno Veronens.

S. Ambros. Hexaëm. iii. 12.

Hugo Card.
Ezek. xv. 2, 3, 4.

rishes best on lofty and rocky ground; that it must needs be exposed to the sun, and be propped up with stakes and poles. And he applies all this to each Christian soul, with sufficiently obvious reference. Of this vineyard, whereof is written, "The vineyard of the LORD of Hosts is the House of Israel, and the men of Judah His pleasant plant," the eventful history is now set before us. GOD brought it *out of Egypt*, away from the darkness of sin, unto the light of grace. *He cast out the heathen*, those seven deadly sins which beset the soul, the evil lusts and passions of the unconverted, before it, *and planted it*, rooted and grounded in love, that it might not creep on the earth, but rise up, twining round the cedars of GOD, the Prophets and Apostles, with the tendrils of charity.

Isa. v. 7.

Hugo Card.

Origen.

9 Thou madest room for it : and when it had taken root, it filled the land.

More exactly, with the A. V., *Thou preparedst room before it*, by clearing away the stones of the vineyard and driving the heathen back. The LXX., *Thou madest a way before it*, may be taken in this sense, but the Vulgate reads, *Thou wast leader of the journey in the sight of it*, seeming rather to refer to the pillar of cloud and fire, which went before the Hebrew camp. S. Augustine, following a reading similar to the LXX., comments: What was the way which was made in the sight of it? "I am," He said, "the Way, the Truth, and the Life." So it was in the fulness of time, but first He gave His people the Law, that they might walk therein, as it is written, "This is the way, walk ye therein." *In the sight of it*. The Vine cannot flourish except it see the Husbandman, and receive from Him the rain of instruction, that it may bear fruit abundantly. The soul must not only be led by CHRIST through this present life to the better country, but must keep Him ever in view by contemplation, if it would follow Him closely. *And when it had taken root*. The older Versions agree with the A. V. in referring the action still directly to GOD. *Thou plantedst its roots*, is their reading. In one sense all the princes of the house of Israel, the heads of tribes, were *roots* of the Vine, as the progenitors of the Jewish Church. In a deeper manner, the Lawgivers and Prophets of the earlier Covenant, the Apostles and Doctors of the New Testament, are roots of the Church grounded in love. Nay, faith, hope, and charity, are the very roots of the life of the soul, without which it can never be fruitful. Most truly of all, you may take the words of Him Who is the Root of Jesse, and yet a Branch growing out of that root, going down in His humility to death and hell, ascending in His glory to the highest heaven, truly that "Plant of renown"

Cd.

Ay.

A.

Z.

Isa. xxx. 21.

C.

Ric. Hamp.

D. C.

C.

Pet. Lomb.

Ric. Hamp.

L.

Ezek. xxxiv. 29.

Virg. Georg. ii. 291.

quæ, quantum vertice ad auras
Æthereas, tantum radice in tartara tendit.

It filled the land. First, with its shoots, as is written, Le Blanc. "It grew, and became a spreading vine of low stature." Ezek. xvii. 6. Secondly, with its grapes, which are perfumed, "As the vine Ecclus. xxiv. brought I forth pleasant savour," large, abundant, and com- 17. mon to all parts of the world. And this last because, as one Father says: "The earth is the LORD's, everywhere GOD the S. Ambros. FATHER is served, everywhere CHRIST is worshipped: this 10 in S. Luc. xx. is our vintage;" and as another speaks, "The banners of S. Hieron. the Cross shine throughout the world." So that Vine began S. Alb. Mag. to fill the land, when three thousand received the Word on one day, and when "Samaria had received the Word of GOD," Acts viii. 14. and the prophecy entered on its completion, "The earth Isa. xi. 9. shall be full of the knowledge of the LORD, as the waters cover the sea."

10 The hills were covered with the shadow of it : and the boughs thereof were like the goodly cedar-trees.

"Who are the *hills?* The Prophets. Why did its *shadow* A. cover them? Because they spake darkly the things foretold as yet to come. Thou hearest from the Prophets, Keep the Sabbath day, on the eighth day circumcise a child, offer sacrifice of a ram, a calf, a he-goat. Be not troubled; its shadow covers the hills of GOD; after the shadow there will come a manifestation." Again, taking the *hills,* as often, to imply the proud and mighty, they explain the words of the Ay. conquest of mountainous Palestine, of the fall of Sihon and Og, of the sons of Anak, and of all the tribes whom David subdued, and over whom Solomon ruled peacefully. And, most truly of all; taking the hills to denote the heights of Christian love and contemplation, they are said to be under the shadow of that Vine whereof the Bride speaks, "I sat down under His shadow with great delight, and His fruit Cant. ii. 3. was sweet to my taste:" sweet indeed, as the Holy Eastern Church sings of S. Longinus:

> Looking on the fruitful Vine Menæa, Oct.
> As upon the Tree it hung, 16.
> Streaming life's and pardon's wine,
> With thy heart's lips thou hast clung
> Closely, Saint, to drink thy fill
> Of that joy which knows no ill.

The boughs thereof were like the goodly cedar-trees. The S. Alb. Mag. Targum adds here, "Behold the mighty teachers, who are D. C. likened to the stateliest cedars." And then we shall under-stand the words to denote the equality or superiority in spiritual things of the humblest Christian to the mightiest Saints of the elder Covenant. "Verily, I say unto you, S. Matt. xi. Among them that are born of women there hath not risen 11. a greater than John the Baptist: notwithstanding, he that is

C.

Ric. Hamp.

least in the kingdom of heaven is greater than he." The LXX. and Vulgate read here, *The boughs thereof [covered] the cedars of God.* That is, observes Cassiodorus, the Church is the home and shelter of the Martyrs whom she hath reared in her bosom. Or, as another will have it, she has brought the kings and rulers of the earth, lofty and proud though they were, under her sway.

11 She stretched out her branches unto the sea: and her boughs unto the river.

Z.

Theodoret.

Honorius.

C.

L.

P.

The literal reference is to the furthest limits attained by the Jewish monarchy, when, under Solomon, it extended from the Mediterranean to the Euphrates. Mystically, they explain the *branches* to be the Jewish members of the Church; the *boughs,* Gentile proselytes. The *sea,* in like manner, they take to be the heathen world, barren, unresting, and sinful, to which the *branches* were stretched out, when the True Vine sent His Apostles to preach the Gospel. And as they for the most part suppose the *river* to be the Jordan, they interpret this clause of the Jewish people, to which only the lesser position (*boughs* as compared with *branches*) was destined under the new dispensation. Once more, they explain the *sea* to denote tears of repentance, and the *river* the cleansing waters of Baptism.

Besides those tropological interpretations, verses 8—11 have also been explained of the external history of the Christian Church, brought out of heathen darkness and bondage, victorious over Paganism, filling the whole Roman Empire, subjugating kings and sages, rearing Saints equal to the greatest of the Prophets, spreading from the Eastern to the Western Sea, to the Nile and to the Ganges.

12 Why hast thou then broken down her hedge : that all they that go by pluck off her grapes.

Isa. v. 4.

Le Blanc.

S. Ambros.
in S. Luc.
Lib. ix. 30.

S. Greg.
Nyss. Hom.
vii. in Cant.

Why? We are not left in doubt as to the reason, for GOD has answered the question Himself: "Wherefore, when I looked that it should bring forth grapes, brought it forth wild grapes? And now, go to; I will tell you what I will do to My vineyard : I will take away the hedge thereof, and it shall be eaten up ; and break down the wall thereof, and it shall be trodden down." What the *hedge* is which He has thus destroyed, they vary in explaining. The Hebrew גְּדֵרֶיהָ is plural, *fences,* whence they remind us that there are many such. First and best, they take this hedge to be the Presence of GOD Himself. "Far be it from us to dread any peril for this vineyard, which the ever-wakeful guard of the LORD of Salvation hath fenced with the wall of eternal life against all the lures of worldly iniquity, and hath stretched out her branches unto the sea." Next, it denotes

the Angel guard: Thirdly, the Saints: then, God's com- *S. Basil.*
mandments and the virtues which spring from keeping them, *Magn. Hom.*
especially obedience. Or it may be taken of Holy Scripture. *V.*
After this, prayer, according to that saying of a Saint: *Honorius.*
"Prayer is the wall of the Church, which cannot be breached, *S. Chrysost.*
an unshaken bulwark, terrible to evil spirits, but safe and *De Orando*
sheltering to the holy." Lastly, prelates, doctors, and *Deo. Lib. ii.*
preachers are the wall of the congregation. "When the
tower falls," observes Cardinal Hugo, "it is not for its own *Hugo Card.*
ruin alone, but for that of the whole city. For if the tower *in Cant. iv.*
be taken or razed, the entire city is easily stormed. So
when the assembly of the Doctors falls into sin, the city of
the Church lies exposed and defenceless before its enemies."
They dwell on the Vulgate word *maceria*, which denotes a *Cato de*
dry stone wall, built without mortar, and thus easily pulled *Re Rust. 15.*
down, and draw thence the inference that no barrier of prayer, *C.*
of good works, or the like, can stand firmly, unless cemented
with the Blood of Christ. S. Bonaventura, looking at the *S. Bonaven-*
word from a somewhat different point of view, says that there *tura.*
is no *maceria* whatever except Christ, and that this name is
given to Him Who is the chief corner-stone, as Begotten by
God only, and in no human manner.

> Non ex virili semine,   *S. Ambros.*
> Sed mystico spiramine,   *The Hymn,*
> Verbum Dei factum est caro -   *Veni Re-*
> Fructusque ventris floruit.   *demptor Gentium.*

All they that go by. The A.V. more fully, with LXX. and Vul- *C.*
gate, *All they that pass by the way.* Those who pass by the *Way*
are the heathen and unbelievers, who serve idols of their own
framing, and neglect the worship of Christ. Or it may be *Honorius.*
taken of heretics, who, after they have pulled down the wall
of Holy Scripture by their false interpretation of it, lay waste
the Church. *Pluck off her grapes.* They note that this *L.*
phrase shows that unfaithful labourers in the vineyard, hypocrites, and false Christians are intended. They do not destroy
the vine, but turn it to their own profit alone, seeking fruit
for themselves, and not for God.

13 The wild boar out of the wood doth root it
up : and the wild beasts of the field devour it.

The destroyer is called a *wild boar*, not only to denote his *A.*
savage fury, but also his unclean Gentilism, an abomination,
like the flesh of swine, to the Jews. He comes *out of the
wood*, because the Gentiles, uncultured by the Divine Husbandman, are thus contrasted with the sedulously tended
vineyard of Israel. But when they at length believed, what
was said? "Then shall all the trees of the wood rejoice *Ps. xcvi. 12.*
before the Lord." They dispute about the literal applica- *C.*

B.
Ven. Bede.
R.

tion. S. Jerome, followed by many others, interprets the passage of the Roman devastation under Vespasian and Titus. But though the boar was once included amongst the military ensigns of the Romans, it was laid aside in the time of Marius. If we are to see a reference to the Romans here at all, we should therefore apply the words to Hadrian, whose crowning insult to the Jews was carving a boar's head over the chief gate of Ælia Capitolina, that they might shrink from so much as entering it. The Carthusian aptly points

D. C.

out that a far earlier date must be assigned, because the Jewish nation, after the rejection of CHRIST, had no further claim to the title of GOD's vine. The Carmelite, while men-

Ay.

tioning the view of S. Jerome, ingeniously suggests that Nebuchadnezzar is meant, and called the *boar of the wood*,

Dan. iv. 25.
Le Blanc.

because he was driven from men, and had his dwelling with the beasts of the field. Others, again, take it of Antiochus Epiphanes. But in truth, the most satisfactory explanation is that which sees here the captivity of the northern kingdom under Shalmaneser, not only from the express mention of

2 Kings xvii. 6.

tribes (Ephraim, Benjamin,[1] and Manasses) which formed part of it, but because of the absence of any hint of the profanation and destruction of the Temple, such as occurs in Psalm lxxiv., and certain to be here repeated if any sack of Jerusalem were referred to. *The wild beasts of the field.*

B.
Ay.

The reading of the LXX. and Vulgate is, *The singular wild beast.* They who refer this Psalm to the Roman conquest say here, that Vespasian, because of his strength and his foul and sordid life, is styled the *wild boar;* and that Titus, who devoured what his father had merely *uprooted,* is the *singular beast.*

D. C.

The Carthusian, basing his objection on the apostasy of the Jews, declares that the latter epithet is merely emphatic and iterative of the former, and must refer to some much earlier oppressor. Mystically, the truest re-

Arnobius.

ference is that of Arnobius, who sees here the slaying of CHRIST, the True Vine, by the combination of Roman soldiers and Jewish Priests; so that the FATHER might truly say of

L.
Gen. xxxvii. 33.

Him, "It is My SON's coat; an evil beast hath devoured Him." Next, they take the words of the Church, vexed by the devil, typified by the *boar,* as the emblem of brutal pas-

Cd.

sions, and by Antichrist, the *singular beast.* The Chaldee Targum reads, instead of the latter phrase, *The cock of the woods shall feed on it,* wherein they note the fierceness, pride, and boastfulness of the bird, as fit emblems of the sin which drove Lucifer, Adam, and Nebuchadnezzar from their high estate.

---

[1] Only a small part of Benjamin adhered to the house of David. The majority of the tribe, and all its greatest cities, Ramah, Bethel, and Jericho, belonged to the northern kingdom. Note also, that only *one* tribe is promised to the Davidic family in the prophecy of Ahijah. 1 Kings xi. 32, 36.

TheRhythm,
*Multi sunt
presbyteri.*

Quasi rex in capite gallus coronatur;
In pede calcaribus, ut miles, armatur;
Quanto plus fit senior pennis deauratur;
In nocte dum concinat leo perturbatur.

More specifically, they refer the *boar* to Mohammed, uproot- **D. C.**
ing the Eastern Church in so many places, and threatening
even the West till comparatively recent times. Or, going
back to earlier times, they remind us of the slaughter of the
martyrs, the living wall of the Church Militant, and the con- **R.**
sequent devastation wrought by tyrants like Valerian and
Diocletian. And another commentator sees in the *singular
beast* the type of a king, nominally Catholic, oppressing and
plundering the Church.[1] One lesson of comfort, however, **Hugo Card.**
underlies the sorrow of these verses. The wild beast cannot
make its way in so long as the wall stands; the wall will
stand so long as we are desirous that it should. Then we
are safe, as the heathen poet sings, under the protection of
an ever-wakeful Guard, Who tells us:

Ipse seram vites, pangamque ex ordine colles, **Propert.**
Quos carpent nullæ, me vigilante, feræ. **Eleg. iv. 16, 15.**

14 Turn thee again, thou GOD of Hosts, look
down from heaven : behold, and visit this vine;

Here is set forth the perfect state of the Church after the **Ay.**
Advent of CHRIST. And it is divided into six parts, in ac-
cordance with which the Psalmist utters six prophecies.
First; that the Church shall be reconciled to GOD. Secondly;
that it shall be founded on CHRIST. Thirdly; that the Synagogue shall come to an end. Fourthly; that the SON of GOD
shall be Incarnate. Fifthly; that faith shall be confirmed.
Sixthly; that the Church shall be made blessed. *Turn Thee.*
Observe that GOD is said in Holy Writ to *turn* in many ways. **S. Luke xxii.**
First; by converting sinners, as when He turned and looked **61.**
on Peter. Secondly; by delivering the afflicted, as it is
written, "O what great troubles and adversities hast Thou **Ps. lxxi. 18.**
showed me! and yet didst Thou turn and refresh me, yea,
and broughtest me from the deep of the earth again."
Thirdly; by raising up the dead, first the souls from the
death of sin, and then their bodies from the death of nature,
of which turning is said, "I am my Beloved's, and His desire **Cant. vii. 10.**
[*Vulg.* turning] is toward me." And also, "Wilt thou not
turn again, and quicken us, O LORD?" Fourthly; by com- **Ps. lxxxv. 6.**
forting the sorrowful. "O LORD, I will praise Thee: though **Isa. xii. 1.**

[1] When we bear in mind how often the epithet "boar" was given in contempt to Germans in the middle age, and how Erasmus has in set terms applied it to Luther; and note how this gloss of Hugo de S. Cher fits in with the character of Henry VIII.; we may well see here a type of the calamity which befell the Church of England in the disastrous sixteenth century.

Thou wast angry with me. Thine anger is turned away, and Thou comfortedst me." Lastly ; by punishing the obstinate, for then "the sun shall be turned into darkness, and the moon into blood." *Look down*, that is, call us to repentance and grace, because "a King that sitteth on the throne of judgment scattereth away all evil with his eyes." *From heaven*, that is, in the Person of the Mediator CHRIST JESUS, *behold*, that it may see and know Thee, and then learn to see and know its own sins, *and visit*, in Thine own Person, as the great Physician coming to a patient, *this vine*. And note, that to a wise man, his own life, his own mind, his own conscience, is a vineyard. In this vineyard the LORD planted every good seed, but the devil turns it into a garden of pot-herbs. "Ahab spake unto Naboth, saying, Give me thy vineyard, that I may have it for a garden of herbs." He makes the soul a garden of herbs, when he plants there the wisdom of the world, the flesh, and the devil, herbs which will quickly wither. Some are only too ready to yield over this vineyard to the devil, so that it is turned into a desert. "I went by the vineyard of the man void of understanding ; and, lo, it was all grown over with thorns, and nettles had covered the face thereof, and the stone wall thereof was broken down."

Marginal notes: Joel ii. 31. / Prov. xx. 8. / B. / Honorius. / Ric. Hamp. / Ay. / S. Albertus Magnus. / S. Bern. / S. Albertus Magnus. / 1 Kings xxi. 2. / Prov. xxiv. 30.

15 And the place of the vineyard that thy right hand hath planted : and the branch that thou madest so strong for thyself.

The word כַּנָּה, here and in A. V. translated *vineyard*, (as also by the Syriac Psalter) is taken by the LXX., Vulgate, and all the chief modern critics, as a verb in the imperative. The first reads καταρτισαι, the second *perfice*, the remainder *protect* or *shelter* this vine. *Perfect*, then, O LORD, *this vine*. Plant not any other, but make this one perfect. For she is the very seed of Abraham, she is the very seed in whom all nations shall be blessed ; there is the root whereon the grafted wild olive is borne. *The branch*. The Hebrew is בֵּן, and the old versions are agreed in translating it more literally, *the Son of man*, wherein they are confirmed by the Targum, which reads here, "Messiah the King." The metaphor, however, comes to the same thing, for He is spoken of Who is the "rod out of the stem of Jesse, the branch out of his roots." He thus grows out of that very vine which His own right hand had planted, as He grows Himself, the Tree of Life, in the midst of His garden the Church, which He hath planted in faith and love. *Whom Thou madest so strong for Thyself*. A mighty stronghold, build as you may, "for other foundation can no man lay than that is laid, which is JESUS CHRIST." And because He came to fulfil, expand, and glorify the Law, not to destroy it, the

Marginal notes: A. / Isa. xi. 1. / D. C. / A. / 1 Cor. iii. 11. / Ay.

Psalmist calls on Him to perfect His vine, on Him Whom the
FATHER *hath made so strong* by the hypostatic union of Godhead and Manhood, so that "the Branch of the LORD" is Isa. iv. 2,
Marg.
"beauty and glory."

16 It is burnt with fire, and cut down : and they
shall perish at the rebuke of thy countenance.

Let us take it still of the Only-begotten, and we shall see
His Passion shadowed here, the *burning with fire* in the wood
for the burnt-offering of Abraham, the *cutting down* in the Arnobius.
knife which he lifted against Isaac. And as GOD the FA-
THER sware by Himself for this thing to stablish Isaac, that
in him all the nations of the earth should be blessed, so we
beseech Him now to remember His oath, for the sake of the
One Sacrifice, consumed with the fire of Divine love, cut
down by the hands of sinners, that we may never go back
from Him. So taking it, *they* who pierced Him, when they
look on Him again, *shall perish at the rebuke of His countenance.* But the Vulgate reading, from its ambiguity, has led
to a different interpretation: *Things burnt with fire and dug
up shall perish at the rebuke of Thy countenance.*[1] The A.
Pet. Lomb.
most general gloss on these words is, that sins are denoted,
some kindled by ardent desire, others dug by grovelling fear.
These *perish* and disappear in the souls of penitents, who bow
before the *rebuke of God's countenance*, that is, at the preach- Honorius.
ing of the Gospel of CHRIST, whether they be open sins of
passion, hot and conspicuous as fire, or hidden sins of fear, B.
Hesychius.
Ay.
lying, as it were, in a trench. Again, it is explained of the
fall of the Jewish dispensation. *Things burnt with fire,* the
holocausts of the Temple, *things dug up,* the ashes and offal
flung into pits and trenches, perished and ceased after CHRIST,
the Countenance of GOD, appeared to the world. Yet again, Philip de la
Grève.
you may take it of the spiritual temple, burnt and dug up by
ghostly foes. The digging can be countermined by the might
of the five wounds wherewith CHRIST'S Sacred Body was
dug ; the fire may be quenched with the water from His
pierced side.

17 Let thy hand be upon the man of thy right
hand : and upon the son of man, whom thou madest
so strong for thine own self.

And surely His hand was on that Man, so that He might
say, with holy Job, in His Passion: "Have pity upon me, Job xix. 21.
have pity upon me, O ye my friends ; for the hand of GOD
hath touched me. Why do ye persecute me as GOD, and are

---

[1] The LXX., continuing to
speak of the vine, has ἐμπε-
πυρισμένη πυρὶ καὶ ἀνεσκαμμένη,
ἀπὸ ἐπιτιμήσεως τοῦ προσώπου σου
ἀπολοῦνται. The Vulgate, trans- | lating this literally, appears as
though the neuter plural through-
out : *Incensa igne et suffossâ, ab
increpatione vultûs tui peribunt.*

not satisfied with my flesh?" In that Passion He was at first Benoni, the Child of mourning, "a Man of sorrows and acquainted with grief," but the hand of the LORD was still on Him to strengthen Him, like Elijah, to run His course, so that by His Resurrection and Ascension, He became Benjamin, the SON of the Right Hand of GOD. Ayguan prefers to see here the Incarnation, rather than the Passion, of CHRIST, and sees the miraculous nature of that mystery implied in the phrase the *hand of God*. He was *confirmed* by His FATHER when, at His Baptism in Jordan there was heard, " a voice from heaven, saying, This is My beloved SON, in Whom I am well-pleased." He is the *Man of God's right hand* for three reasons. First; He is inseparably united with the FATHER. Next; He has perfect fruition of Him, as is written, "At Thy right hand there is pleasure for evermore." Lastly; He is seated on the FATHER's right, for " the LORD said unto my LORD, Sit Thou on My right hand," where His Proto-martyr beheld Him in the glory of GOD.

18 And so will not we go back from thee : O let us live, and we shall call upon thy Name.

We will not go back, but when others do so because He utters some hard saying which they cannot hear, we shall say with S. Peter, "LORD, to whom shall we go? Thou hast the words of eternal life." We, strengthened by the HOLY GHOST, will not fall away from Thee, but will abide as did Thine Apostles, for "neither death, nor life, nor angels, nor principalities, nor powers, nor things present, nor things to come, nor height, nor depth, nor any other creature, shall be able to separate us from the love of GOD, which is in JESUS CHRIST our LORD." *O let us live.* The LXX. and Vulgate take it in the future, *Thou shalt quicken us*, in the regenerat- ing waters of baptism, wherein our sins are remitted. *Thou shalt quicken us*, by lifting us from love of earthly things, wherein we were dead, and love of Thee, by conversion, turn- ing our faces to Thine, wherein is the light of life; by giving us the true Bread from heaven; with the life of grace here, and that of glory hereafter; with Thyself, Who art alone the Life of all things. *And we shall call upon Thy Name.* Cassiodorus explains it of the daily recitation of the Our FA- THER by all Christians, but the majority take it of that Name which is dearest of all to the Saints of GOD, the Name which is ever on their lips, the Name of their Brother, their Teacher, their King, their Ransom, their Reward. O most beloved Name, let us call on Thee with the passionate cry of Thy servant in days long past :

Jesu, Jesu, Jesu, Jesu, cortese,
Jesu, Jesu, Jesu, Jesu, amore,
Jesu, Jesu, Jesu, d' amor m' accese;
Jesu, Jesu, sì m' ha furato 'l cuore,

Margin notes:
L.
Isa. liii. 3.

Ay.

C.

S. Matt. iii. 17.

S. Albertus Magnus.

Ps. xvi. 12.
Ps. cx. 1.
Acts vii. 55.

S. Albertus Magnus.
S. John vi. 68.
Ay.
Rom. viii. 38.

C.

A.

Arnobius.
Pseudo-Hieron.
D. C.
Haymo.
C.

Bianco da Siena.

Jesu, Jesu, Jesu, mi fa le spese,
Jesu, Jesu, sie 'l mio salvatore,
Jesu, Jesu, Jesu, desideroso,
Jesu, Jesu, sie 'l mio riposo.

19 Turn us again, O LORD GOD of hosts : show
the light of thy countenance, and we shall be whole.

The triple repetition of this verse denotes the mystery of **B.**
the Most Holy Trinity. It sums up all Christian prayer, for **A.**
it asks first for conversion, next for the light of GOD's countenance, which is His loving-kindness, and then for salvation.
It is triply uttered for another reason, that as the first cry
was for the Nativity of CHRIST, and the second for His Pas- **Lu.**
sion and Resurrection, so the third is for His Second Advent
to Judgment. Let Him come, that we may see the King in
His beauty. "For what is so good, so lovely, so sweet, so **D. C.**
fair, so healthful, so pleasant, and so noble, as to look on the
Face of GOD? O beauteous Face, O boundless loveliness,
O measureless bliss! Blessed then are the pure in heart, **S. Matt. v. 8.**
for they shall see GOD."
Wherefore :
Glory be to the FATHER, the LORD GOD of Hosts; and to
the SON, the Shepherd of Israel, the Man of His right hand;
and to the HOLY GHOST, the Sevenfold Light of the Countenance of GOD.
As it was in the beginning, is now, and ever shall be :
world without end. Amen.

COLLECTS.

Visit, O LORD, this Vine, which Thou hast brought out of **Ludolph.**
the Egypt of troubles with Thy strong right hand; that
quickened by the light of Thy countenance, it may be glad
with the plenteousness of good fruits in Thee. Through. (1.)
Almighty GOD, Who hast sent Thine Only-begotten SON, **Acta**
and hast revealed Him as Creator of all things, look upon **S. Damasi.**
this Vine, which Thy right hand hath planted, prune away the
thorns from it, bring forth its branches in might, and give
them the fruit of truth. (2.)
O GOD, Who hast rooted up the thorns of superstition, **Missale**
and set plants in Thy Church with the deep root of faith, **Mozarabic. Easter Day.**
hearken to the prayer of Thy servants; look down from
heaven, behold, and visit this Vine, and grant that it, which
received increase in the bud by Thy planting, may receive
fruit in abundance by Thy watering. Through. (11.)
Hear, O LORD, Who rulest Israel, Thou Who leadest Jo- **Mozarabic.**
seph like a sheep, apply the guidance of a shepherd and the
help of a protector, turn us, and show Thy countenance, and
we shall be whole, Thou Who, though Most High, beholdest
the lowly, and mercifully hearest the prayer of them which
call on Thee. Through Thy mercy. (11.)

Mozarabic.

Come, O LORD most merciful, come; and vouchsafe freedom to the oppressed; stir up Thy strength, and possess the people Thou hast gained, direct that vine which Thou hast planted by the Man of Thy right hand; and hear, as our Advocate, the Son of Man Whom Thou madest so strong for Thyself, that the bread of tears may have measure in its scourges, and the drink of our compunction may not reduce in strength, but nourish our souls. Through Thy mercy. (11.)

Mozarabic.

O LORD of Hosts, receive in mercy, not in anger, the prayers of Thy servants, and vouchsafe to show us how we ought to pray; strengthen them with eternal food whom the bread of tears troubles, and let our eyes shed rivers of tears with such piteous weeping, that they may turn the abundance of Thy mercies upon the sins we have committed, so that we who tremble in dust at the coming of our Redeemer, may look, when He comes, on His glorious countenance in the most peaceful aspect. (11.)

Mozarabic.

Come and deliver us, O LORD GOD of hosts; turn us, and show us Thy countenance, and we shall be whole, that we, purified by Thy gift of worthy repentance, may stand by Thee at Thy judgment. (11.)

Mozarabic.

Stir up Thy strength, O LORD GOD, and come to deliver us, that we, who are overborne by the whirlwinds of temptation may be uplifted by Thy mighty help. Let not the legions of the enemies prevail against us who are sheltered by Thy majesty, but evermore grant us assistance, and inflict punishment on our foes. (11.)

Mozarabic.
For unbe-
lievers.

Hear, Thou Who rulest Israel, Who leadest Joseph like a sheep, stir up Thy strength, and save them for whom Thou camest to be born on earth. Thou Who hast vouchsafed to gain the multitude of the Gentiles by stretching forth to them the worship of faith, deliver by the swift act of Thy lovingkindness the souls of unbelievers from the pit of false doctrine, and bring them to Thyself to please Thee and trust in Thee. Through. (11.)

S. Jerome.

Turn us, O LORD GOD of hosts, show us Thy countenance, and we shall be whole; Him Who is Thine Image, Him Who is Thy Face, Who is the Light of Thy countenance, in Whom Thou dwellest, and Who dwelleth in Thee, that He may vouchsafe to glide into our cleansed souls, show us Himself as the SAVIOUR of the world, and save us by His sacred glance. To Him be glory and power with Thee and the HOLY GHOST, now and for ages of ages. Amen.

D. C.

O GOD, the FATHER of might, graciously vouchsafe to be the Leader in the right way before the people, redeemed with the Blood of Thy SON, that, planted by Thee with the strong root of Christian profession, it may fill the Land of Eternal promise. Through the same. (2.)

J. MASTERS AND SON, PRINTERS, ALDERSGATE STREET.